HEALTH CARE SUPPLY CHAIN MANAGEMENT

Elements, Operations, and Strategies

Gerald (Jerry) R. Ledlow, PhD, MHA, FACHE
Professor and Chair, Department of Health Policy & Management
Jiann-Ping Hsu College of Public Health
Georgia Southern University

Karl B. Manrodt, PhD
Director, Master of Logistics and Supply Chain Management Program
Georgia College & State University

David E. Schott, DrPH
Jiann-Ping Hsu College of Public Health
Georgia Southern University

JONES & BARTLETT
LEARNING

World Headquarters
Jones & Bartlett Learning
5 Wall Street
Burlington, MA 01803
978-443-5000
info@jblearning.com
www.jblearning.com

Jones & Bartlett Learning books and products are available through most bookstores and online booksellers. To contact Jones & Bartlett Learning directly, call 800-832-0034, fax 978-443-8000, or visit our website, www.jblearning.com.

Substantial discounts on bulk quantities of Jones & Bartlett Learning publications are available to corporations, professional associations, and other qualified organizations. For details and specific discount information, contact the special sales department at Jones & Bartlett Learning via the above contact information or send an email to specialsales@jblearning.com.

Production Credits
VP, Executive Publisher: David D. Cella
Publisher: Michael Brown
Associate Editor: Danielle Bessette
Vendor Manager: Nora Menzi
Senior Marketing Manager: Sophie Fleck Teague
Manufacturing and Inventory Control Supervisor: Amy Bacus
Composition and Project Management: Integra Software Services Pvt. Ltd.
Cover Design: Kristin E. Parker
Associate Director of Rights & Media: Joanna Lundeen
Rights & Media Specialist: Merideth Tumasz
Media Development Editor: Shannon Sheehan
Cover Image: © Egorov Artem/Shutterstock
Printing and Binding: Edwards Brothers Malloy
Cover Printing: Edwards Brothers Malloy

Library of Congress Cataloging-in-Publication Data

Names: Ledlow, Gerald R. | Manrodt, Karl B., 1957. |
  Schott, David, 1985.
Title: Health care supply chain management : elements, operations, and
  strategies / Gerald Ledlow, Karl Manrodt, David Schott.
Description: Burlington, Massachusetts : Jones & Bartlett Learning, [2017] |
  Includes bibliographical references and index.
Identifiers: LCCN 2016011901 | ISBN 9781284081855
Subjects: | MESH: Materials Management, Hospital | Purchasing,
  Hospital–organization & administration | Economics, Hospital |
  Efficiency, Organizational
Classification: LCC RA971.3 | NLM WX 147 | DDC 362.11068/1–dc23 LC record available at http://lccn.loc.
gov/2016011901

6048

Printed in the United States of America
20 19 18 17 16   10 9 8 7 6 5 4 3 2 1

CONTENTS

AUTHORS

Dr. Gerald (Jerry) Ledlow

Dr. Ledlow has earned a PhD in Organizational Leadership (University of Oklahoma, 1999), a Master of Healthcare Administration (Baylor University, 1996), and a B.A. in Economics (Virginia Military Institute, 1987). He is a board certified fellow in healthcare administration from the American College of Healthcare Executives (ACHE).

He has twenty-eight years of healthcare management experience in leadership positions in managed care, supply-chain management, operations and in academia. Before returning to academia, Dr. Ledlow was the Corporate Vice President for Supply Chain Operations for the Sisters of Mercy Health System within the Genesis Project and previously was the director and tenured faculty for the Doctor of Health Administration program at Central Michigan University. Earlier in his career, he was the executive director of corporate services at Central Michigan University and a commissioned United States Army officer in the Medical Service Corps where he earned experience in both field and fixed facility operations and deployed as the healthcare supply chain leader in the former Yugoslavia to support the United Nations operations and in combat divisions in Louisiana and Panama (Operation Just Cause). Dr. Ledlow was also a National Registry Certified Emergency Medical Technician (volunteered in both emergency departments and ambulance) in the late 1980s and early 1990s.

He has been awarded two ACHE Regent's Awards (1997 and 2003), the Federal Sector Managed Care Executive of the Year Award (1998) and the Boone Powell Award (1996). Previously, he has served on two ACHE Regent's Advisory Councils.

Dr. Ledlow serves on the Executive Board of the Global Business and Technology Association, the Editorial Board for the association's peer review journal and has served as reviewer for several peer reviewed publications, and is a grant reviewer for the National Institutes of Health, National Cancer Institute, and National Eye Institute as a health administration expert.

He has edited and authored several books; notably a national textbook on Healthcare Leadership (2nd edition published on June 3rd, 2013), a healthcare supply chain book for Health Administration Press, and four volumes on community preparedness and terrorism prevention. Dr. Ledlow has authored nearly two dozen book chapters and numerous articles and manuscripts. Dr. Ledlow's interests are leadership and management, healthcare supply chain operations improvement, emergency preparedness, and healthcare delivery systems.

Dr. Ledlow is the chair of the Health Policy and Management Department and a tenured professor of Health Policy and Management within the Jiann-Ping Hsu College of Public Health at Georgia Southern University.

Dr. Ledlow is married to his wonderful wife of over 21 years and is the father of three daughters (yes, he is outnumbered four to one at home), enjoys watching football, building analytical operational computer-based models, shuttling to various ball fields and courts with his children, and, on rare occasions, fishing.

Dr. Karl Manrodt

Dr. Karl Manrodt serves as Professor in the Department of Management at Georgia College and State University, located in Milledgeville, Georgia. He is also the Director of the online Master of Logistics and Supply Chain Management program.

Dr. Manrodt has nearly 20 years in logistics, transportation, and supply chain research. These research projects have been funded by a wide range of participants in the supply chain, ranging from consulting firms, associations, carriers, software providers, and shippers. He serves on the editorial advisor board for several leading practitioner-based journals.

As the first Executive Director, Office of Corporate Partnerships, at the University of Tennessee, Karl was responsible for efforts to develop strategic partnerships with business and industry for the purposes of sharing research expertise, enhancing student-learning experiences and increasing the level of external funding support.

Dr. Manrodt also had served the profession in several forums. He served on the Board of Directors for the Council of Supply Chain Management Professionals (CSCMP, formerly CLM). He was the Executive Director for the Flat Glass Logistics Council, which promotes safety in the production and fabrication supply chain. He also served on the College-Industry Council on Material Handling Education (CICMHE), which prepares and provides information, teaching materials and various events in support of material handling education and research. Dr. Manrodt served as the 2004 Program Chair for the Council of Logistics Management's annual conference, as well as a Track Chairperson for the annual meetings of the Warehouse Education & Research Council. He was recognized as a "2004 Rainmaker" by DC Velocity Magazine and in 2005 was awarded the Eugene Bishop Award for Sustained Academic Excellence by the College of Business at Georgia Southern University.

Teaching and research interests include information technology and its impact on supply-chain management, performance measurement, CEO perceptions of logistics and supply-chain management, customer service, and corporate strategy. His research has appeared in such journals as the *Journal of Business Logistics, Transportation Journal*, the *International Journal of Physical Distribution and Materials Management, Journal of Transportation Management and Interfaces*. His research on top shippers has appeared in *Logistics Management* for the last 20 years. His survey of warehousing metrics is now in its ninth year, and is done in partnership with WERC and DC Velocity magazine. Dr. Manrodt is a recognized speaker, making over one hundred presentations to government, industry and academic groups in Sweden, Austria, Brazil, Denmark, China, Germany, Canada, Australia, Africa, Turkey, and the United States. He coauthored his first book, *Customer Responsive Management: The Flexible Advantage* in 1992. His second book on logistics and supply chain measurement—*Keeping Score: Measuring the Business Value of Logistics in the Supply Chain*—was published in 1999. Palgrave Macmillan published his first book on vested, *Vested Outsourcing*, in February 2010. The second edition was printed in April 2013. This was followed with *The Vested Way: How a "What's in it for We" Mindset Revolutionizes Business Relationships* in March 2012. His newest book, *Vested: How P&G, McDonald's, and Microsoft Are Redefining Winning in*

Business Relationships, was released in September 2012. Two other books, *The Power Paradox: Strategic Sourcing in The New Economy* and *Healthcare Supply Chain Management Fundamentals: Elements, Operations and Strategies* are due for release in 2015 and 2016 respectively.

Karl resides in Statesboro, GA and travels extensively.

Dr. David Schott

Dr. Schott has earned a DrPH in Public Health Leadership (Georgia Southern University, 2016), a Master of Business Administration (Georgia Southern University, 2016), a Master of Science in Public Health (Tulane University, 2010), and a B.A. in Economics (The Ohio State University, 2008). He is board certified in public health by the National Board of Public Health Examiners and holds a Lean Six Sigma Black Belt.

Dr. Schott has nearly 10 years' experience as an entrepreneur as well as several years' experience within health systems at both the facility and corporate level. His interests include organizational leadership, strategic planning, healthcare supply chain, and process improvement.

CONTRIBUTORS

Sarah Storey

Sarah Storey earned her Master of Healthcare Administration at Georgia Southern University. She also received her Bachelor of Science in Psychology at Georgia Southern University. During her MHA program, she took an interest in Healthcare Supply Chain. After graduation she began a career with a Group Purchasing Organization representing multiple health systems across the Southeast United States.

Dr. James Stephens

Dr. Stephens earned a Doctor of Health Administration at Central Michigan University's School of Health Sciences, a Master of Health Administration at Indiana University's School of Medicine, and a Bachelor of Science in Business Administration at Indiana University's School of Business. He is a Fellow in the American College of Healthcare Executives (ACHE) and is Board Certified. He has held senior executive positions in large medical centers and health systems for 25 years, with 18 years at the President and CEO level. Before joining the Georgia Southern University faculty, he held faculty/staff positions at University of Kentucky, Ohio University, University of Indianapolis, and Butler University. Dr. Stephens has served on many healthcare and civic organizational governing boards to include the Kentucky  and Indiana Hospital Associations, Chamber of Commerce, United Way, Boy Scouts, and the International Rotary Club. He has been awarded Excellence in Teaching at Georgia Southern University, Excellence in Service Award at Ohio University, Sagamore of the Wabash (highest award from the Governor of Indiana), Kentucky Colonel (highest award from the Governor of Kentucky), Indiana Governor's Award for Volunteerism, Indiana University Alumni Association President's Award, Lincoln Trail Red Cross Award, and Equal Opportunity Award of Merit by the Urban League. He is also a Paul Harris Fellow in International Rotary. He and his wife have been recognized as Special Donations by International Rotary for their contribution to the Polio-Plus Program. Dr. Stephens' interests include healthcare systems, disparity issues in urban/rural communities, CEO leadership development and succession planning, healthcare governance, strategic planning, and new healthcare delivery models. Dr. Stephens is an Associate Professor and Distinguished Fellow in Healthcare Leadership and the Director for the Master of Healthcare Administration Program within the Jiann-Ping Hsu College of Public Health at Georgia Southern University. He teaches only doctoral and master's courses to include Healthcare Finance, Healthcare Economics, Leadership and Strategic Planning, and Communication in Healthcare Organizations. Dr. Stephens has published many articles, book chapters, and case studies in additional to national and international academic presentations.

Dr. Jeff Jones

Dr. Jeff Jones is an Assistant Professor in the Department of Health Policy and Management at the Jiann-Ping Hsu College of Public Health, Georgia Southern University as well as adjunct faculty for the Biomedical Informatics Program at the College of Osteopathic Medicine, Nova Southeastern University. He brings more than 16 years of experience in public health research. Having served as principal investigator (PI) on more than thirty studies, Dr. Jones has received more than $6.5 million in funded research awards. Through joint, funded research initiatives, he has built collaborative partnerships with many of the leading national public health policy and practice organizations in the country such as ASTHO, NACCHO, NALBOH, NNPHI, and the Public Health Foundation. These efforts include conducting a national data harmonization and integration project collecting demographic and services data on every state health agency, local health department and board of health in the United States in 2010 and 2011. As
co-PI, he formerly directed data informatics for the National Center for Public Health Services and Systems Research. Dr. Jones continues to work with state and local urban and/or minority community groups, hospitals, school systems, and agencies in Georgia and Kentucky to provide program evaluation, health education, survey design, program analysis, and grant-writing support through community based participatory research. As PI, he collected Kentucky's Youth Risk Behavior Survey (YRBS) data and other behavioral data for the US Centers for Disease Control and Prevention (CDC) for over a decade. His expertise includes harmonizing large databases with other national data sets as well as spatial analysis, survey research, and health informatics using GIS (Geographic Information Systems). Much of his state-level work involves program evaluation of physical activity, nutrition, and obesity prevention programming involving children and adolescents, program evaluation of HIV care systems, and community health assessments among minority populations.

Dr. Julie Reagan

Julie Reagan is an assistant professor at the Jiann-Ping Hsu College of Public Health at Georgia Southern University. She holds a PhD in Management, Policy, and Community Health from the University of Texas Health Science Center, School of Public Health in Houston, Texas. Dr. Reagan is also an attorney with over 20 years of practice experience in state government, primarily at public health agencies. Her work focuses on the areas of health policy and management, health law, public health law, and healthcare governance.

Andrew Blues

Andrew Blues serves as the Associate Director for Facilities Information Services (FIS) under the Vice President for Facilities Management at the University of Kentucky. Andrew has worked for over 20 years at the university in a variety of information technology roles and has spent the last five years growing FIS into an independently funded department. He has worked to expand the thinking of what an information service department can be by consolidating a variety of information technology and geospatial based services, along with Enterprise Resource Planning (ERP) support, into a one-stop service offering. Under his leadership, the department has continued to expand while also adding new departments to their support umbrella, even during public university budget cuts.

Andrew holds a Bachelor of Science degree in Computer Science and has served as the lead programmer for the university's enterprise mapping solutions since its inception. Throughout his tenure with the university, Andrew has built a reputation for making lean principles a core value in what he builds and manages. He leads the team that was recognized with the ESRI Vision Award and the ESRI International Special Achievement in GIS (SAG) Award. He also makes time to share endeavors with colleagues and enjoys helping others expand their usage of innovative technologies in their day-to-day activities.

Michelle Ellington

Michelle Ellington serves as the GIS Coordinator for FIS at the University of Kentucky. She is known as a technical evangelist for the development and adoption of innovative geospatial products that support the university community. Michelle manages and continues to expand a data-rich geospatial library used for a variety of needs including campus planning and analysis, Master Planning, space reporting, asset management, and wayfinding. Data is published through custom designed web and mobile solutions that utilize modern and innovative graphical mapping techniques. These solutions have been used to support hospital occupancy, analyze classroom utilization and building efficiencies, and for space analysis in support of the university's new budget modeling process.

Michelle is a frequent guest speaker for multiple university courses, local and international conferences, TEDx speaker, and invited plenary speaker at the 2014 Esri International Education Conference. Most recently, Michelle received the 2014 University of Kentucky Supervisor of the Year Award for her leadership and appreciation for "inspiring us to greatness."

Dr. Schott, Sarah Storey and Dr. Ledlow

CHAPTER 11 CONTRIBUTORS

Acknowledgements

The authors would like to thank the University of Tennessee, the Sourcing Interest Group (SIG), the Center for Outsourcing Research and Education, and the International Association for Contracting and Commercial Management for collaborating on this chapter. By joining forces, the organizations hope to educate practitioners about the importance of procurement, contracting, and business groups working together to determine that the right sourcing business model is matched to the right business environment and needs.

About the Contributors

Kate Vitasek is an international authority for her award-winning research and Vested® business model for highly collaborative relationships. Vitasek, a faculty member at the University of Tennessee, has been lauded by *World Trade Magazine* as one of the "Fabulous 50+1" most influential people impacting global commerce. Her pioneering work has led to five books, including: *Vested Outsourcing: Five Rules That Will Transform Outsourcing*, *Vested: How P&G, McDonald's and Microsoft Are Redefining Winning in Business Relationships* and *Getting to We: Negotiating Agreements for Highly Collaborative Relationships*. Vitasek's work also won the Supply Chain Council's Academic Advancement award for its impact in advancing the business. Vitasek is internationally recognized for her practical and research-based advice for driving transformation and innovation through highly collaborative and strategic partnerships. She has appeared on Bloomberg radio multiple times, NPR, and on Fox Business News. Her work has been featured in over 300 articles in publications like *Forbes*, *Chief Executive Magazine*, *CIO Magazine*, *The Wall Street Journal*, *Journal of Commerce*, *World Trade Magazine* and *Outsource Magazine*.

    Bonnie Keith is an adjunct faculty in the University of Tennessee's Center for Executive Education and is the President of The Forefront Group, LLC, an international leader in Strategic Sourcing Transformation concepts. Bonnie's business experience includes corporate executive and officer positions for three Fortune 100 companies and two Fortune 500 companies where she provided international, successful procurement and supply management strategies. She served as a member of the White House Year 2000 Advisory Council for the Pharmaceutical Industry. Bonnie teaches all over the world and is an executive coach.

    Jim Eckler is the COO of Health Services BC, the provider of shared services for the healthcare system across British Columbia. Prior to joining Health Services, BC, Jim was President and CEO of SCI Group Inc., a leading outsourcing services company. Jim is a founding member and a Director of the Center for Outsourcing Research and Education and is a past chairman of the Supply Chain and Logistics Association of Canada. He has authored numerous articles and is the author of a textbook on transportation issued by the Purchasing Management Association of Canada. He is a frequent speaker at industry conferences and is a popular guest lecturer at universities.

Dawn Tiura Evans is the SIG's President and Chief Executive Officer. She has more than 20 years' leadership experience in large and small organizations, with the past 14 years focused on the sourcing and outsourcing industry. In 2007, Dawn joined SIG as CEO, but has been active in SIG as a speaker and trusted advisor since 1999, bringing the latest developments in sourcing and outsourcing to SIG members. Prior to joining SIG, Dawn held leadership positions as CEO of Denali Group and before that as a partner in a CPA firm. Dawn is actively involved in a number of boards promoting civic, health, and children's issues in the Jacksonville, Florida area. Dawn is a licensed CPA and has a BA from the University of Michigan and an MS in taxation from Golden Gate University.

Jaqui Crawford is the Commercial Excellence Manager for BP leading the development of contracting processes, capability, and contracting best practice for the exploration and production segment. She is an internationally respected dealmaker, thought leader, and creative commercial leader. Jacqui's deal portfolio includes many complex agreements. The core of her success is her focus on outcomes, fair play, and mutual gain. Over the past 25 years, Jacqui has worked extensively in the UK, United States, Japan, Thailand, Singapore, Africa (Egypt), and Europe, and her open and direct approach has gained her an international reputation for fair dealing. Jacqui is on the Board of Directors of the International Association for Contract and Commercial Management (IACCM) and is a co-author of The Vested Outsourcing Manual.

Srinivas Krishna is Director, Finance Operations—Global Vendor Management for the Microsoft Corporation where he is responsible for managing all global outsourced relationships within finance operations, specifically focusing on the business, commercial, and contractual structuring of these partnerships. His corporate experience spans Fortune 100 organizations across the United States, UK, Europe and the emerging markets. Srinivas is also a Sloan Fellow of the London Business School.

Katherine Kawamoto is the Vice President of Research and Advisory Services at the International Association for Contracts and Commercial Management (IACCM), a worldwide nonprofit association with members representing more than 4,000 organizations in more than 120 countries. Katherine works with leading corporations, public, and academic bodies, supporting executive awareness and understanding of the role that contracting and relationship management capabilities increasingly play in 21st-century business performance and public policy. Prior to joining IACCM in 2006, Katherine was the Worldwide Director of Contract Management at NCR Corporation. She has also held leadership positions at Teradata Corporation and Hughes Aircraft Company in Los Angeles. She is a frequent speaker at industry conferences, researcher, thought leader, and author of articles on current contracting topics.

FOREWORD

The time to improve the healthcare supply chain with efficient, effective, and efficacious systems is now! Our greatest challenge today in the healthcare supply chain is a shortage of talent. While the profession of provider-centered supply chain has been formally recognized for nearly 40 years, the market and technological changes in recent times have yielded an unprecedented demand for new skills. As in many industries, the rate of business model changes and market disruptions in the healthcare industry have accelerated in recent years. Traditional healthcare supply-chain skill sets and knowledge are no longer  adequate to keep pace with the greater needs of the organization in the areas of clinical, operational, and financial viability.

The healthcare provider-based supply-chain enterprise lags other industries by 10 or more years in adoption of new methods, technologies, and strategies. While the healthcare provider supply chain is dramatically differentiated from other industrial supply chains—we care for patients—the time is right for adoption of cross-industry supply chain solutions into the healthcare industry. Hospital Boards of Directors and Executive teams are elevating Supply Chain to the "Board-Level Agenda." At the John Hopkins Health Systems we consistently receive invitations to collaborate with other provider organizations. One of the top three collaborative initiative requests from these provider organizations is supply-chain management.

With continued market disruptions, accelerating interest in supply chain collaboration, board-level actions in supply chain, and growing interest—and shortage—of supply chain talent, the timing of this textbook could not be better. This textbook will prove to be a market catalyst for educating the next generation of healthcare executives on the strategies, opportunities, and methods for healthcare supply chain and effective management of these systems.

Supply-chain management is a significant contributor to improving patient safety, quality of care, and at the same time achieving cost reduction objectives. In fact, as we have seen in John Hopkins, supply-chain management can be the catalyst and common thread to align each of these efforts. While there has been continuous improvement in healthcare supply chain methods and solutions, there remains much opportunity yet to be realized by the industry sector. The need to develop new methods, share knowledge, and train the next generation of leaders is well served by this textbook and curriculum materials.

The structure of this textbook's approach to supply-chain management is effectively built upon Michael Porter's Value Chain Model. The basic elements, which provide the groundwork for supply chain, are established in Chapters 1–5. Building upon those basic elements Chapters 6–10 take the readers into the operations of supply chain with specific emphasis on leadership, and the final section of this textbook provides the reader with key strategies and strategic thinking with regard to sourcing, contracting, supply-chain models, and clinical integration in Chapters 11–14. The layout and organization of this text book will serve the reader initially through a comprehensive, sequential learning and into the future as a sourcebook for topical content and reference material. The authors of this book have a combined 65 years of experience in leadership, management and academic roles to include healthcare supply chain and other industry supply-chain programs. Their direct experience, real-world accomplishments, and proven, practical methods provide added value in the content of this impactful presentation.

The goal of improving the healthcare supply chain is paramount in today's health industry. For a well-prepared health professional, knowledge to improve the healthcare supply chain from the bed to the boardroom is critical to achieve success in the dynamic health industry. Success can no longer be myopically located in a single functional area, be it surgery, ER, or oncology. In order to achieve sustainable high-quality patient outcomes, all components in the system must practice excellence. This book helps those of us in supply-chain management to understand what excellence looks like, and provides a way of getting there.

I am delighted that the authors have taken the initiative to develop a formal approach to graduate-level education in healthcare supply-chain management. For those of us in the practice of supply-chain management our greatest challenge today in the healthcare supply chain is talent. The authors' efforts in producing this textbook and accompanying instructional materials will make a significant contribution in the development of knowledgeable healthcare professionals and the advancement of supply-chain knowledge into the future.

Gary F. Dowling
Enterprise Supply Chain Management
The Johns Hopkins Health System
Baltimore, Maryland

INTRODUCTION

The healthcare supply chain is a critical core business component of the healthcare delivery system. The supply chain ensures that the technology of care is available to the physician, surgeon, nurse, clinician, or caregiver at the right time, at the right place, and in sufficient quantity and quality for superior health outcomes for patients within the health system. As, from various sources, the healthcare supply chain comprises between 30 – 45% of annual operating expense, the absolute necessity for efficient, effective and efficacious healthcare supply chain operations and strategic leadership is evident. With pressure to deliver care with higher quality, better outcomes, and with fewer resources, the healthcare supply chain is a major opportunity for health system improvement and further maturation.

This textbook and associated materials bring an overview of the healthcare supply chain through the elements of the supply chain in the first five chapters, the operational aspects in Chapters 6 through 10 and then strategic aspects in Chapters 11 through 13. Chapter 14 wraps the discussion with integration of the supply chain with the clinical delivery of care. The intent is to provide a sound basis of knowledge for students and early careerists so that healthcare supply-chain improvements can be achieved for the mutual benefit of the healthcare industry.

The concept of the Value Chain by Porter introduces the healthcare supply chain in the first part of the textbook, Chapters 1 through 5, and is reinforced with learning aids such as "Follow the Cotton Ball" and a student's perspective on each chapter in a "Sarah Says" segment. The method called Focused Content Cycling has been used to establish a foundation, called the elements in part one (Chapters 1–5), of concepts, approaches, and tools then is further built upon and explored in the operational section of the text (Chapters 6–10 as part two). Part three, Chapters 11 through 13, explores strategic concepts before Chapter 14 brings an integration to the text in the interface between the supply chain and the clinical operations of care. In addition, Chapters 9 and 10 add leadership and management concepts, topics, and applications to the operational part of the text. Supplements, presentation material, journal items, assignments (for most chapters), and test banks augment each chapter of the text.

The authors have considerable (over 60 years' combined) academic, healthcare delivery, supply-chain, and managed-care experience, and have designed this textbook as part of a learning system for enhanced mastery of the healthcare supply chain. We wish you well in your journey!

THE HEALTHCARE SUPPLY CHAIN

LEARNING OBJECTIVES

1. Outline and explain the concept of a supply chain and supply chain management.
2. Discuss and give examples of categories involved in the healthcare supply chain.
3. Explain the concept of the Value Chain.
4. Distinguish the functional areas of the Value Chain in the healthcare supply chain.
5. "Follow the Cotton Ball" – Relate the processing of cotton into a medical/surgical supply item to the functional areas of the healthcare supply chain.
6. Consider the benefits of improved healthcare supply chain management.

Introduction

This chapter presents the basics of the healthcare supply chain. Using the Value Chain model as a structure, the healthcare supply chain is presented by functional areas to provide a foundation for the rest of the textbook. First, we will start with the concept of the supply chain and supply chain management specific to the healthcare industry.

The Supply Chain and Supply Chain Management

While the term "supply chain management" (SCM) may be a new term for you, it can trace its roots back at least thirty years. It was not until the 1990s that SCM captured the attention of most executives in the business community, and another decade till some of the key concepts started to be seen in healthcare.

Yet SCM really is not a new concept. From the beginning of time, people have thought about and used two key components of SCM, logistics and transportation, in their lives. Farmers looked for ways to store their produce and take them to market. Ships sailed to all parts of the world trading spices, silk, cotton, coffee, and other goods. Even military campaigns depended on the success or failure of logistics and transportation.

The modern supply chain has its roots in the industrial revolution during the 1800s. One of the

> Supply chain management is the integration of the flows of products, information, services, and finances from the point of origin to the final customer.

first examples of supply chain commonly cited is the Ford Motor Company, which introduced the Model T in 1908. To increase production of the Model T, Henry Ford installed the first moving assembly line in 1913. This innovation was important for the development of the supply chain because, as materials were used more quickly, the ability to resupply required materials became more critical.

Supply chain management is the integration of the flows of products, information, services, and finances from the point of origin to the final customer. This includes the transport and storage of raw materials, work in progress, and finished goods from production to the point of usage. A supply chain is an interconnected network of people and organizations that are involved in the production of products and services. Every organization is part of a supply chain, whether they produce a product or a service.

Logistics is a more popular term, especially since UPS's "I Love Logistics" commercials hit the airways and YouTube. As defined by the Council of Supply Chain Management Professionals, logistics management "is that part of supply chain management that plans, implements, and controls the efficient, effective forward and reverse flow and storage of goods, services, and related information between the point of origin and the point of consumption in order to meet customers' requirements."[1] This encompasses procurement, raw materials, work in progress,

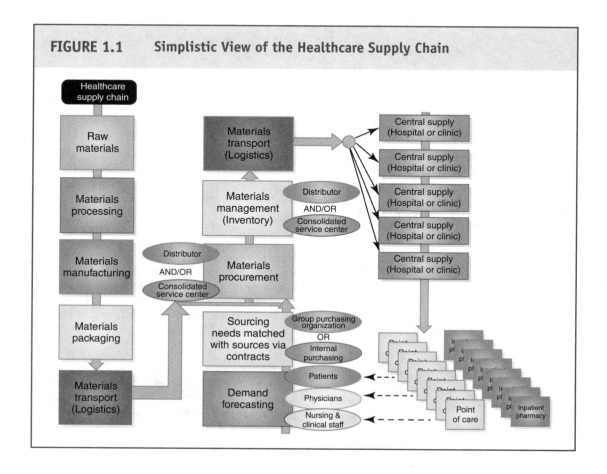

FIGURE 1.1   Simplistic View of the Healthcare Supply Chain

Walmart's Supply Chain

Managing Walmart's supply chain has provided several sustainable competitive advantages in

- Lower product costs;
- Reduced inventory / inventory carrying costs;
- Improved in-store selection; and
- Competitive pricing for consumers

Modified from "Walmart: Keys to Successful Supply Chain Management" by University Alliance. Found at http://www.usanfranonline.com/resources/supply-chain -management/walmart-keys-to-successful-supply-chain -management/#.VCr_ySlkF10.

---

warehousing, packaging, transportation, inventory management, inventory control, forecasting, and customer service. This includes the transport and storage of raw materials, work in progress, and finished goods from production to the point of usage. A supply chain is an interconnected network of people and organizations that are involved in the production of products and services. Logistics management is how one firm—or a customer and supplier—manage these flows to maximize efficiency and effectiveness. In contrast with logistics, supply chains are much broader and would include more than two companies in the movement and storage of goods and services. SCM integrates the major business functions and processes within and across multiple firms. Based on the definition below, all vendors, service providers and customers are links in the supply chain.[2] Every organization is part of a supply chain, whether it produces a product or a service.

In the healthcare sector, logistics is often referred to by an older name: materials management. The difference between materials management (logistics) and supply chain management is one of perspective and depth. Materials management in healthcare is the procurement, storage, inventory control, quality control, and operational management of supplies, pharmaceuticals, equipment, and other items used in the delivery of patient care or the management of the patient care system. Take, for instance, a suture, which is usually received, stored, and then pulled when needed for a patient. How much suture to order, where to keep it (operating room (OR), surgery, storeroom), what types of suture to order all fall in purchasing under the broader area of materials management. Purchasing could even work with a group-purchasing organization (GPO) in order to get a better price on the suture and other goods.

As important as these activities are, they are still within the domain of materials management (logistics) within the healthcare supply chain. The processes do not transcend multiple organizations; the decisions made are primarily within the domain of the firm or hospital. To be a true supply chain process, the hospital, the GPO, and the manufacturer of the suture would all work together to better understand how much suture is being sold, when it is being sold, where and how it should be stored, etc. In some cases the doctors at the hospital could provide feedback on the performance of the suture and collaborate on developing new products to better meet patient needs. This collaboration, coordination, and communication are critical to successful, well-managed supply chains. SCM is critical to the healthcare sector.

How are Healthcare Supply Chains Different?

Healthcare supply chains have similarities and differences from other industries, yet it is these differences that significantly impact the cost and delivery of care to the patient. Healthcare supply chains face specific challenges not present in many commercial supply chains. In the healthcare supply chain, these statements are generally true:

- "Providers control a very small portion of the cost of products used in their facilities;
- Providers have very little control or impact on the quality of supply service; and
- Providers believe that the supply chain is a necessary evil and does not play a significant role in the quality of patient care."[3]

"Supply Chain Management (SCM) encompasses the planning and management of all activities involved in sourcing and procurement, conversion, and all logistics management activities. This includes coordination and collaboration with channel partners such as: suppliers, intermediaries, third-party providers, and customers. SCM drives coordination of processes and activities with and across marketing, sales, product design, finance, operations, and information technology. In essence, supply chain management integrates supply and demand management within and across companies."

Modified from http://cscmp.org/sites/default/files/user_uploads/resources/downloads/glossary-. Page 187. Definitions compiled by Kate Vitasek. www.scvisions.com

Four basic differences between industry supply chains and the healthcare supply chains are summarized in the following discussion.

First, the consequences of failure are very different. Failure to deliver a can of beans to the grocery store does not leave the lasting consequence of a failure in a facility that could result in the loss of life. As a medical device manufacturer noted in an interview, if FedEx did not get a delivery right, someone might not get their Victoria's Secret order on time; if FedEx did not ship the right product on time to a hospital, a patient could die. This consequences of a failure leads to more inventory, premium levels of transportation, and, ultimately, higher costs.

Second, the healthcare industry faces unprecedented regulation. Physicians, nurses, and other workers are examined and certified as to their qualifications. Surgical equipment and medical devices used face similar tests and trials before being adopted. According to a recent Forbes article, bringing a new drug to the market can cost in excess of $4 billion dollars. If you take into account all of the drugs that do not make it, the number balloons to $11 billion dollars.[4] No other industry spends as much on research and development (R&D).

Third, the healthcare industry's supply chains have greater levels of variation. That is, some product and service flows are relatively simple to manage. An example of this, for instance, is food services or laundry services. Others, like surgical

equipment or medical or diagnostic imaging, are much more complex. Logistics managers in other industries would not face the same degree of variation in their supply chains.

How are healthcare supply chains different from other supply chains?

1. Consequences of failure.
2. Unprecedented regulation.
3. Variation in demand for supplies.
4. Many assets utilized are not under the direct control of the hospital.

Finally, many of the assets utilized in the delivery of a service by a hospital are not directly controlled by the hospital. Hospitals provide privileges to physicians and surgeons to operate on patients at their hospital. In the past, the surgeon was not an employee of the hospital and could not have a financial stake in the profitability of the hospital. If there were two hospitals in the area, the surgeon could hold privileges in both and operate in both. Revenue for the hospital was derived from the use of the operating suite, nurses, number of days the patient stayed at the hospital, etc. Surgeons schedule a time when they want to operate, regardless of the cost to the hospital. This scheduling could impact the overall capacity utilization of the facility, increasing costs for the hospital. While the hospital and its administrators can make suggestions as to when surgeons may want to schedule their operations, it is imperative that the hospital keep the surgeons as happy as possible. After all, surgeons drive revenue to the facility.

What are some of the consequences of these differences? If running out of a product could harm a patient or lead to a fatality, hospitals will err on having too much inventory on hand. This means costs will go up, especially the cost of holding additional safety stock. This does not mean that there is not room for improvement; inventory levels should be realistic and take into account the high level of service available in the unforeseen event like a stock-out. Like other logistics managers in other industries, management of the supply chain is viewed as a support function; more progressive firms view their supply chains as a means of creating a strategic advantage.

Because of the complexity and variety of supply chains utilized in healthcare purchasing, healthcare is significantly different from other industries. In healthcare, purchasing is typically dependent on GPOs. A GPO is an entity that is formed by its members to leverage their combined purchasing power to obtain discounts from its vendors. Forming a partnership with a supplier instead of working with a GPO to purchase goods directly is not common in healthcare. In other sectors, group purchasing is not used, and it is common for partnerships to form between suppliers and customers.

Finally, these challenges encourage the use of metrics to evaluate performance. However, in healthcare, organizations are usually benchmarked against their peers, whereas, in other industries, benchmarks and best practices are compared regardless of industry. For instance, a bank may study a retailer to benchmark and measure customer service. In addition, other industries use scorecards and other tools to manage supplier performance. Process improvement such as lean, six sigma, lean six sigma, SCOR, and other tools are commonplace.

The leading professional association, the Association for Healthcare Resource and Materials Management, or AHRMM, lists common functions that purchasing traditionally controls or participates in as follows:

- Budgeting.
- Inventory replenishment.
- Capital evaluation and selection.
- Negotiating.
- Maintenance of the materials management information system (MMIS).
- Product utilization review and value analysis.
- Maintenance of the vendor relationships in the organization.
- Monitoring the product selection process to assure selection is competitive.
- Coordinating with finance to insure procured products and equipment are reimbursable.
- Providing information to end users regarding product utilization, costs, and alternative products.[5]

What does that mean? Medical and surgical supplies, as well as pharmaceuticals and equipment, are the "products" and "technologies" that enable the delivery of healthcare services. These products and technologies, coupled with clinician knowledge and expertise, provide efficacious services to patients who need or demand care. **Figure 1.2** is an example of the "technologies" associated with material management. If a loved one were to have a procedure in that operating suite, how would you want it "supplied?"

The healthcare supply chain is a vital component of the healthcare Value Chain concept in the delivery of healthcare services. The healthcare supply chain is comprised of several elements: medical and surgical supplies (sutures, gauze, cotton balls, and syringes, sometimes called "Med/Surg"); pharmaceuticals (medicinal and biological treatments such as tablets, pills, injections, and the like, called "pharma"); equipment used in healthcare services; linen services (scrubs, lab coats, bed items, towels, etc.); contracts for services (such as housekeeping); and facilities (such as maintenance of buildings and areas and gas services such as liquid oxygen). In addition, the healthcare supply chain provides several overarching functions as

---

FIGURE 1.2   Technologies supported by the supply chain; stent, pacemaker and pharmaceuticals

  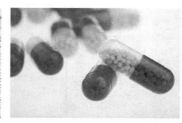

© hywards/Shutterstock, © Swapan Photography/Shutterstock, © Tiplyashin Anatoly/Shutterstock

---

The supply chain integrates with the healthcare provider to diagnose, treat, and care for a patient; take either the supply chain or the provider of care out of the equation and healthcare is significantly less effective, less efficient, and less efficacious. Patient safety, cost of care, quality of care, and access to care are intimately connected to the healthcare supply chain.

part of the Value Chain system: sourcing, moving, storing, and dispensing. Providing the right item at the right time, at the right place, and with quality into healthcare providers' able hands is the focus of the healthcare supply chain. Simply put, the healthcare supply chain plays a critical role in the production of healthcare services.

Why is Supply Chain Management Important in Healthcare?

Healthcare is the diagnosing, treating, caring, and supporting of patients that need services for illness, injury, disability, and for services focused at the prevention of illness, injury, and disability.[6] Healthcare reduces or eliminates pain and suffering, improves the quality of individual life, increases the health status of communities, and enhances productivity in those communities. Healthcare, as a continuum, starts with self-care and prevention and continues to primary care, secondary care, tertiary care, rehabilitative care, long-term care, and to hospice care; each component of the continuum of care has a supply chain aspect associated with that level of appropriate care. The technology of healthcare, supplies, pharmaceuticals, and equipment to diagnose, treat, care for, and support patients comes from the healthcare supply chain. The "technology of care" is coupled with the trained, experienced, credentialed, privileged, and compassionate healthcare providers within the industry to produce healthcare services and positive outcomes.

These outcomes and services would not be possible without the operation of the physical movement of goods through the healthcare supply chain. Lab coats and scrubs are needed for surgeons and nurses. Sheets are needed for the hospital bed. Scalpels and other devices, depending on the procedure, are needed in the operating room. Pain medication is needed post-op. The healthcare supply chain is concerned with a wide range of products, from bed pans, cotton balls, syringes, towels, medications, joints, prosthetics, to meals, contracts for services (such as housekeeping), and facilities (such as maintenance of buildings and areas and gas services such as liquid oxygen). The healthcare supply chain plays a large—and usually hidden—role in the production and delivery of healthcare services.

As the cost of medical supplies and devices continues to increase, the total expense associated with the supply chain increases as well. Currently, supply chain management is second only to labor in terms of expense for the average health system. It is estimated, that if the cost of supply chain management continues to increase at the current rate, this cost could exceed the cost of labor by 2022.[7] Technological advances are enabling organizations to more efficiently and consistently manage supply chain operations, billing practices, and compliance while providing flexibility for different processes within the system of care. "In all industries, not just healthcare, three out of four chief executive officers consider their supply chains to be essential to gaining competitive advantage within their markets."[8] Vance Moore, CEO of ROi (the supply chain entity within the Sisters of Mercy Health System based in St. Louis, Missouri) suggested that this trend could happen between 2020 and 2025.[9] Clearly, maximizing efficiency of the healthcare supply chain is an increasing concern amid increasing costs but with increasing quality.

Increased cost can best be understood by thinking about the total cost of ownership. In economics and accounting, the total cost of ownership is the complete cost of an item or procedure, including direct and indirect costs during the life of the product or service. An example of direct cost is the price a person pays for a printer. However, there are usually additional "hidden" costs associated with the purchase, which are called indirect costs. An example of an indirect cost in the case of the printer is the cost of the replacement ink cartridges. In healthcare, an example would be additional training for physicians or specialized storage needs of new medical devices or supply items.

The total cost of ownership can also impact how patients are treated. An example of this is stents used in percutaneous coronary intervention (PCI), a procedure used to treat narrowing of the coronary arteries in patients with coronary heart disease.

The first stent was implanted during a PCI procedure in the mid-1980s.[10] Because of the success of the procedure, the use of stents became more commonplace. In 2001, improved drug-eluting stents were introduced, which means that they are coated in a medication, or secrete medication, which reduces the risk of complications from the procedure that were associated with the older type of stent. The increased level of efficacy and effectiveness associated with drug-eluting stents (DES) comes at a price. PCI procedures done with DES cost about $2,500 more per procedure than they would have if basic, older-version stents were used.[11] The improvement in the quality of care is now accepted as the standard of care (that is, the level and type of care expected in the industry that produces outcomes of higher quality than before). And while the direct costs are higher, the total cost of ownership is much lower, because the care is better and fewer procedures have to be performed on the same patient.

Healthcare organizations have to be diligent when it comes to managing their supply chain, and they have to be especially mindful concerning the disruptions. The consequences of supply chain disruptions in healthcare organizations, be they weather related or errors in judgment, can prove deadly for patients. Because of the consequences associated with running out of items necessary for patient care, all hospitals attempt to maintain a reserve level of important items, called safety stock, in storage. This can add additional administrative costs to the delivery of care, leaving the hospital less able to invest monies in areas that would provide a service to the market. A streamlined supply chain can create a competitive advantage for an organization through the elimination of waste found in too much inventory or through even purchasing the wrong products. A competitive advantage is an attribute or process that outperforms competitors in a specific area. An example of a business that has competitive advantage because of its supply chain is Walmart. Can the healthcare supply chain provide the same competitive advantage for healthcare organizations and increase value to the delivery of care? The answer to both questions is yes, provided the health industry focuses on improving the supply chain.

Healthcare organizations, individually and as an industry, are lagging behind other industries in the areas of supply chain structure, coordination, management, and value creation. Industry leaders understand a simple reality: funds, information, services, and products are closely linked together. It is imperative for healthcare, using a team approach, to make improvements to the supply chain operations and to the management and information systems that drive their care delivery processes by providing the "technology of care" to providers of care.

An excerpt from a healthcare supply chain book written for senior healthcare executives describing today's healthcare supply chain can be found in the text box; recently completed situational assessments reveal similar findings.[12]

While not overly comprehensive this section should start to give you a new perspective as to the importance of the healthcare supply chain and some of the unique challenges it faces. Healthcare professionals can learn a lot from other industries, provided they are mindful of the regulatory environment surrounding them.

The Value Chain

Any discussion of logistics, transportation, or supply chain management would be incomplete without discussing the importance of creating value for the ultimate customer. Value is an underlying theme of the actions of logistics and supply chain managers. Firms that do not create value will not stay

---

"Today's Healthcare Supply Chain Characteristics

- *Multiple systems, multiple processes that lack cohesiveness and uniformity* – Many health systems, if not stand-alone facilities, use different materials management information systems and different processes across facilities and departments.
- *High distributor fees* – Most healthcare organizations spend hundreds of thousands of dollars, if not millions each year, with outside parties for supply (medical/surgical and pharmaceutical) distribution.
- *Service quality failures & service frequency did not match need* – Distributors commonly fill at 80% to 90% of the order. This causes a tremendous number of product shortages for clinicians each day. At times, distributors overfill orders, causing excessive stock on shelves and higher costs (for the overage and cost of storing the items). As for frequency, many healthcare organizations receive supplies based on distributors' schedules not based on clinical needs.
- *Wholesalers lead pharmacy processes* – The medications obtained, primarily from outside distributors /wholesalers, control the systems and processes for medication sourcing, ordering, receiving, and distribution.
- *Inconsistent management processes* – Many healthcare organizations manage the supply chain operation in different ways within the same facility. In some cases, each department seems to be a unique entity with regard to supply chain operations.
- *Limited usable data* – In many healthcare organizations, identical products are named differently, depending on facility and/or department. This reality limits the ability to aggregate data for decision making, volume purchasing, and bulk ordering (thus impacting the bottom line).
- *Many intermediaries or middle-men* – The majority of distributors service many customers and stock what sells for **them** best (not necessarily what you need or want). This means that most healthcare organizations get supplies, or are sourced, from many different distribution facilities to meet their needs or are directed to use what the distributor stocks in that particular service region."

Optimize your healthcare supply chain performance: a strategic approach by LEDLOW, GERALD R.; CORRY, ALLISON, pp. 2-4. Reproduced with permission of Health Administration Press

in business very long. Value is generated through a chain of actions or processes. The concept of a Value Chain was first introduced by Michael Porter in his 1985 book *Competitive Advantage: Creating and Sustaining Superior Performance*. The Value Chain concept originated in the idea that an organization is more than a random collection of individuals or functions performing different activities. The central idea is that a chain of specific activities, when done correctly, can add more value to an organization than the cost of each activity individually. The value added to the organization is in the form of competitive advantage. Because of the potential to generate a competitive advantage, the Value Chain can be used as a tool for strategic planning and process improvement.

The Value Chain categorizes activities as primary and support.[13] The primary activities include Inbound Logistics, Operations, Outbound Logistics, Marketing and Sales, and Service. The support activities include Infrastructure, Human Resource Management, Technology Development, and Procurement. The primary and support activities are listed in **Figure 1.3** below.[14]

Primary activities can be related to either the market or the product. Product-related activities are what enable the organization to add value to products and services. The product-related activities are service, operations, and inbound logistics. Services are what the organization offers after the primary product or service has been purchased. An example of a service provided is the warranty that comes with a new car. Operations include the activities related to the production of a product or the provisioning of a service. Examples of activities related to operations are assembly line maintenance in a manufacturing plant or providing patient care in a hospital. The final product-related area in the Value Chain is inbound logistics. Inbound logistics is an area that includes all activities related to sourcing, moving, and dispensing items used to provide a service or manufacture goods.[15]

In the healthcare Value Chain, inbound logistics is, or should be, supported through information systems, quality control, regulatory compliance, and management. The support of inbound logistics through information systems or technology development as a broader category enables healthcare

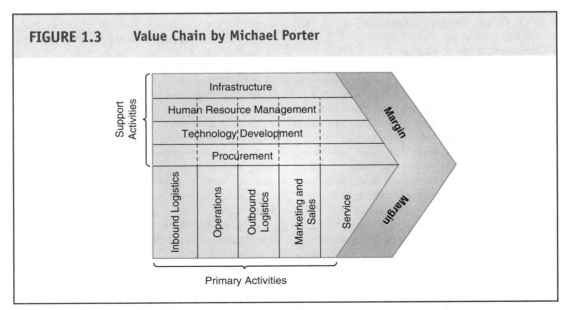

FIGURE 1.3   Value Chain by Michael Porter

organizations to comply with required inventory levels while minimizing warehouse space and maximizing patient treatment areas. Materials Management Information Systems (MMIS) will be presented in this textbook; MMIS is a component of Enterprise Resource Planning (ERP) systems used in many health organizations.

The remaining two primary activities—outbound logistics, marketing and sales—are considered to be market related. Market-related activities are what organizations do to transfer goods and services to customers. Marketing and sales are essential for completing the transfer of products and services to the customer. This is because they are how customers find out about the organization. Marketing and sales activities include pricing, advertising, selling, promoting, and other various functions. Proper marketing and sales activities are important because they ensure that individuals who visit a business to buy a product or receive a service will be interested in what the business provides. If a hospital were advertising a sale on new cars, the individuals who responded to the advertising would be interested in new cars, not medical care. Although, admittedly, this is an exaggerated example, even small inconsistences in advertising as to what the business is offering will lead to the loss of potential customers and, in this case, patients.

Outbound logistics focuses on order fulfillment to the customer once a service has been ordered or a product purchased.[16] In other industries, this could include the transfer of finished goods to a customer and could require transportation and distribution services after the order has been placed. In a hospital, outbound logistics occurs internally when a physician places an order for a procedure or test. In these cases, the patient may be transferred to the "distribution center" and have the X-ray or other procedure completed.

Support activities are those activities a firm does to help the organization gain a competitive advantage. These include human resources, infrastructure, procurement, and technology management.

Human resource management involves advocating for employees and maintaining a comfortable work environment. Business functions that are a part of human resource management include hiring, termination, employee development, and recognition. Maintaining staff with the proper skills is essential to all of the primary activities, although it is not itself a primary activity of the business.

Infrastructure, in terms of the Value Chain, includes public relations, finance, general management, and other such activities. If the infrastructure were not in place, then the business would not be able to move forward and increase value through the primary activities.[17]

Procurement is the planning and purchasing of components required to perform a service or create a product; this is sometimes referred to as "strategic sourcing" in other industries. Strategic sourcing is "an organized approach or method that allows a supply chain function to systematically work on spend areas or processes that can result in cost saving benefits."[18] The value added from procurement comes from using the proper or best sourcing business model to create the best value for both the supplier and the buyer.

In addition to procurement, technology management is playing an ever-increasing role in adding value to organizations. **Figure 1.4** shows some of the technology present in today's modern surgical suite. Value is added through technology primarily by supporting other business functions and making them more efficient. In healthcare, technology is starting to play a larger role through government regulation such as the electronic medical record (EMR) mandate. Under the EMR mandate, hospitals are required to show meaningful use of electronic medical records or face a penalty on their Medicare reimbursement.

Porter's Value Chain model is a helpful tool to better understand how a firm's competencies and activities can be used to gain a competitive advantage in the marketplace. This is accomplished by configuring the Value Chain to meet the strategic objectives of the organization. Firms normally compete using two strategies. One is to gain a cost advantage by reducing costs as much as possible and passing on those savings to their customers. Or companies can adopt a differentiation strategy, where the firm focuses on activities around their core competencies that they can do better than their competitors. Differentiation could be

FIGURE 1.4   **Typical Operating Suite**

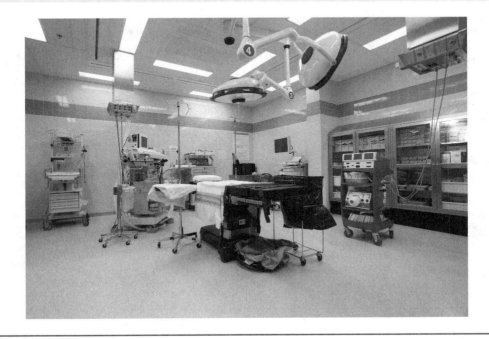

© Tyler Olson/Shutterstock

accomplished by scale, location, policies, learning, or integration, to name a few.[19]

Healthcare Value Chain

Logistics within the supply chain is a major component of the Value Chain in healthcare. Applying logistics and supply chain principles to gain efficiencies and analyzing and evaluating the inbound processes for improvement are vital to healthcare leaders given the complex regulatory environment and ever-squeezed reimbursements. While healthcare leaders and managers are aware of activities related to inbound logistics, typically this process is not optimized. The underutilization of inbound logistics is a huge opportunity for creating competitive advantage and building more value, efficiency, effectiveness, and contributing

to greater efficacy. Before discussing the specifics of the healthcare Value Chain, we need to define some of the common terminology associated with inbound logistics.

Moving is the component of a supply chain that deals with the transportation of products from their point of origin to the place where they are needed. There are important cost trade-offs made in this area; speed usually results in higher costs. A manager in moving asks "will shipping the product this way meet our service requirements?"

Storing is the storage of materials used in patient care. There are a multitude of variations for this from just-in-time inventory for noncritical goods to having many days of stock on hand for critical items (known as safety stock). While having more safety stock on hand than is needed may sound like a reasonable solution, it is costly.

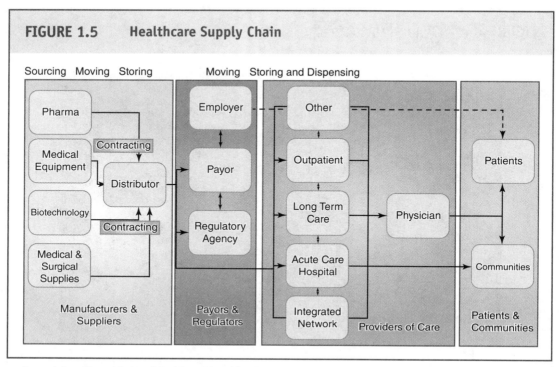

FIGURE 1.5   Healthcare Supply Chain

By permission of Harvard Business School Press. Adapted from Porter, M. E. & Teisberg, E. O. (2006). Redefining health care: Creating value based competition on results, pp. 203–213. Boston: Harvard Business School Press.

A manager in this area asks "What is the right amount of this item we should stock?"

Storing has come a long way. The technology exists to be able to trace products back to their origin, track recall notices, and keep a record of contract pricing.[20] Instituting data standards for information systems will enable hospitals to actively implement and measure success of "the Seven Rs."

1. Right product.
2. Right quantity.
3. Right condition.
4. Right place.
5. Right time.
6. Right customer/patient.
7. Right price.

One example of instituting data standards is the barcode, a technology that has been around for decades but whose adoption was resisted in healthcare.[21] As the healthcare supply chain increases in complexity, the apparent value in adopting and implementing inter-industry-standard techniques for supply chain management is becoming clear to healthcare organizations. The change in attitudes is accelerated by government regulatory changes that reward the use of electronic systems, resulting in quickening the adoption of data standards.[22]

Dispensing is the process of delivering the technology of care (supply chain items) to the points of the care process where those items are utilized efficaciously for patient diagnosis, treatment, and care. In a hospital, dispensing can be as simple as restocking supply cabinets on each floor or as complicated as dosing out pharmaceuticals in a liquid bench for inclusion in intravenous (IV) solutions to be given to a patient and insuring they are administered to the correct patient at the correct time.

As you can see, the management of inbound logistics impacts the operations areas of the healthcare organization such as medical and surgical patient areas. Inefficient management of inbound logistics can result in a reduced capacity to treat patients, as well as increased costs, and it can be fatal if the right items are not stocked. Even with the impact that inbound logistics and supply chain has on operations, there seems to be a lack of knowledge regarding supply chain management within healthcare today. Given the potential value of these improvements, why have they not been achieved across the industry?

A recent survey found that only 51% of hospitals have a senior supply chain leader on their executive team.[23] The study further identified several challenges to improving the supply chain in healthcare organizations. The study found there is significant underutilization of supply chain data standards, which results in a lack of information that creates ongoing inefficiencies across the entire supply chain. A lack of data standards means that information flows within and between parts of the supply chain can be delayed, miscommunicated, or lost. When the lack of data standards results in manual intervention in the process, costs and the potential for error increase. Second, it is still common for organizations to operate separate supply chains for individual departments and service lines so that economics of scope and scale cannot be achieved. In these cases, the various departments buy what they want from whomever they want, and usually at very different prices. This limits health organizations' ability to coordinate purchasing and manage supply chain costs through volume purchasing. The final finding of the study was that clinicians are typically loyal to particular products or brands and are resistant to change, even if a similar good is available for a reduced cost.[24] Applying the principles of the value chain, each of these situations can be improved in a way that is beneficial to the healthcare organization, the health industry, communities, and patients.

Products in the Healthcare Supply Chain

As we noted earlier, healthcare is unique as an industry because of the consequences, span of services, control of products, and number of stakeholders involved. The consequences for mistakes in healthcare are quite literally life and death. Mistakes commonly result in the injury or death of patients, and, as such, healthcare as an industry is very intolerant of mistakes. It is not just physician error that can have dire consequences in healthcare. Facility maintenance, power outages, natural disasters, and supply chain disruptions can also lead to serious consequences for patients. This leads healthcare organizations to create contingency plans in case of emergencies. Backup generators for power outages, emergency plans for natural disasters, taking extra care to ensure facility maintenance is done correctly, and having safety levels (excess quantities of commonly used supplies) and backup equipment in case of supply chain interruption are common remedies to these potential disasters.

Healthcare organizations provide many different services with relative levels of complexity. Such complexity creates a challenge in terms of the supply chain because different services typically require specialized equipment and supplies. Such a challenge is a common problem for industries that have a service-shop type of operation. However, hospitals and other healthcare organizations exemplify this situation. Basic commodity items, such as paper clips and copy paper, and clinical commodities, Band-Aids, gauze, and cotton balls are usually interchangeable among departments, as mentioned earlier. By centralizing many of these processes, fewer employees need to be involved in the ordering process, storage locations can be combined, and costs can be more easily controlled. Integration can also lead to better pricing on bulk purchases, improving quality control, and realizing economies of scope and scale that enable the health organization to invest in better clinical technology; these improvements further enhance competitive advantage and potentially improve patient care.

Generally speaking, there are four types of items commonly utilized in health organizations: commodities, clinical commodities, clinical staff preference items, and physician preference items (PPI). Physician preference items are usually high volume/dollar items.

Commodities are not used for patient care. They are items that are easily substituted with another brand or have different alternatives. An example of a commodity is printer paper. As long as the paper is of a standard size, it is likely no one will even notice if a different brand is ordered.

Clinical commodities are used for patient care and are items or devices common to every hospital, and they are needed to operate efficiently and effectively. As with commodities, there are several different brands and alternatives. Examples of clinical commodities are cotton balls or bandages.

Clinical staff can have a preference for some items used in the care of patients. These are called clinical staff preference items and can include things such as gloves or needles. While there may be a cheaper alternative available, it is usually advised to order the items that the clinical staff prefers or selects. Doing so may cost slightly more, but it will add value to the operations and assist with provider morale in the healthcare organization.

PPIs are things such as medical devices like replacement joints, drug-eluting stents, and diagnostic or treatment-oriented equipment. PPIs are actually bought by the hospital, but it is the physicians and surgeons that actually determine which device to use for a specific patient. Their decisions can be based on factors other than cost, such as past experience, relationship with the particular manufacturer's representative, or how well they believe the product will work for the patient. These items are usually highly specialized and costly; one study found that up to 61% of the total supply expenditures are for items which physicians have a strong preference.[25]

Physicians diagnose, treat, and care for patients in hospitals that give physicians "practice rights" at their facility; this is called privileging. Importantly, physicians in privileged practice create health services that serve patients and communities and allow revenue into the health organization in reimbursements. This process enables patient care and reimbursement. In many ways, physicians are both customers of the services provided by the hospital, as well as a supplier of patients to be served by the hospital. Failure to provide physicians with the PPIs they want will result in them taking their patients to a competing hospital. For this reason, the control of products is much more limited for healthcare organizations than what is typical for other businesses. Healthcare organizations typically provide the infrastructure, equipment, supplies, and other diagnostic and treatment components.

In addition to physicians, healthcare organizations have a variety of stakeholders which should be considered, if not involved, in the sourcing process. Major stakeholders in healthcare, in addition to physicians, include nurses, pharmacists, technicians, allied health workers, patients and their families, and the community. Clinicians and supply chain professionals work together in their respective areas to ensure that the needs of the patient are met. Clinicians express what is important to them and what they need to deliver quality care. Supply chain managers translate this critical information and determine how best to serve the clinicians and ultimately the patient.

It is important for healthcare professionals to understand the language of the supply chain, such as knowing what a packaging string means and knowing that processes in the supply chain are important for efficient, effective, and efficacious healthcare operations focused on patients and their improvement. The following is an example of the importance of understanding supply chain terms; can you see the importance?

A **packaging string** is a common and standard series of packaging of supply items. The American National Standards Institute (ANSI) sets packaging and volumetric standards.[26,27] With regard to a pharmaceutical item, "an example of a packaging string would be BOX/10 VIAL/10 ML. This string indicates that there are 10 milliliters (MLs) in a VIAL and 10 VIALS in a BOX."[28] With cotton balls, you could have 100 cotton balls in a package, 50 packages in a box, 25 boxes in a case and 20 cases to a pallet. So, basically, "packaging string is what determines how inventory is tracked and in what form it is purchased from the vendor."[29] It is important to know the medical product that is needed because a package, together with its associated costs, is far different from a case or a pallet. In addition, knowing the size of the item or product is important for storage and space considerations. That is why **volumetric tables** (based on ANSI Standards) are important to understand as well.[30] Volumetric tables basically count the total volume of the item in its package. For example, 1 square foot or 0.25 square feet is what you would see in the table based on the packaging (box, case, etc.).

Follow the Cotton Ball

For purposes of learning and illustration, the "Follow the Cotton Ball" theme will be utilized in the first two parts of the textbook. The cotton ball and cotton products in general are heavily used in healthcare services.

The cotton ball is commonly used in healthcare facilities and seems to be a simple product. However, the transformation from raw cotton fibers on the cotton plant to the finished product is a multistep process that involves many different businesses: farmers, transportation companies, raw material processing, intermediate vendors, manufacturers, wholesalers, and end users. Cotton is used in the provision of healthcare services tens of millions of times a year.

Native to tropical and subtropical areas of the world, cotton has been cultivated by man for centuries. Cotton fibers are spun into yarn or thread and used to make fabric; cotton fiber is the most widely used natural fiber cloth in clothing today, and it is critical to the care of patients. Yet how does it go from a cotton boll to a cotton ball?

Cotton bolls arrive at a cotton gin in either a trailer or a compact compressed module. The cotton boll is put in a dryer to remove excess moisture and is then cycled through a cleaner that removes twigs and leaves. The cotton gin itself uses the teeth of rotating saws to pull the fibers off the cotton seed. These fibers are then baled and sent to be bleached. Then the cotton is fed through a wide array of equipment, including feeders, openers, carders, and slitters. The cotton is then sterilized and packaged. Johnson & Johnson was a key innovator of creating sterile, absorbent cotton. Interestingly, the company made the decision not to patent these new developments so that they would be as widely available as possible to the medical profession because of the great help the new developments would be to surgeons and patients.[31]

FIGURE 1.6   Cotton Ready for Harvest

Courtesy of Sarah Ledlow

Benefits of Improved Healthcare Supply Chain Management

The supply chain integrates with the healthcare provider to diagnose, treat, and care for a patient; if you take either the supply chain or the provider of care out of the equation, healthcare is significantly less effective, less efficient, and less efficacious. Patient safety, cost of care, quality of care, and access to care are intimately connected to the healthcare supply chain.

Supply chain management is an important area of growth for healthcare organizations for several reasons; the most obvious being the cost associated with mismanagement of the supply chain. It is estimated that, in the United States, supply chain costs in healthcare are typically around 40–45% of the operating cost of the organization[32] and that the associated costs are likely to continue to increase. Other estimates suggest the healthcare supply chain is attributed to 30–35% of the annual operating costs of healthcare organizations.[33] Recent estimates suggest there may be as much as $20 billion ($30 billion with adjustments for inflation and utilization) in efficiencies gained by improving healthcare supply chain operations and management across the health industry.[34]

Steve Banker at *Logistics Viewpoints* writes: "The health care industry in the US is undergoing transformation driven by the Affordable Care Act (Obamacare) and the increasing impact of consumerism. Healthcare providers historically have had prepaid plans where the cost of care was paid up front and the more procedures a hospital did, the more they got paid. Consequently providers felt little need to practice even the basic tenets of supply chain management or even understand the total cost of particular procedures.

Now reimbursements are not only going down, they are becoming incentive based. If a hospital does a procedure and the patient is released but then has to be readmitted, the provider takes a major hit on what they are paid. That means the industry needs a lower cost structure even as they improve the quality of patient outcomes.

Typically, if the network has more than four hospitals, savings in procurement become a major opportunity. Historically, many integrated delivery networks ordered from large medical supply distributors like Cardinal Health or Owens & Minor. Those distributors bought in quantity, broke the bulk, delivered smaller quantities to their clients, and earned a 3-6 percent markup for their efforts.

"Now larger healthcare chains are building warehouses, automating them, ordering direct from the manufacturers, and eliminating the middle man markup."[35]

Opportunities clearly exist in the healthcare supply chain for improvement, resulting in better and more affordable patient care. By reading this book and learning more about the healthcare supply chain, you will be prepared to assist in this important industry effort.

In the United States, the healthcare industry is highly regulated by federal, state, and local governments because of the consequences of poor performance. An example of a recent government regulation is the Hospital Value-Based Purchasing program (VBP), which is associated with federal reimbursement, such as Medicare. VBP is designed to incentivize hospitals based on the quality of care with increased reimbursements and penalizing those hospitals who underperform with lower payments and reimbursements. One of the measures included in the VBP program is efficiency of care.[36] Through supply chain management, healthcare organizations are able to not only gain a competitive advantage but also to provide care more efficiently. In essence, government programs such as VBP are designed to increase what hospitals have to gain or lose based on performance in an effort to encourage process improvement.

Organization of this Textbook

The textbook is organized in three distinct yet integrated parts. Part One covers the basic elements of the healthcare supply chain in the first five chapters. Part Two focuses on operations and the integration of healthcare supply chain elements that were presented in Part One. In addition, Part Two focuses on flows of items and information and also introduces the essential function of management of the supply chain. Part Three presents strategies, models, and decision making concerning the healthcare supply chain. In each part, the essential components of the supply chain and integration with the Value Chain in healthcare are presented. The intent is to improve your ability to apply sound supply chain principles and make important supply chain decisions to increase the effectiveness, efficiency, and efficacy of the healthcare Value Chain through the supply chain, its operations, leadership, and management.

Progressing from basic elements in Part One to operations in Part Two to strategies in Part Three, the information builds upon itself in complexity and context. This is called focused content cycling; in this approach, the reader will see foundational concepts and topics early in the textbook (Part One); those topics are further expanded and in context in Part Two of the text and further integrated and built upon in Part Three of the textbook. In addition, the learning objectives, discussion questions, and exercises are constructed using Bloom's Taxonomy of the Cognitive Domain. In Bloom's model, early stages of knowledge and comprehension are established in the reader/learner in order to progress to the application, analysis, synthesis, and, lastly, evaluation stages. Each chapter is set up in Bloom's model to mirror the focused content cycling approach of the entire textbook. Each chapter ends with a "Statement from Sarah" (Sarah is a graduate student in the Masters of Healthcare Administration Program) to get a student's perspective, discussion questions, exercises, and a series of journal items to provide an avenue for additional mastery of healthcare supply chain material. We hope you learn much and improve the healthcare supply chain in your organization or future organization while providing efficient, effective, and efficacious care to your communities.

Summary

In this chapter, the healthcare supply chain was introduced as a vital component of the healthcare Value Chain concept in providing the "technology of care" in the delivery of healthcare services. Providing the right item, at the right time, at the right place, and with quality into healthcare providers' able hands is the focus of the supply chain. The healthcare supply chain comprises several elements: medical and surgical supplies (sutures, gauze, cotton balls, and syringes, sometimes called "Med/Surg"); pharmaceuticals (medicinal and biological treatments such as tablets, pills, and injections, called "pharma"); equipment used in healthcare services; linen services (scrubs, lab coats, bed items, towels, etc.); contracts for services (such as housekeeping); and facilities (such as maintenance of buildings and areas and gas services such as liquid oxygen). In addition, the healthcare supply chain provides several overarching functions as part of the Value Chain system: sourcing, moving, storing, and dispensing. Simply, the healthcare supply chain plays a large role in the production of healthcare services.

The potential for increased effectiveness, efficiency, and efficacy of the healthcare supply chain is great. As much as $20 billion in value could be achieved from improved supply chain operations and management. This starts with increasing the knowledge and understanding of the health industry and its workforce to achieve greater value within the system.

Sarah Says: A Student's Perspective

FIGURE 1.7   Sarah Storey

At the end of each chapter, you will find a summary called "Sarah Says." This is a summary about what you should be getting out of each chapter. If you missed something, then go back and reread that part of the chapter before you continue. The goal is to make sure you are on track, and reinforce the key concepts. I hope you find it helpful!

Sarah Says

Chapter one provides an overview of the healthcare supply chain. It expresses the need for improvement in the healthcare industry with regard to the supply chain while providing examples of these potential improvements. It is important to understand the concepts and operation of the healthcare supply chain as part of the Value Chain. Several terms, such as sourcing, acquiring, moving, storing, and dispensing, are important to learn and understand as they relate to healthcare specifically. The "Follow the Cotton Ball" theme is a great tool to help with the learning of how products move through the supply chain. Following this example will help connect the concepts later in the book and allow an understanding of how different concepts work simultaneously to create as efficient and efficacious supply chain as a whole.

Discussion Questions

1. Outline and explain the concept of a supply chain.
2. How is a healthcare supply chain different from many other types of supply chains?
3. Discuss and give examples of categories of items involved in and functions provided by the healthcare supply chain.
4. Relate, discuss, and provide an example where the Value Chain integrates with healthcare supply chain operations and management.
5. Distinguish the functional areas of the Value Chain in the healthcare supply chain.
6. Relate the processing of cotton into a medical/surgical supply item with the functional areas of the healthcare supply chain.
7. Evaluate the benefits of improved healthcare supply chain operations and management in terms of a healthcare organization, a patient, a community, and from the health industry standpoints.

Exercises

1. Outline the Healthcare Value Chain and identify important supply chain functions in the delivery of healthcare services.
2. Discuss healthcare supply chain item categories, provide examples, and identify stakeholders who would have significant preferences for those categorical items.
3. Relate the sequence of the healthcare supply chain to sourcing, acquiring, moving, storing, and dispensing cotton balls.
4. Distinguish the key concerns and incentives for manufacturers, distributors, and providers of care in sourcing and acquiring healthcare supply chain items.
5. Relate costs of supply chain to potential improvements in efficiency, effectiveness, and efficacy in the healthcare supply chain with examples of industry-wide change.
6. Evaluate the "value" of the healthcare supply chain to the healthcare delivery process.

Journal Items

Chapter 1 Journal

Define:

Supply chain management:

Strategic sourcing:

Dispensing:

Privileging:

PPIs:

Value Chain:

Value Chain analysis:

Answer the following questions in one to three sentences.

Answer: What are the functions of the healthcare supply chain?
Answer: What is similar and what is different between the healthcare supply chain and other industry supply chains?
Search: *Search items may give you great assistance in understanding the healthcare supply chain; provide the website/URL and provide a one paragraph summary of what you found.*

Strategic Market Initiative, AHRMM:

References

1. http://cscmp.org/sites/default/files/user_uploads/resources/downloads/glossary-2013.pdf

2. http://cscmp.org/sites/default/files/user_uploads/resources/downloads/glossary-2013.pdf

3. Michael McCurry, and Vance Moore. Sisters of Mercy Supply Chain Summit 2005, Resource Optimization and Innovation, a subsidiary of Sisters of Mercy Health System of Saint Louis, Missouri, Branson, MO, October 20–21.

4. http://www.forbes.com/sites/matthewherper/2012/02/10/the-truly-staggering-cost-of-inventing-new-drugs/

5. Danny Blount et al., *Materials Management Review Guide*, 4th ed., (Chicago: Association for Healthcare Resource & Materials Management of the American Hospital Association, 2012), 12.

6. World Health Organization, "Primary health care - World Health Organization," http://www.who.int/topics/primary_health_care/en/ (accessed 8 Oct. 2014)

7. Jasmine Pennic "5 Ways Supply Chain Can Reduce Rising Healthcare Costs." http://hitconsultant.net/2013/05/13/5-ways-supply-chain-can-reduce-rising-healthcare-costs/ (accessed 25 Aug. 2014).

8. Gerald Ledlow, Allison Corry, and Mark Cwiek, *Optimize Your Healthcare Supply Chain Performance: A Strategic Approach* (Chicago: Health Administration Press, 2007), 2.

9. Vance Moore, "Clinical Supply Chain," A presentation at the American College of Healthcare Executives National Congress, (Chicago, 2008)

10. Lisa T. Newsome et al., *History of Coronary Stents* (2010) http://www.apsf.org/newsletters/html/2007/winter/12_protocol.htm (accessed 2010)

11. Jason Ryan, David J. Cohen. Ryan, J. "Are Drug-Eluting Stents Cost-Effective?" *Circulation*. (2006). http://circ.ahajournals.org/content/114/16/1736.full.

12. Gerald Ledlow, Allison Corry, and Mark Cwiek, *Optimize Your Healthcare Supply Chain Performance: A Strategic Approach* (Chicago: Health Administration Press, 2007), 2–4.

13. Dagmar Recklies. *The Value Chain* (2011) http://www.fao.org/fileadmin/user_upload/fisheries/docs/ValueChain.pdf (accessed 25 Aug. 2014)

14. Dagmar Recklies. *The Value Chain*

15. Avijit Saha, *Mapping of Porter's value chain activities into business* (2011) http://www.managementexchange.com/hack/mapping-porter%E2%80%99s-value-chain-activities-business-functional-units (accessed 2 Sep. 2014).

16. Avijit Saha, *Mapping of Porter's value chain activities into business*

17. Avijit Saha, *Mapping of Porter's value chain activities into business*

18. Bonnie Keith et al., *Strategic Sourcing in the New Economy: Harnessing Sourcing Business Models in Modern Procurement* (Palgrave, 2015).

19. http://www.netmba.com/strategy/value-chain/ (accessed 13 Jun. 2015)

20. Lee Ann Jarousse, "Data standards in the supply chain." (2012). *H&HN: Hospitals & Health Networks* 86, no. 6 (2012), 41–43.

21. Lee Ann Jarousse, "Data standards in the supply chain."

22. Lee Ann Jarousse, "Data standards in the supply chain."

23. Lee Ann Jarousse, "Strategic Supply Chain Management." *H&Hn: Hospitals & Health Networks*, 85, no. 12 (2011), 39–43.

24. Lee Ann Jarousse, "Strategic Supply Chain Management."

25. Eugene S. Schneller, Larry R. Smeltzer, *Strategic Management of the Health Care Supply Chain* (San Francisco: Jossey-Bass, 2006)

26. http://webstore.ansi.org/?source=google&adgroup=ansi_standards&gclid=CLeojpDln8ECFRJp7Aod2CcAyw (accessed 9 Oct. 2014).

27. http://meditech2.com/prpha/materials/PHAxbASmmphainterface.pdf (accessed 9 Oct. 2014).

28. http://meditech2.com/prpha/materials/PHAxbASmmphainterface.pdf (accessed 9 Oct. 2014).

29. http://meditech2.com/prpha/materials/PHAxbASmmphainterface.pdf (accessed 9 Oct. 2014).

30. http://webstore.ansi.org/?source=google&adgroup=ansi_standards&gclid=CLeojpDln8ECFRJp7Aod2CcAyw (accessed 9 Oct. 2014).

31. RED CROSS® Notes, No. 4, August, 1897, (New Brunswick, NJ: Johnson & Johnson Laboratories, 1897), 2.

32. Jasmine Pennic, "5 Ways Supply Chain Can Reduce Rising Healthcare Costs." (2014) http://hitconsultant.net/2013/05/13/5-ways-supply-chain-can-reduce-rising-healthcare-costs/ (accessed 25 Aug. 2014).

33. Vance Moore, "Clinical Supply Chain," A presentation at the American College of Healthcare Executives National Congress, Chicago, 2008.

34. Gerald Ledlow, Allison Corry, and Mark Cwiek, *Optimize Your Healthcare Supply Chain Performance: A Strategic Approach* (Chicago: Health Administration Press, 2007), 2–5.

35. Steve Banker, "Leading Healthcare Systems Respond to Obamacare by Making Supply Chain a Critical Differentiator," *Logistics Viewpoints*, 13 October 2014, http://logisticsviewpoints.com/2014/10/13/leading-healthcare-systems-respond-to-obamacare-by-making-supply-chain-a-critical-differentiator/ (accessed 14 Jun. 2015).

36. Department of Health and Human Services. *Hospital Value-Based Purchasing Program* http://www.cms.gov/Outreach-and-Education/Medicare-Learning-Network-MLN/MLNProducts/downloads/Hospital_VBPurchasing_Fact_Sheet_ICN907664.pdf (accessed 1 Sep. 2014).

CHAPTER 2

ACQUIRING

1. Outline and explain the concept and process of sourcing in the healthcare supply chain.
2. Discuss and give examples of segmentation of supply chain items and the stakeholders involved with influence within each of those segments.
3. Relate, discuss, and provide an example where the Value Chain integrates with healthcare supply chain sourcing and purchasing.
4. Distinguish the functional areas of vendor management in the context of the request for proposal and/or quote and shipping terms.
5. Relate the sourcing of a medical/surgical item, such as cotton balls, to the identification codes and electronic data interchange catalogs and why those codes and catalogs are important.
6. Evaluate the benefits of improved sourcing with regard to outsourcing as compared to insourcing for healthcare supply chain operations and management in terms of stakeholders' perceptions and incentives and healthcare organization capabilities.

Introduction

Acquiring the "technology of care" within the healthcare supply chain is known as procurement. Procurement starts with determining a need for an item, forecasting demand, and then sourcing that item. Sourcing is finding the ability to acquire the needed item. Items in the procurement process include capital equipment such as robotic surgery units, medical devices such as pacemakers for the heart, pharmaceuticals, medical and surgical items, computer equipment, services, and the like. Sourcing is the first step in the procurement function. Coupled with purchasing, that is transacting business through purchase orders or contracts

with manufacturers, vendors and distributors, the function of sourcing is vital in that the evaluation of value and benefit are continuously required to acquire items for care delivery. Stakeholders play a significant role in this process to relative degrees determined by the type and cost of medical and surgical items, pharmaceuticals, medical devices, equipment, and service contracts; preferences those stakeholders have in the overall system of patient care delivery are valuable for the efficient, effective, and efficacious function of acquiring the "technology of care." In addition, the purchasing function is responsible for vendor selection, management and monitoring. In order to acquire supply chain items, healthcare organizations have an array of options that are available based on their missions, strategies, capabilities, and partnerships. The utilization of outsourcing, with group purchasing organizations (GPOs) and distributors, has a stable foundation in the health industry, however insourcing options are available based on resources and capabilities of the healthcare organization. Mixed models of outsourcing and insourcing are common considering the dynamic nature of the industry; for example, pharmaceuticals in the supply chain may be outsourced, while the medical and surgical items could be insourced with regard to contracting, storing, and logistics. This chapter focuses on these essential functions of acquiring supply chain items and their elements.

Procurement

The traditional methods healthcare organizations have used to conduct business transactions are economically unsustainable due to tighter reimbursement, focused on Value Based Purchasing, for healthcare services and increased costs of labor, equipment, and supplies. To set the context for the previous statement, let's consider reimbursement of federal programs. The Centers for Medicare and Medicaid Services (CMS) has raised the bar on quality and patient perception of care. The risk of total lost Medicare reimbursement could be as high as 5–7 % for those hospitals that are unable to measure up. Therefore, it is increasingly important for healthcare organizations everywhere to develop a laser focus on system-level clinical performance and patient experience improvement opportunities. Facilities will need the right tools and support to respond to the current requirements and prepare for even tougher ones in the future. In FY 2015 (discharges from October 1, 2014, to September 30, 2015) the Value-Based Purchasing performance score will be calculated based on four domain scores: Clinical Process of Care (20% weight), Patient Experience of Care – HCAHPS (30% weight), Patient Outcomes (30% weight) and the addition of the Efficiency domain (20% weight).[1] Hospitals account for nearly half

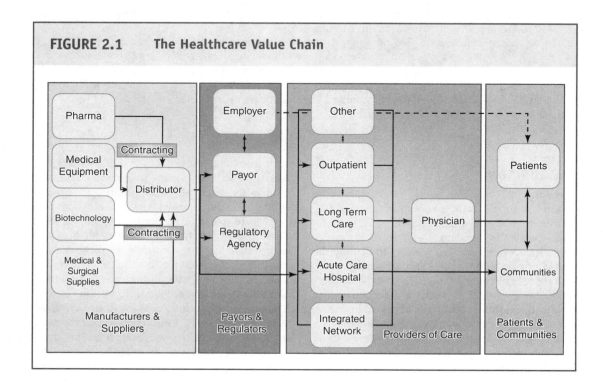

FIGURE 2.1   The Healthcare Value Chain

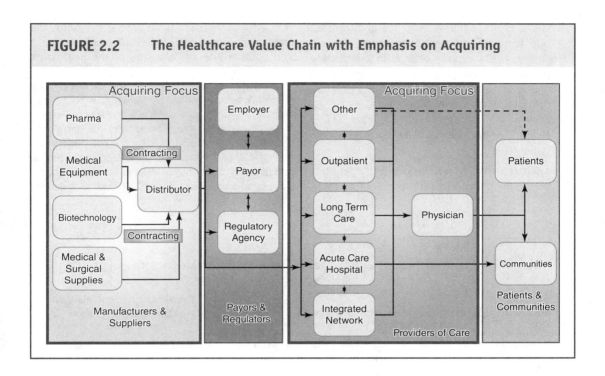

FIGURE 2.2   The Healthcare Value Chain with Emphasis on Acquiring

the cost of spending within a health system. One of the best practices for effectively lowering hospital costs quickly is improving procurement.[2] Considering the Healthcare Value Chain, depicted in figure 2.1, is the basis for the presentation of acquiring, the figure 2.2, for the healthcare supply chain.

The focus for the remainder of this chapter will be how acquiring the "technology of care" is accomplished. Acquiring is known as procurement.

Acquiring/ Procurement = Sourcing + Purchasing

Where

> Sourcing = Need and Vendor Assessment + Value Analysis
>
> Purchasing = Value Analysis + Business Transactions + Vendor Management

Procurement is a business activity which includes all the activities and processes to acquire goods and services.[3] Procurement is just as important in a service industry, like healthcare, as it is in a manufacturing business. Both types of businesses need certain items to continue to operate. In manufacturing, these items can be raw materials or components which are assembled into a new product. In a service business, equipment and tools used by the business to provide the service need to be procured. Understanding the perspectives and incentives of various stakeholders within the supply chain process, specifically considering procurement, is critically important to efficiently, effectively, and efficaciously utilize scarce resources of the healthcare organization. To make quality decisions about your healthcare organization's supply chain, it is important to understand the mission, process, goals, and incentives of these stakeholders: Manufacturers; distributors; group purchasing organizations (GPOs) transportation organizations; and healthcare organizations (also known as provider organizations) are presented below.

- Manufacturers of medical equipment, devices, pharmaceuticals, and supply items.
- Distributors of healthcare supply chain materials.

- GPOs. For an administrative fee and transaction fees charged to the healthcare organization, GPOs usually offer both contracting functions (negotiating volume-based agreements with discounts) and use two or more distributors for supply items.
- Distribution/Transportation/Logistics.
- Health System/Hospital Operations (Providers of Care).

To summarize the differences of the entities that physically "touch" (make, contract for, transport, or warehouse) supply items, the following table gives examples of the different incentives and goals of the stakeholders of the healthcare supply chain.

With the general understanding of stakeholder differences and similarities, knowing what type of item needs to be procured is an essential step in the procurement cycle. Segmenting the items that need to be purchased according to cost, preference, and clinical preference and utilization is a common practice. It is important to understand that clinicians, surgeons, physicians, nurses, clinical technicians,

TABLE 2.1   Healthcare Supply Chain Model Stakeholder Incentive Conflicts

Manufacturers want . . .	Distributors want . . .	Providers (Hospitals and Health Systems) want . . .
To reduce costs of production and distribution to enhance margins.	To store/carry the fewest number of profitable items as possible in the lowest quantities as possible.	Minimize their purchase points and reduce distribution fees.
To produce in large batch sizes to reduce production costs.	To be the collector of usage data so that they can sell it to the manufacturer (sold as Sales Tracing Reports—used to pay sales representatives and as decision support information).	Deal with people they can trust.
Ship their product to the fewest locations as possible.	Sell the most profitable products to the customer.	Minimize counter selling efforts of sales reps in using their departments.
Ship the product in pallet or truckload quantities.	Augment their offering with self-manufactured items that can be positioned for the bait and switch.	Reduce the number of items to store and manage (stock keeping units [SKUs]) and reduce inventory.
The customer to buy their entire product line exclusively.	High turn-over of their inventory.	Be innovative.
Real-time data on how and where their products are being used and in what quantities.	For their customers to use them as the "one-stop shop" for healthcare items and not compete with other distributors for same or similar items.	Obtain guarantees on service and product availability.

Data from McCurry, Michael & Moore, Vance (2005). Sisters of Mercy Supply Chain Summit 2005, Resource Optimization and Innovation, a subsidiary of Sisters of Mercy Health System of Saint Louis, Missouri, Branson, Missouri, October 20–21.

and clinical support staff are essential to provide care to patients, to bill for services, and to seek and receive reimbursement for those services. The healthcare supply chain is responsible to provide the 'technology of care' to these professional care providers in the most efficient, effective, and efficacious manner. For example, a much-lower-cost item that is essential to the care process that is not wanted, liked, or used by the clinical team will, in the end, be a financial, social, and morale problem. Working with the clinical team appropriately to determine the best set of "technology of care" items to purchase is vital to holistic healthcare supply chain operations. An overview of a segmentation method used by a large healthcare system for healthcare supply chain items is presented in the following section.

Healthcare Segmentation of Purchases[4]

Healthcare supply chain items could be identified and linked to one of the following four categories:

Basic Commodity Items (BCI)

Interchangeable with equivalent products with no measurable decrease in value to the end user. Products within this category are office supplies, plastic patient care items, etc. These items tend to have a low priority from a contracting perspective with high potential for bundled contracting. These items have potential to repackage and/or brand (royalty for organizational brand/logo) to reduce costs and touch points in supply chain.

Clinical Commodity Items (CCI)

Interchangeable with equivalent products that justify clinical evaluation due to intended use; most evaluation by nursing and clinical technician staff. Products within the category are needles, syringes, general wound care, etc. These items are targeted as low-to-medium items from a contracting perspective. These items have potential to repackage and/or brand (royalty for organizational brand/logo) to reduce costs and touch points in supply chain.

Clinical Preference Items (CPI)

Specialty products requiring clinical/physician/nurse input and a significant degree of evaluation.

Products types are custom packs, balloon catheters, wound closures, etc. Contracting efforts for these items are considered medium-to-high with high organizational benefit for compression to two or three vendors.

Physician Preference Items (PPI)

Highly specialized products selected as a result of a physician preference. These items are of high value. These item types are implants, cardiac interventional items, orthopedic implants, etc. Contracting efforts are high-to-very-high for these items. The organizational benefit for selection and compression to one-to-two vendors/manufacturers are critical to reducing supply chain costs.

All items should be evaluated from the transaction history and item master files, then cross-referenced by vendor master files (for contracts). In addition, items must be cross-referenced by manufacturer code in order to create an environment that allows for generic equivalent or substitute item identification for substitute assessment. Volume and expenditure evaluation (annual) is critical for contracting and partnering. Providing the basic definitions and information to the files mentioned, the following are provided as basic components: A) the supply item master file; B) the charge description master file; C) the vendor master file; and D) the transaction history file.

A. The supply item master file is a list (hard copy or electronic) of all items used in the delivery of care for a health organization that can be requested by healthcare services providers and managers. This file typically contains between 30,000 and 100,000 items. As a practical example, this would be similar to your grocery list of all items you need, would need, or have bought in the past year.

B. The charge description master file is a list of all prices for services (for example, Diagnosis-Related Groups [DRG][5], Healthcare Common Procedure Coding System [HCPCS][6], Common Procedural Terminology [CPT][7]) or goods that are provided to patients and that serve as the basis for billing. A practical example is the list of prices of all items and services you utilize in your home, office, or grocery store.

FIGURE 2.3 Sample Item Master File in a Spreadsheet View

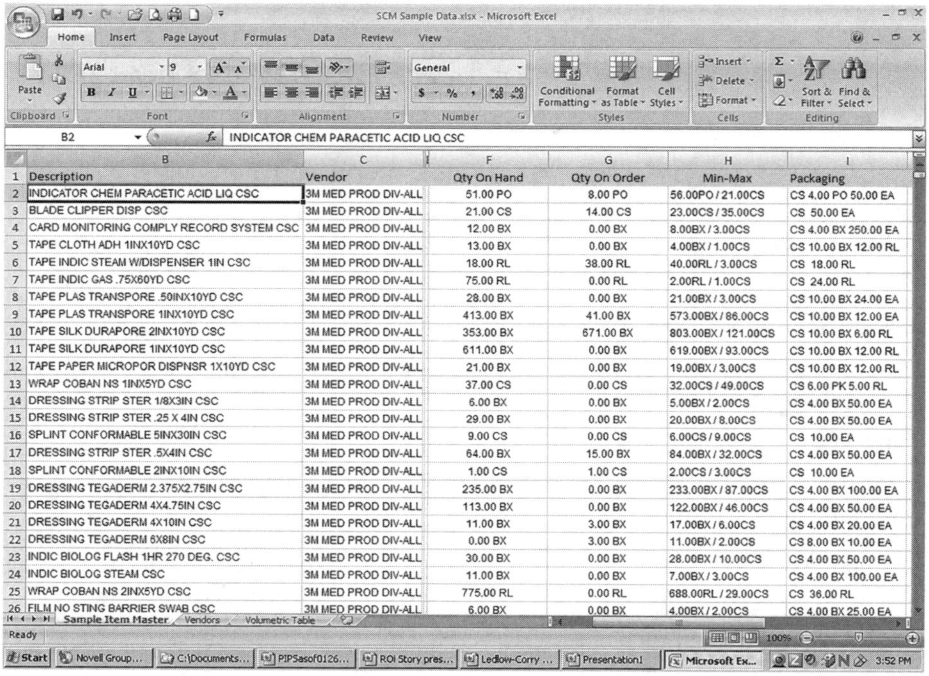

	Description	Vendor	Qty On Hand	Qty On Order	Min-Max	Packaging
2	INDICATOR CHEM PARACETIC ACID LIQ CSC	3M MED PROD DIV-ALL	51.00 PO	8.00 PO	56.00PO / 21.00CS	CS 4.00 PO 50.00 EA
3	BLADE CLIPPER DISP CSC	3M MED PROD DIV-ALL	21.00 CS	14.00 CS	23.00CS / 35.00CS	CS 50.00 EA
4	CARD MONITORING COMPLY RECORD SYSTEM CSC	3M MED PROD DIV-ALL	12.00 BX	0.00 BX	8.00BX / 3.00CS	CS 4.00 BX 250.00 EA
5	TAPE CLOTH ADH 1INX10YD CSC	3M MED PROD DIV-ALL	13.00 BX	0.00 BX	4.00BX / 1.00CS	CS 10.00 BX 12.00 RL
6	TAPE INDIC STEAM W/DISPENSER 1IN CSC	3M MED PROD DIV-ALL	18.00 RL	38.00 RL	40.00RL / 3.00CS	CS 18.00 RL
7	TAPE INDIC GAS .75X60YD CSC	3M MED PROD DIV-ALL	75.00 RL	0.00 RL	2.00RL / 1.00CS	CS 24.00 RL
8	TAPE PLAS TRANSPORE .50INX10YD CSC	3M MED PROD DIV-ALL	28.00 BX	0.00 BX	21.00BX / 3.00CS	CS 10.00 BX 24.00 EA
9	TAPE PLAS TRANSPORE 1INX10YD CSC	3M MED PROD DIV-ALL	413.00 BX	41.00 BX	573.00BX / 86.00CS	CS 10.00 BX 12.00 EA
10	TAPE SILK DURAPORE 2INX10YD CSC	3M MED PROD DIV-ALL	353.00 BX	671.00 BX	803.00BX / 121.00CS	CS 10.00 BX 6.00 RL
11	TAPE SILK DURAPORE 1INX10YD CSC	3M MED PROD DIV-ALL	611.00 BX	0.00 BX	619.00BX / 93.00CS	CS 10.00 BX 12.00 RL
12	TAPE PAPER MICROPOR DISPNSR 1X10YD CSC	3M MED PROD DIV-ALL	21.00 BX	0.00 BX	19.00BX / 3.00CS	CS 10.00 BX 12.00 RL
13	WRAP COBAN NS 1INX5YD CSC	3M MED PROD DIV-ALL	37.00 CS	0.00 CS	32.00CS / 49.00CS	CS 6.00 PK 5.00 RL
14	DRESSING STRIP STER 1/8X3IN CSC	3M MED PROD DIV-ALL	6.00 BX	0.00 BX	5.00BX / 2.00CS	CS 4.00 BX 50.00 EA
15	DRESSING STRIP STER .25 X 4IN CSC	3M MED PROD DIV-ALL	29.00 BX	0.00 BX	20.00BX / 8.00CS	CS 4.00 BX 50.00 EA
16	SPLINT CONFORMABLE 5INX30IN CSC	3M MED PROD DIV-ALL	9.00 CS	0.00 CS	6.00CS / 9.00CS	CS 10.00 EA
17	DRESSING STRIP STER .5X4IN CSC	3M MED PROD DIV-ALL	64.00 BX	15.00 BX	84.00BX / 32.00CS	CS 4.00 BX 50.00 EA
18	SPLINT CONFORMABLE 2INX10IN CSC	3M MED PROD DIV-ALL	1.00 CS	1.00 CS	2.00CS / 3.00CS	CS 10.00 EA
19	DRESSING TEGADERM 2.375X2.75IN CSC	3M MED PROD DIV-ALL	235.00 BX	0.00 BX	233.00BX / 87.00CS	CS 4.00 BX 100.00 EA
20	DRESSING TEGADERM 4X4.75IN CSC	3M MED PROD DIV-ALL	113.00 BX	0.00 BX	122.00BX / 46.00CS	CS 4.00 BX 50.00 EA
21	DRESSING TEGADERM 4X10IN CSC	3M MED PROD DIV-ALL	11.00 BX	3.00 BX	17.00BX / 6.00CS	CS 4.00 BX 20.00 EA
22	DRESSING TEGADERM 6X8IN CSC	3M MED PROD DIV-ALL	0.00 BX	3.00 BX	11.00BX / 2.00CS	CS 8.00 BX 10.00 EA
23	INDIC BIOLOG FLASH 1HR 270 DEG. CSC	3M MED PROD DIV-ALL	30.00 BX	0.00 BX	28.00BX / 10.00CS	CS 4.00 BX 50.00 EA
24	INDIC BIOLOG STEAM CSC	3M MED PROD DIV-ALL	11.00 BX	0.00 BX	7.00BX / 3.00CS	CS 4.00 BX 100.00 EA
25	WRAP COBAN NS 2INX5YD CSC	3M MED PROD DIV-ALL	775.00 RL	0.00 RL	688.00RL / 29.00CS	CS 36.00 RL
26	FILM NO STING BARRIER SWAB CSC	3M MED PROD DIV-ALL	6.00 BX	0.00 BX	4.00BX / 2.00CS	CS 4.00 BX 25.00 EA

C. The vendor master file is a list of all manufacturers or distributors (vendors) who provide the materials needed for the healthcare organization and contain the associated contract terms and prices for specific items. It typically contains from 250 to 600 different vendors/suppliers. As an example, this would be a list of all business and vendors you utilize in your home or office.

D. The transaction history file is a running log of all supply chain material transactions of the healthcare organization. As an example, this would be a list of your purchases such as those in your checkbook ledger.

Items must be identified on pricing agreements as "Contract Preferred" for primary vendor/manufacturer or "Contract Available" for backup contracts. Compliance targets must be established and included in the contract negotiations for added value in rebates or discounts for each item. Heavy scrutiny is required for Sole Source items. If deemed necessary, an item may also be linked to a third contract or a price quote from a third supplier.

Procurement in business is similar to an individual looking for the best price and quality (in essence, best value) of a particular product and then going to a certain store to purchase it. However, due to the wide range of items used in a business, the procurement process has evolved specialized systems and processes so that a business can achieve the best price on a product. The procurement process can be broken down into an eleven-step process, known as the procurement cycle.[8] The procurement cycle provides an overview of a generalized procurement process. Like any model, it describes an idealized sequence of events.

FIGURE 2.4   **Typical Item Master on a Healthcare Supply Chain Information System, Classes Tab**

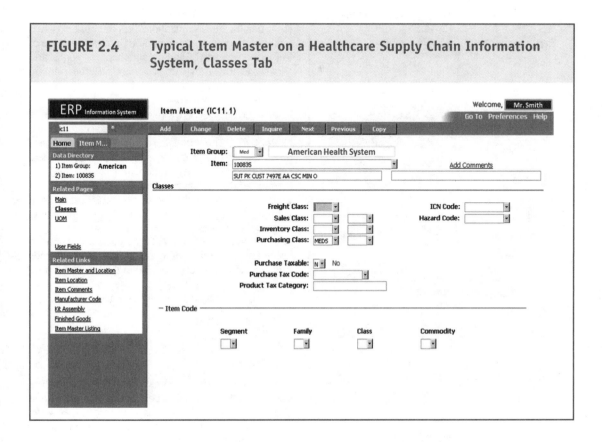

In reality, the procurement process for a particular organization may not contain all eleven steps; some may be combined or absent, but the general sequence of events remains the same.

1. Need: The first step in the procurement process is to identify the need. This can be the need to reorder standard inventory items or an ad hoc purchase.
2. Specify: The second step is to specify how much of the item is needed and what time it is needed.
3. Order or requisition: The order needs to be formally documented through the use of a purchase order for the item or items to be ordered. This is typically done in supply chain management software.
4. Financial authority: Before an order can be placed, authorization is typically required

to make the purchase. Depending on the order, this can be a multistep process or automatic.

5. Research suppliers: Orders that are repeated frequently typically have a set supplier or group of suppliers that the products are ordered from.[9] Special orders or orders for new items may need to be sourced, or researched, in order to insure the organization will receive the best possible price.
6. Choosing the supplier: During this phase the supplier is formally selected.
7. Establishing the terms and price to be paid: Through negotiation with the selected supplier, the price to be paid and terms of delivery are determined.
8. Placing the order with the supplier: Once the price and delivery terms are established, the order is placed with the supplier.

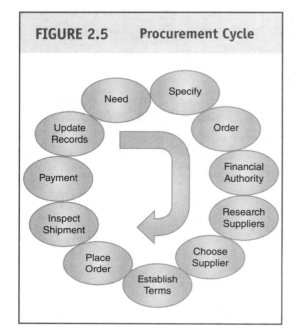

FIGURE 2.5   Procurement Cycle

9. Inspecting the shipment and receiving the order: Before accepting an order, a shipment is usually inspected to ensure it has the correct items and that they have arrived without damage per the terms of the order.
10. Approval and payment: Depending on how the order was negotiated, payment will typically happen within 30 days of when the goods are received.
11. Updating records: Updating records is typically done through a computer system. Before automation, orders were tracked in purchasing ledger that tracked the items, what was paid for them, and when the purchase occurred.[10]

The procurement cycle can have variations, depending on what is ordered within the industry, but the process remains relatively the same. A salient and central question, with regard to all procurement activities, is, how much does it cost?

Cost

In the last chapter, we mentioned that improving the procurement process will decrease the operating cost for a healthcare organization. Procurement has two major components, sourcing and purchasing. **Sourcing** is the process of finding suppliers for goods and services. "How much does it cost?" is the primary question sourcing professionals ask themselves. "How much does it cost?" is an important question to answer because once the total cost of an item is known, it is possible to search for more cost-effective alternatives. "The strategic sourcing process consists of a number of formal steps: identification of need, analysis, sourcing, negotiation and contracting, implementation, measurement and management."[11] Purchasing is actually transacting business with a vendor. "Purchasing is the... acquisition, contracting, and costing arm of the materials management role. It requires an understanding of the clinical areas and the special needs of each of those disciplines and blends the product selection, contracting, and monitoring of the value these products provide on a continuous basis."[12] "Purchasing involves four basic steps:

- Requisitioning;
- Sourcing;
- Negotiating; and
- Ordering."[13]

Total cost is an economic term referring to the sum of fixed and variable cost of an item. Total cost can be represented mathematically as $Tc = Fc + Vc$. In sourcing, the fixed cost is the price paid for a product, and the variable cost consists of all the other costs associated with an item. Examples of variable cost include shipping, associated taxes, storage, and spoilage or waste. It is important to consider variable cost when sourcing products because shipping or other hidden costs can quickly make a product that appeared to be a cheaper alternative much more expensive than the alternative with the higher fixed cost.

Importance: Why Does it Matter?

According to the Healthcare Supply Chain Association, formerly the Health Industry Group Purchasing Organization, hospitals purchase over $275 billion in supplies every year, including more than $30 billion in pharmaceuticals and $50 billion in equipment used in surgery and for medical procedures.[14] Additionally, many healthcare organizations today have an inefficient supply chain.[15] Additionally, the cost of equipment, supplies, and service contracts is important because it is one of the few expenses that a healthcare organization can fully control. Labor costs are dictated by the current labor market; the cost of utilities and maintenance, assuming best practices are used, is also out of the control of the typical healthcare organization.

Costs associated with procurement include, as mentioned in the last section, shipping, taxes, storage, and spoilage, as well as the actual cost of the product. Variable costs are not always avoidable; however, using proper techniques when sourcing products can minimize the risk when making a purchase. Costs can be minimized by finding alternative suppliers, using multiple sources, using "the next-best option," or by taking advantage of economies of scale through group purchasing organizations. When thinking about cost, it is also important to remember whom the products are being purchased for and how they will be used.

Stakeholders: Who Do You Buy for in the Healthcare Organization?

Items are procured for many groups within a healthcare organization, including clinicians, support staff, and facility maintenance. Each one of these groups has specific needs related to the items being purchased for them. Some products may be used infrequently, while others may be used daily. Some items have a government-mandated level, which must be kept on hand in case of emergency. Other items have multiple alternatives, which can be substituted; others are unique. Understanding the group and how they will use the items is critical to insuring that products are correctly sourced. Previously, the concept of supply chain item segmentation was presented. With segmentation and stakeholders preferences in mind, let's briefly overview the stakeholders involved in the sourcing and purchasing process.

Healthcare Supply Chain Stakeholders

The first group of stakeholders within the healthcare organization's supply chain are typically logistics and supply chain professionals. Depending on the size of the organization and their chosen method of managing their supply chain, the size of the supply chain workforce within an organization can vary. Leadership, management, and supervision in the healthcare supply chain have traditionally been confined to lower levels of management within a healthcare organization. In a recent study, it was found that fewer than 15% of United States supply chain managers are in strategic positions within their organization.[16] This creates a challenge for strategic sourcing and carrying out the overall purchasing strategy. Raising healthcare supply chain leadership to executive levels, such as in the C Suite (CEO, COO, CFO, CIO, CMO, and CNO), is in the best interest of the healthcare organization, given the implications the supply chain has to the core business of patient care.

Clinicians and the Supply Chain Workforce: Supply Chain Support of Care

As presented in overview previously, the supply chain supports direct patient care activities by ensuring that the items required to treat the patient are in stock and at the appropriate levels within the healthcare organization. In addition to standard orders, physicians may sometimes place orders for special items. These physician orders are referred to as physician purchase items or PPI. Due to economies of scale, controlling the price of PPI may be difficult for a company that manages their own supply chain. The costs associated with PPI increase every year as medical technology becomes more advanced. Another factor contributing to PPI cost is the service line within the healthcare organization. More specialized areas have the potential to have higher PPI and more frequent ad-hoc orders than service lines that perform more standard procedures.

Healthcare Supply Chain Professional Associations and Professional Groups

There are multiple professional associations and groups involved with supply chain sourcing, operations, and management. Four of the largest associations will be presented: AHRMM, HSCA, CSCMP, and WERC. Professional associations provide individual, organizational, and industry-level development, research, advocacy, and monitoring to the healthcare domain. These associations are a great resource for information, training, trends, and innovation. Each healthcare professional should be aware of and, where appropriate, should join one or more of these organizations for the improvement, development, and sustainment of efficient, effective, and efficacious healthcare supply chain operations and management. A brief overview of each association follows.

The Association for Healthcare Resource & Materials Management (AHRMM) is part of the American Hospital Association and is a professional organization for healthcare supply chain professionals.[17] The Healthcare Supply Chain Association (HSCA), formerly named the Health Industry Group Purchasing Association (HIGPA), is a trade association that represents group purchasing organizations, including for-profit, and not-for-profit corporations, purchasing groups, associations, multi-hospital systems, and healthcare provider alliances.[18] The Council of Supply Chain Management Professionals (CSCMP) is an organization which provides education, research, networking, and professional development for supply chain managers.[19] The Warehouse Education and Research Council (WERC) is a professional association for distribution professionals.[20] These organizations are vital to the growth, development, improvement, and sustainment of the healthcare supply chain.

Healthcare supply chain professionals commonly belong to one or more of these organizations because of the resources provided to members. Just as in any other professional field, it is important to keep up with industry developments, and professional organizations tend to aggregate advances within a field for easy availability and utilization. In essence, these associations compile information, research, advances, and innovations into knowledge for the industry.

Sourcing Models: Big Picture

There are multiple sourcing models for healthcare organizations to choose from based on the mission, strategies, resources, and capabilities of the organization. Healthcare organizations need to purchase goods from suppliers but must also distribute products internally. While it is possible to perform these two functions independently, hospitals typically use "co-sourcing" for both their internal and external sourcing, generally focused around the use of a GPO and other suppliers.[21] One of the advantages of co-sourcing is that the continuity of the supply chain is preserved. If different departments manage the internal and external supply chain for an organization, it creates a potential communication barrier that could lead to supply chain interruption.

While some businesses will handle all ordering and procurement internally, it is more common to outsource some aspects of the procurement process. After evaluation of capabilities and resources, outsourcing can provide a distinct competitive advantage to a healthcare organization that selects that model because it allows the organization to garner additional capabilities without the additional fixed costs traditionally associated with those services if provided internally (or insourced). In the case of outsourcing some or all of the supply chain, a healthcare organization is able to concentrate on activities related to its operation instead of diverting resources to contracting, distributing, or even procuring raw materials if manufacturing is embarked upon within the organization. Depending on the product being sourced, it may be preferable to have one or more suppliers for items to establish redundancy. In the case of healthcare organizations, there is another alternative to a completely self-managed supply chain, the GPO. The decision to outsource to a single supplier, to multi-source, or to join a GPO is central to an organization's supply chain operations and management strategy.

Differing Approaches of the Healthcare Supply Chain: Outsource or Insource?

There are multiple models, hybrids, and configurations within the healthcare supply chain throughout the industry. The key is finding what model, parts of models, or innovative approaches that work best for you and your organization today, right now, and over time. This involves understanding the key components of the models. In this, a very traditional or non-integrated model and a vertically integrated model are presented as extremes of a continuum of potential models. It is important to note that rarely does a healthcare entity use a pure version of either of the two models, but understanding the components are critical to knowing what options you have available to you for decision making and implementation in your efforts to improve. Before we overview the models, what is the role of the supply chain? Simply, in priority, the role is to

- Provide the healthcare organization products at the lowest cost possible.
- Deliver those products with timeliness, accuracy, and in sufficient quantities at lowest logistical cost possible.
- Understand patient and clinician needs, product trends, and the system of sourcing and use that information to plan for, manage, and provide products in the care delivery processes and across the business of care.
- Manage collateral operations as assigned.

The VHA report, Taking Control of Your Supply Chain: The Buck Starts Here[22], and Poirer and Quinn's work, "A Survey of Supply Chain Progress," in *Supply Chain Management Review*,[23] present a clear progression and steps to improve and mature the supply chain. The VHA Report suggests the progression from a functional to an integrated to an extended supply chain management system, and Poirer and Quinn describe steps in the maturation process. The ideas and realities presented are valuable, but only to leaders and their teams who understand the basic models of the supply chain and the factors and principles to achieve improvement. The factors and principles are presented later in this volume. The intent in this book is to provide a foundation of factors and principles for executive level action that enable the improvement and maturation of the healthcare supply chain and thus return greater value in the care delivery process through efficient use of resources, improved patient care and safety, and improved stakeholder satisfaction. First, the tradi-

tional or non-integrated model, then the vertically integrated (also called dis-intermediated) model are described.

Traditional (Outsourced) or Non-Integrated/Non-Intermediated (Insourced) Model

Considering the large supply chain operating expenditure, healthcare organizations have traditionally used a non-integrated supply chain model (called traditional or intermediated model) that emphasizes outsourcing. This model uses group purchasing organizations for contracting of manufactured items, distribution organizations, and transportation organizations that are outsourced. Once the supply items reach the hospital or health system, the internal distribution and management of supplies can be either outsourced or managed by internal labor (insourced). To grasp the full extent of the utilization of this or some form of this model, 98% of healthcare organizations use GPOs to some extent and a vast majority of hospitals rely on them heavily.[24] The traditional model's structure is illustrated in Figure 2.6.

The traditional model creates an environment where multiple entities, group purchasing, distribution and transportation organizations add cost to the supply chain for company profit. This is not necessarily a negative aspect of the model if the hospital or health system gets a quality supply item with quality service at a better price (thus lower cost) than they could achieve themselves. However, understanding that the model layers additional cost as a burden on the supply chain is important to know so that improved service, quality, and pricing can be analyzed and better decisions can be made given the realities of the model. Also, with the various intermediaries involved in this model, incentives are difficult to align to reduce supply chain item and operational costs.

The various separate entities/intermediaries conflict with each other based on dollar flow and processes that maximize their profit margins. This is how the free marketplace works; the intermediaries are not "bad" but merely attempting to maximize their profits. However, it is vital to understand

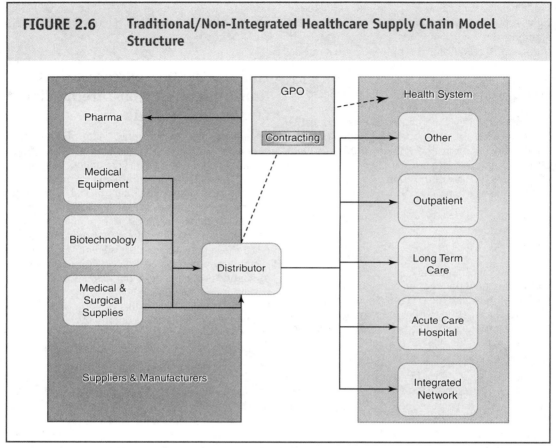

FIGURE 2.6   Traditional/Non-Integrated Healthcare Supply Chain Model Structure

Data from McCurry, Michael & Moore, Vance (2005). Sisters of Mercy Supply Chain Summit 2005, Resource Optimization and Innovation, a subsidiary of Sisters of Mercy Health System of Saint Louis, Missouri, Branson, Missouri, October 20–21.

that misaligned incentives exist in this model since that is where your negotiating power and internal business analyses depends.

Model Decisions

The traditional model's stakeholders clearly have differing incentives and goals within the overall healthcare supply chain. The importance of understanding the structure, cost allocation, and incentives within the traditional model is paramount to make wise decisions about outsourcing or insourcing, structure of the particular hospital or health system supply chain, and where to select different approaches to optimizing supply chain operations to achieve reduced costs, greater patient, physician, and clinical staff satisfaction, and overall improved patient care. So the traditional model, so embedded in healthcare, still allows many improvements to be achieved. The decision to insource or outsource components of the traditional model are situational, but evaluating your particular business case can lead to great improvements. Next, the antithesis or complete opposite model, the vertically integrated supply chain model, is presented.

Vertically Integrated or Dis-Intermediated Model (Insourced)

In contrast to the traditional or non-integrated healthcare supply chain is the vertically integrated supply chain, also called the dis-intermediated model. The vertically integrated model uses insourcing to a much greater extent than the traditional model. The vertically integrated model maintains an internal group purchasing, distribution, transportation, and hospital supply chain organization where the goals and work are coordinated to derive the greatest value for the organization. The below figure depicts the vertically integrated model's structure.

Differences in the vertically integrated model, compared to the traditional model, include the following:

- Eliminating external non-essential supply chain entities (GPOs and distributors).
- "Insourcing" traditional model to speed transition and capture traditional revenue streams.
- Increasing control and accountability for service, pricing, and quality.
- Establishing closer links to manufacturers.

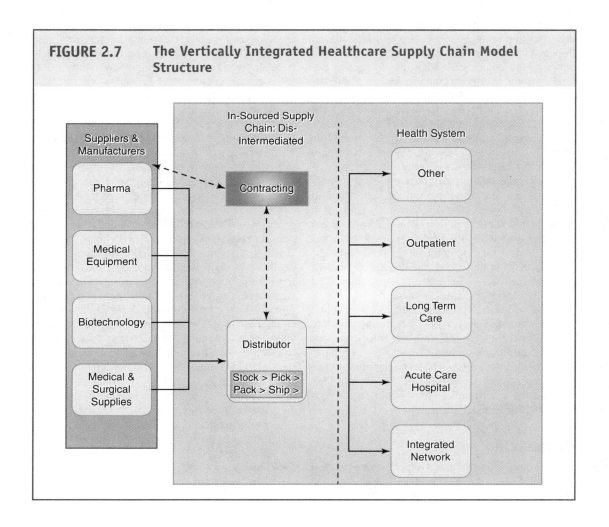

FIGURE 2.7   The Vertically Integrated Healthcare Supply Chain Model Structure

The vertically integrated model can achieve a net savings on supply cost of 15–20% and introduce a revenue stream, from sales tracing reports, of 1–5% (depending on manufacturer). Of course, the larger the operation, the greater the economies of scope and scale that would compete with the traditional model costs of outsourcing. Also, the ability to positively improve patient safety and physician and staff satisfaction are enhanced by improving service (timeliness and accuracy) and leveraging opportunities of compliance. Opportunities of compliance revolve around selecting one or two manufacturer service lines that represent high-priced and high-volume items (such as cardiac rhythm management supplies and implants) and leveraging better pricing due to volume and compliance; this also improves patient saftey (a surgeon who implants the same item a hundred times will be better [more efficiacious] than one using five different brands twenty times each) and clinician satisfaction (by being a decisive factor in the decision process). The vertically integrated model requires the healthcare organization to develop infrastructure, resource, and operate the supply chain. This includes creating and operating an internal group purchasing organization (consult federal regulations for legal status requirements such as for-profit status and external customers), a distribution system with warehousing capabilities such as a consolidated services center, and a transportation fleet over and above the typical in-house localized supply chain operation common in most hospitals. This decision is important but heavily dependent on resources available, internal capabilities, and leadership acceptance and advocacy.

Each option has benefits and risks associated with it, and one model may not be appropriate for all situations. If the sourcing model is not appropriate for the current business environment, it could lead to supply chain interruptions. The next sourcing model we will discuss, outsourcing, has increased dramatically in popularity across many industries in recent years.

Outsourcing

Outsourcing is contracting a project or process to a third party.[25] This model of sourcing has evolved over time, and there are two primary types of outsourcing: single and multi-sourcing. Single-sourcing models involve the outsourcing of purchasing to a single company. Multi-sourcing occurs when a company has multiple suppliers for a particular product or service.

The benefits of single sourcing include a reduction in product variation, no additional training required, and potential cost savings.[26] The reduction in product variation achieved from single sourcing may not be important for products such as paper or hand soap, but for more specialized items, such as surgical equipment or medical devices, standardization becomes important. The reduction in training time from single sourcing goes hand in hand with product standardization; if the items being ordered are all the same, then time and money are saved by avoiding relearning skills on a different product. Cost savings from outsourcing to a single supplier are achieved in a similar way to how a GPO saves cost, by increasing the quantity ordered.

The primary risks associated with single sourcing are failures at the supplier and greater power of the supplier.[27] Failures at the supplier result in inconsistency within the supplied product or late delivery of the product; both situations can be catastrophic in a healthcare environment. Product inconsistency can result in adverse results for patients, whereas late delivery can completely disrupt patient care. Greater supplier power means that an organization can potentially pay more because there is no competition between suppliers. This ability to make its customers pay more is referred to as supplier power. Outsourcing is the "hiring of external resources to perform functions formerly performed 'in house.' Outsourcing agreements are business partnerships where both the provider and receiver of the services share in the risks and benefits [in the relationship]."[28] Outsourcing has been used successfully in several health organizational functional areas, several in the supply chain:

- "Materials management and purchasing;
- Sterile processing;
- [Linen services];
- Printing;
- Laundry;
- Dietary services;
- Custodial services;
- Transportation;

- Waste management;
- Emergency room operations;
- Information services;
- Rehabilitation services;
- Laboratory services; and
- Pharmacy operations."[29]

Multi-Sourcing

As organizations become more complex, outsourcing procurement to a single source can become increasingly difficult. As such, it becomes more common to receive materials from multiple sources; this is referred to as multi-sourcing. The practice of multi-sourcing is also promoted by industry analysts to increase cost savings as well as operational and strategic risk reduction.[30] The successful adoption of multi-sourcing is dependent on the overall sourcing process, which we defined earlier as the process of finding suppliers for goods and services. More specifically, sourcing is a set of organizational practices that facilitate discovering new supply opportunities, evaluating suppliers, developing relationships, coordinating between suppliers, and changing levels of supplier commitment.[31] Multi-sourcing enables the company to choose from several vendors and benefit from competition between the vendors, leading to reduced cost.[32] Having multiple vendors also makes the supply chain more "agile" or adaptable, which reduces potential disruptions. There are potential downsides associated with multi-sourcing as well, including increased interdependence between organizations, an incentive structure that becomes formalized, and a need for alignment of goals and metrics.[33] This stands in contrast to a single-sourcing environment where a supplier may encounter moral-hazard issues related to being a sole supplier. The moral hazard occurs because formal contracts may not be possible due to intermediate steps within the sourcing process not always being directly verifiable with a single supplier. In multi-sourcing environments, intermediate steps can be indirectly verified through the actions of other vendors.[34]

Group Purchasing Organizations

The majority of hospitals are members of GPOs. GPOs are cooperative organizations through which hospitals combine their buying power to obtain better prices by purchasing in bulk. GPOs develop a package of negotiated contracts with one or more distributors and logistics/transportation organizations to provide healthcare organizations with all, most, much, or some of the "technology of care" the healthcare supply chain provides to the providers of care. The strategy adopted by the healthcare organization, to outsource or not (insource), should match the mission, vision, and capabilities of the entity.

The HSCA, formerly HIGPA, says that nearly 80% of hospitals and nursing homes purchase their supplies through a GPO.[35] The primary services a GPO provides to a healthcare organization are contract and price negotiation, but GPOs also provide product standardization, support for safety and quality improvement, revenue cycle management, and labor staffing.[36] It is estimated that GPOs saved hospitals over $36 billion in 2009. This cost savings was split among multiple activities:

- $8.5 billion in medical and surgical purchases.
- $6.8 billion on pharmaceuticals.
- $1.9 billion on supplies for cardiac procedures.
- $1.8 billion in savings on administrative costs.
- $840 million on orthopedic devices.[37]

These cost savings are perhaps why GPOs are so popular with hospitals. GPOs work to negotiate contracts with suppliers, distributors, and manufacturers. In contrast to outsourcing, once a group-purchasing contract has been created, the individual hospital determines which products are most appropriate and make the purchase.[38]

Twenty years ago, a study conducted by Arizona State University found that on average a GPO saved 13.43% on purchases and produced a 767% return on investment. Another one of the findings from this study was that cost savings was the principal reason for companies becoming involved with group purchasing.[39] These cost savings also carry over to the healthcare sector, where GPOs are estimated to save healthcare organizations between 10 and 15% on their total purchases.[40]

When an organization purchases an item, with the exception of special order items, it is typically under contract. The average time for these contracts has been measured to be just over 50 hours. An average GPO has been measured to

TABLE 2.2	Cost Avoidance with Group Purchasing Per Contract		

ACTIVITY	Hospital Self-Contracting Cost	Hospital Contracting Cost with GPO	Cost Avoidance	
Determine Product Requirements	$265	$174	$91	34%
Determine Product Usage	$251	$120	$131	52%
Department Meetings User Input	$208	$109	$99	48%
Access Supplier lists	$68	$20	$40	59%
BID or RFP Preparation	$379	$14	$365	96%
Send Bid or RFP	$40	$2	$38	95%
Respond Suppler Questions	$150	$48	$102	68%
Analyze Bid Proposal	$295	$101	$194	66%
Conduct Product Evaluation	$520	$450	$70	13%
Decision Product Selection	$180	$143	$37	21%
Implementation Contract	$633	$462	$171	27%
Record Retention	$25	$16	$9	36%
Monitor contract compliance	$70	$65	$5	7%
Monitor Market Competitiveness	$33	$26	$7	21%
Total	$3,116	$1,749	$1,367	44%

Reproduced from Schneller, E. (2012). The Value of Group Purchasing in the Health Care Supply Chain, Table 3, p. 7. Arizona State University, School of Health Administration and Policy. Retrieved from https://www.novationco.com/media/industryinfo/GroupPurchasing .pdf., from Value of Group Purchasing Case Studies

save a healthcare organization $1,367 on each new contract, in addition to savings associated with the actual purchase.[41]

Sourcing for Patient Care

Sourcing for patient care refers to sourcing items that will be used in direct patient care, such as medical supplies and surgical equipment. An example of sourcing for patient care in a modern healthcare environment is a physician order for a medication. This type of order is typically sourced internally. When a physician orders a drug, the order is reviewed by a pharmacist to ensure the order is for an appropriate type of medication and quantity. If the pharmacist approves the order, it is entered into the pharmacy order system and copied into the electronic medical record. The nurse sees the medication order and retrieves the medication from the storage system. Before administering the medication to the patient, the nurse checks the identity of the patient by scanning the barcode on the bracelet the patient received at admission. If it is the correct patient and the correct time, the nurse administers the medication. After the medication is administered, a notice is sent to the pharmacy to refill the medication storage system on the patient care floor, and the medical record is updated to show the patient received the medication.

Differences

Sourcing for patient care is different than sourcing other materials because of the consequences of making a mistake in direct patient care. Ordering the wrong paper or an order for light bulbs being delivered late is an inconvenience than may slow down operations until the order is corrected. Running out of an antibiotic or ordering the wrong medical device can lead to medical errors and the injury or death of the patient. In addition to the importance of medical items, many are also highly complex. PPI and pharmaceuticals can cost healthcare organizations millions of dollars a year. As medical care evolves, the cost of new PPI and pharmaceuticals continues to rise and has outpaced Medicare reimbursement by more than five times in the past 20 years.[42] These sourcing challenges combined with the potential cost savings of large orders are what drive healthcare organizations to outsource their sourcing or join forces in a GPO. Once the best sources are identified either though the GPO or some other sourcing method, the healthcare organization must decide which product to purchase and what method to use for purchasing. Depending on the healthcare supply

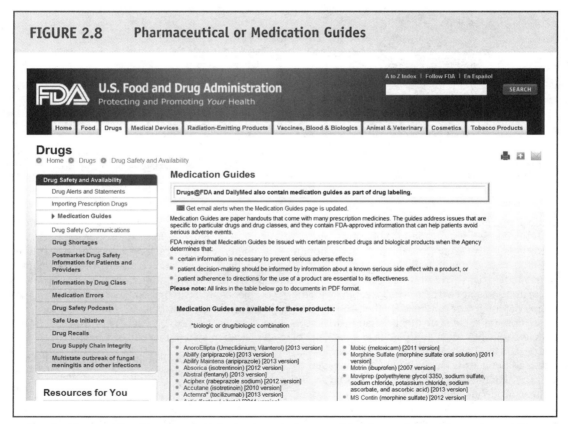

FIGURE 2.8   Pharmaceutical or Medication Guides

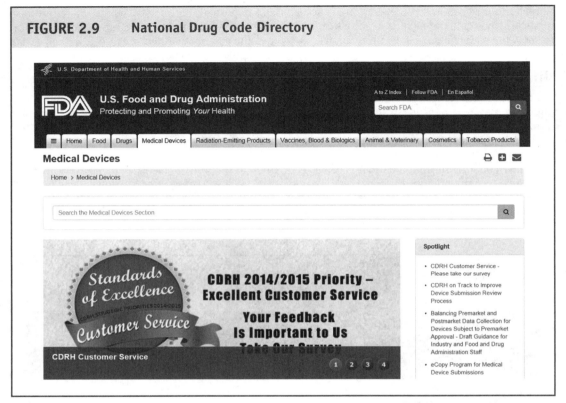

FIGURE 2.9   National Drug Code Directory

Reproduced from National Drug Code Directory http://www.fda.gov/Drugs/InformationOnDrugs/ucm142438.htm?source=govdelivery&utm_medium=email&utm_source=govdelivery, Retrieved September 24, 2014.

chain item, different information sources should be utilized when considering pharmaceuticals, medical/surgical supplies, devices, and equipment. Some example information sources are presented.

To find and source a cotton ball, keeping with the theme of "Follow the Cotton Ball," the UNSPSC code is an important element of information to know. How would you source and purchase a package of cotton balls? "The United Nations Standard Products and Services Code® (UNSPSC®), managed by GS1 US™ for the UN Development Program (UNDP), is an open, global, multi-sector standard for efficient, accurate classification of products and services. The UNSPSC system is an efficient, accurate, and flexible classification system for achieving company-wide visibility of spending analysis, as well as enabling

procurement to deliver on cost-effectiveness demands and allowing full exploitation of electronic commerce capabilities. Encompassing a five-level hierarchical classification code-set, UNSPSC enables expenditure analysis at grouping levels relevant to your needs. You can drill down or up to the code-set to see more or less detail as is necessary for business analysis. The UNSPSC offers a single global classification system that can be used for

- Company-wide visibility of spending analysis;
- Cost-effective procurement optimization; and
- Full exploitation of electronic commerce capabilities."[43]

Part of this task is to find the code for the Cotton Ball from the UNSPSC Code Set on page 1,330 of the January 2014 English Version Code Set:

FIGURE 2.10   Medical Devices

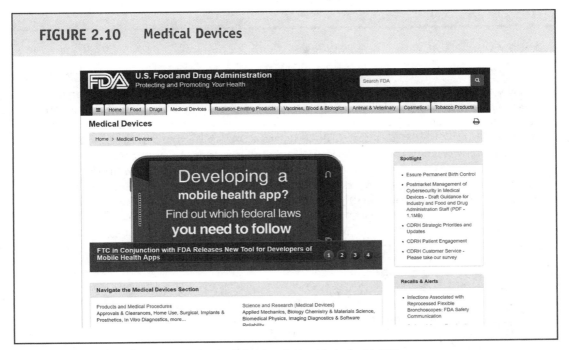

Reproduced from http://www.fda.gov/MedicalDevices/default.htm, Retrieved September 24, 2014.

TABLE 2.3   UNSPSC Code Set: Follow the Cotton Ball

Family: 42140000, Patient care and treatment products and supplies
Class: 42141500, Applicator swabs and **cotton balls**

Code for the Commodity	Commodity Title	Definition
42141501	**Cotton ball** or fiber	
42141502	Fiber tipped sticks	
42141503	Skin preparation wipes	Skin preparation wipes are a liquid, film-forming product that, upon application to intact skin, forms a protective interface that prepares skin attachment sites for drainage tubes, external catheters, surrounding ostomy sites, and adhesive dressings.

Data from http://www.gs1.se/globalassets/unspsc/unv151101.xlsx.

Follow the Cotton Ball

In addition, how items are packaged and specifically labeled is important to understand. A brief overview of GS1 labeling standards follows. GS1 uses a system of standards to promote efficiency amongst an organization's supply chains. GS1 has various systems of standards, which include the GS1 identification keys, GS1 barcodes, GS1 EPCglobal, GTIN, GDSN, and eCOM. One standard that is used in today's healthcare organizations is the GS1 barcode. GS1 barcodes are made up of subscript text with numerical, symbolic, and alphabetical data. The barcodes are read by barcode scanners that read the embedded code and use detailed software that presents product detail information such as the location of the product and helps inform users of exactly what the object's job is. Next, a few examples of what these barcodes actually look like under the GS1 standard.

The most updated barcode to date is the GS1 Data Matrix. The GS1 scanner that scans the barcodes to provide information to the organization looks exactly like a scanner that you would see in

FIGURE 2.11   GS1 Barcode Examples

(01) 0123456 7890128 BAR-CD

(01)01234567890128BAR-CD

01 123-4567

0123-4567

FIGURE 2.12   Example of the GTIN-14 Label

5 2826108992 87 7

your local grocery store, Wal-Mart, etc. Organizations can use barcodes to help them identify products that are low in stock and can inform them on which products have expired or are on the verge of expiring.

Another important GS1 standard that is important to healthcare organizations is the GTIN distribution rules for Healthcare. The GTIN, which stands for Global Trade Item Number, places barcodes on mainly pharmaceutical and medical devices and uses a barcode that is up to fourteen digits long. Organizations use this to look up product information and identify exactly what products the organization purchases and uses on a regular basis. To have this ability, organizations need to implement the software and train subordinates on the use of the GTIN and know how to input and interpret the data used. Below is an example of what a GTIN barcode looks like.

Using this standard could help the organization minimize wasteful spending while promoting efficiency among the organization and could provide exceptional care for their patients. For this standard to fully work to the best of its ability, the organization needs to open its communication lines and inform management teams, internal employers, and external employers on the GTIN standards to make the supply chain more efficient. The use of the GTIN can help healthcare organizations from running out of supplies such as sutures, bandages, first aid kits, over-the-counter pain relievers, and even injectable products. Through the use of the GTIN, organizations can reduce throwing away expired products and can be informed on which products are low and need to be ordered. Using both GS1 barcodes and GTIN can help organizations record and track products to help improve patient safety and efficiency amongst the supply chain side in the organization.

Other Information Sources

There are other sources of healthcare supply chain items and equipment information. One example is the Emergency Care Research Institute (ECRI). There are several organizations that provide detailed information about capital equipment (magnetic resonance imaging [MRI], robotic surgery equipment, hospital beds, etc.), supplies, and other procurement services; GPOs and distributors may have information available for these items as well. ECRI has a healthcare organization customer base of more than 5,000 organizations who utilize their services.[44] "Technology changes rapidly, and as a healthcare organization your patients' lives are impacted by the choices you make. Don't make capital equipment purchases on your own–work with an organization who understands your needs."[45] Information and evaluation sources such as ECRI are important to conduct sourcing and value analysis of supply items, equipment, and medical devices. From the ECRI webpage on healthcare supply evaluation and vendor selection, they state, "Is identifying suppliers and manufacturers to find the best products at an affordable price challenging? As a healthcare organization, you want to select single-use medical supplies that are quality products and also help your bottom-line."[46] There are commercial businesses that assist with the knowledge required to make appropriate sourcing and purchasing decisions.

Once a source, or multiple sources, for a healthcare supply chain item is known, the next consideration is the function of purchasing. Purchasing is where the transaction of business occurs. Purchasing, in general, is comprised of the business transaction for the purchase of healthcare supply chain items, vendor management, and a continuation of value analysis. Within the function of purchasing is determining how much to purchase – demand forecasting.

Demand Forecasting

Demand forecasting is simply determining how much of an item you need for future use. It is important to know the receiving and storage capability of your health organization (you do not want to order and receive more than you can handle, store, or distribute) and the amount of funds available (you do not want to spend more than you have to spend on that item). In addition, you need to know the order-ship time of the item since you may want to cover the time it will take to receive the item at your organization; this is especially true if the item is crucial or a physician or clinical high-preference item. There are several basic variables and methods for determining demand of an item. Time series methods, along with a brief discussion of safety levels, are provided. There are four basic variables you need to apply to a purchasing decision with regard to demand forecasting. Demand forecasting variables:[47]

1. Supply: the amount of product available.
2. Demand: overall market demand for product.
3. Product characteristics: product features that influence demand.
4. Competitive environment: actions of product suppliers in the market.

In addition, you will want to know the order-ship time (time it takes to receive the item after purchase/order). With that information, forecasting methods fall into four basic categories; time series will be presented as an overview. Forecasting methods:[48]

1. Qualitative: relies on a person's intuition of opinion.
2. Causal: assumes that demand is strongly related to certain factors.
3. Time series: based on historical demand patterns [including cyclic patterns].
4. Simulation: combines causal and time series methods.

From these variables, the appropriate methods are applied. It starts with understanding of demand and demand variation within your health organization for the particular supply chain item. "Knowledge of demand and demand variation [changes in demand for an item over time] within the system can enable improved demand forecasting, which, in turn, can allow inventory reductions and greater assurance that something will be available when needed. Bar coding and point-of-use [such as bar code scanner, RFID tag receivers, etc.] systems allow organizations to track when and how many supplies are being consumed, use that information to forecast demand organization-wide, and plan how to meet that demand in the most effective manner."[49] Many organizations utilize averaging (mean of several inputs) to estimate or forecast. Averaging assumes little-to-no variation so that changes in demand, such as growth or decline in a supply item over time, are not any more important than any other input; as in a simple moving average, all inputs are given equal weight or consideration. Where, F_t = forecast for the time period t (or the estimated/forecasted period of time in the future), D_{t-1} = value in the previous time period, and p = the number of time periods (#).

Simple Moving Average:

$$F_t = \frac{D_{t-1} + D_{t-2} + ... + D_{t-p}}{P}$$

So if monthly demand for a package of cotton balls over the past 6 months was: 12, 15, 21, 23, 25, and 30, the simple moving average is:

$$F_t = \frac{12 + 15 + 21 + 23 + 25 + 30}{6}$$

With $F_t = \frac{126}{6}$ or 21 packages of cotton balls.

Common software programs, such as Microsoft Excel ©, can assist in calculations.[50] Using a weighted moving average, inputs are given weights or more importance and influence in the calculation. Usually, more recent inputs are given higher weights or more influence in the calculation, where adding to the simple moving average formula, w_p = weight for time period p and $w_1 + w_2 + w_3 + ... + w_p = 1$. So if monthly demand is the same, expanding on the example, the formula for a weighted moving average would be

$$F_t = .05*12 + .05*15 + .15*21 + .2*23 + .25*25 + .3*30$$

$F_t = .6 + .75 + 3.15 + 4.6 + 6.25 + 9$ or 24.35 packages of cotton balls (in essence 25 packages). Clearly, just by allowing greater influence in data from more

recent months increased the forecast by 3.35 packages. Again, using common software programs, such as Microsoft Excel©, can greatly assist in forecasting.[51] The next method is Economic Order Quantity.

Economic Order Quantity[52, 53]

Another well-known and utilized method is called Economic Order Quantity or EOQ. This method calculates the most cost-effective amount to purchase at a time. Also, EOQ can be combined with a safety level for crucial items, so the health organization always has that item available. The formula is

$$EOQ = \sqrt{\frac{2UO}{hC}}$$

Where U = annual usage rate, O = ordering cost, C = cost per unit (each package, box, carton, etc.), and h = holding cost per year as a percentage of unit cost. An example would be, if an item, say a package of cotton balls, has an annual usage of 1,200, a fixed cost per order of $3.00, a unit cost of $2.50, and an annual holding cost of 20% per unit, the calculation is

$$EOQ = \sqrt{2 \times 1200 \times 3.00 / .2 \times 2.50} = \sqrt{7200 / .5}$$

$$= \sqrt{14,400}$$

Taking the square root = 120 packages of cotton balls to order. To add a simple safety-level method, determine the time it will take to receive the cotton ball packages order, say 1 week, and divide the annual usage by 52 weeks (52 weeks per year) for 1200/52 = 23.077 packages and rounding up = 24 packages. So, using this method, you would order 120 packages of cotton balls, and if you use a simple safety-level method with EOQ on this item, you would purchase 144 cotton ball packages.

Purchasing

Purchasing refers to the process of orders and receiving goods and services.[54] It is the final step in sourcing. "As a department within materials management, there are several functions that purchasing traditionally controls or participates in:

- Budgeting;
- Inventory Replenishment;
- Capital Evaluation and Selection;
- Negotiating;
- Maintenance of the Materials Management Information System (MMIS);
- Product Utilization Review and Value Analysis;
- Maintenance of the Vendor Relationships in the Organization;
- Monitoring the Product Selection Process to Assure Selection is Competitive;
- Coordinating with Finance to Insure Procured Products and Equipment are Reimbursable; and
- Providing Information to End Users Regarding Product Utilization, Costs, and Alternative Products."[55]

How these functions are performed in purchasing are decisions of the healthcare organization leadership and management. There are two types of products that a company buys: 1) direct or strategic materials that are needed to produce products or services the health organization "sells" to patients and customers; and 2) indirect or maintenance, repair and operational products and services a health organization consumes as part of operations.[56] There are several different methods to purchasing with the most common including supplier optimization, total quality methods, risk management, global sourcing, vendor development, and green purchasing.[57] These purchasing strategies are described in terms of the best-case scenario for each, while the best-case scenario may never be reached; it is the goal of each purchasing method to attain the best-case scenario. Supplier optimization requires the firm to select an optimal mix of vendors who provide the best product at the best price. Under supplier optimization, those suppliers who are not able to compete at a given level of service and quality are ignored. This is the most common purchasing strategy. Total Quality Methods (TQM) requires that a vendor provide an increasing quality of service with low or no errors in the fulfillment and service provided. This idea is based on process improvement methodology and utilizes

business tools such as Six Sigma and Lean Sigma; both are quality-improvement methods. Since purchasing's crucial element is the business transaction, it is important to understand that "key attributes of transactions are asset-specificity, uncertainty and frequency."[58] These key attributes link back to the demand-forecasting variables of supply (the amount of product available), demand (market demand for product), product characteristics (product features that influence demand), and the competitive environment (competitive environment and understanding the supply item of product).[59]

"As a purchasing manager, you and your department are responsible for the appropriate acquisition of goods, equipment, and services in your healthcare facility. The terms purchasing and procurement are sometimes used interchangeably; purchasing has been defined as one of the functions under procurement, along with expediting, sourcing, supplier quality, etc."[60] How purchasing is accomplished should be aligned with the mission and strategies of the healthcare organization. Regardless of purchasing approach, the patient population and community needs must be an important consideration. "The procurement and evaluation of products and equipment has to be tailored to these specific populations [based on patient care needs and types of patients, pediatrics to geriatrics]."[61] This is especially true given the federal regulatory environment in the health industry.

Given the patient engagement provisions of the Patient Protection and Affordable Care Act (PPACA) and the Internal Revenue Service (IRS), policy guidelines for not-for-profit status (most healthcare organizations, namely hospitals, are not-for-profit (NFP) or 501(c)(3) status organizations), community needs assessments and meeting those needs are paramount in recent industry operations. The IRS, in its oversight of NFP organizations with IRS Code 501(c)(3) status, has revised policy guidance. The guidance change reflects the requirement that NFP health organizations improve service and connection with the communities they serve. One major element is the requirement for NFP health organizations to conduct community health needs assessments, integrate findings of those assessments into the strategic decision making of the organization and to monitor effectiveness of community health needs initiatives. The organization will have to write and publish a fee assistance policy, a policy written for actions taken in emergency medical conditions, and perform a community needs assessment once every three years.[62] The IRS policy has implications for the supply chain in health organizations given that a third or more of annual operating expense is attributed to the supply chain for health organizations. Accrediting bodies such as the Joint Commission (for many hospitals, it is critical to be Joint Commission accredited to continue to seek federal program, such as Medicare, reimbursement). "The Joint Commission now includes a section for review on specific patient needs and how hospitals address these needs."[63] Thus risk management is also a concern given the inherent nature of healthcare delivery and the regulatory environment.

Risk management strategies that are operationalized in practice are necessary in supply-chain management. "Managing risk and uncertainty is one of the primary objectives of firms operating in a global environment."[64] This is also true of the purchasing function but becomes a strategy unto itself when a company purchases from suppliers with a substantially lower price who are at greater risk of incomplete or low order fulfillment rates. An example of a risk management strategy would be outsourcing manufacturing to a developing nation. While the labor costs will be substantially less, there is greater risk for supply-chain disruption due to the distance raw materials and finished products need to be transported. This example, while given for risk management, also has components of global sourcing. In global sourcing, companies view the world as one global market and seek out the cheapest vendors no matter where they are located; this is also referred to as globalization. Vendor development occurs when companies choose to work with their vendors through developing processes with them in order to enhance their business relationship and improve efficiency. This is common in situations where a company has chosen to go with a single sourcing model. If a vendor is unable to meet the required standards of the purchasing organization, the purchasing company may offer assistance with regard to improving the vendor's purchasing cycle

or aligning it more closely with their own to reduce supply-chain disruption. Green purchasing is not a new concept but has recently become more important in industries where it is possible and especially among governments. In green purchasing, the organization prioritizes the importance of recycling and purchasing products that have a low environmental impact. Regardless of what strategy is chosen, the goal of purchasing is to contribute to procurement best practices, maximize quality, minimize cost, and ensure that high-quality products are delivered on time.[65]

Vendor Selection and Management

Vendor management is a critical purchasing function as well. Purchasing verifies that a vendor can transact business (defined by the U.S. Office of the Inspector General) and monitors vendor performance with regard to order fulfillment, quality of product(s) and service(s), and pays attention to vendor delivery service terms achievement.[66] When selecting a vendor, the capabilities of that vendor must be understood and evaluated; this evaluation includes the value of the vendor's product or service with regard to quality, service levels, delivery terms, and methods and technical support.[67] "Three recent trends in purchasing and supply practices have further served to emphasize the importance of selecting the right supplier. First, the increased use of outsourcing has led to more firms spending a greater proportion of their total revenue on externally sourced goods and services, thereby increasing the impact of suppliers' performance on purchasing. Second, the trend towards supply base reduction has increased the impact that any given supplier is likely to have on a purchaser's performance. Third, and perhaps most important, the trend towards closer relationships between vendors and purchasers based on collaboration and cooperation increases the role and contribution of suppliers in the operations of the purchaser [buyer]."[68]

Monitoring vendor performance, regardless of direct purchasing (insourcing) from a manufacturer or GPO and/or distributor (outsourcing), is a continual element of vendor management. "Purchasing is the link for the clinical, financial, and administrative perspectives for the providers of the products and services; purchasing provides reports and guidance to product utilization and costs that maintain the hospital's [efficiency and] efficacy."[69] Supplier performance affects the buyer's continued commitment to the relationship.[70] "With the increasing significance of the purchasing function, purchasing decisions become more important. As organisations become more dependent on suppliers the direct and indirect consequences of poor decision making become more severe. [...] Globalisation of trade and the Internet enlarge a purchaser's choice set. [...] New organizational forms lead to the involvement of more decision-makers."[71] In addition, "as a general rule, a company [health organization] seeks to narrow down the number of suppliers [vendors] it does business with; this way it can leverage its purchasing power with a few suppliers and get better prices in return for purchasing higher volumes of product."[72] Health organizations have adopted various approaches to vendor management and control;[73] the basic functions are presented.

"[Other than the procurement function], purchasing has several specific tasks:

- Vendor Control – Monitoring vendor visitations, coordinating with the compliance office, ensuring vendors are credentialed for the departments they are to visit, have completed and up to date Business Associate Agreements, and are properly identified, especially in patient care and clinical areas; and
- Process Management – Monitoring, conducting value analyses/assessments, and developing and maintaining financial controls on costs associated with ordering supplies, pharmaceuticals, capital equipment and services [This directly links to Williamson's TCE concepts and models]. The process has to be efficient and effective from the identification of the need for the item all the way through payment of the invoice(s) for the items to include tracking of rebates, sales tracing fees (if appropriate) and administrative fees. This is especially true considering systematic audits."[74]
- Strategic Process: "...purchasing is moving from a clerical function towards a strategic process."[75]

Embodied in the mission statement of the UNC Health Care System are the principles of vendor relationships: "Our mission is to provide services adding value and improvement in support of the patient care mission of UNC Health Care System.

The Purchasing Department strives to become an acknowledged leader among service providers, recognized for innovative, high quality, and cost effective approaches to meeting and exceeding our customers' expectations.

The Purchasing Department takes pride in applying our core values:

- Seeking, establishing, and maintaining supplier relationships that foster the premise of best quality at the lowest total cost;
- Improving processes to facilitate ease of procurement;
- Understanding and responding to our customers' business needs and challenges;
- Remaining open, competitive, and fair in our business practices;
- Retaining the integrity and confidentiality of the information we utilize in compliance with applicable law and accreditation requirements;
- Developing and fostering a dynamic, proactive, and committed relationship with all activities with which we are associated; and
- Continuously supporting the six pillars that are the hallmark of our commitment to caring: people, service, quality, finance, growth and innovation."[76]

Purchase Orders

Once the purchasing function has a system established to acquire healthcare supply chain items, a method to monitor vendors and a method to determine need, preferences, and value of competing items, the next essential step to consider is the purchase order. "A purchase order is a contractual, legally binding document that details the buyer's terms for acquiring products, services, or equipment."[77] There are different types of purchase orders:

- Standing Order: "the automatic delivery of a specific amount of product on a regular basis; a standing order always has a start and end date, total amount, and defined delivery dates and quantities. Standing orders are most useful for delivery of bulk items with predictable, regular usage."[78] A standing order establishes a master account, in most instances, between the buyer and supplier.

- Blanket Orders: "an agreement that is similar to a standing order in that it is pre-negotiated by the purchasing department, but the vendor does not automatically ship [deliver]. In most instances the user department is responsible for calling the vendor to ship quantities of the items as they are needed."[79] Blanket orders establish a master account, in most instances, between buyer and supplier. The buyer must initiate an order for each instance of purchase.
- Open Orders: "are pre-negotiated agreements with suppliers and provide products on demand without the need for purchase orders or requisitions. This type of order is rare in today's supply chain environment and is being replaced by the procurement card or purchasing card method."[80]
- Procurement or Purchasing Card: "is a credit card linked to the departmental general ledger [on the chart of accounts in the financial system to commit and obligate budgeted funds] and allows purchases of goods and services without a requisition or purchase order."[81] This method is used heavily with online/web-based purchases.

In addition, healthcare organizations may require additional elements for the purchase order to include documents such as equipment purchase order addendums and other such supplemental documents/information.[82]

Purchasing Terms and Conditions

Negotiations, contract negotiations many times, must be conducted with individual vendors to determine the specific items, prices, service levels, and delivery terms and conditions.[83] "Purchasing terms include, but are not limited to, freight terms and payment terms. Freight terms describe how freight charges [the cost of delivering a product or equipment] are paid, and where and when the transfer of ownership [of the product or equipment] occurs. Payment terms refer to other specifics about how and when the invoice is paid [and with what discounts, rebates, rates, etc. are valid]."[84] There are different types of freight terms and conditions. "The term FOB (free on board) refers

to the point of delivery for goods, products, and equipment from the supplier to the buyer. FOB also determines the point at which title is passed from the supplier to the delivery site."[85] Determining when "ownership" occurs is important when considering damage or theft (pilferage). "When damages occur before the FOB point, the supplier is responsible. When damages occur after the FOB point, the ordering party is responsible."[86] FOB and the FOB point can be established between the buyer and supplier in several ways:

- FOB Destination: "the supplier absorbs all transportation costs and files claims for damages incurred. The facility [buyer] does not receive title [ownership] until the items are received at the [loading] dock. This is the most advantageous freight term for a facility [buyer]."[87]
- FOB Shipping Point: "the title [ownership] of the goods passes to the facility at the origin of shipping. The facility [buyer] is responsible for all freight costs and for filing any damage claim. This is the most advantageous freight term for a supplier."[88]
- FOB Destination, Prepay Freight, and Add: "the supplier prepays the freight charges and adds this cost to the facility's invoice. The supplier is responsible for filing all damage claims. The title [ownership] does not transfer until the item is received at the facility [loading] dock."[89]
- FOB Shipping Point, Freight Allowed: "the title [ownership] passes to the facility when the carrier picks up the goods, but the supplier reimburses the facility for the cost of shipping."[90]

Payment Terms and Conditions

Negotiations between the buyer and supplier of products, items, and equipment include payment terms. There are a myriad of payment terms; the basic methods[91] are:

- Percent (%), Days, Net such as 3%, 10 days, Net 30: the buyer can deduct a 3% discount from the invoice if paid within 10 days of the invoice date while the full amount is due in 30 days of the invoice date. There could also be late fees if the payment is not received within the time frame based on invoice date.

- COD: or collect on delivery, where the invoice must be paid upon delivery and usually includes the freight/shipping costs.
- Pre-Pay: the payment for products or items or equipment is prior to delivery of the purchased items. In this case the buyer receives credit for payment prior to the invoice.
- Capital Terms: "In large capital purchases for devices and systems, payment terms will be linked to specific phases of the project. It is advisable when purchasing capital to retain some part of the total payment until the capital is operational and/or acceptable."[92]

Purchasing Requests to Make Buying Decisions

In many instances where new purchases are needed or existing purchases need more favorable conditions, price, shipping terms, fulfillment, etc., requests for information (RFI), requests for proposals (RFP), requests for tender (RFT), and requests for quotation (RFQ) are tools utilized in the purchasing process to bring data from suppliers to the buyer/purchaser to make purchase decisions. RFIs, RFPs, RFTs, and RFQs can be made to a few or many suppliers; this will primarily be based on competitive forces in the market. RFIs and RFPs are used most often and are commonplace.

Request for Information: "is a standard business process that collects written information about the capabilities of various suppliers. Normally it follows a format that can be used for comparative purposes. RFIs are primarily used to gather information to help make a decision on what next steps to take. RFIs are seldom the final stage and are instead often used in combination with RFPs, RFTs and RFQs."[93] RFIs generally lead to RFPs.

Request for Proposal: "is an invitation for suppliers, often through a bidding process, to submit a proposal on a specific commodity or service. A bidding process is one of the best methods for leveraging a company's negotiating ability and purchasing power with suppliers. The RFP process brings structure to the procurement decision and allows the risks and benefits to be identified clearly upfront. Effective RFPs typically reflect the strategy and short/long term business objectives, providing detailed insight on which suppliers will be able to offer a matching perspective."[94]

Once enough comparative information is acquired, a value analysis is conducted. "Value analysis is a process that determines the best and most economical procedures, products, equipment, or services that will reliably and technologically meet the needs of the user while reducing overall costs."[95] A value analysis is specific to the health organization as terms, conditions, strategies, and business objectives will be different between health organizations. This also includes physician, nurse, clinical staff, and support staff, typically in that order of priority, preferences for supplies, pharmaceuticals, equipment, and furnishings. The more the item(s) of the purchase decision involve(s) diagnosis, treatment and patient care and patient support, the more emphasis must be placed on the preferences of the clinical care team. Whereas copy paper and other office supplies are important, the selection of a supplier for cardiac rhythm management supplies and equipment (pacemakers, stents, etc.) would involve the cardiac surgeons and physicians heavily as well as consideration of nursing and the patient care team. For example, an important example and point to understand, having five physicians taken out of patient care (and thus seeing patients, diagnosing, and treating them with reimbursement for those services) to review copy paper selection RFPs from four suppliers would be a huge waste of the physicians' time while having five cardiac specialist physicians review RFPs for pacemaker supplier selection is an important, actually critical, aspect of selection and decision making for cardiac rhythm management suppliers/vendors/manufacturers. Use physician, nurse and clinical staff time diligently with extreme focus; without patient care, the health organization is a building, not a place of diagnosis, treatment, and patient care.

With that understood, establishing a value analysis process as part of the purchasing decision culture in the health organization is a wise and prudent step in the supply chain. Tenets of the value analysis process include

- "Creation of a value analysis committee composed of supply-intensive department managers and nurses;

- Inclusion of senior management and physician representatives on the committee;
- Determination of specific aggressive annual goals for cost savings [cost avoidance] from the committee [and to establish a cost index using past years cost data to understand cost increases and inflationary pressures in the market];
- Provision of concrete, quantitative analysis of alternatives (qualitative results are important but, whenever possible, qualitative results should be quantified); and
- Follow-up after ideas are implemented to ensure the projected benefits are realized."[96]

Value Analysis generally follows these steps:

- "Step 1: Assess current product use and variations [establish current state];
- Step 2: Establish quality specifications or best practice;
- Step 3: Analyze costs [all costs of ownership] and establish cost of use;
- Step 4: Develop recommendations and communicate action plan with rationale;
- Step 5: Implement action plan;
- Step 6: Communicate value analysis and success stories; and
- Step 7: Re-evaluate progress [regularly]."[97]

When purchasing any item, understanding the total cost of that item is critically important. This is especially true when considering to do the work yourself within the health organization (insourcing) or outsourcing. Items to consider for total cost of ownership are

- "Costs of placing an order;
- Purchase price of the product or item or service;
- Administrative costs of receiving;
- Warehousing;
- Inventorying;
- Issuing;
- Delivering;
- Holding Costs;
- Pilferage [theft, loss];
- Obsolescence [item is outdated, not up to current standards, wear and tear];
- Disposal costs; and
- Residual value."[98]

Capital purchases also will need the following items considered:

- "Cost of device;
- Useful life of device;
- Cost of service and support;
- Cost of included [required] disposables;
- Cost of labor to use the device;
- [cost of facility renovation required for device]; and [cost of cleaning]."[99]

Transacting the Purchase

In healthcare, over 50% of medical and surgical items, such as cotton balls, are processed and transacted electronically between healthcare organizations and vendors by GHX (Global Health Exchange), which is the electronic business-to-business system run by the GHX Corporation.[100] Now the vendor is linked to the item master and information system for the supply chain operation.

For a best practice when the supply item(s) will be ordered in large quantities, over a long period of time or when the cost of transactions with this vendor will be moderate to high, a contract should be established with this vendor to achieve the best pricing and service terms for ordering, receiving, returning, utilizing, and maintaining our supply items. Although a special order or non-contract or out-of-contract order/requisition/purchase can be made for one time or few time orders, a contract from a vendor should be developed and implemented so that the contract terms can be linked to the vendor, the items from the vendor (from the EDI 832 electronic catalog) and into the supply chain system. Last, electronic data interchange is an important concept to electronic transactions in the healthcare supply chain.

What is EDI? "Electronic Data Interchange (EDI) is a set of standards that collectively provide a common protocol or syntax for transacting business documents electronically. In essence, EDI is to electronic commerce as grammar is to verbal communication – it is a set of rules and guidelines that are applied when developing and implementing software and services designed to transmit business documents electronically. Just as a group of individuals with diverse backgrounds can use a common language (such as English) to converse with

TABLE 2.4   **Examples of Commonly used EDI Transaction Sets**

X12ID Code	Transaction Set	Document Usage
850	Purchase Order (PO)	A trading partner sends a PO to order products from a vendor.
810	Invoice	The vendor sends an invoice back to its trading partner as a bill for the products ordered.
997	Acknowledgement	An acknowledgement is sent as a receipt to the sender upon the retrieval of a document.
856	Advanced Ship Notice (ASN)	The vendor sends an ASN to its trading partner specifying to a mutually agreed level of detail the dates and contents of a shipment. Many businesses require the receipt of an ASN from a supplier before the shipment reaches their receiving docks.
820	Remittance Advice	Remittance advice informs the vendor that its trading partner has made a deposit into its bank account.
852	Product Activity Data	The Product Activity Data is used by trading partners to advise vendors of inventory, sales, and other product activity information.
832	Electronic Product Catalog	An electronic catalog of products/items from a manufacturer, distributor, or vendor.

Reproduced from: TrueCommerce EDI Solutions, "EDI Overview: A Practical Guide to EDI and the TrueCommerce EDI Platform," White Paper, Seven Fields, Pennsylvania, Retrieved from http://www.highjump.com/sites/default/files/Resources/WP-US-EDI.pdf, p. 4

each other, EDI provides a common 'language' that enables businesses with dissimilar computer-based business systems to communicate with each other."[101]

Summary

This chapter has focused on acquiring the "technology of care" within the healthcare supply chain. Acquiring healthcare supply chain items includes the function of procurement that is made up of sourcing and purchasing. Procurement starts with determining a need for an item, forecasting demand, and then sourcing is finding the ability to acquire that needed item. Sourcing is the first step in the procurement function. Coupled with purchasing, that is, transacting business through purchase orders or contracts with manufacturers, vendors, and distributors, the function of sourcing is vital in that the evaluation of value and benefit is continuously required to acquire items for care delivery. Stakeholders play a significant role in this process to relative degrees determined by the type and cost of medical and surgical items, pharmaceuticals, medical devices, equipment, and service contracts; preferences those stakeholders have in the overall system of patient care delivery are valuable for the efficient, effective, and efficacious function of acquiring the "technology of care." In addition, the purchasing function is responsible for vendor management and monitoring. In order to acquire supply chain items, healthcare organizations have an array of options that are available based on their mission, strategies, capabilities, and partnerships. The utilization of outsourcing, with GPOs and distributors, has a stable foundation in the industry; however, insourcing options are available based on resources and capabilities of the healthcare organization. Mixed models of outsourcing and insourcing are common, considering the dynamic nature of the industry. This chapter focused on these essential functions and their elements.

Sarah Says: A Student's Perspective

Chapter 2 focuses on acquiring the "technology of care." Acquiring is a combination of Sourcing and procurement. This chapter is quite long and detailed, but the concepts are easy to break down. Procurement starts with determining a need for an item, forecasting demand, and then sourcing that item. First, it is important to ask the following questions: What items does the hospital need in order to successfully care for the patients? How much of each item does the hospital need? What is the most reliable and cost-saving method to get these items to the hospital? Second, it is important to understand what part acquiring plays in the healthcare Value Chain and how it can impact the hospital system as a whole. Cost is a major factor in determining value. One of the best methods for successfully lowering hospital costs quickly is improving procurement and processes associated with the acquiring function.

Stakeholders are very important to the function of acquiring. It is imperative that the stakeholders play a role in the procurement process. Some stakeholders include physicians, nurses, support staff, and facility maintenance personnel. These stakeholders, especially physicians and nurses, are going to use the majority of the items acquired by the hospital. Each physician might have preference on the item; it is best to consider these opinions when acquiring an item. Value is the key to these high-preference items, and you should not just focus on the cost of an item as a single factor. Acquiring is an essential step in the healthcare Value Chain.

Discussion Questions

1. Outline and explain the concept and process of sourcing in the healthcare supply chain.
2. Discuss and give examples of segmentation of supply chain items and the stakeholders involved with influence within each segmentation.
3. Relate, discuss, and provide an example where the Value Chain integrates with healthcare supply-chain sourcing and purchasing.
4. Distinguish the functional areas of vendor management in the context of the request for proposal and/or quote and shipping terms.
5. Relate the sourcing of a medical/surgical item, such as cotton balls, to the identification codes and electronic data interchange catalogs.
6. Evaluate the benefits of improved sourcing with regard to outsourcing as compared to insourcing for healthcare supply chain operations and management in terms of stakeholders' perceptions and incentives.

Exercises

1. What methods would you use for determining a demand forecast for cotton balls?
2. Where would you start to search for a supplier for cotton balls? What is the UNSPSC Code for a cotton ball?
3. How would you categorize supplies based on your health organization's situation?
4. What would be the difference if you outsourced through a GPO and distributor versus insourcing through a manufacturer?
5. What considerations (such as volume needed, delivery terms, quality, cost) are important and why?
6. What considerations are important if you contracted with a vendor for cotton balls?

Journal Items

Define:

Intermediated Supply Chain:

Dis-intermediated Supply Chain:

Distributor:

Strategic Sourcing:

Supply Chain Management:

810 Transaction:

832 Electronic Catalog:

Medical/Surgical Supplies:

Pharmaceutical Supplies and Equipment:

Manufacturer:

Distributor:

Group Purchasing Organization (GPO):

Answer the following questions with one to three sentences:

What are the differences between an Intermediated and a Dis-intermediated Supply Chain? Give examples.

What do manufacturers, distributors, and providers of care, such as hospitals, health systems, physician offices, want from a supply chain transaction and why?

Why are long-term strategic sourcing relationships important to the health organization (consider the need for the "technology of care")?

Search: *Search items may give you great assistance in understanding the healthcare supply chain; provide the website/URL, and provide a one-paragraph summary of what you found.*

GHX: http://www.ghx.com/
ANSI: http://www.ansi.org/about_ansi/overview/overview.aspx?menuid=1

References

1. Hospital Consumer Assessment of Healthcare Providers and Systems survey (HCAHPS)"Source: http ://www.amerinet-gpo.com/quality/value-based -purchasing.aspx, (accessed 8 Jul. 2014)

2. "How sourcing excellence can lower hospital costs." 2013. https://www.mckinsey.com/~/media/mckinsey /dotcom/client_service/Healthcare%20Systems%20 and%20Services/Health%20International/HI10_lower-ing_hospital_costs.ashx (accessed 18 Sep. 2014)

3. (2010). Definition of Procurement - Purchasing Insight. http://purchasinginsight.com/resources/what-is /definition-of-procurement-procurement-vs -purchasing/ (accessed 17 Sep. 2014).

4. Gerald Ledlow, Allison Corry, and Mark Cwiek, *Optimize Your Healthcare Supply Chain Performance: A Strategic Approach* (Chicago: Health Administration Press, 2007), 80.

5. https://oig.hhs.gov/oei/reports/oei-09-00-00200.pdf (accessed 25 Sep. 2014).

6. http://www.cms.gov/Medicare/Coding/MedHCPCS GenInfo/index.html?redirect=/medhcpcsgeninfo / (accessed 25 Sep. 2014).

7. https://www.aapc.com/medical-coding -books/2014/2014-cpt-book.aspx?gclid=CKPjlNzP _MACFSkA7AodMyUACA (accessed 25 Sep. 2014).

8. "The Purchasing Cycle," *Purchasing and Procurement Center*, (2010), http://www.purchasing-procurement -center.com/purchasing-cycle.html (accessed 25 Sep. 2014).

9. "The Purchasing Cycle," *Purchasing and Procurement Center*

10. "The Purchasing Cycle," *Purchasing and Procurement Center*

11. Wendy L. Tate and Lisa M. Ellram "Offshore Outsourcing: A Managerial Framework," *Journal of Business and Industrial Marketing*, 24, no. 3/4 (2009), 257.

12. Danny Blount et al., *Materials Management Review Guide*, 4th ed., (Chicago: Association for Healthcare Resource & Materials Management of the American Hospital Association, 2012), 12.

13. Danny Blount et al., *Materials Management Review Guide*, 14.

14. Richard K. Miller and K. D. Washington & Richard K. Miller & Associates, *The 2009 healthcare business market research handbook* (Loganville, GA: Richard K. Miller & Associates, 2010), 51–52.

15. McKesson, *Paving a new way for procurement* (2014) http://www.mckesson.com/documents/providers /health-systems/department-solutions/paving-a -new-way-for-procurement/ (accessed 17 Sep. 2014).

16. Eugene S. Schneller. "A guide to successful Strategic Sourcing." *Materials Management in Healthcare*, (June 2010), 26.

17. AHRMM Home. http://www.ahrmm.org/ (accessed 20 Sep. 2014).

18. Healthcare Supply Chain Association (HSCA). (2011). http://www.supplychainassociation.org/ (accessed 20 Sep. 2014).

19. Council of Supply Chain Management Professionals (2005) http://cscmp.org/ (accessed 23 Sep. 2014).

20. About WERC | WERC (2010) http://www.werc.org /about/about_werc.aspx (accessed 20 Sep. 2014).

21. Schneller. "A guide to successful Strategic Sourcing," 26.

22. Center for Research and Innovation (2004). *Taking Control of Your Supply Chain: The Buck Starts Here,*

VHA Research Series, VHA, www.vha.com (accessed 19 Apr. 2006).

23. Charles Poirer, and Francis Quinn, "A Survey of Supply Chain Progress," *Supply Chain Management Review*, Sept./Oct. 2003, http://www.manufacturing .net/scm/index.asp?layout=article&articleid =CA323602 (accessed 19 Apr. 2006).

24. Mark McKenna, "Transforming American Health Care Through Supply Chain Excellence," *Transforming American Healthcare Over the Next Decade National Symposium* (Biltmore Resort, Phoenix, AZ, March 23 2006).

25. EMS Industry Terms and Definitions, *VentureOutsource.com*, (2013), https://www.ventureoutsource .com/contract-manufacturing/information-center /terms-and-definitions (accessed 17 Sep. 2014).

26. Benefits and Risks of Single Sourcing - SCM | Supply Chain, (2011), http://scm.ncsu.edu/scm-articles /article/benefits-and-risks-of-single-sourcing (accessed 21 Sep. 2014).

27. Benefits and Risks of Single Sourcing - SCM | Supply Chain, (2011)

28. Danny Blount et al., *Materials Management Review Guide*, 28.

29. Danny Blount et al., *Materials Management Review Guide*, 27.

30. Natalia Levina and Ning Su. "Global Multisourcing Strategy: The Emergence of a Supplier Portfolio in Services Offshoring." *Decision Sciences*, 39, no. 3 (2008), 541–570. doi:10.1111/j.1540-5915.2008.00202.x

31. Natalia Levina and Ning Su. "Global Multisourcing Strategy: The Emergence of a Supplier Portfolio in Services Offshoring."

32. "Single Sourcing versus" Multisourcing," *Insead*, (2012), http://www.insead.edu/facultyresearch/research /doc.cfm?did=49453 (accessed 25 Sep. 2014).

33. "Single Sourcing versus Multisourcing" *Insead*,

34. "Single Sourcing versus Multisourcing" *Insead*,

35. Richard K. Miller and K. D. Washington, *The 2009 healthcare business market research handbook*, 51–52.

36. Richard K. Miller and K. D. Washington, *The 2009 healthcare business market research handbook*, 51–52.

37. Richard K. Miller and K. D. Washington, *The 2009 healthcare business market research handbook*, 51–52.

38. Frequently Asked Questions - Healthcare Supply Chain, (2011), http://www.supplychainassociation.org/?page =FAQ (accessed 25 Sep. 2014).

39. Eugene S. Schneller, The value of group purchasing in the health care supply chain. *School of Health Administration and Policy, Arizona State University College of Business, Tempe.* (2000).

40. Schneller, The value of group purchasing in the health care supply chain.

41. Eugene S. Schneller, "The Value of Group Purchasing," *Novation*, (2012), https://www.novationco .com/media/industryinfo/GroupPurchasing.pdf.

42. High Complexity and Pharmaceuticals — *BravoSolution*, (2010), https://www.bravosolution.com/cms/us /healthcare/high-complexity. (accessed 25 Sep. 2014).

43. http://www.unspsc.org/, (accessed 8 Jul. 2014).

44. https://www.ecri.org/Products/Pages/default.aspx (accessed 26 Sep. 2014).

45. https://www.ecri.org/Products/TechnologyAcquisition /CapitalEquipment/Pages/default.aspx (accessed 26 Sep. 2014).

46. https://www.ecri.org/Products/TechnologyAcquisition/Supplies/Pages/default.aspx (accessed 26 Sep. 2014).

47. Michael H. Hugos, *Essentials of Supply Chain Management*, 3rd ed. (Hoboken, NJ: John Wiley and Sons , 2011), 47.

48. Hugos, *Essentials of Supply Chain Management*, 47.

49. Daniel B. McLaughlin and Julie M. Hays, *Healthcare Operations Management* (Chicago : Health Administration Press, 2008), 378.

50. Refer to http://www.excel-easy.com/examples /moving-average.html.

51. Refer to http://www.excel-easy.com/examples /exponential-smoothing.html.

52. Hugos, *Essentials of Supply Chain Management*, 53.

53. McLaughlin and Hays, *Healthcare Operations Management*, 379.

54. "Definition of Procurement," *Purchasing Insight*, (2010). http://purchasinginsight.com/resources/what -is/definition-of-procurement-procurement-vs -purchasing/ (accessed 17 Sep. 2014).

55. Danny Blount et al., *Materials Management Review Guide*, 12.

56. Hugos, *Essentials of Supply Chain Management*, 63.

57. 6 Core Purchasing Strategies, (2010), http://www .purchasing-procurement-center.com/purchasing -strategies.html (accessed 24 Sep. 2014).

58. Oliver E. Williamson, "Outsourcing: Transaction Cost Economics and Supply Chain Management," *Journal of Supply Chain Management*, 44, no. 2, (2008), 8.

59. Hugos, *Essentials of Supply Chain Management*, 47.

60. Danny Blount et al., *Materials Management Review Guide*, 11.

61. Danny Blount et al., *Materials Management Review Guide*, 11.

62. Sarah H. Ingram, Department of the Treasury, Internal Revenue Service. (2012). *Additional requirements for charitable hospitals* (2012-15537)

63. Danny Blount et al., *Materials Management Review Guide*, 11.

64. Tate and Ellram "Offshore Outsourcing," 259.

65. 6 Core Purchasing Strategies, (2010), http://www.purchasing-procurement-center.com/purchasing-strategies.html (accessed 24 Sep. 2014).

66. Danny Blount et al., *Materials Management Review Guide*, 13.

67. Hugos, *Essentials of Supply Chain Management*, 65.

68. Xinxing Luo et al., "Supplier Selection in Agile Supply Chains: An Information-processing Model and an Illustration," *Journal of Purchasing and Supply Management*, 15, 249–262, (2009), 249.

69. Danny Blount et al., *Materials Management Review Guide*, 13.

70. Joseph P Cannon et al., "Building Long- Term Orientation in Buyer-Supplier Relationships: The Moderating Role of Culture," *Journal of Operations Management*, 28, (2010), 506–521.

71. Luitzen de Boer, Eva Labro, and Pierangela Morlacchi, "A Review of Methods Supporting Supplier Selection," *European Journal of Purchasing & Supply Management*, 7, (2001), 75.

72. Hugos, *Essentials of Supply Chain Management*, 65.

73. Refer to https://www.unchealthcare.org/site/purchasing/vendorpolicy.pdf (accessed 30 Sep. 2014).

74. Danny Blount et al., *Materials Management Review Guide*, 13.

75. Paul D Cousins and Robert Spekman, "Strategic Supply and the Management of Inter – and Intra-organizational Relationships," *Journal of Purchasing & Supply Management*, 9, 19–29, (2003), 19.

76. https://www.unchealthcare.org/site/purchasing/mission_html (accessed 30 Sep. 2014).

77. Danny Blount et al., *Materials Management Review Guide*, 15.

78. Danny Blount et al., *Materials Management Review Guide*, 15.

79. Danny Blount et al., *Materials Management Review Guide*, 15.

80. Danny Blount et al., *Materials Management Review Guide*, 16.

81. Danny Blount et al., *Materials Management Review Guide*, 17.

82. https://www.unchealthcare.org/site/purchasing/equipmentaddendum.pdf/view (accessed 30 Sep. 2014).

83. Hugos, *Essentials of Supply Chain Management*, 65.

84. Danny Blount et al., *Materials Management Review Guide*, 16.

85. Danny Blount et al., *Materials Management Review Guide*, 16.

86. Danny Blount et al., *Materials Management Review Guide*, 17.

87. Danny Blount et al., *Materials Management Review Guide*, 17.

88. Danny Blount et al., *Materials Management Review Guide*, 17.

89. Danny Blount et al., *Materials Management Review Guide*, 17.

90. Danny Blount et al., *Materials Management Review Guide*, 17.

91. Danny Blount et al., *Materials Management Review Guide*, 17.

92. Danny Blount et al., *Materials Management Review Guide*, 18.

93. Danny Blount et al., *Materials Management Review Guide*, 22.

94. Danny Blount et al., *Materials Management Review Guide*, 22.

95. Danny Blount et al., *Materials Management Review Guide*, 24.

96. Danny Blount et al., *Materials Management Review Guide*, 24.

97. Danny Blount et al., *Materials Management Review Guide*, 24–25.

98. Danny Blount et al., *Materials Management Review Guide*, 26.

99. Danny Blount et al., *Materials Management Review Guide*, 26.

100. http://www.ghx.com/ (accessed 8 Jul. 2014).

101. TrueCommerce EDI Solutions, "EDI Overview: A Practical Guide to EDI and the TrueCommerce EDI Platform," White Paper, Seven Fields, PA. http://www.highjump.com/sites/default/files/Resources/WP-US-EDI.pdf (accessed 8 Jul. 2014).

MOVING, STORING, AND DISPENSING

LEARNING OBJECTIVES

1. Outline and explain the concepts of logistics in the healthcare supply chain.
2. Discuss and give examples of different storing (inventory management) models and different dispensing models.
3. Relate, discuss, and provide an example where the Value Chain integrates with healthcare supply chain warehousing/storing, transportation/moving and distribution/dispensing.
4. Distinguish the functional areas of logistics in the context of the healthcare supply chain.
5. Relate the storage in a warehouse of a medical/surgical item, such as cotton balls, to bulk, pick, and cross-docking areas and discuss the differences.
6. Evaluate the organizational capabilities necessary for optimal logistics operations in healthcare with regard to warehousing, transportation, and distribution.

Introduction

Now What?

Moving healthcare supply-chain material and products, as well as storing those items, are the foci of this chapter. Regarding moving and storing, the healthcare Value Chain applied to the supply chain is made operational with the functions of logistics and inventory management. The concept of logistics is based on information and material/product flow, movement, and management. This chapter intends to provide an overview of the healthcare supply chain in the functional aspects of moving, storing, and dispensing products, material, items, equipment, and devices. Moving from the Value Chain to the specific aspects of this chapter, the following graphics provide a visual concept of this chapter's content.

Logistics in the Healthcare Supply Chain

Logistics includes the integrated planning, control, realization, and monitoring of all internal and network-wide material, parts, and product flow, including the necessary information flow, industrial, and trading companies along the complete value-added chain (and product life cycle) for the purpose of conforming to customer requirements.[1] In more common terms, logistics is managing the flow of materials between their point of origin and their point of delivery. By this definition, you can see that logistics is an integral part of supply chain management.

Looking at the healthcare Value Chain, logistics fits in between suppliers and distributors as well as distributors and providers of care. The importance of logistics is not limited to healthcare and is not even a new idea.

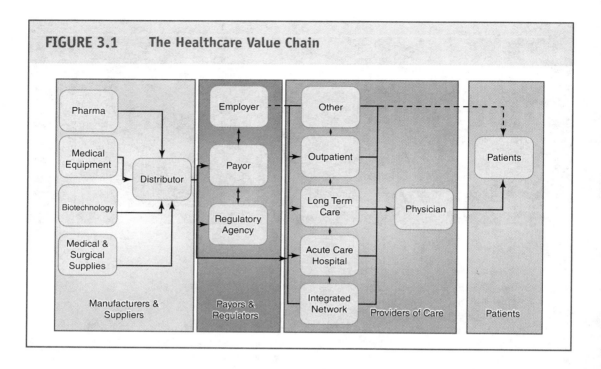

FIGURE 3.1   The Healthcare Value Chain

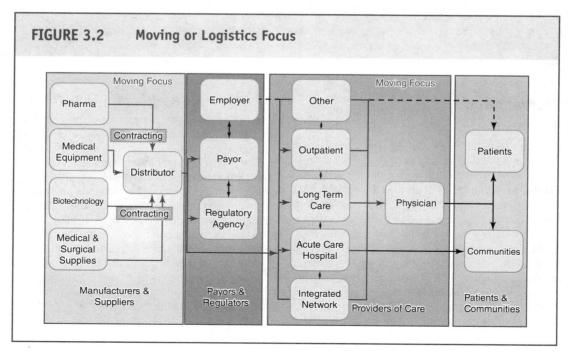

FIGURE 3.2   Moving or Logistics Focus

History and Overview

Logistics has been an important part of global development for nearly 5,000 years. One of the first large scale uses of logistics and materials handling was the construction of the Great Pyramid of Giza. The term "logistics" was used by Greek generals to describe the procedure of procuring supplies for their armies. Up until relatively recently, logistics was primarily an issue for generals and warfare because these were the largest scale operations of the time. As business practices evolved during the industrial revolution, the need for managing inputs and supply chain contributed to the evolution of the science of logistics. Post-World War II, many factors such as deregulation, globalization, information technology, and competition continues to push the evolution of logistics into what it is today.[2] At its core, logistics is making sure that items are where they need to be when they are needed.

Transportation

Why Does Transportation Matter?

Transportation matters because when items are ordered, the items typically must be shipped from the manufacturer to the customer or point of sale. **Transportation** refers to all the movement of raw materials, finished goods, and everything in between in a supply chain. In this factor the tradeoff between efficiency and responsiveness is controlled by mode of transport. To increase responsiveness, you must also decrease the cost effectiveness. While lower rates of responsiveness are more cost efficient, that lack of responsiveness can negatively affect the supply chain. There are advantages and disadvantages associated with all of the types of transportation commonly used to ship items, but before looking at the economics of transport, let's take a short look at the history of transportation.

History and Overview

The history of transportation is based on technological advancement. As technology improved, it became possible to go further, faster, and carry more weight. The history of transportation has many advances and spans thousands of years, but the history of modern transportation in the United States begins in the mid-1800s. Around this time, the rail system in the United States began to be developed and eventually played a key role in the industrial revolution and westward expansion of the country. In 1898, Gottlieb Daimler built the first truck in Germany, and, the next year, Autocar produced the first truck in the United States.[3] In 1903, the Wright brothers successfully flew the first motorized aircraft, but it would be nearly ten years before the first airmail service and nearly twenty years before the first cargo aircraft. In 1908, Henry Ford began to mass produce the Ford Model T, which made transportation by car accessible to the majority of Americans. As the years progressed, the technology associated with transportation continued to improve. In the years following World War II, the highway system in the United States was begun and was expanded continuously. As of 2012, there were over 47,000 miles of interstate highway in the United States.[4]

Common Transportation Modes Used in Healthcare

Economics of Transportation

The method and quantity of material shipped affect the price of shipping. There are five main types of transportation: air, truck, rail, ship, and pipeline. We will concentrate on air, truck, and rail because these methods are more important for the healthcare industry.

Common modes used to transport items in healthcare include air, ground parcel, less than truck load (LTL), and truckload (TL).

Air

Air and express delivery services are the most common way to send expedited, time-sensitive, and end-to-end service for high-value items and small packages.[5]

Rail

Rail is used to transport high volumes of heavy cargo and products over long distances. In the United States, freight rail moves more than 70% of the coal, 58% of the raw metal ore, and more than 30% of the grain.[6]

Rail transport is safer and lower cost when compared to other land-based vehicle transportation methods. Transportation by rail is capable of high levels of cargo utilization and is very energy efficient, although more capital intensive than transport by truck. The cost per ton shipped is much less

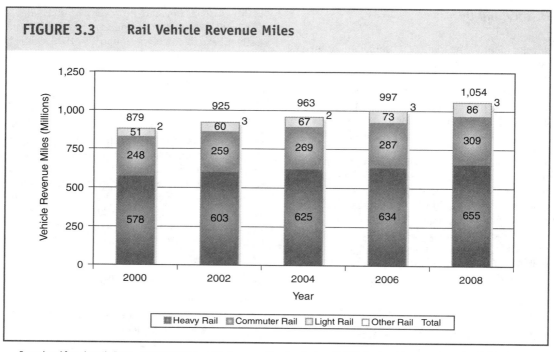

FIGURE 3.3   Rail Vehicle Revenue Miles

Reproduced from (2012). FHWA - 2010 Conditions and Performance: Chapter : System, (2012). Retrieved October 14, 2014, from http://www.fhwa.dot.gov/policy/2010cpr/chap2.htm.

than truck or air, and this makes rail transport the preferred choice for transporting large loads over long distances.[7] Disadvantages associated with rail transport include

- Lack of versatility of transport by truck because trains require fixed rails to operate.
  - Station to station, instead of point to point.
- Being slower than some other alternatives[8].

Ground Parcel

According to the United States Department of Transportation, shipment by truck accounts for nearly 70% of all shipping by volume and 65% by value.[9]

By 2012, the there was a daily average of 54 million tons shipped per day with a value of almost $48 Billion.**

Shipping via truck, as with other forms of shipping, can be outsourced. However, it is not uncommon for organizations to purchase their own

**http://www.ops.fhwa.dot.gov/freight/freight_analysis/nat_freight_stats/docs/13factsfigures/table2_01.htm

trucks for shipping. If an organization decides to purchase its own vehicles, there are several items which must be considered prior to purchase. The advantages associated with an organization owning its own fleet of trucks include

- The vehicles can be designed to carry a specific product, including whatever specialized equipment is needed for handling materials on the vehicle.
- The driver can be trained to act as an advocate or sales person for the organization.
- Vehicles can be branded with the organization's logo, providing low-cost, high-visibility advertising.
- The organization remains in full control over the vehicle and its operation.[10]

The disadvantages associated with owning a fleet of trucks is that trucks take time to manage, require expertise which an organization may be lacking, and can be a significant capital outlay for an organization.[11]

As previously mentioned, the other option for shipping via truck is outsourcing to a third party. The main advantage associated with outsourcing shipping is that an organization's shipping needs are easy to manage even through periods of rapid fluctuation of volumes being shipped. Sometimes, outsourcing shipping is necessary even if the company owns its own vehicles. This occurs when the need to ship goods exceeds the organization's ability to do so; greater flexibility in shipping volume is

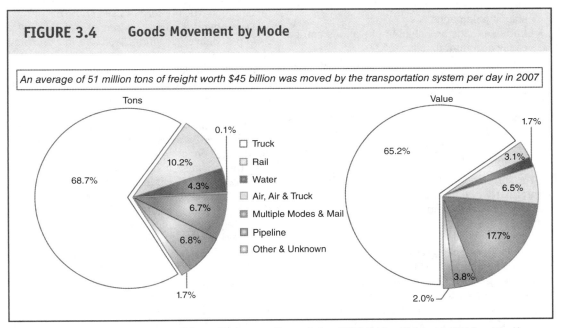

FIGURE 3.4   Goods Movement by Mode

An average of 51 million tons of freight worth $45 billion was moved by the transportation system per day in 2007

Reproduced from (2012). FHWA - 2010 Conditions and Performance: Chapter: System, (2012). Retrieved October 14, 2014, from http://www.fhwa.dot.gov/policy/2010cpr/chap2.htm.

Weight of Shipments by Transportation Mode***				
2012				
	Total	**Domestic**	**Exports**	**Imports**
Total	**19,662**	**17,523**	**901**	**1,238**
Truck	13,182	12,973	118	92
Rail	2,018	1,855	82	82
Water	975	542	95	338
Air, air & truck	15	3	5	7
Multiple modes and mail	1,588	453	540	595
Pipeline	1,546	1,421	13	112
Other and unknown	338	277	47	14

***http://www.ops.fhwa.dot.gov/freight/freight_analysis/nat_freight_stats/docs/13factsfigures/table2_01.htm

obtained by the organization through outsourcing rather than purchasing vehicles due to the shared capacity of the third-party logistics company.[12]

The advantages associated with using a third party company to ship products include the following:

- Organizations can accommodate fluctuating shipping demands.
- Variable loads and shipping locations can be easily accommodated.
- The logistics company may be able to provide lower-cost service to the organization due to economies of scale.
- The organization is able to concentrate more resources on revenue-generating activities because administration of the vehicles and drivers is no longer the responsibility of the organization.

The primary disadvantage of shipping with a third party is that a level of control is given up with regard to the chain of custody for items being shipped.[13]

Less than Truck Load (LTL) vs. Truck Load (TL)

LTL is a shipping method that is typically set up in a hub-and-spoke arrangement and can be local or regional. Typically ten pallets or less is considered LTL. When items are shipped LTL, they share truck space with freight from another company. So, for example, if your company needs to ship four pallets of equipment, the shipping company would come to your warehouse and pick up the four pallets, then go to another business that is also shipping goods and pick up pallets from them, and so on, until the truck is full. Once the truck is full, the shipment is sent to a central processing facility, where it is grouped with pallets going to the same area. The trucks are then reloaded with the pallets going to the same area and delivered to the processing facility.[14] As you may have guessed, the risk for damage to the products being shipped is increased due to the unloading and reloading of trucks that occurs in LTL shipping.

A full truck load or FTL shipping avoids the multiple loading and unloading of trucks associated with LTL but is usually for larger items or large volumes. Full truckload pricing is very dependent on supply and demand. Depending on the capacity available, the price to ship via FTL will fluctuate.

In logistics, capacity generally refers to how many empty trucks are available at a given time. Truck load pricing is typically more straightforward than LTL pricing because the distance between two locations can be determined and broken down into a cost per mile or similar metric. Additional charges that may occur in both TL and LTL include detainment, truck order not used (TONU).

Detainment is when a shipment is delayed at a pickup or delivery location. Typically, in a shipping contract, there is a certain amount of time allotted for pickup and delivery; if that time is exceeded, it can create delays throughout the shipping process. For this reason, a fee is charged for delays in loading and unloading. TONU occurs when a truck is sent to a location to pick up products for shipment but the order is canceled after the truck is already en route. There is typically a TONU fee associated with this because it costs the shipping company resources to send a truck to a location to make a pickup. The TONU fee recovers these costs for the shipper.[15]

LTL pricing is typically pre-negotiated and can be determined easily knowing just a few simple pieces of information: origin zip code, destination zip code, weight, shipping class, and special requirements for delivery. The LTL shipping for a business is nearly identical to the process of an individual shipping a package, except that instead of going to a shipping store, the truck comes to the business. The primary difference between personal shipping and business LTL shipping is that, in LTL shipping, the business is sent a bill once the shipping is complete. Since the pricing is pre-negotiated for LTL, in some cases the rates will increase, and the company shipping the goods will not know about the price increase until the bill arrives; this adds uncertainty to the shipping process. Other additional charges that may occur during LTL shipping are special requests from the delivery location and surcharges due to size and weight of the package.[16]

Weight in TL is typically fine up to 45,000 pounds. If the weight is not exactly correct in TL, as long as the total weight of the product being shipped is less than 45,000 pounds, it usually will not result in an extra charge from the shipping company. In contract, LTL is very sensitive to weight. This is because LTL shippers are attempting to maximize the available space in their trucks.[17]

Trade-offs and Selection Criteria

The primary selection criteria between shipping methods are

- Speed
- Reliability
- Flexibility
- Comparative unit cost

Trends and Issues in Transportation

Compliance Safety Act (CSA)of 2010

CSA is a major safety measurement and reporting initiative run by the Federal Motor Carrier Safety Administration (FMCSA).[18] The 2010 update to the CSA program contains no new regulations; however, nearly every aspect of the commercial freight industry in the United States is subject to expanded safety reporting and enforcement measures. The goal of the data collection is to reduce accidents by locating and addressing areas of concern.[19]

Hours of Service (HOS)

Most commercial drivers must follow HOS regulations. A vehicle is considered commercial if it is used for a business or interstate commerce and can be described by any of the following:

- Transports hazardous materials in a quantity that requires placards on the vehicles;
- Is designed to transport sixteen or more individuals, including the driver, without compensation;

TABLE 3.1   Shipment modes and order winning criteria

	Truck	Rail	Air
Speed	Medium	Medium	High
Reliability	Medium	Medium	High
Cost per ton per mile	Medium	Low	High
Flexibility	High	Low	Medium
Advantages	• Relatively quick • Direct delivery • Flexibility • Cost	• Large load capacity • Good range and speed • Economical	• Fast • Reliable • Direct • Easy to track
Disadvantages	• Roads may be dangerous or blocked	• Difficulty locating freight cars • Delays • Transshipment • Inflexible • Tracking	• High cost • Need to travel between airports • Restricted loading capacity
Other	• Short to medium distances	• Large consignments • Usually from port of discharge to operation site or warehouse • Ecological ("green")	• Emergency phase • Expensive goods • Fragile or perishable goods • Cold chain • No alternative option • Small shipment

- Is designed to transport nine or more individuals, including the driver, for compensation;
- Has a weight or weight rating of 10,001 pounds or more[20].

Hours of service regulations are important to take note of when scheduling deliveries and estimating shipping time.

Driver Shortage

There has been an ongoing shortage of truck drivers for the past decades. Interestingly, studies have determined that these shortages are not due to a lack of potential employees. A study that analyzed trucking between 1992 and 1999 found that even though employment in the trucking industry grew about 11% more than the overall economy, turnover in the industry was between 100 and 200% of the national average.[21] In order to entice drivers to stay in an organization once hired, trucking companies have been increasing driver wages.[22, 23] Long term, paying higher salaries is actually a cost-saving measure for trucking companies because of the costs associated with recruiting and training new drivers.[24]

Trade-offs between Transportation and Inventory

Cost Trade-Offs

There are cost trade-offs associated with storing and transporting items as well as other "hidden costs." Total logistics costs include storing, shipping, administration, and order-processing costs. The administration and order-processing costs are typically related to the volume of items being handled. Depending on the logistics strategies being used, the cost to transport and warehouse items will vary for the same volume of items. A strategy to minimize cost and maximize return on purchases is classifying the items stored or used by an organization.

Inventory

Inventory consists of the items or materials that a company has on hand. Inventory is a buffer between a company's use of products and its need to produce or purchase more goods.[25] In industries such as retail, items not being in inventory, or out of stock, result in back orders. Back-ordered items can lower customer satisfaction and reduce sales.

In manufacturing, running out of raw materials results in a slowing or complete stop in production. In service industries, such as healthcare, when equipment or supplies needed to perform a service are not available, the organization cannot perform the service. As such, inventory management is crucial for all types of businesses. In healthcare, depending on the size of the organization, there can be thousands of types of items that need to be kept on hand. At first glance, managing inventory seems as if it should be as easy as ensuring that there are at least N number of all items on hand at all times. Unfortunately, this is not a feasible solution due to the cost of keeping so many items in inventory.

Item Classification

There are many systems for classifying and recording items. All of these systems were designed to meet different challenges with keeping items on hand. Although designed for different circumstances, there are two major variables common to all inventory control systems: order quantity and order frequency. Depending on the industry, it may be more important to have a specific number of items on hand or to order less frequently.[26] A perpetual review system holds order size constant and allows the order frequency to fluctuate based on usage patterns. For example, if a healthcare organization preferred to order cotton balls by the pallet, they would use a perpetual review system and reorder when they required a full pallet of cotton balls. The other method, the periodic review system, holds the frequency of orders constant and adjusts the quantity ordered as needed. Under this system, the healthcare organization may order cotton balls every Friday, regardless of the quantity needed and simply adjust the amount of cotton balls ordered.

The perpetual review system requires stock to be monitored either continually or after an item is used. When the number of items available reaches the re-order level, a standard number of the product is reordered. This system works best for high-cost items which need close attention. Advantages associated with the perpetual review system include

- An efficient, meaningful order size;
- Safety stock needed only for the lead-time of the reorder;
- Less attention required for items that are infrequently used;

- A relative insensitivity to forecast and parameter change.[27]

Disadvantages associated with the perpetual review system include

- A requirement for a perpetual auditing of inventory levels;
- Potentially reducing the cost savings associated with ordering multiple items in bulk at one time.

In contrast, when using a periodic review system, inventory levels are reviewed at fixed intervals. When ordering, an amount equal to the amount of the item used is reordered. This system is well suited for situations where there is a central supplier and the items being ordered are expensive. In comparison to the perpetual review, periodic review does not have a re-order point but instead uses a target inventory level. Second, order size may not be economical to ship since the quantity ordered varies according to the demand for the item. Finally, the order interval is fixed, not the order quantity.[28] Advantages associated with the periodic review include

- Less record keeping is needed because of the scheduled replenishment.
- Multiple items can be ordered from the same supplier and delivered in the same shipment.

The disadvantages associated with periodic review systems include

- A requirement for safety stock levels to protect against demand fluctuations during the review and lead period. This results in a larger safety stock when compared with the perpetual review system.[29]

The most common variants of item classification are summarized below:

ABC Analysis

ABC analysis is a common technique for inventory control used in materials management. The "ABC" classification system groups items based on need and importance. This system was developed out of another model, which asserted that 80% of total sales by a company were made up by only 20% of the total product inventory.[30] This means that a small portion of the items in storage are used most frequently. Through grouping inventory items via ABC analysis, a company is able to optimize its inventory levels. The breakdown of the three categories in ABC analysis is as follows:

- A items – 80% of total items used;
- B Items – 15% of total items used;
- C items – 5% of total items used.

TABLE 3.2   Classification of Inventory Control

Abbreviation	Inventory Control Type	Criteria Used
ABC	Always Better Control	Minimize the carrying costs of inventory
FSN	Fast Slow Non Moving	Grouped based on how quickly the items are turned over
GOLD	Government Ordinary Local Foreign	Items grouped based on the place of origin
HML	High Medium Low	Grouping items based on their value
SDE	Scarce Difficult Easy	Items grouped based on difficulty obtaining
SOS	Seasonal Off Seasonal	Items grouped based on seasonal availability
VED	Vital Essential Desirable	Categorizing items based on their importance
XYZ	High Medium Very Low Demand	Grouped based on level of investment required to carry the inventory

Data from Indiaclass. Selective Inventory Control. Retrieved October 15, 2014, from http://www.indiaclass.com/selective-inventory-control/

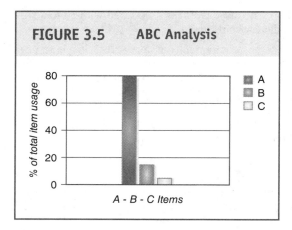

FIGURE 3.5   ABC Analysis

ABC analysis on items in a warehouse produces a report such as the following:

According to the example, ten items were used 80% of the time, these items were assigned A. Similarly, twenty-six items were used 15% of the time and assigned B. Finally, 133 items were used 5% of the time or less and assigned a C designation. It is important to note that if ABC analysis was done for just the first month in the example, only five items would be listed as high importance and if the period from January to May was included, then ten items would be listed as high importance. When classifying items using the ABC method, it is important to use an appropriate time period to ensure that inventory levels will be appropriate.[31] Using a tool like the ABC method to determine which items are high usage allows for potentially reducing holding costs associated with keeping high inventory levels of items that are not commonly used.

Holding Costs and Trade-Offs

Holding costs include all the costs associated with keeping an item in storage. Holding costs typically run between 5% and 45% in business. All holding costs can be assigned one of three different categories:

1. The costs of capital to finance the inventory;
2. The costs of storing and handling the inventory;
3. The costs associated with risk.[32]

The costs of capital

The costs associated with capital have several common interpretations. One common method for calculating the costs associated with capital is to take the rates banks are charging for lending money.

Returns on investment or returns on net assets are also commonly used. The most common method of calculating capital costs is called the Weighted Average Cost of Capital (WACC).

$$WACC = \frac{E}{V} * R_E + \frac{D}{V} * R_E * \left(1 - T_C\right)$$

Where

E = Market value for the company's equity

R_E = Cost of equity

D = Market value of a company's debt

$V = E + D$

T_C = Corporate tax rate[33]

The costs of storing and handling inventory

The costs associated with storing and handling inventory fall into two categories, depending on whether organizations outsource

Length of analysis	Time Period	Total Items	% Difference	A	B	C
1 Month	January	67	–	5	13	60
2 Months	January – February	103	54%	7	16	96
3 Months	January – March	131	27%	10	22	98
4 Months	January – April	143	9%	10	26	119
5 Months	January – May	161	13%	10	26	133

their warehouses or own their own. For companies who rent warehouse space from a third party, the costs come down to cost per pallet. It is important to note that the cost per pallet does not refer to the value of the inventory, which can vary greatly, depending on the value of goods being stored in different areas of the warehouse.[34]

For companies who own their own warehouses, the storage costs are fixed based on the size of the warehouse. The fixed cost of the warehouse includes not only the cost to maintain the area but the opportunity cost associated with using the warehouse for activities related to operations. This opportunity cost exists because, while the items stored within a warehouse are needed for primary business activities, their storage does not generate revenue for an organization. For example if a hospital has a 10,000 square foot warehouse, that space has upkeep costs associated with it and economic costs of not using at least part of that space for additional patient treatment areas.

Two techniques for the valuation of inventory, first in first out (FIFO) and last in first out (LIFO), originated in cost accounting. This is the branch of accounting that is associated with a company's financial information.[35] Depending on the external situation, either FIFO or LIFO may be a more accurate representation of the cost of items stored in inventory.[36] This is important because it is useful for a business to track not only units sold but also the cost of items that are purchased for resale.[37] In the case of healthcare, this is the cost of items used to perform a procedure.

First in First Out (FIFO)

There are several advantages associated with FIFO inventory systems. First, items stored using an FIFO system are less likely to become outdated or to spoil. This is because, under FIFO, the oldest items in inventory are used first. This is beneficial for products that have short shelf lives, such as medication with special storage needs. Since inventory needs to be tracked and managed for accounting purposes, FIFO offers the advantage of knowing exactly what is in inventory and its current market value. This is not the case under LIFO, which uses the latest items first. The final advantage of FIFO is one of simplicity. FIFO is a less complicated system than its counterpart, LIFO. More businesses use FIFO than LIFO as well, which results in less confusion during the training process for new employees. The major disadvantage associated with the FIFO system with regard to inventory is clerical errors as to quantity and storage location of items.[38]

Last In First Out (LIFO)

The LIFO system is used only in the United States, because its use for accounting applications is not allowed under International Financial Reporting Standards (IFRS). This system can be considered the opposite of FIFO because items that are most recently acquired are the first ones used. The primary benefit of LIFO is to reduce the cost of inventory on paper in times of inflation; however, this system also makes items much more prone to spoilage while in storage.[39] Despite the tax benefits of the LIFO system, the United States is considering banning the use of LIFO.[40]

A similarity between FIFO and LIFO methods is that they depend on the type of product to be the same, with only fluctuations in the price. FIFO and LIFO both influence a company's earnings on paper. FIFO is based on the price of the cost of the earlier products purchased, and ignores the future price changes affecting those products. This is most effective in industries where the price of products remains steady and the oldest products are sold or used first. LIFO works best in industries with rapid price fulgurations in which the newest units are sold first.[41]

Receiving

Receiving is unloading and processing a shipment.

Receiving Methods

There are two basic methods for receiving: centralized and decentralized receiving of purchased healthcare supply chain products, materials, items, equipment, and devices. An overview of each method follows.

Centralized: "uses a single point for the physical delivery of products. Then from the single point, products are moved to end-use areas. This method results in a central storage inventory system."[42]

Decentralized: "uses multiple points of physical delivery of products and physical delivery of the product is either at or near end-use areas. This system is more conducive to a stockless inventory system."[43]

Trade-Offs Between Logistics and Transportation

As described in the previous section, there are trade-offs associated with transportation cost and the speed of order delivery. However, there is not one single best solution for all organizations.

What Matters

Determining the best logistics solution for an organization depends on a variety of factors, many of which have already been outlined in this chapter.

Additional concerns include the volume of a shipment and how it is packed into the container in which it will be shipped.

Volume

Weight and volume are the key measurements when determining the correct shipping method for an order. Weight is relatively simple to obtain using a scale. Volume is typically calculated in cubic meters (CBM). CBM can be calculated as:

$$\text{Length(CM)} \times \text{Width(CM)} \times \text{Height(CM)} / 1{,}000{,}000 =$$

$$\text{Length(M)} \times \text{Width(M)} \times \text{Height(M)} = \text{Cubic Meters (M3)}^{[44]}$$

Volumetric weight is calculated as:

$$(\text{Length(CM)} \times \text{Width(CM)} \times \text{Height(CM)}) / 5000 =$$

$$\text{Volumetric weight in kilograms}^{[45]}$$

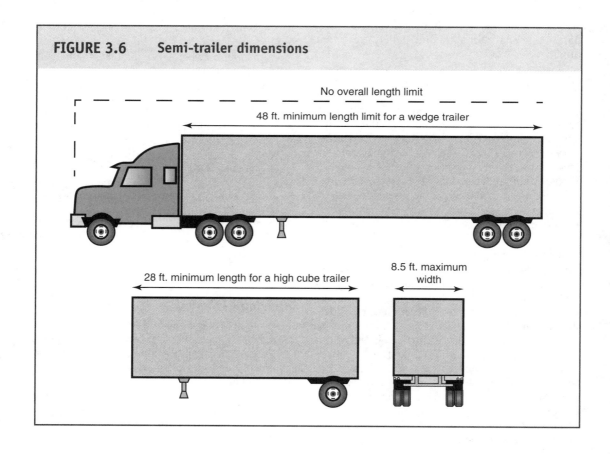

FIGURE 3.6   Semi-trailer dimensions

No overall length limit

48 ft. minimum length limit for a wedge trailer

28 ft. minimum length for a high cube trailer

8.5 ft. maximum width

TABLE 3.3   Standard Trailer Dimensions

Standard Trailer Dimensions	
Standard Lengths	45, 48, or 53 feet
Interior Height	9 feet 4 inches (110 inches)
Overall Height (from road)	13 feet 6 inches (162 inches)
Interior Width	8 feet 4 inches (100 Inches)
Exterior Width	8 feet 6 inches (102 Inches)
Swing door opening	98 inches by 110 inches
Roll door opening	94 inches by 104 inches

Data from http://www.truckscales.com/semi53.jpg

The volume of a shipment or warehouse can then be used for further calculations such as product density.

How to Measure
Measuring of different shipping containers is done using the inside volume of the container. For semi-trailer dimensions[46] the figure on page 70 is provided.

The dimensions of standard trailer are listed in table 3.3.

Packaging

Packing items efficiently to maximize space during shipping and warehouse storage is the primary way to control the volume of items being shipped. When packing pallets, there are several guideline to follow. A pallet should never be overloaded. The maximum capacity of a pallet is rated by manufacturers to be around 3,300 pounds, although it is advisable to not load a pallet to the maximum capacity.[47] The other consideration when packing items is the stability of the package. Instability can be avoided by ensuring that heavier items are loaded closer to the bottom of the pallet if there is any variation in weight. Items should also fit within the dimensions of the pallet. Overhanging items should be split between two pallets. If items are overhanging during shipping, there is a higher chance of damaging the items being shipped. Once a pallet is completely loaded, it is typically covered in shrink wrap or some other packing material to keep it together during shipping. When wrapping the items on a pallet, it is also important to continue down the load and wrap around the base of the pallet as well. This contributes to the stability of the pallet.

Aside from the "don't" list of pallet packing, there are several steps which should always be done when loading a pallet. First, a pallet should be in good condition, or it may not support the items being loaded onto it. Second, it is advisable to place a protective sheet, typically wooden, on top of the pallet to protect it from the weight of other items being stacked upon the pallet. Third, before applying the final wrap with shrink wrap, fragile goods can be wrapped in bubble wrap or some other protective product. Very heavy items should be strapped to the pallet to prevent damage associated with movement during shipping. Just as with personal shipping, any old labels on the items being shipped should be removed to prevent items being lost or delivered to the wrong address.[48]

Cost

Incorrectly packing or measuring can lead to an increase in cost as well as delays in shipping or damage to items being shipped. Controlling costs associated with shipping is a priority for any business that ships items, whether regularly or only occasionally. The supply chain of healthcare organizations can seem distant or even unrelated to the revenue-generating activities of healthcare organizations, and this makes the healthcare supply chain at risk for cost increases within their supply chain. There are several cost-cutting strategies than can be utilized to reduce shipping costs within an organization. The main methods for reducing cost have already been discussed, but they include negotiating with multiple suppliers for the best price, bulk ordering, and joining a group purchasing organization (GPO).

Packaging Strings and Volumetric Tables

As presented in a previous chapter, packaging strings are important to understand as are volumetric tables. For purposes of transporting, receiving, storing, and "picking" items for a customer, both of these concepts are vital to grasp. A packaging string is a common and standard series of packaging of supply items. The American National Standards Institute (ANSI) sets packaging and volumetric standards. With regard to a pharmaceutical item, "an example of a packaging string would be BOX/10 VIAL/10 ML. This string indicates that there are 10 milliliters (MLs) in a VIAL and 10 VIALS in a BOX." With cotton balls, you could have 100 cotton balls in a package, 50 packages in a box, 25 boxes in a case and 20 cases to a pallet. So, basically, "packaging string is what determines how inventory is tracked and in what form it is purchased from the vendor." It is important to know what medical product is needed since a package, together with its associated costs, is far different from a case or a pallet. In addition, knowing the size of the item or product is important for storage and space considerations. That is why volumetric tables (based on ANSI standards) are important to understand as well. Volumetric tables basically count the total volume of the item in its package. For example, 1 square foot, .25 square feet, is what you would see in the table based on the packaging (box, case, etc.).

Storage

Storage is defined as putting away materials used in patient care for future use.

Logistical Considerations in Healthcare

Healthcare logistics has additional concerns associated with it due to the nature of the healthcare industry. Some items used in healthcare, especially pharmaceuticals, must be kept at a certain temperature. For some items, this means maintaining a cold chain while the item is in shipment. A **cold chain** is shipping an item in a temperature-controlled environment. Keeping items cold in shipping was documented back to 1797 and British fishermen, but using the technology for pharmaceuticals is a relatively new development.[49] The practice of shipping pharmaceuticals began on a wide scale in the 1950s. Before then, cold chain for shipping of temperature-sensitive pharmaceuticals was primarily local from a manufacturer to their point of use. Originally, the process of cold-chain shipping was regulated internally by organizations. In the United States, the Food and Drug Administration now regulates cold-chain shipments. This has caused many companies who ship products requiring a cold chain to rely on specialty third-party shipping organizations. According to the Healthcare Distribution Management Association, around 10% of drugs are temperature sensitive.[50] If temperature-sensitive medications are not properly shipped, they may become ineffective or harmful to patients.

Material Handling Equipment

Storage and Handling Equipment

Storage equipment is usually limited to non-automated examples, which are grouped in with engineered systems. Storage equipment is used to hold or buffer materials during "downtimes," or times when materials are not being transported. These periods could refer to temporary pauses during long-term transportation or long-term storage designed to allow the buildup of stock. The majority of storage equipment refers to pallets, shelves, or racks onto which materials may be stacked in an orderly manner to await transportation or consumption. Many companies have investigated increased efficiency possibilities in storage equipment by designing proprietary packaging that allows materials or products of a certain type to conserve space while in inventory. Examples of storage and handling equipment include

- Racks, such as pallet racks, drive-through or drive-in racks, push-back racks, and sliding racks;
- Stacking frames;
- Shelves, bins, and drawers;
- Mezzanines;
- Engineered Systems.

Engineered systems cover a variety of units that work cohesively to enable storage and transportation. They are often automated. A good example of an engineered system is an Automated Storage and Retrieval System, often abbreviated AS/RS, which is a large automated organizational structure involving racks, aisles, and shelves accessible by a "shuttle" system of retrieval. The shuttle system is a mechanized cherry picker that can be used by a worker or can perform fully automated functions to quickly locate a storage item and quickly retrieve it for other uses. Other types of engineered systems include:

- Conveyor systems;
- Robotic delivery systems;
- Automatic guided vehicles (AGV).

Industrial Trucks

Industrial trucks refer to the different kinds of transportation items and vehicles used to move materials and products in materials handling. These transportation devices can include small hand-operated trucks, pallet-jacks, and various kinds of forklifts. These trucks have a variety of characteristics to make them suitable for different operations. Some trucks have forks, as in a fork-lift, or a flat surface with which to lift items, while some trucks require a separate piece of equipment for loading. Trucks can also be manual or powered lift, and operation can be walk or ride, requiring a user to manually push them or to ride along on the truck. A stack truck can be used to stack items, while a non-stack truck is typically used for transportation and not for loading. There are many types of industrial trucks:

- Hand trucks;
- Pallet jacks;
- Pallet trucks;
- "Walkie" stackers;
- Platform trucks;
- Order pickers;
- Slide-loaders;

Bulk material handling refers to the storing, transportation, and control of materials in loose bulk form. These materials can include food, liquid, or minerals, amongst others. Generally, these pieces of equipment deal with the items in loose form, such as conveyor belts or elevators designed to move large quantities of material, or in packaged form, through the use of drums and hoppers. Examples are

- Conveyor belts.
- Stackers.
- Reclaimers.
- Bucket elevators.

Materials Management

Materials management is a branch of logistics that deals with the tangible components of a supply chain. Where dispensing is providing items to a single patient or location, materials management focuses on the overall system of distribution and materials within the facility, specifically, the acquisition of items, quantity control of purchasing and standards related to warehousing, ordering, and shipping.[51] The key functions of materials management can be broken down to the five Rs of material management:

- Is it the right quality?
- Is it the right quantity?
- Is it the right time?
- Is this the right source?
- Is it the right price?[52]

Keeping the five Rs in mind when dealing with moving materials will provide a guide for decision making and allow the materials management professionals to meet their goals. The general goals of materials management are summarized below:

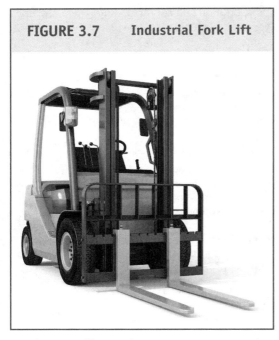

FIGURE 3.7 **Industrial Fork Lift**

© Supertrooper/Shutterstock

- Acquire items of the appropriate level of quality for the best possible price.
- Provide input on make-or-buy decisions.
- Keep inventory turning over. A constant turnover rate for inventory will reduce carrying costs and inventory loss due to damage or spoilage.
- Promote internal cooperation with regard to inventory coordination.
- Maintain high quality records and controls.
- Prevent supply chain disruptions.
- Develop relationships with vendors to create reliable alternative sources.[53]

Material Handling Equipment[54]

As a brief overview, warehouses or consolidated service centers use material handling equipment to move supply chain items within the warehouse. Clearly there are different types of material handling equipment. Material handling encompasses a diverse range of tools, vehicles, storage units, appliances, and accessories involved in transporting, storing, controlling, enumerating, and protecting products at any stage of manufacturing, distribution, consumption, or disposal. The four main categories of material handling equipment include storage, engineered systems, industrial trucks, and bulk material handling.

Receiving and Distribution Methods

"Receiving operations are usually thought of as the physical receipt of material into the facility. However, receiving operations are more than simply receiving goods. There are several other important processes directly or indirectly related to the physician receipt of material. The most important of these is the accounts payable process."[55] "Accounts payable collects data from the receiving process to facilitate payments to vendors. The receiving services function ensures the entire inventory transaction works smoothly."[56] Three-way matching between invoice, receipts/receiving documents, and requisition/order documents to ensure proper payment is essential to an effective and efficient process to link receiving to accounts payable.

Considerations with Shelving and Storage Options

Storing and Dispensing Models

"The supply chain includes all of the processes involved in getting supplies and equipment from the manufacturer to use in patient care areas. SCM [supply chain management] is the management of all activities and the processes related to both upstream vendors and downstream customers in the Value Chain. Because SCM requires managing relationships outside as well as inside an organization, SCM is a broad field of thought."[57] Storage functions and facilities, warehouses, and consolidated service centers are an integral component of the supply chain operation.

Inventory Management

Inventory management is concerned with managing the amount of items that are stored in a warehouse. It is important because if a company has insufficient raw materials or inputs in inventory, that organization will have interruptions in production. In situations where determining the level of demand would be difficult, there are several inventory management models which can be used to approximate needed inventory levels. Warehouses or consolidated service centers are used to store healthcare supply-chain products, items, equipment, and devices (medical and surgical items, pharmaceuticals, and medical equipment). Consolidated service centers are warehouse operations that handle and store multiple types of healthcare supply chain items and are most usually owned or internal to the healthcare system (insourced vs. outsourced). Warehouses have longer term storage capability with a receiving area near a receiving dock, a smaller item loose pick (to pick items that have been ordered to send to the customer) area, a longer-term bulk storage area, and different levels of security for certain items that can be stolen easily (called pilferage) or that require statutory/regulatory storage security requirements such as with federal schedule pharmaceutical items. First, the discussion will focus on the type of inventory models that are

utilized and then will be followed by a discussion on warehouse models.

The **single-period model** is used for one-time orders such as purchasing items for a one-time event.

A **fixed-order quantity model** can be used to maintain a specific level of an item in stock. Under this system, inventory levels are monitored, and when they reach a certain level, the item is reordered.

The **fixed-time period model** is similar to the fixed-order quantity model, but the key difference is that, instead of monitoring the inventory level and reordering when the inventory reaches a critically low level, the item is ordered regularly on a specific day regardless of the quantity needed.[58]

Inventory is important to all businesses, including those using just-in-time (JIT) ordering, for three main reasons. First, inventory allows businesses to remain independent in their operations.

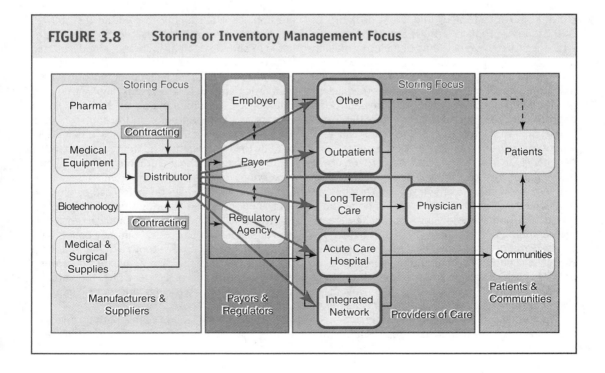

FIGURE 3.8 **Storing or Inventory Management Focus**

This is because there are costs associated with changing processes due to running out of supplies. Second, inventory allows an organization to continue operating during sharp increases in demand for its product or service. In healthcare, increases in demand may be associated with the seasonality of disease or natural disaster. Inventory also allows for flexibility in production scheduling. Having items on hand in a manufacturing business means that there is less pressure on the production system when orders increase. In healthcare and other service industries, it allows for flexibility in ordering products. Inventory also allows for bulk purchases, which can increase order costs due to pricing discounts, as well as the costs associated with placing the order. Examples of costs associated with placing orders are equipment required to place the order, such as phones, additional office space, salaries for employees, and transportation costs.[59] Storage and inventory management also include warehouse or consolidated service-center cost based on the model utilized.

Warehouses have three basic, yet different, approaches to formation: stock keeping unit (SKU) storage, job lot storage, and cross-docking. In SKU storage, products are separated by specific type and stored together, thus reducing confusion and increasing efficiency. Job lot storage employs the idea of storing a product related to a certain job stored together, providing a more efficient picking and packing method. The cross-docking approach uses a different system where the warehouse does not store the product; instead it is where trucks from suppliers drop off large quantities of a given product and it is then broken down into smaller lots and repackaged "on the dock" and not brought into inventory or storage but immediately shipped to the final location. These production and warehousing approaches create the beginning of the supply chain at the distributor or warehouse or consolidated service center (which is a warehouse with multiple product storage). A basic principle is "increase throughput while simultaneously reducing both inventory and operating expense."[60]

Traditionally, the goal of inventory management has been to ensure that supplies are available and accessible to clinical staff at all times. Stock-outs are to be avoided because they can require costly emergency shipments and extra labor. When a key supply is missing, nurses spend precious time tracking it down, sometimes poaching from other stations. The risks are so great that, in many cases, nurses have been known to hoard supplies in order to avoid stock-outs. However, maintaining large inventories and multiple storage areas (the solution of the past) is a suboptimal response because it presents its own set of problems, including high inventory carrying costs; cost of space devoted to supplies; opportunity cost of capital tied up in unused supplies and space that could be used to increase procedures and generate revenue; and cost of shrinkage due to obsolescence, pilferage, and lost inventory. When combined with a system of periodic physical inventory and replenishment, overstocking provides little protection against spikes in demand, which again send nurses on search-and-poach missions. Over time, accuracy of the inventory is questioned without proper systems and management.

Storage locations and identification of SKUs are important basic concepts within the storage function. In storage facilities, locations are numbered; some use alpha-numeric identifications, by section (bulk, "pick" or "loose," cross-docking, etc.), aisle and shelf, or pallet riser location where the particular item is stored. It is similar to a card catalog or electronic catalog in a library when you are looking for a book on the shelves. Some warehouses utilize radio frequency transmitters or RFID to identify items and item locations in the healthcare supply chain warehouse or consolidated service center. "RFID [radio frequency identification] is a tool for identifying objects, collecting data about them, and storing that data in a computer system with little human involvement. RFID tags are similar to bar codes, but they emit a data signal that can be read without actually scanning the tag. RFID tags can also be used to determine that location of the object to which they are attached. However, RFID tags are more expensive than bar coding."[61]

After receiving, followed by putting away or storing the healthcare supply-chain items and

FIGURE 3.9   Warehouse

© Dmitry Kalinovsky/Shutterstock

products, the process of inventory management continues. Dispensing or distributing the supply chain items and products to end users, customers, and providers of care is the next major function that we will discuss in the next section.

Dispensing

In response to these challenges, most hospitals have some type of centralized materials management and have adopted supply distribution systems designed to limit the risk of stock-outs and reduce inventory without incurring the costs of overstocking. In the healthcare Value Chain terminology, dispensing is the operative term for distribution. Some of these basic distribution systems include

- PAR (periodic automatic replenishment) systems involve setting and maintaining optimal levels of stock for each item (based on usage history) at the point of care. Periodically, PAR level shortages are identified, and items are restocked from a central storage location. Often, the process is facilitated by using handheld scanners to read product barcodes. PAR systems are best suited for patient care units and for high-use, low-cost items.

- JIT delivery, where the goal is to provide supplies as close to the time and point of use as possible. These systems generally require that contracts be established with selected prime vendors for more frequent delivery of supplies.

- Stockless or Low Unit of Measure (LUM) systems extend the concept of JIT by allowing hospitals to receive products at the loading dock already packaged in unit-of-use quantities for delivery directly to the point of use. PAR levels are established and closely monitored through a systems contract with the outside vendor. Stockless or LIM systems have been most successful when supported by vendor automation systems.

- A more recent development has been the case cart system, which utilizes the JIT concept to deliver supplies to surgery departments. A case cart is a vehicle stocked with instruments and supplies designated for a single surgical procedure. The carts are filled in central storage, using a standard supply list and a preference list specific to the surgical procedure and the physician and delivered to the operating room.

- Another recent development has been the Two-Bin Replenishment model, which provides an alternative to the PAR system. Inspired by the Japanese Kanban inventory system developed in 1950 by Toyota, it has been used in some healthcare settings since 2000. Units of each low-cost item stored in a clinical department are divided equally between a primary/active bin and a backup/safety bin. Supplies are picked from the primary bin until depleted. The backup bin then becomes the primary/active bin, and the depleted bin is replenished and becomes the new backup.

- Two further ways that hospitals have reduced inventory and cut costs are standardization and consolidation to limit the broad range of products, manufacturers, sizes, and packaging. Often this has been accomplished through limiting the number of preferred vendors. These supply-distribution systems have brought cost savings to many hospitals through significant inventory reduction. As computer technology

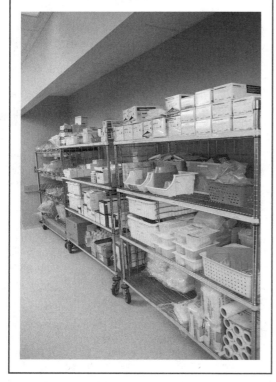

FIGURE 3.10 **Healthcare Supply Storage**

© Tyler Olson/Shutterstock

has advanced, automation and software have been incorporated to improve and streamline these supply-distribution systems, providing better information to support decision making. System-wide computer applications, called enterprise resource planning (ERP) systems are becoming commonplace. ERP systems are a set of software applications that organize, define, and standardize the business processes necessary to effectively plan and control an organization so the organization can use its internal knowledge to seek external advantage. Likewise, more experience has yielded tweaks here and there to adapt the systems

to the realities of day-to-day usage. However, in some cases, technology and "workaround" solutions have simply added further layers of complexity and confusion to the process. In order to leverage inventory management to drive real and lasting improvements in efficiency, effectiveness, and efficacy, hospitals must systematically shift away from the "supply distribution" mind-set, toward a "demand-pull" vision of inventory management. This shift requires genuine innovations in applying value analysis, process engineering systems, and robust technology solutions.

Distribution Services

"Distribution is the physical movement of products to end-use areas. Often the inventory system used will dictate which distribution system is selected."[62] There are several distribution methods, presented in overview as follows:

- Random request system: "supplies are delivered to the user based on demand, by requisition, from an ordering department."[63]
- Emergency requisition system: "the requester of the supply item travels to the site where the item is stored and then hand carries the item back to the department [end-user area]."[64]
- PAR: "is the maximum volume or quantity established for specific items. PAR levels should be determined by historical usage and in conjunction with available space. The PAR level can either be filled by the user or materials management [supply chain] staff."[65]
- Exchange cart system: Carts used for short-term storage of healthcare supply items are exchanged and reloaded with supplies; this process replaces an empty cart with a fully loaded supply cart for specific healthcare delivery areas such as the perioperative areas and procedure areas.

The Demand-Pull Vision

Mike Duffy, Executive VP of Operations at Cardinal Health, has written convincingly about the need

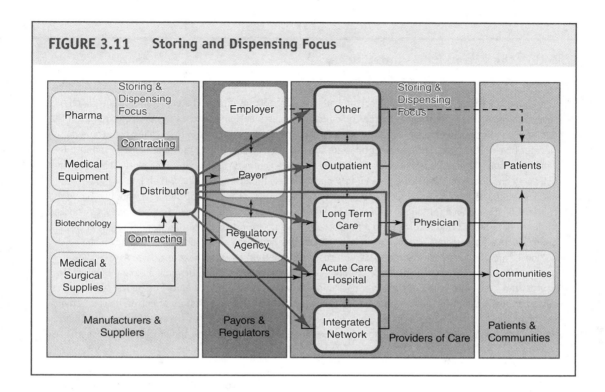

FIGURE 3.11   Storing and Dispensing Focus

to shift how healthcare organizations view the supply chain. "Our culture had to shift from one in which we pushed products into the market to one focused on improving product availability at the retailer's shelf. That mindset had to permeate our organization and embed itself in all that we did-from developing packaging to creating responsive supply-side systems that reacted quickly to changes in consumer demand."[66]

The healthcare industry presents particular challenges because it is more fragmented and less inclined to adopt technology than other industries (e.g., consumer package goods and retail). However, Duffy (who moved to healthcare supply chain management in 2006) and other healthcare SCM leaders argue that the demand-pull "model is not only possible; it is essential. As supply chain leaders, we must break through silo thinking, challenge old paradigms and push ourselves

to find solutions for the industry's issues. In doing so, we will provide the necessary leadership for transforming our industry." This cultural shift will demand greater utilization of value chain analysis, process engineering, and leveraging of technology to improve information transparency. Duffy also discusses the critical role of building trust and a collaboration mind-set among stakeholders mainly by aligning goals and incentives.

Dispensing Equipment

Dispensing equipment used in the last one hundred feet, from central storage to the patient room, is much different from the equipment used earlier in the process. In the last one hundred feet, dispensing equipment takes the form of storage lockers, carts, refrigerators, and medication dispensing units such as Pyxis and Accudose.

Follow the Cotton Ball – Ordering

Continuing the theme of following the cotton ball, the transport, receipt, and storage of cotton balls take several steps. After strategic sourcing the cotton balls, procurement, and purchasing, the cotton balls in the packaging and quantity ordered will arrive at their place of storage. The cotton balls that were acquired are a "receipt line" in the warehouse. Receipt lines are the number of items [lines] processed or received into inventory in that particular warehouse or consolidated service center. If usually or permanently stored, cotton balls are considered an SKU. If the packaging string is pallet, then case, then box, then bag, a typical scenario would be as follows. Bulk, such as a pallet of twenty or more cases of cotton balls, would be brought to the bulk storage area for longer-term storage. Some cases may be broken down to boxes and cross-docked for immediate receipt and loading onto a transportation vehicle for delivery to the hospital or physician group practice for customer use now while other cases may be broken down into boxes or bags in the "pick" or "loose" area for customer loading (based on customer ordering) over the next few days. As the "pick" or "loose" area for cotton balls decreases, supply-chain team members go to the bulk area and break down another few cases into boxes or the lower packaging string, bags, to refill the "pick" or "loose" area. As customer orders diminish the warehouse or consolidated service center's inventory of cotton balls, strategic sourcing more cotton balls is necessary through sourcing and purchasing. Thus the healthcare Value Chain model of strategic sourcing, moving, storing, dispensing comes full circle, and the process begins again.

Summary

Moving healthcare supply-chain material and products, storing those items, as well as dispensing those items were the foci of this chapter. Regarding moving, storing, and dispensing, the healthcare Value Chain applied to the supply chain is made operational with the functions of logistics and inventory management. The concept of logistics is based on information and material/product flow, movement, and management. Considerable coordination is required for efficient and effective movement, storage, and distribution of healthcare supply chain products, items, equipment, and devices. This chapter provided an overview of the healthcare supply chain in the functional aspects of moving, storing, and dispensing products, material, items, equipment, and devices.

Sarah Says: A Student's Perspective

Chapter 3 can be broken down into three sections: Moving (Logistics), Storing (Inventory Management), and Dispensing. These are vital aspects after the strategic sourcing function of the healthcare supply chain. Each aspect has an important role within the supply chain.

Logistics is managing the flow of materials between their point of origin and their point of delivery. Transportation plays a large part in logistics. There are many forms of transportation. The three main forms of transportation used in healthcare are train (rail), trucks, and air. Each different mode of transportation is associated with different advantages and disadvantages. It is important to determine which is best for each healthcare system.

Inventory consists of the items or materials that a company has on hand. It is imperative that each healthcare system has an exceptional inventory management system. Properly controlling inventory can be extremely cost saving to the healthcare system. Also, it prevents stock-outs and ordering unnecessary quantities of supplies.

Dispensing is an operative term for distribution. There are many distribution systems that can benefit a healthcare system. Some basic distribution systems include: PAR, JIT delivery, stockless or LUM, case cart systems, and the Two-Bin Replenishment model. These systems have brought many cost saving advantages to healthcare systems by significantly reducing unnecessary inventory.

Coordination of these three components is crucial for excellent SCM in healthcare systems. Hospitals must find a way to incorporate efficient, effective, and efficacious methods for moving, storing, and dispensing within their operation. Significant cost-saving methods within their health systems can be found and achieved with improved processes and management in these areas.

Discussion Questions

1. Outline and explain the concepts of logistics in the healthcare supply chain.
2. Discuss and give examples of different storing (inventory management) models and different dispensing models.
3. Relate, discuss, and provide an example where the Value Chain integrates with healthcare supply chain warehousing/storing, transportation/moving, and distribution/dispensing.
4. Distinguish the functional areas of logistics in the context of the healthcare supply chain.
5. Relate the storage in a warehouse of a medical/surgical item, such as cotton balls, to bulk, pick and cross-docking areas, and discuss the differences.
6. Evaluate the organizational capabilities necessary for optimal logistics operations in healthcare with regard to warehousing, transportation, and distribution.

Exercises

1. Outline the healthcare Value Chain and identify important logistical supply-chain functions in the delivery of healthcare services.
2. Discuss healthcare supply chain warehousing/storing models, provide examples, and identify differences in bulk, "pick" or "loose," or cross-docking concerning those models.
3. Relate the sequence of the healthcare supply chain to sourcing, strategic sourcing, moving, storing, and dispensing cotton balls with emphasis on the warehouse or consolidated service center aspect of the sequence.
4. Distinguish the key concerns regarding transportation options with consideration of speed, cost, and reliability.
5. Relate costs of storing items in the healthcare supply chain to potential improvements in efficiency, effectiveness, and efficacy in the healthcare supply chain with examples.
6. Evaluate the "value" of the healthcare supply chain inventory management function to the healthcare delivery process.

Journal Items

Define:

Enterprise Resource Planning (ERP) Systems:

Consolidated Service Center:

Cross-Docking:

Receipt Lines:

SKUs (in supply-chain context):

PAR:

Answer the following questions with one to three sentences:

What does the Packaging String mean?
What does FTL and LTL mean, and does it matter?
Using a Volumetric Table (ANSI may be a good place to look), what are the cubic feet approximation for an "Each," for a "Case," and for a "Roll," and why does it matter what space an item takes to store?

Search: *Search items may give you great assistance in understanding the healthcare supply chain; provide the website/URL, and provide a one-paragraph summary of what you found.*

1. Warehouse Education and Research Council http://www.werc.org/
2. Food and Drug Administration (2 URLs) http://www.fda.gov/
3. Techsys (Warehousing and Inventory Management Information Systems) http://www.tecsys .com/?gclid=COTl7v_e27QCFQcHnQodbXEAQg
4. Manhattan Supply Chain Solutions (Warehousing and Inventory Management Information Systems) http://www.manh.com/solutions/distribution-management/warehouse-management

References

1. Logistic, *GRK-International Courier & Cargo*, (2014), http://www.grk-co.com/EN/logistic/ (accessed 6 Oct. 2014).

2. Chapter 2 Logistics: Basic Concepts & Characteristics, (2011), http://www.adam-europe.eu/prj/7095 /prj/CourieL_WP2_Chapter2_final.pdf (accessed 14 Oct. 2014).

3. Company - Autocar, (2014), http://www.autocartruck .com/Page/Company (accessed 20 Oct. 2014).

4. Table HM-20 – Office of Highway Policy Information (OHPI), (2013), http://www.fhwa.dot.gov/policy information/statistics/2012/hm20.cfm (accessed 20 Oct. 2014).

5. "The Logistics and Transportation Industry in the United States," (2011) http://selectusa.commerce. gov/industry-snapshots/logistics-and-transporta-tion-industry-united-states (accessed 9 Oct. 2014).

6. "The Logistics and Transportation Industry in the United States," (2011)

7. Transport - Logistics Operational Guide, *Logistics Cluster*, (2011), http://log.logcluster.org/mobile/response /transport/index.html (accessed 14 Oct. 2014).

8. Transport - Logistics Operational Guide, *Logistics Cluster*

9. FHWA - 2010 Conditions and Performance

10. Transport - Logistics Operational Guide, *Logistics Cluster*

11. Transport - Logistics Operational Guide, *Logistics Cluster*

12. Transport - Logistics Operational Guide, *Logistics Cluster*

13. Transport - Logistics Operational Guide, *Logistics Cluster*

14. FreightPros, (2013), http://www.freightpros.com/video /tl-ltl-freight-differences-part-i/ (accessed 12 Oct. 2014).

15. FreightPros, (2013)

16. FreightPros, (2013)

17. FreightPros, (2013)

18. What Is CSA? - CSA 2010 DOT Regulations Overview, (2011), http://www.whatiscsa.com/overview/ (accessed 3 Jul. 2014).

19. What Is CSA? - CSA 2010 DOT Regulations Overview

20. Hours of Service | Federal Motor Carrier Safety Administration, (2014), http://www.fmcsa.dot.gov /regulations/hours-of-service (accessed 3 Jul. 2014).

21. Hickey Min and Thomas Lambert, "Truck Driver Shortage Revisited." *Transportation Journal*, 42, no. 2, (2002), 5–16.

22. Hunter, D. (2000). Driver Shortage Pushes Up Wages. Chemical Week, 162(9), 44.

23. Richard Beilock and Russell Capelle Jr. "Occupational Loyalties Among Truck Drivers." *Transportation Journal*, 29 no. 3 (1990), 20–28.

24. David Hunter. "Driver Shortage Pushes Up Wages." *Chemical Week*, 162, no.9 (2000), 44.

25. What is inventory? *AccountingCoach*, (2013), http ://www.accountingcoach.com/blog/what-is -inventory (accessed 14 Oct. 2014).

26. Annexure F. (2014), http://saiindia.gov.in/english /home/our_products/audit_report/government_wise /union_audit/recent_reports/union_compliance /2000/Defence/2000_book3/annexuref.htm (accessed 16 Oct. 2014).

27. Annexure F. (2014)

28. Annexure F. (2014)

29. Annexure F. (2014)

30. Dinesh Dhoka, D and Y. Lokeswara Choudary, "ABC Classification for Inventory Optimization" (PhD diss.)

31. Dhoka and Choudary, "ABC Classification for Inventory Optimization"

32. "Inventory and Holding costs," *Durlinger*, (2013) 15 Oct. 2014 http://www.durlinger.nl/files/artikelen /Inventory-and-Holding-Costs.pdf (accessed 15 Oct. 2014).

33. Weighted Average Cost of Capital (WACC), *Investopedia*, (2012), http://www.investopedia.com /walkthrough/corporate-finance/5/cost-capital /wacc.aspx (accessed 15 Oct. 2014).

34. "Inventory and Holding costs," *Durlinger*.

35. FIFO vs LIFO: The Disadvantages and Advantages..., *Udemy*, (2014), https://www.udemy.com/blog /fifo-vs-lifo/ (accessed 18 Nov. 2014).

36. Murdoch, B. (2013). Comparing LIFO and FIFO: An Empirical Test of Representational Faithfulness. *Conflict Resolution & Negotiation Journal*, *2013*, (1).

37. FIFO vs. LIFO: What is the Difference? *Business News Daily*, (2013), http://www.businessnewsdaily. com/5514-fifo-lifo-differences.html (accessed 18 Nov. 2014).

38. FIFO vs LIFO: The Disadvantages and Advantages

39. FIFO vs LIFO: Difference and Comparison, *Diffen*, (2012), Retrieved November 18, 2014, from http ://www.diffen.com/difference/FIFO_vs_LIFO(accessed 18 Nov. 2014).

40. FIFO vs. LIFO: What is the Difference? *Business News Daily*

41. FIFO vs. LIFO: What is the Difference? *Business News Daily*

42. Danny Blount et al., *Materials Management Review Guide*, 4th ed., (Chicago: Association for Healthcare Resource & Materials Management of the American Hospital Association, 2012), 32.

43. Blount et al., *Materials Management Review Guide*, 32.

44. CBM Calculator, calculate CBM, volume and quantity per... (2008), http://www.ginifab.com/feeds/cbm / (accessed 19 Oct. 2014).

45. CBM Calculator.

46. YRC Freight Trailer Dimensions, *YRC Freight*, (2014), http://yrc.com/trailer-dimensions/ (accessed 17 Oct. 2014).

47. Peter Macleod, "ASK DAN: What is the weight capacity of a pallet?" *SHDLogistics*, (2012), http://www .shdlogistics.com/news/view/ask-dan-what-is-the -weight-capacity-of-a-pallet (accessed 17 Oct. 2014).

48. How to pack your pallet for delivery, *ParcelsPlease*, (2012), http://www.parcelsplease.co.uk/delivery-information /uk-pallet-delivery/pallet-packaging-advice / (accessed 17 Oct. 2014).

49. Jean-Paul Rodrigue and Theo Notteboom "The Cold Chain and its Logistics," *Hofstra*, (2006), http ://people.hofstra.edu/geotrans/eng/ch5en /appl5en/ch5a5en.html (accessed 15 Oct. 2014).

50. Rodrigue and Notteboom, "The Cold Chain and its Logistics."

51. Principles of Material Management - EIILM University, (2014), http://www.eiilmuniversity.ac.in/coursepack /Management/Principles_of_Material_Management .pdf (accessed 16 Oct. 2014).

52. "Definition and Scope of Materials Management," *Materials Management* (2009), http://www .materialsmanagement.info/defscope/ (accessed 16 Oct. 2014).

53. "Definition and Scope of Materials Management," *Materials Management*

54. http://www.thomasnet.com/products/material -handling-equipment-50140409-1.html?WTZO =NTKG+Body+Link (accessed 20 Oct. 2014).

55. Blount et al., *Materials Management Review Guide*, 32.

56. Blount et al., *Materials Management Review Guide*, 32.

57. Daniel B. McLaughlin and Julie M. Hays, *Healthcare Operations Management* (Chicago : Health Administration Press, 2008), 375.

58. Chapter 11 - Inventory Management, *McGraw-Hill Education*, (2014), http://highered.mheducation.com /sites/dl/free/0073525235/940447/jacobs3e _sample_ch11.pdf (accessed 16 Oct. 2014).

59. Chapter 11 - Inventory Management, *McGraw-Hill Education*

60. Michael H. Hugos, *Essentials of Supply Chain Management*, 3rd ed. (Hoboken, NJ: John Wiley and Sons, 2011).

61. McLaughlin and Hays, *Healthcare Operations Management* , 377.

62. Blount et al., *Materials Management Review Guide*, 33.

63. Blount et al., *Materials Management Review Guide*, 33.

64. Blount et al., *Materials Management Review Guide*, 33.

65. Blount et al., *Materials Management Review Guide*, 34.

66. Michael Duffy, "Is Supply Chain the Cure for Rising Healthcare Costs?" *Supply Chain Management Review*, (2009).

CHAPTER 4

DISPENSING AT POINTS OF CARE, SECURITY, AND COMPLIANCE IN THE SUPPLY CHAIN

LEARNING OBJECTIVES

1. Discuss dispensing at the points of care in the healthcare supply chain.
2. Discuss and give examples of several dispensing/distribution models.
3. Discuss security, storage, and chain of custody requirements of sensitive or legally designated items in the healthcare supply chain.
4. Distinguish the functional requirements of pharmaceutical supply-chain items from medical and surgical supply-chain items in terms.
5. Describe the differences and similarities of an outsourced dispensing/distribution system to an insourced system.
6. Evaluate the organizational capabilities necessary for optimal supply chain and logistics operations in healthcare with regard to dispensing/distribution to points of care in a hospital or clinic environment.

Introduction

Dispensing healthcare supply chain items to the care providers and patients, or at points of care, is an essential continuation of the healthcare Value Chain. In essence this is stocking of supplies used in patient care. To keep the supply items available to care providers, restocking is accomplished to replenish supplies used in the care process. The healthcare supply chain provides the "technology of care" in a variety of methods and models. Healthcare organizations can either insource (provide the functional capability within the organization by employing supply chain technicians, equipment, and facilities) or outsource (hire an organization outside of the healthcare organization to provide the functional

capability) the distribution of supply chain items to points of care within the health organization. There are several models of distribution of supply chain items; the different models are selected based on the point of care (medical and surgical ward, clinic, operating room, etc.) and the operational needs of the health organization. In addition, security and compliance within the supply chain is essential in healthcare in order to provide care with the highest level of efficacy and safety for patients while meeting legal requirements and statutes. These statutory or legal requirements include chain of custody of sensitive, high-pilferage, or highly addictive items through the components of the supply chain. Due to the complexity of the items used within most

FIGURE 4.1   Healthcare Value Chain with Emphasis on Dispensing to Points of Care

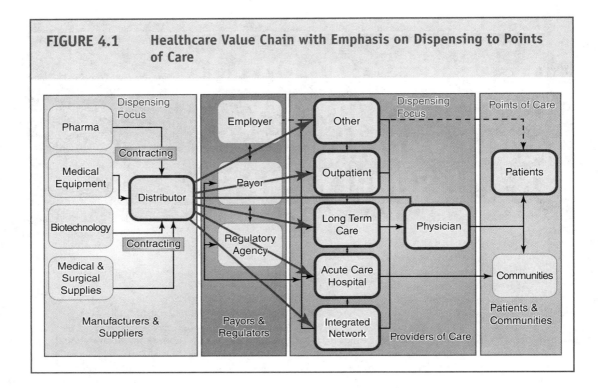

healthcare facilities, there are a myriad of regulations and protocols for the storage, chain of custody (that is who is in control of the items), and dispensing of medications/pharmaceuticals and medical supplies. This chapter will focus on dispensing/distribution of healthcare supply chain items and will give overview of statutory requirements associated with these processes.

There are different systems for dispensing items within an organization. General purpose inventory dispensing systems such as PAR, JIT, Perpetual Inventory or Kanban systems are commonly used. It can be a myriad of "alphabet soup" but the overview provided will explain the different models. Outsourced or vendor specific solutions are often used as well. The most common dispensing or distribution outsourced/vendor solutions are discussed after a brief introduction to PAR, JIT, Perpetual Inventory, and Kanban dispensing models. These models have widespread use in healthcare.

Periodic Automatic Replenishment (PAR)

The PAR system is a method of managing inventory that requires items be restocked to a specific level. In a PAR system, each of the items stored in central storage and the department storage areas are assigned a stock requirement or PAR level. At a certain time, sometimes continuously, through the use of automation, or every few days, the items are counted and restocked based on the number of items used.

When implemented within a healthcare organization, a PAR system requires a staff member to count all of the supplies in a storage area. When counting the supplies, the employee notes which items need to be restocked or "brought up to PAR level." Once the counting is complete, the employee retrieves the items required from central storage to restock the department storage area.[1]

FIGURE 4.2   PAR Bins with Scales

Courtesy of PAR Excellence Systems. http://www.parexcellencesystems.com/par-bins.aspx.

Just in Time (JIT)

JIT is a system to reduce inventory and minimize spoilage while still meeting the needs of customers. The central theme of JIT is essentially "items in inventory is wasted cash that cannot be used for other activities." Items in inventory do not add value to the company until they are sold, used for manufacturing, or provide a service. In addition, items in inventory are subject to damage, loss, or spoilage while in storage. The JIT system was developed in the 1970s to address these issues. Taiichi Ohno of Toyota developed the system for manufacturing to minimize waste and improve quality.[2] The key benefits of the JIT system are

- Low inventory;
- Low waste;
- High quality production;
- High customer responsiveness.

Keeping low inventory levels leads to low waste levels as discussed, but the reasons JIT creates high quality production and high customer responsiveness may be more elusive. The responsiveness and production quality are due to the closer alignment of production with the demands of customers. An organization with high inventory levels typically needs to use their current inventory before they are able to receive new inventory. This creates a lag time between customer demand and what the company is able to produce. For example, a company with a 14-day inventory of a raw material needs to produce those materials even if the marketplace is demanding production of another item not using this ingredient. This is applicable to service industries such as healthcare as well as manufacturing. Healthcare is a field of rapid innovation, and if a company has large quantities of a certain item, it can be negatively affected if that item is made obsolete by a technological advancement.

Perpetual Inventory

In a typical hospital, the perioperative department (operating room/suite and recovery area post procedure) typically generates between 50 and 60% of the revenue for the organization while accounting for 30 to 40% of the total expenses; the costs are mostly related to the use of supplies. Due to pressure from the market, the majority of healthcare organizations are looking for ways to reduce supply costs while increasing safety, efficiency, and productivity.[3] Due to the high priority, high urgency needs within the operating room, the power of information technology can be utilized to improve the accuracy and efficiency of the operating room supply chain. This is accomplished through electronically requesting supplies from the materials management department and automatically receiving the supplies requested in the correct quantities. When done optimally, the perioperative supply chain can be converted to a perpetual style system that is based on consumption. This eliminates the need for counting of bins, spot checks, or other manual inventory management.[4]

A subset of perpetual inventory is the case-cart system for managing operating room supplies on a case-by-case basis. When a case-cart system is used by a surgical services department, equipment and supplies for surgical cases are prepared in a central processing area and sent to the operating room on case carts. The purpose of a case cart is to ensure that the correct supplies and equipment are available in the correct quantity for the procedure being performed. After the case is complete, the cart is returned for cleaning and restocking for the next case.[5] In addition, consignment is typically used on perioperative areas of the health organization as well. In consignment, the manufacturer or distributor of perioperative items (examples include surgical screws, cardiac rhythm management items such as pacemakers, stents.) provides an assortment of items for use in patient procedures in the perioperative area. Consignment is a method where a vendor's or supplier's stock of supply or durable medical items (such as implants for surgery) are

stored and the healthcare organization is invoiced/billed for what they utilize based on a pre-arranged price schedule of those items. The manufacturer or vendor/supplier or distributor will inventory items used in a given time period (weekly, monthly, or quarter) and charge the health organization for the used consigned items. It is wise for a dual inventory process where the health organization representative and the manufacturer or distributor count items used in procedures and come to consensus on the number to charge/bill to the health organization.

Kanban

Another common method for dispensing is the use of a Kanban system which originated in manufacturing. "Kanban" is a Japanese word for card and is a signal or permit for action. The Kanban system was developed by Toyota in the late 1940s and was modeled after a process observed at grocery stores. They noticed that items on the shelf of a typical grocery store were restocked from inventory held within the store, not from an external source. Items were only ordered from vendors when the internal inventory levels reached a certain point; they referred to this point as a visual signal. This visual signal served to reduce waste due to spoilage and maximize value for the grocery stores and Toyota as well.[6]

The same principal can be easily applied to healthcare. Hospitals typically have a central storage area where shipments are stored upon delivery from the supplier. Since the size of all but the smallest hospitals makes it impractical to go to the central storage area every time supplies are needed, each department or ward will usually have a local storage room with just the supplies that are typically used for the procedures performed in that area of the hospital. When the inventory levels in the department storage area reach a certain level, there is a signal to restock that item. The type of signal can vary, but no matter what the signal is, the response to it is to restock the item in the local storage area.

An example of the Kanban system in practice is the Kanban two-bin supply system. A two-bin Kanban system uses RFID stock cards and a red signal card. The two-bin Kanban system is typically part of a medical shelving system that stocks a variety of supplies, either in a partitioned bin or in two separate bins. A black item card with an imbedded RFID specific to the items in the bin is placed in the front of each supply bin. When the last item in the primary bin is used, the user removes the item card and places it into an RFID reader equipped box. When the RIFD tag is read, it sends a signal to central storage indicating the item needs to be restocked. After the black item card is removed, the red card indicating that the restock is in progress is visible so that staff knows to use the stock in the secondary bin until the stock is replenished. When the employee responsible for refilling the bins comes to replenish the supply, the black cards are replaced in front of the storage bins, and all items are restocked. In order to reduce spoilage of supplies, any items remaining in the secondary bin at the time of restocking are moved to the primary bin, and the new supplies are placed in the secondary bin.[7]

The effectiveness of any inventory management system is situational, and no single solution works best for all locations. However, among our example cases, there are clear benefits to the two-bin Kanban system. One of the benefits in our example includes the elimination of trips back and forth between departmental supply locations and central storage. Another benefit is a potential reduction in inventory as well as a reduction in shortage levels. These reduction and inventory and shortage levels are made possible through the standardization of the replenishment procedure.[8] Standard procedures for replenishment are also subject to process improvement measures, which can further increase efficiency over time.

Medical/Surgical dispensing requires the storage of a mix of devices, sterile and non-sterile equipment, and medications. Some of these items, commonly medications, need to be stored securely and administered accurately to ensure patient safety and speed of treatment. The restock system can be based on PAR, Kanban, or some other system, but some system should be used to manage the deceptive complexity of the storage requirements in these areas.

Pharmaceutical dispensing is different from other items within a healthcare organization because of the added chain of custody issues, access controlled substances, and safety issues associated

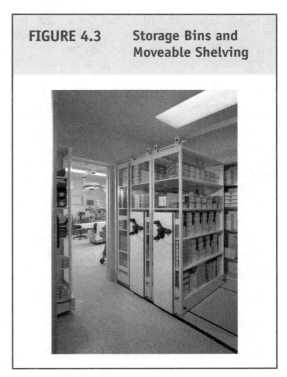

FIGURE 4.3 **Storage Bins and Moveable Shelving**

Courtesy of Southwest Solutions. Retrieved from: http://www .southwestsolutions.com/equipment/hospital-operating -room-storage-cabinets-medical-supplies-shelving.

with medications. Since many pharmaceuticals are controlled by law (requiring a secure area for storage) and can only be given to a patient by a licensed physician's prescription, special storage and security controls, such as locked storage and chain of custody, must be utilized. A chain of custody is a method that clearly lists who is responsible and accountable for specific items within the healthcare organization.

Point of Use

Point of use is a supply chain solution based on modern technology. The point of use system integrates bar code scanning or radio frequency identification (RFID) chips to help manage high-cost items primarily, but it can be used with any item in the supply chain. In addition to RFID, the point of use system uses GS1-128 and HIBC codes to track lot, serial number, and expiration dates of items.

Like most other vendor-based systems, it has the ability to integrate with other systems to provide a more complete logistics solution for a facility. Computerized systems such as point of use can be used as part of a JIT inventory system to track high-cost items as well as simplifying access to lower-cost items. Access to low-cost items is simplified through the use of stock tracking and automatic discovery of items that are in need of replenishment.[9] Point of use is important to understand since that is the place where the supply item is utilized for patient diagnosis, treatment and/or care. The method of distribution, JIT or Kanban or PAR, is dictated to a large degree by the specific needs of the patient at the point of use.

Pharmaceutical-Specific Solution Models

Many inpatient and outpatient (to include retail pharmacies) pharmacies utilize cabinet systems integrated with the patient care process and the supply chain system. These are computerized systems, in most cases, that are linked to computerized physician order entry (called CPOE systems) where physicians order/prescribe pharmaceuticals to patients as per the patient's plan of care. The CPOE system alerts the pharmacy where the computerized cabinet decrements the pharmaceutical item stock on hand (such as a tablet or pill) in the cabinet when the pharmacist prepares the prescription for the patient. The system links to the supply chain system to electronically "order" the item that was used for the patient for resupply of that item. Typical and commonplace pharmaceutical systems are overviewed in the next section.

Omnicell

The manufacturer, Omnicell, is a popular solution for managing central pharmacy automation. The primary advantages of an automated system such as Omnicell are increases in efficiency, support for the prevention of medication errors, and documentation for regulatory compliance.[10] The system maintains a locked-cabinet environment to ensure chain of custody and security of the pharmaceutical items.

Pyxis

The Pyxis system is a brand name for one of the most commonly used automated medication dispensing systems. Automated medication

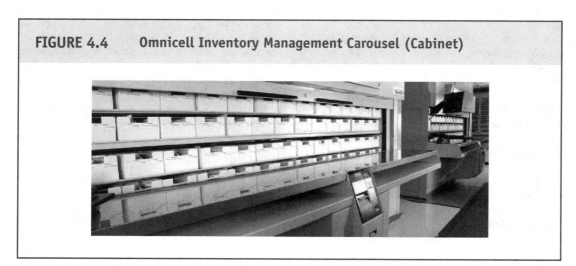

FIGURE 4.4   Omnicell Inventory Management Carousel (Cabinet)

Courtesy of Omnicell. Retrieved from: http://www.omnicell.com/Products/Central_Pharmacy_Automation/WorkflowRx_System/Inventory_Management_Carousel.aspx dispensing systems such as Pyxis support decentralized medication management, which leads to greater efficiency within the pharmacy department. The system utilizes barcode scanning to ensure accurate medication dispensing as well as features which help prevent the loading of incorrect medication into the system. These storage units are maintained in the inpatient pharmacy and possibly in the patient care areas of the healthcare organization. The systems are linked to the enterprise resource planning system to prompt automatic replenishment once a specific pharmaceutical item falls below the re-order point. Additionally, the Pyxis system has an alert system which provides an added level of safety when dealing with high-risk medications. According the manufacturer, some hospitals were able to reduce the average patient's

time-to-first-dose by more than 90%. These time savings are accomplished through the decentralization of medication management. An added benefit from the decentralization of medication management is that pharmacists are available for other duties.[11] As with any system, quality control is of paramount concern.

Quality Control

Quality control is a key issue in the storage of medication, medical supplies, and equipment. All of the inventory control systems mentioned above increase quality of care and reduce the total variable cost of operations.[12]

It is not uncommon for items used in healthcare to have specific storage needs such as a certain temperature range or humidity that the items need to be stored at. Some of these requirements are designed to prevent the spread of infection, such as storing linens and gowns at a certain temperature. Others, such as storing insulin in a secure refrigerator, extend the shelf life of the medication. Some tests are sensitive to humidity and lose their accuracy when stored outside of the manufacturer recommended range. In addition to storage requirements, items need to be stored safely to prevent damage. While it is advantageous to all industries that have inventory to store it in a way to prevent damage to the item, it is especially critical in healthcare, where damaged items may cause harm to patients.

An example of an item-specific requirement common within healthcare organizations is the need to refrigerate medications during storage. Insulin, a medication used in the treatment of diabetes, is one such example. According to the three United States-based manufacturers of insulin, it is recommended that insulin be stored in a refrigerator at between 36 and 42 degrees Fahrenheit. Storing medications according to their guidelines is important to ensure that their potency and safety is maintained until the expiration date on the package.[13]

Expiration dates on medications have been required since 1979. The expiration date on medication is the date until which the manufacturer guarantees the full potency and safety of the medication. The majority of the information

FIGURE 4.5   Pyxis MedStation System (Cabinet)

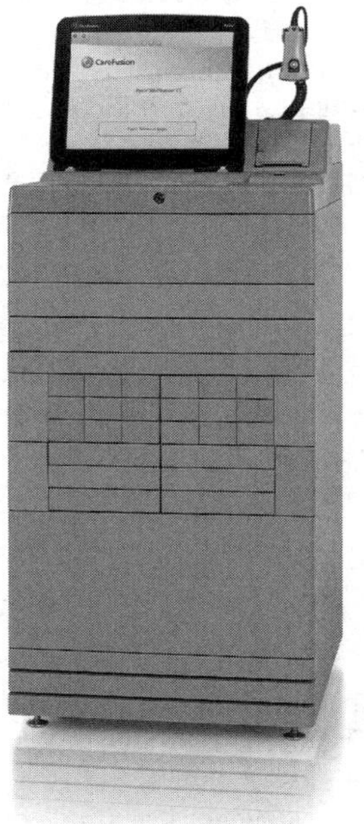

Courtesy of CareFusion. Retrieved from: http://www.carefusion .com/medical-products/medication-management/medication -technologies/pyxis-medstation-system.aspx

regarding drug expiration dates can be traced back to a study conducted by the FDA for the military. The situation was that because the military had a large stockpile of drugs, there were huge costs associated with the maintenance of their supply. According to the researchers involved in the study, nearly 90% of more than a hundred medications studied were effective up to fifteen years after their listed expiration date.[14] However, there are some exceptions to this rule, such as tetracycline, an antibiotic, though the majority of medications in pill form are safe and effective long after the expiration date.[15] Medications in other forms, such as nitroglycerin, insulin, and liquid antibiotics, are typically much more volatile than medications in pill form and, as such, have much shorter shelf lives.[16] In a healthcare environment, the extension of drugs past their written expiration date is a decision made by the pharmacists, as the storage of medication requires specific conditions to maximize their effective lifespan.

Lot Size

Lot sizing has both storage and ordering implications. Ordering in large quantities can result in reduced per-unit-price due to economies of scale, but if the item is not used in high volume, the storage costs for the item can be more than the savings from ordering in bulk. One method for determining the "best" amount of an item to order is to calculate the economic order quantity or EOQ.

It is important to also note that an EOQ quantity usually has a safety level added to that quantity. The more important the item, to not have a stock out or have none available or on hand, the greater the safety level. Safety levels can be the amount of the item needed to cover the days it takes to order and ship the item to your location, or it can be a percentage of the use of that item. A safe level of stock is necessary to provide coverage for unexpected customer/patient demand, damage in the warehouse or quality issues found in production.

Another implication of lot size is the potential for spoilage of items in storage. Spoilage is not a problem limited to grocery stores; medications, as well as sterile supplies, also have expiration dates. Depending on the product, these dates may be flexible, but spoilage is still a very real concern.[17]

Another item to consider with regard to lot size is the potential for goods to be damaged in storage, particularly with large lot sizes. A large lot size may take more space than was expected, leading to potential damage. Even if items ordered in large quantities are stored properly, they are still at an increased risk for damage simply because of the increased time items purchased in bulk are held in storage when compared to items purchased in a smaller lot size.

Healthcare Supply Chain Impact to Quality and Efficacy of Care

Consider the following statements. How does the complexity of the healthcare supply chain contribute to quality of care? Efficacy, security, and quality go hand in hand. It is important to keep quality imperatives in mind, along with security and compliance requirements.

- There are several logistical impacts of the varied shelf lives and storage requirements of medications.
- Inventory management, as discussed in a previous chapter, is a critical component in the supply chain.
- Additional complexity is added to the sourcing and procurement component of the supply chain for medications due to the variation in shelf life.
- Depending on the agreement a healthcare organization has with its vendors, it may be possible to return expired products to receive credit on a future order.

Security in the Healthcare Supply Chain

The healthcare supply chain has many items that require security due to mandates from government regulating agencies or that are stored in a secure area due to their cost. Several examples of items that are stored securely due to government regulation are pharmaceuticals on the federal schedule of narcotics and radioactive materials. Items such as medical devices may be stored securely due to their value and the potential for damage if they were not stored in a secure environment. Other items such as food or office supplies may also require some level of secure storage due to pilferage. The Department of Justice oversees the security and chain of custody requirements of various identified healthcare supply chain items. It is imperative to follow and comply with these guidelines and statutes; they can be found at: http://www.deadiversion.usdoj.gov/index.html. The sections that follow provide an overview of the requirements regarding security in the healthcare supply chain.

Federal Schedule of Narcotics

The federal schedule of narcotics is a system for categorizing narcotics and was created as part of Title II of the Comprehensive Abuse Prevention and Control Act of 1970. Title II of this law, more commonly known as the Controlled Substances Act (CSA), is jointly enforced by the Food and Drug Administration (FDA) as well as the Drug Enforcement Agency (DEA). There are five levels, designated CI through CV, within the federal schedule of narcotics. This designation is based on the abuse potential of the medication, medical applications, and safety. Organizations that distribute, store, handle, or order medications on the schedule of narcotics are required to be registered with the DEA. In addition to registration, there are requirements to maintain accurate inventories, security, and records of the controlled substances.[18]

CI drugs have a high potential for abuse and currently have no accepted medical use for treatment in the United States. Since there is no currently accepted medical use for CI drugs, these are substances for which physicians cannot write prescriptions. In addition, there is a lack of accepted safety for the use of CI drugs even while under medical supervision. Examples of CI drugs include heroin, LSD, MDMA, GHB, and psilocybin.[19]

CII drugs also have a high potential for abuse, but they do have a currently accepted medical use for treatment in the United States. Due to their high potential for abuse, CII drugs typically have severe restrictions on their use. Abusing a CII drug can result in either psychological or physical dependence on the substance. Examples of CII drugs include hydrocodone, morphine, and Adderall.[20]

CIII drugs have less potential for abuse than CI or CII substances. CIII drugs have an accepted medical use for treatment within the United States. However, abusing a CIII drug may still lead to moderate physical dependence or a strong psychological dependence. Examples of CIII drugs include codeine combined with aspirin as well as synthetic testosterone and its precursors.[21]

CIV drugs have a low abuse potential relative to drugs classified as CIII. These substances also have an accepted medical use within the United States and are widely used. Abusing a CIV drug may lead to minor physical or psychological dependence. CV drugs have an even lower potential for abuse even when compared to CIV drugs. CIV and CV drugs are less commonly known by the general public than CI, CII, and CIII drugs. Examples include medications such as diazepam, a CIV drug used to treat anxiety, and Notuss-PE, a CV drug used to treat cold and flu symptoms.[22, 23, 24]

Non-Provider Requirements

There are various non-provider requirements with regard to handling controlled substances outlined by the United States Department of Justice. Non-providers are healthcare organizations or affiliated employees who do not provide direct patient care; patient care is provided by physicians, nurses, and other clinical staff. Special considerations are needed when non-providers have access to medical supplies and pharmaceuticals as defined by law. These requirements apply to organizations that handle class 1 through 5 (CI through CV) drugs as outlined in the CSA. Non-practitioners include manufacturers, packagers, labelers, distributors, importers, exporters, narcotic treatment programs, and compounders for narcotic treatment programs.[25] Classes of drugs/pharmaceuticals are categorized, with associated levels of security and storage requirements, by law and the potential for addiction and black market activity of a particular drug.

FIGURE 4.6   Security Cage for Storage

© C Berry Ottaway/Shutterstock

Minimum Standards: Handlers of CI and CII Controlled Substances

Small quantities of CI and CII raw materials, bulk materials awaiting further processing, and finishing products must be stored in an underwriters lab (UL) listed burglary-resistant safe with a Group 1-R lock or in a General Services Administration (GSA) Class V-rated security container or in the equivalent, which affords the following security protection:

1. 30 man minutes against surreptitious entry,
2. 10 man minutes against forced entry,
3. 20 man hours against lock manipulation,
4. 20 man hours against radiological attack.[26]

This safe, or security container, must be bolted, strapped, or otherwise securely fastened to the floor or wall in such a way that it cannot be readily removed if it weighs less than 750 pounds. Depending upon the quantities and types of controlled substances stored, this safe, or security container, must be equipped with an alarm system which, upon attempted unauthorized entry, transmits a signal directly to a central protection company, a local or state police agency, which has a legal obligation to respond, a 24-hour proprietary central station operated by the registrant, or such other protection as DEA may approve.[27]

Large quantities of such controlled substances that do not permit storage in a safe or security container may be stored in a vault meeting the following specifications or their equivalent, if constructed after September 1, 1971:

1. The walls, floor, and ceiling are constructed of at least eight inches of reinforced concrete or other substantial masonry reinforced vertically and horizontally with #4 (half-inch) steel rods tied six inches on center or UL-listed modular vault panels.
2. The door and frame unit are UL-listed burglary-resistant, GSA Class V-rated or the equivalent, i.e., the multiple-position Group 1-R combination lock, the relocking device, the special metal alloy that resists carbide drilling and in general affords the overall security protection set forth above for safes and security containers.
3. If operations require the vault/container to remain open to frequent access, the door is required to

be equipped with a day gate which is self-closing and self-locking. If the operation requires only that the vault be opened infrequently, such as to remove raw material in the morning and return it at night and is always relocked immediately after use, a day gate is not required.

4. The walls or perimeter are equipped with an alarm system that, upon attempted unauthorized entry, must transmit an alarm directly to a central protection company, a local or state police agency that has a legal obligation to respond, a 24-hour proprietary central station operated by the registrant, or such other protection as DEA may approve. If necessary, due to local conditions or other problems, holdup buttons may be required to be placed at strategic points of entry or exit from the perimeter.

5. The door is equipped with a contact switch or contact switches, and there is complete electrical lacing of the walls, floors, and ceiling, sensitive ultrasonic or infrared sensors within, a sensitive sound accumulator system, or other such devices or equipment designed to detect unauthorized entry as may be approved by the DEA.

Vaults constructed before or under construction on September 1, 1971, and approved by the Bureau of Narcotics and Dangerous Drugs or its predecessor agencies may be of substantial construction with a steel door, combination or key lock, and alarm system.[28]

The DEA evaluates a registrant security system on an element-by-element basis and on an overall basis, measuring the system against the potential theft or diversion problem the registrant might encounter at the registered location. Thus, DEA may approve a security system although some of the specific standards are not met, e.g., a registrant who provides 24-hour guard surveillance may not need the full alarm protection as set forth in the regulations. A registrant who handles large quantities of in-process liquids running through a pipe system may not need to vault this form of controlled substances because of the difficulties in containing or diverting the liquids and their possible non-restrictability. The minimum standards and general security requirements set forth above and below are used by the DEA as a basis for making decisions on the specific security needs of each registrant.[29]

Minimum Standards: Handlers of CIII–V Controlled Substances

Controlled substances are those deemed by federal law to be highly susceptible to pilferage (theft) due to the addictive qualities of the substance and/or the high probability of illegal sale of the items (illegal sales on the black market). Small quantities of C III–V controlled substances may be stored in a UL-listed burglary-resistant safe or a GSA Class V-rated security container or equivalent, which complies with the requirements for storing CI and CII substances. Large quantities of such controlled substances that do not permit storage in a safe or in a security container may be stored in

1. A building or an area within a building having perimeter security that limits access during working hours, provides adequate security after working hours, and has the following security controls:

   a. An electronic alarm system as described above for CI and CII controlled substances.

   b. Substantially constructed self-closing and self-locking doors employing either multiple-position combination or key lock type-locking mechanism. In lieu of self-locking/closing doors, a door that is kept closed and locked at all times when not in use and that, when in use, is kept under direct observation of a responsible employee of the registrant is permitted.

   c. Requisite key control, combination limitations, and change procedures.

2. A cage within a building on the premises meeting the following specifications:

   a. Walls constructed of not less than ten-gauge steel fabric mounted on steel posts which are

      1. at least one inch in diameter;
      2. set in concrete or installed with lag bolts that are pinned or brazed; and
      3. placed no more than ten feet apart with horizontal one-and-one-half-inch reinforcement every sixty inches.

   b. Mesh construction with openings not more than two and one half inches across the square.

    c. A ceiling constructed of the same material or walls extending to and firmly attached to the structural ceiling.

    d. A door constructed of the same gauge steel fabric on a metal door frame in a metal door flange.

    e. An alarm system protecting the perimeter and interior as described above.

3. An enclosure of masonry or other such materials or secure storage area which has been approved by the DEA.[30]

Collocating CIII–V with CI and CII Controlled Substances

In order to save money, sometimes classes of products are stored together, or collocated together. Schedule III–V controlled substances may be stored with CI and CII substances under the security measures required for the higher-class substances (CIII–V with higher-security requirements). CIII–V substances may be stored in the vault provided that access to the area is not substantially increased and that permission for such storage is obtained in advance from the appropriate DEA Field Office.[31]

Multiple Storage Areas

On occasion it may be necessary for non-practitioner registrants to handle several classes of controlled substances separately. Some examples of these special circumstances are damaged goods, returned goods, and goods in processing. In these circumstances, controlled substances may be stored apart from the main stock of controlled substances provided that each storage area complies with the security requirement set forth in the previously described minimum standards.[32]

Accessibility to Storage Areas

In order to minimize the possibility of diversion, the registrant must limit access to the storage areas for controlled substances to a minimum number of authorized employees. Although not specifically required, it may be necessary to institute some type of security pass system if the size, type, or other characteristic factors specific to the organization dictate the need. Where it is necessary for employee or non-employee maintenance personnel, business guests, or other visitors to have access to or to pass through a controlled substances storage area, the registrant needs to provide authorization to those individuals. The authorization should be in writing, and the specially authorized individuals should be held under adequate observation during the time they are in the storage area.[33]

Compounding and Manufacturing Areas

Processing and manufacturing medical substances are part of the supply chain in that raw or elemental substances must be processed to produce a usable medical substance. Compounding pharmacies (those that produce substances from raw or elemental material for patient use based on a physician's prescription for the patient) and manufacturing organizations also fall under the requirements of the federal law for controlled substances. Manufacturing activities (include processing, packaging, and labeling) involving controlled substances listed in any schedule, as well as all compounders, must implement the following security controls:

1. All in-process substances must be returned to the controlled substances storage area at the termination of the process. If the process is not completed at the end of the work day, the processing area or tanks, vessels, bins, or bulk containers holding controlled substances must be securely locked inside an area or building which affords adequate security.

2. Manufacturing activities with controlled substances must be conducted in an area or areas with limited access and must be kept under surveillance by one or more employees designated in writing by management to be responsible for the area. The designated employee or employees must be able to provide continuous surveillance of the area in order that unauthorized persons may not enter or leave the area without the designated employee's knowledge. Access may be

limited by the use of physical dividers such as walls or partitions, by traffic control lines, or by restricted space designations.

3. During controlled substances production, the manufacturing areas should be accessible only to those employees necessary for efficient operation. If it becomes necessary for employee or non-employee maintenance personnel, business guests, or visitors to be present or to pass through manufacturing areas during production, it is in the best interest of the registrant to have an employee designated in writing as being responsible for providing adequate surveillance of the area.[34]

Public Warehouses

Registrants, those with access rights to the storage areas, who store controlled substances in public warehouses are responsible for selecting a facility that will provide adequate security to guard against losses and thefts. Whenever possible, the registrant should select a storage warehouse or terminal that meets the physical security requirement and controls set forth above and below, with the knowledge that it is the registrant, not the warehouseman, who is responsible for the security of the controlled substances. Other aspects of warehouse or terminal security which the registrant might consider are

1. Adequacy of fencing, lighting, electronic security, checkpoints, and other perimeter controls.
2. Type of order tracking or tracing system in use, if any.
3. Personnel screening, hiring, and control programs.
4. Hours of operation.
5. Use of contract or proprietary guards.
6. Procedures and systems in use to control inbound and outbound tractors, trailers, containers, etc.
7. Yard control of drivers, tractors, trailers, containers, etc.[35]

Common or Contract Carriers

Registrants are also responsible for selecting common or contract carriers that will provide adequate security against in-transit losses or thefts. This includes parcel delivery from vendors such as the U.S. Postal Service, FedEx, UPS, and DHL. If the registrant has substantial quantities of controlled substances lost or stolen in transit when using a particular common or contract carrier, steps should be taken to obtain another secure carrier or means of transport. When evaluating common or contract carriers, in addition to evaluating warehouses or terminal security, the registrant might consider the following:

1. Physical security of the vehicles, e.g.
   a. Adequate vehicle and trailer locks subject to proper key control, and locking of vehicles at all times when unattended.
   b. Vehicular alarm systems in use at all times when vehicles and trailers are unattended.
   c. Fuel lock alarm devices.
   d. Page alert alarm systems carried by drivers when away from vehicles and trailers to alert them to unauthorized opening of doors, hoods, etc.
2. Route variations to avoid patterns.
3. Vehicles equipped with CBs or other radios to communicate with local law enforcement agencies or the company warehouse or terminal in the event of an emergency or other duress condition.
4. Special code numbers or symbols painted on or otherwise affixed to the roof.
5. Driver screening, hiring, and control programs.
6. Overall priority and security afforded controlled substances shipments.
7. Use of subcontracted carriers.

These security aspects and procedures are also applicable when delivering and picking up controlled substances using company-owned or leased vehicles operated by company employees. Although not required, precautions such as securely wrapping and sealing packages containing controlled substances and using unmarked or coded boxes or shipping containers are strongly recommended for guarding against in-transit losses.[36]

Theft or Loss

Registrants must notify the appropriate DEA field office of theft or significant loss of any controlled substance. Furthermore, the supplier is responsible for reporting in-transit losses of controlled substances by a common or contract carrier. The registrant must then promptly complete and submit the DEA Form 106 regarding such losses or thefts. Thefts must be reported whether or not the controlled substances are subsequently recovered and/or the responsible parties identified and action taken against them.[37]

Radioactive Materials

Radioactive materials are being used with increasing frequency in medicine. The use of radioactive materials is common in fields such as nuclear medicine, radiology, and oncology. There are two broad categories of medicine that use radioactive materials: diagnostic and therapeutic. Approximately one-third of all the patients admitted to hospitals are diagnosed or treated using radioactive materials.[38] Generally speaking, diagnostic nuclear medicine procedures use a small amount of radioactive material that is administered to the patient though either injection, inhalation or orally. The administered radioactive compound collects in the organ or area of the body being analyzed and emits radiation. This radiation is collected by a device that provides information on the function and structure of the organ, which allows physicians to locate and identify tumors or functional organ problems. Therapeutic use of radiation follows similar procedures for administration. However, instead of being used to visualize a problem, the radioactive material collects in an area of the body for the purpose of killing cancerous tissues, reducing tumor size, or relieving pain.[39]

Due to the potential harmful effects of radiation, the use, storage, and disposal of radioactive materials is controlled within the healthcare environment. The Nuclear Regulatory Commission (NRC) is responsible the regulation of radioactive materials. According to the NRC, organizations that offer nuclear medicine services must be licensed. In addition to licensing, facilities are also required to have a radiation safety officer on site. The radiation safety officer is responsible for the proper security and handling of all radioactive materials in the possession of the facility. Locations where radioactive materials are stored are required to have warning signs to show the public that radioactive materials are stored nearby. This requirement is shared by vehicles which transport radioactive materials. When storing, shipping, or handling radioactive materials, they are kept inside special containers that are shielded to protect those nearby from the radiation.[40]

Pilferage

Employee pilferage affects nearly all businesses and cuts across all job classifications. The U.S. Chamber of Commerce estimates that employee theft costs businesses in the United States $40 billion annually.[41] Pilferage includes anything from embezzlement, taking office supplies, making personal copies or calls from work, taking extended lunch breaks, or taking more food than what is paid for. It is estimated that a company typically loses an amount comparable to between 1 and 3% of its annual revenue due to pilferage.[42] Food pilferage can be an issue whether an organization feeds thousands of people a day or a few hundred a week. The use of inventory control systems can help detect discrepancies that may indicate pilferage is occurring. Some pilferage issues can be addressed through the use of a point of sale (POS) system to track which items have been sold in close to real time. Using such a system, it can be more easily determined which items were sold to customers or used in the production of meals. Implementing a system such as PAR to determine the number of items in stock and to record their use can also help identify pilferage.[43]

In addition to measures to help prevent pilferage, companies typically have systems in place to keep potential thieves out of an organization as well as deal with employees caught stealing. A long-term solution to pilferage is culture change. Changing the attitudes and perceptions of pilferage activities can be an effective tool to combat the theft. The primary tool in this process is education regarding the activities and the types of behavior that the organization wants to promote. The education process will need to be reinforced over time to continue to encourage the behavior changes.[44]

Chain of Custody

The chain of custody is an unbroken path a product takes from the first stage in the supply chain to the end customer, including raw commodity materials, conversion, transformation, distribution, and logistics.[45] There are several elements to maintaining a proper chain of custody. However, custody chains for items vary slightly based on the type of item. A common example of chain of custody is the pre-employment drug screening and is outlined below:

- The donor is either directly or indirectly supervised while they deliver the specimen.
- The specimen container should be handed directly to whoever is supervising the collection and then sealed.
- The container is initialed by both the donor and the individual supervising to show that both individuals agree as to the contents of the container.
- The names of everyone who has access to the specimen should be recorded on a form which accompanies the specimen.
- The specimen should be stored in a secure location until testing or being sent to the laboratory.
- In situations where testing is done on-site, the testing should be completed in a secure environment to avoid the possibility of the sample being switched out prior to testing.
- In the event that a specimen is transported to an external laboratory, it should be mailed in a sealed container by a licensed carrier.
- Proper labeling is essential to prevent confusion with other samples.[46]

Chain of Custody for Pharmaceuticals

Maintaining the chain of custody for pharmaceuticals is essential for maintaining the efficacy and safety of the medications. Maintaining the chain of custody for sensitive products such as pharmaceuticals or other products is the same general process outlined in the previous section's example. With the real-world example in mind, a more generalized description of chain of custody requirements can be laid out.

The first step in developing a chain of custody is creating key control points. This process includes analyzing the process to determine where there is a potential for contamination, theft, or damage to products within the chain of custody. The next step in the process is to identify the product through unique markings using a system that is uniformly applied. This is a simple way to assure that there is no cross contamination, damage, or injury due to misidentification of pharmaceuticals in the chain of custody. All activities should be documented for the purpose of accountability and monitoring within the supply chain. Proper documentation within the chain of custody will make compliance audits easier to carry out. The fifth step is to audit the process using both internal and external auditors to ensure process as well as product integrity. The final step is integration within the supply chain. Typically, the supply chain is integrated downstream in the supply chain. An example of downstream integration of the supply chain for pharmaceuticals is medications which, as well as items that do not require a strict chain of custody, may eventually end up on the same medical/surgical floor of a hospital.[47]

In summary,

Step 1: Develop key control points.
Step 2: Create a product identification and unique marking system.
Step 3: Institute a record-keeping process and document all activities.
Step 4: Assign responsibility, accountability, and authority (RAA) to ensure compliance.
Step 5: Audit procedures.
Step 6: Integrate the supply chain.[48]

Additionally, there are some special needs within the pharmaceutical supply chain as outlined previously. These include the need of a cold chain for some products (such as insulin) and security requirements for controlled substances.

Chain of Custody for Implants

Medical implants have their own special storage and tracking requirements. The FDA requires manufacturers to track certain items from the point of manufacture through the distribution throughout the supply chain. The tracking of medical devices became federal law in 1993 and included devices that were implanted inside the human body for a period of more than one year or devices that could cause serious health consequences if they failed. The purpose of this tracking is to ensure that these devices can be located quickly. The tracking information facilitates any notifications or recalls that the FDA orders in the case of medical devices that can cause serious health risks. Prior to 1998, the FDA had automatic mandatory tracking procedures in place for medical devices. However, this regulation was changed as a part of legislation aimed at the modernization of the regulation of medical devices. Instead of tracking all devices, the FDA now mandates manufacturers of certain classes of medical devices to track their items down to the patient level.[49] This requirement demands a patient-specific implant log that includes manufacturer of the implant information, serial number of the implant, and a system of recall and advice tracking from the FDA. In addition, the health organization and supply chain must have a method to inform providers of care using those implants for patient care and procedures and patients with those embedded implants of important information from the manufacturer of the implant and FDA guidance.

Outsourcing and Vendor Contract Services

From these few examples, the complexity of the healthcare supply chain with regard to security and compliance should be apparent. As you may have guessed, this complexity fosters a large industry of consultants and companies which provide services for healthcare organizations that would rather outsource an activity than perform it internally or insource. A few examples of vendor organizations are provided to provide a sense of outsourcing options in the healthcare supply chain. Outsourcing can be for the entire supply chain or components of the supply chain such as medical and surgical, pharmaceutical, and other commodities. The security requirements are to be maintained throughout the "chain" from production to patient utilization.

Cardinal Health

Cardinal Health started as a distribution company in 1971; for nearly a decade, the organization was primarily a food distributor until 1979, when the company began to distribute pharmaceuticals. Today, Cardinal Health is a leading distributor of pharmaceuticals but also provides other services to hospitals.[50] The services provided by Cardinal Health include pharmacy solutions, automation technology, distribution, and perioperative products.[51]

Owens and Minor

Owens and Minor has a history dating back to the late 1880s. At this time, Richmond, Virginia, was the center of drug wholesaling in the southern part of the United States. Otho Owens and Gilmer Minor worked for competing drug wholesalers who eventually began working together and formed their own company in 1882.[52] Since then, the company has continued to expand; they now distribute around 220,000 medical-surgical products and have over fifty distribution centers across the United States. Similar to Cardinal Health, they also offer analytic tools as well as assistance with logistics and supply chain.[53]

Amerisource Bergen

Amerisource Bergen was formed in 2001 through a merger of AmeriSource Health Corporation and Bergen Brunswig Corporation. Just like Cardinal Health and Owens and Minor, they have a large network of distribution centers and employees.[54] Amerisource Bergen has a focus on pharmacy solutions and offers services such as purchasing, consulting, packaging, and global sourcing and distribution.[55]

While all of these companies promise to increase efficiency and cost savings, potential problems can arise from the use of contract services.

Contract Compliance

Contract compliance is important in industries such as healthcare because portions of the business operations tend to be conducted by another party.

This can lead to control, expense, and revenue risks for the organization. Examples of business operations conducted by a third party in healthcare include contracting with a physician or physician group to provide care to patients, outsourcing purchasing, or shipping. When the risks associated with contracted activities are not appropriately monitored, problems can arise depending on the regulatory and security requirement associated with the contract.[56]

Compliance with security guidelines applies to all of the items previously discussed, including laboratory samples, CSA medications, and radioactive materials.

Regulatory compliance was discussed in part earlier with regard to radioactive materials, medical implants, medications, and laboratory samples. Regulatory compliance with these varying requirements is typically related to secure storage within manufacturer guidelines to ensure the safety and efficacy of the medication, device, or supplies.

Benefits associated with contract compliance reviews typically affect multiple areas. Financially, money recovered through the investigation of contracts can be spread throughout the organization, and detecting errors can reduce future expenses. In the process of reviewing a contract, the language of the contract can be enhanced to reduce ambiguity, include or increase performance requirements, or measure variables. Examining current contracts for compliance can lead to future business process improvement initiatives such as streamlining the contracting process. Finally, contract auditing ensures all members involved in the contract are aware of their obligations. All of this leads to an increased return on investment for present and future contracts.[57]

An example of contract compliance is an agreement between the hospital and its vendor to not accept drugs that have less than an existing 60-day shelf life. The hospital only accepting medications with a 60-day or greater shelf life may reduce spoilage for the hospital and reduce expenses incurred by the vendor due to orders returned. Some items have a very short shelf life, such as biologicals that need refrigeration, and tend to have separate contract terms (carved-out contract items).

Drug Recalls

Recalls are actions taken by a company to remove a product it produces from the marketplace. Drug recalls can be initiated by a company, a request from the FDA, or an FDA order under statutory authority. There are three types of drug recalls categorized as class I, II, and III.[58]

Class I recalls are situations where there is a reasonable probability that the use of or exposure to a volative product (product in violation of FDA regulations) will cause serious adverse health consequences or death.

Class II recalls are situations where the use of or exposure to a volative product may cause temporary or medically revisable adverse health consequences or where the probability of serious adverse health consequences is remote.

Class III recalls are situations in which the use of or exposure to a volatile product is not likely to cause adverse health consequences.

A **market withdrawal** is a situation that occurs when a product has a minor violation that would not be subject to FDA legal action. The firm removes the product from the market or corrects the violation. An example of this would be a product that is removed from the market due to tampering, even if there is no evidence of a manufacturing or distribution problem.

A **medical device safety alert** is a notification that is issued in situations where a medical device may present an unacceptable risk of substantial harm to patients. In some cases, these situations are considered recalls as well.[59]

Lot and Batch Number

You may have heard news stories about product recalls due to contamination or manufacturing defect. Common examples of this are food recalls due to contamination or automobile recalls due to manufacturing defects. These recalls are made possible through batch numbers associated with the contaminated shipments or the VIN on a vehicle. Tracking or batch numbers are used in a similar way in healthcare. Medications, devices, and supplies all have associated identification numbers.

The lot or batch number system can be used to track to whom and when items are dispensed. Tracking items can be used for purposes beyond product recalls and restocking of items. Supply chain compliance can be audited periodically to determine who removed items that are tracked, for what purpose they were removed, and when they were removed.

Hazardous Waste Disposal

The disposal of hazardous materials is regulated by multiple federal agencies. There are eight general steps for the disposal of hazardous waste. Depending on the step in the process and type of material, different regulations may apply. Some of the specialized regulations already discussed also apply to disposal. For example, controlled substance and radioactive material still must be disposed of through a secure process that minimizes risk to the public and environmental impact. The eight general steps to hazardous waste management and disposal are as follows:

1. Evaluate the waste material.
2. Apply for the appropriate licenses and hazardous waste identification number if needed.
3. Store and label waste properly.
4. Transport and dispose of waste properly.
5. Manifest shipments of hazardous waste.
6. Have a contingency or emergency plan in place.
7. Train personnel and reinforce the training.
8. Keep documentation on the entire process.[60]

An example of hazardous waste disposal common to hospitals is the disposal of medical sharps, which is regulated in part by the Environmental Protection Agency (EPA). The improper management of discarded needles or other sharps can pose a public health risk and a personal risk to individuals involved in the disposal process. An example of this hazard is the potential for exposure to needle stick injuries which can lead to infection. Exposure risk is increased in situations where the sharps containers break open during transport or if the container is accidentally sent to the incorrect facility for disposal.[61] Other personnel at risk include janitorial staff if the container is punctured. The primary risk posed

from needle stick injuries are diseases such as hepatitis or HIV. In order to minimize these risks, the EPA established the Coalition for Safe Community Needle Disposal. The coalition was made up of businesses, community groups, and other organizations to promote awareness and design solutions for safe disposal of sharps. The coalition created several recommendations for programs to encourage the safe disposal of sharps, both within a healthcare organization and in the community for individuals who self-inject such as insulin users. The coalition recommended areas to be focused upon within the supply chain system of health organizations:

Supervised Collection Sites or Drop Box Locations

Individuals who need to dispose of sharps can take their own containers filled with used needles to collection sites such as physician's offices, hospitals, or health departments. These services are either offered free of charge or for a small disposal fee.

The Group Also Recommended Mail-Back Programs

Participating sharps users would place their sharps in a special container and return them via mail to be disposed of properly. This service typically has a fee associated to mail the package.

Syringe Exchange Programs

Syringe exchange programs are a popular choice to control the use of dirty needles by IV-drug users. However, syringe exchange programs are also effective for the disposal of sharps used for medical purposes. Depending on the purpose of the program and the target audience, there may or may not be a fee associated with a needle exchange program.

In-Home Needle Destruction Devices

The final recommendation of the coalition was the use of in-home needle destruction devices. Several manufacturers offer products for this purpose. Depending on the manufacturer, these devices will either melt or cut the needle, making it safe for disposal.[62]

Follow the Cotton Ball

Cotton balls in storage or within the replenishment process will not need the level of security and chain of custody requirements that controlled substances will require. However, can you imagine the process of storing cotton balls in bulk storage versus a controlled and secure area? How difficult would distributing a "controlled cotton ball" be compared to an uncontrolled cotton ball? Regarding chain of custody, can you imagine a positive control of a cotton ball (a chain of custody of responsibility and accountability) versus what is required without a chain of custody requirement for this item of supply? As you can see, the labor, storage, and financial equation changes drastically as levels of security, control, and chain of custody increase.

Summary

Dispensing or distributing healthcare supply chain items to the care providers and patients, or at points of care, is an essential continuation of the healthcare Value Chain. The healthcare supply chain provides the "technology of care" in a variety of methods and models. Healthcare organizations can either insource or outsource the distribution of supply-chain items to points of care within the health organization. There are several models to accomplish the distribution of supply-chain items; the different models are selected based on the point-of-care situational requirements focused on patient care quality and efficacy. Meeting regulatory requirements is also essential.

Security and compliance within the supply chain are paramount in providing healthcare services with the highest level of efficacy and safety for patients while meeting legal requirements and statutes. These statutory or legal or law requirements include chain of custody of sensitive, high-pilferage or highly addictive items through the components of the supply chain. Due to the complexity of the items used within most healthcare facilities, there are a myriad of regulations and protocols for the storage, chain of custody, and dispensing of medications/pharmaceuticals and medical supplies. This chapter focused on dispensing/distribution of healthcare supply chain items and an overview of statutory requirements associated with these processes.

Sarah Says: A Student's Perspective

A variety of methods and models can be utilized for inventory management and dispensing when hospitals provide the "technology of care" to its patients. Healthcare organizations can either insource or outsource the distribution of supply-chain items to points of care within the healthcare organization. The different models are selected based on the point of care and the needs of that particular service. There are many different methods a healthcare organization can use to manage their inventory. Some methods include: Periodic Automatic PAR, JIT, or Kanban. Each method has advantages and disadvantages; having a system and strategy that is efficient and effective is paramount. Each healthcare organization should pick the best overall method for its particular healthcare organization and services within the organization.

In addition, security and compliance within the supply chain is essential and required in order to provide care with the highest level of efficacy for patients. Dispensing and storing high-pilferage or highly addictive items (narcotics) require a chain of custody and adherence to numerous other specific regulations based on the individual drugs. Drugs are categorized, based on potential for addiction and pilferage, in different groups to determine which regulations must be followed. Companies such as Omnicell provide automatic dispensing machines for hospitals to assist in following these regulations and track the different pharmaceuticals and medical supplies. Furthermore, there are different protocols that must be followed in order to properly dispose of hazardous waste (such as used needles). These important aspects are crucial to know and apply to get the "technology of care" to the patient.

Discussion Questions

1. Outline and explain the concepts of dispensing at the points of care in the healthcare supply chain.
2. Discuss and give examples of points of care of different dispensing/distribution models.
3. Relate by providing an example of security storage and chain of custody requirements of sensitive or legally designated items in the healthcare supply chain.
4. Distinguish the functional requirements of pharmaceutical supply chain items from medical and surgical supply chain items in terms of dispensing/distributing to points of care.
5. Relate the differences and similarities of an outsourced dispensing/distribution system to an insourced system.
6. Evaluate the organizational capabilities necessary for optimal supply chain and logistics operations in healthcare with regard to dispensing/distribution to points of care in a hospital or clinic environment.

Exercises

1. Outline the healthcare Value Chain and identify important logistical supply chain functions in the delivery of healthcare services to points of care.
2. Discuss healthcare supply chain dispensing/distribution models, provide examples, and identify differences in outsourcing versus insourcing.
3. Relate the sequence of the healthcare supply chain to dispensing/distribution to points of care for cotton balls with emphasis on the different dispensing/distribution models (PAR, JIT, etc.).
4. Distinguish the key concerns regarding outsourcing dispensing/distribution to points of care with consideration of speed, cost, and reliability.
5. Relate issues of quality of care, access to care, and costs of stock-outs of items in the healthcare supply chain.
6. Evaluate the "value" of the healthcare supply chain with regard to dispensing/distribution to the perioperative points of care (operating room, recovery room, etc.), considering quality of care and efficacy of care in the "value" analysis.

Journal Items

Define:

Restocking:

PAR:

Just-in-Time Delivery:

Safety Level:

Economic Order Quantity:

Class I recalls:

Class II recalls:

Class III recalls:

Perpetual Inventory:

Answer the following question with one to three sentences:

How does PAR restocking work?

Search: *Search items may give you great assistance in understanding the healthcare supply chain; provide the website/URL and provide a one paragraph summary of what you found.*

Omnicell http://www.omnicell.com/Solutions/Supply_Chain-Materials_Management.aspx And http://www.omnicell.com/Solutions/Pharmacy.aspx

Pyxis http://www.carefusion.com/medical-products/medication-management/

Department of Justice Controlled Substance Schedules http://www.deadiversion.usdoj.gov /schedules/index.html

References

1. Par vs Kanban Hospital Inventory, *Two Bin Supply System*, (2014), http://www.southwestsolutions.com /healthcare/par-vs-kanban-hospital-inventory-two -bin-supply-system-for-nursing-supplies (accessed 12 Nov. 2014).

2. Just In Time (JIT) - Strategy Skills Training, *MindTools*, (2007), http://www.mindtools.com/pages/article /newSTR_78.htm (accessed 14 Nov. 2014)

3. Perioperative Supply Chain White Paper - *GE Healthcare*, (2014), http://www3.gehealthcare.com.au /~/media/downloads/anz/products/hcit/centricity _perioperative/perpetual_perioperative_supply _chain_whitepaper_anz_doc1170848.pdf.

4. Perioperative Supply Chain White Paper - *GE Healthcare*

5. Making a Case for a Case Cart System – *hermanmiller*, (2012), http://www.hermanmiller.com/research

/research-summaries/making-a-case-for-a-case-cart-system.html (accessed 14 Nov. 2014).

6. What is Kanban?, *LeanKit*, (2013), http://leankit.com/kanban/what-is-kanban/ (accessed 12 Nov. 2014).

7. Par vs Kanban Hospital Inventory, *Two Bin Supply System*

8. Par vs Kanban Hospital Inventory, *Two Bin Supply System*

9. McKesson, *Point of Use Supply*, http://www.mckesson.com/providers/health-systems/department-solutions/supply-chain-management/mckesson-point-of-use-supply/ (accessed 12 Nov. 2014).

10. Central Pharmacy Automation Systems – *Omnicell*, (2011), http://www.omnicell.com/Products/Central_Pharmacy_Automation.aspx (accessed 12 Nov. 2014).

11. Pyxis MedStation® system - Medication Management, *carefusion*, (2011), http://www.carefusion.com/medical-products/medication-management/medication-technologies/pyxis-medstation-system.aspx (accessed 12 Nov. 2014).

12. (2012). Medical stores management - World Health Organization. http://apps.who.int/medicinedocs/documents/s19621en/s19621en.pdf (accessed 12 Nov. 2014).

13. (2009). Emergency Preparedness > Information Regarding Insulin ... http://www.fda.gov/Drugs/EmergencyPreparedness/ucm085213.htm (accessed 12 Nov. 2014).

14. (2003). Drug Expiration Dates - Harvard Health Publications. http://www.health.harvard.edu/fhg/updates/update1103a.shtml (accessed 12 Nov. 2014).

15. Sumycin (Tetracycline) Patient Information: Side Effects, *rxlist*, (2011), http://www.rxlist.com/sumycin-drug/patient-images-side-effects.htm (accessed 12 Nov. 2014).

16. Drug Expiration Dates - *Harvard Health Publications*, (2003), http://www.health.harvard.edu/fhg/updates/update1103a.shtml (accessed 12 Nov. 2014).

17. Y. Perlman and I. Levner Perishable Inventory Management in Healthcare. *Journal of Service Science and Management*, 7 (2014), 11.

18. CSA Schedules - *Drugs.com*, (2010), http://www.drugs.com/csa-schedule.html (accessed 11 Nov. 2014).

19. List of Schedule 1 Drugs - *Drugs.com*, (2012), http://www.drugs.com/article/csa-schedule-1.html (accessed 11 Nov. 2014).

20. List of Schedule 2 (II) Drugs - *Drugs.com*, (2012), http://www.drugs.com/schedule-2-drugs.html (accessed 11 Nov. 2014).

21. List of Schedule 3 (III) Drugs - *Drugs.com*, (2012), http://www.drugs.com/schedule-3-drugs.html (accessed 11 Nov. 2014).

22. (2009). Notuss-PE liquid: Indications, Side Effects, Warnings - Drugs http://www.drugs.com/cdi/notuss-pe-liquid.html (accessed 12 Nov. 2014).

23. (2003). Diazepam: Drug Uses, Dosage & Side Effects - Drugs.com. http://www.drugs.com/diazepam.html (accessed 12 Nov. 2014).

24. CSA Schedules - *Drugs.com*

25. Controlled Substances Security Manual – DEA Diversion, http://www.deadiversion.usdoj.gov/pubs/manuals/sec/sec_non_prac.htm (accessed 14 Nov. 2014).

26. Controlled Substances Security Manual – DEA Diversion

27. Controlled Substances Security Manual – DEA Diversion

28. Controlled Substances Security Manual – DEA Diversion

29. Controlled Substances Security Manual – DEA Diversion

30. Controlled Substances Security Manual – DEA Diversion

31. Controlled Substances Security Manual – DEA Diversion

32. Controlled Substances Security Manual – DEA Diversion

33. Controlled Substances Security Manual – DEA Diversion

34. Controlled Substances Security Manual – DEA Diversion

35. Controlled Substances Security Manual – DEA Diversion

36. Controlled Substances Security Manual – DEA Diversion

37. Controlled Substances Security Manual – DEA Diversion

38. NRC: Fact Sheet on Medical Use of Radioactive Materials, (2008), http://www.nrc.gov/reading-rm/doc-collections/fact-sheets/med-use-radactiv-mat-fs.html (accessed 12 Nov. 2014).

39. NRC: Fact Sheet on Medical Use of Radioactive Materials

40. NRC: Fact Sheet on Medical Use of Radioactive Materials

41. A. Gross-Schaefer et al., "Ethics education in the workplace: An effective tool to combat employee theft." *Journal of Business Ethics*, 26, no. 2 (2000), 89-100.

42. Gross-Schaefer et al., "Ethics education in the workplace."

43. Theft in Foodservice, *Foodservice Director*, (2014), http://www.foodservicedirector.com/managing-your-business/controlling-costs/articles/theft-foodservice (accessed 12 Nov. 2014).

44. Gross-Schaefer et al., "Ethics education in the workplace."

45. Managing the Chain of Custody, *Institute for Supply*, (2009), http://www.ism.ws/files/Pubs/Proceedings/09ProcBC-Michels.pdf (accessed 13 Nov. 2014).

46. Chain-of-Custody - *Siemens Healthcare Global*, (2013), http://www.healthcare.siemens.com/drug-testing-diagnostics/syva-drug-testing-online-campus/drug-testing-education/chain-of-custody (accessed 12 Nov. 2014).

47. Managing the Chain of Custody, *Institute for Supply*

48. 6 steps for managing the supply chain of custody - *Ann Arbor*, (2009), http://www.annarbor.com /business-review/6-steps-for-managing-the-supply -chain-of-custody/.

49. Medical Device Tracking, *Food and Drug Administration*, (2013), http://www.fda.gov/medicaldevices /deviceregulationandguidance/postmarketrequirements/medicaldevicetracking/default.htm (accessed 12 Nov. 2014).

50. Our history, *Cardinal Health*, (2011), http://cardinal-health.com/us/en/aboutus/ourhistory (accessed 14 Nov. 2014).

51. Hospitals, *Cardinal Health*, (2010), http://www.cardinal .com/us/en/hospitals (accessed 14 Nov. 2014).

52. Our Heritage, *Owens & Minor* (2009), http://www .owens-minor.com/companyinfo/whoisom/Pages /OurHistory.aspx (accessed 14 Nov. 2014).

53. Hospitals - *Owens & Minor*, (2009), http://www .owens-minor.com/Hospitals/Pages/default.aspx (accessed 14 Nov. 2014).

54. AmerisourceBergen | About, (2014), http://www .amerisourcebergen.com/abcnew/about.aspx (accessed 14 Nov. 2014).

55. AmerisourceBergen | Pharmacies, (2014), http://www .amerisourcebergen.com/abcnew/pharmacies.aspx (accessed 14 Nov. 2014).

56. Presentation Slides: Health Care Contracts, (2013), http://www.claconnect.com/State-and-Local -Government/Health-Care-Contract-Compliance .aspx (accessed 12 Nov. 2014).

57. Presentation Slides: Health Care Contracts

58. FDA Drug Recalls - *Food and Drug Administration*, (2013), http://www.fda.gov/Drugs/drugsafety/DrugRecalls /default.htm (accessed 11 Nov. 2014).

59. Recalls, Market Withdrawals, & Safety Alerts, *Food and Drug Administration*, (2009), http://www.fda .gov/Safety/Recalls/ucm165546.htm (accessed 11 Nov. 2014).

60. 8 Step Hazardous Waste Management Guide, *Rethink*, (2014), https://www.rethinkrecycling.com/businesses /waste-management-guide/hazardous-waste/8 -step-hazardous-waste-management-guide (accessed 12 Nov. 2014).

61. Disposal of Medical Sharps, *EPA*, (2008), http://www .epa.gov/osw/nonhaz/industrial/medical/disposal .htm (accessed 12 Nov. 2014).

62. Disposal of Medical Sharps, *EPA*.

CHAPTER 5

INFORMING: INFORMATION SYSTEMS IN THE HEALTHCARE SUPPLY CHAIN

LEARNING OBJECTIVES

1. Outline and explain the utilization of information systems in the healthcare supply chain.
2. Discuss and give examples of the different uses of information systems and technology of those systems in the operation of the supply chain.
3. Relate, discuss, and provide examples where information systems in the healthcare supply chain provide the availability of performance metrics and statistics to inform decision making for improved efficiency, effectiveness, and efficacy of the supply operation in the healthcare organization.
4. Distinguish the functional areas of information systems, such as sourcing, EDI, vendor management, warehousing/storage, and dispensing to points of care with regard to the healthcare supply chain.
5. Relate the business operation, how work is accomplished, to the information systems, how information and data from operations flow, within the healthcare supply chain.
6. Evaluate the benefits of improved information systems and utilization of metrics for healthcare supply chain operations and management in terms of performance, health outcomes, and stakeholders' perceptions.

Introduction

Information systems are valuable assets to healthcare organizations. Data, an enormous amount of data, in context, called information, enables quality decision making at the operational and strategic levels. Data in context, such as a healthcare supply chain context, is information: information that is "actionable" or useable is knowledge. Information systems foster knowledge for operators, managers, leaders, and strategists. Efficient, effective, and most importantly, efficacious business practices (how professionals process and get work accomplished) are reinforced and complemented by well-developed, built and deployed information systems for a trained team of professionals across the healthcare personnel continuum. Good and high-quality business practices must first be in place with high standards and low levels of deviation or variance in order to realize the full potential of information systems. This is especially true in healthcare supply chain management, operations or in strategic decision making. Information systems are vital since:

- Clinical complexity is reality: Over 10,000 unique situations (diseases, injuries, etc.) can be presented by patients to the healthcare organization.
- Complexity of knowledge is reality: Over 500,000 new additions to the knowledge base (literature of medicine and healthcare) each year and increasing each year given that 460,000 additions were available in 2003–2004.
- Operational complexity is reality: Multiple players in the healthcare Value Chain with hospitals, physicians, health plans, pharmacy benefit management companies (PBM), disease management companies, commercial laboratories, etc. when all combined translate into a navigational nightmare for a consumer of healthcare services.
- Technological convergence and integration is reality: Medical devices, equipment, and software applications are converging to create new technological innovations coupled with changes to the professional standard of care due to technological innovation.

In addition to information systems, leaders and managers must make high-quality decisions with efficacy, efficiency, and effectiveness in mind at all times. The use of metrics, made available in a timely fashion and enabled by information systems, informs the decision makers to improve operations and strategies of the healthcare organization and the supply chain that supports the delivery of care by providing the technology of care to the care givers within the Value Chain.

The healthcare supply chain must keep pace, and in actuality forecast needs and demands, of this dynamic industry of healthcare. This chapter will provide an overview of information systems, metrics and improvement opportunities that are enabled by robust and integrated information systems.

Information Systems in Healthcare Supply Chain

Computers and information technology has an important role in healthcare. This is especially true for complex systems that integrate with all other functions within the healthcare organization. However, due to the rapid changes that occur in both the healthcare and computer technology industries, it can be difficult to take full advantages of the opportunities for process improvement that occur through a partnership between healthcare and information technology. Today there are a multitude of information systems available with applications for the healthcare industry, ranging from process simulation to metric tracking and supply chain optimization. As the scope and complexity of the healthcare industry continue to increase, the use of appropriate information technology will continue to be important for health systems to remain profitable. Understanding the evolution of healthcare information systems will allow for a more complete understanding as to the importance of their use in the modern supply chain.

Pencils to Keyboards to Touchpads and Electronic Systems

The evolution of hospital information systems can be traced back nearly to the start of computing. In the 1960s the main force behind healthcare information systems was Medicare and Medicaid. At this time computers, were large and very expensive, so the systems were usually shared between multiple facilities. Some of the earliest hospital information systems (IS) applications date back to this time, including shared hospital accounting systems.[1] By the 1970s computer technology had advanced to a point where computers decreased in price and became small enough for a system to be installed for each key department within a healthcare organization. These systems revolutionized the way work was done, especially in the laboratory and pharmacy, but the systems primarily operated as data silos within departments. As the use of departmental systems proliferated, the need for interdepartmental communication between systems became apparent.[2] The 1980s saw the largest changes to the healthcare system in the United States since Medicare and Medicaid. These changes focused on diagnosis-related groups (DRG) and reimbursement rates for Medicare and Medicaid patients. As a result, hospitals had a need to collect data from the separate clinical and financial systems scattered between departments in order to receive reimbursement payments. While these regulatory changes were being enacted, the personal computing era began. As employees began to have wide-spread access to computing, the systems were connected together via networks.[3] Throughout the 1990s, increased competition in healthcare led to consolidation of health systems, resulting in the need to integrate hospitals and providers. Technological advances during the 1990s gave hospitals access to ever increasing computing power and advanced networks. This in turn gave way to integrated data and reporting capabilities.[4] The 2000s saw the focus of healthcare systems start to shift to an outcomes-based approach. For the first time, the technology was available to create a real-time clinical decision support system (CDS).[5] A CDS system provides clinicians, staff, and patients appropriate information to enhance health care and positively impact health outcomes.[6] The use of technology in healthcare is likely to continue to increase given past history and current government programs such as Healthy People 2020. Healthy People 2020 is a multi-faceted government program designed to improve health outcomes for the United States. One of these objectives is to utilize health communication strategies and health information technology to improve population health outcomes and health care quality, and to achieve health equity.[7] As mentioned earlier, the healthcare supply chain is an often overlooked area that is critical for providing effective patient care. The increased focus on improving quality of care through public health programs and governmental healthcare legislation are the primary driving forces behind the implementation of new technology within healthcare and the healthcare supply chain.

There are other motivating factors for health systems to adopt information technology advances besides government programs. It simply makes business sense to take advantage of technological advances where appropriate because of the potential cost savings. Supply chain costs in health systems average between 30 and 40%, second only to personnel costs.[8] In order to reduce costs, both adaptive and technical changes need to be considered. It has been reported that for every $1.00 spent in supporting supply chain operations, there is a $6.00 return to the health system.[9]

In addition to the cost savings, utilizing information systems is critical because of the complexity of the healthcare system, both in clinical and support areas. This complexity is perhaps best illustrated with a flow diagram, designed to show the movement of information within the supply chain.

Figure 5.1 shows more than twenty separate systems that all have to work together and share information appropriately in order for the supply chain to function effectively. After reviewing the figure, it should be apparent that the foundation of managing the supply chain is the management of data.

Data Management and Information Flow

Managing data and the flow of information in the healthcare supply chain is a continuous challenge. There are a variety of data types that need to be tracked for daily activities in the supply chain. Information flows in the organization are affected by both the functional layout of the organization and the task at hand. Managing this flow of information through the organization is important in the healthcare supply chain in order to prevent stock-outs or excess inventory. With process improvement plans, methods such as lean that push inventory levels down, problems with information flow in the supply chain are quickly uncovered. Some basic information that can prevent supply chain issues is easily communicated across the supply chain by some variation of three questions:

- What needs to be ordered next?
- What has not yet been delivered?
- What types of products will we need in the future?

FIGURE 5.1   Interface Map

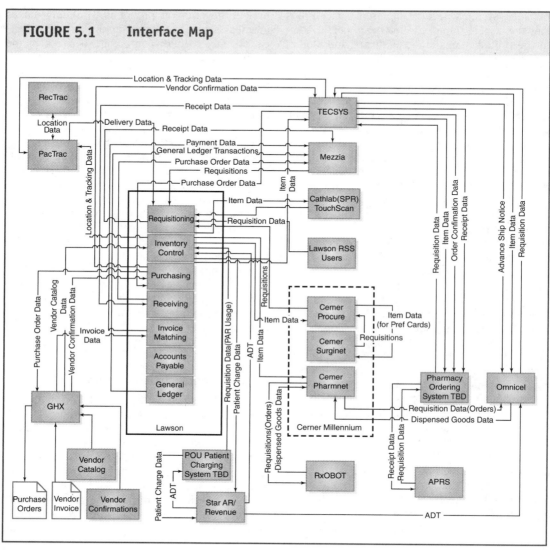

How Does Information Flow in the Organization?

The information flow in a typical organization can take several forms, both informal and formal. For the purposes of communicating information related to the supply chain, we will concentrate on formal communication channels. The formal communication network includes all communication along official lines of authority within an organization. These formal channels typically have certain functional communication barriers.[10] These functional barriers to communication result when information needs to pass between various divisions of the supply chain. For example, without the aid of an information system, passing information about a stock-out from departmental storage to central storage and then to acquisitions is a slow process that moves forward step by step. Through the use of an information system, the level in the departmental storage area can be remotely monitored and restocked from central storage without risk of a stock out. The same is true for central storage; items and their use can be monitored electronically and an order placed automatically without risk of stock out or the use of a large number of employees to hand count stock. This flow of information is typically described in a process flow chart, such as **Figure 5.2**. Information systems in the healthcare supply chain merge with the use of an interface with clinical, revenue management (reimbursement for services or payment), financial and human resource systems. Interfaces connect one information system with another and share data. A one-direction (uni-direction) interface sends information from one system to another while a two-direction (bi-direction) interface sends and receives information from one information system to another.

What Data Should Be Managed?

Information to be managed within the supply chain includes inventory, vendor information, transaction history, and contract-related information. This information is usually managed through the use of an enterprise resource planning software package or ERP. ERP technology is currently more popular in industries not related to healthcare such as financial accounting, human resources, and supply-chain management outside of the healthcare arena.[11] For those healthcare

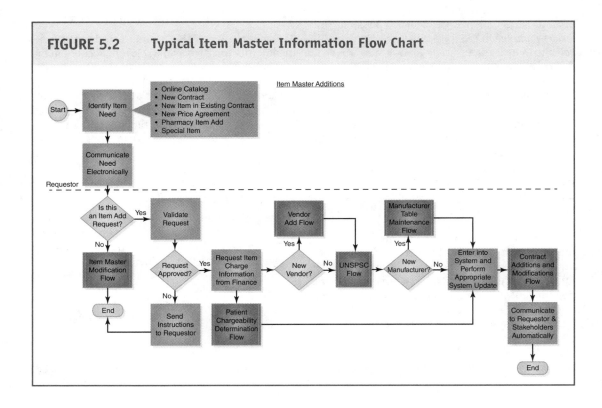

FIGURE 5.2   Typical Item Master Information Flow Chart

organizations that have an ERP system, there is a tendency for organizations to focus on their clinical systems while ignoring their older support system such as ERP. There are multiple vendors for ERP software solutions that specialize in different types of business with the major players in the general business ERP industry being SAP and Oracle. Some examples of healthcare ERP vendors include McKesson, SYSPRO, QAD, and Lawson.

SYSPRO is the vendor for an ERP system, used primarily in the medical device industry and the pharmaceuticals industry with specific modules for each industry. Its ERP system for medical device companies is designed to encourage collaboration with physicians and allows for materials to be tracked throughout the supply chain. As is common with commercial products, the software is also designed to meet the quality and safety standards of the medical device and pharmaceutical industry.

The McKesson system is designed to serve both the health and medical practice industry through its ERP offering. The primary target of this system is to improve operational efficiency for the purpose of improving patient care decision making. The QAD system is an ERP package targeted at the life science industry, specifically laboratories, medical device manufacturers, and pharmaceutical companies.[12]

The Lawson ERP offering is a system that was not specifically designed for the healthcare industry originally. Through the acquisition of other companies such as Healthvision Solutions, its ERP system gained the functionality to become a leading ERP option for healthcare organizations. The Healthvision software was combined into one of the existing ERP systems distributed by Lawson: S3, a general purpose ERP package aimed at service industry businesses.[13,14]

Additionally, data in the information system must be predetermined to work with and reinforce the business practice utilized for a particular function of the supply chain. Data standards are determined within the project management, building and deploying/launching of the supply chain information system or the ERP aspect of the supply chain operation. The following table gives an illustration of data standards for specific elements of an ERP information system for the healthcare supply chain.

Item Master

An item master is a master record for a particular item kept in inventory. This includes the description, warehouse specific information, fulfillment, sales, and handling specifications.

Within an item-master system, there are various functions such as managing serial and batch numbers, defining alternative items, and changing the item valuation.

Vendor Master

A vendor-master system contains information about the vendors that supply an organization. Typically, this information is stored in individual vendor-master records. The master record for a vendor includes the vendor's name and address as well as additional information such as:

- The contact information for important individuals associated with the account, typically sales representatives.
- Terms of payment.
- Currency used for order from the vendor.[15]

This information is also usually linked to accounting information such as the relevant account in the general ledger because to the accounting department, vendors are typically creditors.[16]

Another advantage associated with the vendor master is that the data only needs to be entered into the system once. By storing information within a central vendor master and updating the information regularly, inconsistencies can be prevented throughout the ERP system.[17]

Transaction History File

The transaction history file is a part of the ERP system that tracks the status of customers based on the frequency of orders they place within the organization and what business transactions have occurred with the health organization to external suppliers and vendors. Typical statuses are new, recent, lost, and dormant. The time duration for each status bucket is specific to an organization.[18]

Contract Elements

Various contract elements must also be managed. Contract elements are linked specifically to the

TABLE 5.1   Data Standards in ERP System Development for the Healthcare Supply Chain

Line No	Form	Form Name	Field Name	Standardized?	Function	Data Define	Recommendations
1010	PC20.1	Patient Charges	Charge Date	Y	IC	Autopopulates	Defaults to todays date, otherwise can be overrode
1009	PC20.1	Patient Charges	Source Location	Y	IC	ex: 1) 40101 2) 04001 3) P101A	equal to Requesting location, Build to match PAR or issuing inventory location
1008	PC20.1	Patient Charges	Revenue Center	Y	IC	ex: 1) 40101 2) 04001 3) P101A	equal to the From Location
1007	PC20.1	Patient Charges	Visit Nbr	Y	IC	ex: 0500100001	Patient ADT interface from Revenue system. Up to 10 digits. First two annum, next three Julian date, next five sequential numbering 0500100001 (first patient jan 05)
1005	PC10.1	Patient Charge Items	Patient Price	Y	IC	LEAVE BLANK	LEAVE BLANK
1004	PC10.1	Patient Charge Items	Price Class	Y	IC	NA	NA - NOT APPLICABLE
1002	PC10.1	Patient Charge Items	Charge Number	Y	IC	SIM code	Received from Revenue Team
1001	PC10.1	Patient Charge Items	Revenue Center	Y	IC	ex: 1) 40101 2) 04001 3) P101A	equal to the From Location
999	RQ04.1	Requesters	Allow Dropship	Y	RQ	N	NO
998	RQ04.1	Requesters	List only internal Items	Y	RQ	LEAVE BLANK	Blank = defaults to Company Level

(continued)

Line No	Form	Form Name	Field Name	Standardized?	Function	Data Define	Recommendations
997	RQ04.1	Requesters	List only Contract Items	Y	RQ	LEAVE BLANK	Blank = defaults to Company Level
996	RQ04.1	Requesters	Categories	Y	RQ	5 or 4	IF Specials and Services are Blank then 4
995	RQ04.1	Requesters	Punchout	Y	RQ	LEAVE BLANK	LEAVE BLANK
994	RQ04.1	Requesters	Specials and Services	Y	RQ	4 or Blan	MAY BE BLANK PER REQUESTOR
993	RQ04.1	Requesters	Express Order	Y	RQ	3	Always 3
992	RQ04.1	Requesters	Shopping List	Y	RQ	2	Always 2
991	RQ04.1	Requesters	Catalog Search	Y	RQ	1	Always 1
989	RQ04.1	Requesters	Minor	Y	RQ	Blank or schedule status if RX	-For MS or OS, no minor classes exist yet -For PHAR, NON - Non-scheduled Drug I - Schedule I Drug II- Schedule II Drug IIN- Schedule IIN Drug III- Schedule III Drug IIIN- Schedule IIIN Drug IV- Schedule IV Drug V- Schedule V Drug
988	RQ04.1	Requesters	Major	Y	RQ	MS, OF, or RX	MS - Medical Surgical Product OS - Office Supplies RX - Pharmaceutical product

vendors in the Vendor Master File and are used to set parameters on operational transactions between the vendors and the healthcare organization. We will focus on the administration of existing contracts as contract writing is a separate subject. Once a contract is drafted and agreed upon, it must be properly administered to ensure that all the benefits anticipated when it was created are collected by the organization.[19] Management of contract elements allows for the early identification of performance problems. This is important to avoid delays within the supply chain.[20] An additional concern with contracts is the administration of any amendments to existing contracts.[21] Both the monitoring of contracts for performance problems and the managing of amendments can be administered through most ERP systems. Contract information such as delivery and payment terms, items to transact and other elements are loaded in the ERP system and linked to the vendor master to ensure that the negotiated contract terms are utilized when business is conducted.

What Is Linked to the Information System?

Links to information systems can be found throughout the healthcare supply chain. Information systems can be used to track the movement of goods from the manufacturer to central storage to the floors through their use in patient care. Performing tracking without the use of information systems would be an extremely time consuming and error prone process.

Clinical links to information systems include pharmaceutical usage, medical/surgical supplies, and usage information.

Acquiring and Procurement: Sourcing and Purchasing

Many healthcare supply chains in the industry are linked to an "external hub" to conduct transactions. This means the health organization information system is connected or interfaced (electronically, through the use of human/personnel keyboard input, etc.) to a "business to business" organization such as Global Health Exchange (GHX). GHX connects manufacturers, distributors,

suppliers, and vendors to healthcare organizations' supply chains to efficiently transact the business of purchasing. The "perfect order" concept is where electronic preset decisions are made to order, purchase, deliver and receive, and then pay the invoice with minimal human interaction; this concept was first conceived by Lynn Britton, Mike McCurry, and Shannon Sock of Mercy Health Systems nearly twenty years ago. A transaction hub enables the potential of ever increasing "perfect orders" or "perfect transactions." The language of the interaction is the Electronic Data Interchange or EDI. As presented in a previous chapter, EDI is presented in the context of information systems.

In healthcare over 50% of medical and surgical items, such as cotton balls, are processed and transacted electronically between healthcare organizations and vendors by GHX, which is the electronic business-to-business system run by the GHX Corporation.[22] Now the vendor is linked to the item master and information system for the supply-chain operation.

For a best practice when the supply item(s) are ordered in large quantities, over a long period of time or when the cost of transactions with this vendor are moderate to high, a contract should be established with this vendor to achieve the best pricing and service terms for ordering, receiving, returning, utilizing and maintaining our supply items. Although a special order or non-contract or out of contract order/requisition/purchase can be made for one time or few time orders, a contract from a vendor should be developed and implemented so that the contract terms can be linked to the vendor, the items from the vendor (from the EDI 832 electronic catalog) and into the supply chain system. Lastly, electronic data interchange is an important concept to electronic transactions in the healthcare supply chain.

What is EDI? "Electronic Data Interchange (EDI) is a set of standards that collectively provide a common protocol or syntax for transacting business documents electronically. In essence, EDI is to electronic commerce as grammar is to verbal communication – it is a set of rules and guidelines that are applied when developing and implementing software and services designed to transmit business documents electronically. Just as a group of individuals with diverse backgrounds can use

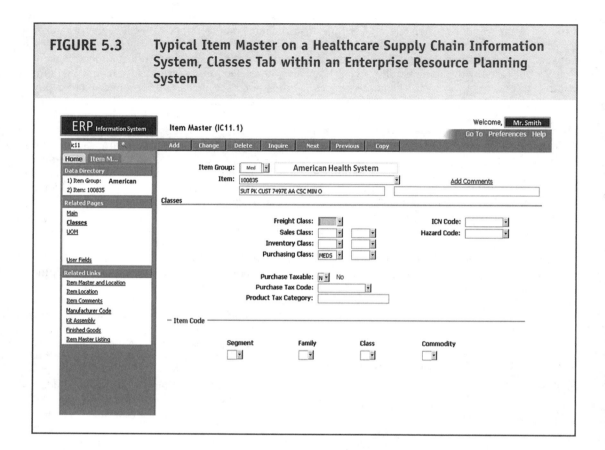

FIGURE 5.3 **Typical Item Master on a Healthcare Supply Chain Information System, Classes Tab within an Enterprise Resource Planning System**

a common language (such as English) to converse with each other, EDI provides a common 'language' that enables businesses with dissimilar computer-based business systems to communicate with each other."[23]

Transportation

Tracking the transportation of products using information systems has been commonplace for years. A sophisticated example of this is the UPS package tracking system. When a package is delivered to UPS, a barcode is attached to the item. As the package is moved from location to location during the shipping process, the barcode is scanned and the information system updates the location of the package on the route. The barcode is either scanned by hand or an automated system.[24]

Warehousing/Storing

Storage and inventory that is managed in a warehouse, consolidated service center, or within central supply in the hospital provides critical information that must be linked to the rest of the healthcare supply chain system. The purchases that are received, where information systems provide critical information on the requisition, the invoice, and the actual count of items received (called a three-way match) is an important quality control and fiduciary step in the receiving function. Once received, items are stored in either bulk storage (usually in intermediate packages such as pallets of multiple cases or boxes) or in loose/small "pick" locations for easy access for quick customer/care giver order fulfillment. Items received can also be cross-docked for immediate routing to

TABLE 5.2	Examples of Commonly used EDI Transaction Sets	
X12ID Code	**Transaction Set**	**Document Usage**
850	Purchase Order (PO)	A trading partner sends a PO to order products from a vendor.
810	Invoice	The vendor sends an invoice back to their trading partner as a bill for the products ordered.
997	Acknowledgement	An acknowledgement is sent as a receipt to the sender upon the retrieval of a document.
856	Advanced Ship Notice (ASN)	The vendor sends an ASN to their trading partner specifying to a mutually agreed level of detail the dates and contents of a shipment. Many businesses require the receipt of an ASN from a supplier before the shipment reaches their receiving docks.
820	Remittance Advice	Remittance advice informs the vendor that their trading partner has made a deposit into their bank account.
852	Product Activity Data	The Product Activity Data is used by trading partners to advise vendors of inventory, sales and other product activity information.
832	Electronic Product Catalog	An electronic catalog of products/items from a manufacturer, distributor or vendor.

TrueCommerce EDI Solutions, "EDI Overview: A Practical Guide to EDI and the TrueCommerce EDI Platform," White Paper, Seven Fields, Pennsylvania, Retrieved from http://www.highjump.com/sites/default/files/Resources/WP-US-EDI.pdf (accessed 8 Jul. 2014).

the health organization for use by the care givers. All this information, on hand quantities for SKUs (stock keeping units) stored in the warehouse, received items, cross-docked items, requisitions/orders received that are confirmed with a three-way match for invoice payment, etc., are all resident in the information system. This system, the storing/warehouse functions, is connected to dispensing and distribution systems such as perpetual inventories, PAR locations and for patient custom orders (such as supply charge capture items). Two of the most popular warehousing/consolidated service center information systems (in many instances

these are interfaced to the healthcare organization ERP system) are TecSys and Manhattan.

"TECSYS is a visionary and technology leader in warehouse management software. TECSYS has an unrivaled staff of warehouse experts who serve the Government, Healthcare Supply Chain and High-Volume Distribution industries with game-changing supply chain management solutions. TECSYS is currently powering the supply chains of numerous companies."[25]

"Manhattan Associates supports supply chains operating on platforms of visibility, holistic intelligence, flexible workflows and shared common elements create enduring competitive market advantage for their customers. Platform thinking gives operational executives unprecedented business agility in managing their supply chains, while also grounding and orchestrating logistical functions in a unified structure that, over time, can slash millions of dollars in deployment costs, maintenance fees and upgrade investments."[26]

Examples of Best Enterprise Information System Practices in Industry[27]

In the 1990s through the early 2000s the healthcare supply chain found at Sisters of Mercy Health System was much like those found at many organizations. The fragmented and duplicative systems across Mercy were dependent on six different information

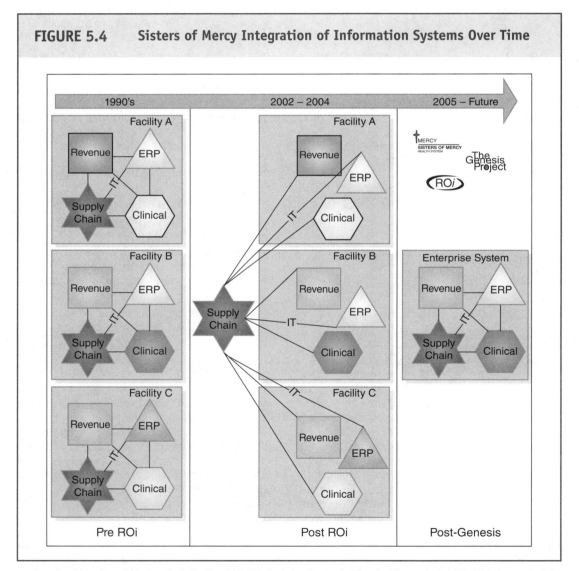

FIGURE 5.4   Sisters of Mercy Integration of Information Systems Over Time

technology (IT) materials management software solutions, were unable to negotiate the maximization of supplier discounts, and were heavily relying on outside vendors to help facilitate the management of the health system's supply chains.

The decentralized work found in the mimicking of similar processes at each health system wasn't managed for process efficiency or cost savings at the enterprise level. This realization created a new organization at the system level, with the intent to create an integrated supply chain that better utilized available technologies for inventory management and implemented supply chain best practices from inside and outside the industry. With the creation of a new centralized supply chain, departmental data could then be shared across the system, and Mercy's reliance on outside vendor information was dramatically lessened. This progression in strategy led to a project called "Genesis" within the health system to integrate and leverage strategic units for increased efficiency, effectiveness, efficacy, and competitive advantage.

Prior to the Genesis Project the healthcare supply chain elevated in importance to the healthcare system. The creation of the entity called Resource Optimization and Innovation (ROI) helped consolidate the supply chain throughout Mercy at the corporate level, align major processes utilizing a shared materials management software solution, create an internal group purchasing organization, and allow for the enterprise-wide management of supply chain distribution and repackaging processes within Mercy.[28]

In addition, the creation of an internally owned and managed repackaging and distribution facility, the Consolidated Services Center (CSC), permitted improved supply chain responsiveness by better catering to customer hospitals; improving fill rates over the 85% to 90% that other distributors achieved, streamlining the receiving process, and reducing complexity by 70% through combined deliveries of medical/surgical supplies and pharmaceuticals; created standard inventory management metrics such as fill rate percentage to measure departmental and centralized performance; permitted more timely deliveries to facilities (with an internal truck fleet), improving cost savings by eliminating third-party markup

fees (approximately $3 million annually) and by purchasing directly from manufacturers; and permitted bulk purchasing and contracting for economies of scope and scale.[29]

The system sought to leverage similar gains from integration, standardized business practices and improved information systems across the domains of clinical practice, revenue management, human resources, and finance along with the supply chain. In the supply chain, with these efficiency improvements and by taking advantage of economies of scope and scale, the Sisters of Mercy supply chain now returns $6 for every $1 invested in this core business function.[30]

Distribution

Item distribution within a facility works much the same way as the package tracking system described in the previous section, just on a smaller scale. Internal to a facility, products may be tracked with an RFID system such as what was described in a previous chapter. When an item is removed from the shelf an RFID tag either in a signal card or the item packaging is read by a RFID reader attached to the storage shelf. This RFID signal informs central storage that the particular product was used and needs to be replaced.

Alternatively, the use of products in departmental storage locations may be tracked by weight. In systems that track the quantity remaining by weight, the trays containing items have a built-in scale; when the weight of the tray drops below a certain level, central storage is notified to restock the item.

Why Is All This Important?

Information technology provides the tools necessary to efficiently manage the transportation and distribution of items within the supply chain through the use of automation. The process automation made possible through the use of information systems, when implemented appropriately, has the effect of decreasing workload. Decreases in workload related to support activities allow employees to perform activities that generate revenue for the organization, such as providing patient care. This is important because employee salaries are the number one expense in healthcare and supply chain expenses are typically the second

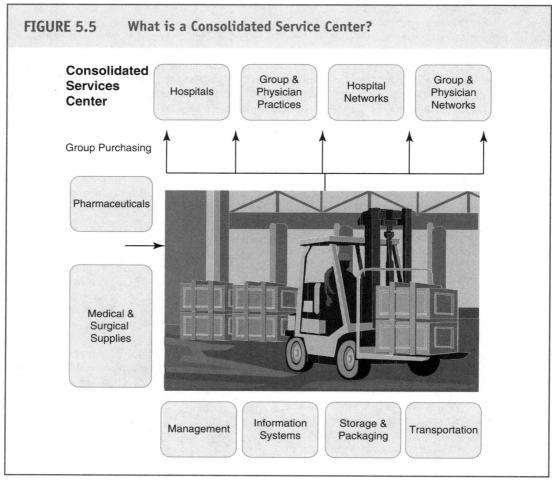

FIGURE 5.5   What is a Consolidated Service Center?

Sisters of Mercy Health System, Supply Chain Summit, Branson, MO, October 20–21, 2005.

highest. Since automation of supply chain activities can potentially reduce costs in both of these areas, the supply chain is an excellent choice for automation and process improvement activities.

Visualizing the Flow of Items

One of the primary advantages of using information systems to monitor the healthcare supply chain is that it allows decision makers to visualize the flow of items from vendor to storage and their usage in providing care. This visualization allows

for the easy determination of bottlenecks and efficient areas within the system.

Information Systems Facilitate Metrics and Performance Statistics

The ability to visualize items and information flow opens the discussion on metrics. Selecting appropriate metrics is critical to process improvement efforts. The benefits of using metrics in healthcare include the fact that their use promotes accountability, clarity, and brings into focus objectives while promoting systems thinking and problem solving.[31] The typical steps in using metrics include: collecting data, analyzing data, making decisions based on the data, evaluating results, and repeating the cycle to improve the accuracy of the metrics.[32]

Selecting appropriate metrics typically goes back to the question, "What does my customer value?" The customer in this context is whomever the service is being directly provided to. For example, the customer of central storage is the departments that they restock and the customer of the delivery truck is central storage or whoever is receiving the shipment. The data that is being used for a particular metric should be verified to ensure that it is correct and presented in an easy-to-comprehend format.[33] Properly selected metrics provide both an internal and external perspective and are clearly defined. The definition of a metric can include what is being measured, why it is being measure, who uses the data, and how the data is utilized to determine if the metric is relevant to the organization.[34]

For all the benefits of performance metrics, there are several common problems that arise from their use. One of the most common is the desire of managers to "look good" on the measures they are accountable for. This creates problems because managers are more likely to track measures that they score highly on and are less likely to track measures that need serious improvement. Especially if there is a financial component attached to their performance on the metric.[35] Another common source of problems with the use of metrics is allowing the metrics to be defined by the concerns of the individual department instead of the organization as a whole. It may seem counterintuitive for departments not to track the measures that the managers feel are most important, but this way of thinking can lead to suboptimal performance for the organization.[36] As mentioned earlier, it is important to create metrics that track value-added activities from your customer's perspective. It is a common pitfall to track items that either do not matter to the customer or only address a small part of what the customer wants.[37] To prevent this from occurring it is important to have an open flow of information throughout the healthcare supply chain.

Basic Metrics

Information systems give healthcare organizations the ability to better track metrics used to improve patient care, profitability, and efficiency. Examples of some basic healthcare supply chain metrics include inventory turnover, contract utilization, supply cost per adjusted case mix, and pharmaceutical supply cost per adjusted case mix. Inventory turnover rate is the measure of capital invested in the storing of goods and the value of the goods in storage. This metric should be evaluated in the context of reordering and restocking while taking into account risks such as stock outs. This metric allows for the more complete utilization of inventory, which is important because the cash value of inventory is money not available for other value-adding purposes.

$$Inventory\ Turnover\ Rate = \frac{Total\ annual\ expense\ on\ stock\ items}{Average\ inventory\ value\ in\ stock}$$

Contract-utilization rate is a measure of the percentage of spending for contracted supply chain items as compared to total supply chain purchases. This is a critical metric because supplies purchased utilizing a valid contract from a vendor encourage standardization, typically cost less, and result in increased contract compliance. This can potentially impact contract discounts or rebates based on compliance and vendor satisfaction.

$$Contract\ Utilization\ Rate = \frac{Amount\ of\ dollar\ value\ in\ purchases\ using\ a\ valid\ contract}{Amount\ of\ total\ dollar\ value\ of\ all\ purchases} \times 100$$

Supply attribution value is a measure of the supply cost intensity for the patient population of a particular hospital. It uses supply cost weighting, which is similar to case mix index (CMI). This is important to a healthcare organization because the metric indicates the intensity of supply use for a facility. Understanding the intensity of supply use allows an organization to create better benchmark grouping. Additionally, the standard supply costs for each diagnosis relate group (DRG) can also be used to calculate a predicted total supply cost.

$$\text{Supply Attribution Value} = \frac{\text{Standard supply cost per DRG} \times \text{number of patients in each DRG}}{\text{Total number of inpatients in all DRGs}}$$

Stock inventory fill rate is a measure of the fill rate for each supply location, typically including item master, stock, and standard items. This ratio allows the tracking of the level of customer service provided by a stock inventory location. A higher fill ratio indicates a higher level of service with the trade-off of either a higher stock inventory value, storage cost, management cost, or a more intense management of time sequencing the stock line.

$$\text{Stock Inventory Fill Rate} = \frac{\text{Number of stock item requisition lines filled complete the first time}}{\text{Number of total stock item requisitions}} \times 100$$

Pharmacy inventory fill rate is a measure of the pharmaceutical stock inventory for each supply location. Similar to the stock inventory fill rate, this measure makes use of information from item master, stock, and standard items. The pharmacy inventory fill rate is used to measure the level of customer service provided by the pharmaceutical stock inventory location.

$$\text{Pharmacy Inventory Fill Rate} = \frac{\text{Number of Pharmaceutical stock item requisition lines filled complete the first time}}{\text{Number of total Pharmaceutical stock item requisition}} \times 100$$

Delivery date accuracy is a measure of the item delivery performance to customer on time or early as compared to the required or expected delivery date. This is compared to the line level on purchased orders.

$$\text{Delivery Date Accuracy} = \frac{\text{Purchase order line delivery date item deliveries on or before expected delivery date}}{\text{Total number of purchase order delivery line}} \times 100$$

These basic metrics all provide operational information to decision makers. In addition to these operational metrics, it is also important to track so-called "soft metrics." These soft metrics include information related to activities that may not be as easy to quantify, such as employee performance.[38]

Operational Management Enabled by Metrics, Statistics and Information

Improvements to operations, informed management, and quality leadership strategic decision making are facilitated with the availability of timely metrics, operational statistics, cost reports and integrated information. Data in context is used as information. That information is used to make decisions and take action to improve the operation and strategies of the health organization. This is very applicable to the healthcare supply chain as a core business element in the healthcare organization.

In many healthcare organizations, the use of dashboard reports are commonplace. This trend of timely if not "real time" information system reports is the essence of decision support for managers and leaders. At the operational level, information systems inform replenishment as in a perpetual inventory system or PAR system for restocking of supply chain items.

Systems: *Cloud versus Server Based*

Information systems have traditionally been run from servers stored either locally or in a specialized facility housing servers called a data center. A sever is a computer specifically designed to store or process large amounts of data. It has the same components as a personal computer, except the components in a server are typically able to store more information, run more programs, or process data much faster than a personal computer. An alternative to running an application system on a traditional server is cloud computing.

Cloud computing is a system in which groups of remote servers are connected together on a network to share resources. The concept of cloud computing has been around since the 1950s when programs were run on large computers called mainframes that were accessed through remote terminals. However, the term "cloud computing" originated in the mid-1990s. In technical diagrams the symbol for the internet was a stylized cloud. The term "cloud computing" was coined by the Compaq Computer Company in 1996 as a way to refer to the future of business on the internet.[39] It was not until ten years later in 2006 when the term began to increase in popularity following the release of the Elastic Compute Cloud by Amazon.com.[40] Recently advances in computer power and networking have paved the way for the increased use of cloud computing in all types of business. From the end user perspective, these cloud systems operate essentially the same as a traditional server but at a fraction of the cost and with a higher level of reliability. The cost savings are achieved through the use of shared services and system resources over multiple physical computers. Even though cloud computing has advantages with regard to cost and redundancy, there are security concerns with using cloud-based systems. These security concerns stem from the fact that the cloud systems are accessed over the internet and who has access to the servers making up the cloud is not always clear to the end users of the system.

Simulation for Process Improvement and Optimization

With information system utilization, valuable tools such as simulation can offer decision support information to improve the healthcare supply chain operation and how it is managed. Simulation can be a powerful tool for process improvement and optimization within the healthcare supply chain. There are two main categories of simulation: discrete and dynamic simulation.

Discrete Event Simulation

Discrete event simulation (DES) is a way to model the operation of a system as a series of events over time. In this modeling system, each event is considered to change the system. Between each event, it is assumed that no changes to the system occur. An example of a DES application is AutoCAD.

AutoCAD is a system that is used for drafting and modeling by engineers. The models created in AutoCAD can be run through other models to simulate how the particular item or building layout will function once built. Another DES in a process simulation application is MedModel.

MedModel software was designed to allow decision makers within a healthcare system to visualize processes and optimize their function through in-depth analysis.[41] MedModel allows the creation of an animated computer model of the clinical environment from value stream maps, process simulator models, or CAD files. This allows decision makers to see the current clinical processes in action. Any proposed changes to the process can be run through the model to gain a more complete understanding as to their potential effects in a specific area or with regard to patient flow.[42] The ability to run multiple scenarios through the model in order to test potential improvements can quickly improve the delivery of care within an institution. This is because instead of doing a great deal of analysis and followed by a trial of a proposed change in a particular department, many potential process changes can be tested simultaneously without any impact on day-to-day operations. Once complete, the output from each simulation can be compared to one other using standard statistical methods. This comparison allows for the optimization of the model chosen. Several common issues that can be addressed through this type of simulation include:

- Patient Flow.
- Bed Management.
- Facility Design.
- Low Productivity.
- Transition Planning.

- Future Staffing Requirements.
- Equipment Planning.
- Logistical Analysis.
- Emergency Preparedness.
- Planning for Future Changes.

Through modeling the important elements of a healthcare organization, decision makers are able to experiment with different solutions to determine the best result for their patients.[43]

Dynamic simulations are a type of modeling where a computer program is used to model the changing behavior of the system over time. In contrast to DES modeling, dynamic simulations are based on continuous activity, not discrete events. Because dynamic simulations analyze time periods instead of discrete events, they are typically much slower to run than discrete event simulations.

Follow the Cotton Ball

Can you imagine how a requisition for a box of cotton balls in the ERP system (from the item master) for a medical/surgical nursing ward unit in a hospital is compiled with other cotton ball box requisitions? Can you imagine how that compiled set of requisitions gets ordered using the terms of the contract (terms of the contract are in the ERP system linked to the vendor master to apply to this order)? Can you imagine how that order from the healthcare organization goes through the GHX transaction hub in "cyberspace" using the appropriate EDI transaction code? Can you imagine how that order is received while an EDI confirmation is sent back to the healthcare organization that ordered the cotton balls? Can you imagine how the cotton balls are delivered to

FIGURE 5.6   **Cotton From the Field**

Courtesy of Sarah Ledlow

the CSC, where a three-way match is done, the invoice is paid and the cotton balls are then sent to the healthcare organization customers who requisitioned the items and some cotton balls are placed in the pick area and the bulk storage area of the CSC or warehouse? Can you image how the transaction history file is updated to document the transaction? If you can "follow the cotton ball" through the information system, then you are starting to understand the flow of data and the flow of tangible items in the healthcare supply chain.

Summary

Information systems are valuable assets to healthcare organizations. This chapter provided an overview of this truth. Data, an enormous amount of data, in context, called information, enables quality decision making at the operational and strategic levels. Data in context, such as a healthcare supply chain context, is information; information that is "actionable" or useable is knowledge. Information systems foster knowledge for operators, managers, leaders, and strategists. Efficient, effective, and most importantly, efficacious business practices are reinforced and complemented by well developed, built and deployed information systems for a trained team of professionals across the healthcare personnel continuum. Good and high-quality business practices must be in place first with high standards and low levels of deviation or variance in order to realize the full potential of information systems. This is especially true in healthcare supply chain management, operations or in strategic decision making. Technological convergence and integration is reality; medical devices, equipment, and software applications are converging to create new technological innovations coupled with changes to the professional standard of care due to technological innovation.

In addition to information systems, leaders and managers must make high-quality decisions with efficacy, efficiency, and effectiveness in mind at all times. The use of metrics, made available in a timely fashion and enabled by information systems, informs the decision makers to improve operations and strategies of the healthcare organization and the supply chain that supports the delivery of care by providing the technology of care to the care givers within the Value Chain.

The healthcare supply chain must keep pace with, and in actuality forecast needs and demands of, this dynamic industry of healthcare. This chapter provided an overview of information systems, metrics, and improvement opportunities that are enabled by robust and integrated information systems. The domain of information systems will continue to grow and develop over the course of your lifetime. It is important to keep up to date on technological improvements, and this includes information systems, software packages, and the integration (or interface) between these systems.

Sarah Says: A Student's Perspective

This chapter focuses on the implementation and use of information systems in healthcare organizations. Information systems foster knowledge to leaders and enhance quality decision making at the operational and strategic levels.

It is important to stay up to date on these information systems. Technological advances occur rapidly in the industry, and it is imperative that healthcare organizations keep up with technology in order to efficiently, effectively, and most importantly, efficaciously run their business practices.

Information technology provides the tools necessary to efficiently manage the transportation and distribution of items within the supply chain through the use of automation. Automation has the effect of decreasing employee compensation. Cost of labor, or personnel, is the top operating cost to healthcare organizations, followed by cost of supplies. Since automation of supply-chain activities can potentially reduce costs in both of these areas, the supply chain is an excellent choice for automation and process-improvement activities.

Discussion Questions

1. Outline and explain the utilization of information systems in the healthcare supply chain.
2. Discuss and give examples of the different uses of information systems and technology of those systems in the operation of the supply chain.
3. Relate, discuss, and provide examples where information systems in the healthcare supply chain provide the availability of performance metrics and statistics to inform decision making for improved efficiency, effectiveness, and efficacy of the supply operation in the healthcare organization.
4. Distinguish the functional areas of information systems, such as sourcing, EDI, vendor management, warehousing/storage, and dispensing to points of care with regard to the healthcare supply chain.
5. Relate the business operation, how work is accomplished, to the information systems, how information and data from operations flow, within the healthcare supply chain.
6. Evaluate the benefits of improved information systems and utilization of metrics for healthcare supply-chain operations and management in terms of performance, health outcomes, and stakeholders' perceptions.

Exercises

1. Outline three different applications and explain the utilization of information systems in the healthcare supply chain.
2. Discuss and give three examples of the different uses of information systems and technology of those systems in the operation of the supply chain.
3. Relate, discuss, and provide two examples where information systems in the healthcare supply chain provide the availability of performance metrics and statistics to inform decision making for improved efficiency, effectiveness, and efficacy of the supply operation in the healthcare organization.
4. Distinguish the functional areas of two different aspects of information systems, such as sourcing, EDI, vendor management, warehousing/storage, and dispensing to points of care with regard to the healthcare supply chain.
5. Relate one business operation such as warehousing or storing or dispensing to points of care, how work is accomplished, to the information systems, how information and data from operations flow, within the healthcare supply chain.
6. Evaluate three different benefits of improved information systems and utilization of at least three metrics for healthcare supply chain operations and management in terms of performance, health outcomes, and stakeholders' perceptions.

Journal Items

Define:

Enterprise Resource Planning (ERP) Systems:

Metrics:

Information System Interface:

Consolidated Service Center:

Supply Chain – Clinical Integration:

Supply Chain – Revenue Management Integration:

Search: *Search items may give you great assistance in understanding the healthcare supply chain; provide the website/URL and provide a one paragraph summary of what you found.*

Lawson INFOR ERP Systems http://www.infor.com/product_summary/scm/scm-for-healthcare/

McKesson ERP Systems http://www.mckesson.com/en_us/McKesson.com/

Techsys (Warehousing and Inventory Management Information Systems) http://www.tecsys.com/?gclid=COTl7v_e27QCFQcHnQodbXEAQg

Manhattan Supply Chain Solutions (Warehousing and Inventory Management Information Systems) http://www.manh.com/solutions/distribution-management/warehouse-management

References

1. Healthcare Information Systems: Past, Present, Future, *Healthcatalyst*, (2014), https://www.healthcatalyst.com/healthcare-information-systems-past-present-future (accessed 3 Dec. 2014).

2. Healthcare Information Systems: Past, Present, Future, *Healthcatalyst*.

3. Healthcare Information Systems: Past, Present, Future, *Healthcatalyst*.

4. Healthcare Information Systems: Past, Present, Future, *Healthcatalyst*.

5. Healthcare Information Systems: Past, Present, Future, *Healthcatalyst*.

6. What is Clinical Decision Support (CDS)?, HealthIT.gov, (2012), Retrieved December 4, 2014, from http://www.healthit.gov/policy-researchers-implementers/clinical-decision-support-cds (accessed 4 Dec. 2014).

7. Health Communication and Health Information Technology, *healthypeople.gov*, (2014), https://www.healthypeople.gov/2020/topics-objectives/topic/health-communication-and-health-information-technology (accessed 7 Dec. 2014).

8. Designing the Standard for a Healthy Supply Chain, *mThink*, (2012), http://mthink.com/article/designing-standard-for-healthy-supply-chain/ (accessed 7 Dec. 2014).

9. Designing the Standard for a Healthy Supply Chain, *mThink*.

10. 8.5 Communication Channels, *Flat World Knowledge*, (2012), http://catalog.flatworldknowledge.com/bookhub/7?e=collins-ch08_s05 (accessed 8Dec. 2014).

11. A Few Thoughts on ERP in Healthcare – *Tribridge*, (2013), http://www.tribridge.com/knowledge-center

/tribridge/posts/p2/2013/06/09/a-few-thoughts-on
-erp-in-healthcare (accessed 8 Dec. 2014).

12. Healthcare & Medical ERP: Major Products & Players,
(2013), http://www.erpfocus.com/healthcare-medical
-erp-products-players-1352.html (accessed 8 Dec. 2014).

13. Lawson Bets More Heavily on Healthcare, *ITJungle*, (2010),
http://www.itjungle.com/tfh/tfh011810-story05
.html (accessed 8 Dec. 2014).

14. Lawson software, *Software Advice*, (2014), http
://www.softwareadvice.com/erp/lawson-software
-brand/ (accessed 8 Dec. 2014).

15. Vendor Master Data, *SAP Help Portal*, (2005), http://help
.sap.com/saphelp_47x200/helpdata/en/75
/ee0b1c55c811d189900000e8322d00/content.htm
(accessed 8 Dec. 2014).

16. Vendor Master Data, *SAP Help Portal*

17. Vendor Master - *South Carolina Enterprise Information System*, (2009), http://www.sceis.sc.gov/page
.aspx?id=95 (accessed 8 Dec. 2014).

18. 6 Configuring Oracle Supply Chain and Order Management, (2014), https://docs.oracle.com/cd/E14223_01
/bia.796/e14216/anyimp_enterprisesales.htm   (accessed 8 Dec. 2014).

19. Contracting Writing and Management for Supply
Chain, (2006), http://www.ism.ws/files/Pubs/Pro-
ceedings/CBDBGabbard.pdf (accessed 7 Dec. 2014).

20. Contracting Writing and Management for Supply Chain

21. Contracting Writing and Management for Supply Chain

22. http://www.ghx.com/ (accessed 8 Jul. 2014).

23. TrueCommerce EDI Solutions, "EDI Overview: A Practical Guide to EDI and the TrueCommerce EDI Platform,"
White Paper, Seven Fields, PA, http://www.highjump
.com/sites/default/files/Resources/WP-US-EDI.pdf
(accessed 8 Jul. 2014).

24. How Does the UPS Tracking System Work? - *Pack-
ageFox.* (2014), http://www.packagefox.com/blog
/how-does-the-ups-tracking-system-work/ (accessed
7 Dec. 2014).

25. http://www.tecsys.com/?gclid=COTI7v
_e27QCFQcHnQodbXEAQg (accessed 10 Dec. 2014).

26. http://www.manh.com/solutions/distribution
-management/warehouse-management   (accessed
10 Dec. 2014).

27. A. Corry, G. Ledlow, and S. Shockley. (2005). "Designing the standard for a healthy supply chain." In *Achieving
supply chain excellence through technology (ASCET)* 6., pp.
199–202). San Francisco, CA: Montgomery Research.

28. A. Corry, G. Ledlow, and S. Shockley. (2005). "Designing the standard for a healthy supply chain." In *Achieving supply chain excellence through technology (ASCET)*

6., pp. 199–202). San Francisco, CA: Montgomery
Research.

29. A. Corry, G. Ledlow, and S. Shockley. (2005). "Designing the standard for a healthy supply chain." In *Achieving supply chain excellence through technology (ASCET)*
6., pp. 199–202). San Francisco, CA: Montgomery Research.

30. A. Corry, G. Ledlow, and S. Shockley. (2005). "Designing the standard for a healthy supply chain." In
*Achieving supply chain excellence through technology
(ASCET)* 6., pp. 199–202). San Francisco, CA: Montgomery Research.

31. Selecting Effective Metrics and Dashboards for Process, *processexcellencenetwork.com* (2011), http://www
.processexcellencenetwork.com/business-process
-management-bpm/columns/selecting-effective
-metrics-and-dashboards-for-pro/ (accessed 7 Dec. 2014).

32. Selecting Effective Metrics and Dashboards for Process,
processexcellencenetwork.com

33. Selecting Effective Metrics and Dashboards for Process,
processexcellencenetwork.com

34. Selecting Effective Metrics and Dashboards for Process,
processexcellencenetwork.com

35. The 7 Deadly Sins of Performance Measurement,
innovationlabs.com, (2008), http://www.innovationlabs
.com/summit/summit6/pre/reading_materials
/0407_SMR_7DeadlySinsPerfMeas.pdf   (accessed   8
Dec. 2014).

36. The 7 Deadly Sins of Performance Measurement,
innovationlabs.com.

37. The 7 Deadly Sins of Performance Measurement,
innovationlabs.com.

38. A hard look at the soft side of performance
–   Strategy,   *supplychainquarterly.com*,   (2011),
http://www.supplychainquarterly.com/topics
/Strategy/201104people/ (accessed 4 Dec. 2014).

39. Who Coined "Cloud Computing"?, *MIT Technology
Review*, (2012), http://www.technologyreview.com
/news/425970/who-coined-cloud-computing/ (accessed 23 Nov. 2014).

40. Announcing Amazon Elastic Compute Cloud, *Amazon EC2*, (2008), http://aws.amazon.com/about-aws
/whats-new/2006/08/24/announcing-amazon
-elastic-compute-cloud-amazon-ec2---beta/ (accessed
23 Nov. 2014).

41. MedModel - *Promodel Corporation*, (2014), https
://www.promodel.com/Products/MedModel (accessed
7 Dec. 2014).

42. MedModel - *Promodel Corporation.*

43. MedModel - *Promodel Corporation.*

CHAPTER 6

OPERATIONS OF ACQUIRING

LEARNING OBJECTIVES

1. Outline and explain the concept and process of sourcing selection in the healthcare supply chain.
2. Discuss and give examples of the process of segmentation of supply chain items and the stakeholders involved with influence within each of those segments.
3. Relate, discuss, and provide an example where the tools of source selection and legal components of agreements integrate with healthcare supply chain sourcing and purchasing.
4. Distinguish the operational areas of vendor management in the context of the request for proposal and/or quote and negotiations.
5. Relate the sourcing of a medical/surgical item, such as cotton balls versus a cardiac pacemaker, to the categorization of suppliers/sourcing and why categorization is important.
6. Evaluate the benefits of improved sourcing with regard to outsourcing as compared to insourcing for healthcare supply chain operations and management in terms of stakeholders' perceptions, incentives, and healthcare organization capabilities.

Introduction

Turning to operations, leadership, and management of the healthcare supply chain as a core business of healthcare, this chapter will focus on acquiring the "technologies of care" for health organizations. Included in this chapter are tools for analysis, categorization, and legal considerations to establish a quality acquisition function or operation within the context of the healthcare supply chain. The premise used in the operations section of this textbook is based on the principles of high-performing organizations.

Operational Focus

The next chapters will take the concepts introduced in the first section of the textbook and expand upon them with a focus on healthcare organization operations. This chapter focuses on acquiring functions of sourcing and purchasing of items within the healthcare organization. Chapter 7 moves into the storage and management of the purchased commodities. Chapter 8 details several methods for the distribution of stored items at the points of care. Chapters 9 and 10 will drill down on various components of managing the supply chain and provide a more in-depth discussion of the use of metrics and strategic and operational planning.

Introduction to Operations

Business operations are the process through which an organization gains value from assets controlled by the organization and in turn provide value to customers. Customers are patients, family members of those patients, and the community the health organization serves. In a hospital setting, this includes all aspects of the business that provide care or support the care of patients with focus on the supply chain. From day-to-day management of the supply chain to strategic integration of supply-chain operations into the health organization, the essential knowledge of important functions of the supply chain will serve you well in your career. Leading and managing to be "high-performing" individually, and more importantly, as a unit or team must be the mind-set of the health professional. Many organizations, in various industries, leverage their supply chain operation to add greater value to customers; that means delivering items of quality, proven performance and durability at reasonable costs and in mass quantities. You have that opportunity in health organizations as well, and this opportunity, if implemented successfully, can be a lasting cornerstone to your career and legacy as a professional in the health industry.

In order to better understand the operation decisions you will be making for your hospital or system, it is best to put these decisions in context. Operational decisions, to be effective, must align with and support the firm's strategy. A firm's strategy is both impacted by and impacts overall corporate strategy. High-performing firms understand this dynamic; it is imperative that today's managers take this into account.

The Basics of High-Performing Organizations

High-performing organizations are focused on achieving results and outcomes. These organizations have a result-oriented organizational culture which fosters and reinforces their focus.[1] Moving an organization from low to high-performing requires a shift in culture that moves from:

- Outputs to results.
- Stovepipes to matrixes.
- Hierarchical to a more flat, horizontal structure.
- An inward to external focus on clients, customers, partners, and other stakeholders.
- Moving from micromanagement to employee empowerment.
- Reactive behavior to proactive approaches.
- Avoiding new technologies to embracing and leveraging them.
- Moving from hoarding knowledge in data silos to sharing knowledge.
- Avoiding risk to managing risk.
- Protecting "kingdoms" to forming partnerships.
- Moving from adversarial to constructive leader-member relations.[2]

As you can see, there are many changes that can help an organization increase its level of performance. High-performing organizations have four general themes in common, regardless of industry. First, **high-performing organizations have a clear, well-articulated, and compelling mission and vision**. Defining the mission and vision for an organization is important to the strategic planning process and, along with senior leadership, defines the culture of an organization. The vision of an organization can be thought of as "where we want to go" and the mission is a short statement of "what we do." The mission and vision are supported with goals and individual objectives which help to move the organization closer to its vision while keeping in line with the mission statement. High-performing organizations will also have a performance management system that is aligned to the goals and objectives of the organization. This creates an alignment between the vision of an organization and the day-to-day activities. The alignment is further reinforced through regular, clear, consistent communication with employees, customers, and key stakeholders to achieve a higher level of performance.[3] Do your team members know what their mission is every day? Do your team members know the importance of accomplishing their mission and how it contributes to the value in the health organization? Do your team members know what the future looks like for your team and operation? Are your team members inspired to accomplish their mission and strive for the vision of an improved future?

High-performing organizations also make strategic use of partnerships. Partnerships allow organizations to more efficiently achieve results and also have important implications across a range of management functions. Two key benefits provided by partnerships are shared accountability and an increased knowledge network. While shared accountability for projects has benefits with regard to sharing workload and project oversight, some managers find it difficult to hold partners accountable. The expansion of an organization's knowledge network is critical because it results in new connections within the network that provide an organization with a new outlet with which to share and learn best practices.[4] Can you categorize partnerships for your health organization based on cultural fit between the organization's aligned goals and increasing value? Who are your most important suppliers? Do you have "back-up" suppliers? Have you categorized essential (high-preference or high-volume /high-cost supply items) supply-chain items by supplier or vendor?

Strategic partnerships in healthcare can take the form of partnerships between clinics and acute-care hospitals where patients are referred to a particular facility based on their needs. In healthcare supply chain, there are many examples of strategic partnerships. They may be as simple as an agreement between two hospitals to sell supplies to each other in case of an emergency stock out at a particular facility. There are also much more complex strategic partnerships, such as those formed through a group purchasing organization. As previously discussed, the power of the Group Purchasing Organization (GPO) comes from the increased buying capacity of the organization when compared to a single facility. Each member healthcare organization is faced with purchasing trade-offs as part of the GPO. The best-priced item may be a brand that was not used within the hospital prior to joining the GPO. Do you have direct GPO supply relationships? Do you have direct manufacturer relationships? Do you have distributor

relationships? What items are associated with what suppliers?

They focus on the needs of clients and their customers. A clear focus on the needs of their customers is often mentioned when interviewing employees within a high-performing organization. At a minimum this customer focus includes a concerted effort to understand and respond to customer needs, tracking progress towards meeting the needs of their customers, and reporting out on that progress to increase accountability.[5] What supply items are "sensitive" to surgeons, physicians, nurses, and other clinical staff?

In healthcare, there are two primary customers, the patients and the physicians working within the healthcare facility. Balancing the needs of these two customer groups is central to all aspects of hospital operations. In the healthcare supply chain, the needs of both these customer groups is apparent in balancing the cost of preference items with substitutes. Balancing the needs of physicians and patients will be discussed further in a later chapter on leadership theory.

Finally, **high-performing organizations strategically manage people**. This is critical because people are the key resource of high-performing organizations. Without a high-performing staff, the other objectives of high-performing organizations cannot be met. The United States Government Accountability Office (GAO) has repeatedly noted that people are the center of any serious transformation initiative or change in management. Strong, charismatic, visionary leaders empower their employees to achieve results and manage risks to the benefits of the organization's customers and clients. Another aspect of strategically managing people is providing education and growth opportunities for all employees to allow them to excel. Organizations that fail to provide growth opportunities for employees will lose talent early and fail to develop top leaders within the organization. Even within the federal government, effective training and development programs are an integral part of enhancing the government's ability to attract and retain quality employees.[6] Do you have a "plan" for each team member and have you determined how that team member fits within the bigger picture of the supply-chain operation? How do your team members assist in achieving the vision of the health organization? What surgeons, physicians, nurses, clinical staff, and administrative staff influence the supply chain operation? Who are your stakeholders?

Transforming into a high performing organization takes concerted effort and a well-thought-out plan because it is not a short term goal. GAO made some suggestions to this point in a recent analysis of governmental performance. Even though these points were directed towards the federal government, the principles can be applied in all types of business, including healthcare. Its first suggestion was to establish a transformation fund which would award money for short-term targeted investments, based on a well-developed business case.[7] In the private sector this is analogous to investing in new equipment or office space as appropriate. The GAO's second suggestion was to appoint an individual to the role of chief operating officer or to empower an employee to provide attention and focus to management issues and work towards transformational change. Its third suggestion was to provide more oversight of existing programs and the budget reform process.[8] Budget reform is, once again, universally applicable to business. While private businesses do not obtain funding through the same means as a public entity, oversight of spending and reducing waste is mutually beneficial to both private and public entities. High-performing organizations produce, deliver, and conduct their work with quality; those organizations exceed expectations!

Specific to Healthcare Supply Chain

Gene Schneller, Professor at Arizona State University and supply-chain management expert, suggests that there are several keys to better supply-chain performance. Those keys are:

- Senior management involvement.
- Supply-chain optimization is a strategic goal.
- Integrated financial and clinical decision making.
- Organization cost management focus.
- Tracking of performance measures.
- End-user accountability for supply-cost management.
- Physicians are involved in supply chain activities.

- Control of new technology.
- Business skills, information and processes are in place.
- Supplier involvement.
- Aligned incentives.[9]

Strategically, leadership must concentrate on growing seven strategic factors and taking action on ten supply-chain value principles to form the necessary foundation that will enable the improved vision to develop. In *Optimize Your Healthcare Supply Chain: A Strategic Approach* by Health Administration Press, Dr. Gerald (Jerry) Ledlow provided a solid rubric for healthcare supply-chain "high-performance:"

Strategic Supply-Chain Factors in Order of Importance

1. **Information System Usefulness, Electronic Purchasing, and Integration**: Good data working in good systems create information that can be turned into knowledge for decision support, decision making, and action. Supply chain or materials management information systems should be integrated for the major functions of finance, clinical, cost accounting, and revenue in such a way that the healthcare team can speak the same language, use integrative data for joint analyses, decision making, and present individual and aggregated data for transactions. Electronic purchasing reduces errors and discrepancies significantly, especially with use of an electronic catalog.

2. **C-Staff Supply Chain Expertise**: Every leader in the organization should have a working understanding of the supply-chain strategic and operational fundamentals to find areas for improvement and have the ability, as a team, to implement good ideas. This must start with the CEO, COO, CFO, and CIO. Starting with language, each member of the leadership team must "talk" the same language. It is apparent that this does not happen on its own; indeed, the language of supply chain is foreign to clinicians, financial staff, and administration. Simply gather five supply items commonly used in your facility and ask different people on your team the name, unit of measure and use of the items, and chances are, you will get very different

answers (all the answers may very well be correct in the context of the team member). Creating a common language takes effort and a cross fertilization of contexts and understanding.

3. **Supply Chain Expenditure**: The more an organization spends, the greater its power in the marketplace for negotiations of pricing, service, quality, and payment terms.

4. **Physician and Surgeon Level of Collaboration**: The greater the level of surgeon and physician collaboration with the leadership, strategically, and supply chain management team, operationally, the greater an organization's ability to compress high-cost and high-volume supplies into one or two manufacturers' or vendors' item lines and thus improve bargaining leverage.

5. **Nurse and Clinical Staff Level of Collaboration**: The greater the level of nurse and clinician collaboration with the leadership, strategically, and supply chain management team, operationally, the greater an organization's ability to compress high-cost and high-volume supplies into one or two manufacturers' or vendors' item lines and thus improve bargaining leverage

6. **Leadership Team's Political and Social Capital**: The ability for leadership to positively influence the five items above is paramount.

7. **Capital Funds Availability**: The more capital funds that are available, the greater the ability for an organization to purchase necessary information systems, insource, or vertically integrate key components of the supply chain (only after a thorough business case analysis).

These tenets will be expanded upon in later chapters in the sections on strategy.

Sourcing and Purchasing

Operationalizing sourcing, procurement, and purchasing requires the healthcare professional in supply chain operations to understand the needs and wants of the health organization. Understanding needs and wants of clinical staff and administrative staff and what items the supply chain must provide to deliver healthcare is essential.

The starting point to understand needs and wants begins with the item master, vendor master and transaction history files. The power of electronic and computerized records allows the supply chain professional to analyze trends, needs, wants, and cycles of various supply chain items. Sourcing and purchasing are initial steps to fulfill wants and needs of the clinical and administrative professionals in the delivery of healthcare services.

Insource versus Outsource

Most health organizations outsource sourcing and purchasing through GPOs and distributors and do not have internal functions (some may have small purchasing sections for special or non-routine supply items to order and purchase) to satisfy the large quantity and variety of health supply items utilized by health organizations. With regard to insourcing, some health organizations, mostly health systems of several hospitals and clinics, do have internal capability for sourcing and purchasing of health supply chain items.

Shared Services

The shared services model for organization and delivery operations was developed in the 1980s as a way to increase organizational efficiency. This model came about due to concerns regarding productivity, globalization, and technological improvements which required companies to produce more at a lower cost to stay competitive.[10] GPOs are a form of shared services where many health organizations utilize GPOs and distributors to supply their needs. This provides lower cost due to the quantity of items the GPO and distributor passes through to the health organization. Negotiating with manufacturers for cost, service, delivery etc. is a function the GPO provides and thus frees the individual health organization from having negotiating capacity and mastery. In essence this is like a cooperative such as a Sam's Club or Costco for health supply chain items.

Intermediaries

Intermediaries are organizations that act as a channel for products or services in the supply chain. Typically, an intermediary will add some value to the supply chain that cannot be obtained if, for example, the manufacturer sold directly to the customer. A common example of an intermediary in the healthcare supply chain is the GPO. A GPO adds additional value for both supplier and consumer. The value added to the supplier comes from the ability of the GPO to sell products in bulk, which generates more revenue with less time for the manufacturer or distributor than if they sold direct. Value is added from the customer's perspective through bulk pricing discounts available to the GPO that are out of reach for most stand-alone facilities.

Even More Sourcing Models

There are several configurations for sourcing. A health organization can insource the medical and surgical supply chain while outsourcing the pharmaceutical supply chain. A health organization can outsource all but medical devices and equipment. The health organization must consider its capabilities, resources, and strategic plan, to include strategies, goals, and objectives, to determine what specific sourcing and supply chain model to use to best fit their needs and capabilities. Decisions are made through situational, strategic, and operational analyses.

Total Cost Analysis

Total cost analysis is a tool to identify all relevant costs over the entire life of a product or project. The concept originated in logistics within the domain of Total Cost Economics, based on the idea that if all logistical options provide equal service, the option that minimizes the total cost is preferred.[11] In supply chain management, the total cost is the sum of all the associated costs within the supply chain. This provides insights with regard to the hidden costs, in addition to the acquisition costs associated with insourcing part of the supply chain.[12] Another example of where total cost analysis can be used is in the determination of the actual cost of purchasing an item that requires regular maintenance over its lifespan or specialized training to operate.

Rebates

Rebates are price discounts offered by manufacturers to attract customers. Rebates are commonly offered for consumer products as well as supplies ordered by businesses and serve the same function. Rebates are favored by manufacturers over temporary price reduction because unless every customer claims the rebate, the rebate always benefits the manufacturer.[13] **Slippage** is the proportion of customers who purchase a product as a result of a rebate but fail to request a refund. The greater the slippage, the more beneficial the rebate is to the manufacturer. It has been reported that slippage rates of 70% are common, especially in the case of a "mail-in rebate."[14]

Value Chain

The Value Chain is a series of activities that a business performs to provide their product. The concept is based on manufacturing, but it is applicable to all forms of business. The Value Chain can be applied to a high-performing healthcare supply chain through a focus on sustainability, which will add value from the perspective of the healthcare organization and the patient. This sustainability is achieved through the management of environmental, social, and economic impacts while encouraging good governance practices throughout the Value Chain.[15] It is common for organizations to think of sustainability as a cost center for the organization. However, there are opportunities for cost savings, creating new partnerships and managing risk through the focus on supply chain sustainability from the perspective of the patient's Value Chain.

The healthcare supply chain can slowly be moved to one that is sustainable and creates value from the customer's perspective through the creation and following of a roadmap with goals that align with the mission of the organization.[16] There are several techniques that can be used when creating the roadmap to transform an organization's supply chain; some of these were discussed throughout the introductory section of this text. Some of the key techniques are reviewed here from an operational perspective. Let's turn from the supply chain as a whole to the functions of acquiring (sourcing and purchasing).

Want versus Need

Identifying want versus need within an organization is an important part of sourcing. For many types of commodities it will be clear if the item is a want or a need. However, for some items this distinction may not be as clear as for others. A tool that can be used for this purpose is Pareto analysis. Wants and needs also bring fulfillment into the discussion. Fulfillment is the availability and delivery of a supply-chain item to a customer (clinician, such as a surgeon or nurse, or support staff, such as a laboratory technician) in the process of care delivery or support of care delivery. Knowing the expected or essential level of fulfillment for a supply item is an important aspect of understanding wants and needs. The following graphic may explain the concept. In essence, at what level of availability does each supply item need to be stored and distributed (90%, 95%, 99% or all the time at 100%)?

The quantity acquired of any supply chain item has a cost associated with it. The simple cost of the item multiplied by quantity is one issue, but also the receiving, storing, loss rate, or pilferage and shrinkage rate, and quality control have costs associated with it. Knowing what availability or fulfillment rate is necessary, what is perceived to be necessary, and what is actually delivered are salient aspects of acquiring supply chain items. Understanding the true need (asking the direct question of what level of availability is expected to

stakeholders) of a supply chain item and communicating the cost of that level of fulfillment are serious operational concerns of the healthcare supply chain. Transaction history adds information to this picture; analysis of the transaction history of each supply item develops a common picture of need and want. It is essential that this is understood when the supply chain item is being acquired.

It is vital to understand the collection of wants and needs for each item in the item master based on transaction history, also called demand history. The suppliers and vendors selected by your health organization based on this demand information the most are very important to your organization. This includes high-volume, high-cost and clinician-preference items and the associated suppliers and vendors. These high-volume, high-cost and preference suppliers and vendors should require a high level of serious focus to negotiate and sign supplier contracts between your health organization and the supplier. This includes services like linen cleaning, case-cart processing, housekeeping, maintenance services, and the like. It may also include device and equipment suppliers as well.

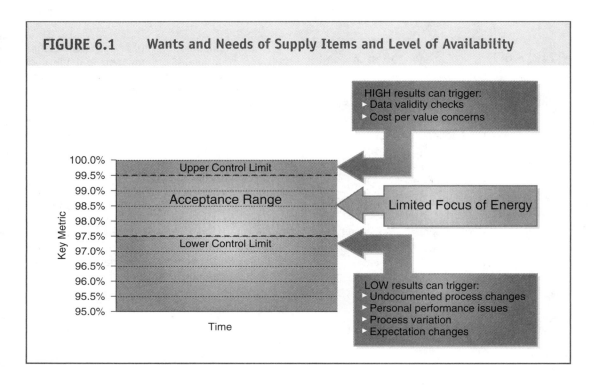

FIGURE 6.1   Wants and Needs of Supply Items and Level of Availability

FIGURE 6.2   Cost of Availability or Fulfillment Rates

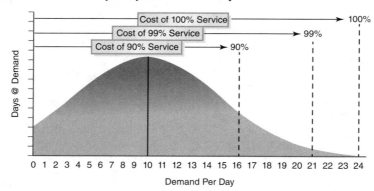

- 100% Fill Rate is Easy... it just takes Money...

Cost of Service:	100%	99%	90%
$ 1,000 item =	$1,440	$1,260	$960
$1 item =	$1.44	$1.26	$0.96
(Based on a holding cost of 6%)			

- It costs 3.5% more per service level point to go from 90% to 99% fill rate.

- It costs four times that rate to go the final 1%

TABLE 6.1   Categorization of Goods

High cost	Predominantly PP	Mix of items
	5% of all items	25% of all items
	40% of dollars spent	10% of dollars spent
	medium importance on fill rate	100% fill rates
Low Cost	Predominantly CC	Predominantly BC
	25% of all items	45% of all items
	30% of dollars spent	10% of dollars spent
	No need for high fill rate	same as above
	Commodity products	
	Low volume	High volume

The strategic relationship, or even partnership, between your health organization and the supplier or vendor can create "win-win" situations for both parties based on long term commitments and volume or high-dollar purchases. Gaining and ensuring contract compliance (physician, surgeon, nurse, and clinical staff concordance) from your health organization will be paramount and critical for your organization to reap the benefits from such relationships. To assist in this analysis, or demand forecasting, of supply chain items, there are various analytical methods and techniques that are important to making informed decisions and meeting stakeholder expectations. A few techniques and models have been presented earlier in the textbook but are shown again below along with additional models and techniques.

Demand Forecasting

Demand forecasting is simply determining how much of an item you need for future use. It is important to know the receiving and storage capability of your health organization (you do not want to order and receive more than you can handle, store, or distribute) and the amount of funds available (you do not want to spend more than you have to spend on that item). In addition, you need to know the order/ship time of the item since you may want to cover the time it will take to receive the item at your organization; this is especially true if the item is crucial or a physician or clinical high-preference item. There are several basic variables and methods for determining demand of an item. Time series methods along with a brief discussion of safety levels are provided. There are four basic variables you need to apply to a purchasing decision with regard to demand forecasting. Demand forecasting variables:[17]

1. Supply: the amount of product available.
2. Demand: overall market demand for product.
3. Product characteristics: product features that influence demand.
4. Competitive environment: actions of product suppliers in the market.

In addition, you will want to know the order/ship time (time it takes to receive the item after purchase/order). With that information, forecasting methods fall into four basic categories; time series will be presented as an overview. Forecasting methods:[18]

1. Qualitative: relies on a person's intuition or opinion.
2. Causal: assumes that demand is strongly related to certain factors.
3. Time series: based on historical demand patterns (including cyclic patterns).
4. Simulation: combines causal and time series methods.

From these variables, the appropriate methods are applied. It starts with understanding of demand and demand variation within your health organization for the particular supply chain item. "Knowledge of demand and demand variation [changes in demand for an item over time] within the system can enable improved demand forecasting, which, in turn, can allow inventory reductions and greater assurance that something will be available when needed. Barcoding and point-of-use [such as bar-

code scanner, RFID tag receivers] systems allow organizations to track when and how many supplies are being consumed, use that information to forecast demand organization-wide, and plan how to meet that demand in the most effective manner."[19] Many organizations utilize averaging (mean of several inputs) to estimate or forecast. Averaging assumes little to no variation, so changes in demand such as growth or decline in a supply item over time are not any more important than any other input; as in a simple moving average, all inputs are given equal weight or consideration. Where, F_t = forecast for the time period t (or the estimated/forecasted period of time in the future), D_{t-1} = value in the previous time period, and p = the number of time periods (#).

$$\text{Simple Moving Average: } F_t = \frac{D_{t-1} + D_{t-2} + \ldots + D_{t-p}}{P}$$

So if monthly demand for a package of cotton balls over the past six months was: 12, 15, 21, 23, 25, and 30, the simple moving average is:

$$F_t = \frac{12 + 15 + 21 + 23 + 25 + 30}{6}$$

With $F_t = \dfrac{126}{6}$ or 21 packages of cotton balls.

Common software programs, such as Microsoft Excel ©, can assist in calculations.[20] Using a weighted moving average, inputs are given weights or more importance and influence in the calculation. Usually, more recent inputs are given higher weights or more influence in the calculation. Where, adding to the simple moving average formula, w_p = weight for time period p and $w_1 + w_2 + w_3 + \ldots + w_p = 1$. So if monthly demand is the same, expanding on the example, the formula for a weighted moving average would be:

$$F_t = \frac{.05 * 12 + .05 * 15 + .15 * 21 + .2 * 23 + .25 * 25 + .3 * 30}{}$$

$$F_t = .6 + .75 + 3.15 + 4.6 + 6.25 + 9$$

or 24.35 packages of cotton balls (in essence 25 packages). Clearly, just by allowing greater influence in data from more recent months increased the forecast by 3.35 packages. Again, using common software programs, such as Microsoft Excel©, can greatly assist in forecasting.[21] The next method is economic order quantity.

Economic Order Quantity[22, 23]

Another well-known and utilized method is called economic order quantity or EOQ. This method calculates the most cost-effective amount to purchase at a time. Also, EOQ can be combined with a safety level for crucial items, so the health organization always has that item available. The formula is:

$$EOQ = \sqrt{\frac{2UO}{hC}}$$

Where U = annual usage rate, O = ordering cost, C = cost per unit (each, package, box, carton, etc.) and h = holding cost per year as a percentage of unit cost. An example would be if an item, say a package of cotton balls, has an annual usage of 1200, a fixed cost per order of $3.00, a unit cost of $2.50 and an annual holding cost of 20% per unit, the calculation is:

$$EOQ = \sqrt{2 \times 1200 \times 3.00 / .2 \times 2.50}$$
$$= \sqrt{7200 / .5} = \sqrt{14,400}$$

Taking the square root = 120 packages of cotton balls to order. To add a simple safety level method, determine the time it will take to receive the cotton ball packages order, say 1 week, and divide the annual usage by 52 weeks (52 weeks per year) for 1200/52 = 23.077 packages and rounding up = 24 packages. So you, using this method, would order 120 packages of cotton balls, and if you use a simple safety level method with EOQ on this item, you would purchase 144 cotton ball packages.

Pareto Analysis

How would you know where you are spending funds, with whom and for what items? Pareto analysis is a decision-making technique based on the Pareto principal, otherwise known as the 80–20 rule. Pareto analysis allows for this by statistically separating the input factors that have the greatest

impact on an outcome. The thought behind this is that 80% of something can be traced to 20% of another. An example of this principle in practice is that 20% of the items purchased by a health organization account for 80% of the sourcing costs.[24] There are several situations when Pareto analysis should be used:

- To analyze data regarding frequency.
- If there are many potential causes and there is a need to focus on the most significant cause.
- To analyze a potential cause and see what components have the greatest effect.
- To communicate data to others.[25]

The steps to perform a Pareto chart analysis are:

1. Group items into categories.
2. Decide what measurement is appropriate; common measurements include frequency, time, cost, and quantity.

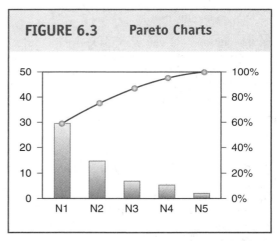

FIGURE 6.3   Pareto Charts

The charts above display categories of data and their relative frequency, that is, how often they occur. In the first chart, the total of all columns adds to 100%; this relationship is shown by the line above the bars. The line shows the sum of the categories directly below and to the left of the current position. The second chart displays relative frequency of occurrence by number of occurrences, not percentage of total occurrences; however this method also allows for Pareto analysis.

FIGURE 6.4   Healthcare Supply Item Categorization Schema

Product Area	Examples	Contracting Effort	Clinical Input (in Blue) ◔
Commodity Interchangeable with equivalent products and no measurable decrease in value to end user	Industrial paper, office supplies, patient care plastics	Very Low	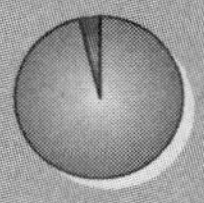
Clinical Commodity Interchangeable with equivalent products that warrant clinical evaluation due to intended use	Needles & Syringes, ostomy supplies, general wound care	Low to Medium	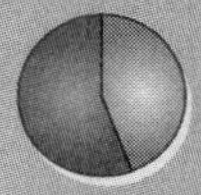
High Preference Specialty products requiring clinical/ physician input and a significant degree of clinical evaluation	Anesthesia circuits custom packs, balloon catheters, wound closure	Medium to High	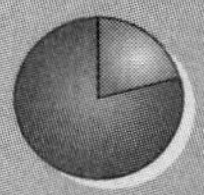
High Cost / High Preference Highly specialized products selected as a result of physician preference	Cardiac Rhythm Mgmt., cardiac interventional, ortho. implants	High to Very High	

3. Determine the time period for analysis.
4. Collect data for each category.
5. Total the measurements in each category.
6. Determine the appropriate scale to use. The highest value on the scale is the largest total from step 5.
7. Create the bar chart, the largest value on the left.
8. Calculate percentages and cumulative sums.[26, 27]

Once you have conducted a Pareto analysis of transactions in the supply chain to identify the top suppliers/sources of vital items, categorization of healthcare supply items is another important step. The following tool or model, adapted from a healthcare system based in St. Louis, Missouri, assists in this categorization process.

The basic notion is to categorize what types of supplies fall into each category. The items with more clinical input from physicians, surgeons, nurses, and technical professionals are most likely to be more costly and could be problematic if the wrong item is purchased for use in patient care. Seeking and gaining clinician input on high-preference and high-cost items is crucial, but it is in these areas where significant cost savings can be gained. Through compression (selection of one–two sources/vendors/suppliers rather than four–five vendors can gain steep discounts if volume targets are reached in the contract with the selected one–two vendors), significant savings on supplies (cost avoidance) can be achieved. Once these tools, techniques and models are utilized to categorize items, coupled with Pareto Analysis, selection of suppliers/sources of supply items can be achieved through one of two models, the Kraljic model and the CAAVE model. The following analysis focuses on supplier or vendor relationships with your health organization. Now that you have a good understanding of wants and needs, demand forecasts for supply chain items, and a good picture of high-volume, high-dollar, and preference supply-chain items, developing strategic relationships and partnerships is important. Having your wants and needs, demand forecasting, and historical purchase information at hand and analyzed, your health organization is ready to collaborate to build relationships with suppliers or vendors, improve existing relationships or find new relationships.

Strategic Relationships

Strategic relationships are bi-directional. This means both parties, in this case your health organization and the supplier or vendor, gain from the relationship over long time periods. Two models are presented to assist you in determining which suppliers or vendors should be "strategic" for your health organization.

The Kraljic Model

Purchasing portfolio models are a hot topic in professional purchasing. One of the most famous of the purchasing portfolio models is the Kraljic model. According to Kraljic, supply strategy depends on two key factors: profit impact and supply risk.[28] The popularity of the Kraljic model has caused scholars to introduce variations of the original model. However, they are typically very similar to the Kraljic and as such result in similar recommendations to the end user.[29]

The Kraljic model for managing a purchasing portfolio organizes items into four categories: routine, bottleneck, leverage, and strategic. Items categorized as routine generally have a low impact on profit and have a low risk of supply shortage. Bottleneck products also have a low impact on profit but have a high degree of difficulty of sourcing associated with them. Leverage products are items that have a high potential to impact profit but a low risk of stock-out. Strategic products are items that have a high difficulty in sourcing associated with them and also a high potential to impact profitability.

FIGURE 6.5 **Product Purchasing Classification Matrix**

By permission of Harvard Business School Press. Adapted from Exhibit II in Kraljic, P. (September 1983). Purchasing must become supply management. Boston: Harvard Business School Press.

The basic recommendations for products in each quadrant of the model are:

- Form partnerships for products deemed strategic.
- Assure supply for bottleneck products.
- Use market power for leverage products.
- Ensuring the efficient processing of non-critical products.[30]

However, in addition to the generalized recommendations for each quadrant of the model, there are also several strategies within each quadrant. These strategies can be broken into two broad categories: strategies to hold position within a quadrant and strategies to move to another position.[31] The situation in which each strategy would be used is specific to each situation, and as such only general guidance can be given in this regard. Any decision to change market position for a particular product should be guided by the mission and vision of the organization. Ensuring this will maximize the positive impact for the organization and move it closer to its goals.

Products can be correctly placed within the Kraljic model using a four-stage approach to develop supply strategies for one or more products.

1. Classify all purchased products by their impact on profit and the associated risk of a stock out.
2. The bargaining power of an organization is then compared to that of its competitors.
3. Next, the products identified as both strategic and high risk are placed in the matrix position corresponding to both high profit impact and high supply risk.
4. The final step is to develop an action plan and purchasing strategy for the strategic products.[32]

The plan that an organization develops will be based on the particular market and the strength of the organization within that market. Whatever the organization decides, its purchasing plan will fall into one of three categories: exploit, balance, or diversify. An exploit strategy is chosen in situations where the organization has a dominant position in the market. In the other extreme case, supplier dominance, a diversify approach should be taken. In a more balanced market, a balanced approach consisting of diversification and exploitation where possible should be taken.[33] This process is repeated for each category of product within the Kraljic matrix. The Kraljic model is one method to categorize suppliers (sources of supply); the CAAVE model is another approach based on value and links well with the Value Chain concepts.

The CAAVE Model

Another more contemporary model to use in strategic relationship determination is called the CAAVE model. Let's compare the Kraljic model and the CAAVE model in the following graphic.

In comparing the two models, several concepts are presented to support the need to evolve to a more contemporary model. "Following these elaborations of Kraljic's model, another line of development can be observed. This second wave focuses on classifying the content of buyer-supplier relationships as opposed to the initial focus set by Kraljic."[34] Moreover, in the results of research findings by Cousins and Spekman[35] "the interviews highlighted two clear relationship clusters, which we called 'Opportunistic' and 'Collaborative.' Opportunistic relationships are focused mainly on short term price reduction technique; the strategy is to create a competitive advantage via leveraging the supply market but only on the ability to extract a price concession. This approach usually utilized Kraljic's Strategic Positioning matrix and was in

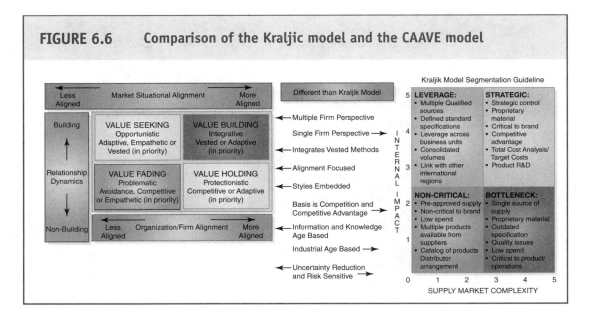

FIGURE 6.6   **Comparison of the Kraljic model and the CAAVE model**

most cases initiated by the use of corporate consultants. The problem, as the majority indicated, was that in the medium to long term this strategy could not be sustained. Interviewees who wanted to sustain cost reduction used the collaborative relationship model. This model clearly shows that there are ranges of aspects that are important when looking at how a firm deals with its relationships."[36] Dubois and Pedersen offer, "…we argue that using 'given' [power-dependence models] products as a port of departure, in addition to a dyadic perspective on purchasing management, may be counterproductive when purchasing efficiency is concerned. First, the object of exchange is not 'given' when firms interact, but may be subject to continuous joint development. Second, the dyadic perspective may obscure potentials for enhancing productivity and

innovativeness since both parties have other relationships that impact on the collaboration between them."[37] Lastly, "How could one deduce strategies from a portfolio analysis that is based on just two dimensions"[38] and often the supplier's side is disregarded with the Kraljic model. Considering the current evidence, the CAAVE approach minimizes the concerns raised and incorporates contemporary constructs necessary for thorough evaluation of strategic relationships in a parsimonious framework. The CAAVE model rests on four quadrants while integrating market and relationship dynamics as well as firm compatibility based on assessment of each the set of axes' constructs.

In support of these quadrants, DuBois and Pedersen in 2002 offer, "we argue that these problems [using Kraljic as compared to the industrial

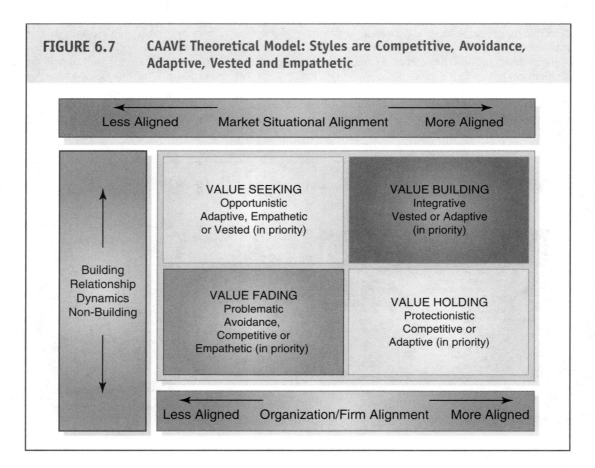

FIGURE 6.7   CAAVE Theoretical Model: Styles are Competitive, Avoidance, Adaptive, Vested and Empathetic

network approach] and solutions may lead much further, as they are not concerned with optimization, or resource allocation, but with 'total' cost considerations and joint value creation."[39] Integrating TCE and "win-win" approaches in strategic relationships, the operational issue of sourcing and supply chain evidently come to light. "It is encouraging to note, however, that there is a very strong trend toward integrating theory in SSCM research."[40]

Integrating organizational theory, human dynamics, communication and leadership as relationship dynamics and compatibility constructs in the evolution of strategic relationships into the Nash and Williamson framework is evident as suggested by the CAAVE model. However, operationalization is key; "talking about the 'black box' of transaction cost economics, ...prioritization, conceptualization and operationalization are needed."[41]

Utilizing the Kraljic or CAAVE models will assist the health organization in determining what suppliers/sources of supply can be strong strategic partners as vendors to the health organization. These models can also be used for both insource and outsource sourcing models.

Group Purchasing Organization

GPOs save the US healthcare industry more than $36 billion dollars a year. This saving is accomplished through discounts offered for bulk purchases that GPOs make possible because they are purchasing for multiple facilities. GPOs typically charge a small administrative fee to the vendors who provide services to hospitals, although some GPOs charge fees to the hospitals. There are even GPOs that charge a fee to both the vendor and hospital. Whatever the selected fee structure, the fees are used by the GPO to fulfill its mission to encourage competition and reduce overall costs for healthcare organizations.[42] In addition to the leverage and bulk-buying power provided by GPOs, they also allow healthcare organizations to save time and money that would normally be spent negotiating and executing, potentially, thousands of individual contracts. Hospitals are able to select the most cost effective GPO available, and this produces a strong incentive for GPOs to be as efficient as possible.

Distributors

In industries where their products are made continuously or in large batches, shipments are also large in order to maximize profit. These shipments are usually much larger than what the end user of the product can use or store. Due to the need for large shipments from manufacturers and smaller shipments to the end user of the product, there is a need for an intermediary in the supply chain to receive large quantities and ship out many smaller loads of the product; the distributor fulfills this role. Distributors are different from brokers, who do not take delivery or ownership of the product, and surplus buyers, who usually buy older material to resell at a discount.[43]

Sales Tracing Fees

Sales tracing fees are fees paid by manufacturers to distributors for rectifying payment to the manufacturer's sales force or sales representatives. Knowing where the item was "bought" and "sold" allows a commission payment to be made to the sale representative. Typically the distributor (as an outsourcer) or the health organization or system (if insourcing the acquiring function) is paid between 0.5–1% of the value of the items transacted (bought and sold) within the domain of a particular

TABLE 6.2	GPO and Distributor Attributes	
Attribute	**GPO**	**Distributor**
Takes physical possession of goods	Not usually	Yes
Shared services	Yes	No
Sells to everyone	No	Yes
Can represent a single manufacturer	No	Yes

manufacturer's sale representative. Sales tracing fees can be a point in acquiring supply items during negotiations if the distributor or health organization can provide sales tracing reports to the manufacturer as part of a contract for supply-item sourcing; this would be a service provided for payment.

Comparative Trade-offs

Comparative trade-offs are a result of scarcity. Scarcity is an economic term referring to the unlimited wants of an individual or organization and the limited resources available to fulfill those wants. Trade-offs are how the limited resources available are allocated to best satisfy those wants. In short, trade-offs occur because resources devoted to one task cannot be used for another task. The choice to allocate resources between two options is represented in economics by the production–possibility frontier (PPF), shown here in **Figure 6.8.**

The PPF is typically represented as a curved line to account for marginal opportunity costs associated with choosing one product over another. This means that due to the nonlinear relationship between production choices, the production of one additional unit of item X reduces the number of units of product Y that can be produced.

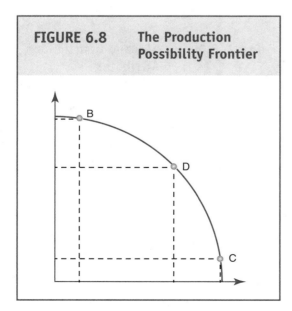

FIGURE 6.8   **The Production Possibility Frontier**

Figure 6.8 displays the PPF for two products, one on the X axis and the other on the Y axis. Points B, C, and D (as well as any other point along the curve) represent optimal production efficiency for the firm. At each point along the curve, the product mix produced is different, represented by the dashed lines. For example, at point D the same amount of the product on the X axis is produced as the product on the Y axis. When the firm moves along the PPF to point C, additional units of product X are produced at the expense of the Y axis product.

In sourcing, the trade-offs between one product and another include all the variables associated with the sourcing, storage, and distribution of the products. In situations where the usage of a product exceeds the ability of the supply chain to provide that product, a shortage can occur. Pharmaceutical shortages are more commonplace and greatly impact the functions of acquiring (sourcing and purchasing).

Transacting the Purchase

With the demand forecasts and supplier/vendor relationships understood and, hopefully, established with an agreement or contract, it is time to make the purchases necessary to fulfill demands of healthcare supply chain items. This can be accomplished with "hardcopy" purchase orders (called POs) or electronically. In some cases orders may be written up by a sales representative, or a customer calls and orders a product. Electronic purchasing with electronic data interchange (EDI) transaction is commonplace and growing in the industry. In healthcare over 50% of medical and surgical items, such as cotton balls, are processed and transacted electronically between healthcare organizations and vendors by GHX (Global Health Exchange), which is the electronic business-to-business system run by the GHX Corporation.[44] Now the vendor is linked to the item master and information system for the supply chain operation.

For a best practice, when the supply item(s) are ordered in large quantities over a long period of time or when the cost of transactions with this vendor is moderate to high, a contract should be established with this vendor to achieve the best pricing and service terms for ordering, receiving, returning, utilizing, and maintaining our supply items. Although a special order or non-contract or out of contract order/requisition/purchase can be made for one time or few time orders, a contract from a vendor should be developed and implemented so that the contract terms can be linked to the vendor, the items from the vendor (from the EDI 832 electronic catalog) and into the supply chain system. Lastly, electronic data interchange is an important concept to electronic transactions in the healthcare supply chain.

The Basics of EDI

What is EDI? "Electronic Data Interchange (EDI) is a set of standards that collectively provide a common protocol or syntax for transacting business documents electronically. In essence, EDI is to electronic commerce as grammar is to verbal communication –

it is a set of rules and guidelines that are applied when developing and implementing software and services designed to transmit business documents electronically. Just as a group of individuals with diverse backgrounds can use a common language (such as English) to converse with each other, EDI provides a common 'language' that enables businesses with dissimilar computer-based business systems to communicate with each other."[45]

The Healthcare Supply Chain Information System

How does a healthcare organization add an item or modify an item into the item master so the item can be ordered/requisitioned by the patient care team? How is a supplier/vendor contract entered or modified? The next sections discuss these issues as an overview.

TABLE 6.3	Examples of Commonly used EDI Transaction Sets	
X12ID Code	**Transaction Set**	**Document Usage**
850	Purchase Order (PO)	A trading partner sends a PO to order products from a vendor.
810	Invoice	The vendor sends an invoice back to its trading partner as a bill for the products ordered.
997	Acknowledgement	An acknowledgement is sent as a receipt to the sender upon the retrieval of a document.
856	Advanced Ship Notice (ASN)	The vendor sends an ASN to its trading partner specifying to a mutually agreed level of detail the dates and contents of a shipment. Many businesses require the receipt of an ASN from a supplier before the shipment reaches their receiving docks.
820	Remittance Advice	Remittance advice informs the vendor that its trading partner has made a deposit into its bank account.
852	Product Activity Data	The Product Activity Data is used by trading partners to advise vendors of inventory, sales and other product activity information.
832	Electronic Product Catalog	An electronic catalog of products/items from a manufacturer, distributor or vendor.

Modified from TrueCommerce EDI Solutions, "EDI Overview: A Practical Guide to EDI and the TrueCommerce EDI Platform," White Paper, Seven Fields, Pennsylvania, Retrieved from http://www.highjump.com/sites/default/files/Resources/WP-US-EDI.pdf, retrieved July 8, 2014.

Item Master Additions

The requester identifies the need or want for a new item. The need or want is analyzed and a demand forecast is developed. The person or team responsible for the item master file is notified of the item addition(s) (usually this is done electronically in a specified load format). The request is reviewed to validate the item's status. Item modifications are usually taken through a defined process that may resemble this flow:

- The item "add" request is validated and approved. If the item "add" request is rejected, the requestor is notified why and given further instructions as needed. If the request is approved, the finance department (usually the revenue management section) is contacted to determine the chargeability of the item and obtain the appropriate revenue and expense codes.
- While waiting for the financial information, the item's supplier/vendor is evaluated and if necessary sent though the "vendor add" flow.
- Then a United Nations Standard Products and Services Code (UNSPSC) code is identified and the manufacturer is checked and added if necessary. Once the supplier/vendor, UNSPSC code, patient chargeability, and manufacturer are prepared, the items are loaded into the information system.
- Once complete, the requestor is automatically notified of the items' availability.

Supplier/Vendor Addition or Modification

The next salient issue is establishing the supplier/vendor in the system to link to the specific item master file supply chain item. The following flow gives a description of that sequence of events in the information system and business processes associated with this action:

- The person or team responsible for the item master is notified of a vendor addition via the accounts payable section.
- That want or need is received and validated and then communicated to the third party administrator (such as GHX) for supplier/vendor setup in the information system. The third party administrator determines whether the supplier/vendor is capable of conducting EDI transactions. If the supplier/vendor is EDI capable, then the third party administrator sends a pre-established standard format supplier/vendor specifications file with complete EDI data for loading into the information system to establish the setup. The system flags are set up to handle EDI transactions.
- If the supplier/vendor is determined to be incapable of EDI transactions, then the item master responsible person or team is notified. At that time the item master team must create the supplier/vendor system setup file and the supplier/vendor flag is selected appropriately (fax, email, etc.).
- The requestor is notified automatically of the supplier/vendor addition and availability. If there is a change to the vendor's information, the item file team is notified of needed supplier/vendor table modifications. If the supplier/vendor is not handled via EDI, then the changes are validated and then updated within the information system. If the vendor is handled via EDI, and the source of that communication is the EDI third party administrator, then the changes are updated within the information system.

Contract Additions and Modifications

The last major event in this sequence of activities in the information system is a change to an existing supplier/vendor contract. The general flow of activities would be similar to those described below:

- A new or modified contract is identified and communicated to the contract administration section/team electronically in a specified information format.
- The request is validated against the contract agreement and approval for the contract changes is sought. If the contract change is rejected, the requestor is notified why and given further instructions as needed. If the request is approved, the contract is checked to see if it is new or existing. If the contract is existing, then the items are checked to see if they indeed exist in the system. If the contract is new, then the contract type is identified as either a product contract (GPO, distributor, manufacturer direct or local), a service contract (GPO or local) or a capital contract. Whatever the contract type, the finance section/team is contacted to obtain the appropriate account information for

that contract and the request is forwarded on through the patient chargeability process.

- At the same time, the items within the contract are checked to ensure they exist within the contract. If the items are in the system, then the key systems information (supplier/vendor, manufacturer, unit of measure, appropriate codes like the UNSPSC code, etc.) are validated. If the items are not in the system, the item is sent to be added in the item additions process (item master file addition).
- Once all the items are in the system and are validated, the contract is entered into the system. Once the contract is in the system, all requestors and stakeholders are automatically notified of the items' availability.
- The system must also set a "ship to" location (where the supplier/vendor will ship/transport orders to the healthcare organization) in the system for the vendor. System support is notified of ship-to, inventory path, or location changes needed in the system.

Those requested changes are validated in the system. The information is entered into the system and the requestor is automatically notified of the completion of the task.

That is the basic process for acquiring with the functions of sourcing and purchasing. Next the discussion will focus on some areas important to acquiring functions in the areas of pharmaceutical shortages and emergency preparedness.

Pharmaceutical Shortages

Pharmaceutical shortages are defined as a change in drug supply that could potentially compromise patient care. Changes in supply can alter the way that a pharmacy needs to prepare medications; such changes may change the way medications are administered and in extreme cases determine if the patient can even receive medication.[46] In recent years, drug shortages have been an increasing problem for healthcare organizations because they typically appear with little warning and greatly increase

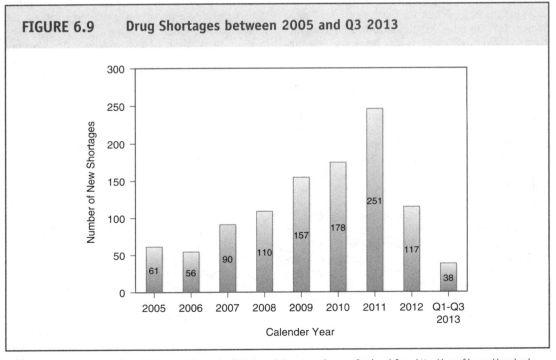

FIGURE 6.9   Drug Shortages between 2005 and Q3 2013

resources needed to manage patients when certain treatment options are not available.[47] When data collection on drug shortages began in 1996, there were less than five drug shortages per year. Between 1997 and 2000, the number of shortages increased to twenty per year.[48] The number of shortages continued to increase nearly every year until 2011, when the number of shortages reached 251.[49]

The US Food and Drug Administration (FDA) takes several actions to help limit the effects of drug shortages by responding to potential shortages and addressing their underlying causes. The specific action taken depends on the situation and potential severity of the shortage.

For shortages related to manufacturing or quality, the FDA will work with the business to address the issues in the manufacturing process. These problems range from low-risk situations such as an incorrect exportation date on a product to high-risk situations such as product contamination. In some cases the FDA may take regulatory action to mitigate any significant risk to patients.[50]

If it is not possible for manufacturers in the United States to immediately resolve a shortage and the drug is critically needed for patients in the United States, the FDA may look towards foreign manufacturers of the drug. In these situations, the FDA has a list of criteria to ensure the efficacy and safety of the imported product. However, there are a number of factors that can cause or contribute to drug shortages that are out of the control of the FDA.[51] For this reason it is important that healthcare organizations take steps to safeguard themselves as much as possible from the threat of drug shortages. It has been estimated that healthcare organizations may spend between one half-time and three full-time equivalent employees on the management of drug shortages.[52] The duties of these employees include finding alternative sources for products, determining alternative products, investigating the reason for the shortage, or creating a replacement internally.[53]

There are several reasons why drug shortages occur. Some of the more common reasons are: regulatory non-compliance, voluntary recalls, raw material shortage, manufacturer rationing, restricted distribution, product discontinuation, and natural disasters.[54]

Regulatory non-compliance results in a shortage if the FDA determines the manufacturing of a particular substance to be outside of good manufacturing practices. Regulatory non-compliance can potentially affect the supply of multiple products depending on if the facility has production lines for more than one product.

Voluntary recalls can result in shortages depending on their scope, especially when there is only one manufacturer of a specific product. Voluntary recalls have a similar effect as temporary manufacturer rationing. In both situations the supply is reduced for a specific period of time. Occasionally, manufacturers will permanently reduce the quantity of a drug supplied. This may occur in situations where there are alternative products or if the manufacturer is switching production resources to another product. In cases where the production of a drug is no longer in the best interest of the manufacturer, production may be completely discontinued. The most common reasons for this is a lack of profitability or if a more effective drug is created for the same purpose.

Raw material shortage has the potential to impact multiple drugs and create widespread shortage due to their position in the supply chain. Since raw materials may be used in multiple products, their shortage can have a huge effect on the pharmaceutical market.

The distribution of pharmaceuticals is sometimes restricted to select patient populations that will receive the most benefit from the drug. This is usually a short-term shortage that ends when the market surveillance program is complete.[55]

Natural disasters can cause a shortage by affecting key production facilities that manufacture drugs or raw materials used in their production. Emergency preparedness is also a concern of the sourcing and procurement function.

Recalls

The FDA will also work with other manufacturers that produce drugs in short supply to help increase production. Often this support includes approving new production lines or new sources of raw materials. In these situations, the FDA will expedite the review of permit applications; however, the FDA cannot require manufacturers to increase production.[56] If a shortage has already occurred and there is available inventory that has expired or is close to expiration, the FDA can extend the expiration date in cases where the safety and efficacy of use past the listed expiration date has been established.

Emergency Preparedness

Being prepared for the effects of disasters on the healthcare supply chain is of central importance given the complexity of the modern supply chain. Alternate sources should be identified and emergency stockpiles in place for key items. Many of the safeguards related to emergency preparedness have federal guidelines as to the minimum standards that must be met, such as safety stock levels. Above and beyond the minimum standards set by the federal government, there are several best practices for supply chains:

1. Plan ahead.
2. Set aside funds.
3. Designate a crisis team.
4. Know who should be called for specific situations.
5. Line up suppliers.
6. Diversify transportation modes.
7. Have process documentation in place.
8. Know what will be needed.
9. Anticipate future demand.
10. Be prepared to make changes to the plan.[57]

After September 11, the Council of Logistics Management sponsored research on supply chain management during times of crisis.[58] Their research was focused on the summarization of existing techniques for disaster management. The traditional approach to disaster management was created by the Federal Emergency Management Agency (FEMA). The FEMA plan consisted of a series of guidelines designed to aid in disaster manage-

TABLE 6.4   Helferich and Cook Disaster Management Process Overview*†

Stages	Planning	Mitigation	Detection	Response	Recovery
Major Steps	1. Establish a Planning team 2. Analyze capabilities and hazards 3. Develop the plan 4. Implement the plan	1. Define mitigation opportunities 2. Develop mitigation plan 3. Initiate development 4. Continuous improvement program	1. Develop detection plan 2. Acknowledge warnings 3. Evaluate and act on observations 4. Decide on need for further action 5. Continuous improvement	1. Implement response plan 2. Evaluate direction and control 3. Evaluate Communications 4. Evaluate life safety 5. Evaluate property protection 6. Evaluate public services 7. Evaluate Community outreach	1. Review and implement recovery plans 2. Ensure continuity of management 3. Maintain employee support 4. Resume operations

*T. Hale, Improving supply chain disaster preparedness.

†Helferich and Cook, "Securing the Supply Chain".

ment and was divided into three categories: planning, response, and recovery.[59] Helferich and Cook extended the FEMA guidelines in 2002 by adding two additional stages in order to provide a better fit for increasing complexity within the supply chain.[60]

According to Helferich and Cook, mitigation is an important step because it is crucial to reduce the potential impact of disasters on the supply chain in order to reduce the length of any disruption that does occur. Detection was added as well because if a potential disaster is identified early enough, it may be possible to avoid or take additional steps to mitigate its impact.[61, 62]

However, it is impossible to plan for every scenario in emergency planning. Ochsner Medical Center in New Orleans was reminded of this on August 28, 2005. During Hurricane Katrina the city of New Orleans was inundated with storm surge after flood waters breached the levees and overpowered the pumps protecting the city. Ochsner Medical Center was outfitted with the typical emergency preparedness equipment found in a hospital, items such as a safety stock of key supplies and backup generators. As flood waters approached the medical center, they began to flow into basement levels of the facility. Eventually, the water level increased to the level of the ventilation pipes for the hospital's generators and flooded them; this resulted in Ochsner losing electricity during one of the hottest months of the year.[63] This situation, unfortunately, was not unique to Ochsner; Tulane medical center and other New Orleans hospitals were in similar situations. Before Hurricane Katrina, it seemed impossible that a major US city could be flooded to such an extent. After Hurricane Katrina, many hospitals moved their backup generators to higher levels of the facility to prevent this particular risk. However, in some hospitals, the equipment that supports the generator such as fuel pumps and tanks remained in the basement. On October 29, 2012, the decision to keep fuel tanks in the basement resulted in the evacuation of nearly 1,000 patients from two major hospitals in an unlikely location: New York City.[64] Hurricane Katrina in New Orleans and Hurricane Sandy in New York City are examples of the unpredictability of nature and show that despite best efforts to prepare for emergencies, there will always be unforeseen events that occur in times of crisis. For more information on emergency preparedness, the health professional should refer to the Healthcare Preparedness Program (HPP), the Public Health Preparedness Program (PHEP) and the Strategic National Stockpile (SNS), (this is heavily associated with the healthcare supply chain).

Legal Considerations of Sourcing and Purchasing

The healthcare supply-chain professional, as all health leaders, should be well versed in the basics of contracts. In the functions of acquiring, contract principles and tenets are essential knowledge. The following section is provided by a legal professional with many years of experience in law.

Contracting for the Healthcare Supply Chain

The following section on contracting was developed by Dr. Julie Reagan. Dr. Reagan has an extensive background in healthcare and public health law as a practitioner and scholar.

Contracts provide a central foundation for business relationships in healthcare. Our healthcare system is built upon many different types of contracts between government agencies, insurers, physicians, and other healthcare professionals, institutional providers, GPOs, distributors, and numerous types of suppliers of services. For this reason, the business of healthcare has a strong connection with contract law.

The process of contracting is integral to the procurement of a healthcare organization's supplies and products. Hospitals and other providers purchase a tremendous amount of supplies annually as part of business dealings between healthcare organizations, intermediaries, and suppliers. To illustrate the essential role of contracting for supply chain purposes, a discussion of the various aspects of contracting will be presented next.

What Is a Contract?

A contract is a legally binding agreement between two or more parties. It is defined as an "agreement, upon sufficient consideration, to do or not to do a particular thing."[65] The primary purpose of a contract is to specify and define an agreement. It provides one or more of the parties with a legal remedy if the other party does not carry out his or her obligation as outlined in the terms of the contract.

Healthcare agreements are guided by the principles and rules of contract law. The law upon which contracts are based is predominantly judge made—common law established by judicial decisions that resolve disputes between parties.[66] In contractual disputes or cases involving a breach of contract, attorneys and judges will look to previously decided court cases (precedent) as guidance. Statutory laws (laws enacted by legislatures) also play a large role. Additionally, the Restatement (Second) of Contracts may also be utilized as a persuasive authority.[67] The Restatement is a synthesis of existing case law and serves as a guide for the drafting of contracts. It is not a state or federal law (unless recognized by a court). However, it is frequently relied upon by lawyers as persuasive authority.

Various types of contracts are used in the healthcare industry. A short list of some of the more common types includes the following:

- Employment and professional service agreements with physicians and other healthcare professionals.
- Recruitment/relocation agreements.
- Supervision agreements.
- Management services arrangements.
- Partnership agreements.
- Shareholder agreements.
- Licensing agreements.
- Business mergers and acquisitions.
- Joint venture contracts.
- Real estate purchase contracts.
- Medical directorships.
- Transfer agreements.
- Under-arrangement agreements.
- Operating agreements.
- Many more.

Examples of contracts used for supply chain purposes include:

- Distribution contracts.
- Service and maintenance contracts.
- Technology licensing.
- Equipment sales and leases.
- Purchased services agreements.
- Vendor contracts.
- Contracts for the purchase of pharmaceuticals.

Parties of Supply Chain Contracts

Of primary consideration are the **parties** involved in the agreement. Three primary groups are usually involved as parties in the supply-chain process: (1) producers and vendors, (2) intermediaries, and (3) providers. Each of these three groups has a different role in the supply chain contracting process. Producers and vendors are the companies producing healthcare products and supplies. They may supply products such as pharmaceuticals, medical devices, or a large array of other healthcare-related products. Intermediaries include wholesale distributors and GPOs. In essence, intermediaries are the middlemen that bring products to the healthcare industry. Providers consist of the various types of healthcare organizations that purchase products and supplies: physicians' offices and other types of medical practices, hospitals, large integrated delivery networks (IDNs), and various other healthcare institutions such as outpatient care centers and long-term care facilities.

In some situations, a provider may contract directly with a producer or vendor to purchase supplies. In today's healthcare market of competitive pricing, however, the more likely scenario involves the use of an intermediary (wholesale distributor or GPO) for negotiating contracts with producers on behalf of the providers. The intermediary, who will have numerous member provider organizations, will be able to negotiate lower prices than a single provider would receive on its own.

The two types of intermediaries—wholesale distributors and GPOs—have differing means of doing business. A wholesale distributor operates by purchasing products and supplies at wholesale, and then sells to providers at retail prices. In contrast, a GPO negotiates contracts with vendors and producers on behalf of their provider members. They do not purchase the products but instead issue catalogs from which their members can place orders.[68, 69] Thus, because it has numerous purchasing providers, a GPO operates on a larger scale by aggregating the buying power of many healthcare organizations. It can realize savings and efficiency by aggregating purchasing volume and using that leverage to negotiate discounts with manufacturers, distributors, and other vendors.[70] As a result, the GPO can offer supplies at a greatly reduced price as compared to what an individual provider could achieve.[71] Although this GPO contracting method is commonly used by providers, they are still free to enter into non-GPO contracts.[72]

Required Elements

Contracts must contain certain elements to be legally enforceable. For a contract to be legally valid, there must be an **offer** and **acceptance**. "An offer is a promise by one party to do (or not do) something if the other party agrees to do (or not to do) something" in return.[73] For example, in a supply-chain situation, a supplier may agree to provide supplies (offer) and a hospital agrees to pay (acceptance) for the supplies.

Mutual assent, also called a meeting of the minds, refers to the parties' mutual understanding and assent to the contents or expression of their agreement. The parties must understand and agree to the terms of the contract. The details, rights, and obligations of the contract must be clear to both parties.

An acceptance must not change the terms of an original offer. The terms presented by both parties must be identical. If the acceptance does not mirror the offer exactly, then it is not an acceptance, and the original offer will be considered rejected.

A valid contract must also be supported by **consideration**. Consideration is the price paid (or something of value given) for the contract. Each party to the contract must promise to provide something of value to the other party. For example, in a supply-chain contract for the purchase of supplies, the agreement for a monetary payment (the price paid) for the supplies provided (value given) illustrates consideration from both parties.

Referred to as **legality of purpose**, the objective of a contract must be legal. For example, a contract involving an illegal distribution of drugs will not be binding because the underlying purpose is not legal.

The parties to a contract must have the **capacity** to enter into the contract. They must comprehend and understand (be legally competent) to enter into the contract. For example, a contract entered into by a mentally incompetent person may be deemed invalid because of the person's incapacity. Certain people have traditionally been considered to lack the legal capacity to form a legally binding agreement. This list has typically included minors, people with mental illness, and prisoners.

Does a Contract Have to Be in Writing?

Contracts do not always have to be in writing; they may be oral (spoken) or written (a written document). In fact, there are only a few situations when a contract must be in writing to be legally valid. For example, state laws commonly require contracts lasting more than one year to be in writing. Also, contracts involving the sale of real estate normally require written documentation to be legally enforceable.

Even though a supply chain contract need not legally be required to be in written form, it is highly recommended to put all business contracts in writing. The general purpose of any written contract is to provide a reference document that sets forth the terms to an agreement. In many cases, especially in large healthcare organizations or systems where many contracts are created, memories of contract terms may wane, resulting in misunderstandings at a later date. Oral agreements may also be difficult to prove. Thus, a contract in writing with complete terms will serve to bring clarity and will prevent any misunderstandings or conflicts at a later date.

Terms and Conditions

In addition to the required elements for a contract to be legally valid, the other terms and conditions of a contract must be legally defined. Contracts will usually contain numerous terms and conditions. These are often called **boilerplate** or **standard terms and conditions**. For example, contracts commonly include the following clauses:

- Introductory information (sometimes referred to as recitals).
- Definitions of key terms.
- A statement of purpose or purposes.
- Obligations of the parties.
- Scope of work.
- Price, payment, and delivery.
- Contract term (dates involved).
- Abandonment or default.
- Duty to mitigate (lessen damages caused by a possible breach of contract).
- Arbitration (out-of-court proceeding to resolve disputes in the event of a breach).
- Termination and dispute resolution choices.
- Signature block.
- Exhibits or attachments.

Although the above terms and conditions are common, others will vary depending on the type of contract and subject matter. For example, federal and state laws may also impose other requirements. Examples of other variable types of terms and conditions include clauses or provisions related to:

- Antitrust.
- Technology access.
- Confidential information.
- Right to audit.
- Ownership of intellectual property, such as rights to data, documents, and computer software.
- Risk.

Supply-chain contracts frequently contain terms and conditions specific to cost savings and efficiency. Supply-acquisition costs can constitute a significant portion of a healthcare organization's operating budget. Organizations can reduce these costs significantly by including clauses for **rebates, discounts, or other competitive sourcing strategies**. These types of clauses can favorably impact the organization's profitability by maximizing business leverage and taking advantage of economies of scale.

Stages of the Contract Process

The process of contracting involves several different stages. It includes contract planning, negotiation, contract preparation, performance of the agreed upon terms, and contract execution. Each stage can be critical for procurement.

Contract planning involves assessing provider needs and is an important stage for cost savings and reduction of ordering errors. In the procurement of supplies, it involves assessing the need for products, supplies, or equipment. Also prospective contracting arrangements, such as whether the provider will be purchasing from a GPO or directly with a supplier, should be analyzed. Contract planning involves planning and forecasting needs for the future, identifying prices, determining if the products are to be purchased using a written contract or off-contract (without a formal written agreement), and deciding how or from what entity the items will be purchased.

Negotiation is a critical stage for providers to make connections with suppliers, vendors, and intermediaries. After supply needs have been assessed and the provider has decided on the entity supplies will be purchased from, the parties will negotiate and agree on terms. Healthcare contracting involves multiple parties and can be very complex. Thus, negotiation skills are needed to achieve the best value and to build positive relationships and strategic alliances. Proper negotiation of terms will support beneficial relationships between providers and the supply chain community. The amicable relationships formed will result in flexibility in contracting, better options, lower cost solutions, and overall efficiency of procurement.

During negotiations, it is critically important to review and negotiate the terms and conditions of the agreement to be made. While the performance of the agreed elements of the contract by each party is also an important focus, it is the legal terms and conditions that determine control, costs, standardization, and risk avoidance. Therefore, terms should be negotiated prior to drafting the contract.

The process of **contract preparation and drafting** necessarily requires the involvement of an expert such as a contract specialist or attorney. Healthcare organizations will usually have a contract specialist on staff (or a contract services team). Contract specialists have unique skills and an important role in supply-chain management. They maintain the various service, product, IT, and capital equipment contracts for the organization. They consult with managers, directors, and team members to learn what products and services are necessary to run the organization. Moreover, they are also closely aligned with accounts payable to ensure proper bills are paid to ensure contract compliance.

To ensure regulatory compliance, involving or consulting with attorneys for drafting and finalizing contracts is an essential component of supply-chain management. The healthcare attorneys involved should have substantial knowledge and experience in providing legal advice for these types of contracts. The attorney should be involved during certain crucial points of supply-chain management and operations such as determining facility needs, purchasing transactions, and negotiating and drafting contracts.

Performance is the act of fulfilling the obligations as agreed to in the contract. Once an agreement has been made, the parties are legally required and bound by its terms and conditions. Parties must perform their mutual obligations as formalized in the agreement.

There are certain legal defenses to nonperformance. Examples include:

- Fraud (one party intentionally misrepresents a material fact or term of the contract and intends that the other party will rely on the misrepresentation).
- Mistake of fact (a mistake in the contract).
- Duress (using unlawful threats or pressure to force someone to enter into the contract against his will); illegal contracts (illegal purposes).
- Impossibility (a contract that is impossible to perform).
- Statute of limitations (one party does not take action to enforce contract rights within a required period).

Contracts are binding on the parties named in the agreement. If one of the parties does not do what is promised in the contract, a **breach** has occurred. As a result, the other party will have legal remedies available, including the right to bring a lawsuit and receive damages. Thus, in negotiating and drafting agreements between providers and suppliers, contracts have to be structured to minimize exposure to liability.

In some situations, a contract may be terminated when one of the parties concludes that the other has failed to perform as agreed to in the contract, make sufficient progress towards the terms and conditions, or otherwise breaches the contract in some way. One example is when a contract is terminated for default when the failure to perform is the result of an excusable cause. In this scenario, the cause must be beyond the control and without fault or negligence of the party seeking to be excused from the contract. Examples may include: fires, floods, epidemics, labor strikes, freight embargoes, or unusually severe weather.

Contracts often include **force majeure** clauses. Force majeure is a French word meaning "irresistible power." It is an event that results from the elements of nature, as opposed to one caused by human behavior. Force majeure clauses protect the parties if an event outside the control of one of the parties occurs. The event must be one that could not have been avoided through the exercise of due care, and, as a result, the party cannot perform as previously agreed in the contract.

Another method of discharging a claim of nonperformance is called **accord and satisfaction**.

This remedy is used when there is an actual controversy between the parties. Examples may include: a failure to deliver products ordered and paid for, an accident during delivery, or the failure to finish a project. There must be a genuine dispute regarding the contractual arrangement, a subsequent meeting of the minds between the parties, along with an intent to compromise. The party with the legal claim releases the other party from its contractual obligations in return for compensation of some form. The agreement between the parties to resolve the matter is referred to as the accord, and the compensation made is the satisfaction.

An **executed contract** is one in which all terms and conditions of the contract have been met through the performance of all parties. At this point, the obligations between the parties have ended.

Contract Management

Contract management is an essential component of all provider operations. Basic contract management has been defined "as the execution and monitoring of a contract for the purpose of maximizing financial and operational performance and minimizing risks."[74] In the normal course of business, hospitals and other healthcare organizations will have many contracts that must be tracked and managed.

Of utmost concern is managing the cost of products and increasing efficiency. New healthcare reforms mandated by the Patient Protection and Affordable Care Act require hospitals and other healthcare organizations to discover new ways to cut costs and increase effectiveness. Because supply-chain purchases affect an organization's bottom line, it is essential to manage properly and track each contract. Additionally, healthcare organizations are searching for innovative ways to cut costs to deal with economic uncertainties. As a result, contracting, as a means of reducing costs associated with supplies, services, and equipment, has become increasingly important.

In addition to cost savings, proper contract management is imperative for a healthcare organization's comprehensive approach to supply-chain processing. Contract management will ultimately save the organization funds, decrease waste, and create a more effective and efficient healthcare system. Having a contract management system in place helps to achieve the following goals:

- **Management of on- and off-contract purchases**: Managing supplies that are purchased with the use of a written contract, as compared to those purchased without a contract, can be beneficial to an organization. In many cases, off-contract purchases can be consolidated with those made with on-contract items purchased through a GPO or other supplier. This management will not only lead to cost reductions by managing and detecting repeat purchases and overcharges, but may also encourage supplier partnerships and strategic alliances through controlled and consistent purchasing.

- **Tracking of tiered-pricing contracts**: Contracts containing tiered pricing can be difficult to track. Management of these types of contracts will result in workload reductions and is a viable method of checking for errors and/or credits.

- **Notification of contract renewals and expiration dates**: A contract management system will alert managers of upcoming automatic contract renewals (evergreen contracts). This allows providers to renegotiate contracts (if necessary) before they automatically renew. Similarly, notifications can be set up to alert providers of expiration dates.

- **Reductions of contractual nonperformance**: Likewise, a contract management system can alert providers of vendor nonperformance. For example, if a vendor has inadvertently failed to comply with the terms of the agreed-upon contract, such as delivering supplies by an agreed-upon date or for a

certain amount, a management system with alerts will remind the manager of the agreed-upon timing and terms.

- **Spending and performance analytics**: Management protects against duplicate contracts and ensures consistent pricing. Spending and performance analyses serve to accurately compare forecasted expenditures with resulting purchases.

- **Rebate management**: Rebates and other price incentives are commonly used for supply purchases. A management system will help to ensure incentives negotiated between the parties have been properly captured. In this manner, delinquent rebate payments can be easily discovered and addressed by the contract team. These efforts will also support compliance efforts.[75]

- **Providing a central repository**: Contractual management enables an organization to maintain contracts in a central location for easier access and control. This allows managers to review, control, and be aware of spending. It also allows for quicker access to work with suppliers for payments and invoicing.

- **Enhanced audit preparations**: Contract management improves auditing procedures. A central aspect of audit preparation is the chief financial officer's (CFO's) knowledge of hospital contractual performance as compared to vendor performance.[76] Effective contract management will help the CFO ascertain if the hospital is meeting vendor expectations or in compliance with contractual terms and conditions.[77]

Follow the Cotton Ball

With an operational focus on acquiring, how would you source a cotton ball? What methods would you use for determining a demand forecast for cotton balls? Where would you start to search for a supplier for cotton balls? What is the UNSPSC Code for a cotton ball? Can you find an EDI 832 Catalog from more than one supplier or vendor of cotton balls? How would you categorize the supplier or vendor based on your health organization's situation? What would be the difference if you outsourced through a GPO and distributor versus insourcing through a manufacturer? What considerations (such as volume needed, delivery terms, quality, cost) are important? What legal considerations are important if you contracted with a vendor for cotton balls?

Summary

This chapter has focused on acquiring the "technology of care" within the healthcare supply chain with an operational and analytical focus. Acquiring healthcare supply chain items includes the function of procurement that is made up of sourcing and purchasing. Procurement starts with determining a need for an item, forecasting demand, and then sourcing is finding the ability to acquire that needed item. Sourcing is the first step in the procurement function. Coupled with purchasing, that is transacting business through purchase orders or contracts with manufacturers, vendors, and distributors, the function of sourcing is vital in that the evaluation of value and benefit is continuously required to acquire items for care delivery. Stakeholders play a significant role in this process to relative degrees determined by the type and cost of medical and surgical items, pharmaceuticals, medical devices, equipment, and service contracts; preferences those stakeholders have in the overall system of patient care delivery are valuable for the efficient, effective, and efficacious function of acquiring the "technology of care." In addition, the purchasing function is responsible for vendor management and monitoring. In order to acquire supply-chain items, healthcare organizations have an array of options that are available based on their mission, strategies, capabilities, and partnerships. The utilization of outsourcing, with GPOs and distributors, has a stable foundation in the industry; however, insourcing options are available based on resources and capabilities of the healthcare organization. Mixed models of outsourcing and insourcing are common, considering the dynamic nature of the industry. This chapter focused on these essential functions in an operational context.

Sarah Says: A Student's Perspective

This chapter focuses on acquiring the "technologies of care" for healthcare organizations. An organization can gain value from assets through business operations, which in turn provides value to customers. Leading and managing to be a "high-performing" organization is vital. In order for your organization to be "high performing," there are certain characteristics that your organization should strive to accomplish. The characteristics are as follows: high-performing organizations have a clear, well-articulated, and compelling mission and vision; high-performing organizations also make strategic use of partnerships; they focus on the needs of clients and their customers; high-performing organizations strategically manage people.

Furthermore, a healthcare organization can leverage their supply chain to add greater value to their customers. In order to leverage your organization's supply chain to better provide quality of care to patients, you must deliver items of quality and durability at a reasonable cost and in mass quantities. This can be accomplished by managing all of the business related to providing care to patients that focus on the aspect of the supply chain. Knowledge of important functions related to supply chain management and the ability to strategically integrate supply chain operations into your healthcare organization will serve you well in your career.

Discussion Questions

1. Outline and explain the concept and process of sourcing selection in the healthcare supply chain. How are insource and outsource options different?
2. Discuss and give examples of the process of segmentation of supply-chain items and the stakeholders involved with influence within each of those segments. What segments involve greater clinician (surgeon, physician, nurse, clinical technician) involvement?
3. Relate, discuss, and provide an example where the tools of analysis of supply items integrate with healthcare supply chain sourcing and purchasing.
4. Distinguish the operational areas of law (legal contract principles) and vendor management in the context of the request for proposal and/or quote and negotiations.
5. Relate the sourcing and stakeholder involvement of a medical/surgical item, such as cotton balls versus a cardiac pacemaker, to the categorization of suppliers/sourcing and why categorization is important.
6. Evaluate the benefits of improved sourcing with regard to outsourcing as compared to insourcing for healthcare supply-chain operations and management in terms of stakeholders' perceptions, incentives, and healthcare organization capabilities.

Exercises

1. What methods would you use for determining a demand forecast for cotton balls (be careful about unit of measure and packaging string)?
2. Where would you start to search for a supplier for cotton balls? What is the UNSPSC code for a cotton ball? Can you find an EDI 832 catalog from more than one supplier or vendor of cotton balls?
3. How would you categorize the supplier or vendor based on your health organization's situation?
4. What would be the difference if you outsourced through a GPO and distributor versus insourcing through a manufacturer?
5. What considerations (such as volume needed, delivery terms, quality, cost) are important and why?
6. What legal considerations are important if you contracted with a vendor for cotton balls? How would you ensure contract compliance with your health organization team members?

Journal Items

List the tools, models, or techniques of demand forecasting with a short summary that make the most sense to you.

Explain how the transaction history file is used to determine high-volume, high-dollar, or clinician-preference items and why knowing this information is important.

Explain how you would categorize or segment healthcare supply-chain items and which segments need clinician interaction and communication.

Explain what can be done to limit the impact of drug shortages.

What contract principles are important in supplier or vendor legal agreements?

References

1. U.S. Government Accountability Office. High-Performing Organizations: Metrics, Means, and Mechanisms for Achieving High Performance in the 21st Century Public Management Environment. (2004, February). (Publication No. GAO-04-343SP). GAO Reports Main Page via GPO Access database: http://www.gpoaccess.gov/gaoreports/index.html

2. U.S. Government Accountability Office. High-Performing Organizations.

3. U.S. Government Accountability Office. High-Performing Organizations.

4. U.S. Government Accountability Office. High-Performing Organizations.

5. U.S. Government Accountability Office. High-Performing Organizations.

6. U.S. Government Accountability Office. High-Performing Organizations.

7. U.S. Government Accountability Office. High-Performing Organizations.

8. U.S. Government Accountability Office. High-Performing Organizations.

9. Eugene Schneller, "Transforming American Health Care Through Supply Chain Excellence," *Transforming American Healthcare Over the Next Decade National Symposium* (Biltmore Resort, Phoenix, AZ, March 23 2006).

10. Shared Services in Procurement and Supply Chain, *CIPS*, (2014), https://www.cips.org/en/Knowledge/Procurement-topics-and-skills/Efficiency/Collaborative-Working1/Shared-Services-in-Procurement-and-Supply-Chain-Management/ (accessed 26 Jan. 2015).

11. What is Total Cost Concept? *Demand Solutions*, http://www.demandsolutions.com/resource-center/supply-chain-glossary/supply-chain-glossary-t/total-cost-concept.html (accessed 26 Jan. 2015).

12. What is Total Cost Concept? *Demand Solutions*, http://www.demandsolutions.com/resource-center/supply-chain-glossary/supply-chain-glossary-t/total-cost-concept.html (accessed 26 Jan. 2015).

13. X. Chen (2007) http://publish.illinois.edu/xinchen/files/2012/12/NRL2007.pdf.

14. X. Chen (2007)

15. Operationalising Sustainability in Value Chain, *Yes Bank*, (2014), http://www.yesbank.in/images/all_pdf/OperationalisingValueChainSustainability_Report.pdf (accessed 26 Jan. 2015).

16. Operationalising Sustainability in Value Chain, *Yes Bank*

17. Michael H. Hugos, *Essentials of Supply Chain Management*, 3rd ed. (Hoboken, NJ: John Wiley and Sons, 2011), 47.

18. Hugos, *Essentials of Supply Chain Management*, 47.

19. Daniel B. McLaughlin and Julie M. Hays, *Healthcare Operations Management* (Chicago : Health Administration Press, 2008), 378.

20. http://www.excel-easy.com/examples/moving-average.html.

21. http://www.excel-easy.com/examples/exponential-smoothing.html.

22. Hugos, *Essentials of Supply Chain Management*, 53.

23. McLaughlin and Hays, *Healthcare Operations Management*, 379.

24. Pareto Analysis Definition, *Investopedia*, (2009), http://www.investopedia.com/terms/p/pareto-analysis.asp (accessed 28 Jan. 2015).

25. Pareto Chart Analysis (Pareto Diagram), *ASQ*, (2006), http://asq.org/learn-about-quality/cause-analysis-tools/overview/pareto.html (accessed 25 Jan. 2015).

26. N. Tague, *The quality toolbox* (Milwaukee: ASQ Quality Press, 2005).

27. Pareto Chart Analysis (Pareto Diagram), *ASQ*

28. M. C. Caniels and C. J. Gelderman, "Purchasing strategies in the Kraljic matrix—A power and dependence perspective." *Journal of Purchasing and Supply Management*, 11 no. 2, (2005), 141–155.

29. Caniels and Gelderman, "Purchasing strategies in the Kraljic matrix."

30. Caniels and Gelderman, "Purchasing strategies in the Kraljic matrix."

31. Caniels and Gelderman, "Purchasing strategies in the Kraljic matrix."

32. Caniels and Gelderman, "Purchasing strategies in the Kraljic matrix."

33. Caniels and Gelderman, "Purchasing strategies in the Kraljic matrix."

34. Anna Dubois and Ann-Charlott Pedersen, "Why Relationships do not Fit into Purchasing Portfolio Models: A Comparison Between the Portfolio and Industrial Network Approaches," *European Journal of Purchasing and Supply Management*, 8, (2002), 35–42.

35. Paul D Cousins and Robert Spekman, "Strategic Supply and the Management of Inter – and Intra-organizational Relationships," *Journal of Purchasing & Supply Management*, 9, (2003), 19–29.

36. Cousins and Spekman, "Strategic Supply and the Management of Inter – and Intra-organizational Relationships," 23.

37. Dubois and Pedersen, "Why Relationships do not Fit into Purchasing Portfolio Models," 35.

38. Cees J. Gelderman and Arjan Van Weele, "Handling Measurement Issues and Strategic Directions in Kraljic's Purchasing Portfolio Model," *Journal of Purchasing and Supply Management*, 9 (2003), 208.

39. Dubois and Pedersen, "Why Relationships do not Fit into Purchasing Portfolio Models," 41.

40. Craig R Carter and P. Liane Easton "Sustainable Supply Chain Management: Evolution and Future Directions," *International Journal of Physical Distribution & Logistics Management*, 41, no. 1 (2011), 55.

41. Oliver E. Williamson, "Outsourcing: Transaction Cost Economics and Supply Chain Management," *Journal of Supply Chain Management*, 44, no. 2, (2008), 6.

42. Understanding Administrative Fees - Healthcare Supply, (2011), http://www.supplychainassociation.org/resource/resmgr/research/admin_fees.pdf (accessed 19 Jan. 2015).

43. Distributors and their role, *CompositesWorld*, (2010), http://www.compositesworld.com/articles/distributors-and-their-role (accessed 26 Jan. 2015).

44. http://www.ghx.com/ (accessed 8 Jul. 2015).

45. TrueCommerce EDI Solutions, "EDI Overview: A Practical Guide to EDI and the TrueCommerce EDI Platform," White Paper, Seven Fields, PA. http://www.highjump.com/sites/default/files/Resources/WP-US-EDI.pdf (accessed 8 Jul. 2014)

46. Understanding and Managing Drug Shortages, *ASHP*, (2011), http://www.ashp.org/DocLibrary/Policy/DrugShortages/DShort-abbott-drug.aspx (accessed 24 Jan. 2015).

47. Understanding and Managing Drug Shortages, *ASHP*

48. Understanding and Managing Drug Shortages, *ASHP*

49. P. Law, REPORT TO CONGRESS, (2014), http://www.fda.gov/downloads/Drugs/DrugSafety/DrugShortages/UCM384892.pdf.

50. (2009). Drug Shortages > Frequently Asked Questions About the ... Retrieved January 24, 2015, from http://www.fda.gov/Drugs/DrugSafety/DrugShortages/ucm050796.htm.

51. Drug Shortages, Frequently Asked Questions, *FDA*, (2009), http://www.fda.gov/Drugs/DrugSafety/DrugShortages/ucm050796.htm (accessed 26 Jan. 2015).

52. Understanding and Managing Drug Shortages, *ASHP*

53. Understanding and Managing Drug Shortages, *ASHP*

54. Understanding and Managing Drug Shortages, *ASHP*

55. Understanding and Managing Drug Shortages, *ASHP*

56. Drug Shortages, Frequently Asked Questions, *FDA*

57. Disaster Preparedness for Modern Supply Chains, *Ryder*, http://www.ryder.com/~/media/Ryder/Files/KnowledgeCenter/WhitePapers/RSC449EBookDisasterPrep102013LoRes.pdf (accessed 24 Jan. 2015).

58. O.K. Helferich and R.L. Cook, "Securing the Supply Chain," *Management Report* (Oak Brook, IL: CLM Publications, 2002).

59. T. Hale, Improving supply chain disaster preparedness – *nyu.edu* http://www.nyu.edu/intercep/lapietra/Hale&Moberg_ImprovingSupplyChainDisasterPreparedness.pdf

60. T. Hale, Improving supply chain disaster preparedness

61. Helferich and Cook, "Securing the Supply Chain"

62. T. Hale, Improving supply chain disaster preparedness

63. Fink, *Five days at Memorial: life and death in a storm-ravaged hospital*. (New York: Crown Publishers, 2013).

64. What caused generators to fail at NYC hospitals? - *CBS News*, http://www.cbsnews.com/news/what-caused-generators-to-fail-at-nyc-hospitals/ (accessed 24 Jan. 2015).

65. Henry C. Black, *Black's Law Dictionary, 10th ed*. St. Paul, MN. Vol. 10, (2014). pg. 261

66. Robert A. Hillman. *Principles of Contract Law*, 3rd ed. (West Academic Publishing. 2014).

67. The American Law Institute created the Restatement (First) of Contracts in 1932. A second version, called the Restatement (Second) of Contracts was drafted in 1981.

68. A Primer on Group Purchasing Organizations. Supply Chain Association. http://c.ymcdn.com/sites/www.supplychainassociation.org/resource/resmgr/research/gpo_primer.pdf (accessed 30 May, 2015).

69. Carl A. Johnston and Curtis D. Rooney. GPOs and the Health Care Supply Chain: Market-Based Solutions and Real-world Recommendations to Reduce Pricing Secrecy and Benefit Health Care Providers. *The Journal of Contemporary Health Law and Policy*, XXIX, no. 1 (2012), 72-88.

70. A Primer on Group Purchasing Organizations. Supply Chain Association.

71. Johnston and Rooney. GPOs and the Health Care Supply Chain.

72. A Primer on Group Purchasing Organizations. Supply Chain Association.

73. George D. Pozgar. *Legal and Ethical Issues for Health Professionals*, 4th ed. (Jones & Bartlett Learning, LLC, 2016).

74. Lisa T. Miller. "Contract Management Best Practices: Avoiding the Common Mistakes that Cost Hospitals Millions of Dollars Annually." *Becker's Hospital Review*, February 23, 2011. http://www.beckershospitalreview.com/hospital-management-administration/contract-management-best-practices-avoiding-the-common-mistakes-that-cost-hospitals-millions-of-dollars-annually.html. (accessed 20 May, 2015)

75. Miller. Contract Management Best Practices.

76. Miller. Contract Management Best Practices.

77. Miller. Contract Management Best Practices.

CHAPTER 7

OPERATIONS OF STORING: STORAGE AND INVENTORY MANAGEMENT

LEARNING OBJECTIVES

1. Outline and explain the concepts and processes associated with storage and inventory management in the healthcare supply chain.
2. Discuss and give examples of the process of storage and inventory management of various supply chain items (medical and surgical, pharmaceutical, office supplies, etc.).
3. Relate, discuss, and provide examples of how the tools and resources of storage and inventory management integrate with healthcare supply-chain sourcing and purchasing.
4. Distinguish the operational areas of a healthcare supply-chain storage facility.
5. Relate the storage and inventory management of a medical/surgical item, such as cotton balls versus a cardiac pacemaker, versus federal schedule pharmaceutical narcotics to the healthcare supply-chain operation.
6. Evaluate the benefits of improved storage and inventory management practices for healthcare supply-chain operations and management in terms of healthcare organization capabilities.

Introduction

The operational functions of storing and inventory management are the focus of this chapter. The ability to store, secure, and manage inventory are critical core business skills of the healthcare supply chain. From warehouses or consolidated services centers (CSC) to central supply storerooms in specific hospitals or clinics, the ability to provide adequate storage, security for highly pilferable or federal schedule items (security cages, secure rooms, and vaults with limited access for personnel) are the essential aspects of the "storing" functions.

Multiple Supply Chain Methods Within the Organization

The modern healthcare organization has multiple supply chains that provide the equipment, supplies, and medications needed to provide services to patients. These three distinct supply chains have some overlapping features, but their specialized needs are what define the categories. It is important to understand the storage requirements of each of these supply chain components as well as the space requirements to store these items. Storage space is a function of, but not limited to, the following:

- Number of stock keeping units (SKUs).
- Number of turns of the stock (number of times a year the SKUs stored are distributed and restocked/received back into inventory).
- Number of facilities the warehouse of CSC supports.
- The safety level of SKUs kept in inventory.
- The layout of the storage facility (bulk storage, small pick locations where bulk is broken down to smaller units of measure like boxes or "eaches" versus full pallets or cases).
- The material handling equipment utilized (small forklifts take smaller space to move and turn around in an aisle while large forklifts take more space).
- The size of secure cages and vault space for items that require limited access (only screened and designated personnel; refer to FDA requirements for non-clinician personnel access of sensitive items) and more security.
- The size of the receiving and loading dock and pack-out areas (to prepare for distribution and loading of trucks or vans for use at the points of care).
- Space for specialty storage such as refrigeration units and radioactive material storage (such as lead-lined storage cases).
- Space needed for any repackaging or item processing.

Materials Management

Materials management is a branch of logistics that deals with the tangible components of a supply chain. Specifically, the acquisition of items, quantity control of purchasing and standards related to warehousing, ordering, and shipping.[1] The key functions of materials management can be broken down to the five Rs of material management:

- Is it the right quality?
- Is it the right quantity?
- Is it the right time?
- Is this the right source?
- Is it the right price?[2]

Keeping the five Rs in mind when dealing with moving materials will provide a guide for decision making and allow the materials management professionals to meet their goals. The general goals of materials management are summarized below:

- Acquire items of the appropriate level of quality for the best possible price.
- Provide input on make-or-buy decisions.
- Keep inventory turning over. A constant turnover rate for inventory will reduce carrying costs and inventory loss due to damage or spoilage.
- Promote internal cooperation with regard to inventory coordination.
- Maintain high-quality records and controls.
- Prevent supply-chain disruptions.
- Develop relationships with vendors to create reliable alternative sources.[3]

Inventory Management

"The supply chain includes all of the processes involved in getting supplies and equipment from the manufacturer to use in patient care areas. SCM [supply-chain management] is the management of all activities and the processes related to both upstream vendors and downstream customers in the Value Chain. Because SCM requires managing relationships outside as well as inside an organization, SCM is a broad field of thought."[4] Storage functions and facilities, warehouses, and consolidated service centers are an integral component of the supply chain operation.

Inventory management is concerned with managing the amount of items that are stored in a warehouse. It is important because if a company has insufficient raw materials or inputs in inventory, that organization will have interruptions in production. In situations where determining the level of demand would be difficult, there are several inventory management models which can be used to approximate needed inventory levels. Warehouses or consolidated service centers are used to store healthcare supply-chain products, items, equipment, and devices (medical and surgical items, pharmaceuticals, and medical equipment). Consolidated service centers are warehouse operations that handle and store multiple types of healthcare supply-chain items and are most usually owned by or internal to the healthcare system (insourced versus outsourced). Warehouses have longer-term storage capability with a receiving area near a receiving dock, a smaller item loose pick (to pick items that have been ordered to send to the customer) area, a longer-term bulk storage area and different levels of security for certain items that can be stolen easily (pilferage) or that require statutory/regulatory storage security requirements such as with federal schedule pharmaceutical items. First, the discussion will focus on the type of inventory models that are utilized and then be followed by a discussion on warehouse models.

The **single-period model** is used for one-time orders such as purchasing items for a one-time event. A **fixed-order-quantity model** can be used to maintain a specific level of an item in stock. Under this system, inventory levels are monitored and when they reach a certain level, the item is reordered. The **fixed-time-period model** is similar to the fixed-order-quantity model, but the key difference is that instead of monitoring the inventory level and reordering when the inventory reaches a critically low level, the item is ordered regularly on a specific day regardless of the quantity needed.[5]

Inventory is important to all businesses, including those using just-in-time (JIT) ordering, for three main reasons. First, inventory allows businesses to maintain independence in their operations. This is because there are costs associated with changing processes due to running out of supplies. Second, inventory allows an organization to continue operating during sharp increases in demand for its product or service. In healthcare, increases in demand may be associated with the seasonality of disease or natural disaster. Inventory also allows for flexibility in production scheduling. Having items on hand in a manufacturing business means that there is less pressure on the production system when orders increase. In healthcare, and other service industries, it allows for flexibility in ordering products. Inventory also allows for bulk purchases which can increase order costs due to

pricing discounts as well as the costs associated with placing the order. Examples of costs associated with placing orders are equipment required to place the order such as phones, additional office space, salaries for employees, and transportation costs.[6] Storage and inventory management also include warehouse or CSC cost based on the model utilized.

Warehouses have three basic, yet different, approaches to formation: stock keeping unit (SKU) storage, job lot storage, and cross-docking. In SKU storage, products are separated by specific type and stored together, thus reducing confusion and increasing efficiency. Job lot storage employs the idea of storing a product related to a certain job stored together, providing a more efficient picking and packing method. The cross-docking approach uses a different system where the warehouse does not store the product; instead it is where trucks from suppliers drop off large quantities of a given product and it is then broken down into smaller lots and repackaged "on the dock" and not brought into inventory or storage but immediately shipped to the final location. These production and warehousing approaches create the beginning of the supply chain at the distributor or warehouse or consolidated service center (which is a warehouse with multiple product storage). A basic principle is "increase throughput while simultaneously reducing both inventory and operating expense."[7]

Traditionally, the goal of inventory management has been to ensure that supplies are available and accessible to clinical staff at all times. Stock-outs are to be avoided because they can require costly emergency shipments and extra labor. When a key supply is missing, nurses spend precious time tracking it down, sometimes poaching from other stations. The risks are so great that, in many cases, nurses have been known to hoard supplies in order to avoid stock-outs. However, maintaining large inventories and multiple storage areas (the solution of the past) is a suboptimal response as it presents its own set of problems, including high inventory carrying costs, cost of space devoted to supplies, opportunity cost of capital tied up in unused supplies and space that could be used to increase procedures and generate revenue, and cost of shrinkage due to obsolescence, pilferage, and lost inventory. When combined with a system of periodic physical inventory and replenishment, overstocking provides little protection against spikes in demand, which again send nurses on search-and-poach missions. Over time, accuracy of the inventory is questioned without proper systems and management.

Storage locations and identification of SKUs are important basic concepts within the storage function. In storage facilities, locations are numbered, some use alpha-numeric identifications, by section (bulk, "pick" or "loose," cross-docking, etc.), aisle and shelf or pallet riser location where the particular item is stored. It is similar to a card catalog or electronic catalog in a library when you are looking for a book on the shelves. Some warehouses utilize radio frequency transmitters or RFID to identify items and item locations in the healthcare supply-chain warehouse or CSC. "RFID [radio frequency identification] is a tool for identifying objects, collecting data about them, and storing that data in a computer system with little human involvement. RFID tags are similar to bar codes, but they emit a data signal that can be read without actually scanning the tag. RFID tags can also be used to determine that location of the object to which they are attached. However, RFID tags are more expensive than bar coding."[8]

Medical and Surgical Devices

Medical and surgical devices are the most "basic" type of supply chain in a healthcare organization. These items include, for example, scalpels, bandages, sutures, and splints. Essentially, anything that is not a medication or equipment falls into this category. As you may imagine, the medical surgical supply chain is quite complex and requires the monitoring, storing, and distributing of thousands of items throughout the healthcare facility. Medical/surgical items are typically stored in a large storage area within a hospital referred to as central storage. Items are distributed from central storage to storage rooms near the point of use and restocked using various methods.

Pharmaceuticals

Pharmaceuticals tend to have more specialized storage requirements than other items in a healthcare organization. These storage requirements may be as a result of increased security requirements for narcotics or the need for a cold chain for certain types of medication. This is particularly true for biological that need refrigeration and for radioactive material that need special handling and storage such as lead-lined cases.

Capital Equipment

Capital equipment includes large, expensive items such as robotic surgery stations, MRI machines, specialized equipment for the heart catheterization lab, and other such equipment. The supply chain for these items is typically less complicated than for medical/surgical and for pharmaceuticals. Typically, capital equipment is ordered directly from the manufacturer or a cleaning house for capital equipment. However, the complexities associated with installing the capital equipment are much greater than storing smaller items in central storage.

Strategy

Integrating the three distinct supply chains present in most healthcare organizations takes strategic planning and adjusting the plan as needed to stay on target. Properly managed, the supply chain is nearly transparent to those who use the items supplied to treat patients. However, when the supply chain is incorrectly managed, the importance of an efficient supply chain becomes apparent to everyone within the organization. Ensuring that items are available when and where they are needed can be expensive. Reflecting this, supply chain costs within a typical organization are second only to the cost of labor. In order to minimize supply-chain costs, the efficient storage and distribution of inventory is paramount in today's healthcare environment.

The opportunities for healthcare organizations to improve the efficiency of their supply chain activities extend from bedside to distribution center.

Supply Chain Point of Use Capture

The point of use for the majority of items in the healthcare supply chain is bedside in patient treatment rooms. There are many ways to manage the usage of materials bedside, but, no matter the system, they all come down to monitoring the usage of supplies and replenishing them as needed. A popular choice for this purpose is periodic automatic replenishment (PAR), the details of which were discussed in Chapter 4 and will again be presented in Chapter 8. When implemented within a healthcare organization, a PAR system requires a staff member to count all of the supplies in a storage area. When counting the supplies, the employee notes which items need to be restocked or "brought up to par level." Once the counting is complete, the employee goes to central storage and retrieves the items required to restock the department storage area.[9]

Storage Bins

Storage bins are a common way of storing smaller items within a stock room or central storage. There are a myriad of different storage options that cater to the needs of the storage items and the organization. The basic elements to consider in storage such as number of SKUs, bulk versus small item pick storage, inventory turns, will dictate the type of storage units utilized. Storage will most likely be pallet risers (for pallets to be placed into with bulk items in cases on the pallets, for example) to shelves to small tub-like bins. Storage of sensitive items in security cages and vaults is also important to consider.

Interstitial Space

Interstitial space is space in the area between walls or floors of the building. Some hospitals have been able to take advantage of this space in existing facilities or plan storage locations in key interstitial areas around the facility. An advantage of using interstitial space is that supplies can be located closer to the point of use while not occupying space that could be used for patient care.

Central Storage

Central storage acts as the internal warehouse for a healthcare organization. This storage is in addition to a warehouse or CSC (either as a distribution center in an intermediated supply-chain model or as an intra-organizational storage facility like a CSC in a disintermediated supply chain) but is at the hospital or clinic level, closer to the points of care.

Organizations must make a decision as to how often to replenish the stock within central storage. This decision has a huge impact on business operations for an organization.

Distributor Warehouse

Examples of companies which operate distribution warehouses for the healthcare industry include Cardinal Health and Owens & Minor.

When a healthcare organization decides to contract services with an external distributor warehouse, there are several choices. Prominent examples include Cardinal Health and Owens & Minor. Both organizations provide supplies and equipment to healthcare organizations. Owens & Minor stocks over 220,000 medical/surgical products and has fifty-five distribution centers located around the United States.[10] Similarly, Cardinal Health is a multinational healthcare industry service provider that operates distribution centers for pharmaceuticals as well as medical/surgical supplies.[11]

Pros and Cons to External Distribution Centers

External distribution centers are able to fulfill orders at all levels of the supply chain, including PAR, operative, and central storage. The argument for outsourcing supply chain activities is that it can result in a competitive advantage for the healthcare organization because supply-chain management is a multifaceted system that requires wide ranging expertise to be efficient. Just as the outsourcing of transportation fleets to companies such as DHL and UPS allowed organizations to focus on their primary business activities, outsourcing of distribution will further allow an organization to focus on their primary business activities.[12]

A major argument against the use of an external distribution center is the control given up over the supply chain by the organization when it is outsourced. This loss of control can result in unanticipated fees and potentially increased shipping costs from the distribution center to the hospital. These problems can be magnified if the organization handing the supply chain creates unrealistic timelines with regard to distribution. The worst case scenario is the potential for stock outs of key items due to missing shipments.[13]

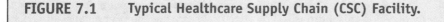

FIGURE 7.1   **Typical Healthcare Supply Chain (CSC) Facility.**

This being said, outsourcing high-level supply-chain functions is becoming an economically effective strategic option for organizations. In order to facilitate decision making with regard to outsourcing, a decision making framework can be utilized. An example of such a framework is as follows:

Prior to deciding to outsource, the following four questions should be carefully examined:

1. Is the function a core competency?
2. Is the knowledge management strategy associated with the function fully understood and aligned with the goals of the organization?
3. Who will improve the function most in the future?
4. What is the externalization risk?[14]

Based on the answers to these questions, the decision to outsource or keep supply-chain activities in-house can be made. If it is decided that the organization will operate its own distribution centers, the next step is to ask:

What Does Your Own Distribution Center Look Like?

There are three primary types of distribution centers:

1. Conventional.
2. Mechanized.
3. Automated.

A conventional distribution center moves materials round the facility through the use of people and mobile equipment. A mechanized distribution center has equipment that helps move materials throughout the facility such as sorting or conveyer systems. Finally, an automated distribution center moves materials totally, or in part, through the use of robotics.[15]

About 20% of healthcare organizations have their own distribution centers. The advantages of owning the distribution center are primarily long term cost savings; simplified ordering and logistics. As you may have guessed, building a distribution centers is extremely expensive. Due to the costs, typically only large organizations or a group of smaller organizations build their own distribution centers. In the wake of the Great Recession, a group of four healthcare organizations in Washington State decided to take advantage of the potential cost savings associated with running their own distribution centers. Swedish Medical Center in Seattle and Providence Health and Services, Multicare Health System in Tacoma, and Central Washington Hospital worked together on the distribution center. The health systems expected to order about $10 million per month in supplies through the distribution center.[16] Due to the large quantities of supplies used by these four organizations, senior leadership decided that designing and building a distribution center would be more economical than continuing to contract services to a third party.

In addition to potential cost savings, there are some considerations that go along with operating, expanding, or building a distribution center. Examples of things to consider include machinery to move pallets, types of pallets, how high to stack the pallets, and the overall layout of the facility.

The Cost of Storing and Handling Inventory

The costs associated with storing and handling inventory fall into two categories, depending on whether an organization outsources their warehouse or owns their own. For companies who rent warehouse space from a third party, the costs come down to cost per pallet. It is important to note that the cost per pallet is not referring to the value of the inventory, which can vary greatly, depending on the value of goods being stored in different areas of the warehouse.[17]

For companies who own their own warehouse, the storage costs are fixed based on the size of the warehouse. The fixed cost of the warehouse includes not only the cost to maintain the area but the opportunity cost associated with using the warehouse for activities related to operations.

This opportunity cost exists because while the items stored within a warehouse are needed for primary business activities, their storage does not generate revenue for an organization. For example, if a hospital has a 10,000 square foot warehouse, that space has upkeep costs associated with it and economic costs of not using at least part of that space for additional patient treatment areas.

Two techniques for the valuation of inventory, first in first out (FIFO) and last in first out (LILO), originated in cost accounting. This is the branch of accounting that is associated with a company's financial information.[18] Depending on the external situation, either FIFO or LIFO may be a more accurate representation of the cost of items stored in inventory.[19] It is important for a business to track not only units sold, but the cost of items that are purchased for resale.[20] In the case of healthcare, this is the cost of items used to perform a procedure.

First in First Out (FIFO)

There are several advantages associated with FIFO inventory systems. First, items stored using a FIFO system are less likely to become outdated or to spoil. This is because under FIFO, the oldest items in inventory are used first. This is beneficial for products which have short shelf lives such as medication with special storage needs. Since inventory needs to be tracked and managed for accounting purposes, FIFO offers the advantage of knowing exactly what is in inventory and its current market value. This is not the case under LIFO, which uses the latest items first. The final advantage to FIFO is one of simplicity. FIFO is a less complicated system than its counterpart, LIFO. More businesses use FIFO than LIFO as well, which results in less confusion during the training process for new employees. The major disadvantage associated with the FIFO system with regard to inventory is clerical errors as to quantity and storage location of items.[21]

Last In First Out (LIFO)

The LIFO system is only used in the United States as its use for accounting applications is not allowed under International Financial Reporting Standards (IFRS). This system can be considered the opposite of FIFO because items that are most recently acquired are the first ones used. The primary benefit of LIFO is to reduce the cost of inventory on paper in times of inflation; however, this system also makes items much more prone to spoilage while in storage.[22] Despite the tax benefits of the LIFO system, the United States is considering banning the use of LIFO.[23]

A similarity between FIFO and LIFO methods is that they depend on the type of product to be the same, with only fluctuations in the price. FIFO and LIFO both influence a company's earnings on paper. FIFO is based on the price of the cost of the earlier products purchased and ignores the future price changes affecting those products. This is most effective in industries where the price of products remains steady and the oldest products are sold or used first. LIFO works best in industries with rapid price fulgurations in which the newest units are sold first.[24]

Inventories

Inventory or supplies, equipment and pharmaceuticals on hand, should occur at each level of the supply chain; from the warehouse or CSC to central supply, the stock on hand should be inventoried at regular intervals. The intervals depend on the security concerns associated with the items. Regular SKUs may be inventoried yearly while vault items, such as federal schedule pharmaceuticals, require monthly (or more frequent) inventories. Inventories match registered on-hand stock items to actual items in storage locations. This can be done as a percentage each month such as 8–9% of all inventory per month or done as a 100% item inventory. Again, security-oriented items much be inventoried at a much higher rate. In addition, security-oriented items must be inventoried by personnel that have been screened for clearance for access to those sensitive items, and the inventory must be conducted by at least two individuals (for cross checking and security reasons) who do not regularly manage and process the sensitive supply items.

Inventories contribute to a larger financial function called audits, where orders, requisitions, invoices, receipt documents, and the like are compared to stock on hand and items registered/documented as utilized.

Equipment

The availability of appropriate equipment for each job in the distribution center or warehouse is a critical component within the supply chain. Workers using incorrect equipment or using the correct equipment incorrectly leads to inefficiencies and creates a hazardous working environment for employees. Best practices for warehousing are outlined by government agencies, with respect to worker safety, and by consultants and industry leaders, with respect to operational efficiency. Many of these best practices are a moving target, but they are introduced here as a starting point, with the current state information being just a click away.

Pallets

Pallets are the most basic part of any materials handling system. Documenting the dimensions, quantity, size, and type of pallets is of central importance. This information is used when purchasing new equipment to make sure it is compatible, that materials are correctly stored on the pallet and that there is a sufficient number of pallets in the facility to handle the storage and throughput of items.[25] There are several methods for the storage of pallets, called racking, within a facility. The most common are outlined in **Table 7.1**:

Facility Layout

How will you know if the distribution center is no longer functional for the organization?

How can the distribution center be improved?

Does it make financial sense to expand the current facility to increase capacity or build a new distribution center?

A common problem with distribution centers is that they were not built to anticipate current needs and are now running over capacity. An over-capacity distribution center is a problem because it can result in slow order fulfillment, potentially unsafe working conditions for employees, and cost the organization additional time and money. Managing current levels of utilization and planning for future growth is best done through a comprehensive supply chain optimization process. There are three broad categories that problems effecting capacity fall into: personnel, pick locations, and reserve storage.[26]

TABLE 7.1   Pallet Storage Systems

System of Storage	Details
Static shelves and case flow racks	Storage location for less than full cases of products. These can be free standing units or part of a racking system.
Bulk floor storage	Pallets are typically stored in deep lanes and stacked vertically between two and four pallets depending on pallet stability.
Selective pallet racks	This is a fixed racking system that typically allows for pallets to be stored to a depth of one or two.
Cantilever racks	Stores oversized items and may or may not use pallets.
Sustainable racks	Racking system that can also be used as storage containers. This allows them to be vertically stacked to hold oversized items.
Drive-in racks	Multiple pallet storage depth system that allows trucks to access the pallets directly.
Push-back racks	LIFO rotation of items stored multiple pallets deep.
Flow through racks	FIFO rotation of items stored multiple pallets deep.
Shuttle system racks	FIFO rotation of items using a robotic pallet shuttle carrier.

*Adapted from (2012). Distribution Center Design Concepts Explained ... - *MWPVL*. Retrieved February 21, 2015, from http://www.mwpvl .com/html/distribution_center_design_concepts_explained.html.

Problems with reserve storage occur when a facility operates at, or close to, capacity on a continual basis. This is different from a seasonal rush, which is common in the retail industry. The "optimal" level for facility utilization during every-day operations is about 80 to 85% of total reserve space. This allows for easier access to items for faster order fulfillment as well as providing excess capacity for peak usage periods.[27] When picking locations are no longer sufficient to support the number of products or SKUs within the facility, it may be time to consider expanding or planning a new facility. This is especially true in cases where an automated system is already in place and the space is being highly utilized. Typical signs a facility does not have enough pick locations include if there are delays due to the volume of products requested by customers or if the current pick locations cannot be replenished fast enough. Finally, if additional personnel or shifts are not allowing the facility to meet demand, it may be time

to consider expanding the current distribution center. Common signs that this is the case are extreme levels of growth or when only two shifts are able to pick products because the third shift needs to replenish.[28]

In addition, each location of storage in a facility has a location number that is a logical numbering or alpha-numeric system. Each aisle and each location on each side of the aisle as well as the level of the aisle (some storage locations can be several stories high) are identified with a method of identification. This is a storage location, and within storage facilities, bin locations are also unique as well as secure cages and vault areas.

Planning a New Facility

If a new facility is necessary for the continued growth of the organization, careful planning is critical so that time and effort does not need to be spent retrofitting the facility after it is complete. The phrase "measure twice, cut once" has been

FIGURE 7.2   Storage Bins

used to describe the planning process due to the high cost of adding on additional capital equipment after construction is complete.[29]

Greenfield

Greenfield is a term that refers to a new distribution center. When designing a greenfield distribution center, the material handling system should be designed first and then a building planned around the material handling equipment. This allows for the most efficient use of space within the facility.[30] However, this is typically not the case, and the material handling system needs to be designed around an existing building. An additional point of interest for greenfield construction is that it is generally cheaper to build up than to build out due to the cost of land. Modern forklifts are able to lift nearly 42 feet, which is significantly higher than the typical clear stacking height of around 30 feet found in most facilities. In automated distribution centers, it is common to construct up to 110 feet in North America and up to 150 feet in Europe.[31]

Existing Structure

When a distribution center is housed in a preexisting building there are several considerations with regard to planning the facility layout. In this case, it is important to note the location of building columns and other features that cannot be moved and ensure that they will not be in the operating aisles of the facility. Additionally, the designing of rack systems should be done in a way that building columns have the least impact on racking capacity.

A concern for both greenfield and existing distribution centers is the width of aisles in the facility as the aisle determines the type of equipment that can be used in that space. Generally speaking, there are three designations of aisles: very narrow, narrow, and wide. Very narrow aisles are typically about 72 inches wide and require specialized turret tracks for the handling and storage of pallets, or the use of selector trucks for picking from vertical storage locations. Due to the width of the aisle, an aisle is limited to one vehicle at a time; this creates a constraint on how the facility operates. Very narrow aisles are usually implemented in facilities that demand a high storage density. Another possible use for very narrow aisles is when there are a large number of items to be distributed and this exceeds the number of pick facings on the ground level of the facility.[32] Narrow aisles are usually between 108 and 132 inches wide; this size of aisle allows the use of electric forklifts such as stand-up or reach trucks. Narrow aisles are the most commonly used in North American facilities because they allow two forklifts to pass within the aisle and this creates flexibility as operating requirements change. The last category, wide aisles, is typically aisles that are wider than 156 inches. Wide aisles are common in facilities that store heavy items and need to use sit-down counterbalance lift trucks to move the products throughout the facility. A potential advantage of a wide-aisle facility is it can potentially allow for a single type of vehicle to perform unloading, storage, material handling, and loading activities within the facility. An example of a typical wide-aisle facility is a cross-dock distribution center.[33]

Loading Dock

One often overlooked area of the distribution center is the loading dock. Since the dock is the primary point of entry and exit of products to and from the distribution center, an inefficient dock can cripple the entire facility. Typical dock problems include insufficient space and depth. These issues lead to a dock that is crowded, potentially unsafe for workers, and longer than necessary loading and unloading times. Activities that take place on a loading dock include receiving, inspecting products, quality assurance, pallet building and lumping, sorting, cross docking, flow through, checks and audits,

staging, load consolidation, and loading.[34] A typical dock configuration has two distinct shipping and receiving areas. Performing both of these operations on one dock increases security and allows for easier supervision of goods entering and exiting the facility. As you may have guessed, it is also cheaper to combine shipping and receiving into one dock area. The cost savings comes from needing less space because there is only one dock as well as potentially needing fewer employees to staff the dock. However, depending on the overall strategy and the distributors involved, sometimes it is preferential to have a dock for receiving and a separate dock for shipping. This configuration is typical of facilities that have very high throughput of products or those that frequently cross dock products.[35]

Facility Automation

It is becoming more common for distribution centers to use more complex methods of material handling. The addition of conveyance, sorting, packing, or other automation increases the efficiency of the facility and increases worker safety. There are some basic guidelines that suggest a facility could benefit from additional automation.

TABLE 7.2   Recommended Automation

Metric	Value	Type of automation recommended
Direct labor associates	More than 50 per shift	Mechanization or automation
Fully loaded direct labor wage	More than $30.00 an hour	Semi-automation or automation
Order picking volumes	Picking more than 15,000 items a shift	Mechanization or semi-automated picking systems
High volumes with special storage needs such as refrigeration or freezers	Shipping more than 300 pallets an hour or storing over 10,000 pallets	High bay warehouse
Product variety	Greater than 90,000 items	Automation for slow moving products

*Adapted from (2012). Distribution Center Design Concepts Explained ... - *MWPVL*. Retrieved February 21, 2015, from http://www.mwpvl .com/html/distribution_center_design_concepts_explained.html.

These measures are somewhat of a moving target, changing slightly from year to year.

When the decision is made to add mechanization or increase facility automation, there are a variety of choices.

Automated Storage and Retrieval Systems

An automated storage and retrieval system (ASRS) is typically designed to move materials up to 150 feet in height. There are different ASRS systems depending on the desired pallet depth and many different ASRS machine variations. Examples of these variations include machines with turret forks, single aisle systems, aisle changing systems, and machines that can transport two pallets at once for high volume or oversized items.[36]

A-frame Dispensing Systems

A-frame dispensing systems are automated picking machines that are typically used in distribution centers with a high volume of small products that are roughly the same size. A healthcare example of this is the storage and distribution of pharmaceuticals. The A-frame system automatically picks the product from storage to the conveyor designated for a specific customer order.[37]

Automated Full Case Picking Systems

A completely automated picking system for full cases does not require an operator to integrate multiple systems that can handle full cases or pallets. Vendors that are currently providing full automated case picking systems include Witron, SSI, Schaeferm Symbolic, Nedcon, and Vanderlande.[38]

Automatic Sortation Systems

There are a number of sorting systems that allow for the automatic sorting of items prior to shipping. Examples include tilt tray sorters, Bombay sorters, and conveyor sorters such as cross belt, diverter, quad sorter, and sliding shoe.[39]

Carousel Systems

Carousel systems are mechanized systems that are typically used to store loose items. The machine has several bins that rotate either on a conveyor or on a central axis. When an item stored on a carousel is needed, an employee selects the bin with the needed item, and the carousel system rotates so that the bin is accessible to the employee.[40]

Case / Tote / Unit Conveyor Systems

There are many different types of conveyer systems which can transport items either vertically

---

FIGURE 7.3   Automated Storage Systems

© Baloncici/Shutterstock

FIGURE 7.4   Automated Sorting Systems

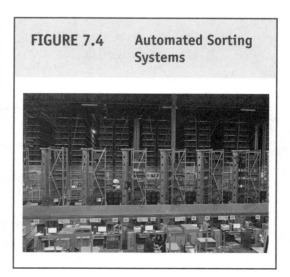

Reprinted courtesy of Cardinal Health.

or horizontally throughout a facility. The primary advantages of these systems are a reduction in travel time and increase in worker safety.[41]

Pallet Conveyor Systems

These conveyor systems are simply larger versions of the smaller conveyor system used for cases or totes. One important difference is that pallet conveyor systems only run horizontally due to the potential weight and size of a loaded pallet as well as how pallets are typically stored within a distribution center.[42]

Robotic Goods to Man Systems (Less than Full Case)

Systems that use robotic vehicles to move products to the equipment operator save the operator time associated with picking, storage, and retrieval for items. Some systems retrieve a tote box for the operator who then selects the desired product from inside the bin. There are many examples of these robot systems such as Kiva Systems, Swisslog AutoStore, Dematic Multishuttle and RapidPick system, Knapp OSR, and Viastore Viapick.[43]

Shuttle Cart Systems

Shuttle cart systems are most commonly used in high bay warehouses in place of an ASRS system to move pallets. These systems are used to move

FIGURE 7.5   **Case/Tote Conveyor System**

Reprinted courtesy of Cardinal Health.

pallets automatically within the chosen racking system. Each shuttle cart serves a designated level of the racking system. The shuttle cart system first transports the pallet to the designated storage lane, then positions the pallet within the lane to allow for the storage of pallets at multiple depths within the lane.[44]

How Is Inventory Received?

There are different methods, used simultaneously in many operations, for receiving inventory. JIT, cross-docking, and regular receiving are some of the methods.

Just in Time (JIT)

There are several methods for receiving the inventory in a distribution center. A common choice is JIT inventory. JIT is a method for optimizing the storage and delivery of materials within an organization. The idea behind JIT is that inventory in storage is not making the organization any money; in fact, due to holding costs, inventory actually costs an organization money! While hospitals are required to have certain levels of items stored as emergency stock, storing inventory above that level does not add any value. JIT inventory increases efficiency and decreases waste by minimizing the amount of inventory held by the organization and receiving shipments of supplies "just-in-time" or as they are needed. By doing so, holding costs are eliminated and money is saved.[45] Holding costs are costs associated with storing inventory.

Standard Replenish

When items are received on the loading dock and placed into storage in the bulk or broken down from bulk to loose pick/small pick item locations and documented in the system as supplies on hand, this is standard replenishment and regular receiving. Most items are received as regular receipts.

Cross-Docking

Cross-docking is when items are received in the loading dock but immediately sent or distributed to the customer without placing the received items into storage as supplies on hand. Cross-docking is an effective method since the items of supply are touched once as they are sent out to the end users.

Worker Safety

Worker safety is a constant concern in a distribution center. Over 145,000 people work in over 7,000 warehouses and distribution centers around the country. The fatal injury rate for warehouses and distribution centers is higher than the national average for all industries. Common hazards for workers in distribution centers include the unsafe use of forklifts, improper stacking of items, failure to use proper personal protective equipment, failure to follow proper lockout procedures, inadequate fire safety measures, and repetitive motion injuries.[46]

Docks

Worker injuries on docks commonly occur when forklifts are run off the dock, products fall on employees, or equipment strikes a worker. The solutions recommended by OSHA to these common problems include:

- Driving forklifts slowly on docks and dock plates.
- Securing the dock plate and ensuring that the plate can safely support the load.
- Keeping the dock edges clear and never backing forklifts or other equipment up to the dock edges.
- Prohibit "dock jumping" by employees. Dock jumping is jumping off the edge of the dock rather than using the stairs.
- Follow additional OSHA guidelines with regard to dock ladders and stairs available on the OSHA website.[47]

Forklifts

Nearly a hundred employees are killed and 100,000 injured every year when operating forklifts. The most significant cause of forklift-related death is forklift turnovers. Preventative measures for these occurrences include:

- Provide additional training and certify all forklift operators to ensure they can do their jobs safely.
- Do not allow anyone under eighteen to operate a forklift.
- Properly maintain forklifts, including proper tire maintenance.
- Inspect forklifts at the start of each shift or prior to use. If anything is found during inspection,

do not use the equipment and place a work order to have it repaired immediately.
- Follow safe procedures for handling of materials with the forklift.
- Do not exceed 5 mph and be aware of congested areas or areas with potentially slippery surfaces.
- Require operators to wear manufacturer-installed seatbelts.
- Never drive up to an individual standing near a fixed object such as a wall or storage rack. This will reduce the chance an individual can be pinned down by the forklift.
- Have a strict policy against stunt driving.
- Ensure that safe clearances for all equipment and the aisles are wide enough for the equipment to be used effectively.
- Ensure that there is adequate ventilation for all equipment to limit the buildup of noxious gas from engine exhaust.
- Cover all open pits, vats, or tanks to ensure that machinery cannot be driven into the uncovered space.
- Continually train employees on hazards associated with forklift operations.[48]

Conveyor Systems

Workers can be injured if they are caught in pinch point or hit by a falling object. Additionally, there is a potential for repetitive motion injuries for employees who continually load or unload the conveyer system. Measures that should be taken to prevent injuries associated with conveyor systems include:

- Inspect the system regularly.
- Ensure that guards are in place to cover pinch points.
- Develop conveyor lockout methods and ensure that employees are properly trained in the procedure.
- Proper lighting and working space should be provided around the conveyor system.[49]

Material Storage

Materials that are stored improperly have the potential to fall, injuring workers. The recommended methods for preventing worker injury from falling objects are:

- Stack products evenly and straight.
- Place heavier items on lower or mid-height shelves.
- Remove one item at a time from shelves.
- Keep aisles and passageways clear and in good repair.

Manual Lifting and Material Handling

Back injuries can occur from the improper lifting of materials or from overextension. The primary way to prevent these injuries is providing general ergonomic training to employees specific to the tasks they will be performing. The need for lifting can also be minimized through the use of good process design and facility engineering. Employees should always be reminded to lift properly and get help from a coworker if a product is too heavy to safely lift alone.[50]

Communication of Hazards

Employees should be made aware of potential hazards in the work environment. Examples of what can happen if workers are uninformed are injuries such as chemical burns if a hazardous material is spilled and needle sticks from sharps. Recommended solutions to prevent these occurrences are as follows:

- Maintain a material safety data sheet, MSDS, for each chemical or hazardous substance to which workers can be exposed within the facility.
- Train workers to follow instructions on the MSDS for handling chemical products.
- Employees should also be trained on the risks associated with improper storage of items.
- Spill cleanup kits should be available in any area where chemicals are stored.
- There should be written guidelines posted with information on what to do in case of a spill.
- Proper personal protective equipment should be available to employees at all times, and the proper use of this equipment should be enforced.
- Chemicals should be stored away from forklift or high traffic areas to reduce the chance of a collision with the storage container resulting in a spill.[51]

Charging Stations

Charging stations for equipment pose a fire or explosion risk if they are not maintained and used properly. OSHA recommends the following steps be taken to increase worker safety around charging stations:

- Prohibit smoking and open flames in and around charging stations.
- Provide adequate ventilation to disperse fumes from gassing batteries.
- Ensure that fire extinguishers are available and properly maintained.
- Provide proper personal protective equipment such as gloves and eye protection.
- Properly position equipment to be charged and apply the break before charging or refueling.
- Provide mechanical assistance for removing batteries from equipment.
- Install an eye washing and safety station for employees exposed to battery acids.[52]

Poor Ergonomics

Poor ergonomics encompasses activities which can result in musculoskeletal disorders in workers. Examples of these include improper lifting, repetitive motion, and poor design of workflow. Recommended solutions to these issues include:

- Using powered equipment whenever possible instead of requiring manual lifting of heavy materials.
- Reducing the number of lifts from holder height and from floor height by repositioning pick locations.
- Provide adequate lighting for tasks.
- Train employees on how to perform their assigned tasks with ergonomics in mind.
- Remind employees to use their legs for lifting while keeping their back straight.
- Encourage the testing of loads to determine size and weight prior to lifting.
- Remind employees to get help when lifting heavy or oversized objects.
- Remind employees not to twist their bodies when carrying heavy loads. Instead, employees should move their feet and take small steps to turn when carrying items.
- Keep floors clean and clear of trip hazards.[53]

Other Hazards

Other potential hazards within a distribution center or warehouse include inadequate safety provisions, the improper use of locking-out procedures, and incorrect use of personal protective equipment (PPE). In case of an emergency, employers should have information positioned around the facility describing what employees should do in an emergency. Examples of this information include exit signs and exit procedures, a method of accounting for all employees and visitors in an emergency, and clearly marked fire extinguishers and other safety equipment. Locking out of equipment is critical to prevent the accidental energizing of equipment, which can result in employee injury. The employees who are responsible for locking out equipment should be trained and practice the procedure regularly. All other employees within the facility should at least be aware of how to shut down equipment in case of an emergency. With regard to PPE, leadership within a facility should regularly review onsite hazards and ensure that the correct personal protective equipment is being worn in the appropriate areas. Additionally, employees within the facility should be trained on the selection of proper PPE as well as the use and maintenance of the equipment.[54]

Simulation and Operations Management

Simulation is a tool for visualizing real-world processes. As computers became more powerful as well as affordable in the 1990s, process simulation became an increasingly important aspect of operations management.[55] Process simulation certainly has a role in all aspects of business, but simulation stands out as a business tool for complex processes such SCM.

Process Improvement

Simulation provides an inexpensive method for trying out new processes. In this way, many possible process improvement plans can be tested rapidly and the most promising can be implemented for real-world testing. There are several software packages for discrete simulation to test process improvements before they are implemented (and the associated costs) in actual practice.

Information Systems for Storing Functions

Storing functions such as those provided in warehouses or CSCs also have specialized information systems for work processing (receiving, storing, inventorying, quality control, and distribution) and inventory management. Two systems with significant market share in the industry are TECSYS and Manhattan. These information systems are interfaced and integrated into the other healthcare organizational systems such as the enterprise resource planning (ERP) systems and clinical systems. The modern healthcare supply chain invests heavily in quality information systems and the design, build, implementation, and training of staff on those important systems.

Follow the Cotton Ball

Can you imagine how you would receive a truck load of cotton balls that have been sourced and purchased and that are now ready to be received? The bulk cases on pallets would be placed in a specific location (with a location number with a cross reference in the computer system or manual system so it can be found easily), and some bulk items would be broken down to replenish the loose pick or small pick locations. Some cotton balls may be cross-docked and resent immediately to the end-user locations. All the actions associated with receiving would be documented in the automated or manual system so the match with the invoice can be completed and the bill to the manufacturer or distributor paid.

Summary

In this chapter the operational functions of storing and inventory management were the focus of the discussion. The ability to store, secure, and manage inventory is a critical core business skill of the healthcare supply chain. From warehouses or CSCs to central supply storerooms in specific hospitals or clinics, the ability to provide adequate storage and security for highly pilferable or federal schedule items (security cages, secure rooms, and vaults with limited access for personnel) is the essential aspect of the "storing" functions. The modern healthcare organization has multiple supply chains that provide the equipment, supplies, and medications needed to provide services to patients. These three distinct supply chains have some overlapping features, but their specialized needs are what define the categories. It is important to understand the storage requirements of each of these supply chain components as well as the space requirements to store these items. Storage space is a function of, but not limited to, the following:

- Number of SKUs.
- Number of turns of the stock (number of times a year the SKUs stored are distributed and restocked/received back into inventory).
- Number of facilities the warehouse or CSC supports.
- The safety level of SKUs kept in inventory.
- The layout of the storage facility (bulk storage, small pick locations where bulk is broken down to smaller units of measure like boxes or "eaches" versus full pallets or cases).

- The material handling equipment utilized (small forklifts require a smaller space to move and turn around in an aisle while large forklifts take more space).
- The size of secure cages and vault space for items that require limited access (only screened and designated personnel; refer to FDA requirements for non-clinician personnel access of sensitive items) and more security.
- The size of the receiving and loading dock and pack-out areas (to prepare for distribution and loading of trucks or vans for use at the points of care).
- Space for specialty storage such as refrigeration units and radioactive material storage (such as lead-lined storage cases).
- Space needed for any repackaging or item processing.

Storing and inventory management processes are crucial elements of the healthcare supply chain. Inventory management and materials management are heavily supported by standardized business processes and information systems. The ability to systematically inventory stock on hand, receive supply items, store those items, and distribute them to providers of care is the essence of storing and inventory management. The more efficient, effective, and efficacious that these functions are performed, the greater the benefit of the healthcare organization supply chain in pursuit of their mission and vision of the organization.

Sarah Says: A Student's Perspective

This chapter focuses on the operational functions of storing and inventory management. The ability to systematically inventory stock on hand, receive supply items, store those items, and distribute them to providers of care is the essence of storing and inventory management. The more efficient, effective, and efficacious that these functions are performed the greater

the benefit of the healthcare organization supply chain. Automation systems can also benefit the organization in many ways. It lowers the amount of employee compensation and also decreases the risks for mistakes in storing and inventory management.

The ability to store, secure, and manage inventory are critical core business skills of the healthcare supply chain. The cost-saving potential is astronomical if the correct skills and procedures are implemented. Storage functions and facilities, warehouses, and consolidated service centers are an essential element of the supply chain operation. Modern healthcare organizations have multiple supply chains that provide the equipment, supplies, and medications needed to provide services to patients. These three distinct supply chains have some overlapping features, but each has specialized storing needs. It is important to understand the storage requirements of each of these supply chain components as well as the space requirements to store these items. These requirements could include temperature control and federal safety guidelines.

Discussion Questions

1. Outline and explain the concepts and processes associated with storage and inventory management in the healthcare supply chain.
2. Discuss and give examples of the process of storage and inventory management of various supply-chain items (medical and surgical, pharmaceutical, office supplies, etc.).
3. Relate, discuss, and provide examples of how the tools and resources of storage and inventory management integrate with healthcare supply-chain sourcing and purchasing.
4. Distinguish the operational areas of a healthcare supply-chain storage facility.
5. Relate the storage and inventory management of a medical/surgical item, such as cotton balls versus a cardiac pacemaker, versus federal schedule pharmaceutical narcotics to the healthcare supply-chain operation.
6. Evaluate the benefits of improved storage and inventory management practices for healthcare supply-chain operations and management in terms of healthcare organization capabilities.

Exercises

1. What considerations would you think about when designing a storage facility?
2. Where would you possibly store cotton balls as compared to a federal schedule narcotic? What would be the storage considerations of each item?
3. How would you explain the difference between regular receiving and cross-docking?
4. What are the differences between a warehouse or CSC and a central supply in a hospital?
5. What considerations for material handling equipment are important and why?
6. What regulatory considerations are important in a storage facility?

Journal Items

Search the Internet and find two or three healthcare storage facility pictures or graphical layouts; what are the differences in layout, security locations and storage equipment?

Search the Internet and find three different material handling equipment types. What are the size differences and how would they impact the storage facility, and what safety and licensure requirements would be required for each equipment type?

Search the Internet and find two warehouse or CSC information management systems (hint: TECSYS and Manhattan: you have seen these earlier in the text). How do these information systems lend themselves to efficient, effective, and efficacious healthcare supply-chain storage?

Discuss how regular supply items (SKUs) are different from highly sensitive or security-oriented supplies or pharmaceuticals with regard to inventory intervals and method of inventory.

References

1. Principles of Material Management, *EIILM University*, (2014), http://www.eiilmuniversity.ac.in/coursepack /Management/Principles_of_Material_Management .pdf (accessed 16 Oct. 2014).

2. Materials Management Definition, *Materials Management*, (2009), http://www.materialsmanagement.info /defscope/ (accessed 16 Oct. 2014).

3. Materials Management Definition, *Materials Management*

4. Daniel B. McLaughlin and Julie M. Hays, *Healthcare Operations Management* (Chicago: Health Administration Press, 2008), 375.

5. Chapter 11 - Inventory Management - *McGraw-Hill Education*, (2014), http://highered.mheducation. com/sites/dl/free/0073525235/940447/jacobs3e _sample_ch11.pdf (accessed 16 Oct. 2014).

6. Chapter 11 - Inventory Management - *McGraw-Hill Education*

7. Michael H. Hugos, *Essentials of Supply Chain Management*, 3rd ed. (Hoboken, NJ: John Wiley and Sons, 2011)

8. McLaughlin and Hays, *Healthcare Operations Management*, 377.

9. Par vs Kanban Hospital Inventory: Two Bin Supply System, *southwestsolutions.com*, (2014), http://www .southwestsolutions.com/healthcare/par-vs-kanban -hospital-inventory-two-bin-supply-system-for-nursing -supplies (accessed 12 Nov. 2014).

10. Hospitals - *Owens & Minor*, (2009), http://www .owens-minor.com/Hospitals/Pages/default.aspx (accessed 25 Feb. 2015).

11. About us, *Cardinal Health*, (2010), http://www .cardinal.com/us/en/AboutUs/ (accessed 25 Feb. 2015).

12. C. Alvarenga, Core Competency 2.0: The Case For..., *Accenture*, http://www.accenture.com/SiteCollection-Documents/PDF/282Accenture_Core_Competency _20_The_Case_For_Outsourcing_Supply_Chain _Management.pdf

13. The Risks and Benefits of Outsourcing Supply Chain ... Retrieved February 25, 2015, from http://www .businessbee.com/resources/operations/supplier -management/the-risks-and-benefits-of-outsourcing -supply-chain-management/ (accessed 25 Feb. 2015).

14. The outsourcing of even high level supply chain functions are become an economically effective strategic option for organizations.

15. Distribution Center Design Concepts Explained ... – *MWPVL*, (2012), http://www.mwpvl.com/html /distribution_center_design_concepts_explained. html (accessed 21 Feb. 2015).

16. Washington hospitals join forces to launch distribution center. http://www.healthcarefinancenews .com/news/washington-hospitals-join-forces -launch-distribution-center (accessed 21 Feb. 2015).

17. Inventory and Holding costs, *Durlinger*, (2013), 15 Oct. 2014 <http://www.durlinger.nl/files/artikelen /Inventory-and-Holding-Costs.pdf (accessed 15 Oct. 2014).

18. FIFO vs LIFO: The Disadvantages and Advantages..., *Udemy*, (2014), https://www.udemy.com/blog/fifo -vs-lifo/ (accessed 18 Nov. 2014).

19. Murdoch, B. "Comparing LIFO and FIFO: An Empirical Test of Representational Faithfulness." *Conflict Resolution & Negotiation Journal*, 1, (2013).

20. FIFO vs. LIFO: What is the Difference? *Business News Daily*, (2013), http://www.businessnewsdaily.com/5514 -fifo-lifo-differences.html (accessed 18 Nov. 2014).

21. FIFO vs LIFO: The Disadvantages and Advantages

22. FIFO vs LIFO: Difference and Comparison, *Diffen*, (2012), Retrieved November 18, 2014, from http ://www.diffen.com/difference/FIFO_vs_LIFO (accessed 18 Nov. 2014).

23. FIFO vs. LIFO: What is the Difference?

24. FIFO vs. LIFO: What is the Difference?

25. Distribution Center Design Concepts Explained, *MWPVL*

26. Planning, Designing & Implementing Distribution Center, *forte-industries.com*, (2012), http://www .forte-industries.com/media/16704/planning __designing_and_implementing_dc_improvements .pdf (accessed 21 Feb. 2015).

27. Planning, Designing & Implementing Distribution Center, *forte-industries.com*

28. Planning, Designing & Implementing Distribution Center, *forte-industries.com*

29. Planning Your Warehouse or Distribution Center, *trifactor*, http://www.trifactor.com/Material-Handling -White-Papers/Seven-Critical-Steps-to-Planning -Your-Warehouse-or-DC (accessed 21 Feb. 2015).

30. Distribution Center Design Concepts Explained, *MWPVL*, (2012), http://www.mwpvl.com/html /distribution_center_design_concepts_explained. html (accessed 21 Feb. 2015).

31. Distribution Center Design Concepts Explained, *MWPVL*.

32. Distribution Center Design Concepts Explained, *MWPVL*.

33. Distribution Center Design Concepts Explained, *MWPVL*.

34. Distribution Center Design Concepts Explained, *MWPVL*.

35. Distribution Center Design Concepts Explained, *MWPVL*.

36. Distribution Center Design Concepts Explained, *MWPVL*.

37. Distribution Center Design Concepts Explained, *MWPVL*.

38. Distribution Center Design Concepts Explained, *MWPVL*.

39. Distribution Center Design Concepts Explained, *MWPVL*.

40. Distribution Center Design Concepts Explained, *MWPVL*.

41. Distribution Center Design Concepts Explained, *MWPVL*.

42. Distribution Center Design Concepts Explained, *MWPVL*.

43. Distribution Center Design Concepts Explained, *MWPVL*.

44. Distribution Center Design Concepts Explained, *MWPVL*.

45. Just In Time (JIT) Definition, *Investopedia*, (2003), http ://www.investopedia.com/terms/j/jit.asp (accessed 25 Feb. 2015).

46. Warehousing, *OSHA*, (2009), https://www.osha.gov /Publications/3220_Warehouse.pdf (accessed 22 Feb. 2015).

47. Warehousing, *OSHA*

48. Warehousing, *OSHA*

49. Warehousing, *OSHA*

50. Warehousing, *OSHA*

51. Warehousing, *OSHA*

52. Warehousing, *OSHA*

53. Warehousing, *OSHA*

54. Warehousing, *OSHA*

55. M. Montazer, "Simulation Modeling in Operations Management," *POMS*, (2015), http://www.poms.org /archive/conferences/Meeting2003/2003A/Papers /PSC-04.4.pdf

CHAPTER 8

OPERATIONS OF DISPENSING: DISTRIBUTION TO POINTS OF CARE

LEARNING OBJECTIVES

1. Outline and explain the concepts and processes associated with distribution to points of care in the healthcare supply chain.
2. Discuss and give examples of the process of distribution and various methods of distribution of the different types of supply chain items (medical and surgical, pharmaceutical, office supplies, etc.).
3. Relate, discuss, and provide examples of the tools and methods of distribution and the link to inventory management within the healthcare supply chain.
4. Distinguish the operational differences of areas within the healthcare organization (perioperative area vs. medical and surgical ward to an outpatient clinic) with regard to restocking of healthcare supply-chain items.
5. Relate the differences of a case cart vs. a PAR location for restocking operations.
6. Evaluate the benefits and limitations of three restocking methods within the health organization to the points of care.

Introduction

The distribution of supplies throughout the healthcare organization is perhaps the most complex portion of the supply chain. Distribution is also a key component to the culture of patient safety. As you read this chapter, keep the idea of patient safety in your mind since errors, even small, can be detrimental to patient care. Earlier stages of the supply chain, from manufacturer to distributor to central storage, are generally linear in nature, and all supply lines converge upon central storage within each hospital in a healthcare organization. From this point, the supply lines become much more complicated, with medical/surgical, pharmaceutical, and capital equipment interwoven throughout the facility. The types of methods used to distribute supply-chain items to the points of care are heavily dependent on the needs of the end user or customer (namely the clinician and patient) and how a particular service operates in the healthcare organization. Rather than creating a "one-size-fits-all" approach, the supply-chain operation must attend to the needs of the particular service of care in the healthcare organization. In this effort, this chapter will cover the typical distribution methods of the supply chain for each common department within a facility, but we will also focus on the perioperative space. Lastly a generic nursing floor will be used as an example.

Different Clinical Areas Matter

Depending on the clinical area the supply chain supports, how that area is restocked, equipped, and the method surrounding distribution to the points of care matter. Several clinical areas are discussed to impart the importance of how the supply chain must support the unique needs of those specific areas.

Operative/Perioperative Space

The distribution of supplies and equipment in the perioperative space is perhaps the most complex aspect of distribution within a hospital. This is because the perioperative environment utilizes high volumes of items from all three categories of supply line: medical/surgical, pharmacy, and capital equipment. In this area, the operating suite with pre-operative and post-operative areas, the ability to deliver the exact items needed with sufficient backup material is essential. Each

| FIGURE 8.1 | Typical Operating Suite Supported by the Supply Chain |

© XiXinXing/iStockphoto.com

procedure, as well as each surgeon, operative team, or specialist, will have a supply and equipment item list that must be prepared in advance of a scheduled operation or procedure. These supply and equipment item lists can be digital (within the information system that when an operation case is scheduled, the supply and equipment list is processed to be filled), or it can be a "hardcopy" index card or sheet. In many health organizations, a case cart is prepared and labeled for that particular scheduled case. In most operative areas, the case cart preparation involves sterilizing equipment, checking for sterilization effectiveness (spore strips, sterilizer, or autoclave report of pressure and heat level, etc.), loading the operative equipment, and stocking supply chain items necessary for an efficient, effective, and efficacious operation or procedure. This is clearly the essence of providing the "technology of care" to assist in patient care.

Medical/Surgical

When you think of surgical supplies, there is a good chance that you immediately think about scalpels, sutures, and protective equipment such as gloves and masks. A more inclusive list of medical/surgical supplies is everything brought into the operating room on the case cart, other than pharmaceuticals. These items are stored in a central storage location that is typically a sterile area connected to the operating rooms.

These stored items are pulled as needed for each case along with reusable equipment that is sterilized and reused for multiple cases. All of these items are placed on a case cart and wheeled into the operating room for each case.

Pharmacy

The perioperative environment utilizes a high volume of pharmaceuticals starting before the procedure and continuing through the operation and recovery. Antibiotics are typically given to patients for a certain time period before and after the operation is complete to prevent infection. The various types of anesthesia used during surgery are also pharmaceuticals. Very often, these items require storage at a specific temperature and always require storage within a secure location. As shown in

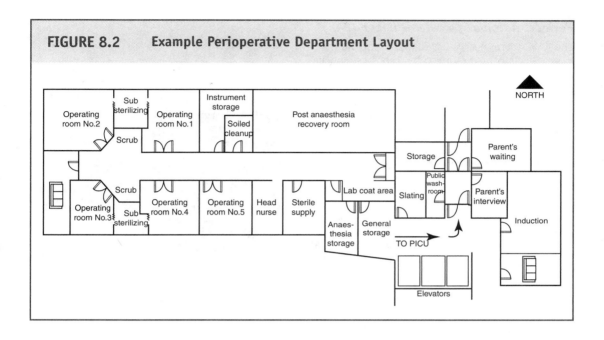

FIGURE 8.2   Example Perioperative Department Layout

Figure 8.2, it is common to store anesthesia supplies and possibly medications with a storage area in the department. Due to the federal schedule of narcotics, many of the medications used for anesthesia have special security requirements associated with their storage and use. These medications are typically stored in a secure cabinet either in a departmental storage area or within the pharmacy and retrieved on a case-by-case or daily basis.

Capital Equipment

An example of capital equipment that is being added to operating rooms across the country is surgical robots. When the da Vinci robot was introduced in 2000, it became the first surgical robot approved for general laparoscopic surgery. While robots had been used for surgical procedures in the past, the da Vinci system was the first complete unit and did not need additional devices to be used effectively.[1] According to the manufacturer, every top-ranked hospital in the United States now has a da Vinci robot.[2] The robot itself is a large piece of equipment, often requiring modifications to the

operating room in which it will be held. Receiving and installing large capital equipment, such as the da Vinci robot, in an operating room is an extremely complex task. Care needs to be taken during the installation to ensure that the environment can be returned to a sterile state once the installation is complete. This involves following procedures exactly to ensure that there are not areas of the operating room or newly installed equipment that cannot be adequately cleaned in between surgical cases.

Earlier, different types of restocking methods were discussed. We are about to go into more depth with regard to the most common methods for restocking in a healthcare organization as well as where they are best utilized.

Restocking

Restocking within a hospital is complex due to the multiple supply lines entering the facility, various usage locations, usage rates, and documented industry-wide issues with capturing item charges. Let's start by reviewing the basics from an earlier chapter in this textbook.

Periodic Automatic Replenishment (PAR)

The PAR system makes use of minimum and maximum levels of inventory to be kept in a specific location. Utilizing a PAR system allows for efficiencies to be created based on price, packing strings, and economic order quantity (EOQ).[3] The PAR system is driven by demand for the products in inventory, and the ultimate goal of the system is to reorder products at a certain point so that just as the item is nearing safety or out-of-stock levels, the new shipment arrives.

The PAR system is a method of managing inventory that requires items be restocked to a specific level. In a PAR system, each of the items stored in central storage and the department storage areas are assigned a stock requirement or PAR level. At a certain time, sometimes continuously, through the use of automation, or every few days, the items are counted and restocked based on the number of items used.

When implemented within a healthcare organization, a PAR system requires a staff member to count all of the supplies in a storage area. When counting the supplies, the employee notes which items need to be restocked or "brought up to par level." Once the counting is complete, the employee goes to central storage and retrieves the items required to restock the department storage area.[4]

Just in Time (JIT)

JIT is a system to reduce inventory and minimize spoilage while still meeting the needs of customers. The central theme of JIT is essentially "items in inventory is wasted cash that cannot be used for other activities." Items in inventory do not add value to the company until they are sold, used for manufacturing, or providing a service. In addition, items in inventory are subject to damage, loss, or spoilage while in storage. The JIT system was developed in the 1970s to address these issues. Taiichi Ohno of Toyota developed the system for manufacturing to minimize waste and improve quality.[5] The key benefits of the JIT system are:

- Low inventory.
- Low waste.
- High quality production.
- High customer responsiveness.

FIGURE 8.3   PAR Bins with Scales

Courtesy of PAR Excellence Systems. Retrieved from: http://www.parexcellencesystems.com/par-bins.aspx

Keeping low inventory levels leads to low waste levels as discussed, but the reasons JIT creates high-quality production and high customer responsiveness may be more elusive. The responsiveness and production quality are due to the closer alignment of production with the demands of customers. An organization with high inventory levels typically needs to use its current inventory before it is able to receive new inventory. This creates a lag time between customer demand and what the company is able to produce. For example, a company with a fourteen-day inventory of raw materials needs to produce using those materials even if the marketplace is demanding production with another type of raw material. This is applicable to service industries such as healthcare as well as manufacturing. Healthcare is field of rapid innovation, and if a company has large quantities of a certain item, they can be negatively affected if that item is made obsolete by a technological advancement.

Perpetual Inventory

In a typical hospital, the perioperative department (operating room (OR)/suite and recovery area postprocedure) typically generates between 50 and 60% of the revenue for the organization while accounting for 30 to 40% of the total expenses; the costs are mostly related to the use of supplies. Due to pressure from the market, the majority of healthcare organizations are looking for ways to reduce supply costs while increasing safety, efficiency, and productivity.[6] Due to the high-priority, high-urgency needs within the OR, the power of information technology can be utilized to improve the accuracy and efficiency of the OR supply chain. This is accomplished through electronically requesting supplies from the materials management department and automatically receiving the supplies requested in the correct quantities. When done optimally, the perioperative supply chain can be converted to a perpetual style system that is based on consumption. This eliminates the need for counting of bins, spot checks or other manual inventory management.[7]

A subset of perpetual inventory is the case cart system for managing operating room supplies on a case-by-case basis. When a case cart system is used by a surgical services department, equipment and supplies for surgical cases are prepared in a central processing area and sent to the operating room on case carts. The purpose of a case cart is to ensure that the correct supplies and equipment are available in the correct quantity for the procedure being performed. After the case is complete, the cart is returned for cleaning and restocking for the next case.[8] In addition, consignment is typically used on perioperative areas of the health organization as well. In consignment, the manufacturer or distributor of perioperative items (surgical screws, cardiac rhythm management items such as pacemakers and stents) provides an assortment of items for use in patient procedures in the perioperative area. The manufacturer or distributor will inventory items used in a given time period (week, month, or quarter) and charge the health organization for the used consigned items. It is wise for a dual inventory process where the health organization representative and the manufacturer or distributor count items used in procedures and come to consensus on the number to charge/bill to the health organization.

The Last Mile

The last mile is a term for the final step in the distribution of products within the supply chain. For a delivery company like UPS or DHL, the last mile is when trucks deliver from the local distribution center to customers' doors. In a healthcare environment, the last mile of distribution is in-house distribution from central storage to departmental or unit storage locations from which items are dispensed for patient care.

Kanban

"Kanban" means symbol or card in Japanese. As discussed in an earlier chapter, kanban was developed at Toyota and is a tool used to maintain a JIT inventory system. The basic idea is that when a product reaches a certain level, a signal is sent that prompts restocking from central storage or an order to be placed to the distributor.

Where Is Kanban Best Utilized?

The kanban system is quite simple but is often misused in spite of this simplicity. In fact, kanban is one of the most incorrectly implemented process improvement or inventory management tools. These difficulties include suboptimal implementations, incorrect implementation, or complete abandonment of kanban.[9] Before implementing a kanban system, it is important to know what a kanban is and what it is not appropriate for. A kanban is a communication device that relays information from the point of use to the supplier. This can take the form of a purchase order from a supplier or a work order for manufacturing. Importantly, kanbans are visual cues to action and eliminate excess paperwork.[10] Kanbans are not appropriate for items that are rarely used, consignment items, safety stock, or as long-term planning tools. Aside from those considerations, kanban fits with typical inventory flow within a hospital. An example of this fit is the kanban supermarket. In manufacturing an intermediate storage area between storage locations, an external distributor has been referred to as a "supermarket." The function of the supermarket is to respond to restocking signals from internal customers (departments) and send a restocking signal to external suppliers (ordering more supplies).[11] The supermarket probably sounds a lot like central storage within a hospital; that's because they both provide the same function, to act as a sort of a buffer.

There are five generalized rules that should be followed when operationalizing a kanban system:

1. A kanban system should not be attempted without involving stakeholders within the Value Chain for the item.
2. A kanban ensures that a quality product is being delivered to the customer. Defective items will deplete the stock prematurely and add pressure to the supply chain.
3. A kanban requires reliable support structure to function. If the kanban is an electronic system, then that system should be maintained and kept up to date.
4. Kanbans should only be created for products with stable delivery requirements, short setups and short lead times. In hospitals with a central

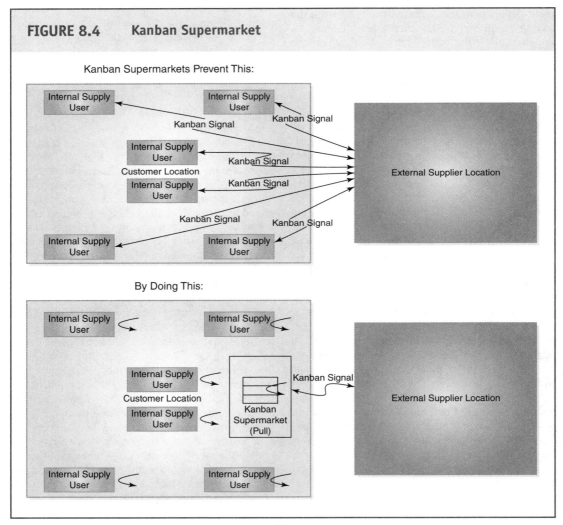

FIGURE 8.4   Kanban Supermarket

Kanban Supermarkets Prevent This:

Internal Supply User

Internal Supply User

Kanban Signal

Kanban Signal

Internal Supply User

Kanban Signal

Customer Location

Internal Supply User

Kanban Signal

Kanban Signal

Kanban Signal

Internal Supply User

Internal Supply User

External Supplier Location

By Doing This:

Internal Supply User

Internal Supply User

Internal Supply User

Customer Location

Kanban Signal

Internal Supply User

Kanban Supermarket (Pull)

External Supplier Location

Internal Supply User

Internal Supply User

(2010). Larry Rubrich, 14 things to keep in mind when implementing kanbans. Retrieved March 9, 2015, from http://www.reliableplant .com/Read/22368/implementing-kanbans-lean. Reprinted by permission of the author.

FIGURE 8.5   Typical Case Carts

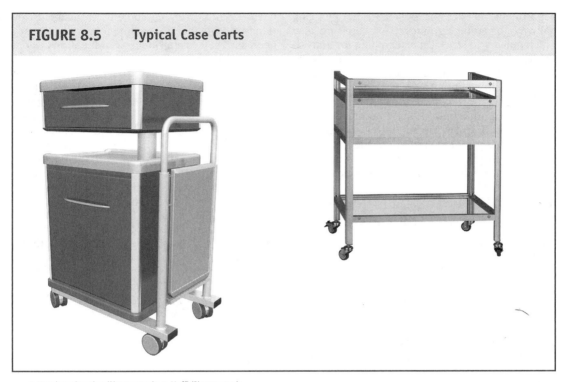

© Morphart Creation/Shutterstock; © Maffi/Shutterstock

storage, kanbans can potentially be implemented in all departmental storage areas.

5. Kanbans may need to be adjusted periodically after implementation. They are simply signals to initiate restocking, and based on usage patterns, the timing of that signal may need to be adjusted.[12]

Case Cart Preparation as Restocking

The cost of supplies used in a surgery is, on average, about 20% of the cost associated with each case. As the OR is potentially one of the largest cost centers for a hospital, the price associated with supplies used in the OR can be significant.[13] Due to these associated costs, case carts were developed as a way to efficiently manage inventory in the OR

as well as procedure rooms. Prior to a procedure, the case cart is loaded with all the typical supplies used for the upcoming procedure as well as physician-preference items. This insures that needed items are available in the OR and that unnecessary supplies are not taken out of storage. After the procedure, the implements used during the procedure are placed back on the cart and, in the case of reusable items, sterilized or else discarded for one-time use items. There are several types of case carts commonly used in hospitals; some examples are shown below.

The use of case carts allows for the better monitoring of PAR levels and allows for automated reordering of standard equipment and supplies. Since case carts allow for a system such as PAR to be used, low-use items can be eliminated and inventory costs can be reduced because fewer items are needed on hand. The space saved will increase efficiency within the perioperative department, as excess supplies are not clogging hallways or storage rooms. Case carts are also much quicker to stock than searching for individual items for each procedure as requested by the surgeon. Of course the surgeon will have preference items in addition to the standardized equipment, but all the supplies for each procedure can be quickly loaded onto the cart and taken to the OR. The case cart system allows the surgical staff to be confident that everything needed for a particular case is already in the room, and this leads to time savings as well as an increased level of patient safety.[14]

Inventory on the Floor

The decision of what inventory to store on a nursing floor is a complicated one. What needs to be stored on patient care floors? Should we just store items used every day? Should we have special-use items that only our department uses stored on the floor or in central storage?

Typically, hospitals will store lower-cost items that have a very high-usage pattern on the nursing floor. These items include, for example, syringes, commonly used pharmaceuticals, gloves, masks, bandages, and emergency equipment. Each of these items has various storage requirements – pharmaceuticals need to be stored in a secure location, whereas it is more important that gloves are stored in an easily accessible location within each patient room. Emergency supplies are stored on specialized case carts, sometimes called crash carts, with all the supplies required to resuscitate an individual.

Consignment of Goods

Consignment inventory is inventory that is owned by a supplier but is in possession of the customer. Consignment inventory allows the customer (in this case the hospital) to avoid tying up capital in inventory. However, consignment does not eliminate holding costs associated with inventory. The costs related to storing and managing inventory are still incurred; only the carrying costs are avoided.[15] Consignment of inventory is used many times in the perioperative areas where supplies,

devices, and even equipment are very costly (high-price items). Consignment has traditionally been used in the retail industry in situations where a supplier has a new or untested product it wishes to put in stores. In these situations, retailers can be hesitant to purchase and stock the items because their sales performance is unknown. In order for the supplier's new product to gain in-store exposure, the supplier will offer to stock the product directly in the stores, under consignment. This arrangement shares the risk between the supplier and the retailer. The retailer is risking the space that is dedicated to selling the product, whereas the supplier is risking the capital investment associated with the inventory. Additionally, when items are consigned to a retailer, neither the retailer nor the supplier will benefit until the items are sold.[16] Consigned inventory requires a structured inventory where both the supplier and user organization are involved in joint inventory so that periodic (monthly, quarterly, etc.) invoices can be agreed to and processed within reasonable time frames.

In a healthcare setting, inventory consignment is best suited to products with a high turnover rate such as implantable medical devices. This includes items such as artificial knees, surgical screws, and other high-value items that have been traditionally handled by medical device representatives. Of the approximately 6,000 medical device or equipment manufacturers, between 50 and 80% of their total revenue comes from products introduced in the past three to five years.[17] While it is true that medical devices are growing in expense, this number is primarily due to the high turnover of products in the marketplace. This high turnover rate is especially troubling given the tight regulations and high liability associated with medical devices. Using a consignment inventory management system, CIMS, is one way that healthcare organizations and medical device companies can work together for an optimal outcome. Utilizing a CIMS for products with high turnover rates insures that the healthcare organization always has the latest implantable technology available. Ensuring that patients have access to the best care, including the latest advances in medical devices, makes sense for the healthcare organization and the medical device company. The medical device company can gain market share with its new products, and the hospital can provide better care and reduce liability by using the latest medical devices for the best possible patient outcomes.[18]

Another potential advantage of using CIMS is that it reduces the workload for supply-chain managers within the organization. It is in the best interest of the representatives of the medical-device company to keep inventory available for the organizations they support because they are usually paid on commission.

In addition to medical-device consignment mediated by device-company representatives, there is a growing trend in healthcare where distributors are consigning medical supplies directly to a healthcare organization. This is occurring for several reasons, all revolving around the bottom line for hospitals in the face of declining Medicare reimbursement rates and recent pay-for-outcome programs. The declining reimbursement rates incentivize hospitals to push back on the long-standing sales model used by medical device and supply companies. This is resulting in changing market conditions which force manufacturers to alter their marketing, sales, and product development strategies.[19] This trend is compounded because declining reimbursement rates are also causing physicians to move from private practice to direct employment within healthcare organizations. This means that there are fewer physicians in private practice for the companies to directly market their products.

In the previous chapter, major companies operating distribution centers for medical/surgical and pharmaceuticals were discussed. Many of these organizations also offer a consignment program in which they place storage cabinets where requested within a hospital and directly manage the inventory for each location. Advantages of moving some inventory to a CIMS model are:

- Products are kept current, and managing expiration dates is managed by the vendor.
- Products are only reconciled and invoiced when they are dispensed.
- A larger quantity of inventory can be stored onsite, eliminating the need for emergency delivery of out-of-stock items.

- Products are sourced directly from the manufacturer, which ensures the highest level of supply-chain integrity.
- The product is always in stock, and the need to borrow inventory from other facilities is eliminated.[20]

Distribution to the Patient

Distribution to the patient occurs when a caregiver retrieves items from departmental supply and uses them at the patient's bedside or at an affiliated pharmacy. Depending on the overall distribution strategy and the type of item being dispensed, the actual process leading up to distributing items to the patient will change. However, some generalizations can be made. Of the three supply lines, medical/surgical, pharmaceutical, and capital equipment, only medical/surgical items and pharmaceuticals are distributed to patients. The distribution can take place either at bedside or from the hospital pharmacy, depending on the patient's position within the continuum of care and the policies of the healthcare organization.

Bedside

Bedside distribution to patients is the end point in the supply chain for many medical/surgical supplies as well as pharmaceuticals. Distributing the correct medication and providing the highest level of care is a constant concern for a healthcare organization. Literally everything done throughout the entire supply chain was done to support this.

Patients are commonly issued a wristband with a barcode containing a unique identification number upon admission to a hospital. These barcodes are part of a barcoding system designed to provide the highest level of safety to patients within the facility. A barcoding system makes use of a barcode scanner located at a patient's bedside, which is used to verify patient care activities. In a fully implemented barcoding system, all single-unit items have a barcode on the packaging which contains information such as a unique identifier, expiration date, lot number, or other information. The bedside scanners are linked to multiple systems within the hospital and show patient information when patients' wristbands are scanned. Typically, this information includes transfer data, pharmacy information, laboratory results, and, if available, a decision support system.

When a physician places an order for a patient to receive a specific medication, a nurse would then scan his or her own identification barcode to document who performed the procedure, the patient's barcode to verify the patient's identity and presence of the order, and the packaging of the medication to be administered.[21] The system automatically verifies that the user is authorized to dispense the medication and that it has not already been administered to the patient, checks for medical alerts, and automatically records the activity within the patient's medical record. The benefits of barcoding extend beyond the basic process flow outlined above.

Benefits and Challenges of Barcoding

Point-of-care systems that are barcode enabled at the most basic level verify what is known as the five rights. Verifying the five rights, right drug, right patient, right dose, right route, and right time, as well as appropriately documenting that a patient received a particular medication or treatment, will increase patient safety and the bottom line for the hospital through accurate charge capture.

There are quite a few challenges associated with barcode technology implementation, although there are fewer challenges related to barcode implementation than other clinical technologies. Some of the main challenges with barcoding technology include:

- Currently, only a minority of drugs contain barcodes directly from the manufacturer, although this number is constantly increasing.
- There is a growing trend where manufacturers are providing fewer medications in a single dose form. This is occurring mostly as a cost saving measure for the manufacturer.
- A lack of standardization of barcodes among the medications which are available as single dose containers from the manufacturer.
- There is no agreed-upon standard for reading barcode technology, and, as such, existing

barcoding systems typically use proprietary technology. This lack of standards among barcoding systems extends to a lack of a standard interface that a healthcare organization could use to connect the system to the existing hospital systems. All this variation creates a need for home-grown solutions to interface systems so that they are able to communicate and function properly.

- Some specialty medication will always need to be bottled by the pharmacy within the hospital due to the needs of certain patients.[22]

Pharmacy

Distribution directly to patients at an in-house or affiliated pharmacy provides a simpler charge-capture mechanism than bedside distribution. The chain of custody is also more secure because items are handled by fewer people before being distributed to the patient. One major concern with distributing to the patient at a pharmacy is that the patient typically needs to go to the pharmacy to fill or retrieve their prescription or medical supplies. Patient noncompliance leads to increased cost to the healthcare organization if the patient is readmitted, as well as unnecessarily jeopardizing the health of the patient.

In recent years, a trend towards mail-order pharmacies has taken hold. In fact, mail-order pharmacies are the fastest-growing provider of prescriptions in the United States to insured individuals.[23] It has been reported that upwards of one-third of all medications for chronic conditions are delivered by mail and that revenue from their sale accounted for nearly 25% of pharmacy revenue in the United States in 2009.[24] Originally, mail-order pharmacies were marketed to consumers by promoting cost savings due to "less overhead" than a traditional pharmacy, referring to the lack of a retail location. However, in recent years studies have been inconclusive as to the actual cost savings associated with mail-order pharmacies. Research does agree on the greater satisfaction patients report with prescription drug benefits and pharmacy services through the mail.[25] Perhaps this satisfaction is the driving force behind the mail-order pharmacy business, even if there are no conclusive cost advantages to consumers.

In a study of patients who used a mail-order pharmacy service to deliver their medication to control their LDL cholesterol, 85% of patients achieved their LDL-C level goals as outlined by their physician as compared to 74.2% of patients using a traditional pharmacy.[26] These study results should be noted by hospital administrators, especially as healthcare reimbursement moves from a fee-for-service model to a performance-based model. Given all the distribution options and their potential implications to both patient satisfaction and the bottom line for the healthcare organization, careful thought should be put into the implementation of any distribution strategy. One tool that can help administrators make the correct decision with regard to distribution strategy is computer simulation.

Simulation

Simulation is a powerful tool for modeling the distribution of items within the supply chain. The most common options listed above may not be the best choices for your particular organization or situation. Even if your organization chooses to use consignment, kanban, or PAR, how is that solution best implemented? These questions are as a result of a fundamental problem in supply-chain management, performance evaluation. How do we choose the best solution and monitor its performance over time against alternatives to ensure we remain competitive? There are three main approaches to performance evaluation:

- Analytical methods.
- Physical experimentations.
- Simulation or emulation.[27]

For today's complex supply chain, the use of analytical methods is considered to be impractical because a mathematical model for a realistic case is too complex to be solved in any realistic time period.[28] Actually implementing all possible scenarios is also impractical due to the time and cost associated with not only running the test but lost productivity due to testing of suboptimal choices. Simulation is the clear option of the three main approaches because it gives an organization the ability to test out many scenarios and choose the best option according to the simulation to implement within the facility.

Some considerations when designing a simulation are the location of storage, capacity, what items are supplied at each level of fulfillment, policies governing the system, and collaboration with stakeholders.[29] Finally, it is important to stress the simulation during testing to ensure that the model holds up in a "worst case" scenario.

Charge-Capture Outcomes

Every year, hospitals lose millions of dollars because patients are not correctly charged for supplies used in their treatment.[30] Typically, supplies kept on the nursing floor are the lowest-cost items in terms of reimbursement, but they are used in high volumes. A study found that only about 36% of medical/surgical supplies were being correctly charged on nursing floors. At one hospital studied, if the top twelve supplies used by volume were correctly captured, gross charges could have been increased by nearly 5 million dollars. Additionally, charges were found to not be captured primarily due to a lack of standardization in the process.[31]

Charge capture is a term referring to the recording of charges for items and services provided. The process through which a hospital captures charge data involves multiple systems, but the final system in the process is the patient account system, where the charge description is entered and ultimately charged to the patient. This process as a whole can be complex, but the accurate capture of charges is critical to the efficiency of a healthcare organization.[32] This inherent complexity of charge capture and the lack of a standardized process combined with the huge financial impact that charge capture has on an organization makes charge capture a critical area for improvement within most healthcare organizations. Any process improvement plan for increasing supply-charge-capture revenue should include the following:

- Developing a standardized process or improving an existing process for the following:
  - Item Master.
  - Selecting stock for nursing unit floors.
  - Accurately capturing supply-item charges within a certain time frame.

- Accountability for staff and nurses.
- Standardizing the replenishment process.
- Reconciliation of supply charges, either daily or each shift.

The reconciliation process for supply charges should take the following into account:

- The needs of each nursing unit.
- Any variations in the physical layout of a unit that may require deviation from a standard process.
- The existing process should be as efficient as possible, with as few "non-value added" steps, before additional technological solutions to the process.
- Above all, there is no "one-size-fits-all" solution.[33]

When standardizing a process, one of the more difficult tasks is balancing trade-offs while the process becomes as uniform as possible. There are likely to be competing goals between various stakeholders within an organization, and there will be trade-offs between these groups in order to find a balanced approach that best meets the needs of everyone. Three common stakeholders that will need to have their interests balanced in this process are nurses, supply chain managers, and shareholders.

Nursing goals:

- Any implemented system does not negatively impact delivering patient care.
- Minimized rework.
- Correct supplies are in the correct place at the correct time.

Supply chain manager goals:

- Efficient use of resources such as labor.
- Accurate recording of supplies used.
- Timeliness of supply consumption.

Shareholder or venue goals:

- Improve the supply-charge-capture rate.
- Improve the timeliness of supply-charge capture.
- Improve capture accuracy.
- Reduce the number of capture-charge items.[34]

It seems that nearly every few months a new process improvement or planning model is introduced promising to help organizations create a balanced process while maximizing the value-added steps in a particular process. The majority of these process improvement models have similar themes between them, and one of the most popular, which has stood the test of time, is lean manufacturing, otherwise known as the Toyota Production System.

The Lean Methodology

The Lean system is based on maximizing value to the customer. In the Lean system, the customer is whomever a particular group is providing services to. For example, the typical customers of a hospital are the patients and physicians. In terms of the nursing floor example, the customers are the patients. From the perspective of supply-chain managers, the nurses on the floor are the customers. Understanding who your primary customer is and what they value is the first step in the Lean process, where the ultimate goal is to provide more value to that customer while using fewer resources. It is a common misconception that Lean only works in manufacturing. While Lean was initially developed by Toyota for the manufacturing of vehicles, the concepts can be applied to any process.[35] Lean enables process improvement through a collection of tools and concepts that can be used to frame and improve processes within an organization. Many of these tools are not new ideas, such as kanban and JIT inventory, which have been discussed at length throughout this text. Another key tool in the Lean process is the overall methodology for implementing improvements.

PDCA, or plan, do, check, act, is an iterative process central to implementing Lean quality improvement programs. According to PDCA, the first step is to develop a plan and determine expected results. Then the plan is implemented, the do step. Once the plan is in place, results are monitored to determine if the desired outcome is being achieved. The final step, act, involves reviewing and assessing, then continuing the process.[36]

In order to carry out a PDCA cycle with the best possible results, a proper team of experts on the topic needs to be selected. One of the central themes of Lean is that there are no bad people, only bad processes. In keeping with this philosophy, the team of experts brought together for an improvement event using PDCA includes the people who do the activity every day: the employees in that particular department and the key stakeholders in the process. Another Lean term for the group of people meeting to discuss issues and how to improve them is a quality circle.

The entire process of the quality circle coming together and using the PDCA methodology is summed up in what is known as A3 thinking. A3 was given this name due to the size of paper the analysis was typically done on, 11 × 17 inches, also known as A3. The A3 report is just an 11 × 17 inch piece of paper with a structured outline made of several sections. Although the exact structure of the report depends on the situation and the needs being addressed, the format is generally the same and includes the following basic sections:

1. Background.
2. Current situation and problem.
3. Goal.
4. Root cause analysis.
5. Action items and implementation plan.
6. Result check.
7. Follow up.

Utilizing this standard form is another way that Lean is able to provide standardization and thus process improvement. Using a standard A3-style report will simplify the writing process for proposals and status updates as well as general purpose reporting. Simplified reporting in turn increases communication and understanding throughout the organization.[37]

There are many more Lean tools as well as process improvement tools of other types that are popular in different industries. Something common to all these process improvement tools is that they require the buy-in from the team as well as senior leadership and commitment. If team members are not committed to the process or the process is abandoned early, then no process improvement program will truly take hold and have positive results for an organization.

Information Systems for Distribution Functions

Distribution functions such as those provided in PAR, perpetual inventor, and case-cart preparation are usually linked and interfaced with enterprise resource planning (ERP) or clinical information systems. For example, case-cart preparation for a surgical procedure case for a patient would most likely be information shared to multiple systems within the information system: 1) patient scheduling and billing in revenue management; 2) supply chain in case-cart preparation and fulfillment; and 3) clinical systems for case-cart-item checklists (to make sure the surgeon has the items needed for a particular case) and matching patient clinical history to the procedure (for example, is the patient allergic to latex where you would not want to use latex gloves?). All of these systems work together down to the points of care to ensure a safe, efficient, effective, and efficacious patient-care environment.

Follow the Cotton Ball

How would a cotton-ball package be restocked in a PAR method, in a kanban method, in a perpetual inventory method, or as a consignment item? Although cotton balls will most likely not be consigned, can you imagine how these various methods would work? From the warehouse to the points of care, can you envision how a cotton ball travels through the system to the eventual assistance of a patient by a clinician or caregiver? Going back to the continuum of care, how would cotton balls move from sourcing to use on a patient at a point of care?

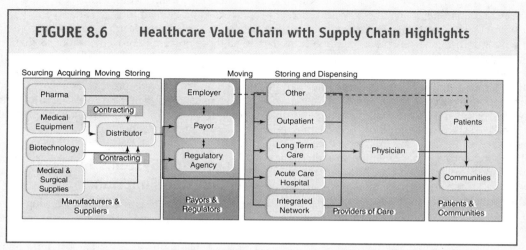

FIGURE 8.6   Healthcare Value Chain with Supply Chain Highlights

By permission of Harvard Business School Press. Adapted from Porter, M. E. & Teisberg, E. O. (2006). Redefining health care: Creating value based competition on results, pp. 203–213. Boston: Harvard Business School Press.

In the movement of the cotton ball, can you meet the tenets of the Value Chain? Information systems clearly play a major role, but can the actual item, the supply chain item, move from source to patient? Is the movement efficient, effective, and efficacious?

FIGURE 8.7   Cotton Field in Bloom Revisted

Courtesy of Sarah Ledlow

FIGURE 8.8   **Cotton from the Field Revisited**

Courtesy of Sarah Ledlow

FIGURE 8.9   **Cotton Balls Ready for Patient Use**

Courtesy of Sarah Ledlow

As the healthcare Value Chain shows us, primary activities add value for an organization when they are properly integrated with the support activities. Information technology is one significant example of supporting and integrating with the healthcare supply chain. The technology exists to be able to trace products back to their origin, track recall notices, and keep a record of contract pricing.[38] Instituting data standards for information systems will enable hospitals to actively implement and measure success of "the seven Rs."

1. Right product.
2. Right quantity.
3. Right condition.
4. Right place.
5. Right time.
6. Right customer/patient (or point of care).
7. Right price.

From the elements of the supply chain to the operations of the supply chain, those tenets must be the goals of the healthcare supply chain.

Summary

The distribution of supplies throughout the healthcare organization is perhaps the most complex portion of the supply chain. Distribution is also a key component to the culture of patient safety. As you read this chapter, keep the idea of patient safety in your mind since errors, even small, can be detrimental to patient care. Earlier stages of the supply chain, from manufacturer to distributor to central storage, are generally linear in nature, and all supply lines converge upon central storage within each hospital in a healthcare organization. From this point, the supply lines become much more complicated, with medical/surgical, pharmaceutical, and capital equipment interwoven throughout the facility. The types of methods used to distribute supply chain items to the points of care are heavily dependent on the needs of the end user or customer (namely, the clinician and the patient) and how a particular service operates in the healthcare organization. Rather than creating a "one-size-fits-all" approach, the supply chain operation must attend to the needs of the particular service of care in the healthcare organization. In this effort, this chapter has covered the typical distribution methods of the supply chain for each common department within a facility.

Sarah Says: A Student's Perspective

This chapter focuses on the distribution of supplies throughout healthcare organizations. The distribution of supplies throughout the healthcare organization is perhaps the most complex portion of the supply chain. Distribution is also a key component to the culture of patient safety. From this point, the supply lines become much more complicated, with medical/surgical, pharmaceutical, and capital equipment interwoven throughout the facility.

In operative spaces, each procedure, as well as each surgeon, operative team, or specialist, will have a supply and equipment item list that must be prepared in advance of a scheduled operation or procedure. Usually case carts with preferred medical/surgical supplies are prepared before each procedure and then brought into the operating room. This does not include pharmaceuticals. The perioperative environment utilizes a high volume of pharmaceuticals starting before the procedure and continuing through the operation and recovery. Pharmaceuticals, especially narcotics, have strict specific guidelines to follow when storing and distributing in the hospital; this adds to the complexity of distributing these items. Furthermore, distributing the correct medication and the correct dose is essential when distributing medications to patients. Using barcoding systems and scanners can dramatically reduce the risk of giving the wrong medication or dose to patients.

Discussion Questions

1. Outline and explain the concepts and processes associated with distribution to points of care in the healthcare supply chain.
2. Discuss and give examples of the process of distribution and the various methods of distribution of the different types of supply chain items (medical and surgical, pharmaceutical, office supplies, etc.).
3. Relate, discuss, and provide examples of the tools and methods of distribution and the link to inventory management within the healthcare supply chain.
4. Distinguish the operational differences of areas within the healthcare organization (perioperative area versus medical and surgical ward to an outpatient clinic) with regard to restocking of healthcare supply-chain items.
5. Relate the differences of a case cart versus a PAR location for restocking operations.
6. Evaluate the benefits and limitations of three restocking methods within the health organization to the points of care.

Exercises

1. What considerations would you think about when selecting a restocking method of distribution within a healthcare facility?
2. How would you possibly distribute cotton balls to points of care in a perioperative area, in a medical and surgical nursing ward, or to an outpatient clinic?
3. How would you explain the difference between PAR and kanban?
4. What would be the differences in a perioperative area vs. an outpatient clinic with regard to distribution to points of care?
5. What considerations would be appropriate for a perpetual inventory system vs. a consignment system?
6. How would you maintain chain of custody and inventory management of supply chain items at points of care?

Journal Items

Search the Internet and write a summary of the following within a healthcare context:

Kanban
Perpetual inventory
Consignment
Lean supply chain
Supply chain and patient safety

References

1. History of Robotic Surgery, *Robotic Oncology*, (2008), http://www.roboticoncology.com/history/ (accessed 8 Mar. 2015)

2. Learn more, *da Vinci Surgery*, (2013), http://www.davincisurgery.com/facts.php (accessed 8 Mar. 2015)

3. What Clinicians Need to Know About Inventory Management, (2014), http://nexerainc.com/97/File.aspx (accessed 9 Mar. 2015)

4. Par vs Kanban Hospital Inventory, *Two Bin Supply System*, (2014), http://www.southwestsolutions.com/healthcare/par-vs-kanban-hospital-inventory-two-bin-supply-system-for-nursing-supplies (accessed 12 Nov. 2014).

5. Just In Time (JIT) - Strategy Skills Training, *MindTools*, (2007), http://www.mindtools.com/pages/article/newSTR_78.htm (accessed 14 Nov. 2014)

6. Perioperative Supply Chain White Paper - *GE Healthcare*, (2014), http://www3.gehealthcare.com.au/~/media/downloads/anz/products/hcit/centricity_perioperative/perpetual_perioperative_supply_chain_whitepaper_anz_doc1170848.pdf.

7. Perioperative Supply Chain White Paper - *GE Healthcare*

8. Making a Case for a Case Cart System – *hermanmiller*, (2012), http://www.hermanmiller.com/research/research-summaries/making-a-case-for-a-case-cart-system.html (accessed 14 Nov. 2014).

9. 14 things to keep in mind when implementing kanbans, *reliableplant.com* (2010), http://www.reliableplant.com/Read/22368/implementing-kanbans-lean (accessed 8 Mar. 2015).

10. 14 things to keep in mind when implementing kanbans, *reliableplant.com*

11. 14 things to keep in mind when implementing kanbans, *reliableplant.com*

12. 14 things to keep in mind when implementing kanbans, *reliableplant.com*

13. Making a Case for a Case Cart System – *hermanmiller*

14. Making a Case for a Case Cart System – *hermanmiller*

15. Consignment Inventory, *InventoryOps.com*, (2004), http://www.inventoryops.com/ConsignmentInventory.htm (accessed 8 Mar. 2015).

16. Consignment Inventory, *InventoryOps.com*,

17. Consigned Inventory Management: The Rx for Ailing, *Inbound Logistics*, http://www.inboundlogistics.com/cms/article/consigned-inventory-management-the-rx-for-ailing-medical-profits/ (accessed 9 Mar. 2015).

18. Consigned Inventory Management: The Rx for Ailing, *Inbound Logistics*

19. Selling hospitals, not doctors, *Modern Healthcare*, (2013), http://www.modernhealthcare.com/article/20131019/MAGAZINE/310199974 (accessed 9 Mar. 2015).

20. Consignment program, *Cardinal Health*, (2013), http://www.cardinal.com/us/en/spd/consignment-program (accessed 9 Mar. 2015).

21. Assessing Bedside Bar-Coding Readiness - *ismp.org*, (2006), http://www.ismp.org/tools/pathwaysection3.pdf (accessed 9 Mar. 2015).

22. Assessing Bedside Bar-Coding Readiness - *ismp.org*

23. Mail Order Pharmacies, *McKesson*, (2013), Retrieved March 9, 2015, from http://www.mckesson.com/pharmacies/mail-order/mail-order-pharmacies/ (accessed 9 Mar. 2015).

24. J. Schmittdiel et al. The Comparative Effectiveness of Mail Order Pharmacy Use vs. Local Pharmacy Use on LDL-C Control in New Statin Users. *JGIM: Journal Of General Internal Medicine* [serial online].; 26, no. 12, (December 2011), 1396–1402. Available from: Academic Search Complete, Ipswich, MA. (accessed 9 Mar. 2015).

25. Schmittdiel et al. The Comparative Effectiveness of Mail Order Pharmacy Use

26. Schmittdiel et al. The Comparative Effectiveness of Mail Order Pharmacy Use

27. C. Thierry, The Role of Modeling and Simulation in Supply Chain, *scs.org*, (2010), http://www.scs.org/magazines/2010-10/index_file/Files/Thierry.pdf.

28. Thierry, The Role of Modeling and Simulation in Supply Chain

29. Thierry, The Role of Modeling and Simulation in Supply Chain

30. G. R. Ledlow, J. H. Stephens and H. H. Fowler, Sticker shock: an exploration of supply charge capture outcomes. *Hospital topics*, 89, no. 1 (2011) 1–8.

31. Improving Patient Charge Capture at Yale-New Haven. http://www.isixsigma.com/implementation/case-studies/improving-patient-charge-capture-yale-new-haven/ (accessed 9 Mar. 2015).

32. Ledlow, Stephens, Fowler, Sticker shock, 1–8.

33. Ledlow, Stephens, Fowler, Sticker shock, 1–8.

34. Ledlow, Stephens, Fowler, Sticker shock, 1–8.

35. What is Lean? *Lean Enterprise Institute*, (2007), http://www.lean.org/whatslean/ (accessed 8 Mar. 2015).

36. Top 25 Lean Tools, *Lean Production*, (2011), http://www.leanproduction.com/top-25-lean-tools.html (accessed 9 Mar. 2015).

37. FAQ's, *A3 Thinking*, (2009), http://a3thinking.com/faq.html (accessed 9 Mar. 2015).

38. Lee Ann Jarousse, "Data standards in the supply chain." (2012). *H&HN: Hospitals & Health Networks* 86, no. 6 (2012), 41–43.

CHAPTER 9

LEADING THE HEALTHCARE SUPPLY CHAIN

1. Describe the concepts, theories, and models of leadership in the context of the healthcare supply chain.
2. Discuss leadership principles and how to implement those principles in leading healthcare supply-chain operations.
3. Relate, discuss, and provide areas of integration between the transformational leadership model and the dynamic culture leadership model.
4. Distinguish the differences between two or more leadership models.
5. Merge principles of leadership to develop a personal leadership framework for leading the healthcare supply-chain team.
6. Evaluate the benefits and limitations of three leadership models within a healthcare supply chain context.

Introduction

How do you lead people and manage resources in the healthcare supply chain? How can you be an excellent leader within the context of healthcare supply chain operations? Leadership theory serves as the basis for understanding the actions of leaders. Throughout the course of this chapter, we will look at several prominent leadership theories and models. Some of these models are stand-alone and work to explain industry phenomenon, and others are designed to be integrated into a personal leadership model. It is important to note that while some theories are more applicable in certain situations, there is no one "best" theory. Instead, theories function as a sort of conceptual model, which describes concepts that may be abstract in nature. In some cases, it may even be appropriate to use parts of one theory, called constructs, with the constructs from another theory. What leadership framework or model would you develop to lead the healthcare supply chain? Several models are presented in this chapter to form a basis to facilitate critical thinking on improving leadership in the healthcare supply chain. The models that have proven salient in healthcare and healthcare supply chain operations were selected to focus that critical thinking for efficient, effective, and efficacious practice.

Motivation and Inspiration

In the healthcare supply chain leader's array of knowledge, skills, and abilities, motivation and inspiration rank high on the list. Carnevale states that "creating a climate that enhances motivation, with the commensurate increase in productivity, is a requirement."[1] Motivation is all about getting a person to start and persist on a task or project. Inspiration is the emotive feeling of value a person experiences while performing a worthy task or project.

Motivation and inspiration in the present day are rooted in the concepts of influence and, to some degree, power. Leaders use motivation and inspiration to influence subordinate actions. Traditionally, leadership thinking rested in the concepts of power and influence. However, the modern-day art of leadership requires a more subtle approach to the misconception of aggressive power and "arm-twisting" influence. The well-educated and complex health workforce will resist the use of errant influence and positional power.

Perhaps not surprisingly, many leaders, academics, and scholars disagree about the best use of power and influence. "There is more conceptual confusion about influence processes than about any other facet of leadership."[2] First this section presents a brief discussion of where influence "exists" for a person; it is followed by a discussion on group affiliation, and then influence as a concept is explored.

Subordinates in health organizations look to leaders, especially senior executives, as champions and sources of inspiration. Inspirational motivation in health organizations can be achieved when the leader passionately believes in the vision and is able to motivate others through this passion. The leadership team plays an important role in ensuring the success of the organization. This team determines the direction of the organization, while also ensuring that the details behind each event are managed well. Leaders have the responsibility of being concerned about the task of the organization and the support of the organization's stakeholders. Successful health organizations have leaders who not only provide the overall vision for the organization but also step in and play a pivotal role by motivating and recognizing the efforts of subordinates that contribute to success.[3]

Ethics and morality play a key role in motivating others as well; collectively, they represent a crucial characteristic for a leader to possess. The success of the organization may rise and fall on the perception of the community regarding the morals of the organization. Subordinates and the community expect leaders to use their best judgment and to do what is right. Although leadership distinctions may depend on the execution of skills and abilities, such as charisma, the distinction of authentic leadership rests heavily on perceptions of morality.[4] To gain widespread support, the organization must demonstrate the sincerity of its mission and stay true to the values it supports as an organization.

Locus of Control

To understand where or how people are motivated and inspired, it is important to recognize each person's perspective on influence. Rotter used a personality scale that measured locus of control orientation as a means of assessing influence.[5] People with a strong internal locus of control orientation (a belief that they control their own destiny and success) believe that events in their lives are determined more by their own actions than by chance or uncontrollable forces (leaders and managers tend to be "internals"). In contrast, people with a strong external control orientation believe that events are determined mostly by chance or fate and that they can do little to improve their lives. Research by Miller and Toulouse associated effective (leadership) management with (leaders) managers with an internal locus of control orientation.[6,7] According to this research, some people are influenced inside themselves (internalizers) and some are influenced outside of themselves (externalizers). In reality, both an internalizer and an externalizer are present inside each person. As a health leader, it is important to understand those people you lead—specifically, to understand which subordinates are more internally oriented and which are more externally oriented.

Group Affiliation

Schutz's theory of affiliation suggests that individuals form groups in response to three kinds of needs:

- Inclusion need: need to be included.
- Control need: need for status and power.
- Affection need: need to give and receive warmth and closeness.

These needs are cyclical; groups pass through observable phases of inclusion, control, and affection.[8] When a leader balances a subordinate's need for inclusion with his or her needs for control and affection within a group environment, the seeds of a powerful organizational or group culture are planted. In a study published in the research literature in 2007, charismatic leadership attributes used by leaders positively contributed to social

identification processes and to social identity applied to the workplace.[9] This suggests that leaders can positively influence group affiliation.

Goal-Setting Theory: A Motivational Theory

As described in Chapter 3, goal-setting theory,[10,11,12] which was originally developed by Edwin Locke, is an effective motivational and inspirational leadership approach. Goals are the aim of an action or behavior. They can be set for any verifiable or measurable outcome. "Goals provide order and structure, measure progress, give a sense of achievement, and provide closure."[13] Locke's basic assumption is that goals are immediate regulators of human action. An individual synthesizes direction, effort, and persistence to accomplish goals (**Figure 9.1**).

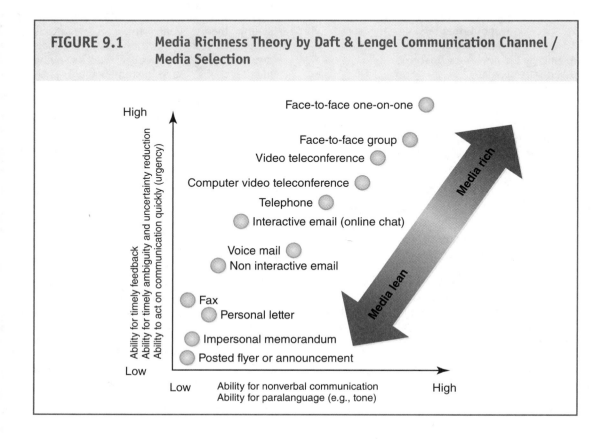

FIGURE 9.1   **Media Richness Theory by Daft & Lengel Communication Channel / Media Selection**

To maximize the effectiveness of goal setting, specific and challenging goals should be established to focus action and effort over time so as to accomplish tasks. From 1968 to 1980, 90% of all studies conducted in this area showed that specific, well-defined, and challenging goals led to greater improvements in performance as compared to vague and easy goals.[14] Individuals must commit to set goals to produce results; the more difficult (challenging yet reasonable) the goal, the better the individual will perform.

Individuals need leadership support (feedback, reward mechanisms, and required resources (time, training, and material goods)) to maximize performance when applying goal setting. "Goal setting and regular communication increase the challenge of the job, make it clear to workers precisely what they are expected to do, and deliver a sense of pride and achievement."[15] Locke suggests seven steps to follow to apply and optimize goal setting:

1. Specify objectives or tasks to be done.
2. Specify how performance will be measured.
3. Specify the standard to be reached.
4. Specify the time frame involved.
5. Prioritize goals.
6. Rate goals as to difficulty and importance.
7. Determine the coordination requirements.[16]

Leaders must ensure that the goals they set do not conflict with one another or with organizational goals. For groups, every group member should have verifiable specific goals, as well as an overall group goal to counter social loafing. Smaller groups (three to eight people) are more effective than larger ones in goal setting.[17] The use of management by objectives (MBO) is an approach to utilize goal setting[18] by leaders, whereby mutually acceptable goals can be developed with subordinates.[19] Locke's model coupled with SMART goals is an excellent model; SMART is an acronym for specific, measurable, attainable, relevant and time-bound.[20]

Leaders should be cognizant of risks of goal setting, which include excessive risk taking and excessive competitiveness. Indeed, goal failure can reduce subordinate confidence and create unwanted stress. However, the benefits of goal setting outweigh the negative potential aspects of applying the theory. "Goal-setting theories provide specific explanations for why people are motivated.

Difficult, specific, and mutually developed goals will assist individuals in being motivated. Although goal setting is extremely useful, many individuals are motivated more by climate [current atmosphere or "feeling" of the workplace; an easily changed phenomenon], culture, and affiliation."[21]

Goal setting integrates well with other motivational theories. Although goal setting is a principal component of many motivational and performance theories, research in this genre has largely focused on locus of control influences and expectancy theory relationships. For the health leader, the merging or synthesis of related theories provides a powerful repertoire for utilization in a multitude of situations. Following are some examples of results from the evaluation of merged theories:

- Considering the theory of locus of control, internalizers tend to have better performance than externalizers with regard to goal setting and applying goal setting.[22]
- In the merger of expectancy theory and goal setting theory, goal setting is negatively related to valence (setting low-level goals does not satisfy individuals as well as setting high-level goals), and instrumentality is positively related to goal setting (difficult goals give the individual a greater sense of achievement, self-efficacy, and skill improvement than easy goals).[23]

Clearly, motivation and influence are critical to leadership success. The understanding, application, and enhanced skill and ability a leader gains by using applied theories such as goal setting are invaluable.

Interpersonal Relationships[24]

Building relationships while in a leadership role is not always easy. Nevertheless, you can build relationships in a professional manner while maintaining your position of power and authority. If honesty, inclusion, and sincerity (the building blocks of trust) are the basis of your quality communication, and if that communication is culturally competent, then you can maintain your role while building relationships. You can gauge the nature of each relationship based on disclosure levels; leaders must consciously draw the line when determining their personal level of disclosure. Disclosing too much or too soon or too often can reduce your position of power and authority; being personally "disclosure conservative" is a good initial approach when building new relationships.

For health leaders (or any other leaders, for that matter), interpersonal relationships are required, are beneficial, and enhance leadership capability and success. Certain elements or factors facilitate improved, positive, and mutually beneficial relationships. In 1989, Yukl proposed a taxonomy of managerial behaviors in which one of the four major domains of managerial life was "building relationships;" in this construct, managing conflict, team building, networking, supporting, developing, and mentoring were the actual behaviors and activities leaders were recommended to engage in to strengthen relationships.[25] A health organization leader should establish, enhance, and grow relationships with a myriad of organizational stakeholders both internal and external to the organization. There is no better method to build relationships than going to visit people in their own environment or location; this kind of "management by walking around" is a powerful approach.

The next subsection provides an overview of four key factors that will enhance relationships. Each factor described has monumental importance, though many factors play a role in forging and maintaining solid relationships.

Factors to Strengthen Relationships

A relationship encompasses the feelings, roles, norms, status, and trust that both affect and reflect the quality of communication between members of a group.[26] Relational communication theorists assert that every message has both a content and relationship dimension:

- Content contains specific information conveyed to someone.
- Relationship messages provide hints about whether the sender/receiver likes or dislikes the other person. Communicating with someone in a manner that provides both content and positive relationship information is important. Language, tone, and nonverbal communication all work together to provide communicative meaning that is interpreted by another person.[27,28]
- Nonverbal communication is more prevalent than verbal communication and consists of the following:
  - Eye contact.
  - Facial expressions.
  - Body posture.
  - Movement.
- People believe nonverbal communication more than verbal communication.
  - Sixty-five percent of meaning is derived from nonverbal communication.
- People communicate emotions primarily through nonverbal communication.
  - Ninety-five percent of emotions are communicated nonverbally.

Frequency of communication that is timely, useful, accurate, and in reasonable quantity is needed to reinforce and validate the relationship. Thus one important factor in developing quality interpersonal relationships is quality communication of sufficient and desired frequency.

A second factor is disclosure, which was mentioned briefly earlier in this chapter. Disclosure relates to the type of information you and the other person in the relationship share with each other; disclosure is one factor that can help you "measure" or evaluate the depth and breadth of a relationship. The "deeper" the information disclosed, the closer the bond of the relationship. Also, the broader the topics of information and experience sharing (e.g., family, work, fishing together, or playing golf) between people, the closer the bond of the relationship. Disclosure or self-disclosure is strongly and positively correlated with trust; that is, more trust means more disclosure. Again, trust starts with quality communication.

Self-disclosure can be categorized and measured. In Powell's model[29] level 5 illustrates a weak relationship bond, whereas level 1 shows a strong relationship bond:

- Level 5: cliché communication.
- Level 4: facts and biographical information.
- Level 3: personal attitudes and ideas.
- Level 2: personal feelings.
- Level 1: peak communication (rare; usually with family or close friends).

Self-disclosure can be summarized as having the following characteristics:[30]

- A function of ongoing relationships.
- Reciprocal.
- Timed to what is happening in the relationship (contextual/situational/relational).
- Should be relevant to what is happening among people present.
- Usually moves in small increments.

A third factor in building strong interpersonal relationships is trust (mentioned briefly in relation to self-disclosure). Trust is built and earned over time through honest interaction (communication and experiences). It is an essential component of a quality, positive relationship. Honesty, inclusion, and sincerity are directly linked to building trust. Honesty means being truthful and open concerning important pieces of information that you share with another person. Inclusion entails including the other person in the relationship in activities and experiences that are important to the other person, to you, and to both of you. Inclusion is also about making sure the other person is part of the "group" in the organization. Sincerity is meaning what you say, meaning what you do, and not keeping record or account of the relationship (not keeping score). Over time, if honesty, inclusion, and sincerity are the basis of your interactions with others, positive and quality relationships will begin to grow.

A fourth factor in forging successful relationships is cultural competence. This factor is based not only on ethnical or national dimensions but also on socioeconomic factors. For instance, consider the cultural differences in surgeons as opposed to nurses as opposed to facility technicians or linen staff or consultants. Every stakeholder group, and every individual, has a varying culture of uniqueness. Understanding those cultural issues—"walking a mile in someone else's shoes"—is a factor important to building solid interpersonal relationships. Understanding and modifying your approach to relationship building and enhancement based on cultural differences will serve you well in leadership positions.

Communication and Culture

Health leaders need to have exceptional communication skills. They must learn the techniques for clarifying what someone else is saying and for being clear in their own communication. Mintzberg's study on managerial work revealed that managers' activity was characterized by "brevity, variety, and fragmentation"; managers were continually seeking information preferring oral communications to written reports.[31,32] This finding applies to leaders as well. The preference for oral communication may be difficult for health leaders to enact, but it is nonetheless important. As an example of personal preference for oral communication, it has been noted that within his first seven months in office, Barack Obama had more White House press conferences than George W. Bush did in his eight years as president.[33] Although verbal communication may be time consuming, given employees' and the public's need for such communication, it is a very valuable tool that is essential to achieve success.

Simply put, communication is the process of acting on information.[34] Communication contributes tremendously to the culture and climate of the health organization. A response—feedback—is an essential aspect of the communication process. Obstacles to communication, called noise, either in the channel or in the mind of the receiver, may contribute to an inaccurate understanding of the intended message. Communication is the main catalyst behind the motivation efforts and strategies utilized by leaders.[35] "Various management [leadership] practices, including goal setting, reinforcement, feedback, and evaluation, require communication."[36] There are three goals of communication:

- Understanding.
- Achieving the intended effect.
- Being ethical (moral).

Communication is a process of active transaction (transactive), which means messages are sent and received simultaneously. Everything you do or do not do, say or do not say, communicates something. You cannot *not* communicate. Communication media, which encompasses what and how to communicate, is discussed next.

Media-Richness Theory

Media-richness theory[37,38,39] which was originally developed by Daft and Lengel and then later updated with the inclusion of computer-mediated communication[40] by D'Ambra and Rice, explains and predicts why certain types of technologies, called media channels or media, are effective (or not effective) in communication efforts. This theory is important to health leaders in that selecting the appropriate communication media channel, such as a face-to-face meeting, a telephone call, or an email, can predict the likelihood of successful communication to others, such as superiors, subordinates, and peers. Today, it is all too easy to send off an email. In many situations, however, email, as a media channel, is not a good choice to have your communication understood as you meant and, in that, receivers of your message may not take the proper action you expect.

In media-richness theory, various media are placed on a "richness" continuum based on the following factors:

- Potential for instant feedback.
- Verbal and nonverbal cues that can be processed by senders and receivers.
- Use of natural language versus stilted or formal language.
- Level of focus on an individual versus a group or mass of people.

This theory indicates that ambiguous or potentially ambiguous messages should be sent with richer media to reduce the level of potential (or actual) misunderstanding. Ambiguity—also called equivocality—is based on the ability of the receiver, in this context, to ask questions. In other words, does the receiver know which questions to ask and how to get started?

Different from ambiguity is uncertainty, although these two constructs complement each other. Certainty is "having the question answered" and having the appropriate information to proceed with an action, task, or project. Uncertainty is a measure of the organization's ignorance of a value for a variable in the [information] space; equivocality is a measure of the organization's ignorance of whether a variable exists in the [information] space.[41] More information reduces uncertainty.[42] In the workplace, the more similar the work performed by subordinates (or the workforce in general) is, the more ambiguity exists, whereas the more dependent each segment of the work process or work flow is on other segments, the more uncertainty exists.

It is vital for leaders to reduce ambiguity and uncertainty to the greatest extent possible. The richer the media utilized, the greater the chance of leader communication success, the greater the chance of reducing ambiguity, and the greater the chance of reducing uncertainty. Unfortunately, richer media, such as face-to-face communication, costs more in terms of resources (e.g., time, travel, meeting space) than less rich media.

Health leaders will be more effective if they master the basics of the media-richness theory. Following are some important points to reflect on for leadership success:

- Select media channels to reduce ambiguity.
- Select media channels to reduce uncertainty.
- The more complex the issues, the more group members like face-to-face meetings.
- Computer-mediated communication (CMC) deals more with tasks but less with group relationships.
- CMC may increase polarization.
- CMC works best with linear, structured tasks.
- CMC increases individual "information processing" requirements.
- People with technological skills gain more power in CMC group communication.
- More cliques and coalitions form with CMC than with face-to-face communication.

Burns's Transformational Leadership Model (1978)

Two of the more recent theories of leadership discussed a great deal are transactional and transformational leadership theories. Transactional leadership was first described by Max Weber in 1947 and was resurfaced in 1981 by Benjamin Bass, who hypothesized that transactional leaders believe workers are motivated by rewards. That is similar to McGregor's Theory X description of one type of subordinate. The transformational-leadership model is a situation-influenced theory that suggests the situation influences the leader to adopt a style most fitting to the specific circumstances at hand. This style may be transactional or transformational, or some combination of the two. In practice, a combination of these approaches is the most practical leadership strategy to undertake in health organizations. The knowledge, skills, and abilities of a health leader to use transformational and transactional leadership are critical for success in today's environment.

The descriptors applied to transactional leadership are "working to achieve specific goals, rewarding employees, [responding] to employees and [their] self-interests. Because a trade—an exchange of work and effort for rewards—occurs, transactional leadership is perceived as an economic model of leadership."[43] A potential negative outcome with this model is that employees may not be motivated to accomplish certain tasks if there is no reward attached to performance and positive outcomes.

James MacGregor Burns, around 1978, distinguished between transactional- and transformational-leadership styles. Burns based his theories on other sources, such as Maslow's hierarchy of needs and Kohlberg's theories of moral development.[44] Burns believed the transactional leader lived in keeping with certain values, such as fairness, responsibility, and integrity. Transformational leadership is sometimes viewed as the opposite end of the pole from transactional leadership, though in reality that perception is inaccurate. Transformational leaders are charismatic; they have vision, empathy, self-assurance, commitment, and the ability to assure others of their own competence; and they are willing to take risks.[45,46] "Transformational leadership refers to the process of building commitment to the organization's objectives and empowering followers to accomplish these objectives."[47]

Burns compared and contrasted transactional with transformational leadership. Transactional leadership involves values, but they are values relevant to the exchange process such as honesty, fairness, responsibility, and reciprocity, and bureaucratic organizations enforce the use of legitimate power and respect for rules and tradition rather

than influence based on inspiration. For Burns, leadership is a process, not a set of discrete acts. Burns (1978) described leadership as "a stream of evolving interrelationships in which leaders are continuously evoking motivational responses from followers and modifying their behavior as they meet responsiveness or resistance, in a ceaseless process of flow and counter-flow." At the macro-level of analysis, transformational leadership involves shaping, expressing, and mediating conflict among groups of people in addition to motivating individuals.[48]

Building on Burns's work, Bernard Bass argued that rather than the two leadership styles being polar opposites, there was a linear progression from transactional to transformational leadership. Bass also believed that transformational leadership should be measured in terms of how it affects employees, such as how much they trust and respect the leader. According to Bass, transformational leadership must be grounded in moral foundations that include inspirational motivation, individualized consideration, intellectual stimulation, and idealized influence. These concepts position the transformational leader in a place similar to that identified in servant-leader models such as the model proposed by Greenleaf.[49]

From this discourse, Bass (1985) proposed a theory of transformational leadership that is measured in terms of the leader's influence on subordinates or followers. Subordinates or followers "connect" to the transformational leader through trust, admiration, a sense of loyalty, and respect for the leader. Transformational leaders, in turn, create an environment that propels subordinates and followers to greater performance and greater deeds[50] than previously expected, in three ways: (1) by making followers aware of the importance of their performance and task outcomes; (2) by replacing their own self-interest with the good of the group, team, and organization; and (3) by energizing and motivating followers' higher-order needs.[51] In more recent research, transformational leadership has been identified as the most important predictor of individual success and active involvement in healthcare delivery teams (multidisciplinary teams).[52]

In summary, transformational leadership focuses on four constructs. Bass's original theory included three behaviors of transformational leaders, while the fourth was added later to transformational behaviors:

- Charisma: The leader influences followers by arousing strong emotions and identification with the leader.
- Intellectual stimulation: The leader increases follower awareness of problems and influences followers to view problems from a new perspective.
- Individualized consideration: The leader provides support, encouragement, and developmental experiences for followers.
- Inspirational motivation: The leader communicates an appealing vision using symbols to focus subordinate effort and to model appropriate behavior (role modeling, Bandera's social learning theory).[53,54]

In support of this theory, Fairholm, in an assessment of empowering leadership techniques that closely resemble transformational leadership, suggests that leaders fulfill the following responsibilities:

- Utilize goal setting.
- Delegate to followers.
- Encourage participation.
- Encourage self-reliance.
- Challenge followers.
- Focus on followers.
- Specify followers' role.[55]

Transformational leadership can be measured by an instrument called the Multifactor Leadership Questionnaire (MLQ). Using this tool, global attributes, specific traits, and combinations of assessments have been applied to validate forecasts of retrospective and concurrent transformational leadership through measurement.[56] Several different approaches have been used to confirm the reliability and validity of MLQ assessments. Under situational or contingency theory, transformational leadership and transactional leadership are viewed as encompassing a range of viable styles that a leader can select from depending on the situation. Like Burns, Bass considers transactional leadership to entail an exchange of rewards for compliance. Transactional behaviors include the following:

- Contingent reward: clarification of work required to obtain rewards.

- Active management by exception: monitoring subordinates and corrective action to ensure that the work is effectively accomplished.
- Passive management by exception: use of contingent punishments and other corrective action in response to obvious deviations from acceptable performance standards.[57,58]

Bass regards theories such as leader–member exchange theory and path–goal theory as descriptions of transactional leadership. He views transformational and transactional leadership as distinct but not mutually exclusive processes; the same leader may use both types of leadership at different times in different situations.[59]

Leadership as Managing Organizational Culture

There is a growing trend to incorporate organizational culture into leadership theories and models. This is a rather new emphasis, but a critically important one. Leaders build culture in everything they do—from role modeling, to assigning responsibilities, to communicating with others, including how they communicate and what they do not do or do not say. Models with an organizational-culture emphasis require leaders to determine, develop, and maintain an organizational culture that can best meet the expectations—if not thrive—in the external environment. This perspective envisions a more important and dramatic role for organizational culture as a construct—a leadership role—compared to that assigned under the situational leadership philosophy. *Leaders must now create culture!* The dynamic culture leadership model enables leaders to create the culture of excellence that is required in the healthcare supply chain.

The Dynamic Culture Leadership Model[60]

Superb leadership is required at all levels of the health organization due to the increasingly dynamic nature of the health environment. This reality was the catalyst for the development of the dynamic culture leadership (DCL) model. Leadership in this model is recognized at three levels as the critical ingredient in the recipe for overall success: at the personal level, at the team level, and at the organizational level. The challenge is to focus the knowledge, skills, and abilities of organizational leaders appropriately and to empower the total organization to complete its mission, reach its vision, and compete successfully in an environment that constantly changes. This model is built on various theories and models from the leadership literature and related research. An overview of the DCL model is presented; this model is intended to fit within the situational and transformational leadership paradigm with an emphasis on organizational culture development. This model is appropriate for organizational, department, system, subsystem, or program leadership and should be used as a basis for developing a personal leadership plan or model.

The DCL model[61] provides both a descriptive and a high-level prescriptive process model of leadership. This model emphasizes a sense of balance that needs to be maintained to achieve a sustainable and continuing level of optimized leadership based on the changing macro and micro factors in the external environment.

"Optimized leadership," like the concept "high quality," is not necessarily a norm to be achieved at all times. Rather, it is a worthy goal, an ideal state. No individual (and certainly no organization) can in all situations and at all times enjoy a steady state of higher-level leadership. Nevertheless, many individuals and organizations continuously optimize their ability to function at high leadership levels by consciously (and even unconsciously) cultivating the various elements of the model.

The basic assumptions of the DCL model are as follows:

- Due to the very dynamic nature of the environment (in this case, the health industry), it is critical for the leadership and management team to bring multiple knowledge, skills, abilities, perspectives, and backgrounds (DCL leadership alignment assessment) to the organization to enable it to successfully and proactively navigate the external environment and focus the internal people and resources on the mission, vision, strategies, goals, and objectives of the organization.
- Leadership is defined as the ability to assess, develop, maintain, and change the organizational culture to optimally meet the needs and expectations of the external environment

through focusing the collective energy of the organization on the mission, vision, strategies, goals, and objectives of the organization.
- The leadership and management team should consciously determine the culture of the organization and guide and direct culture through communication improvement, organization-wide strategic planning, decision making alignment, employee assessment and empowerment, and knowledge management and organizational learning (process constructs).
- Based on the predetermined organizational culture, mission, vision, and strategies, consistency of leadership and management are paramount.
- Situational and environmental assessment and scanning are key to adjusting organizational culture, mission, vision, and strategies.
- Transformational leadership and management (including transactional leadership approaches), where both the science and art leadership and management are in concert with the external environment expectations, provide the best approach to lead people and manage resources in a dynamic world.

Optimized leadership is certainly attainable for any person and any organization, but it usually requires concentrated effort to overcome past habits, ideas, and tendencies. Ultimately, individual leaders make up the leadership team. The team, therefore, must be diverse in style and competencies while being anchored to a set of values and operating principles of the organization. The assessment instrument for individuals and teams for this model is based on a leadership–management continuum and an art–science continuum.

The characteristics of "leadership" as compared to "management," and "science" as compared to "art," are described in **Tables 9.1** and **9.2**. It is important to note that organizations need leaders, managers, scientists, and artists working together to achieve success over the long term. Figure 9.5 illustrates the macro descriptive model, while Figure 9.6 shows the prescription (or processes) associated with the model.

The differences in leadership versus management are shown in Table 9.1; the differences in science versus art are shown in Table 9.2. It is important to keep in mind that organizations need leadership as well as management mentality/capabilities,

FIGURE 9.2   Dynamic Culture Leadership Model

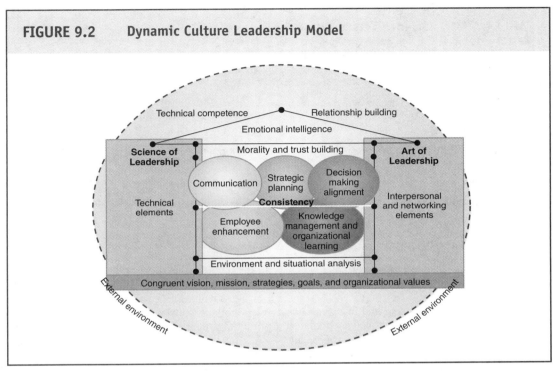

Reproduced from Ledlow, G., & Cwiek, M. (2005, July). The process of leading: Assessment and comparison of leadership team style, operating climate, and expectation of the external environment. Proceedings of Global Business and Technology Association. Lisbon, Portugal.

TABLE 9.1   Leadership Versus Management

Leadership	Management
Longer Time Horizon	Shorter Time Horizon
Vision the Mission Oriented	Mission Oriented
Organizational Validity (Are we doing the right things?) – Environmetnal scanning and Intuition	Organizational Reliability (Are we doing things correctly and consistently?) Compliance to Rules and Policies and Rule Development
Does the Organization Have the Correct Components (People, Resources, Expertise) to Meet Future as well as Current Needs?	How Can Current Components Work Best Now?
Developing and Refining Organizational Culture to meet External Environment Needs	Maintaining Organizational Climate to Ensure Performance
Timing and Tempo of Initiatives and Projects	Scheduling of Initiatives and Projects

Reproduced from Ledlow, G., & Cwiek, M. (2005, July). The process of leading: Assessment and comparison of leadership team style, operating climate, and expectation of the external environment. Proceedings of Global Business and Technology Association. Lisbon, Portugal.

TABLE 9.2	Science Versus Art	

Science	Art
Techincal Skills Orientation – Forecasting, Budgeting, etc...	Relationship Oriented – Networking Interpersonal Relationships
Decision Based More on Analysis	Decisions Based More on Perceptions of People
Developing Systems – Important to Organizations	Developing Relationships and Networks – Important to Organizations
Expert Systems	Experts as People
Cost Control and Evaluation of Value Important	Image and Customer Relationships Important

Reproduced from Ledlow, G., & Cwiek, M. (2005, July). The process of leading: Assessment and comparison of leadership team style, operating climate, and expectation of the external environment. Proceedings of Global Business and Technology Association. Lisbon, Portugal.

as well as science and art mentality/capabilities, if they are to survive and thrive in their external environment.

The DCL model entails a leadership process, as shown in **Figure 9.3**, that emphasizes leadership team assessment, communication improvement, strategic planning, decision making alignment, employee enhancement, and learning organization improvement. Leaders who regularly follow the sequence shown in Figure 9.3 have the best potential to deal with change in their environment, while building a culture that will be effective even

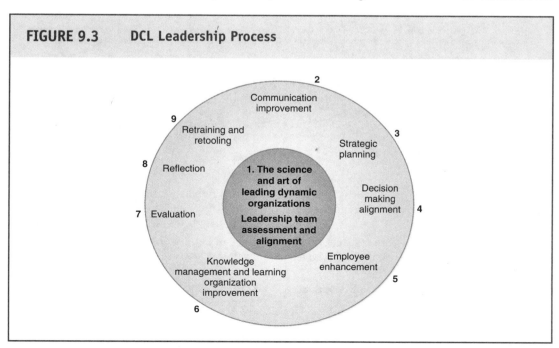

FIGURE 9.3 **DCL Leadership Process**

Reproduced from Ledlow, G., & Cwiek, M. (2005, July). The process of leading: Assessment and comparison of leadership team style, operating climate, and expectation of the external environment. Proceedings of Global Business and Technology Association. Lisbon, Portugal.

during times of change. Members of the leadership team must be ever thoughtful in maintaining their consistency relative to the organizational mission, vision, strategies, goals, and values, but also in terms of the model's constructs and process constructs. Examples of inconsistency might include instituting a defensive and disconfirming communication environment within a customer or patient service and care excellence (differentiation) strategy; using a subordinate decision making tactic (i.e., pushing down decisions to the lowest level appropriate) without involving subordinates in strategic and operational planning; or maintaining a leadership team that is heavily skewed toward "leadership" and "art" while the external environment demands "management" and "science." Examples of consistency would be creating a culture based on a supportive and confirming communication environment; using a subordinate-involved planning process with decision making made at the lowest appropriate level; and initiating a customer-service and patient-care

excellence strategy if the external environment expects such a strategy (today, excellent service and care are expected). The overriding theme is that leadership envisions, develops, and maintains an organizational culture that works amid a dynamic environment. A summary of model constructs and process constructs follows.

Briefly, the DCL model incorporates both constructs and "process" constructs as part of the DCL system. In essence, model constructs are primarily the descriptive model. Model constructs include the following:

- Science of leadership includes all technical elements involved in leading and managing an organization, such as quantitative and qualitative analysis, decision making assessments, finance, and budgeting, job analysis and design, planning structures and processes, computer skills, and the like. Each process construct of the model has both science and art aspects; an integration of the two must be

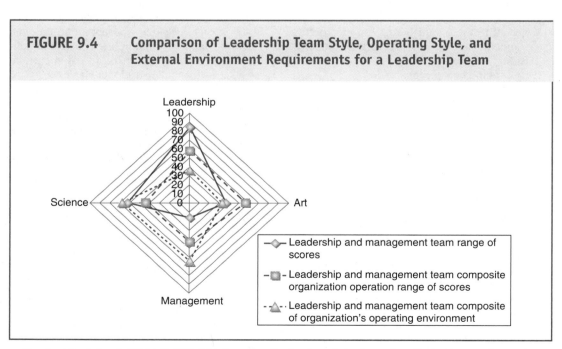

FIGURE 9.4   Comparison of Leadership Team Style, Operating Style, and External Environment Requirements for a Leadership Team

consistently used to ensure successful leadership of an organization.

- Art of leadership includes the elements involved in interpersonal relationships, network building and maintenance, intuition, coalition development, and the like.
- Technical competence, relationship building, emotional intelligence, morality and trust building, and environmental and situational analyses are required at sufficient levels (and should be at high levels) across the leadership and management team to successfully lead people and manage the resources of the health organization.
- Congruent vision, mission, strategies, goals, and organizational values are essential so that a culture of consistency is developed throughout the organization. The leadership and management team must consciously assess the external environment (macro and micro factors) and predetermine these directional, competitive, adaptive, and cultural development strategies for the organization.
- The external environment comprises all organizational stakeholders (anyone or any group that influences, serves, gets service, or is connected to the organization), the macro environmental factors, the micro environmental factors, and the synthesized set of expectations of the health organization.

Prescriptive elements of the model include assessing and aligning a robust leadership and management team that can utilize the knowledge, skills, abilities, and perspectives of all quadrants of the assessment instrument "diamond," being consistent in developing and maintaining an appropriate culture and the sequential and building utilization of the model's process constructs. Process constructs include the following elements:

- Communication improvement is the leadership and management team engagement in predetermined modeling, training, rewarding, and assimilating of the communication environment into the organization in the means that best contributes to an effective organizational culture. In health organizations, a confirming and supportive communication environment that is cognizant of media richness of communication channels and competent in conflict management should be the most effective, efficient, and efficacious.
- Strategic planning (includes operational planning) is the structured, inclusive process of planning to determine a mission, vision, strategies, goals, objectives, and action steps that are consistent with organizational values and that meet the external environment's expectations of the organization. Subordinate, internal, and external stakeholders should be included, as appropriate to level and responsibilities, in the planning process. Continuous and "living" planning is a cultural imperative in dynamic environments.
- Decision making alignment involves aligning decisions with the strategic and operational plan while understanding reality-based decision making (i.e., pushing down decisions appropriately and using policies and standing operating procedures for routine and consistent decisions).
- Employee enhancement is the assessment of employee knowledge, skills, abilities, experience, and trustworthiness and the practice of increasing or reducing responsibilities (such as making decisions) appropriate to the unit, group, and individual in line with the organizational culture as part of development and the strategic and operational plans.
- Knowledge management and organizational learning involves capturing what the organization knows and what it has learned so that improvements to effectiveness, efficiency, and efficacy can be achieved. Leadership, willingness, planning, and training are facilitators of organizational learning.[62]
- Evaluating, reflecting, and retooling are the leadership and management team's honest assessment of the DCL model cycle and ways to improve the cycle in the next repetition.

Using this process consistently will not only improve the organization's ability to use these processes and produce an organizational culture that reflects the leadership's vision, but will enable the organization to maneuver in dynamic/changing situations.

Leadership team assessment and alignment are important. Figure 9.4 illustrates the leadership team assessment (Step 1 in Figure 9.3) for ten members of a hospital leadership team as it compares to the current operational environment and the expectations of the external environment. As shown in Figure 9.4, there is a tension between what the leadership team tends to be (more leadership oriented with a reasonable science and art balance) and the more management and science emphasis in leadership demanded by the external environment; the operating environment can be found between that tension. The external environment requirements, as perceived by the leadership team, are skewed toward management and science (the "analytical manager" quadrant). The perception of leadership would lead one to believe that the external environment requires greater cost control, accountability, and adherence to policies and rules, although relationships are still important, as is some leadership focus.

Assessing an organization's leadership team is essential. Aligning the team to bring diversity of style, skills, experience, and abilities is essential for organizations if they are to maintain a robust and resilient, and even opportunistic, personality. In this model and assessment, both cultural diversity and individual diversity are valued because they enable the organization to better respond to dynamic organizational and external environments. In contrast, diversity of focus and diversity of organizational goals are not advantageous; a diverse leadership team brings robustness to solving organizational problems as long as the focus on the vision, mission, and goals are similar across the leadership team. An assessment that looks at leadership as a team, across organizational levels, operating environments, and external environment needs, is far better than simply relying on only individual leader assessments.[63]

Leaders are gifted in different ways, with different personalities and varying skill sets. All leaders can grow and become more balanced and achieve greater effectiveness. Notably, some common factors found in those who succeed in becoming dynamic culture leaders, including the desire to learn more about themselves, the motivation to learn and practice new skill sets, and the need to grow and to become more tomorrow than what the person is today. This is not the easiest path to

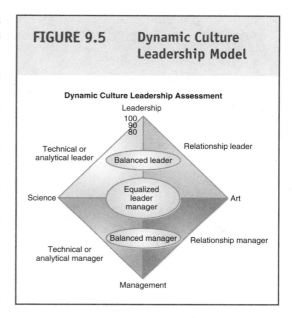

FIGURE 9.5   Dynamic Culture Leadership Model

Dynamic Culture Leadership Assessment

travel, but it is the path that optimizes the likelihood of leadership effectiveness and success.

The DCL model categorizes leaders and managers, scientists and artists, based on the diamond configuration of the assessment tool. Overlaying this categorization scheme on top of the assessment are the following classifications: relationship leader, relationship manager, technical or analytic leader, technical or analytic manager, balanced leader, equalized leader-manager, and balanced manager (**Figure 9.5**). In which category would you put yourself? This same schema can be used in assessing the operating style of the organization (such as relationship-led operation or relationship-managed operation) and the external environment expectations (such as technical or analytically led environment or technical or analytically managed environment). A comparison of two hospital leadership teams is presented to demonstrate the assessment from the DCL model.

Comparison: Two Community-Based Hospitals

Two community hospital leadership teams were assessed using the DCL leadership alignment assessment tool. The first hospital is a military

TABLE 9.3	Hospital Comparisons

Type of Facility:	Hospital A: Short Term Acute Care Hospital B: Short Term Acute Care
Type of Control:	Hospital A: Governmental, Federal Hospital B: Voluntary, Nonprofit
Total Staffed Beds:	Hospital A: 76 Hospital B: 88

community hospital in the Western United States, and the other hospital is in the North Central/Midwest United States. The two hospitals, with similar services and case mix indexes, are highlighted.

When comparing the two hospitals, both Hospital A (federal) and Hospital B (nonprofit) are skewed strongly towards "leadership" and somewhat towards "science." Hospital A is slightly higher on both areas than Hospital B. There is a moderate amount of diversity in the area of "art" and little in the "management" area for both hospitals, with Hospital B having slightly higher scores. Both hospitals leadership teams demonstrate the analytical leader, as compared to the relationship leader or relationship manger team composites. The perceived operating environment for both Hospital A and Hospital B is fairly balanced. However, Hospital B is now slightly skewed towards "art" and Hospital A towards "science."

The external environment requirements, as perceived by Hospital A, are skewed toward "management" and "science" (the analytical manger quadrant), and for Hospital B, slightly skewed toward "leadership" and "science" (analytical leader). For Hospital A, the perception is that the external environment requires greater cost control, accountability and adherence to policies and rules, whereas with Hospital B, there is a balanced focus on vision and decision making based on analysis.

When leadership style by organizational level is compared, there is much more propensity for "leadership" than "management" as you go down the organizational hierarchy. However, and most interestingly, Level 3 and Level 4 are balanced with a slight skew for "art" and "science" for both Hospital A and Hospital B. At this level of the organization, both scientist and artist are needed to deal with dynamic environments. The DCL leadership alignment assessment summaries and charts follow.

TABLE 9.4	Hospital A DCL Scores

Hospital A	Levels	Level	Level	Level
Organizational Level (levels from CEO)	**0–1**	**2**	**3**	**4**
Leadership	100	85	70	80
Art	40	25	50	40
Management	0	15	30	20
Science	50	75	50	60
Number in Category	**1**	**2**	**1**	**1**

TABLE 9.5 Hospital B DCL Scores

Hospital B	Levels	Level	Level	Level
Organizational Level (levels from CEO)	**0–1**	**2**	**3**	**4**
Leadership	100	80	74	80
Art	40	35	50	50
Management	0	20	26	20
Science	50	60	50	50
Number in Category	**1**	**2**	**5**	**2**

Hospital 'A' Charts – Government, Federal

Hospital B Charts – Voluntary, Not for Profit

Which hospital leadership team is more "diverse?" Which hospital leadership team is more aligned with the operating climate and external environment expectations?

DCL and Organizational Culture

Organizations are more dynamic today than ever before. With the advent of the Information Age, the fluidity of professional and family life, and the competitive nature of the global marketplace, more of

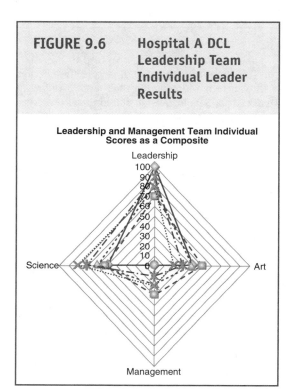

FIGURE 9.6 Hospital A DCL Leadership Team Individual Leader Results

Leadership and Management Team Individual Scores as a Composite

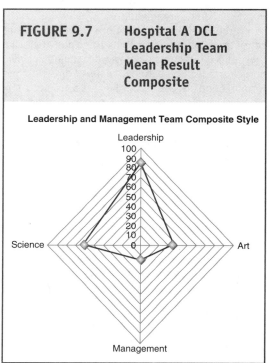

FIGURE 9.7 Hospital A DCL Leadership Team Mean Result Composite

Leadership and Management Team Composite Style

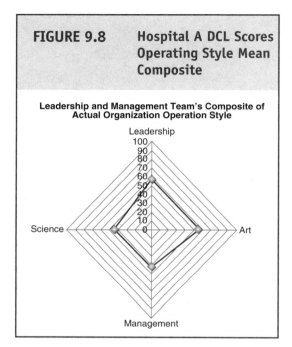

FIGURE 9.8   Hospital A DCL Scores Operating Style Mean Composite

Leadership and Management Team's Composite of Actual Organization Operation Style

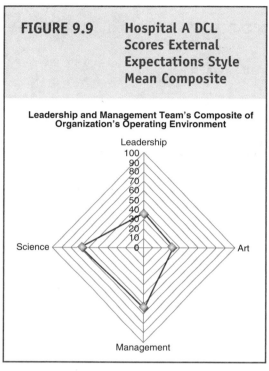

FIGURE 9.9   Hospital A DCL Scores External Expectations Style Mean Composite

Leadership and Management Team's Composite of Organization's Operating Environment

an entrepreneurial environment can be found in many of today's organizations.

Entrepreneurial organizations reflect a different set of underlying assumptions principally because they shift the focus away from producing specific, predetermined behavior by means of direction and formal controls. Instead, they encourage coordination through the shared understanding that will enable individuals to choose effective actions themselves. Organization structure and control systems can no longer be depicted as tools that mechanically determine members' behaviors. We, too, must shift our thinking about organizations away from the organization as an entity, to members' choice and understanding.[64]

Leaders in this environment cannot rest on the laurels of "cookie-cutter" methods, but must instead learn and become effective in developing teams of professionals within dynamic cultures. To see the reality of the dynamic nature of organizations today, one need simply consider the changes wrought by increased human diversity, information overload, the evolution of technology, the increasing sophistication of the consumer, and the introduction of e-commerce.

Leaders need to have a firm grasp of how they can develop an organizational culture that creates a thriving environment for their organization. In 1999, Edgar Schein defined "culture" as the basic assumptions and beliefs shared by members of a group or organization.[65] "A major function of culture is to help us understand the environment and determine how to respond to it, thereby reducing anxiety, uncertainty, and confusion."[66] The key question then becomes, how do leaders shape culture? Schein suggests that leaders have the greatest potential for embedding and reinforcing aspects of culture with the following five primary mechanisms.[67]

- Attention: leaders communicate their priorities, values, and concerns by their choice of things to ask about, measure, comment on, praise, and criticize.
- Reaction to crisis: this reaction increases the potential for learning about values and assumptions.
- Role modeling.
- Allocation of resources.

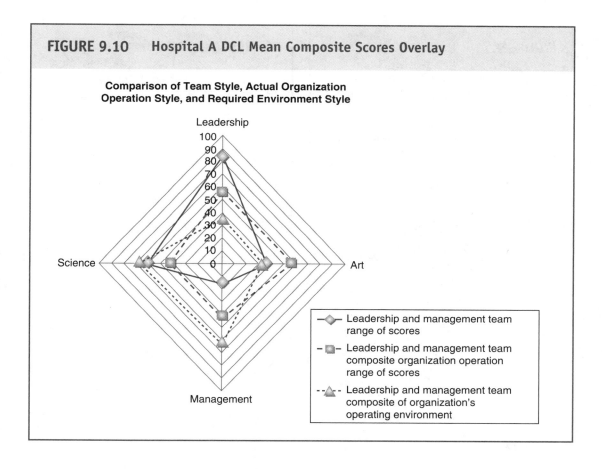

FIGURE 9.10   Hospital A DCL Mean Composite Scores Overlay

Comparison of Team Style, Actual Organization
Operation Style, and Required Environment Style

- Leadership and management team range of scores
- Leadership and management team composite organization operation range of scores
- Leadership and management team composite of organization's operating environment

TABLE 9.6   Hospital A DCL Mean Composite Scores

Hospital A Scores:	Leadership and Management team range of scores	Leadership & Management team composite organization operation range of scores	Leadership and Management team composite of organization's operating environment
Leadership	84.00	56.92	36.00
Art	36.00	56.00	32.00
Management	16.00	43.08	64.00
Science	62.00	44.00	68.00

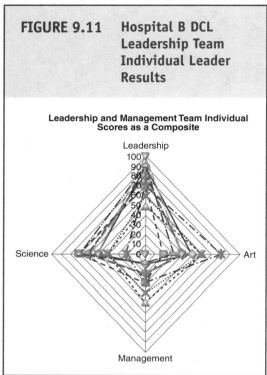

FIGURE 9.11 Hospital B DCL Leadership Team Individual Leader Results

Leadership and Management Team Individual Scores as a Composite

FIGURE 9.12 Hospital B DCL Leadership Team Mean Result Composite

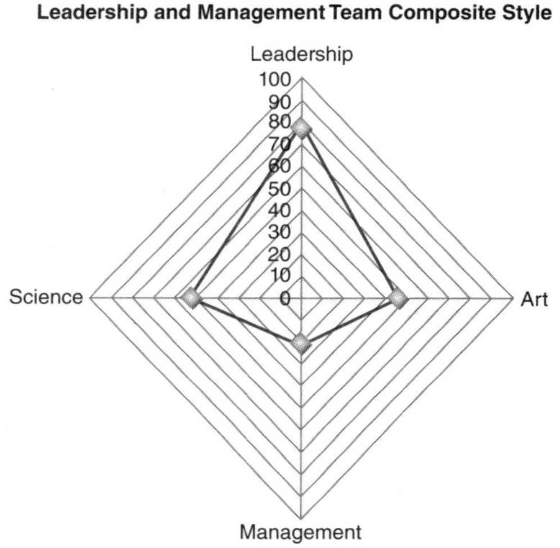

Leadership and Management Team Composite Style

- Criteria for selection and dismissal: leaders can influence culture by recruiting people who have particular values, skills, and traits, and then by promoting (or firing) them

Schein also described five secondary mechanisms:[68]

- Design of organizational structure: a centralized structure indicates that only the leader can determine what is important; a decentralized structure reinforces individual initiative and sharing.
- Design of systems and procedures: where emphasis is placed shows concern and ambiguity reduction issues.

TABLE 9.7 Hospital B DCL Mean Composite Scores

Hospital B Scores:	Leadership and management team range of scores	Leadership and Management team composite organization operation range of scores	Leadership and Management team composite of organization's operating environment
Leadership	79.00	60.38	54.00
Art	46.00	44.00	44.00
Management	21.00	39.62	46.00
Science	52.00	56.00	56.00

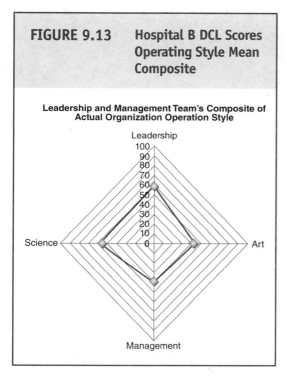

FIGURE 9.13 **Hospital B DCL Scores Operating Style Mean Composite**

Leadership and Management Team's Composite of Actual Organization Operation Style

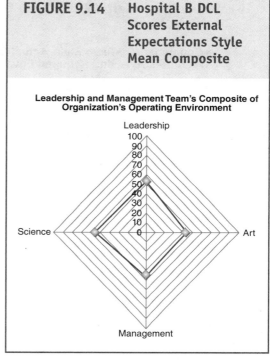

FIGURE 9.14 **Hospital B DCL Scores External Expectations Style Mean Composite**

Leadership and Management Team's Composite of Organization's Operating Environment

- Design of facilities.
- Stories, legends, and myths.
- Formal statements.

It is imperative that health organization leaders understand the various factors that influence culture. Culture is more stable and more difficult to change than "climate," because climate usually does not remain stable over time. Whether employees are "happy" today (a climate indicator) is only of temporal importance. By comparison, culture indicators (e.g., processes, incentive systems, communication environment, understanding of goals and how they fit into the work to achieve success) are much more meaningful and important.

The DCL model is a set of constructs for which its goal is to unify the various leadership theories that previously have received attention. Further, the DCL model can be studied immediately and put to work by leaders and organizational scholars intent on developing highly effective leadership. In their book *The Success Paradigm*[69] Mike Friesen and James Johnson discuss the importance of leadership in the integration of quality and strategy to achieve organizational success. In this book, the leadership process is described as critical for success. The DCL model is presented as an application of theory to advance existing contingency leadership theories, coupled with a strategic process. It is, therefore, presented as a prescriptive model.

Today's complex, ever-changing organizations are experiencing a shortage in leadership effectiveness, not because of a lack of talent or goodwill, but because of the demanding balancing act required for success. This balance of scientist and artist attributes defined in the DCL model provides the pathway for success. According to experts, leadership is the pivotal issue in organizational success. The DCL model is intended to become central to the understanding of leadership in organizations and the people who lead them.

The DCL model, in its current state of development, is being tested in both theoretical and practical ways. It currently provides a conceptual framework for the better understanding of complex organizations and serves as a model for advancing leader effectiveness. Further, tools for

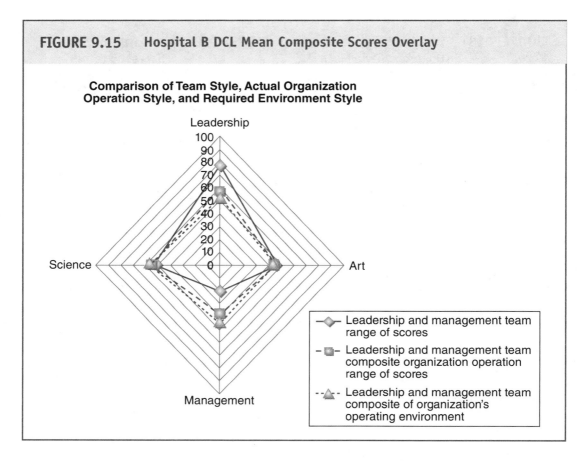

FIGURE 9.15   Hospital B DCL Mean Composite Scores Overlay

Comparison of Team Style, Actual Organization Operation Style, and Required Environment Style

— ◇ — Leadership and management team range of scores

– ▣ – Leadership and management team composite organization operation range of scores

– – ▲ – – Leadership and management team composite of organization's operating environment

leadership assessment and direct application are being refined to advance the practical utility of this model in all organizational settings. In summary, the DCL model includes the following recommendations:

- An assessment of the organization's leadership team and ultimately the development of a team should focus on building a team that is diverse in terms of the leadership, management, art, and science attributes, while simultaneously being rooted in the fundamental values, beliefs, and mission of the organization.
- An organization's leadership should focus on communication improvement, strategic planning, decision making alignment, employee enhancement, and learning organization improvement, in a regular, cyclical sequence.

- Leaders should become competent in the use of the process constructs (e.g., communication improvement, strategic planning) included in this model, so that predetermined and consistent alternative strategies and applications can be selected based on the situation.
- The sequence should be repeated based on the tempo of change in the environment: Rapid change creates a need to work through the sequence at a faster pace. It is estimated that in healthcare today, this sequence should be planned for every three to four years.

The DCL model, as a leadership team alignment, macro, and culture creation model, integrates well with the "reframing leadership and management in organizations" model, an episodic leader style selection and "frame" emphasis platform developed by Bolman and Deal. Both models possess descriptive and prescriptive elements that can be learned and embedded into the organization culture of health organizations.

Organizational Culture and Supply Chain

An effective supply chain requires the support of all staff within a healthcare organization. One area of the healthcare supply chain where this is most evident is charge capture. The most modern systems have an automatic charge capture when items are removed from PAR locations or bedside charge capture when items are scanned prior to use. However, some organizations do centralized charge capture, which requires the charges to be recorded on a document that is sent to the materials management department for recording. Without buy-in from the clinical staff, such a system can add enormous hidden expense to the supply chain from items not being recorded prior to use. Understanding your organizational culture as well as your power as a leader to change that culture is the first step in resolving situations such as these, and a model such as the DCL provides a proscriptive as well as descriptive framework for overcoming the challenge.

Bolman and Deal's Reframing Leadership and Management in Organizations Model[70]

Bolman and Deal suggest that leaders must be situational/contingency oriented. Critical variables assist leaders in choosing the emphasis and style they need to use to be successful. Four constructs are considered important in this model: structural, human resources, political, and symbolic. Each of these constructs is important in its own right, but some are more important than others at critical times. Recent research literature from late 2008 used Bolman and Deal's model to suggest several applications for this model in an academic healthcare organization.[71]

With Bolman and Deal's model, a leader must pay attention to the four organizational constructs, each of which has assumptions, attributes, and imperatives for the leader to consider. This section summarizes each of these dimensions. As we progress through this model, pay close attention to its application.

The structural construct (called a "frame") deals with how organizations "structure" work processes, how they establish formal relationships, and how groups facilitate coupling (coupling is the level of adherence to organizational policies, rules, procedures, and social expectations). The structural frame assumptions are outlined here:

- Organizations exist to accomplish established goals.
- Organizational design/structural form can be designed to "fit" the situation.
- Organizations work best when governed by rationality and norms.
- Specialization permits more productivity and individual expertise.
- Coordination and control are essential to effectiveness.
- Problems originate from inappropriate structures and inadequate systems that can be resolved through restructuring and developing new systems (modern reengineering).

The human resources construct or frame embraces McGregor's Theory Y model. This dimension is critical to focus and synergize human energy in an organization. Human resources frame assumptions are as follows:

- "Organizations exist to serve human needs (rather than the reverse).
- Organizations and people need each other.
- When the fit between the individual and the organization is poor, one or both will suffer: individuals will be exploited, or will seek to exploit the organization, or both.
- A good fit between individual and organization benefits both: human beings find meaningful and satisfying work, and organizations get the human talent and energy that they need."[58] "Moreover, the idea that people have needs is a central element in commonsense psychology."[72]

This model's essential theme regarding human-resources management is best summed up in the following quotations: The theories of Maslow, McGregor, and Argyris suggested that conflict between individual and organization would get worse as organizations became larger (with greater impersonality, longer chains of command, and

TABLE 9.8	Bolman and Deal: Choosing a Frame

Frame	Conditions for Salience
Structural:	Clear goals and information; well-understood cause–effect relationships; strong technologies and information systems; low conflict; low ambiguity; low uncertainty; stable legitimate authority
Human resources:	High or increasing employee leverage; low or declining employee morale and motivation; relatively abundant or increasing resources; low or moderate conflict and uncertainty; low or moderate diversity
Political:	Scarce or declining resources; goal and value conflicts; high or increasing diversity; diffuse or unstable distribution of power
Symbolic:	Unclear and ambiguous goals and information; poorly understood cause–effect relationships; weak technologies and information systems; culturally diverse

Data from Bolman, L.G., & Deal, T. E. (1991). Reframing organizations: Artistry, choice, and leadership. San Francisco: Jossey-Bass, p. 315.

more complex rules and control systems) and as society became better educated and more affluent (producing more people whose higher-level needs are salient).[73]

One solution to that problem (treating employees as children) is participation—giving workers more opportunity to influence decisions.[74]

The political construct or frame deals with resource allocation within an organization. The interesting aspect of this construct is that people create interesting webs of relationships to gain and reallocate resources. Political frame assumptions are based on power, conflict, and coalitions:

- "The propositions of the political frame do not attribute politics to individual selfishness, myopia, or incompetence. They assert that interdependence, difference, scarcity, and power relations will inevitably produce political forces, regardless of the players. It is naive and romantic to hope that politics can be eliminated in organizations. [Leaders and managers] can, however, learn to understand and manage political processes."[75]
- This frame suggests that organizational goals are set through negotiations among members of coalitions. A typical organization has a confusing set of multiple goals, many of which are in conflict with one another.
- "The political perspective suggests that the goals, structure, and policies of an organization emerge from an ongoing process of bargaining and negotiation among the major interest groups. . . . the political view suggests that the exercise of power is a natural part of an ongoing contest."[76]

The symbolic construct or frame deals with meaning. This dimension gets at the heart of what organizational members feel about issues and events. Specifically, the meaning of the event is more important than the event. A symbol is something that stands for or means something else.

The symbolic frame seeks to interpret and illuminate the basic issues of meaning and faith that make symbols so powerful in every aspect of the human experience, including life in organizations. This frame presents a world that departs significantly from traditional canons of organizational theories: rationality, certainty, and linearity. It is based on the following unconventional assumptions:

- What is important is not the event but what it means.
- Events and meaning are loosely coupled.

TABLE 9.9 Bolman and Deal: Assessing Frame Selection

Question	Structural Frame	Human Resources Frame	Political Frame	Symbolic Frame
How important are commitment and motivation?	Unimportant	Important	?	Important
How important is the technical quality of the decision?	Important	?	Unimportant	Unimportant
How much ambiguity and uncertainty are present?	Low to moderate	Moderate	Moderate to high	High
How scarce are resources?	Moderately scarce	Moderately abundant to abundant	Scarce or increasingly scarce	Scarce to abundant
How much conflict and diversity are present?	Low to moderate	Moderate	Moderate to high	Moderate to high
Are we working in a top-down or bottom-up manner?	Top down	Top down	Bottom up	Top down or bottom up

Data from Bolman, L.G., & Deal, T. E. (1991). Reframing organizations: Artistry, choice, and leadership. San Francisco: Jossey-Bass, p. 326.

- Most significant events and processes in organizations are ambiguous and uncertain.
- The greater the ambiguity and uncertainty, the harder rationality and logical approaches to analysis, problem solving, and decision making are to use.
- Faced with ambiguity and uncertainty, humans create symbols to decrease confusion, increase predictability, and provide direction.
- Many organizational events and processes are important for what they express than for what they produce: secular myths, rituals, ceremonies, and sagas that help people find meaning and order in experiences.

Symbolic phenomena are particularly visible in organizations with unclear goals and uncertain technologies; in such organizations, most things are ambiguous. Who has power? What is success? Why was a decision made? What are the goals? The answers are often veiled in a fog of uncertainty.[77]

Utilization of the symbolic frame focuses on three types of concepts:

- Concepts of meaning.
- Dilemmas and paradoxes are everywhere.
- Organizations are full of questions that have no answers.
- Organizations are full of problems that cannot be solved.

- Organizations have many events that cannot be understood fully.
- Concepts of beliefs.
- Concepts of faith

The leader uses the following tools within the symbolic frame:

- Myths—to reconcile differences and resolve dilemmas.
- Fairy tales.
- Stories.
- Metaphors—to make confusion comprehensible.
- Scenarios and symbolic activities—to provide direction amidst uncertainty, to provide forums for socialization, to reduce anxiety and ambiguity, and to convey messages to external constituencies.
- Rituals.
- Ceremonies.
- Heroes, heroines, shamans, priests, and storytellers—to provide guides to and interpretations of what life in organizations really means.

Historically, all human cultures have used ritual and ceremony to create order, clarity, and predictability, particularly in dealing with issues or problems that are too complex, mysterious, or random to be controlled in any other way. We all create rituals to reduce uncertainty and anxiety.[78]

Important to the understanding of organizations and leading organizations, then, is culture. The four frames, when integrated, form a unique culture for each organization.

How do leaders effectively utilize Bolman and Deal's model? First we need to understand which actions leaders use in each frame. Let's look at each frame in an overview.

- Leaders do their homework.
- Leaders develop a new model of the relationship of structure, strategy, and environment for their organization.
- Leaders focus on implementation.
- Leaders continually experiment, evaluate, and adapt.

Though structural leadership has received less attention than it deserves, it can be a very powerful approach. Structural leaders lead through analysis and design rather than charisma and inspiration.

Their success depends on developing the right blueprint for the relationship between their organization's structure and strategy, as well as on finding ways to get that blueprint accepted.[79]

Human Resources Leadership

- Leaders believe in people and communicate that belief.
- Leaders are visible and accessible.
- Leaders empower: they increase participation, provide support, share information, and move decision making as far down the organization as possible.

Human-resource leadership has generated an enormous amount of attention. Until very recently, in fact, human resource concepts dominated the literature on managerial leadership. The human-resource literature has focused particularly on interpersonal relationships between superiors and subordinates and on the value of openness, sensitivity, and participation. When they are successful, human resource leaders become catalysts and servant-leaders.[80]

Political Leadership

- Leaders clarify what they want and what they can get.
- Leaders assess the distribution of power and interests.
- Leaders build linkages to other stakeholders.
- Leaders persuade first, negotiate second, and use coercion only as a last resort.

Effective political leaders are advocates who are clear about their agenda and sensitive to political reality and who build the alliances that they need to move their organization forward.[81]

Symbolic Leadership

- Leaders interpret experience (transactional [exchange theory] versus transforming [inspire to reach higher needs and purposes]).
- Leaders are transforming leaders who are visionaries.
- Leaders use symbols to capture attention.
- Leaders frame experience (i.e., reduce the ambiguity and uncertainty through symbolism).
- Leaders discover and communicate a vision.
- Leaders tell stories.

Symbolic leaders are artists, poets, or prophets who use symbols and stories to communicate a vision that builds faith and loyalty among an organization's employees and other stakeholders.[82]

"Wise leaders understand their own strengths, work to expand them, and build teams that together can provide leadership in all four modes—structural, political, human resource, and symbolic."[83] In essence, a situational leader is what is advocated. "Leadership is always an interactive process between the leader and the led. Organizations need leaders who can provide a persuasive and durable sense of purpose and direction, rooted deeply in human values and the human spirit.[84]

The prescriptive aspect of the Bolman and Deal model is summarized in Tables 9.8 and 9.9. Upon reviewing the tables, you may notice that this model has significant connections to other theories, such as media-richness theory.

Bolman and Deal propose that pluralism slows research by impeding communication, in that different disciplines and theories use different languages. Because they used interdisciplinary research on leadership to create their model, Bolman and Deal had to develop their own "language" and a common understanding for people to utilize the model. By doing so, these scholars reduced the "Tower of Babel" problem. When you apply, analyze, synthesize, and evaluate leadership theories and models in your own unique circumstances, it will be important to understand and create a common language (and be consistent).

Summary

How do you lead people and manage resources in the healthcare supply chain? How can you be an excellent leader within the context of healthcare supply chain operations? As presented, various practical theories and models serve as the basis for understanding the actions of leaders. Throughout the course of this chapter, we looked at several prominent leadership theories and models. Some of these models are stand-alone and work to explain industry phenomenon, and others are designed to be integrated into a personal leadership model. It is important to note that while some theories are more applicable in certain situations, there is no one "best" theory. Instead, theories function as a conceptual model, which describe concepts that may be abstract in nature. In some cases, it may even be appropriate to use parts of one theory, called constructs, with the constructs from another. What leadership framework or model would you develop to lead the healthcare supply chain? Several models were presented in this chapter to form a basis to facilitate your critical thinking on improving leadership in the healthcare supply chain. The models that have proven salience in healthcare and healthcare supply-chain operations were selected to focus that critical thinking for efficient, effective, and efficacious practice. What is your leadership model to lead the healthcare supply chain?

Sarah Says: A Student's Perspective

Leadership theories and their application to direct the supply chain are the focus of this chapter. In order to successfully lead in an organization, leaders must passionately believe in the vision of the organization. This will help when motivating others through this passion.

In order to gain support from subordinates, leaders must provide motivation and inspiration. Leadership should also focus on building trust with their subordinates. Trust is built over time and through honest interaction. Leaders must be consistent and moral agents.

Disclosure is an important aspect when trying to build successful relationships in the organization. Disclosure relates to the type of information you and the other person in the relationship share with each other. Disclosure is one factor that can help "measure" the strength of the relationship.

It is important to note, that there is no one "best theory." In some instances, parts, or constructs, of one theory may be used simultaneously with other constructs from different theories. It is up to the healthcare leader to decide which theory, or construct, works best for them personally and for their organization.

Discussion Questions

1. Describe the concepts, theories, and models of leadership presented in this chapter in the context of the healthcare supply chain.
2. Discuss leadership principles and how to implement those principles in leading healthcare supply-chain operations.
3. Relate, discuss, and provide areas of integration between the transformational leadership model and the dynamic culture leadership model.
4. Distinguish the differences between two or more leadership-related models.
5. Merge principles of leadership to develop a personal leadership framework for leading the healthcare supply-chain team.
6. Evaluate the benefits and limitations of three leadership models within a healthcare supply-chain context.

Exercises

1. Describe the concepts, theories, and models of leadership most important to you in the context of the healthcare supply chain.
2. Discuss leadership principles and how to implement those principles in leading healthcare supply-chain operations based on your "leadership model."
3. Relate, discuss, and provide two areas of integration between the transformational leadership model and the dynamic culture leadership model, and support your areas of integration.
4. Distinguish the differences between two or more leadership models in a one-page summary.
5. Merge principles of leadership to develop a personal leadership framework for leading the healthcare supply-chain team in two pages or less.
6. Evaluate the benefits and limitations of three leadership models within a healthcare supply-chain context.

Journal Items

Answer the following:

What leadership and management principles presented in the chapter would work best for leading the healthcare supply chain?

In one to two pages, what type of leadership model and management model (it is fine to create a synergistic model for yourself) would you utilize for leading people and managing resources in the healthcare supply chain?

References

1. A. P. Carnevale, *America and the new economy.* (Washington, DC: Department of Labor, 1991).

2. G. Yukl, *Leadership in organizations*, 3rd ed. (Englewood Cliffs, NJ: Prentice Hall, 1994), 193.

3. M. Sorcher and J. Brant, "Are you picking the right leaders?" *Harvard Business Review* (2002, February), 78.

4. T. L. Cooper, *The responsible administrator: An approach to ethics for the administrative role* (San Francisco: Jossey-Bass, 1998).

5. J. B. Rotter, Generalized expectancies for internal versus external control of reinforcement. *Psychological Monographs*, 80 (1966), 609.

6. D. Miller and J. Toulouse, "Chief executive personality and corporate strategy and structure in small firms." *Management Science*, 32, (1986), 1389–1409.

7. D. Miller, M. Kets de Vries, J. Toulouse, "Locus of control and its relationship to strategy, environment, and structure." *Academy of Management Journal*, 25, (1982), 237–253.

8. S. A. Beebe and J. T. Masterson, *Communicating in small groups: Principles and practices*, 5th ed. (New York: Addison-Wesley Educational Publishers, 1997).

9. L. Cicero and A. Pierro, Charismatic leadership and organizational outcomes: The mediating role of employees' work-group identification. *International Journal of Psychology*, 42, no. 5 (2007), 297–306.

10. E. A. Locke, "Toward a theory of task motivation and incentives." *Organizational Behavior and Human Performance*, (1968, May), 157–189.

11. E. A. Locke et al., "Goal setting and task performance: 1969–1980." *Psychological Bulletin*, 90, no. 1 (1981), 125–152.

12. E. A. Locke and G. P. Latham, Goal setting: A motivational technique that works! (Englewood Cliffs, NJ: Prentice-Hall, 1984).

13. T. L. Quick, *The manager's motivation desk book*. (New York: Wiley, 1985), 124.

14. Locke and Latham, Goal setting: A motivational technique that works!

15. Rosenbaum, B. L. (1982). How to motivate today's workers. New York: Wiley, p. 103.

16. Locke and Latham, Goal setting: A motivational technique that works!

17. E. A. Locke and A. A. Chesney, Relationships among goal difficulty, business strategies, and performance on a complex management simulation task. *Academy of Management Journal*, 34, no. 2 (1991), 400–424.

18. G. P. Latham and J. J. Baldes, The practical significance of Locke's theory of goal setting. *Journal of Applied Psychology*, (1975), 60, 122–138.

19. R. A. Baron, *Behavior in organizations: Understanding and managing the human side of work*. (Boston: Allyn & Bacon, 1983).

20. Motivation and management: Vroom's expectancy theory, *Value Based Management.net*, 2007, http://www.valuebasedmanagement.net/methods_vroom_expectancy_theory.html (accessed 27 Jul. 2009)

21. T. E. Harris, *Applied organizational communication: Perspectives, principles and pragmatics.* Hillsdale, (NJ: Lawrence Erlbaum Associates, 1993), 454.

22. Locke and Latham, Goal setting: A motivational technique that works!

23. A. J. Mento, E. A. Locke, and H. J. Klein, "Relationship of goal level to valence and instrumentality." *Journal of Applied Psychology*, 77, no. 4, (1992), 395–405.

24. G. R. Ledlow, "Conflict and interpersonal relations," in *Health organizations: Theory, behavior, and development*, ed. J. A. Johnson (Sudbury, MA: Jones and Bartlett, 2009), 158–163.

25. G. Yukl, *Leadership in organizations*, 3rd ed. (Englewood Cliffs, NJ: Prentice Hall, 1994), 193.

26. Beebe and Masterson, *Communicating in small groups*, 71

27. O'Hair, D., Friedrich, G. W., Wiemann, J. M., & Wiemann, M. O. (1997). Competent communication (2nd ed.). New York: St. Martin's Press.

28. Beebe and Masterson, *Communicating in small groups*

29. Beebe and Masterson, *Communicating in small groups*

30. Beebe and Masterson, *Communicating in small groups*

31. H. Mintzberg, *Mintzberg on management: Inside our strange world of organizations* (New York: Free Press, 1989).

32. Mintzberg, *Mintzberg on management.*

33. Obama going prime time to help ailing health initiative, *CBS Evening News*, (2009), http://www.cbsnews .com/blogs/2009/07/22/politics/politicalhotsheet /entry5179382.shtml (accessed 25 Jul. 2009)

34. Beebe and Masterson, *Communicating in small groups*, 3

35. L. P. Cusella, "Feedback, motivation, and performance," in *Handbook of organizational communication*, ed F. M. Jablin et al. (Newbury Park, CA: Sage 1987), 624–679.

36. Harris, *Applied organizational communication:* 454.

37. R. L. Daft, R. H. Lengel, and L. K. Trevino, "Message equivocality, media selection, and manager performance: Implications for information systems," *MIS Quarterly*, 11, no. 3, (1987), 355–366.

38. R. L. Daft, R. H. Lengel, "Organizational information requirements, media richness, and structural design, *Management Science*, 22, no. 5, (1986), 554–571.

39. R. L. Daft and J. Wiginton, Language and organization. *Academy of Management Review*, 4 no. 2, (1979). 179–191.

40. J., D'Ambra and R. E. Rice, "Multimethod approaches for the study of computer-mediated communication, equivocality, and media selection." *IEEE Transactions on Professional Communication*, 37, no. 4, (1994), 231–339.

41. Daft and Lengel, "Organizational information requirements," 557

42. Daft, Lengel, and Trevino, "Message equivocality, media selection, and manager performance."

43. S. E. Bryant, "he role of transformational and transactional leadership in creating, sharing and exploiting organizational knowledge." *Journal of Leadership & Organizational Studies*, 9, no. 4, (2003, Spring), 32–45.

44. J. Burns, *Leadership* (New York: Harper & Row, 1978).

45. B. A. Tucker and R. F. Russell, The influence of transformational leadership. *Journal of Leadership & Organizational Studies*, (2004, March 22), http://goliath .ecnext.com/coms2/summary_0199-2375126_ITM (accessed 16 Jun. 2009).

46. B. Bass, *Bass & Stogdill's handbook of leadership: Theory, research and managerial applications*, 3rd ed. (New York: Free Press, 1990), p. 38.

47. G. Yukl, *Leadership in organizations*, 3rd ed. (Englewood Cliffs, NJ: Prentice Hall, 1994), 350.

48. R. A. Baron, *Behavior in organizations: Understanding and managing the human side of work.* (Boston: Allyn & Bacon, 1983).

49. http://www.12manage.com/methods_greenleaf _servant_leadership.html (accessed 11 Jul. 2009).

50. Harris, *Applied organizational communication:* 454.

51. Locke and Latham, Goal setting: A motivational technique that works!

52. B. S. Savic, and M. Pagon, "Individual involvement in health care organizations: Differences between professional groups, leaders, and employees." *Stress & Health: Journal of the International Society for the Investigation of Stress*, 24,no. 1, (2008), 71–84; Valter Moreno, Mateus Hickman, and Flavia Cavazotte, "Effects of leader intelligence, personality and emotional intelligence on transformational leadership and managerial performance." *Leadership Quarterly*, 23, no. 3 (2012).

53. G. Yukl, *Leadership in organizations*, 3rd ed. (Englewood Cliffs, NJ: Prentice Hall, 1994), 256. Marc H. Anderson and Peter Y.T. Sun, "Civic capacity: Building on transformational leadership to explain successful integrative public leadership." *Leadership Quarterly*, 23, no, 3 (2012).

54. Bass, *Bass & Stogdill's handbook of leadership*, 38

55. G. Fairholm, *The techniques of inner leadership: Making inner leadership work* (Westport, CT: Praeger, 2003).

56. B. Bass, *Transformational leadership: Industrial, military, and educational impact.* (Mahwah, NJ: Lawrence Erlbaum Associates, 1998).

57. Yukl, G. (1994). *Leadership in organizations* (3rd ed.). Englewood Cliffs, NJ: Prentice Hall, p. 256.

58. Bass, *Bass & Stogdill's handbook of leadership*, 38

59. Yukl, G. (1994). *Leadership in organizations* (3rd ed.). Englewood Cliffs, NJ: Prentice Hall, p. 352.

60. G. Ledlow, N. Coppola, and M. Cwiek, "Leadership and Transformation." *Organizational theory, behavior and* In *Organizational theory, behavior and development*, ed. J. A. Johnson (Sudbury, MA: Jones and Bartlett, 2008), 193–212.

61. G. Ledlow, M. Cwiek, and J. Johnson, "Dynamic culture leadership: Effective leader as both scientist and artist." Global Business and Technology Association (GBATA) International Conference; *Beyond Boundaries: Challenges of Leadership, Innovation, Integration and Technology*, eds N. Delener & C-n. Chao (2002), 694–740. First reported in the GBATA publication.

62. M. Busch, & C. Hostetter, "Examining organizational learning for application in human service organizations." *Administration in Social Work*, 33 no. 3 (2009), 297–318.

63. J. Conger and G. Toegel, "A story of missed opportunities: Qualitative methods for leadership research and practice," in *Grounding leadership theory and research: Issues, perspectives, and methods*, eds. K. W. Parry and J. R. Meindl (Greenwich, CT: Information Age Publishing, 2002), 175–197.

64. M., Jelinek, and J. A. Litterer, "Toward entrepreneurial organizations: Meeting ambiguity with engagement." *Entrepreneurship: Theory and Practice*, 19, no. 3, (1995), 137–169. 168

65. E. H. Schein, *The corporate culture survival guide: Sense and nonsense about culture change.* (San Francisco, CA: Jossey-Bass, 1999).

66. Yukl, G. (1994). *Leadership in organizations* (3rd ed.). Englewood Cliffs, NJ: Prentice Hall, p. 355.

67. Schein, *The corporate culture survival guide.*

68. Schein, *The corporate culture survival guide.*

69. Friesen, M., & Johnson, J. (1995). *The success paradigm.* London: Quorum Books.

70. Harris, *Applied organizational communication:* 454.

71. Locke and Latham, Goal setting: A motivational technique that works!

72. L. G. Bolman and T. E. Deal, *Reframing organizations: Artistry, choice, and leadership.* (San Francisco: Jossey-Bass 1991), 121–122.

73. Bolman and Deal, *Reframing organizations*, 152–153.

74. Fairholm, *The techniques of inner leadership.*

75. Bass, *Transformational leadership: Industrial, military, and educational impact.*

76. G. Yukl, *Leadership in organizations*, 3rd ed. (Englewood Cliffs, NJ: Prentice Hall, 1994), 256.

77. Bolman and Deal, *Reframing organizations*, 244–245.

78. G. Yukl, *Leadership in organizations*, 3rd ed. (Englewood Cliffs, NJ: Prentice Hall, 1994), 352.

79. Bolman and Deal, *Reframing organizations*, 434.

80. Bolman and Deal, *Reframing organizations*, 435.

81. Bolman and Deal, *Reframing organizations*, 445.

82. Bolman and Deal, *Reframing organizations*, 445.

83. Bolman and Deal, *Reframing organizations*, 445.

84. Bolman and Deal, *Reframing organizations*, 448–449.

CHAPTER 10

BUILDING A CULTURE OF HEALTHCARE SUPPLY-CHAIN EXCELLENCE: LEADING, PLANNING, MANAGING, DECIDING, AND LEARNING

LEARNING OBJECTIVES

1. Describe the concepts and models of planning and decision making in the context of the healthcare supply chain.
2. Discuss the importance of situational factors (trends, environmental issues, technology, regulatory compliance, etc.) in the planning process and how leadership principles, metrics, and improvement tenets can be used to positively impact the organizational culture of healthcare supply-chain operations.
3. Relate, discuss, and provide areas of integration between planning and decision making amid continuous operations of the healthcare supply chain to include the use of metrics and improvement strategies.
4. Distinguish the differences between planning and contingency planning.
5. Merge principles of leadership, planning, and decision making to develop a personal plan for operating in a fast-paced healthcare supply-chain environment.
6. Evaluate the benefits for organizational operations with a solid planning process and standing operating procedures as part of the healthcare supply-chain culture to include outside sales representatives.

Introduction

Planning and decision making are essential to efficient, effective, and efficacious healthcare supply-chain operations and strategies. Leaders and managers must structure and facilitate plans that integrate well with the healthcare organization's strategic plan and must make consistent decisions in alignment with those plans. Creating standing operating procedures for routine and consistent operations of the supply chain allows leaders and managers to spread the operational culture at all levels of the supply-chain enterprise. Contingency planning, that is planning for the unexpected and unwanted such as natural and man-made disasters, is necessary for organizational longevity and survival during chaotic and stressful situations.

Will intermediated or dis-intermediated aspects of the supply chain work best for medical and surgical items or pharmaceutical items, considering the healthcare organization's strategic plan? How does technology impact planning and operational as well as strategic decisions? This chapter provides an overview of planning, improvement strategies, metrics, regulatory compliance, and decision making. These constructs should be reviewed and placed in context for integration into the supply chain's overall operational plan for providing the "technology of care" to the caregivers.

How Are You Leading and Managing the Healthcare Supply-Chain?

The "big" picture is a great starting point for our discussion on planning. Healthcare spending in the United States is projected to reach $4.8 trillion by 2021 according to the Centers for Medicare and Medicaid Services.[1] Second only to labor costs, the healthcare supply chain is a much overlooked source of huge expense for every healthcare organization. In addition to increased expenses, there are several areas driving change as identified by the Pain in the (Supply) Chain survey.

Figure 10.1 shows there are many changes on the horizon for healthcare supply-chain professionals. In order to meet these and future challenges, there are several strategies for efficiently managing the supply chain. Key to meeting future challenges is the controlling of costs within the supply chain. Even though controlling cost is key to meeting challenges such as regulatory compliance, concerns about cost management have decreased significantly since

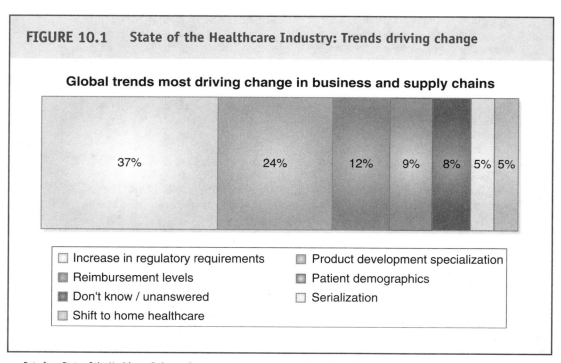

FIGURE 10.1   State of the Healthcare Industry: Trends driving change

Global trends most driving change in business and supply chains

| 37% | 24% | 12% | 9% | 8% | 5% | 5% |

☐ Increase in regulatory requirements   ▨ Product development specialization
▨ Reimbursement levels   ▨ Patient demographics
■ Don't know / unanswered   ☐ Serialization
▨ Shift to home healthcare

Data from State of the Healthcare Industry: Cost management concerns (n.d.). Retrieved from http://thenewlogistics.ups.com/healthcare /healthcare-survey-results/UPS-PITC-Executive-Summary-North-America.pdf, p.7 (accessed 23 Mar. 2015).

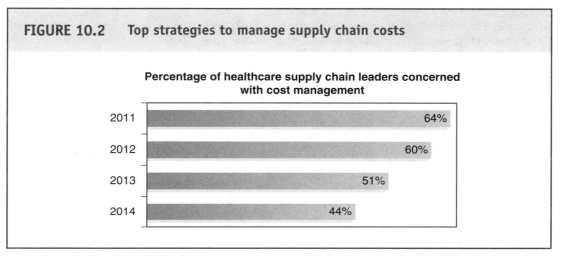

FIGURE 10.2   **Top strategies to manage supply chain costs**

Percentage of healthcare supply chain leaders concerned with cost management

Year	Percentage
2011	64%
2012	60%
2013	51%
2014	44%

Data from State of the Healthcare Industry: Cost management concerns (n.d.). Retrieved from http://thenewlogistics.ups.com/healthcare/healthcare-survey-results/UPS-PITC-Executive-Summary-North-America.pdf, p.7 (accessed 23 Mar. 2015).

2011.[2] One thought as to the acceptance of these increased costs is that supply-chain executives are slowly accepting that cost constraints are here to stay. Another possibility is that new, innovative methods to control cost are being successfully implemented.[3] Some of the leading strategies for controlling supply-chain costs are listed in **figure 10.2**.

Logistics and distribution partnerships include options like vendor-managed inventory and participating in a group purchasing organization, which are discussed later in the chapter.

Continued investment in information technology has the potential to dramatically reduce costs if done appropriately. However, there are associated pitfalls such as incorrectly utilizing technology or using that technology to track erroneous data.

Outsourcing transportation management can save healthcare organizations a significant amount of money depending on the type and amount of transporting done by the organization. These choices should be made with the mission, vision, and strategy of the organization in mind.

Managing Regulatory Compliance

Managing regulatory compliance is a top concern for healthcare supply-chain professionals according to a study by UPS.[4] Interestingly, regulatory compliance concerns have ranked as the number one issue for survey respondents three years in a row. The continued concern among supply-chain executives is also reflected in another result of the survey: 78% of those surveyed said regulatory compliance and increasing regulation are a top trend driving both business and supply-chain changes.[5]

In the 1990s regulatory compliance on the supply chain was minimal. However, the FDA began to increase oversight after a series of high-profile recalls, removing items from the market that were damaged after being shipped from the manufacturer. The result of this oversight was an in-depth assessment of the distribution practices of medical devices and other items. These assessments resulted in regulatory increases designed to increase consumer safety.[6]

Some healthcare organizations are having success in addressing regulatory requirements through partnering with other organizations that have expertise in regulatory compliance. Of supply-chain executives surveyed by UPS, only 12% said that they were happy with their companies' performance in meeting regulatory challenges.

Metrics

Metrics are used to drive performance within an organization. A lack of informative, unified metrics is often cited as a common pitfall of supply-chain management.[7] The performance of the supply-chain depends on the joint performance of all aspects of the supply chain. However, even in a vertically integrated supply chain, each site is typically managed in a fairly autonomous way. As such, each site has its own objectives and mission, which may not always be completely aligned with the goals of the organization as a whole. The end result is that each site in the supply chain is striving to meet individual goals that, when met, may achieve suboptimal results for the chain as a whole due to created inefficiencies.[8]

Another concern is that supply-chain managers select the correct metrics to measure. As we have seen, supply-chain management, particularly in healthcare, is extremely complex. This complexity, coupled with the use of technology, produces massive amounts of data – all of which can be tracked, but should it be? The answer is no. Selecting appropriate metrics is necessary for understanding the advantages, disadvantages, and limitations of the supply chain.[9] Metrics can be both qualitative and quantitative. Metrics can be focused on the individual unit or the supply chain as a whole. While there are several tools for selecting and appropriately displaying metrics, we will focus on one of the most popular: the balanced scorecard.

The concept of the balanced scorecard was introduced in the early 1990s by Kaplan and Norton as a method for communicating strategy.[10] In a typical implementation, metrics are selected for the scorecard that supports the mission and vision of the organization. These metrics are further supported by subsequent "lower level" scorecards that track subcomponents of the larger metrics on the balanced scorecard. An example of this is a healthcare organization that has the reduction of patient readmission rates as part of its core strategy. The balanced scorecard may show the total readmission rate and the lower level scorecard may have readmission rates broken down by condition. In a supply-chain context, the balanced scorecard may track restock times for unit storage locations. The lower level scorecard may display individual metrics such as availability of supplies in central storage or how often the supply care is returned to the correct location. What metrics should you utilize to lead the healthcare supply chain?

Warehousing Education and Research Council (WERC) Data

WERC's mission statement is "To provide leadership in the warehousing/distribution field in its evolving role in the supply chain, to advance the art and science of warehousing management, and to enhance individual development." WERC is the recognized leader in education and research for the warehousing and logistics management field and its role in the supply chain. WERC focuses on advancing the art and science of distribution by helping warehousing professionals be more effective and efficient.

As part of this mission WERC has sponsored a study on distribution metrics for over a dozen years. The DC Measures Study is designed to benchmark performance with DCs and share best practices so the industry can be more efficient. The study captures forty-five key operational metrics that are close to the heart of most distribution center professionals. The measures have been grouped into five balanced sets – customer, operational, financial, capacity/quality, and employee/safety – plus the additional sets related to perfect order and cash-to-cash cycle measurement.

TABLE 10.1   **Healthcare Supply Chain Metrics**

Healthcare Supply-Chain Metric	Numeric	Calculation/ Formula	Target	Variance (add and subtract to target for range)	Definition	Importance
Inventory Turnover Rate	#	Total annual expense on stock items / average inventory value in stock.	>15	range : +8 to –2%	Measures the capital invested in storing goods and in the value of those goods but should be evaluated in the context of reordering and restocking and the risk of stock outs.	Inventory is an asset that should be utilized often since dollars tied into inventory represent funds not available for other purposes.
Contract Utilization Rate	%	Amount of dollar value in purchases using a valid contract / Amount of total dollar value of all purchases × 100	>79%	range: +11 to –4%	Measures the percentage of supply-chain item spending for contracted items as compared to total supply-chain purchases.	Supplies purchased utilizing a valid contract from a vendor promote standardization, typically cost less and promote contract compliance and may impact contract compliance discounts or rebates and contract satisfaction.
Total Supply Cost per Adjusted Case Mix Indexed Discharge	$	Total Supply Cost/Total number of Adjusted Discharges (CMI weighted)	$853.37	$507.98	Measures the medical/surgical, pharmaceutical and other supplies cost per adjusted patient discharges weighted by Case Mix Index	This metric establishes the non-labor expense by cost per adjusted patient discharge as weighted by all payer case mix index and represents price, utilization and technology impacts on non-labor costs of care.

(continued)

TABLE 10.1 Healthcare Supply Chain Metrics (Continued)

Healthcare Supply-Chain Metric	Numeric	Calculation/ Formula	Target	Variance (add and subtract to target for range)	Definition	Importance
Medical/ Surgical Supply Cost per Adjusted Case Mix Indexed Discharge	$	Medical/ Surgical Supply Cost/Total number of Adjusted Discharges (CMI weighted)	$108.00	$82.00	Measures the medical/surgical supplies cost per adjusted patient discharges weighted by Case Mix Index	This metric establishes the non-labor expense attributed to medical/ surgical supplies by cost per adjusted patient discharge as weighted by all payer case mix index and represents price, utilization and technology impacts on non-labor costs of care.
Pharmaceutical Supply Cost per Adjusted Case Mix Indexed Discharge	$	Pharmaceutical Supply Cost/Total number of Adjusted Discharges (CMI weighted)	$744.14	$425.00	Measures the pharmaceutical supplies cost per adjusted patient discharges weighted by Case Mix Index	This metric establishes the non-labor expense attributed to pharmaceuticals by cost per adjusted patient discharge as weighted by all payer case mix index and represents price, utilization and technology impacts on non-labor costs of care.

Metric	Unit	Calculation	BM	BM	Measures	Description
Other Supply Cost per Adjusted Case Mix Indexed Discharge	$	Other Supply Cost/Total number of Adjusted Discharges (CMI weighted)	$1.22	$0.98	Measures the other supplies cost per adjusted patient discharges weighted by Case Mix Index	This metric establishes the non-labor expense attributed by other supplies by cost per adjusted patient discharge as weighted by all payer case mix index and represents price, utilization and technology impacts on non-labor costs of care.
Supply Charge Capture Rate	%	Total Dollar value of supplies charged to a patient/total dollar value of all supplies purchased × 100	Organization Specific	Organization Specific	Measures the percentage of supply dollars captured in a patient charge as compared to total supply dollars purchased	This ratio measures the effectiveness of supply charge capture processes.
Supply Attribution Value	$	(Standard supply cost per DRG x number of patients in each DRG) / total number of inpatients in all DRGs	Must Establish BM	Based on BM	Measures the supply cost intensity for the patient population of a particular hospital (using Supply costs as weighting similar to CMI weighting)	This metric indicates the intensity of supplies a facility is using and is then used to create better benchmark groupings. Additionally, the same standard supply costs per DRG that are used to calculate the SAV are used to calculate a predicted total supply spend.

(continued)

TABLE 10.1   Healthcare Supply Chain Metrics (Continued)

Healthcare Supply-Chain Metric	Numeric	Calculation/ Formula	Target	Variance (add and subtract to target for range)	Definition	Importance
Stock Inventory Fill Rate	%	Number of stock item requisition lines filled complete the first time/ Number of total stock item requisitions × 100	>96%	2%	Measures the stock inventory (item master, stock and standard item) fill rate for each supply location.	This ratio measures the level of customer service provided by a stock inventory location where a higher fill rate ratio indicates a higher level of service with a trade-off of either a higher stock inventory value and storage cost, management cost or more intense management of time sequencing of the stock line.
Pharmacy Inventory Fill Rate	%	Number of pharmaceutical stock item requisition lines filled complete the first time/ Number of total pharmaceutical stock item requisitions × 100	>97%	1%	Measures the pharmaceutical stock inventory (item master, stock and standard item) fill rate for each supply location.	This ratio measures the level of customer service provided by a pharmaceutical stock inventory location where a higher fill rate ratio indicates a higher level of service with a trade-off of either a higher pharmaceutical stock inventory value and storage cost, management cost or more intense management of time sequencing of the stock line.

Delivery Date Accuracy	%	Number of purchase order line delivery date item deliveries on or before expected delivery date/total number of purchase order delivery lines × 100	>85%	2%	Measures the item delivery performance to customers on time or before time as compared to the required or expected delivery date as compared by line level on purchase orders.	This ratio measures the vendor delivery performance for on time or before time deliveries of items by comparing the actual delivery date of a purchase order line to the required or expected delivery date
Purchase Order Accuracy	%	Number of discrepant purchase order lines / total number of purchase order lines × 100	<3%	1%	Measures the percentage of discrepant purchase order lines (lines with errors or are non-compliant) as compared to total invoiced purchase order lines. Most discrepancies are a result of pricing, missing data, or receiving error problems.	This ratio is used to assess the success of matching invoices to the proper purchase order, compliance with contract pricing in the item master and vendor-master files, and the accuracy of receiving processes.
Catalog Purchase Order Rate	%	Number of purchase order lines generated via catalog / total number of purchase order lines generated × 100	>89%	2%	Measures the percentage of purchase order lines created by the electronic catalog for regular items	A non-catalog item is a special order item that is not in inventory or available in the item master resulting in more intervention and effort by the requester and buyer and can negatively impact contract compliance.

(continued)

TABLE 10.1 Healthcare Supply Chain Metrics (Continued)

Healthcare Supply-Chain Metric	Numeric	Calculation/ Formula	Target	Variance (add and subtract to target for range)	Definition	Importance
PAR or Cart Stock Out Rate	%	Total number of Stock Outs at PAR or Cart Level / Total number of Replenishments × 100	>3%	1%	Measures the ability to get the right supply to the right location for patient care purposes	This metric maintains emphasis on supply chain support of the patient care system
PAR or Cart Fill Rate	%	Number of Stock items replenished at the PAR or cart level / Total number of items ordered by an end user customer × 100	>97%	1%	Measures the supply chain operation's ability to support the clinician and the patient care mission for stock items	This measure focusses on meeting patient and clinician needs and demands for stock items.
Annual Purchase Order Cost	$	Annual operating expense for supply chain operation and management / Total number of Annual Purchase Orders	Est BM	Based on BM	Measures the efficiency of the supply chain operation and management by the number of purchase orders	This cost maintains focus on supply chain operation and management efficiency.

Metric	Unit	Formula			Measures	Description
Average Lines per Purchase Order	#	Total number of Purchase Order Lines Issued / Total number of Purchase Orders	20	5	Measures the purchasing process efficiency and can impact number of invoices processed	This measure intends to improve the efficiency of the purchase order process and reduce the number of invoices by increasing the number of Purchase Order Lines for Purchase Order and per Invoice
Electronic Requisitions Rate	%	Number of Requisitions Electronically Sent to Purchasing Function / Total number of Requisitions × 100	Est BM	Based on BM	Measures the use of internal information systems to leverage efficiencies.	This metric focuses on the time spent processing requisitions manually.
Electronic Purchase Order Rate	%	Number of Purchase Orders Sent Electronically / Total number of Purchase Orders × 100	Est BM	Based on BM	Measures the electronic purchase order rate for purposes of efficiency	This measure assesses the use of information systems utilization in the purchasing function intent on reducing purchasing process costs to both the supply chain and suppliers or vendors.

(continued)

TABLE 10.1   Healthcare Supply Chain Metrics (Continued)

Healthcare Supply-Chain Metric	Numeric	Calculation/ Formula	Target	Variance (add and subtract to target for range)	Definition	Importance
Electronic Funds Transfer (EFT) Paid Invoices Rate	%	Number of Invoices Paid Electronically / Total number of Invoices × 100	Est BM	Based on BM	Measures the utilization of information systems and EFT for supply transactions with suppliers and vendors	This metric intends to illustrate improvement to supplier relationships and reduction of costs associated with paying invoices while improving cash flow management.
Invoice Pay Compliance Rate	%	Number of Invoices Paid within Agreed Contract Terms / Total number of Invoices paid × 100	>97%	1%	Measures the invoice pay processes of the organization and the potential to avoid late payment add on charges and taking advantage of discounts while maintaining good supplier and vendor relations	This metric maintains focus on avoiding late payment charges and taking advantage of on time or early pay discounts while ensuring good supplier and vendor relationships.
Supply Charge Capture Value	$	Total Dollar value of supplies charged to a patient	Organization Specific	Organization Specific	Measures the total dollar value of supply charge capture efforts.	Supply charge capture success and accuracy positively impacts the financial success of the organization.

Supply Charge Capture Yield	%	Total Dollar value of reimbursement realized / Total Dollar value of supplies charged to a patient × 100	>39%	5%	Measures the reimbursement yield rate realized from supply charge capture efforts.	Supply charge capture success and accuracy positively impacts the financial success of the organization.
Automated Purchase Order Rate	%	Number of automated regular purchase orders/total number of regular purchase orders × 100	>59%	5%	Measures the percentage of line items ordered on a purchase order through automated means (via EDI or automatic fax) for regular orders that require no human intervention	This ratio evaluates the information system capabilities and leverage utilized by the organization and thus reducing labor resources
Purchase Order Rate Per Supplier	#	Total number of Purchase Orders / Number of Suppliers or Vendors	Est BM	Based on BM	Measures the transactional volume per supplier or vendor.	This measure assists in identifying and evaluating large transactional volumes of specific supplies and/or vendors to find opportunities for supply item and supplier and / or vendor compression and to reduce the number of Purchase Orders Issued.

(continued)

TABLE 10.1   Healthcare Supply Chain Metrics (Continued)

Healthcare Supply-Chain Metric	Numeric	Calculation/ Formula	Target	Variance (add and subtract to target for range)	Definition	Importance
Low Dollar Value Purchase Order Rate	%	Number of Low Value Purchase Order Transactions (under $100 or $200 or $300) / Total number of Purchase Orders × 100	>5%	2%	Measures the amount of small purchases within the supply chain process.	This ratio focuses on the ability to use alternative purchasing methods (unit credit cards and purchasing cards) for low value purchases to remove the added overhead supply chain cost from low value purchases.
Item Master Growth Rate	%	Total number of items added to an organization's item master file over the past year / Total number of items on the organization's item master file at the start of the year assessed × 100	Organization Specific	Organization Specific	Measures the expansion of the items on the organization's item master file	This metric gauges the management of the item master file and the expansion of the purchasing capability to include new products and suppliers

Metric	Unit	Calculation	Target	Measures	Description
Item Master Contraction Rate	%	Total number of active items deleted from the organization's item master file over one year / Total number of items on the organization's item master file at the start of the year assessed × 100	Organization Specific	Measures the contraction/reduction of the items on the organization's item master file	This metric gauges the management of the item master file and the contraction of the file to remove inactive and obsolete items
Customer Awareness Rate	%	Total number of active end users or customers with completed supply chain and commercial awareness training / Total number of active end users or customers × 100	>95%	2%	Measures the end user/customer training rate for assessment of efficiency and commercial vendor compliance in the organization	This measure assesses the ability or potential to manage supplier interactions and requisition to purchase order processes.
Number of Active Suppliers	#	Number of active suppliers and vendors where at least one transaction was processed	Organization Specific	Measures the number of suppliers and vendors of the organization	This metric shows the landscape and complexity of suppliers and vendors of the organization

How to Lead People and Manage Resources

The leader's application of empirically based skill tools and abilities is applicable to small groups and to all members of the entire organization. Strategies for leaders in effecting planning and situational assessment, decision making, and training that result in positive outcomes are addressed; these strategies, in turn, result in practical leadership actions and applications based in "active" leadership.

Planning

Planning is an essential leadership skill that requires knowledge about planning and the ability to structure and develop a system of planning. Planning is an essential and critical component, such as in palliative care programs, to successful leadership; effective planning and consistent leadership practice are vital to linking the clinical and administrative domains.[11] Health leaders plan at all levels of an organization. Specifically, they plan the operational actions necessary within their area of responsibility to implement the senior leadership team's strategic or operational plans. Health leaders who can understand, apply, and evaluate planning will have advantages over those who haphazardly plan or fail to plan. Starting from the highest level health organizational strategic and operational plans, leaders at subordinate levels should (and many say "must") take the high-level plans and develop strategies and operational practices that achieve the goals and objectives of the high-level plans at their level (the subordinate level) of the organization. Each level of the organization should (again, many say "must") have goals and objectives, measureable objectives with time lines and accountable "owners," that contribute to the mission and in achieving the vision of the health organization. Wise leaders at all levels of the organization should ("must") acquire the strategic and operational plans of the organization and seek counsel with their supervisory leader on how to best contribute to the organization's mission in vision at the level of their leadership. Wise leaders also hold themselves accountable to fulfill goals and objectives at their level and report

results regularly (monthly, quarterly, etc.) to those they lead and those they report to in the leadership hierarchy.

For some scholars, such as Yukl, planning is a step in decision making.[12] For others, planning is a cultural imperative and a method for leaders to guide the organization to its most effective, efficient, and efficacious outcomes.[13,14] Planning occurs formally, informally, strategically (how the organization can best serve its purpose in the external environment), and operationally (how the internal capabilities and resources of an organization can be used effectively, efficiently, and efficaciously to achieve the strategies and goals of the organization as documented in the strategic plan).

A set of basic definitions will assist in understanding the differences in the term "planning":

- Planning is a process that uses macro- and micro-environmental factors and internal information to engage stakeholders to create a framework, template, and outline for section, branch, or organizational success. Planning can be strategic, operational, or a combination of both.
- Strategic planning is concerned with finding the best future for the organization and determining how the organization will evolve to realize that future. It is a stream of organizational decisions focused in a specific direction based on organizational values, strategies, and goals. The focus is on external considerations and how the organization can best serve the external markets' expectations, demands, and needs.
- Operational planning is about finding the best methods, processes, and systems to accomplish the mission/purpose, strategies, goals, and objectives of the organization in the most effective, efficient, and efficacious way possible. The focus in operational planning concerns internal resources, systems, processes, methods, and considerations.

Planning is vital to the survival of the organization. Indeed, creating a plan is an investment in improving the organization. Improvement is realized through internal change and evolution. Developing and focusing the organization to best meet the needs and demands of its customers and others (stakeholders) that affect the organization lies at the heart of planning. Because the environment, technology, information, people, financing, and governmental policies and laws are constantly changing, the organization itself must evolve to survive, succeed, and prosper. Planning is a journey—but this journey must have a destination, and it must be planned. In other words, it is a planned journey forward in time. In that light, planning includes both a process (developing and achieving goals and objectives) and an outcome (the plan itself).

Planning is a process. This process involves moving an organization along a predetermined path based on its values. Similar to the decisions involved in planning a real-world trip (e.g., which road to take, which stops to make, and who will drive), the organizational planning process entails deciding which goals are important to the organization and which objectives must be met to reach those goals.

Planning has an outcome. This outcome paves the way to a better future state based on organizational values and the external environment. Improving effectiveness, efficiency, efficacy, customer satisfaction, employee satisfaction, financial performance, and many other possible improvements are a part of moving the organization to reach a better future state.

The desired future state constitutes the vision of the organization; the vision is what the combined staff of the organization strive to achieve. If you know where you are going, then planning the trip and getting commitment from your staff becomes much easier. Also, organizational resources (including your energy and time) can be devoted to reaching set goals and having a positive outcome (turning the vision of your organization into a reality).

In this light, the process comprises a journey that must be planned knowing that different ways of doing things, different stops, and different issues will be encountered along the way. The vision represents the final destination. The destination must be determined and the journey must be planned. As a health leader, you are critical in determining the vision (outcome/destination) and the process (journey/goals and objectives) that will ensure the organization reaches its intended vision.

For all health organizations, mergers, departmental restructuring, implementation of new technologies, and market changes may indicate a need for the organization to develop a strategic plan to support its overall plan. Strategic planning can be described as an organizational planning process that analyzes the current situation of an organization and forecasts how the organization will change or evolve over a specified period of time. The health leader is an integral part of a successful strategic plan. Strategic planning on the part of an organization and its leaders require both thought and action, however. In health organizations, strategic thought includes the "ideas, reasons, and processes for changing the future state of your organization."[15] Within the component of strategic thought exists the vision, intent, and planning affecting the path that the organization takes in moving toward its future.

If the strategic plan is a road map, then the organizational vision is the final destination, describing "where the organization is going." The vision depicts a perfect situation in which the future destination can be obtained. The health leader must energize his or her followers to "buy into" the vision so that the organization can begin its strategic journey on the correct path. The strategic vision must be tested and retested to ensure that it has won "buy-in" from all stakeholders (both external and internal).

A vision may require many drafts and revisions to ensure that the needs of all stakeholders are met. In the dynamic world of the health industry, leaders need to recognize that the strategic vision should be tangible. To be tangible, the vision should be stated in the form of concrete ideals rather than using generalizations, should identify a direct relationship between the organizational values and culture to the future direction of the organization, and should communicate a unique future to stakeholders.[16]

Once an organizational vision is developed, intent must be established. Intent describes how the organization will be affected if change does not occur. Organizational leaders must outline how these "impacts" or "crises" could potentially influence the viability of the organization. Examples of crises might include market changes, technological advances that cause older technology to become obsolete, personnel shortages, and decreased reimbursement from payers. From the roadmap perspective, the wrong intent is analogous to driving in the wrong direction without a roadmap.

Once the vision and intent have been established, the strategic plan needs to be developed; that is, from the road map perspective, the quickest, most efficient route must be drawn to the final destination (i.e., the vision). One can assume that a good plan will lead to an effective outcome—namely, achieving the vision.

Strategic thought is followed by the component of tactical action, which includes commitment, execution, and accountability. In the health industry, tactical action encompasses the feelings, practices, and metrics for changing the future state of the organization.[17] If strategic thought is the plan for the journey to reach the final destination, then tactical action is the journey itself, including the mechanism for getting there. Tactical action requires commitment within the organization, execution of the plan, and accountability for this effort within organizational leadership.

Commitment, like the strategic vision, requires "buy-in" by the organization and its internal and external stakeholders. It involves a relationship between organizational leaders and followers; in contrast, each party has a clear understanding of the strategic vision and his or her role in reaching this vision. Without commitment on all levels, it will be impossible to achieve the strategic vision effectively and efficiently. From a leadership perspective, a leader can foster commitment within his or her team by serving as a model and demonstrating a strong commitment to the plan and vision. A leader cannot expect to achieve buy-in from followers if he or she has not fully committed to the vision.

During the execution phase of the strategic plan, each team member performs his or her assigned duty. Without a strong, unified commitment, execution of the plan will be a dismal failure. It is the leader's responsibility to enhance motivation and maintain commitment within the team, particularly when team members encounter obstacles. The health leader must be supportive of his or her team members, supporting them by providing them with the needed skills, equipment, and materials to effectively carry out their roles in the plan. In many ways, the health leader's effort in this phase echoes the precepts of House's path–goal theory.

Leaders and followers require consistent feedback about performance during execution of the plan. To ensure that they receive this information, measures must be put in place to gauge successes (or lack thereof) during this time. Successes should be acknowledged between leaders and followers. After all, employees want to know that the plan is working correctly. Lack of success should be analyzed and modified to determine inconsistencies within the execution of the plan.

The Leader's Role in Planning

Most people look for leaders who have a vision and someone who can direct them in the path of the mission. There can be many leaders within a single organization, and each leader will have a vision for his or her own tasks or responsibilities. The morale of the organization can sometimes depend on the attitudes espoused by visionaries of the organization. Staff members of an organization look for the visionaries to lead by example. In planning, leadership should come from within the organization; the effort should be exciting, where followers are excited to follow. Health leaders provide the structure, process, macro-direction, shared outcome for all stakeholders, motivation, accountability, influence, obstacle removal, resources, and persistence in the overall effort of directing, staffing, organizing, controlling, and rewarding.

Planning is the fundamental function of leadership from which all other outcomes are derived.

The first step in planning is establishing the organizational situational assessment; the vision, mission, strategies, goals, objectives, and action steps are then developed. Without this structure and signposts as first steps, the organization cannot move forward.

The vision provides the motivational guidance for the organization and typically is defined and promoted by senior leadership. It explains how the organization intends to achieve its goals, whereas the mission defines why the organization pursues the goals it does. Both vision and mission are "directional strategies."

The mission statement is the organization's reason for being. It provides guidance in decision making as well, ensuring that the organization stays on the track that its leaders have predetermined. From the mission statement, strategies to achieve the mission and, ultimately, the vision are devised. Goals are broad statements of direction that come from strategies. This multilevel approach focuses and narrows effort for each section within the health organization. Objectives, in pursuit of achieving goals, are very specific.

Goals further refine the strategies focused on the mission. They are expected to be general, observable, challenging, and untimed.[18] Goals are general in nature; in contrast, objectives are highly specific. Notably, different perspectives often switch goals with objectives and objectives with goals. Whatever framework you select for your organization, try to be consistent. It is not important if goals are at a higher level than objectives, or vice versa; what matters is the process of planning—a planning and execution culture should grow and mature in your health organization. Erven promotes objective development within the "SMART" framework; to be SMART, objectives must be "specific, measurable, attainable, rewarding, and timed."

The phase in which action steps or tactics are established and implemented follows all of the preceding activity. Action steps or tactics represent a fifth level of planning; they provide the most specific approach for describing the who, what, when, where, and how elements of the activities needed to accomplish an objective.

Planning can be described as an ongoing process of thinking and implementing at multiple levels. At each level, health leaders engage in directing, staffing, organizing, and controlling. Along the way, such leaders must remember that "what gets measured gets done"; thus all planning objectives and action steps must be measurable, assigned to an accountable and responsible person, and set within a time period. Periodic progress reviews, either monthly or quarterly, are essential to see the movement toward success.

In addition to this effort of directing, staffing, organization, and controlling, rewarding is important. These five elements are crucial as leaders embrace the foundations and functions of planning. Health leaders must publicly praise success and reward those who have achieved predetermined action steps, objectives, and goals.

As U.S. General and President Dwight Eisenhower once said, the plan is important but the process of planning is even more important. The team building, achievement, and success orientation that a culture of planning and implementation brings to an organization is invaluable in ensuring its success over both the short and long term. Situational assessment and environmental scanning are vital elements to establish, be successful, and maintain a "culture of planning" in a health organization.

Contingency Planning

An important aspect of planning is contingency planning. Contingency planning is planning for unexpected or unwanted events such as natural (tornados, hurricanes, storms, or floods) and man-made (terrorism, accidents, chemical spills, or explosions) disasters. How will your operation continue to provide the "technology of care" to caregivers during these chaotic and stressful situations? How will your information systems be brought back "online" and operate effectively (do you have backups of data and systems?)? In major disasters, the state government will declare a state of emergency and request federal assistance. The federal government has plans and stockpiles of medical and surgical and pharmaceutical items to assist along with durable and semi-permanent items (such as cots, temporary buildings, and modular and moveable structures). Working with local and state healthcare and public health emergency preparedness officials will be important to develop an efficient, effective, and efficacious plan for contingency operations.

Situational Assessment and Environmental Scanning

All health leaders must be able to assess the situation currently facing their organization, which would incorporate an assessment of both internal and external environments. A situational assessment must be an objective and honest look at the diverse factors that could affect the health organization's success in achieving its vision, mission, strategies, and goals. One tool commonly used for the internal assessment is SWOT analysis, which investigates internal strengths and weaknesses and external opportunities and threats.[19]

SWOT analysis offers insight into both the internal and external factors that might affect the organization's performance and success. Every organization needs more information about the environment than just its potential opportunities and threats. Choo reports that it is important to obtain information about relationships, trends, and information in the external environment; health leaders need to know which influences are acting on the industry and even the economy.[20] A focused environmental scan is one that concentrates on specific information, such as how many consumers bought this particular product or that service in the last year. External scanning, whether focused or more general, is essential for planning and forecasting the organization's performance into the future.

Situational assessment and continuous environmental scanning are crucial if organizations hope to survive in the dynamic health industry. A leader's and leadership team's responsibility is to remain current about and relevant to situational and environmental change that can or will affect the organization. Forces that contribute to the health industry's rapid and dynamic environment are varied but are cumulative; as a consequence,

they have a cumulative impact on the industry. "Technology, demography, economics and politics drive change, not only as individual factors but interacting to make the rate of change faster."[21]

Another approach is to look at the dynamic environment as comprising macro-environmental forces and health micro-environmental forces. In an approach that has been validated over the last two decades, Rakich, Longest, and Darr in 1992 outlined a series of categories that leaders can scan (environmental scanning) to keep current and relevant in the industry:

1. Macro-Environmental Forces.
   a. Legal, [regulatory, executive orders, and case law] and ethical forces.
   b. Political (including government policy) forces.
   c. Cultural and sociological (including values [beliefs and attitudes]) forces.
   d. Public expectations (including community, interest groups, and media).
   e. Economic forces.
   f. Ecological forces.

2. Health Care Environmental Forces [also called Micro-Environmental Forces].
   a. Planning and public policy (regulation, licensure, and accreditation) forces.
   b. Competitive forces.
   c. Healthcare financing (third-party payers, public and private, and financial risk).
   d. Technology (equipment, material, and supply entities) forces.
   e. Health research and education.
   f. Health status and health promotion (wellness and disease).
   g. [Integration with other health disciplines and organizations] Public health (sanitation, environmental protection, etc.) forces.[22]

The Rand Corporation suggests that the immense pressure exerted by cost-containment efforts and the rapid speed of change are the major factors influencing the health industry at this time.[23] Multiple forces have cumulatively contributed to change in the health industry in recent decades. Compare the health organizations of the 1960s or 1970s to those of today: There is a vast difference between two temporal organizations. The speed of that change in a mere thirty to forty years is astonishing, as are the gains in the ability of healthcare delivery systems to diagnose, treat, and rehabilitate patients who present with health needs.

For example, consider the life expectancy of people living in the 1960s compared to today. "Between 1961 and 1999, average life expectancy in the [United States] increased from 66.9 to 74.1 years for men and from 73.5 to 79.6 for women."[24] Trends in aging are also tied to life expectancy but have profound implications for health services.[25]

This dynamic whirlwind, often called "whitewater change," frames a picture of the world that the health leader must navigate. Although there have been tremendous successes in this industry, health leaders must continue to recognize the dynamic nature of the industry and challenge their organizations, groups, teams, and individuals to become more efficient, effective, and efficacious, while functioning under significant cost-containment pressure. From a practical viewpoint, Kotter suggests eight steps to transform organizations in dynamic situations (italics added):

1. Establish a sense of urgency by examining market and competitive realities and identifying and discussing crises, potential crises, or major opportunities.
2. Form a powerful guiding coalition by assembling a group with enough power to lead the change effect [from an level of the organization] and encourage the group to work together as a team.
3. Create a vision to help direct the change effort and develop strategies for achieving that vision.
4. Communicate the vision by using every vehicle possible to communicate the new vision and strategies and by teaching new behaviors by the example of the guiding coalition [at lower levels of the organization, the leader translates the senior leadership's vision for his or her section, branch, or unit into understandable and actionable tasks for that level and situation].
5. Empower others to act on the vision by getting rid of obstacles to change, changing systems, or structures that seriously undermine the vision, and encouraging risk taking and nontraditional ideas, activities, and actions.
6. Plan for and create short-term wins by planning for visible performance improvements, creating those improvements, and recognizing and rewarding employees involved in the improvements.
7. Consolidate improvements and produce still more change by using increased credibility to change systems, structures, and policies that do not fit the vision; hiring, promoting, and developing employees who can implement the vision; and reinvigorating the process with new projects, themes, and change agents.
8. Institutionalize new approaches by articulating the connections between the new behaviors and corporate [organizational] success and developing the means to ensure leadership development and succession.[26]

Kotter's eight steps are a sequence of leader actions and are cybernetic; that is, a feedback loop goes from the last step back to the first step. Leaders of health organizations should consider the changes in the macro and micro environments by assessing them against the cost, quality, and access health assessment constructs for those community members whom they serve. This analysis, for the segment of the continuum of care (from self-care and health promotion and prevention to primary, secondary, and tertiary care to long-term care and hospice care) in which the leaders are responsible, should be integrated into the holistic aspect of health and the health infrastructure available (or needed) in the community. Leadership depends on a leader's ability to make quality and consistent decisions. The discussion here now turns to the complexity of decision making and how to develop an efficient, effective, and efficacious decision making culture to dovetail into the organization's planning culture.

Decision Making and Decision Alignment[27]

Decision making occurs in all organizations. Health organizations, for example, face many decisions each day. The decision making process begins with identifying a question or problem—that is, an area needing improvement or an operational issue. Problems, issues, questions, and operational challenges come to leaders and managers from many different people, both within and outside the health organization.

Leaders and managers are usually taught to utilize the rational decision making model, which focuses on analytical (quantitative) methods; when necessary, they may couple this approach with group methods (qualitative) such as the normative group technique (brainstorming, alternative categorization, prioritizing alternatives, and selecting an alternative based on group consensus) to triangulate the final result (using both quantitative and qualitative methods) and identify an effective decision.

In reality, decision making is not as sterile and ordered as most have been taught. Both willful choice (rational) decision making models and reality-based ("garbage can") models are used in organizations amid a myriad of tools and techniques. Thus there are three major domains of decision making:

- Willful choice or rational models.
- Reality-based or garbage can models.
- Combinations of willful choice and reality-based models.

Likewise, three types of decision making methods are used:

- Quantitative methods: tools such as multiple attribute value, probability-based decision trees, analytical mathematical models, linear programming, and similar tools.
- Qualitative methods: tools such as focus groups, interviews (formal and informal), normative group techniques and similar tools.
- Triangulation methods: combinations of quantitative and qualitative methods where, classically, qualitative methods are perceived as "theory building" and quantitative methods are described as "theory testing, validating, or confirming."

A review of bounded rationality, willful choice, and reality-based decision making models is presented next. More time is spent on reality-based models because this decision making method is the least well known, but may be the most applicable to health organizational leaders and managers.

Bounded Rationality In Decision Making

Decision making must occur within the bounded rationality of the environmental context in which the problem must be solved. In modern times, with the advent and availability of the Internet, the bounded rationality of information available for decision making is immense and global. As stated in Chapter 2, the bounded rationality for any problem spans the parameters in which the rational resources are available to the decision maker to accomplish positive outcomes. Organizational culture influences decision making as well. As noted in a study of military officers published in 2009, officers with an embedded "forcefulness" and "decisiveness" culture in team leadership roles were more spontaneous and less rational in decision making than their equally ranked team members.[28] Clearly, then, bounded rationality is influenced by organizational culture.

Prior to the dawn of the Information Age and the widespread use of the Internet, information was considered to be a scarce resource that was difficult to find—a perception that has changed dramatically, to the point that we live in an age characterized by "information overload." Unfortunately, the vast amounts of information available do not always include all the information necessary or completely accurate information with which to make the best decisions. Additionally, information may not be in a form that is immediately useable by those needing it. As a result, the most that the health leader can hope to achieve is the best decision possible based on the information that is known. With any decision at hand, different levels of ambiguity and uncertainty will surround the issue. Decisions made easily and with little risk tend to have less ambiguity and uncertainty associated with them, while complex, difficult, and more risky decisions tend to have much more ambiguity and uncertainty embedded within them.

Complicating this feature of human decision making is the fact that, although much more information is available today, decision makers may not have access to all the proper information regardless of tools available to them. Further, searching out that information may require far more time than decision makers have to arrive at a decision. Not all information or sources will be identifiable, but time will advance in any case. The decision maker will need to arrive at the best decision that can be made at the time. As a consequence, health leaders must often "satisfice" by seeking "a satisfactory reward rather than seeking the maximum reward."[29]

Decision Making

The tools of decision making are the methods by which technology and processes are managed within the organization.

Early careerists need to be aware of the various tools of decision making for future leadership study and practice. Study (e.g., taking a course) and practice of both quantitative and qualitative decision making tools are highly recommended. This section highlights both methods as well as triangulation, which represents a combination of both quantitative and qualitative methods. It is recommended that each tool mentioned here (and those not mentioned) be searched (perhaps on the Internet), discussed, practiced, and role-played with others in the class, group, or organization. Facilitating the decision making process in a group or organization is an essential skill of leaders and managers, and a working familiarity with decision making tools is a prerequisite to such a skill.

Quantitative Methods

Quantitative methods include mathematical and computational analytical models to help leaders understand the decision making situation (data turned into information, which is then turned into knowledge) and produce mathematical outcomes of solutions. Some models are rather simple; others are highly complex. Quantitative models assist in assigning a "number" to uncertainty. Models include multiple-attribute value and multiple-utility methods, linear programming, probability, and decision trees based on Bayes' Theorem, and can be as complex and discrete as dynamic simulation. In general, simulation uses theoretical distributions and probabilities to "model" the real-world situation on the computer. From this computer model, response variables produce "outcomes" that can be evaluated.

Quantitative models take time and understanding of the important elements (also known as factors or variables) associated with the decisions that need to be made. In most health organizations, quantitative models are gaining momentum, though

qualified (highly trained and well-practiced) analysts who understand health processes and can perform a range of quantitative analyses remain difficult to find and hire. Even with quantitative analyses in hand, many times leaders and managers skew decisions toward the qualitative side of decision making.

Six Sigma is a methodology that is growing in prominence in the health industry. Quantitative methods are critical to Six Sigma, which is a fact-based, data-driven philosophy of quality improvement that values defect prevention over detection. The Six Sigma technique drives customer satisfaction and bottom-line results by reducing variation and waste. It can be applied anywhere variation and waste exist, and every employee should be involved in its implementation. Six Sigma is used by many business organizations; health organizations are now using this philosophy as well to improve the work processes in their facilities.

Six Sigma is used to evaluate the capability of a process to perform defect free, where a "defect" is defined as anything that results in customer dissatisfaction.[30] The higher the Sigma level, the lower the number of defects. At the Six Sigma level, there are approximately 3.4 errors per 1 million opportunities, a virtually error-free rate.[31] Among early adopters of this approach are some of the most highly regarded health systems in the country—the Cleveland Clinic, the Mayo Clinic, and Johns Hopkins Medical Center, to name a few. These facilities consistently rank among the best hospitals in the world.[32]

Six Sigma is most successful when senior leadership makes a strong commitment to change, and in institutions where patient satisfaction and error-free care are the driving forces. Health organization staff must be trained by professional Six Sigma trainers. The training includes a "lean" thinking that seeks to drive employees toward perfection. It comprises a set of tools of varying degrees of sophistication that can be helpful for a leader to improve the health organization.[33]

A complementary approach to Six Sigma is Lean Sigma. Lean Sigma focuses on fixing the broken systems and processes that hinder medical professionals from doing what they do best, empowering employees to make improvements, reducing time and costs, synchronizing processes, and improving quality and the patient experience.[34]

This practice helps to create efficient processes and decrease wasted time in a health facility. Lean Sigma provides the roadmap for fast and sustainable improvement while creating a work environment that strengthens and sustains the patient experience and increases the effectiveness of the health service and the provider of care.

Qualitative Methods

Qualitative methods include a variety of tools, ranging from personal intuition, discussions with team members, informal interviews, formal interviews, focus groups, nominal group techniques, and even voting. These methods are very useful in the decision making process, because experience, intuition, and common sense can all be used by individuals as well as by groups.

Study and practice of qualitative methods are essential for leaders to facilitate decision making for themselves, groups, and organizations. The most notable leader decision making tools of the qualitative nature include intuition, consensus, and coalition-based counsel.

Triangulation

The combination of quantitative and qualitative methods results in triangulation, a more thorough (albeit more time-consuming) method with which to make decisions. For example, a group may use nominal group techniques to develop a small set of possible solutions, then analyze each solution quantitatively. From there the leader can make a decision.

Training the group or organization to use triangulation is a good practice for resolving ("resolution" in reality-based models) decisions. Triangulation can also be used to develop standing operating procedures ("oversight" in reality-based models). Lastly, triangulation can be used to make improvements to processes within the organization. Kaizen theory (discussed later in this chapter) utilizes triangulation in the context of continuous quality improvement.

Decision Making in Quality Improvement

Extending the discussion on decision making, quality improvement integrates well into the overall schema of decision systems. In essence, quality improvement is a distinct system characterized by seven phases: (1) decision making (identification of improvement areas); (2) situational assessment; (3) information gathering; (4) decision making (what to do with assessment and information to improve); (5) planning; (6) implementation; and (7) feedback. Quality improvement, as a system, is an organizational culture "flag" found in many excellent health organizations. The connection in this arena is simple: where quality improvement systems exist, decision making systems are embedded throughout the system of continuous quality improvement. Total quality management (TQM), Kaizen theory, and the Shewhart cycle are all quality improvement strategies; they are profiled in the remainder of this section.

Total Quality Management

The TQM principles were initially brought to Japan by Deming after World War II. Consequently, Japanese businesses have been practicing TQM for more than fifty years, with remarkable results: Japan was able to rebuild its war-torn economy and innovate so that it became one of the strongest economies in the world in the latter part of the twentieth century. Despite this proof that TQM can be used over the long term with successful results, many health leaders feel an urgency to adopt new management philosophies every few years.[35,36]

The key with TQM for any leader is to strive for documented and incremental decreases in variation and redundancy. This is a 14-step process:

1. Constantly strive to improve products and services.
2. Adopt a total quality philosophy.
3. Correct defects as they happen, rather than relying on inspection of end products.
4. Award business on factors other than price.
5. Continually improve the systems of production and service.
6. Institute training.
7. Drive out fear.
8. Break down barriers among staff areas.
9. Eliminate superficial slogans and goals.
10. Eliminate standard quotas.
11. Remove barriers to pride of workmanship.
12. Institute vigorous education and retraining.

13. Require that management take action to achieve the transformation.
14. Engage in proactive management.

The prudent health leader will meet in collaboration with fellow leaders in the organization. Working through a facilitator, write down each of Deming's tenets and outline those current organizational policies, practices, and procedures that have an impact on improving or impeding practices in the organization. When all the information has been collected, the leader will then be ready to establish new guidelines and break down barriers as appropriate.

Kaizen Theory

Kaizen theory is another Japanese-originated philosophy that focuses on continuous improvement throughout a system. Because health leaders are ultimately responsible for all aspects of organizational dynamics within the health enterprise, this approach is noteworthy. Kaizen theory is as much of an organizational culture (how things are done here) as a system that can be taught.

Kaizen originated in Japan in 1950 when business management and government acknowledged that there were problems in the then-current confrontational management system, given the pending labor shortage in Japan. This theory considers the initial quality of a project as well as the incremental improvement of quality when planning for quality improvements. Researchers defined Kaizen theory as a strategy to include concepts, systems, and tools within the bigger picture of leadership. This approach involves people (subordinates) and organizational culture, all driven by the customer. Japanese business leaders then involved the workforce in the solution of the problem. A key idea behind this theory is the need to practice reactive problem solving to promote continuous adherence to quality standards.[37]

Kaizen focuses on continuous improvement (CI) in performance, cost, and quality. In fact, some sources use the terms "Kaizen" and "CI" interchangeably, reflecting the nature of the theory. Ellife described Kaizen, or CI, as a method that intensively focuses on improving every small detail of a process, recognizing that lots of small improvements, when executed continuously and embedded in the culture

of an organization, can yield much more benefit than a few "big" programs.[38] The goal when implementing the concepts of this theory in an organization is to promote a culture of consistent standards and quality by addressing small problems or tasks. In other words, "Kaizen" signifies a series of small improvements that have been made in the status quo as a result of ongoing efforts.[39] Others suggest that CI can be generated and sustained through the promotion of a good improvement model and management support.[40]

A "Kaizen event" is a focused and structured improvement project, using a dedicated cross-functional team to improve a targeted work area, with specific goals and objectives, in an accelerated time frame. It is a complex organizational phenomenon, with the potential for altering both a technical system (i.e., work area performance) and a social system (i.e., participating employees and work area employees).[41] Kaizen events are usually short-term projects, sometimes only one week long.

The introduction of a Kaizen event in the health setting may be problematic, given that leaders could face multiple barriers to the proposed change from the start. For example, some have suggested that demarcations are traditionally more stringent in hospital settings; subordinates in different units in the health organization protect "their" territory. It is, therefore, necessary to have personnel from the different groups involved in patient care represented on a Kaizen team. The structure and composition of this team is crucial to the success of a health organization Kaizen event. Kaizen events typically use a semi-autonomous team (a social system) to apply a specific set of technical problem-solving tools.[42]

Benchmarks in Qualitative Decision Making for Leaders

1775: Adam Smith, author of *The Wealth of Nations*, observed a pin factory in 1775 and concluded that the process of making a pin could be separated into fourteen different steps and processes. After observing the process for a period of time, Smith defined the sentinel events of pin making and assigned these tasks to the personnel who showed expertise in each specific stage. The result: The factory went from producing hundreds of pins a week to thousands! However, Smith found that if certain elements of this fledgling assembly line suffered slowdowns, the entire output could be hindered or halted.

1920: Dr. Walter Shewhart of Bell Telephone developed one of the first true control charts. In a paradigm shift from management philosophies, instead of inspecting outcomes, Shewhart began inspecting the process. He developed some of the first process-control methodologies used in the United States. His primary data methods were statistics (outcomes), sampling (convenience), and control charts that could be supplied to management to measure events as they happened.

1950: Kaizen theory resulted in the increase in productivity in Japan after World War II. Before World War II, Japanese products were seen as low quality and cheap; after the war, when Japanese factories and management philosophies were reestablished, Kaizen principles helped the country establish dominance in the global marketplace. Eventually, the word "Japanese" became synonymous with the word "quality" in regard to factory-made items.

1950–2010: W. Edwards Deming applied Shewhart's principles of quality control in his role as a consultant to several organizations while visiting Japan after World War II. From 1950 onward, he often visited Japan as lecturer and consultant (the Japanese honored him by naming the highest Japanese quality award after him). In spite of this popularity in Japan, Deming's principles were not adopted in the United States until the latter part of the 1980s. Today, the demonstration of TQM, Kaizen theory, and Shewhart principles are staples of many accreditation site visits for health leaders.

In the healthcare arena, a Kaizen team should be composed of people from multiple disciplines to accurately address and manage events. Its members may, for example, consist of a physician, nurse, social worker, and physical therapist, depending on the event being addressed. Working as an interdisciplinary team ensures the sustainability of the improvements. Another positive side effect is that the group members can analyze one another's work processes to see how many steps each process actually includes and how much time is spent doing them. Kaizen covers many techniques and processes of CI; one that may be used in the health setting is the Shewhart cycle.[43]

Shewhart Cycle

The Shewhart cycle is also referred to as the Deming model and the plan–do–check–act (PDCA) cycle. This continuous quality improvement model consists of a logical sequence of these four repetitive steps for CI and learning.[44] The Shewhart cycle is a continuous feedback loop that seeks to identify and change process elements so as to reduce variation. The objective of this process is to plan to do something, do it, check for met requirements, and correct the process to achieve acceptable output performance. Performance improvement teams (PIT) are often developed in health organizations to address specific issues and work on problem solving by implementing the Shewhart cycle.

A PIT, which is a multidisciplinary group, may apply a model such as the Shewhart cycle to concentrate on quality improvement issues. Evidence-based data are used to analyze information within a PIT. Evidence-based practice in clinical performance, as well as administrative components, may help to reduce unnecessary tasks and procedures. The PIT can use the Shewhart cycle to tackle issues that affect the quality of care.

Continuing Health Education: Competency Attainment

For the purpose of this summary, we suggest that *knowledge* is recalling information with familiarity gained through education, experience, or association and that comprehension is the understanding of the meaning of the information. A *skill* is the effective and timely utilization of knowledge, and finally, an ability is the physical, cognitive, or legal power to competently perform and achieve positive outcomes. Many of the competencies an early careerist needs to start off a career may be learned in degree programs. However, once an individual moves away from traditional education and enters into professional practice, most, if not all, of these capabilities are learned through CHE. As early careerists will see, whether you are aware or not, you are constantly being evaluated and assessed on a combination of your skills, knowledge, and abilities in any professional practice setting entered!

As we have discussed, the health workforce is a complex assortment of individuals with different backgrounds, educational experiences, certifications, specialties, and work locations. Approximately 12% of the entire US Health Workforce is comprised of those who work in the health professions. As a result, health leaders must continue to use the dynamic nature of the industry to challenge themselves, their organizations, and individuals to become more competent under significant external pressures.

What Is Continuing Health Education?

Continuing education (CE) involves activities, learning events, or individual efforts that result in a combination of recognized (and/or credentialed) and unrecognized (non-credentialed) knowledge. Formal CE consists of those activities that are sponsored through professional organizations or organizations of higher education that award credit towards certification, licensure, accreditation, or apply to annual requirements for practice. These include:

- Formalized continuing health and/or medical education (CHE/CME).
- Certificate, graduate, and doctoral education.
- Recognized didactic instruction.

Some advantages of formal CE include that it is easily recognized and relevant to the current environment. Additionally, it provides a different point of view and adds permanent value to the résumé of the individual, unlike informal CE, which may not hold value between employers. Formal CE, however, is not without its disadvantages. The most common disadvantages of formal CE, include cost, time to complete the education, and potential geographical barriers.

Informal CE consists of those activities, events, and efforts that individuals engage in to maintain proficiency or fill personal gaps in knowledge in personal practice. These may include:

- Mentoring (or being a mentee).
- Heuristics.
- Community volunteerism.
- Professional organizations (networking).

In contrast to formal CE, informal CE is typically low to no cost. However, the disadvantages of informal CE are that it may not be valued between organizations because the skills learned through informal channels may be hard to quantify and measure. An adroit health professional should keep him or herself abreast of several different and ongoing types of CHE in his or her career to maintain appropriate competency within the profession.

Vendor Management

Managing vendors can be a challenge within the healthcare organization. There are several main strategies for vendor management, including group purchasing, sales representatives, and vendor managed inventory. Each method has its use depending on the market conditions and size of the organization.

Group Purchasing Organizations (GPO)

The GPO is an organization that allows healthcare organizations to achieve savings and efficiencies by combining the purchasing volume of multiple organizations to leverage discounts from manufacturers and distributors. Interestingly, GPOs do not actually purchase anything. Their only role is to negotiate contracts which member organizations then use to make their own purchases. The contracts are negotiated with input from the group members. Once the contract is created, each individual organization must still decide which products are most appropriate and only purchase those products which it needs. Typically, purchasing decisions are made through a committee that contains the clinicians who use the items. Hospitals are usually free to purchase outside of the GPO as well, and often do so.[45] The GPO's primary source of income is from administrative fees paid by the members of the organization. Fees are typically only paid when a group member utilizes a contract negotiated by the GPO; however, there are variations to this model.

Vendor Managed Inventory (VMI)

VMI is a system in which instead of sending purchase orders, customers send demand information to the supplier. Based on these objectives, the supplier generates replenishment orders. The entire process is guided on prearranged objectives for customer inventory level, fill rate, and cost per transaction.[46] The benefit to the customer with VMI is the reduction or elimination of stock outs. This is primarily because VMI eliminates the need to reorder items, as the supplier is simply restocking the inventory when it reaches a certain level. A key benefit to the supplier is that VMI will typically secure the customer as long as the suppler is able to keep up with their inventory demands. VMI also allows the supplier to better schedule operations and be more efficient because it will be aware of the usage patterns of the customer.[47]

Sales Representative

New products are typically introduced to healthcare organizations through the use of sales representatives. It is not uncommon for these representatives to also manage inventory and in the case of medical devices, assist in their use. In an effort to cut costs and to reduce manufacturer influence, some hospitals are training their own employees to perform these functions. Loma Linda University Medical Center achieved a 50% reduction in the cost of total hip and total knee implants adopting this model.[48] In the majority of healthcare organizations, sales representatives for medical device and pharmaceutical companies are still welcomed into the facility.

Credentialing of Sales Representatives

The cost of credentialing medical sales representatives adds an estimated $1.7 billion a year to the cost of healthcare in the United States.[49] The process is, however, necessary. Sales rep credentialing is a way to ensure that representatives are insured, oriented, and trained appropriately. Part of the problem with the current credentialing system is that there is a lack of uniformity as to hospital requirements and, as such, there is additional cost associated with accrediting at multiple facilities, and this cost gets added into the cost of the medical devices. In order to reduce associated costs, the Association of peri-Operative Registered Nurses (AORN) has suggested that credentialing focus on the following items:

- Background checks.
- Health vaccinations.
- Hospital orientation as to policies and procedures.
- Product and general liability insurance.
- Training documentation.

Currently, most of the healthcare industry uses similar items, but there is no uniform standard.[50]

Summary

Planning and decision making are essential to efficient, effective, and efficacious healthcare supply-chain operations and strategies. Leaders and managers must structure and facilitate plans that integrate well with the healthcare organization's strategic plan and must make consistent decisions in alignment with those plans. Creating standing operating procedures for routine and consistent operations of the supply chain allows leaders and managers to spread the operational culture at all levels of the supply-chain enterprise. Contingency planning, that is planning for the unexpected and unwanted such as natural and man-made disasters, is necessary for organizational longevity and survival during chaotic and stressful situations. Will intermediated or dis-intermediated aspects of the supply chain work best for medical and surgical items or pharmaceutical items, considering the healthcare organization's strategic plan? How does technology impact planning and operational as well as strategic decisions? This chapter provided an overview of planning, improvement strategies, metrics, regulatory compliance, and decision making. These constructs should be reviewed and placed in context for integration into the supply chain's overall operational plan for providing the "technology of care" to the caregivers.

Healthcare Supply Chain Integration with Geographical Information Systems

The following section was developed by Dr. Jeff Jones, Ms. Ellington, and Mr. Blues. This is a case study in healthcare supply chain and geographical information system integration in a facility building project.

Geographic Information Systems (GIS) and Healthcare Supply Chains: A Case Study in Outfitting a New Hospital Facility

Jeff Jones, Ph.D., Georgia Southern University
Michelle Ellington, GISP, GIS Coordinator, University of Kentucky
Andrew Blues, Associate Director, Facilities Information Services, University of Kentucky

Learning Objectives

1. Describe these terms:
   - Cartography.
   - GIS.
   - Healthcare informatics.
   - Health information technology (HIT).
   - Interoperability.
   - Organizational coupling.
   - Agility.
2. Integrate how GIS affected the interoperability, coupling, and agility of the outfitting supply chain in this chapter's case study.
3. Identify how both the technology and the staff workflow adjusted to create an improved, more efficient supply chain for this building project.

Introduction

The coordination involved in the building, outfitting, and opening of a major new medical facility often costs hundreds of thousands of dollars paid to one or more outside vendors. In 2008, the University of Kentucky (UK) MedCenter began planning the construction of a 1.2 million square foot hospital. Instead of outsourcing the entire coordination of the new hospital to external contractors, UK turned to its existing GIS to help manage the complex supply chain to outfit the hospital with beds, medical instruments, and office equipment needed to operate a health facility. This chapter reviews the uses of GIS in healthcare and how one university hospital leveraged GIS to better meet its

goals. This chapter will introduce you to several key concepts involved in supply chains and then illustrate, in a case study, how these concepts have worked in a healthcare setting.

Key Concepts

The idea of linking geography and health goes back millennia to at least the time of ancient Greece and Hippocrates' classification of disease outbreaks (*pandemic*, *epidemic*, *endemic*) by geographic extent. Often cited as the father of epidemiology, John Snow famously used maps of cholera patients in 19th century London to link cholera to unclean water. And with the advent of modern computers, maps and the science of map-making (*cartography*) grew into GIS as a versatile information tool, indexing data by spatial locations. History credits Roger Tomlinson, a Canadian geographer, with introducing the concept and term GIS to the world in the 1960s.[51] Today, GIS and its sister technologies continue this historic evolution of linking space and data to analyze and visualize patterns and processes within the data.

Geographic information systems such as ESRI's widely used ArcGIS consist of a database with a geographical component to visualize, manage, and analyze spatial data. Widely used in urban and regional planning for decades, today GIS provide a ubiquitous backbone to many of the daily services contemporary residents in industrialized nations take for granted. From the GIS on a smartphone to the 911 emergency routing systems used by ambulances, these systems all build upon a GIS foundation to:

- *Identify* two or more locations by spatial coordinates.
- *Measure* the distance between these locations.
- *Offer* routes between these locations.
- *Layer* new strata of data such as traffic, road conditions, tolls, elevations, etc.
- *Analyze* information for better decision making.

For many users, GIS provide a way to make maps showing spatial patterns within data. GIS, however, also offer a powerful tool for managing data through the software's ability to provide real-time updates to various databases and to overlay multiple layers of data for better visualization, measurement, and analysis of complex patterns. As a result, GIS and its kindred software tools are increasingly used in logistics, supply-chain management, and healthcare informatics.

Standardization and Interoperability

While GIS predate the coining of the term *informatics* by A.I. Mikhailov in 1968 as a branch of linguistics emphasizing biological terminology standardization, GIS and other data management tools represent elements of the constellation of data tools and methodologies increasingly placed under the umbrella of informatics. Indeed, GIS coordinators, health information technology specialists, and electronic health records managers increasingly share the joint professional title of *informatician*. The informatics field in fact began as a branch of linguistics focusing on standardizing data terminology so that data could be better compared and used. This central foundation of standardization applies to GIS as well: a common spatial coordinate system indexes data elements, which allows for the comparison of different locations and numerical data. Within the healthcare branch of informatics, a single hospital may use a variety of HITs such as stand-alone payroll, human resources, and electronic medical record systems divided into silos by department, software incompatibilities, and different staff workflows. These divisions present a problem where these silos cannot communicate with one another. *Interoperability*, the bridging of these divisions and the connection of these silos, represents why GIS can be an asset. If the various systems can export their data to a common format (such as Microsoft Excel or a common-delimited file) and these data have a standardized spatial variable (address, building, county, state, etc.) in common, then GIS can link between systems. The case study describes the interoperability features of GIS that made it attractive to UK project planners.

Bringing Tools and People Together in Transformed Workflows

Employees, tools, and workflows must be matched to work efficiently. Evidence from both clinics' successful and failed adoptions of electronic medical records (EMRs) points to the critical need to adapt employee workflow to using new digital tools when replacing paper records. Simply adopting a new health information technology and expecting it to work with a system designed around paper charts is likely to lead to delays if not outright chaos.[52] Instead, it is critical to transform the work environment to incorporate new data technologies with new work-flow procedures. Look for this same critical element in this chapter's case study.

Lean Supply Chains

This critical work-flow adaptation component to supply-chain management is also found in Toyota's *kanban* (also called the JIT system) manufacturing approach and subsequent expansions to service industries such as Lean Sigma Six Plus.[53] Toyota engineer Taiichi Ohno developed the *kanban* (*signboard* in Japanese) system based on his observations of how grocery stores operate. He observed that Japanese shoppers usually bought only what they needed at a given time. In turn, the grocery stores only stocked enough merchandise to meet current customers' demands. Both customer and supplier, therefore, kept inventories to a minimum, creating a system of minimized waste. Ohno built on these observations to create his *kanban* system where each part of a car was labeled and tracked so that suppliers could provide just enough parts to meet the Toyota factory's immediate production needs.

In subsequent years, the *kanban* method and other concepts have coalesced around the *lean* approach to supply chains, which focuses on reducing waste in terms of costs, time, and efficiencies. Lean principles thus emphasize efficient supply chains that deliver components when needed to manufacturers and then to vendors. Inventories are kept low, and redundancies in work-flows are repeatedly analyzed to cut wasted time and costs. While these concepts originated in the manufacturing sector, the transportation and logistics industries have incorporated many of them into their business models. In turn, logistics companies are using GIS as critical tools in managing their lean supply chains. In fact, GIS are so regularly used now by major shipping firms that an entire subfield of GIS has developed around GIS-T (Geographic Information Systems –Transportation).[54] For some years, health systems have looked to lean models to improve customer satisfaction, improve patient navigation through the clinic environment, and reduce costs. While HIT systems automating payroll and digitizing patient records are increasingly common, GIS use by hospital systems remains in its infancy. Yet, like car parts and transcontinental export containers, the complex flow of patients, lab specimens, and equipment within a hospital supply chain lend themselves nicely to GIS as a tool to facilitate the lean principles of improved communication and reduction in inventories and waste.

Coupling

Another goal of supply-chain management focuses on improving coordination between suppliers outside an organization and workers within an organization. Barut, Faisst, and Kanet call this relationship *coupling* and research ways to measure how well organizations couple through increasingly inexpensive management technologies such as GIS. In areas such as projecting demand, capacity, inventory, and scheduling, efficient supply chains show a higher degree of coupling between organizations than inefficient ones.[55] The UK case study in this chapter has a similarly strong emphasis on the coupling between the primary construction contractor and the internal offices and data systems within the university.

Agility

Finally, we come to the concept of *agility*, the ability of a supply chain to express flexibility when one or more component organizations or work flows run into problems. For example, how well can a hospital and its suppliers respond to both planned (introduction of a new electronic prescriptions system) and unplanned (a fire at a major pharmaceutical factory) events? Some supply-chain analysts view agility and lean principles as contradictory in that lean principles focus on creating a single supply chain with little or no extra *fat*. Such fat is viewed as unnecessary waste. Agile systems, however, often require extra inventories, additional suppliers, and other fat as backups to draw upon during a crisis, when the primary supply chain breaks down.[56]

Developing a supply chain that balances lean with agility has become the goal for many supply-chain developers. This harmonized principle even has earned its own term: *leagility*.[57] Studies looking at HIT and healthcare supply chains find that adoption of such technologies can initially slow work flows, but with proper implementation, they can enhance both leanness and agility.[58,59,60]

GIS and Healthcare

While the GIS tool remains relatively little-used in healthcare outside of its integration into 911 systems, innovative use of this tool is growing among healthcare systems and health-related research. For example, researchers at UK have used interactive GIS mapping tools to communicate tobacco-free policy initiatives (see http://www.uky.edu/TobaccoFree/map) and to measure compliance by plotting cigarette butts on the grounds of the university and its associated medical center.[61] Research in Oregon similarly used GIS to analyze the effects of a clinic's move on vulnerable patients with a chronic disease.[62] Other hospital systems are using GIS in areas such as hospital emergency management and tracking hospital equipment.[63] Also in the area of health, GIS, and supply chains, construction firms are also applying this technology to improve safety, cost estimation, and construction supply chains.[64,65,66]

Case Study

Overview of the Project Overview

The UK Chandler Hospital operates one of Kentucky's two Level-1 trauma centers with almost 1,000 physicians and 3,250 other health professionals. These medical providers support a 473-bed acute care facility in Lexington, Kentucky. In 2008, UK started plans to demolish existing facilities at the hospital and replace them with a state-of-the-art Level-1 trauma center. Expansion plans focused on two 16-story bed towers housing a total of 1.2 million square feet of hospital space. The facility initially opened in July 2010 at a cost of $575 million and is continuing to be fitted out to fill the entire 1.2 million square feet. Key to meeting this ambitious schedule was developing a system to coordinate the complex task of outfitting and occupying the building to be ready for the first patient.

UK's Vice President of Facilities Management, Bob Wiseman, had prior experience with GIS from working with the local government, which operates a GIS office. He championed using in-house solutions, through GIS, to overcome the occupancy challenge, as UK already used Esri's ArcGIS software for campus planning and facilities management. After researching GIS solutions and partners, UK contracted with Esri partner 39°north to build a custom ArcGIS application in conjunction with UK's existing GIS and information technology professionals, Michelle Ellington (UK's GIS Coordinator) and Andrew Blues (UK's Associate Director of Facilities Information Services).

The resulting application was the *Occupancy Module*. This customized module incorporated the new hospital's floor plans as a GIS geodatabase along with CAD (*computer assisted drafting*) plans for the structural elements. The Occupancy Module also included visualization tools such as 360-degree panoramic pictures of each room both before and after drywalling, the pre-drywall picture

Courtesy of Dr. Jones

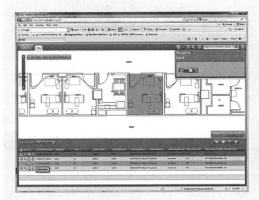

Courtesy of Dr. Jones

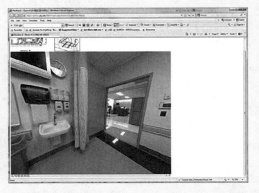

Courtesy of Dr. Jones

Courtesy of Dr. Jones

showing the placement of pipes and wiring in the walls. Access to the Occupancy Module used UK's single, university-wide login system, and security protocols were built into the system, to limit access to individuals in specific departments. In this way, employees and contractors, who did not need access to the entire hospital plan, were still given access to their particular department.

The system allowed employees to view rooms and update and maintain information on outfitting and equipping each room. Each day, staff produced updated room data sheets and taped them to each room's door to assist movers in knowing what equipment went in each of the 206 rooms. The staff updated the Occupancy Module daily so that users university-wide could access live, real-time information on the progress and location of individual equipment pieces and room outfittings in the occupancy supply chain.

Case Study Interview

Michelle Ellington and Andrew Blues oversaw the complex supply line to outfit UK's new hospital. The following interview with them allows a glimpse into the use of GIS.

1. How did UK use GIS in the planning and execution of the move to the new hospital?

   In December of 2008, when occupancy strategies were being identified for the new UK

Patient Care Facility, a Level 1 state-of-the-art trauma facility, the UK Hospital Administration was considering purchasing an industry leading facilities management solution to meet their goals. Administration wanted a system to graphically view and analyze all space and assets in the new hospital and output Room Data Sheets that would be used to track all assets moved into their respective space. At the time, no GIS-centric systems of this magnitude existed. So, instead of investing in an established CAD-based system, UK Facilities Management spearheaded development of a custom GIS solution to support hospital occupancy, which the Hospital Administrations supported. What ensued next was a two-year project of planning, development, and implementation of a robust GIS facility occupancy solution that met the goals 100% as well as gained industry recognition for its innovative design among GIS professionals.

2. What system did UK use before with such moves?

   Typically, construction teams suggest a system to use, which was also the case with this project. However, since this was the largest UK construction project to date, it provided an opportunity to implement something more beneficial for the university than a point-in-time stand-alone application. This was a complex move-in due to the advanced medical equipment, furniture, and technologies needed to fit up a Level 1 state-of-the-art trauma facility.

3. Did the GIS system save money? Time? Have other benefits?

   When the need for a system to support hospital occupancy was first discussed, the top-tiered facilities management systems were identified as possible solutions. These high-dollar systems offered functionality well outside the need of the project so the cost would not have been worth the gains. Plus, out-of-the box systems are not easily customizable, and this project required a flexible system that would support the complex needs of this unique project. The system had to be able to integrate with UK's other computer systems, instead of becoming another, separate system unable to communicate with the other systems. The system UK developed combined multiple university data sets: GIS floor plans, CAD site plans, 360-degree room photo spheres, space usage codes, and asset inventories. All data could be hooked to the GIS floor plans for display, analysis, and graphical output, regardless of the format—hence the power of GIS. This customized system offered a full palette of custom functionality at a third of the price of other systems we evaluated.

4. Were there any challenges or hurdles getting GIS adopted for this project by the administration?

This project was a clear example of the importance of relationships and inter-departmental coupling. UK Facilities Management recommended to the Hospital Administration to move away from external industry-recognized systems and instead go with a custom-built GIS application. Cost savings was one part of the reason for using an internal application, but it was not the most important piece. The key argument to the adoption of GIS was to have a successful, on-time occupancy for the July 14th opening. There was risk in going with a custom system, but there was trust for the Facilities Management vice president by Hospital Administration and trust from the vice president for the internal Facilities Management team managing system development. This project's customization required a well-executed plan to succeed, and it was viewed as an opportunity for all involved. For the Hospital Administration, it was an opportunity to save money while investing in a UK enterprise system. For Facilities Management, it was an opportunity to expand GIS use into the new hospital before it was even built. This project would prove its

value as a key piece for integrating campus enterprise systems into a simple and usable web-based solution.

5. Were there any technical challenges?

The scope of the project included developing new, innovative tools so there were many unknowns going in. The best decision UK made in planning for expected technical challenges was to define that UK was in charge of the business logic, design, and back end database management as a requirement in the project scope while the contractor was responsible for programming the front end. In doing so, the UK team had the ability to code the tools and modify the logic as new technical hurdles were encountered with little to no involvement or support needed from the contractor.

This system was developed in 2008 and used Flash because it offered the best user experience at that time. The system was also designed to render CAD files in GIS, which was an innovative choice in that it allowed publication of the existing floor plan library instead of a duplicated copy for web display. Since then, iOS devices such as iPhones and iPads have become pervasive. Because iOS does not support Flash, these new Apple devices make the original system virtually unusable on most mobile devices. Additionally, Esri software no longer supports rendering CAD files in GIS. These were technical challenges that could not be planned for and, as a result, the system is no longer used as is. Instead, the core features and lessons learned have been migrated to a mobile-friendly, Java Script-based (rather than Flash-based) web application for future use. This shows how unforeseen changes in technology require agility in adapting to new software and hardware devices.

6. How did your office coordinate with vendors, architects, etc.?

Our primary role was to develop a system to support move-in and train the staff on how to use it. Our role was not to coordinate with non-UK personnel. Our secondary role was to manage the Room Data Sheet distribution throughout the hospital and to update the system as rooms were occupied with their necessary assets. The Facilities Information Services staff made scheduled field audits to the hospital and updated the system while in the field on laptops running the system. The advantage of using a GIS graphical interface was that the hospital administration was able to use the system directly to support internal and vendor needs without technical support.

7. If you or another institution were to do this again, what lessons have you learned and what changes would you make?

Do it all internally or buy a package and live with the design. The contractor we partnered with did a good job, but a project of this nature requires institutional knowledge to do it right. Every choice needs to be relevant to the needs of a department or a standard, a campus-wide system. This is knowledge that cannot be quickly acquired or translated easily. Our contractor was very flexible. They were a start-up business and were eager to take a risk on something innovative and new. This project was successful given our extensive involvement in product development, which is a very unique approach and could easily have led to failure. Thus, the right technology coupled with the right institutional knowledge led to success. One without the other would not have worked.

8. Where did the old system create bottlenecks and inefficiencies in the supply chain that this new GIS-powered system improved upon? Did the new system create new bottlenecks?

All out-of-the-box systems, though beneficial, do not meet all needs. So in the past, a team member working to outfit a hospital space would do things manually to fill in where

the system lacked. Being aware of where these bottlenecks were on past projects' supply chains gave us insight into what custom tools the GIS application needed to offer. For example, we wanted the Occupancy Module to have the ability to make custom floor plan maps to provide a vendor during a delivery. Other bottlenecks in older systems were the lack of real-time updating of data and no graphical outputs. The addition of these abilities (customization, real-time updating, and visualizations) were value-added custom tools in the GIS application. The new system was created to not have bottlenecks. However there was an unavoidable limitation: although it integrated data from multiple University systems, it was ultimately not an application that was available to the UK community as a whole given the sensitivity of the hospital data.

The example of the new UK hospital brings together lessons on ways to reduce costs and waste (lean principles) by harnessing existing HIT capabilities for new projects. By using existing GIS expertise coupled well with a GIS consulting firm and construction contractor, UK was able to save thousands of dollars and integrate the new hospital into facilities planning before the first brick was set. By indexing data to a physical point in space, GIS created interoperability between UK's previously separate data systems. The technology alone, however, did not produce the resulting success. It also required an integration of the work flows of the GIS informaticians with the construction firm staff and other HIT professionals on and off campus. Moreover, this project integrated agility by using human beings to conduct daily checks of rooms and to update the Occupancy Module. Through this winning combination of people and technology working together in a flexible, agile, and yet lean supply chain, the university was able to outfit its new hospital in time for its opening deadline using a customized, internal system at a third of the cost of other existing, non-GIS systems.

Summary

This chapter provided a concluding overview of the previous chapters to allow reflection and thinking focused on supply-chain excellence in healthcare. The Value Chain sets the context for the concluding healthcare supply-chain overview. How will you improve the healthcare supply chain to be a valuable core function of healthcare organizations that provide care to patients? How will you provide the "technology of care" to the caregivers, physicians, surgeons, nurses, and other clinical staff to improve the quality of care and efficacy to the care process? How can you develop, improve, and hold to high standards of healthcare supply-chain efficiency, effectiveness, and efficacy? Every health professional serves an important role in healthcare supply-chain operations and management. Thank you for reading and learning to improve the healthcare supply chain. You can and will make a positive and important difference in your health professional career.

Sarah Says: A Student's Perspective

This chapter focuses on leading, planning, managing, deciding, and learning. In order to be an efficient, effective and efficacious healthcare leader, one must incorporate all of the aspects of leading into his or her leadership routine. Having a leadership plan is a critical factor to determine success in leading the supply-chain operation.

As a leader, planning is an essential skill required at all levels of an organization; leaders must obtain knowledge about planning and have the ability to use that knowledge to structure a effective system of planning unique to their organization. Like many other theories in this textbook, no one theory is the best for every organization. Health leaders must decide which method of planning to use that will best benefit their organization. Subordinates will look to health leaders to provide structure, assist in overcoming problems or issues, or answer questions. In order for the health organization to be successful in their planning, it is important for health leaders to stay consistent in their structure.

Leaders are also responsible for decision making. The decision making process begins with identifying a question or problem. Facilitating the decision making process in a group or organization is an essential skill of leaders and managers. It is imperative for the health organizations to work together to make decisions. Each member of the organization can bring different aspects to the decision making process.

Finally, it is important for health leaders and other members of the organization to stay up to date on their education, especially in healthcare, where rapid changes in technology and advances can occur continuously and rapidly. This is mostly, if not all, obtained through CHE.

Discussion Questions

1. Describe the concepts and models of planning and decision making in the context of the healthcare supply chain.
2. Discuss the importance of situational factors (trends, environmental issues, technology, regulatory compliance, etc.) in the planning process and how leadership principles, metrics, and improvement tenets can be used to positively impact the organizational culture of healthcare supply-chain operations.

3. Relate, discuss, and provide areas of integration between planning and decision making amid continuous operations of the healthcare supply chain to include the use of metrics and improvement strategies.
4. Distinguish the differences between planning and contingency planning.
5. Merge principles of leadership, planning, and decision making to develop a personal plan for operating in a fast-paced healthcare supply-chain environment.
6. Evaluate the benefits for organizational operations with a solid planning process and standing operating procedures as part of the healthcare supply-chain culture to include outside sales representatives.

Exercises

1. Describe the concepts and models of planning and decision making in the context of the healthcare supply chain in half a page.
2. Discuss the importance of situational factors (trends, environmental issues, technology, regulatory compliance, etc.) in the planning process and how leadership principles, metrics, and improvement tenets can be used to positively impact the organizational culture of healthcare supply-chain operations; what are the most important factors and why?
3. Relate, discuss, and provide areas of integration between planning and decision making amid continuous operations of the healthcare supply chain to include the use of metrics and improvement strategies. What metrics are most important and why?
4. Distinguish the differences between planning and contingency planning and what the most important contingency planning elements are and why.
5. Merge principles of leadership, planning, and decision making to develop a personal plan for operating in a fast-paced healthcare supply-chain environment; what metrics and improvement tenets would you utilize?
6. Evaluate the benefits for organizational operations with a solid planning process and standing operating procedures as part of the healthcare supply-chain culture to include outside sales representatives.

Journal Items

Answer the following:

Describe the planning process in one page or less.

What metrics would you use and why, to lead, manage and plan within the context of the healthcare supply chain?

Considering chapters 9 and 10, what did you find most helpful in your thinking about leading, managing, and planning within the healthcare supply chain?

References

1. J. Brown, Controlling Costs in the Healthcare Supply Chain, (n.d.), 2015,from http://www.inboundlogistics.com/cms/article/controlling-costs-in-the-healthcare-supply-chain/ (accessed 22 Mar. 2015).

2. State of the Healthcare Industry: Cost management concerns (n.d.). Retrieved from http://thenewlogistics.ups.com/healthcare/healthcare-survey-results/UPS-PITC-Executive-Summary-North-America.pdf, p.7 (accessed 23 Mar. 2015).

3. State of the Healthcare Industry: Cost management concerns (n.d.). Retrieved from http://thenewlogistics.ups.com/healthcare/healthcare-survey-results/UPS-PITC-Executive-Summary-North-America.pdf, p.7 (accessed 23 Mar. 2015).

4. G. Degun, "Regulatory compliance top supply chain concern among healthcare professionals," (2014, September 23), http://www.supplymanagement.com/news/2014/regulatory-compliance-top-supply-chain-concern-among-healthcare-professionals (accessed 22 Mar. 2015).

5. G. Degun, "Regulatory compliance top supply chain concern among healthcare professionals,"

6. Quality Assurance and Regulatory Compliance, *genco*, (n.d.), http://www.genco.com/Healthcare/regulatory-compliance.php (accessed 23 Mar. 2015).

7. A. Gunasekaran, C. Patel, and R. E. McGaughey, "A framework for supply chain performance measurement." *International journal of production economics*, 87, no. 3 (2004), 333–347.

8. Gunasekaran, Patel, and McGaughey, "A framework for supply chain performance measurement." 333–347.

9. C. Elrod, S. Murray, and S. Bande A Review of Performance Metrics for Supply Chain Management. *Engineering Management Journal*, 25, no. 3 (2013), 39–50.

10. A. M. Wicks, L. St. Clair, "Competing Values in Healthcare: Balancing the (Un)Balanced Scorecard." *Journal of Healthcare Management*, 52, no. 5, (2007), 309–324.

11. C. Granda-Cameron et al., Bringing an inpatient palliative care program to a teaching hospital: Lessons in leadership. *Oncology Nursing Forum*, 34, no. 4 (2007), 772–776.

12. G. Yukl, *Leadership in organizations*, 3rd ed. (Englewood Cliffs, NJ: Prentice Hall, 1994)

13. G. Ledlow, and M. Cwiek. "The process of leading: Assessment and comparison of leadership team style, operating climate and expectation of the external environment," in *Global Business and Technology Association Proceedings*, (Lisbon, Portugal, July 1995.)

14. G. Ledlow, M. Cwiek, and J. Johnson, "Dynamic culture leadership: Effective leader as both scientist and artist." Global Business and Technology Association (GBATA) International Conference; *Beyond Boundaries: Challenges of Leadership, Innovation, Integration and Technology*, eds N. Delener & C-n. Chao (2002), 694–740. First reported in the GBATA publication.

15. J. P. Eicher, making strategy happen. *Performance Improvement*, 45, no. 10 (2006), 3148.

16. J. P. Eicher, making strategy happen. *Performance Improvement*.

17. J. P. Eicher, making strategy happen. *Performance Improvement*.

18. J. Higgins, *The management challenge*, 2nd ed. (New York: Macmillan,1994).

19. T. J., Van der Werff and CMC. "Strategic planning for fun and profit," *Global Future* (2009), *Global Future* http://www.globalfuture.com/planning9.htm (accessed 27 Jul. 2015).

20. C. W. Choo, "Environmental scanning as information seeking and organizational learning." *Information Research*, 7, no. 1 (2001, October).

21. J. R. Griffith, *The well-managed healthcare organization*, 4th ed. (Chicago: Health Administration Press, 1999), 1.

22. J. Rakich, B. Longest, and K. Darr, *Managing health services organizations*. (Baltimore, MD: Health Professions Press, 1992), 17.

23. Rand Corporation. http://www.rand.org/cgi-bin/health/showab.cgi?key=1998_77&year=1998 (accessed 11 May 2009).

24. Harvard University School of Public Health. http://www.hsph.harvard.edu/news/press-releases/2008-releases/life-expectancy-worsening-or-stagnating-for-large-segment-of-the-us-population.html (accessed 11 May 2009).

25. Centers for Disease Control and Prevention. http://www.cdc.gov/mmwr/preview/mmwrhtml/mm5206a2.htm (accessed 11 May 2009).

26. J. P. Kotter, "Leading change: Why transformation efforts fail." *Harvard Business Review* (Boston: Harvard Business School Press, 1998), 7.

27. G, Ledlow and J. Stephens, Decision making and communication. In *Organizational theory, behavior*

and development ed. J. A. Johnson (Sudbury, MA: Jones and Bartlett, 2008) 213–232.

28. P. Thunholm Military leaders and followers: Do they have different decision styles? *Scandinavian Journal of Psychology*, 50, no. 4, (2009), 317–324.

29. H. A. Simon, Decision making and problem solving. In *Research briefings 1986: Report of the Research Briefing Panel on Decision Making and Problem Solving.* (Washington, DC: National Academy Press, 1986), http://www.dieoff.org/page163.htm (accessed 8 Jul. 2009).

30. K. Black, and L. Revere, Six Sigma arises from the ashes of TQM with a twist. *International Journal of Health Care Quality Assurance*, 19, no. 3, (2006). 259–266. Retrieved May 2, 2009, from ABI/INFORM Global database. Document ID: 1073443771 (accessed 2 May 2009).

31. S. Morgan, and C. Cooper, "Shoulder work intensity with Six Sigma." *Nursing Management,* 35, no. 3, (2004), 29–32. ABI/INFORM Global database. Document ID: 583229661 (accessed 2 May 2009).

32. R. Hirst and D. Weimer, "Management systems keep hospitals from meeting goals." *Managed Healthcare Executive*, 18, no. 5 (2008), 26–27. ABI/INFORM Global database. Document ID: 1500296291 (accessed 30 Apr. 2009).

33. P. Baker, "Get the right blend." *Works Management*, 58, no. 3 (2005, March), 26–28. ABI/ INFORM Global database. Document ID: 816940421 (accessed 30 Apr. 2009).

34. Hirst and Weimer, "Management systems keep hospitals from meeting goals."

35. J. Burns and M. Sipkoff, *1999 hospital strategies in managed care.* (New York: Faulkner and Gray, 1998).

36. M. N. Coppola, "The hidden value of managing worker's compensation costs in the hospital setting," in *1999 Hospital Strategies in Managed Care*, eds J. Burns and M. Sipkoff (New York: Faulkner and Gray Publishers, 1998), 227–255.

37. J. Singh and H. Singh, "Kaizen philosophy: A review of literature." *ICFAI Journal of Operations Management*, 8, no. 2 (2009). 51–72.

38. S. A. Ellife, "Cutting out the fat." *Journal of Commerce*, (2004, May 3), 22. ABI/INFORM Global database. Document ID: 626516031 (accessed 29 May 2009).

39. Singh and Singh, "Kaizen philosophy: A review of literature."

40. C. I. Chen and C. W. Wu, "A new focus on overcoming the improvement failure." *Technovation,* 24, (2004), 585–591.

41. J. A. Farris et al. Learning from less successful Kaizen events: A case study. *Engineering Management Journal*, 20, no. 3 (2008), 10–20. ABI/INFORM Global database. Document ID: 1582589011 (accessed 27 May 2009).

42. G. Wennecke, "Kaizen–LEAN in a week: How to Implement improvements in healthcare settings within a week." *Medical Laboratory Observer*, 40, no. 8, 28, (2008, August). 30–31. ProQuest Medical Library database. Document ID: 1555010561 (accessed 27 May 2009).

43. Wennecke, "Kaizen–LEAN in a week."

44. Singh and Singh, "Kaizen philosophy: A review of literature."

45. A Primer on GPOs, *Healthcare Supply Chain Association*, (2011), http://www.supplychainassociation.org /resource/resmgr/research/gpo_primer.pdf (accessed 9 Apr. 2015).

46. Vendor Managed Inventory: What is VMI? *Datalliance*, (2008), http://www.datalliance.com/whatisvmi.html (accessed 9 Apr. 2015).

47. Vendor Managed Inventory: What is VMI? *Datalliance*

48. Devicemaker sales reps being replaced in the OR – *Modern Healthcare*, (2014), http://www.modernhealth care.com/article/20140816/MAGAZINE/308169980 (accessed 9 Apr. 2015).

49. The Problem with Medical Sales Rep Credentialing, (2015), https://www.medreps.com/medical-sales -careers/medical-sales-rep-credentialing/ (accessed 9 Apr. 2015).

50. The Problem with Medical Sales Rep Credentialing, (2015).

51. WJ, Drummond and S.P. French, "The future of GIS in planning: converging technologies and diverging interests." *Journal of American Planners Association.* 74, no. 2 (2008),161–174. doi:10 .1080/01944360801982146

52. W. Phillips, "Selection and implementation of EMR systems," in *Health informatics: a systems perspective,* eds G.D. Brown, T.B. Patrick, and K.S. Pasupathy (Chicago, IL: Health Administration Press, 2013), 37–61.

53. "Just-in-time." *Toyota Global.* http://www.toyota -global.com/company/vision_philosophy/toyota _production_system/just-in-time.html (accessed 30. May 2015).

54. HJ. Miller and S. Shih-Lung, *Geographic information systems for transportation: Principles and applications* (New York: Oxford University Press; 2001)

55. M. Barut, W. Faisst, and J.J. Kanet. "Measuring supply chain coupling: an information system perspective." *European Journal of Purchase Supply Management.* 8, no. 3 (2002),161–171. doi:10.1016/S0969-7012(02) 00006-0

56. H. Aronsson, M. Abrahamsson, and K. Spens. "Developing lean and agile health care supply chains." *Supply Chain Management.* 16, no. 3 (2011), 176–183. doi:10.1108/13598541111127164

57. J.B. Naylor, M.M. Naim, and D. Berry, "Legality: integrating the lean and agile manufacturing paradigms in the total supply chain." *International Journal of Production Economics.* 62, no. 1 (1999), 107–118.

58. R, Bi et al. "Developing organizational agility through IT and supply chain capability." *Journal of Global Information Management.* 21, no. 4 (2013), 38–55. doi:10.4018/jgim.2013100103

59. Aronsson, Abrahamsson, and Spens. "Developing lean and agile health care supply chains."

60. Naylor, Naim, and Berry, "Legality: integrating the lean and agile manufacturing paradigms in the total supply chain."

61. A. Fallin et al. "Measuring compliance with tobacco-free campus policy." *Journal of American College Health.* 60, no. 7, (2012), 496–504.

62. A. Bazemore, P. Diller, and M. Carrozza, "The impact of a clinic move on vulnerable patients with chronic disease: a geographic information systems (GIS) analysis." *Journal of the American Board of Family Medice.* 23 no. 1 (2010), 128–130. doi:10.3122/jabfm.2010.01.090103

63. R. Skinner, ed. *GIS in hospital and healthcare emergency management.* (Boca Raton, FL: CRC Press; 2010).

64. V.K. Bansal "Application of geographic information systems in construction safety planning." *International Journal of Project Management*, 29 (2011), 66–77. oi:10.1016/j.ijproman.2010.01.007

65. V.K. Bansal, M. Pal, "Potential of geographic information systems in building cost estimation and visualization." *Automatic Construction*, 16 (2007), 311–322. doi:10.1016/j.autcon.2006.07.002

66. J. Irizarry, E.P. Karan and F. Jalaei, "Integrating BIM and GIS to improve the visual monitoring of construction supply chain management." *Automat Construction*, 31 (2013), 241–254. doi:10.1016/j.autcon.2012.12.005

MEASURING COMPATIBILITY GAPS IN RELATIONSHIPS AND BUSINESS MODELS THAT INFLUENCE STRATEGY

LEARNING OBJECTIVES

1. Describe the concept of value in strategic relationships in healthcare supply-chain sourcing/acquiring.
2. Describe and provide an example to support the Oliver Williamson statement: "There are many hidden transaction costs associated with performing work that is non-core to the organization."
3. Apply the compatibility and trust assessment and model to an ideal hypothetical healthcare supply-chain relationship and to a less-than-ideal hypothetical healthcare supply-chain relationship.
4. Explain and assess the importance of the differences between the CAAVE and Kraljic models.
5. Synthesize the concepts of business models and relationship compatibility and trust with regard to sustainable healthcare supply-chain management practices.
6. Evaluate the application of the different sourcing business models in the context of the healthcare supply chain.

Introduction

Strategic ideas and thinking are the focus for the remainder of the text. This chapter focuses on relationships between supply and buyer (manufacturer/ distributor/GPO and the health organization) models to improve supply-chain relationship decisions and strategic business models that influence those supply-chain relationships. The first section of this chapter develops the concept of value-building relationships (consider the Value Chain) and shows a model of categorization for value relationships and measurement of compatibility and trust between

entities in a supply-chain relationship. Measuring compatibility gaps in strategic relationships was developed by the authors of this textbook and Dr. James Stephens, DHA. The next section of the chapter focuses on business models and strategies associated with those models. The unpacking sourcing business model was revised and integrated into this chapter due to the strategic importance of the concepts, and the work was developed by Kate Vitasek, Bonnie Keith, Jim Eckler, Dawn Evans, Jacqui Crawford, Karl Manrodt PhD, Katherine Kawamato, and Srinivas Krishna.

FIGURE 11.1   Dr. James Stephens

Measuring Compatibility Gaps in Strategic Relationships

"With the increasing significance of the purchasing function, purchasing decisions become more important. As organizations become more dependent on suppliers the direct and indirect consequences of poor decision making become more severe. [...]Globalisation of trade and the Internet enlarge a purchaser's choice set. [...] New organisational forms lead to the involvement of more decision-makers."[1] Have firms evolved to adapt to these modern realities or do firms reenact the medieval "War of the Roses" when negotiating strategic relationships? Are finding and selecting outsourcing partners a "battle" for the "throne?" Do traditional models and concepts of strategic outsourcing rest on tenets of "War" rather than long-term mutual

reward? Is a new integrative model required for modern and dynamic environments?

"The Wars of the Roses were a series of dynastic civil wars fought between supporters of two rival branches of the royal House of Plantagenet: the houses of Lancaster and York (whose heraldic symbols were the 'red' and the 'white' rose, respectively) for the throne of England. They were fought in several sporadic episodes between 1455 and 1485, although there was related fighting both before and after this period. The final victory went to a relatively remote Lancastrian claimant, Henry Tudor, who defeated the last Yorkist king Richard III and married Edward IV's daughter Elizabeth of York to unite the two houses. The House of Tudor subsequently ruled England and Wales for 117 years."[2] In many situations, traditional thought, concepts, and models perpetuate the "War of the Roses" between firms just as the Houses of York and Lancaster perpetuated a power-based, competitive/muscular style, uncertainty and risk-reduction approach to a long-term strategy. Henry Tudor solved the conflict with an approach that mutually benefited both "Houses" or "firms" and became King of England. The strategic relationship lasted 117 years. Could the lessons from the "War of the Roses," and the solution and subsequent success of Henry Tudor and both royal "Houses," apply to strategic outsourcing relationships? A simple historically accurate figure may be best to supply the answer. What approach can you determine from the following figure?

Strategic relationships, networks of outsourcing arrangements, and partnerships are commonplace for businesses given the increasing complexity of globalization, competition, and financial implications. Strategic relationships have grown in number and complexity over the past two decades. Given these realities, have traditional models of strategic relationships, outsourcing arrangements, and partnerships that mimic tenets of the "War of the Roses" become less ecologically valid? Have these traditional models with focus on power, uncertainty reduction, risk, and leverage lost their viability and reliability in contemporary business arrangements? With support of literature, expertise, and experiential knowledge from large firms engaging in Vested Outsourcing and market and relationship

FIGURE 11.2   House of York White Rose, House of Lancaster Red Rose and the Solution, the Tudor Rose

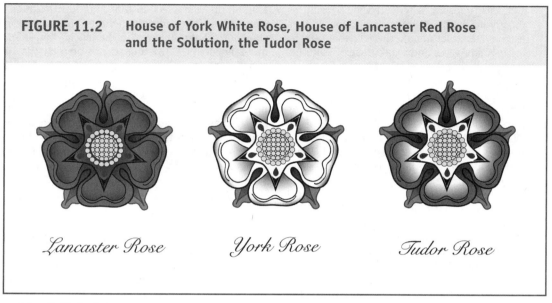

Lancaster Rose   *York Rose*   *Tudor Rose*

© Jane Rix/Shutterstock

dynamics and compatibility assessment, proposed is a set of constructs within a dynamic model that will attend to concerns of globalization, dynamic forces, mutual benefit, and compatibility (organizational culture constructs) in addition to past concerns of uncertainty reduction and risk; leverage, however, is matched with more mutually beneficial arrangements better poised for the environment of modern business. The model also integrates the work of Nash and Williamson, both Nobel Prize recipients. In essence, presented is an application of a "Tudor Rose" for strategic outsourcing relationships and partnerships.

Support for the new set of constructs and model, the CAAVE model (Tudor Rose), begins with prominent scholars of strategic relationships, literature support and followed by case study support as an example from a firm (shown in figures). The journey begins with John Nash in his game-theory based "win-win" cooperative theory to more recent work by Oliver Williamson in his work with "transaction cost economics" or TCE. Given these two scholars' work, the traditional model of Kraljic, used for decades from an industrial age mindset, tends to be one sided and

less than mutually beneficial for both strategic relationship entities. Carter and Easton direct that the traditional purchasing portfolio matrix developed by Kraljic "is not effective within the realm of SSCM."[3] (SSCM is sustainable supply chain management). Likewise, Caniels and Gelderman offer, "...the conditions determining the choice for a specific purchasing strategy within a quadrant are yet unclear [concerning the Kraljic Model]".[4] This is most likely due to the lack of clear measurement in the Kraljic Model. Williamson provides a broad framework with which the CAAVE model partially solidifies.

Williamson provides TCE the following queries for SCM:

1. TCE is based on a pragmatic methodology[5]
2. What is the methodological approach of SCM?[6]
3. What views of human nature are most compatible SCM?[7]
4. What are the implications for research methods and research agendas dealing with SCM?[8]
5. The view of TCE is that governance is the means to infuse order, with the effect of mitigating conflict and realize mutual gains.

6. TCE also describes governance structures, mostly markets both hybrids and hierarchies, as discrete structural alternatives that possess distinct strengths and weaknesses in autonomous and coordinated adaptations.
7. What is the purpose of SCM following a governance structure?
8. How should alternative methods of governance be described?
9. Operationalizing TCE is accomplished through naming key attributes based on which transactions differ, describing governance structures similarly and using the discriminating alignment hypothesis – according to which transactions that differ in their attributes are aligned with governance structures with different their costs and competencies in a transaction cost economizing way.
10. How is SCM operationalized?"[9]

From this support, it is reasonable to migrate from the Kraljic Model to a modern model that allows movement between quadrants based on assessment and measurement, based in both market dynamics and relationship dynamics, and considers firm compatibility. Taken in its entirety, this model must integrate with the forward-thinking work of Nash and the TCE performance considerations of an agreement put forth by Williamson.

Considering the integration with Nash and Williamson, a key premise of the CAAVE model is to answer and tangibly validate Williamson's queries to the supply-chain domain but specifically to embed organizational behavior and theory (namely relationship dynamics and compatibility of firms based on organizational culture constructs) into the framework of Nash's and Williamson's constructs. Tate and Ellram suggest and support the analytical and measurement approach, "the strategic sourcing process consists of a number of formal steps: identification of need, analysis, sourcing, negotiation and contracting, implementation, measurement and management."[10] Compatibility and the measurement of compatibility and relationship dynamics between firms are the tangible evidence necessary to validate the integration of these theories and models into a cohesive whole. These tenets support a long-term and mutually beneficial approach as supported by Cannon, Doney,

Mullen, and Petersen, in that long-term relationships allows firms to be patient and focus less on short-term gains in favor of beneficial long-term mutual benefits.[11] "Existing articles on methods for supplier selection do not sufficiently address this contextual issue [that methods are not useful in all purchasing situations]. Often they assume, explicitly or implicitly, that their method is applicable in all purchasing contexts."[12] The integration of the constructs across these three theories and models can improve success of long-term, modern, mutually beneficial, and financially rewarding strategic relationships.

Model

A more systematic and transparent approach is needed to strategic sourcing.[13] First, an overview of the model is presented followed by compatibility and measurement of compatibility constructs. The higher order model is a migration from the Kraljic Model to a more modern and dynamic structure. The model also proposes strategic partnership or relationship styles; these styles are matched with Williamson's styles to show the evolution of thought in the CAAVE model and the focus on Nash's "win-win" concepts.

In comparing the two models, several concepts are presented to support the need to evolve to a more contemporary model. "Following these elaborations of Kraljic's model, another line of development can be observed. This second wave focuses on classifying the content of buyer-supplier relationships as opposed to the initial focus set by Kraljic."[14] In addition, the results of research findings by Cousins and Spekman offer, "the interviews highlighted two clear relationship clusters, which we called "Opportunistic" and "Collaborative."[15] Opportunistic relationships are focused mainly on short-term price reduction technique; the strategy is to create a competitive advantage via leveraging the supply market but only on the ability to extract a price concession. This approach usually utilized Kraljic's strategic positioning matrix and was in most cases initiated by the use of corporate consultants. The problem, as the majority indicated, was that in the medium to long term this strategy could not be sustained. Interviewees who wanted to sustain cost reduction used the collaborative relationship model. This model

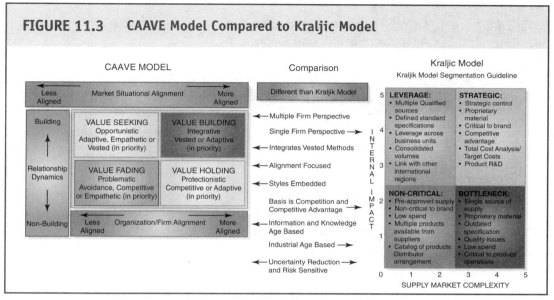

FIGURE 11.3   CAAVE Model Compared to Kraljic Model

Reproduced from Ledlow, J. R., Manrodt, K. B., Stephens, J. H. (2012). Measuring Compatibility Gaps in Strategic Relationships. In Dr. Leonora Fuxman (Ed.), GBATA (1st ed., vol. 14, pp. 10). New York, New York: Global Business and Technology Association.

clearly shows that there are ranges of aspects that are important when looking at how a firm deals with its relationships. Dubois and Pedersen offer, "…we argue that using 'given' [power-dependence models] products as a port of departure, in addition to a dyadic perspective on purchasing management, may be counterproductive when purchasing efficiency is concerned.[16] First, the object of exchange is not 'given' when firms interact, but may be subject to continuous joint development. Second, the dyadic perspective may obscure potentials for enhancing productivity and innovativeness since both parties have other relationships that impact on the collaboration between them." Lastly, "How could one deduce strategies from a portfolio analysis that is based on just two dimensions" and often the supplier's side is disregarded with the Kraljic model.[17] Considering the current evidence, the CAAVE approach minimizes the concerns raised and incorporates contemporary constructs necessary for thorough evaluation of strategic relationships in a parsimonious framework. The CAAVE model rests on four quadrants while integrating market and relationship dynamics as well as firm compatibility based on assessment of each the set of axes' constructs.

In support of these quadrants, DuBois and Pedersen offer, "we argue that these problems [using Kraljic as compared to the industrial-network approach] and solutions may lead much further, as they are not concerned with optimization, or resource allocation, but with 'total' cost considerations and joint value creation."[18] Integrating TCE and "win-win" approaches in strategic relationships, the operational issue of sourcing and supply chain evidently come to light. "It is encouraging to note, however, that there is a very strong trend toward integrating theory in SSCM research."[19]

However, it is necessary to validate the inclusion of organizational theory, human dynamics, communication, and leadership into the genre of outsourcing as firms strategically seek relationships for purposes of contracts and partnerships. Williamson supports that strategic relationships need development and evolution to incorporate relationship constructs, "James Buchanan advises that economics as a science of contract is underdeveloped and that this should be rectified"[20] and "…additional gains can be realized if order-preserving mechanisms are devised that enable the parties to preserve cooperation during contract execution."[21] Carter and Easton

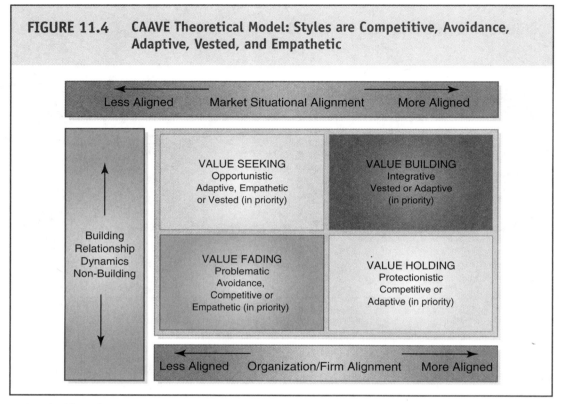

FIGURE 11.4 CAAVE Theoretical Model: Styles are Competitive, Avoidance, Adaptive, Vested, and Empathetic

Reproduced from Ledlow, J. R., Manrodt, K. B., Stephens, J. H. (2012). Measuring Compatibility Gaps in Strategic Relationships. In Dr. Leonora Fuxman (Ed.), GBATA (1st ed., vol. 14, pp. 10). New York, New York: Global Business and Technology Association.

support the inclusion of constructs of strategy (sustainability), organizational culture, and transparency (stakeholder engagement) with the goal of sustainability into the evolution of the "Tudor Rose" model supported by the CAAVE model.[22] The strongest guidance offered by Williamson follows:

Both the economist Friedrich Hayek and the organization theorist Chester Barnard were in general agreement on this point. Hayek focused on the adaptation of economic players who adjust spontaneously to changes in the market. After looking 'at the price system as…a mechanism for communication information,' the wonder of the market is in 'how little the individual participants need to know to be able to take the right action.' Barnard discussed coordinated adaptation between economic players working through an administrative hierarchy. Therefore, economic

theory meets organizational theory in practice. Adaptation of both autonomous and coordination are both important. However, if autonomous adaptation is confined to economics and coordinated adaptation is related to organization theory, how can these two viewpoints be combined? The answer is through common ground.[23]

Interestingly as a "backwards" argument, TCE has had a similar problem integrating into supply-chain practices. "Interestingly, transaction cost economics is one of the lesser used theories in the SSCM literature that we reviewed. This suggests an opportunity for future research. One particular relevant facet of transaction cost economics is that of the bounded rationality of actors, which occurs due to limits associated with communication and information processing capabilities and relatedly, the potential for opportunistic behavior"[24] It is clear that purchasing, outsourcing,

FIGURE 11.5   Linking Market Dynamics in the CAAVE Model for Style Selection

What Contract & Partnership Style Should I Use in a Specific Situation?
MARKET SITUATIONAL ASSESSMENT

This intends to assess the situational context of the contract or partnership
between organizational parties

Place a capital 'X' in the Appropriate Box

Example: To What Level is this Assessment Easy to Use?

1. The Transaction Costs Are Understood at What Level? (Contract activity cost, logistics cost, storage cost, pilferage cost, security cost, etc...)

2. At What Level is the Dollar Value (Volume) of the Contract or Partnership? (Total value/worth of the relationship under consideration)

3. Did You Have a Prior Relationship with the Other Party and What was the Worth of That Relationship? (Use 'Low' if No Prior Relationship)

4. Are the Items, Material, Supplies, Knowledge, Networks, etc... Substitutable and to What Degree?

5. To What Degree is this Contract or Relationship Critical to Your Organization?

Reproduced from Ledlow, J. R., Manrodt, K. B., Stephens, J. H. (2012). Measuring Compatibility Gaps in Strategic Relationships. In Dr. Leonora Fuxman (Ed.), GBATA (1st ed., vol. 14, pp. 10). New York, New York: Global Business and Technology Association.

relationships, and supply chain are connected; "some firms are recognizing that in order to accommodate the evolution of PSM [purchasing and supply management] to becoming a strategic corporate function, professionals need to change their skill sets from completing transactions and expediting orders to managing their supply chains."[25] For this new reality to emerge, the integration and inclusion of TCE, organizational theory, human dynamics (coupled as relationship dynamics and compatibility of firms) and supply-chain practices and principles into an amalgam of a model based on mutually beneficial "win-win" "Tudor Rose" tenets is at hand in the modern strategic outsourcing and relationship environment.

Critical for relationship dynamics and compatibility determination, communication theory must also be integrated into the discussion. Tate and Ellram provide, "while decision makers often intend to act rationally, they are limited by their own information processing and communication ability."[26] Additionally, "...a learning supply chain could be seen as a response to uncertainty, which drives partners to collaborate and increases the value of information. However, they also state that the same uncertainty that motivates firms to collaborate also offers the partners a chance to behave opportunistically. It follows that risks and benefits in supply relationships can be connected to each other."[27] "Fundamentally, or perhaps ideally, a great part of

managing supply chains essentially has to do with communicating and negotiating effectively with supply-chain members. Without this communication and negotiating, the supply chain ceases to exist, as its *modus operandi* has gone".[28]

Integrating organizational theory, human dynamics, communication and leadership as relationship dynamics and compatibility constructs in the evolution of strategic relationships into the Nash and Williamson framework are evident. However, operationalization is key; "talking about the 'black box' of transaction cost economics,...prioritization, conceptualization and operationalization are needed."[29] Hallikas, et al. (2005) strongly support this view.

Two broad models of supplier classification: Continuum Approach which is based on transaction cost economics, core competencies and governance structures where suppliers are classified into market based (adversarial) relations, partnership relations and joint ventures or hierarchy based relations; second approach is the portfolio approach (such as used by Kraljic) where suppliers are classified according to the strength of the relationship and relative supplier attractiveness (Olsen and Ellram, 1997) while Kraljic (1983) uses purchasing power and supply risk as their criteria. "Finally, most portfolio frameworks neglect the supplier's perspective.

The main driver in terms of entering long-term relationships with customers is often the added value of the supplier rather than reduced purchasing costs."[30]

For relationship dynamics and compatibility, in the recognition of human actors, "Herbert Simon contends that 'Nothing is more important in setting our research agenda and informing our research methods than our view of the nature of the human beings whose behavior we are studying' (1985, p.303)" and "...the effect of which is to facilitate adaptation, preserve continuity and realize mutual gain during contract implementation."[31] From this direction, relationship dynamics and organizational (culture otherwise called compatibility) alignment can be established as essential constructs for measurement of strategic relationships between firms. However, a simple yet accurate model is suggested by Williamson as the need for "useful parsimony to pull out central forces and remove the rest and data matters."[32] In addition, "Ignoring or de-emphasizing the relationship between an organization and its suppliers creates conflict when each firm behaves in a way that maximizes its own interest. Involving the right people and clearly defining roles, responsibilities and accountability across the two organizations could minimize opportunistic behavior, thereby improving the relationship."[33]

Relationship or "negotiating" or "posturing" styles are also an issue to evolve the traditional "War of the Roses" approach to a modern application of a flexible yet efficient model. Styles must be selected and used as dynamic forces change the situation or environment; "If organizations do not adapt to changes, poor alignment with supply chain partners will result".[34] Williamson offers muscular, benign/dysfunctional, and credible styles to the argument. However, "the cumulative forces of competition nevertheless serve as a check upon excesses of muscular contracting".[35] Competitive/muscular as well as avoidance styles can damage relationships; thus more collaborative styles are required. In support of collaborative styles, especially a vested style, "Relationships tend to be more stable and mutually beneficial when both parties will experience a loss if the relationship fails."[36] Caniels and Gelderman also support a value-building approach; in that both buyer and supplier dependence in the relationship are important.[37] "Our findings suggest that relatively high levels of both buyer's and supplier's dependence constitute conditions for engaging in a partnership and thereby follow a strategy aimed at moving to another quadrant [of the Kraljic model]."[38] Cousins and Spekman offer, "...purchasing is moving from a clerical function towards a strategic process."[39] In essence, firms should move away from "arms-length" relationships and adopt "obligation"-based approaches.[40] An overview and application context of the CAAVE model styles follow.

TABLE 11.1   CAAVE Styles Examined

Competitive

1. When quick, decisive action is vital to the organization (e.g., emergency situations such as a disaster or terrorism incident or accident).
2. On important issues where unpopular actions need implementing (e.g., cost cutting, enforcing unpopular rules, discipline).
3. On issues vital to company welfare and survival when you know you're right.
4. Against people who take advantage of noncompetitive behavior.

Avoidance

1. When an issue is trivial or more important issues are pressing.
2. When you perceive no chance of satisfying your needs.
3. When potential disruption outweighs the benefits of resolution.

4. To let people cool down and regain perspective.
5. When gathering information supersedes immediate decision.
6. When the relationship could be damaging to the organization and is not critical.
7. When partnering or contracting seems rushed or pushed as a result of other issues; short-term strategy to buy time.

Adaptive

1. When goals are important, but not worth the effort or potential disruption of competing since the situation does not allow a collaborative approach.
2. When opponents with equal power are committed to mutually exclusive goals; you adapt to the contract/partnership situation and create the most advantageous position.
3. To achieve temporary settlements to complex issues.
4. To arrive at expedient solutions under time pressure.
5. As a backup when a vested or competitive style is unsuccessful.

Vested

1. May not always work (takes two to make this style work) and requires trust between parties.
2. Requires the identification of a broader range of strategies, transaction costs and longer term goals.
3. Points for the vested style.
   a. Both parties must have a vested interest in the outcome (the resolution).
   b. Both parties feel a better solution can be achieved through problem-based collaboration.
   c. Both parties recognize the problem is caused by the relationship, not the people involved.
   d. Focus is on solving the problem, not on accommodating differing views.
   e. Both parties are flexible.
   f. Understanding that all solutions have positive and negative aspects.
   g. Both parties understand each other's issues.
   h. Problem is looked at objectively, not personally.
   i. Both parties are knowledgeable about conflict management.
   j. Allow everyone to "save face."
   k. Celebrate successful outcomes openly.
4. To find an integrative solution when both sets of concerns are too important to be compromised.
5. When your objective is to learn and mutually benefit from the relationship.
6. To merge insights from people with different perspectives.
7. To gain commitment by incorporating concerns into a consensus.
8. To work through organizational issues, like transaction costs, service levels, etc. that could harm a relationship.

Empathetic

1. When you find you are wrong; to allow a better position to be heard, to learn, and to show your reasonableness.
2. When issues are more important to others than to you; to satisfy others and maintain cooperation.
3. To build social capital for later issues.
4. To minimize loss when you are outmatched and lack any competitive advantage.
5. When harmony and stability are especially important; when you are building up a weaker partner in the market.
6. To allow subordinates to develop by learning from their mistakes.

Reproduced from Ledlow, J. R., Manrodt, K. B., Stephens, J. H. (2012). Measuring Compatibility Gaps in Strategic Relationships. In Dr. Leonora Fuxman (Ed.), GBATA (1st ed., vol. 14, pp. 10). New York, New York: Global Business and Technology Association.

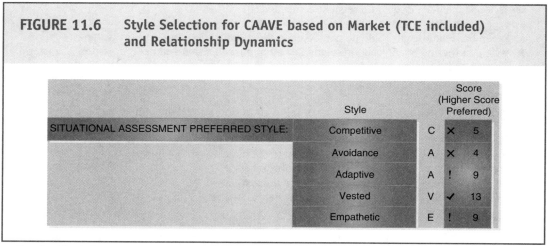

FIGURE 11.6 Style Selection for CAAVE based on Market (TCE included) and Relationship Dynamics

	Style		Score (Higher Score Preferred)	
SITUATIONAL ASSESSMENT PREFERRED STYLE:	Competitive	C	✕	5
	Avoidance	A	✕	4
	Adaptive	A	!	9
	Vested	V	✔	13
	Empathetic	E	!	9

Reproduced from Ledlow, J. R., Manrodt, K. B., Stephens, J. H. (2012). Measuring Compatibility Gaps in Strategic Relationships. In Dr. Leonora Fuxman (Ed.), GBATA (1st ed., vol. 14, pp. 10). New York, New York: Global Business and Technology Association.

The CAAVE model enables assessment, initially based on market dynamics (includes consideration of TCE) and basic relationship dynamics. This assessment offers recommendations of styles for firms to utilize within the buyer-supplier relationship.

The strategic alignment model (in Cousins and Spekman's article) shows how important it is to align strategies.[41] However, it is also equally important to develop these approaches by aligning both the performance measurement systems and the skills and competencies of the individuals involved within

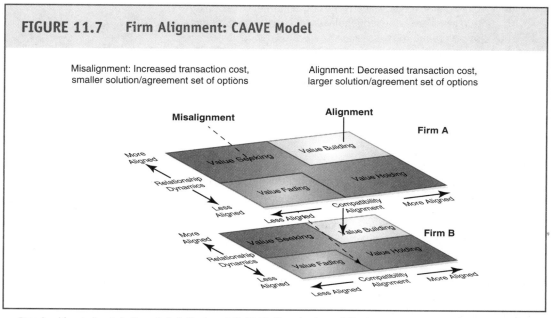

FIGURE 11.7 Firm Alignment: CAAVE Model

Misalignment: Increased transaction cost, smaller solution/agreement set of options

Alignment: Decreased transaction cost, larger solution/agreement set of options

Reproduced from Ledlow, J. R., Manrodt, K. B., Stephens, J. H. (2012). Measuring Compatibility Gaps in Strategic Relationships. In Dr. Leonora Fuxman (Ed.), GBATA (1st ed., vol. 14, pp. 10). New York, New York: Global Business and Technology Association.

FIGURE 11.8 CAAVE Assessment Style Alignment by Firms

Assess alignment of the contract and partnership factors with applicable styles from the CAAVE Model				

Relationship	Non-Building		Building		
	Competitive	Avoidance	Adaptive	Vested	Empathetic
	C	A	A	V	E
Market & Situational Assessment					
Relationship Dynamics Assessment					
Party A Organizational CAAVE Profile					
Party B Organizational CAAVE Profile					
Party C Organizational CAAVE Profile					
ASSESSMENT (type in Yes or NO for each style)					

	Competitive	Avoidance	Adaptive	Vested	Empathetic
	C	A	A	V	E

Reproduced from Ledlow, J. R., Manrodt, K. B., Stephens, J. H. (2012). Measuring Compatibility Gaps in Strategic Relationships. In Dr. Leonora Fuxman (Ed.), GBATA (1st ed., vol. 14, pp. 10). New York, New York: Global Business and Technology Association.

procurement."[42] Alignment of compatible strategies enables the more thorough assessment of relationship dynamics and compatibility between firms.

Integrating CAAVE model styles with Williamson's styles within the quadrants (with suggested styles for each quadrant) is the next focus of the model. Style migration within quadrants is expected in the model. It is important to note that Nash's "win-win" model integrates in the CAAVE Model only in the upper right half of the model (Value Building quadrant specifically).

The CAAVE model integrates Nash's and Williamson's concepts within a flexible framework. Once firms, such as JLL, Coca-Cola, Cardinal Health, Amgen, Cigna, and others, assess their strategic outsourcing relationship in the upper right quadrants with a reasonable level of alignment between styles, deeper relationship dynamics and compatibility, as well as trust, assessments can be conducted. The next section overviews this step in the sequence within the CAAVE model.

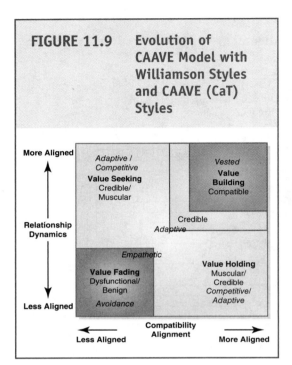

FIGURE 11.9 Evolution of CAAVE Model with Williamson Styles and CAAVE (CaT) Styles

Note: Compatible was added by authors to expand Williamson's Styles.

Reproduced from Ledlow, J. R., Manrodt, K. B., Stephens, J. H. (2012). Measuring Compatibility Gaps in Strategic Relationships. In Dr. Leonora Fuxman (Ed.), *GBATA* (1st ed., vol. 14, pp. 10). New York, New York: Global Business and Technology Association.

Compatibility Measurement

The constructs of relationship dynamics and compatibility between firms have been provided in earlier discussion and are clearly important. Trust, likewise, becomes a key issue in style selection and movement toward a "value building" (upper right quadrant) or "Tudor Rose" approach. "Trust is essential to relationship building."[43] "Awareness or suspicion of opportunistic behavior causes diminished levels of trust in buyer-supplier relationships. The lack of trust, opportunistic behavior and uncertainty in off-shore outsourcing increases the inability to effectively align incentives across the supply chain. It also creates increased purchasing complexity and higher transaction costs."[44] Bringing styles to the forefront of the CAAVE model, Cannon, Doney,

Mullen and Petersen suggest, "the success of this 'global sourcing' strategy depends, in part, on the ability of supply chain partners to create appropriately focused value-adding buyer-supplier relationships."[45] Supporting both trust and communication, "similarly, where trust was examined it was evident that professional services and motor service relationships were characterized by a lack of trust evidenced by a general lack of information sharing, poor levels of communication and non-co-operative behavior".[46]

Considering the previous evidence, relationship dynamics, compatibility between firms, and trust can be parsimoniously measured by sub-constructs of trust, innovation, communication, team orientation, and focus as attributed to a successful strategic relationship. Measuring compatibility for a successful "Tudor Rose," vested style, "win-win" long-term strategic relationship is completed by key stakeholders of the dyadic or triadic or quadratic relationship within an interactive survey tool that examines the key constructs from multiple angles. An example between a large firm buyer and large firm supplier are illustrated.

Cousins and Spekman heavily suggest that relationship assessment and development include relationship assessment within the realm of performance measurement for strategic relationships.[47] "Unquestionably, the supplier's side should be included in any strategic thinking on the field of purchasing and supply management."[48] Unfortunately, more managers have fallen back to qualitative methods of supplier selection [for lack of a better approach].[49] "Key to this research would be placing meaningful measurements on the effect of relationships on a company."[50]

The firms' assessment is plotted on the CAAVE model quadrants to evaluate the potential success of a "vested style" and long-term strategic relationship. The beginnings of a compatibility index for firms can be derived from this assessment. This illustrates the integration of relationship dynamics and compatibility between firms with market dynamics, TCE and "win-win" situations. Once firms engage in strategic partnerships, performance is added to the equation with ongoing relationship dynamics and compatibility assessments.

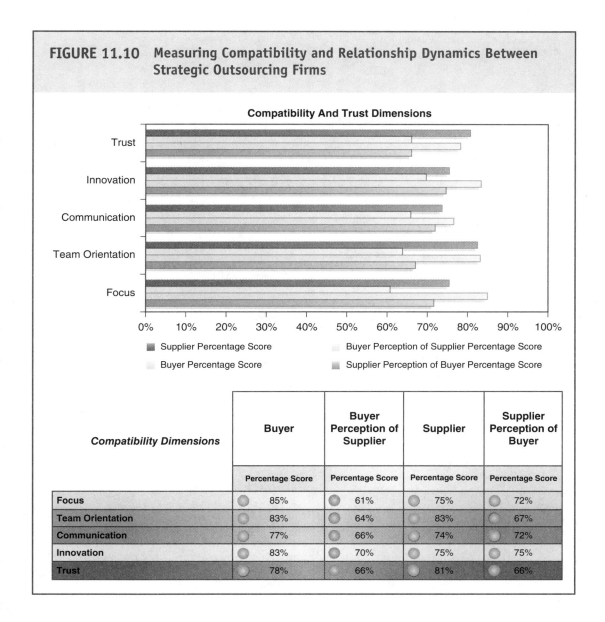

FIGURE 11.10 Measuring Compatibility and Relationship Dynamics Between Strategic Outsourcing Firms

Compatibility And Trust Dimensions

■ Supplier Percentage Score   Buyer Perception of Supplier Percentage Score

Buyer Percentage Score   ■ Supplier Perception of Buyer Percentage Score

Compatibility Dimensions	Buyer	Buyer Perception of Supplier	Supplier	Supplier Perception of Buyer
	Percentage Score	Percentage Score	Percentage Score	Percentage Score
Focus	85%	61%	75%	72%
Team Orientation	83%	64%	83%	67%
Communication	77%	66%	74%	72%
Innovation	83%	70%	75%	75%
Trust	78%	66%	81%	66%

Compatibility Summary

With support and evidence, the CAAVE Model offers a contemporary approach to evaluation of strategic partnerships. From the evidence, it was necessary to develop the relationship dynamics view of strategic partnerships while integrating cooperative game theory, transaction cost economics, and market dynamics into the package of constructs with regard to strategic agreements and partnerships among firms. In addition, research was presented illustrating the evolution of the CAAVE model and the development of a compatibility index, its theoretical

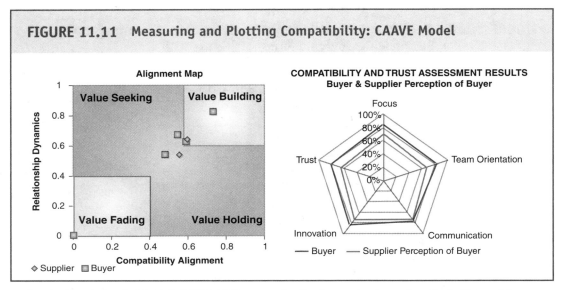

FIGURE 11.11   Measuring and Plotting Compatibility: CAAVE Model

Reproduced from Ledlow, G., & Cwiek, M. (2005, July). The process of leading: Assessment and comparison of leadership team style, operating climate, and expectation of the external environment. Proceedings of Global Business and Technology Association. Lisbon, Portugal.

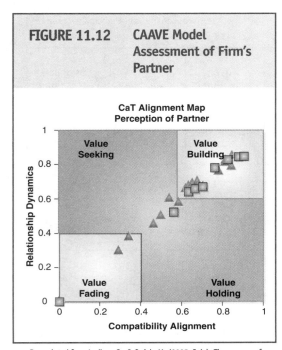

FIGURE 11.12   CAAVE Model Assessment of Firm's Partner

Reproduced from Ledlow, G., & Cwiek, M. (2005, July). The process of leading: Assessment and comparison of leadership team style, operating climate, and expectation of the external environment. Proceedings of Global Business and Technology Association. Lisbon, Portugal.

underpinnings, and how researchers are using the tool to identify gaps in perceptions in the relationship dynamics view of strategic partnerships. The "Tudor Rose" for contemporary, dynamic, and global strategic relationships was presented with hopes of further development, research, and refinement for increased efficacy for firms stuck in the "War of the Roses" environment.

Unpacking Sourcing Business Models

Adam Smith, an eccentric Scottish academician at Glasgow University, observed the human propensity for self-interest and formulated the law of supply and demand in 1776 with the publication of *An Enquiry into the Nature and Causes of the Wealth of Nations*. His theory said that society benefits as a whole from a multiplicity of trading transactions because humans seek what is best for them, resulting in fairness and honesty among equals. As demand for repeat transactions emerged, trading preferences evolved and modern transaction-based business models were born. These transaction-based business models have been the cornerstone of conventional business relationships ever since and created some of the earliest forms of outsourcing.

For the most part, transaction-based approaches served business well through the 20th century. While the concept of outsourcing had been around for decades, the 1990s brought a new spotlight to outsourcing. Business gurus such as Tom Peters and Peter Drucker advised, "Do what you do best and outsource the rest!" and Harvard Business Review featured the leading thinking of Waterman and Peters on outsourcing non-"core" competencies.[51] Many companies jumped on the outsourcing bandwagon by outsourcing complex services normally referred to as "back office" functions such as information technology, finance and accounting, facilities management, logistics and transportation, call-center support, and human resources support.

Today, virtually all businesses use the same transaction-based approach for procuring complex services (i.e., outsourcing) as they do to buy more simple commodities and supplies. Most complex outsourcing efforts fall into conventional agreements that typically focus on detailed per-transaction level pricing, paying either for a business task (cost per warehouse pallet stored, cost per minute of call, or cost per IT server) or on a per headcount basis.

Unfortunately, many business professionals wrongly assume that a transaction-based business model is the only sourcing business model. For simple transactions with abundant supply and low complexity, a transaction-based business model is likely the most efficient model. But the real weakness of a transaction-based approach emerges when any level of complexity, variability, mutual dependency, or customized assets or processes are part of the transaction. A transactional approach cannot produce perfect market-based price equilibrium in variable or multidimensional business agreements. In many instances, other approaches may be more appropriate.

The purpose of this chapter is to drive clarity around outsourcing business models and help procurement, outsourcing professionals, and commercial managers understand and use the appropriate sourcing business model to maximize their desired outcomes.

Section I. Outsourcing is a Continuum

Companies that are looking to outsource generally go through a rigorous make-versus-buy decision process before deciding to outsource. Many assume that the decision to insource versus outsource results in one of two approaches: either

deciding to use "the market" to identify qualified sources to perform the work or retaining or developing the capabilities in-house.

Oliver E. Williamson challenged the traditional make-buy decision process with his work in the area of TCE. Williamson received the Nobel Prize for his work in 2009. One of his key lessons was that companies should view outsourcing as a continuum rather than a simple market-based make-versus-buy decision.

Perhaps the best way to think of Williamson's work is to consider free-market forces on one side and what Williamson refers to as "corporate hierarchies" on the other.

At one end of the continuum is what Williamson referred to as "corporate hierarchy." Companies that use a corporate hierarchy approach to secure goods and services invest to develop capabilities themselves (or insource).

A key factor in the decision to insource versus outsource typically revolves around whether the capability is a "core competency," meaning performing the work provides a competitive differentiation. Unfortunately, it is virtually impossible for a company to be good at all activities, and these inefficiencies drive up the company's cost structures. It is this reason that visionaries such as Drucker, Waterman, and Peters encouraged companies to outsource activities that were not core competencies.

In some cases companies have concluded that they do not want to outsource non-core services.[52] As an alternative to outsourcing many of these

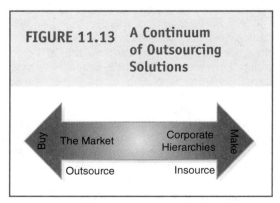

FIGURE 11.13 **A Continuum of Outsourcing Solutions**

Buy — The Market | Corporate Hierarchies — Make

Outsource | Insource

companies have chosen to adopt what is commonly referred to as a "shared services" structure, which is the establishment of an internal organization modeled on an arms-length outsourcing arrangement. Using this approach, processes are typically centralized into a "shared service" organization and departments are cross-charged for the services used.

Williamson's work notes there are many hidden transaction costs associated with performing work that is non-core to the organization. One of the downfalls is that when work is insourced there is not any competition; this provides little incentive to drive inherent improvements in cost and quality. There is also high administrative control and a legal system that is "deferential to the management." As a consequence, innovations that might come from the market or third parties are not shared or developed as rapidly as management typically likes—if at all.

Because these are additional bureaucratic costs, Williamson advises, "The internal organization is usually thought of as the organization of last resort." In other words, if at all possible companies should not insource non-core services.

Using the Market (Outsource)

Companies that choose to outsource typically use what Williamson describes as "the market" for buying goods and services. The market uses the conventional free market economy for determining how companies will do business, including establishing a price. The market mode assumes that free market forces incentivize suppliers to compete on low cost and high service. This approach also features an absence of dependency; if buyers or suppliers are not happy, they can switch at any time with relative ease. Governance of the supply base is typically accomplished by switching suppliers or customers if a better opportunity comes along. As a result, the market approach can rely purely on classical contract law and requires little administrative control.[53]

The big advantage to using the market in the decision to outsource is that it enables a competitive process in determining whether a company is getting a good transaction price. The downside to the market mode is that it often assumes that the service acquired is somewhat standardized and therefore available from a variety of suppliers. Consequently service providers are often "competed" into outsourcing agreements that pose unnecessary risks. For example, Williamson points out that service providers might have "specialized investments" that can easily expose the business to significant loss if the contract fails and for which no safeguards have been provided. Often this investment is made to support innovation, which in turn provides a higher value offering or a more efficient business model. To protect themselves, service providers will raise their price to reflect the level of risk they have taken. To counteract this, and thus provide a more acceptable price to the customer, service providers will often negotiate heavily for contract safeguards in the absence of certainty. This "give and take" is a normal part of market-based negotiations.

The Catch-22

Deciding to insource or outsource is rarely a yes-or-no decision. Although each approach offers advantages, a real Catch-22 has emerged for companies that want to drive innovation and create a competitive advantage, yet still want to outsource a particular activity.[54]

In a transaction-based environment, procurement teams endeavor to limit relationship dependency in an effort to reduce the price of goods or services. Buyers strive to have uniformly available goods and services (e.g. commodities) that can be easily compared across various suppliers. A buyer's goal is often focused around the company's bottom line, which is typically reflected in terms of "price" paid.

As complexity and dependency increase, buyers tend to migrate to an approved provider or a preferred provider sourcing relationship. For the most complex high-risk/high-cost contracts companies will tend to focus on continuity of supply due to extreme mutual dependency. In these cases, an investment-based approach to insourcing is often used. Investment-based approaches can take the form of internal capability development or co-investment such as a joint venture. Under a joint venture a company will often create an equity partnership or other legally binding business arrangement with a firm that gives the company access to the desired capabilities. Another common investment-based option is to centralize the service into a "shared services" group aimed at driving efficiencies. Shared services are discussed in more detail later.

The catch-22 comes into play because companies that are using transactional, approved, or even preferred supplier arrangements are finding that their service providers are meeting contractual obligations and service levels—but they are not driving innovations and efficiencies at the pace they would like to see. Suppliers argue that investing in their customer's business is risky because buyers will simply take their ideas and competitively bid the work. Companies want solutions to close the gaps, but they do not want to make investments in people, processes, and technology where they do not have a core competency. The result is that the industry is at a crossroads, with both buyer and service providers wanting innovation—but neither wanting to make the investment due to the conventional transaction-based commercial structure of how the companies work together.

The Rise of a Hybrid Approach

Because of this catch 22, Williamson advocated for a third "hybrid approach" as the preferred method for dealing with complex services where there is a high level of dependency and the market cannot be used to switch suppliers freely and where an insource solution may not be a good fit.

Companies that use a hybrid approach can apply various approaches with suppliers to create strategic and longer-term relationships that can offset the weaknesses found in a pure market-based or pure insource-based approach. We refer to this hybrid approach as vested indicating that both parties are invested in identifying the best collective solution.

Section II of this chapter outlines seven types of sourcing business models, including the hybrid approach most often referred to as vested outsourcing. These seven sourcing business models should be considered tools in the procurement and outsourcing professional's toolkit. Each of the sourcing business models is discussed in detail on the following pages.

Section II Types of Outsourcing Business Models

Research by the International Association for Contract and Commercial Management shows that most companies operate under conventional transaction-based models that are constrained by a formal, legally oriented, risk-averse, and liability-based culture.[55] There is growing awareness that transactional-based approaches do not always give each party the intended results. University of Tennessee (UT) research and the authors' industry-specific experiences applying alternative outcome-based approaches for complex contracts demonstrate that alternative sourcing business models are a viable alternative to the conventional transactional methods. Outcome-based approaches are gathering momentum as senior leaders see positive results from carefully crafted collaborative agreements.

This section of the white paper outlines seven sourcing business models that fall into four categories. Each model differs from a risk/reward perspective and should be evaluated in the context of what is being procured. The characteristics and attributes for each of these approaches are reviewed in detail below.

Transaction-Based Models

Most companies use transaction-based business models for their commercial agreements when they make a "buy" decision. Conventional approaches to transaction-based models keep service providers at arm's length. Three types of transaction-based sourcing relationships have evolved over time as businesses wrestle with how to create service provider relationships that are better suited for more complex business requirements. The three types are simple transaction providers, approved providers, and preferred providers.

The economics for each of these types of supplier relationships is very similar in that the supplier gets paid by the transaction. There is typically a predefined rate for each transaction, or unit of service. For example, a third party logistics service provider would get paid monthly for the number of pallets stored, the number of units picked, and the number

TABLE 11.2   Sourcing Models

Sourcing Model	Transaction Based	Performance Based/ Managed Services	Vested	Investment Based
		Outcome Based Models		
Simple Transaction Provider	X			
Approved Provider	X			
Preferred Provider	X			
Performance-Based/ Managed Services		X		
Vested Relationship			X	
Shared Services (internal)			X	X
Equitable Partner (external)				X

Reproduced from Vitasek, K et al, Unpacking Sourcing Business Models: 21st century Solutions for Sourcing Services, p. 8, Figure 2.

of orders shipped. A call-center service provider would get paid a price per call or a price per minute.

Transaction-based business models are best suited when a supplier is supplying a standardized service with stable specifications which is easily measured through a commonly understood set of metrics. Payment can be triggered based on successful transactions completed.

The three types of transaction-based providers can be described as follows:

Simple Transaction Provider

A simple transaction provider is a supplier who is one of many available in the marketplace, typically providing a low cost, repetitive service. The services provided by this type of provider are often competitively bid frequently with no interruption of service or impact to the business. Simple transactions are often triggered by a purchase order which signals that the buying company agrees to buy a set quantity of goods or tasks (or hours) outlined in the purchase order. The primary supplier relationship is solely based on a review of performance against standard metrics (did the supplier work that many hours or provide the good or service in the quantities purchased?).

Approved Provider

An approved provider is a supplier who has been identified to offer a unique differentiation from other transactional suppliers and provides a cost or efficiency advantage for the client company. The differentiation could come in the form of geographical location advantage, a cost or quality advantage, or a small disadvantaged business and is ultimately "approved" to assist with meeting the client's goals. An approved provider is identified as a pre-qualified option in the pool of transactional suppliers and has fulfilled preconditions for specified service. Procurement professionals typically turn to approved suppliers as regularly solicited sources of supply when bidding is conducted. An approved supplier may or may not operate under a master services agreement—an overarching contract with the buying company. Approved suppliers may or may not also have volume thresholds to be in an "approved" status. In addition, approved suppliers may or may not participate in supplier management reviews.

Preferred Provider

A preferred provider is a supplier that has been qualified, may have a unique differentiator, and has had demonstrated performance with the buying company. Typical conditions are met such as

- Previous experiences.
- Supplier performance rating (if the client company has a rating system).
- Previous contracts compliance performance.
- Evidence of an external certification (e.g. such as International Organization for Standardization (ISO) certification).

Buying companies often seek to do business with a preferred provider in an effort to streamline their buying process and build relationships with key suppliers. Buying companies often enter into a longer-term contract using a master services agreement that allows for the companies to do repeat business efficiently. It is common for preferred providers to work under a blanket purchase order (PO) with pre-defined rates for work. For example, a labor-staffing firm may have a "rate card" that

has the hourly rate established for various types of staffing needs. The buying company can easily request staffing support from the preferred provider using the pre-determined blanket PO and rate card. Another example might be a facilities management firm having a pre-agreed rate of a certain price per square foot to manage a company's buildings. Often companies will work with a preferred provider under a supplier relationship management plan where both companies agree on improvement or other opportunities.

It is important to point out that a preferred provider is still engaged in a transactional business model, but the nature and efficiencies for how the companies work together goes beyond a simple purchase order.

The table on the following page outlines typical characteristics of each of the transaction-based business model approaches frequently used today.

TABLE 11.3   Attributes of Transaction Based Business Models

Sourcing Relationship	Focus	Interaction	Cooperation Level	Required Trust Level	Characterized by
Simple Transaction Provider	Cost and Efficiency	Standard Terms, Fixed Price	Low-Automated where possible	Minimal – single transaction	Abundant and easy to resource, no need for a relationship
Approved Provider	Economies of Scale, Ease of transactions	Blanket, Negotiated Terms, Pricing Agreements	Medium – based on pricing or specifications	Medium – common terms and price agreement	Managed by category locally and across business sector, purchases bundled for economies of scale
Preferred Provider	Capability, Capacity, and Technology transactions	Contract, SOW, Pricing Agreement, Possible Gain Sharing SLAs	High – Set out in long term service contract	High – defined by contract, high spend zone	Integral supply across business units, delivering added value and capability, not so abundant, a pain to re-source

Outcome-Based Business Models

An outcome-based business model pays a service provider for the realization of a defined set of business outcomes, business results, or achievement of agreed-on key performance indicators. Outcome-based approaches are used most widely in the aerospace and defense industries. Often they are referred to as performance-based logistics because they couple maintenance and support to the procurement of the product. Rolls-Royce PLC was the first known organization to explore outcome-based approaches in the 1960s. However, outcome-based business models did not gain traction until around the year 2000, and the use still is limited. A good example of an outcome-based business model is when an airline pays its outsourced ground crew for achieving a twenty-minute turnaround time after the plane has been parked at the gate. In the simplest form, the service provider does not get paid if it does not deliver results. An outcome-based business model typically shifts some or all risk for achieving the outcome to the service provider.

Outcome-based business models have gained in popularity in the last few years as more companies outside of the aerospace industry have adopted the concepts and have expanded the thinking to pure outsourced service deals. A well-structured outcome-based agreement compensates a service provider's higher risk with a higher reward. However, many companies wrongfully structure deals around "all risk, no reward;" in such cases, a supplier or service provider that does not meet the desired results is penalized.

There are two types of outcome-based business models; a performance-based agreement and a vested agreement. The general rule of thumb for shifting to an outcome-based model is to drive a step function change in performance and costs. Performance-based agreements typically shift risk to the supplier and guarantee savings while a vested sourcing business model is better suited for a highly collaborative supplier relationship with the goal to drive innovation and share risk and reward.

Performance-Based Agreements

The relationship with suppliers under a performance-based agreement is different than with transactional providers. Typically performance-based agreements begin to shift the thinking away from activities to outcomes; however, they often still pay a supplier using transaction-based pricing triggers. These contracts are often also called "pay for performance" because they often have an incentive or a penalty tied to specific service level agreements (SLAs) outlined in the contract.

For example, a company outsourcing call-center services will likely still pay a cost per transaction (most often a cost per call or minute). However, they create incentives or penalties if the service provider does not hit a metric such as answering 80% of the calls within 20 seconds.[56]

Some service industries are seeing an evolution in what is known as a managed service where a supplier typically guarantees a fixed fee with a preagreed price reduction target (e.g. a 3% year-over-year price decrease) with the assumption that the supplier will deliver on productivity targets. These guaranteed savings are often referred to as a "glidepath" because an annual price reduction will be seen over time. Managed services agreements are a form of a performance-based agreement.

Performance-based agreements typically require a higher level of interface between a service provider and a buying company in order to review performance against objectives and determine the reward or penalty options that are typically embedded in the contract. These reviews are periodically scheduled and generally include representatives from the service provider and the client company contracting resources.

Occasionally the buying company's service user(s) participate in the reviews. However, in these relationships there is a great tendency for the client company to solely make the reward determination. If this is not done properly and fairly, it can cause the buyer-supplier relationship to become more adversarial in nature. It can also lead to what the UT researchers term the "Watermelon Scorecard" because it results in a service provider spending all of its time on meeting SLAs and may not lead to overall business needs such as improved flexibility or the ability to focus on process changes that may be valuable—but could risk service levels.

The length of a performance-based relationship is also typically longer in a performance-based agreement. It is not uncommon to see agreements spanning three to five years; however, the contract language may allow for termination at the client company's determination (termination for convenience) within 30, 60, or 90 days.

Vested Outsourcing

Vested outsourcing (vested for short) is a highly collaborative sourcing business model where both the client and service provider have an economic vested interest in each other's success. A good example is Microsoft and Accenture who entered into a seven-year agreement where Accenture was challenged to transform Microsoft's back office procure to pay processes. The agreement is structured so that the more successful Accenture is at achieving Microsoft's goals, the more successful Accenture itself becomes. The Microsoft-Accenture case study is profiled in Section IV.

The term vested outsourcing was originally coined by UT researchers to describe highly successful outcome-based outsourcing agreements the researchers studied as part of a large research project funded by the United Stated Air Force. UT research revealed that the vested outsourcing agreements combined an outcome-based model with the Nobel Prize-winning concepts of behavioral economics[57] and the principles of shared value.[58] Using these concepts, companies enter into highly collaborative arrangements designed to create value for all parties involved above and beyond conventional buy-sell economics of a transaction-based agreement.

The vested sourcing business model is best used when a company has transformational or innovation objectives that it cannot achieve itself or by using conventional transaction-based approaches or performance-based approaches. These transformational or innovation objectives are referred to as desired outcomes; it is these desired outcomes that form the basis of the agreement. A desired outcome is a measurable business objective that focuses on what will be accomplished as a result of the work performed. A desired outcome is not a task-oriented SLA that is often mentioned in a conventional statement of work or a performance-based agreement; rather it is a mutually agreed upon, objective, and measurable deliverable for which the service provider will be rewarded—even

if some of the accountability is shared with the company that is outsourcing. A desired outcome is generally categorized as an improvement to cost, schedule, market share, revenue, customer service levels, or performance.

Another good example of a vested agreement is Jaguar and Unipart. Unipart was inherently incentivized under their ten-year agreement to make heavy investments that would increase dealer support and ultimately improve customer loyalty for service parts management effectiveness and efficiency. Under the agreement, Unipart helped Jaguar move from number 9 in JD Power's customer loyalty to number 1.[59]

Together the companies were able to reduce the number of cars waiting on warranty parts by 98%, while reducing inventory by 35%. The following table outlines the typical characteristics of both performance-based and vested outsourcing approaches.

Shared Services

Companies that struggle to meet complex business requirements using conventional transaction-based or outcome-based approaches typically invest to develop capabilities themselves (or insource). In such cases, many companies have chosen to adopt what is commonly referred to as a "shared services" structure which is the establishment of an internal organization modeled on an arms-length outsourcing arrangement. Using this approach, processes are typically centralized into a "shared service" organization, and departments are cross-charged for the services used.

A key driver when developing a shared services organization or a joint venture structure is to centralize and standardize operations that improve operational efficiencies. The results can be significant. APQC (American Productivity and Quality Center) research shows a direct correlation between low procurement cost and a centralized or shared services procurement function. Specifically, companies with centralized and shared services procurement functions have procurement costs almost one-third of those that have decentralized functions.[60] **Figure 11.14** shows the procurement cost performance of centralized, shared, and decentralized procurement structures.

TABLE 11.4   Attributes of Outcome Based Business Models

Sourcing Relationship	Focus	Interaction	Cooperation Level	Required Trust Level	Characterized by
Performance-Based Relationship/ Managed Services	Outcomes or Performance	SRM Governance, Performance Incentives, Fees at Risk	Integrated	Integrated	Longer term relationship
Vested Relationship	Mutual Gain, Shared Outcomes	Vested Agreement, Vested Governance Framework, Performance Incentives, Margin Matching	Integrated – cooperative, Win-Win	Integrated – behave as single entity	Interdependent outcomes, aligned, mutual gain, managed performance, long term relationship

Reproduced from Vitasek, K et al, Unpacking Sourcing Business Models: 21st century Solutions for Sourcing Services, p. 13, Figure 4.

While these savings are significant, is there a better way to manage shared services? Specifically, can shared services organizations achieve further improvements by better understanding the various sourcing business models? The authors believe the answer is yes.

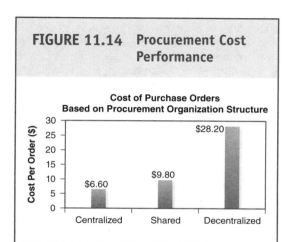

FIGURE 11.14   Procurement Cost Performance

Cost of Purchase Orders Based on Procurement Organization Structure

Cost Per Order ($)

Centralized: $6.60
Shared: $9.80
Decentralized: $28.20

The authors' experiences indicate shared services organizations typically act like an outsourced service provider, performing services and then "charging" their internal customers on a per-transaction or headcount basis. This approach very much mirrors a conventional "preferred supplier" relationship. The authors believe that shared-services organizations could and should consider adopting a vested outsourcing business model for working with their internal customers.

A vested sourcing business model seeks to align the interests of the company with the interest of the service provider by following five "rules" for structuring the buyer-supplier relationship. The authors believe these rules—if followed by shared-services organizations—will better align the interests of internal shares services organizations with their internal customers.

While many shared services organizations are set up to naturally follow some of the vested outsourcing rules, it is the authors' opinion that most shared services do not follow all five of the vested rules. Doing so would create a tighter alignment and further drive effectiveness for the provider.

TABLE 11.5   **Application of Vested Principals in Shared Services Business Models**

Vested Rule	Level of Shared Services Adoption
Outcome-Based vs. Transaction-Based	Low
Focus on the What, not the How	Medium
Clearly Defined and Measurable Desired Outcomes	Medium
Pricing Model with Incentives that Optimize for Cost/Service Tradeoffs	Low
Insight vs. Oversight Governance	Medium

Reproduced from Vitasek, K et al, Unpacking Sourcing Business Models: 21st century Solutions for Sourcing Services, p. 15, Figure 6.

TABLE 11.6   **Attributes of Investment Based Business Models**

Sourcing Relationship	Focus	Interaction	Cooperation Level	Required Trust Level	Characterized by
Shared Services	Leveraging Cost and Investments	Cross Company Services May include multi-company service	Integrated – cooperative, Win-Win	Integrated – dictated by equity sharing	Formal charter, intercompany governance structure, interdependent outcomes, aligned goals and objectives, managed performance, Win-Win relationship
Equity Partner	Equity Sharing	Joint Venture Asset Based Governance Framework	Integrated – cooperative, interrelated structure	Integrated – dictated by equity sharing	Legally bound, formal strategic partnerships, mergers and ac- quisitions, asset sharing/ holding

Reproduced from Vitasek, K et al, Unpacking Sourcing Business Models: 21st century Solutions for Sourcing Services, p. 16, Figure 6.

Specifically, the authors believe that shared services organizations and joint ventures could benefit by applying the lessons of vested outsourcing. The following table provides the authors' viewpoint with regard to maturity of shared services in applying vested principles.

Equity Partner

Some companies decide they do not have the internal capabilities, yet they do not want to outsource for a variety of reasons. In these cases, companies may opt to develop a joint venture or other legal form in an effort to acquire mission-critical goods and services. These equity partnerships can take different legal forms, from buying a service provider, to becoming a subsidiary, to equity-sharing joint ventures. These partnerships often require the strategic interweaving of infrastructure and heavy co-investment. Equity partnerships, by default, bring costs "in house" and create a fixed cost burden. As a result, equity partnerships often conflict with the desires of many organizations to create more variable and flexible cost structures on their balance sheets. Figure 11.6 outlines the typical characteristics of both shared services and joint venture-type investment-based approaches.

Section III Which Sourcing Business Model is Best for Your Situation?

The Conventional Approach—The Kraljic Model

The authors believe understanding the evolution of strategic sourcing is important to helping companies determine the right sourcing business model. It is our belief that many companies have not evolved their approaches to keep pace with the changing business environment, especially as it relates to how they buy and manage strategic outsourcing deals.

The foundations for today's strategic sourcing approaches were birthed in 1983 with Peter Kraljic's portfolio purchasing model. The Kraljic model focuses on helping companies segment their total supply spending into four groupings:

non-critical, leverage, strategic, and bottleneck.[61] Using the Kraljic model to segment supply spending enabled companies to prioritize their time and allocate resources based on two core attributes—internal impact and supply-market complexity. This is mapped in **Figure 15**.

Kraljic described a broad definition and management objective for each group.

- *Non-critical items*. Defined as common in the marketplace with low unit cost and low complexity. The management objective is to identify ways to eliminate management by using a procurement card or a pre-priced catalog from which anyone can buy.
- *Bottleneck items*. Defined as unique or sole source items with low cost and high complexity. The management objective is to identify ways to mitigate supply interruptions or life-cycle transitions.
- *Strategic*. Defined as the most complex to manage and are typically defined as critical to the brand or business objectives. The management approach includes requests for supplier collaboration or "agreed to" value-add activities to protect the company's competitive position. In some instances, the collaborative process is quite entailed but is largely driven by enticing the supplier's participation through the promise of a longer-term contract or additional volume growth.
- *Leverage*. Defined as items that are lower in complexity, yet typically are higher in costs or potential impact to the buying company. The management approach includes standardizing and consolidating items in this quadrant to increase a company's buying leverage in the marketplace.

Kraljic—rightfully so—advocated that companies focus their attention and resources on the strategic and high-cost-leverage category groups.

The Kraljic approach recommends that companies use three approaches to manage overall spending. The model provides several actions or methods for procurement professionals that focus on increasing purchasing power through leverage (or mitigating risk from lack of purchasing power). This "leverage" mentality primarily leads procurement professionals to transactional

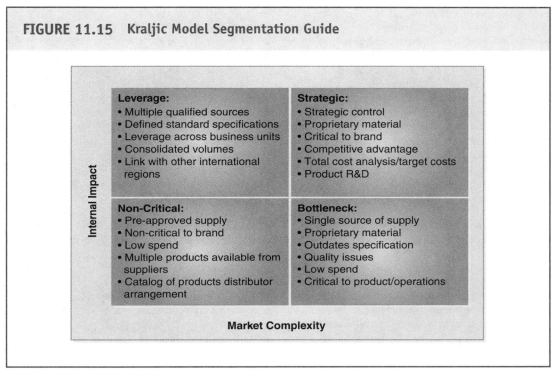

FIGURE 11.15 Kraljic Model Segmentation Guide

Leverage:
- Multiple qualified sources
- Defined standard specifications
- Leverage across business units
- Consolidated volumes
- Link with other international regions

Strategic:
- Strategic control
- Proprietary material
- Critical to brand
- Competitive advantage
- Total cost analysis/target costs
- Product R&D

Non-Critical:
- Pre-approved supply
- Non-critical to brand
- Low spend
- Multiple products available from suppliers
- Catalog of products distributor arrangement

Bottleneck:
- Single source of supply
- Proprietary material
- Outdates specification
- Quality issues
- Low spend
- Critical to product/operations

Internal Impact

Market Complexity

Reproduced from Vitasek, K et al, Unpacking Sourcing Business Models: 21st century Solutions for Sourcing Services, p. 17, Figure 7.

sourcing models. The three approaches are as follows:

1. Exploit—make the most of your high buying power to secure good prices and long-term contracts from a number of suppliers so that you can reduce the supply risk involved in these important items. You may also be able to make "spot purchases" of individual batches of the item, if a particular supplier offers you a good deal.
2. Diversify—reduce the supply risks by seeking alternative suppliers or sources of supply.
3. Balance—take a middle path between the exploitation approach and the diversification approach.

The leverage based philosophies for the Kraljic model quickly became foundation for many companies' strategic sourcing efforts. Companies began to centralize their procurement groups and create "commodity managers" to apply Kraljic's suggested approaches. Procurement organizations rationalized

their supply base and turned to use new tools and technology for competitive bids and in some cases adopted reverse auctions to identify the lowest marketplace price. These efforts helped companies to greatly reduce their spending. While arguably effective, the Kraljic model does have weaknesses.

The first is that Kraljic's model does not address later thinking that emerged around the desire to outsource non-core activities. The model primarily focuses on leveraging the direct spending items versus complex indirect spending items such as outsourced services. As companies increasingly challenged their internal core competencies, a surge in outsourcing occurred. While the Kraljic segmentation matrix does work for segmenting services spending, in many situations movement of work to an outside supplier is completed by procurement without a comprehensive understanding of internal versus external capabilities and interface requirements. Often the work activities are considered business support (assumed to be non-critical or standard) rather than direct product support (identified typically as unique or strategic) without understanding business impact. As a result they are incorrectly classified as non-critical or leveraged. Procurement teams without the involvement and knowledge of other internal functional resources have often assumed that they can leverage a service but later suffer with supplier-performance issues and strained relationships because process considerations and interactive relationships have been insufficiently defined.

The second weakness is that the Kraljic model does not address Williamson's findings that the "market" is not always the best fit for procuring goods and services. The Kraljic approach emphasizes simplifying and standardizing categories to drive all sourcing into a transactional, competitively bid model. The problem is that many outsourced requirements have high impact, are very complex and often require customized solutions and deeper degrees of collaboration for solving business problems. Transactional sourcing models don't easily apply. Using the market inappropriately is like trying to put a square peg in a round hole; it results in suboptimal or less desirable outcomes for these requirements. It is the authors' opinion that the Kraljic model does not account for the fact that a need exists for a hybrid approach, which Williamson points out.

The third weakness is that the Kraljic model suggests companies use leverage as a core sourcing tactic and offers several techniques to drive category purchases into a leverageable market-based approach. Kraljic's "leverage" and "exploit" thinking has grown to be popular over the last three decades. However, Williamson's pioneering work in TCE revealed that using a "muscular" approach as a key tactic does not create mutual advantage and can greatly increase a company's transaction costs and decrease trust levels in supplier relationships. Williamson observed: "Organizations that uses the muscular approach for buying goods and services not only use their suppliers, they often use up their suppliers and discard them. The muscular approach to buying goods and services is myopic and inefficient." Williamson won a Nobel Prize in 2009 for his

insights. It is particularly important to heed Williamson's wisdom during volatile market times when "winners" and "losers" can flip-flop positions rapidly and leverage can switch quickly.

Taking a leveraged approach with all suppliers simply doesn't work. Kraljic himself noted this weakness in a 2008 interview with CPO Agenda. Kraljic was asked if he had chance to rewrite the article in 2008 with the benefit of 25 years' hindsight, if there would be anything he would add. He responded: "I would not change it other than to add trust into the equation—the importance of trust in long-term relationships with suppliers. You need to create win-win."[62]

Since the introduction of the Kraljic model in 1983, strategic guidance and decision support tools have evolved as well. Contemporary companies have responded to economic changes, a global marketplace, and more sophisticated business-management objectives by recognizing the impact of supply requirements and the value of supplier relationships in the business model. In addition, a surge in outsourcing has caused companies to rethink their approaches to supply management. **Figure 16** depicts key milestone influences in the maturity of supply management.

Over time many procurement organizations have sought ways to address the weaknesses in the Kraljic model. Some companies and thought leaders have modified the original model, believing that the original Kraljic attributes are insufficient and do not adequately address the business needs. In the early 1990s some companies began adding supplier relationship as an attribute for consideration in the strategic quadrant to support the need for responsive supply in its global marketplace.[63]

The authors believe the rise of outsourcing—and in particular failures in large outsourcing deals—has created a perfect storm in the strategic sourcing and outsourcing professions. While progressive companies have evolved their use of the Kraljic model, the authors believe today's procurement, outsourcing, and commercial professionals need a more modern approach for determining which sourcing business model to use for which types of outsourcing deals. The next section outlines a simple business mapping model that can help companies select the right sourcing model for what they are buying.

FIGURE 11.16 Maturity Timeline for Supply Management

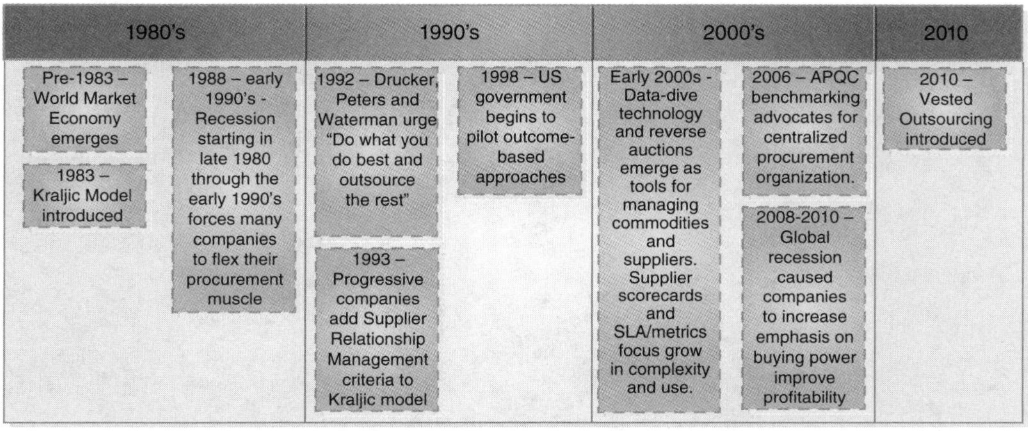

1980's		1990's		2000's		2010
Pre-1983 – World Market Economy emerges	1988 – early 1990's - Recession starting in late 1980 through the early 1990's forces many companies to flex their procurement muscle	1992 – Drucker, Peters and Waterman urge "Do what you do best and outsource the rest"	1998 – US government begins to pilot outcome-based approaches	Early 2000s - Data-dive technology and reverse auctions emerge as tools for managing commodities and suppliers. Supplier scorecards and SLA/metrics focus grow in complexity and use.	2006 – APQC benchmarking advocates for centralized procurement organization.	2010 – Vested Outsourcing introduced
1983 – Kraljic Model introduced		1993 – Progressive companies add Supplier Relationship Management criteria to Kraljic model			2008-2010 – Global recession caused companies to increase emphasis on buying power improve profitability	

Reproduced from Vitasek, K et al, Unpacking Sourcing Business Models: 21st century Solutions for Sourcing Services, p. 20, Figure 8.

Sourcing Business Model Mapping— An Alternative Decision Framework

As mentioned previously, the conventional approach for developing a sourcing strategy is to use a segmentation tool such as the Kraljic model or supplier capability matrix to identify "strategic" focus areas. While this is a good approach for prioritizing spending categories or suppliers, it falls short of ensuring the organization is using the right sourcing model for the right job and does not include consideration for whether the work should be insourced or outsourced.

Our experience is that many companies treat their procurement organizations as functional silos and many procurement professionals perform detailed supply segmentation and develop strategies without the vital input from their business counterparts. On the flip side, procurement professionals complain that all too often business groups throw their requests over the wall and do not spend enough time truly understanding the business needs and requirements. We strongly advise that procurement professionals and business leaders come together and review the overall competencies of the organization as a key strategy for matching the

right sourcing approach to the right business needs. This can be done through a more holistic "sourcing business model mapping" decision framework that allows a company to align its business attributes and the most appropriate sourcing business model.

Figure 17 graphically maps the seven sourcing business models outlined in Section II.[64]

The axes used to classify the business models are that of dependency and shared value. The more dependency, the more the commodity-based market approaches should not be used. The second axis is that of shared value. The more potential reward to an organization, the more a company should strive to use risk/reward incentives that are inherent in outcome-based or investment-based approaches. The Sourcing Business Model Mapping framework (Figure 11.17) provides an excellent tool to help determine where to plot each sourcing category.

The example provided represents a completed map for call-center services for a major credit card issuer. Prior to conducting the sourcing business model mapping review, the credit card issuer was spending in excess of $100 million with multiple call-center suppliers, which they competitively bid on every two years.

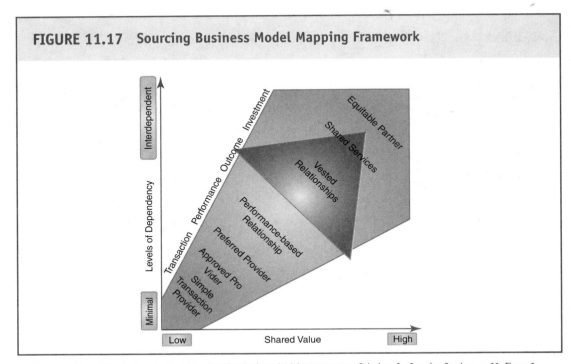

FIGURE 11.17 Sourcing Business Model Mapping Framework

Reproduced from Vitasek, K et al, Unpacking Sourcing Business Models: 21st century Solutions for Sourcing Services, p. 22, Figure 9.

The parties involved modified the business model map to support the business (items in italics and strikethrough). Using the mapping exercise, the company realized it was calling its supplier "strategic" but was using a heavy-handed market-based approach that was focused too much on price per minute rather than achieving the company's desired outcomes—to drive card holder loyalty. The company decided to reduce the number of call center suppliers to two, migrating their primary supplier to a vested-outsourcing business model and keeping their second supplier as a transaction-based preferred supplier.

To complete the sourcing business model map, a company should go through each business attribute and select the appropriate description. The goal is to map the importance of your company's own specific competencies against the desired outcomes for each competency area. For example, you will likely map IT services differently than accounting services and differently than distribution and logistics. The table lists some of the most commonly cited desired outcomes in corporate business plans, and it may be necessary for you to modify this generic list. Remember that outcomes are benefit-based and therefore last longer and do not change as often as tasks, which may be deployed to deliver outcomes. Once completed, the sourcing business Model Map will typically align with one or two of the sourcing models. For example, the sample sourcing business model map above suggests a performance-based or a vested sourcing business model.

Other Influences

Organizational Design and Culture

Organizational design and company culture can greatly influence the sourcing model selection – especially when it comes to deciding if an outcome-based approach is appropriate. Just because the business environment might be conducive to a certain sourcing business model, the organizations may not be cultural compatible or ready. For example,

TABLE 11.7   Attributes of Transaction-Based Business Models

Sourcing Relationship	Focus	Interaction	Cooperation Level	Required Trust level	Characterized By
Simple transaction provider	Cost and efficiency	Standard terms, fixed price	Low: Automated where possible	Minimal: Single transaction	Abundant and easy to resource, no need for a relationship
Approved provider	Economies of scale, ease of transactions	Blanket, negotiated terms, pricing agreements	Medium: Based on pricing or specifications	Medium: Common terms and price agreement	Managed by category locally and across business sector, purchases bundled for economies of scale
Preferred provider	Capability, capacity, and technology transactions	Contract, SOW, pricing agreement, possible gain sharing, SLAs	High: Set out in long-term service contract	High: Defined by contract, high spend zone	Integral supply across business units, delivering added value and capability, not so abundant, a pain to resource

Key: SOW = Statement of Work, SLA = service level agreement

an organization that has a culture of micromanagement will likely struggle deploying vested outsourcing because it will find it hard to move away from telling the supplier "how" to do the work.

Ultimately, organizations have personalities or behaviors that mirror current leadership. Understanding the organizational design and the cultural atmosphere will assist any company in identifying potential roadblocks when selecting the sourcing model that will provide ultimate value.

Procurement Maturity-Review of Experience

A company's experience and maturity in strategic sourcing can also influence a company's choice for the ideal sourcing business model. There are five stages of maturity. The maturity level increases across the five stages companies develop their expertise, knowledge and supplier integration collaboration capabilities. **Figure 18** (following page) outlines a sourcing strategy maturity grid.

Companies with a low level of maturity tend to be tactically focused on executing day-to-day purchase orders. Companies with a high degree of maturity think about sourcing from a more holistic approach, proactively managing the companies' spending and suppliers. Maturity matters when it comes to selecting a sourcing model. Simply

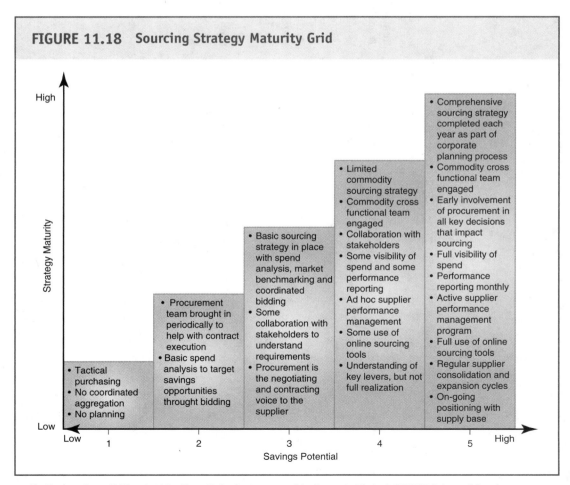

FIGURE 11.18 Sourcing Strategy Maturity Grid

The Forefront Group, LLC found at http://www.theforefrontgroup.com/blog/wp-content/uploads/2015/08/3-Areas-of-Sourcing-Transformation.pdf

put, if a company has a very low level of strategic sourcing maturity it likely will not possess the skill sets needed to manage more complex outcome-based agreements. This skills mismatch can strain an organization and the supplier relationship. For example, let's say that a company's IT department has been working with an IT server provider on many one-off projects and also has a separate infrastructure deal. Under the current agreements, the company has a master service agreement and treats each project as a separate PO. The Chief Information Officer (CIO) is happy with the supplier's performance and wants to move to a vested outsourcing agreement. However, he feels the procurement department "simply does not get it." His procurement representative does not understand the concept of desired outcomes and does not feel the value in establishing a more formal governance structure. In fact, the procurement person on the team thinks governance is "free" and he is not willing to migrate from multiple POs to a broader vested agreement. In this scenario, the organization should not pursue a vested outsourcing approach since the organization is not internally aligned.

Strategic-sourcing maturity does not just pertain to a company's procurement group. More strategic deals demand the procurement and business groups play a more integrated role. We have seen procurement groups who have proactively wanted to shift to more strategic sourcing business models for outsourcing deals and who have become frustrated by mid-level management personnel in the business groups who demonstrate what UT researchers refer to as the junkyard dog syndrome.[65] A classic example of the junkyard dog syndrome occurred when a Telco Company outsourced its facilities management under a performance-based agreement. The majority of the Telco Company's employees transferred to the service provider and "management" remained. The problem? The performance-based agreement had 20% of the service provider's fees at risk based on the service provider's ability to meet detailed SLAs.

The real estate group (the business owners) didn't clearly define the metrics. This led to deep frustration because the group would score the service provider "red" and invoke a penalty on metrics that the companies never agreed to. The service provider consistently found itself never earning the fee at risk portion due to fuzziness over requirements and metrics.

It is important to understand a supplier's ability to operate under a more strategic sourcing business. Performance-based and vested outsourcing agreements rely on the service provider to be more innovative and share in risks/rewards. Some suppliers are simply too risk averse. More importantly, suppliers may not have the capabilities or cultural fit for the more innovative thinking that more strategic sourcing business models demand.

In some cases, companies looking to outsource using more advanced sourcing business models also question whether their service providers can truly bring innovation or process improvements. We have found that buying companies that have low levels of strategic sourcing maturity often suppress their suppliers through rigid contract vehicles. For example, one company complained its suppliers did not bring innovation—yet it did competitive bids every six months to "test the market". Our experience is that often a high level of maturity is never reached, not because the supplier doesn't have the ability, but because the company culture prohibits advancing to more strategic relationships.

When it comes to maturity and the ability to apply more advanced sourcing business models, we advocate that both the company and the service provider self-reflect on their existing relationship. Are the companies saying they want to be more strategic, yet working under a sourcing business model that is driving transactional behaviors? Are both parties capable of adopting a more advanced sourcing model for their outsourcing efforts? We encourage you to stop and reflect to see if you have a mismatch in your sourcing strategy and your sourcing business model. Simply put, saying you want a more strategic partnership with your suppliers and then treating them like a simple commodity is likely to cause frustrations in both parties.

Section IV: Case Studies

The purpose of this section is to provide actual case studies that show how companies are applying each of the seven sourcing business models.

Case Study—Simple Transaction Based

A hospitality company with several properties purchased a variety of low-cost basic food items such as salt, mustard and other condiments, snack items, and pasta. Each property did its own purchasing, and no specific requirements were applied to these basic food items because all items were standard in the marketplace and a number of suppliers provided the products. However, when the company investigated the number of items that were being procured as basic food items, the estimated number of items exceeded 16,000 and multi-millions of dollars of annual spending.

The company believed there was a better way to manage these items. The company sought to put in place a process that would obtain more detailed information across all properties on these items, without adding resources to manage them and to obtain the lowest market price. The company implemented a standard e-auction tool which was used by all properties.

This improved the efficiency of the property procurement process and did not interfere with the quick turnaround needed. Item requirements were entered into the online e-auction tool, the suppliers in the marketplace placed their bids, and the lowest pricing supplier won the order. No negotiations were conducted; a purchase order was generated, using standard terms and conditions and distribution program; and the properties exerted limited effort to manage a multi-million dollar spending, which allowed their purchasing resources to focus on higher-cost items.

Case Study—Approved Supplier

FinanceCo is a financial services firm that is heavily invested in information technology (IT) as part of its product offerings, requiring frequent refreshes in hardware. To support its core business, the company has significant spending in the computer-servers category. The category is critical to the organization, but there are many suppliers available in the market. Therefore the company's sourcing strategy was to select multiple approved suppliers in order to simultaneously take advantage of best-in-class solutions and mitigate risk. The procurement and IT business functions within the organization worked closely together as part of the strategic sourcing initiative. This step in the sourcing process resulted in a market analysis, a needs assessment, and forecasts in annual spending. The two teams worked together to create requirements, build a specification, and identify a diversified supply structure.

After an initial qualification of solution providers and prior to the competitive bid (conducted as a request for proposal), the firm's engineers worked with the solution product engineers to benchmark the firm's current offerings and requirements and to complete an intense evaluation for qualification and proof-of-concept through lab analysis. This step in the process resulted in a ranked list of solution offerings, a shorter list of qualified suppliers, recommendations for improvement in the firm's product offerings, and specific requirements for the competitive bid. Along with those requirements, the firm issued a request for proposal (RFP) with their annual spending forecast.

Following lengthy negotiations with solution providers, the firm selected two suppliers to support the spending category; one supplier supports mission-critical computer servers vital to the firm's own product offerings and a second supplier fills the need for non-critical business applications. Now sourcing happens from a master contract with approved providers operating from proven requirements. Providers are governed through a model that is flexible enough to support future product releases and ongoing procurement. The product/supplier decision was a balance of a total cost of ownership (TCO), which included base product cost and operating cost over the three-year life of the contract and bottom line savings.

Case Study—Preferred Supplier

BankCo is a financial services company that established a successful relationship with Standard Register to consolidate warehousing and inventory management of the bank's forms and marketing materials. The strength of this successful relationship was founded on a flawless execution during transfer of seventeen tractor-trailers of materials into Standard Register's warehouse over a ten-day period, plus the supplier's commitment to reduce the client's baseline costs by 10%. Cost reductions were rapidly achieved through effective sourcing, reduced packaging, process savings, reduced shipping costs, increased inventory turns, on-demand print for selective forms, and storage cost reduction.

Standard Register soon approached its client to beta-test its new technology and process solution to manage commercial print bid and print production management. They collaborated with their client to implement integrated processes for competitive bids and print production management, insourcing a full-time manager into the client organization. Savings were in excess of 25% from previous experience, and the client experienced significant reduction in the previously manual work effort in print production management. For Standard Register, the client became a reputable reference and an enthusiastic spokesperson to its industry analysts.

Case Study—Performance-Based United States Navy

The US Navy was recognized by the Secretary of Defense for their "Performance-Based Logistics" contract with Raytheon for their H-60 FLIR program. The Navy set out to improve the performance of the H-60 FLIR system, which enables the Navy's H-60 helicopter to detect, track, classify, identify, and attack targets like fast-moving patrol boats or mine-laying craft. When first developed, the FLIR was expected to have at least 500 hours of operation before failure but in reality was averaging less than 100 hours. At one point the Atlantic Fleet alone accounted for more than one-third of the 21 deployed H-60 helicopters that had FLIR system failures. This system, made up of three components: a turret unit (TU) electronic unit (EU) and a hand control unit (HCU) was experiencing only 41% TU availability, 17% EU availability and 80% HCU availability.

The Navy and Raytheon implemented a ten-year, fixed-price agreement that was priced per flight hour and valued at $123 million. This fixed price by flight hour contract gave Raytheon incentive to improve reliability and help reduce the necessity for removal of these units from the aircraft. Originally cost savings were projected to be around $31 million but have now been estimated to exceed $42 million.

Raytheon also implemented an online maintenance management information system that allowed for real time data collection by NADEP Jacksonville; an online manual has eliminated the need to have printed copies made and distributed.

In the first three years of the contract the H-60 FLIR components have experienced a 100% availability rate and achieved a 40% growth in system reliability improvement as well as a 65% improvement in repair response time.[66]

Case Study—Vested Outsourcing— Microsoft

The catalyst for changing at Microsoft was simple. Microsoft had grown as an entrepreneurial enterprise, and along the way had cobbled together finance processes on a country-by-country basis. These patchwork processes were floundering under their own weight, threatening future efficiencies. In 2006, Microsoft began a complete reengineering of its major global finance processes and operations. Microsoft thought long and hard and determined that the best path forward for a major transformation would involve outsourcing. Microsoft felt the best approach was a "lift and shift" where the service provider would as quickly as possible determine a clear and accurate baseline that it would be expected to improve with Microsoft. The service provider would then be highly compensated for achieving transformational results.

To accomplish the objective, Microsoft applied a vested outsourcing approach by contracting for transformation instead of contracting for the day-to-day work under a transaction-based or managed services agreement. In short, Microsoft created a relationship where Accenture, the outsource provider, would have a vested interest in achieving Microsoft's desired outcomes. It would shift the economics of the model whereby Microsoft would buy desired outcomes, not individual transactions or service levels for a set book of business. Accenture would be paid based on its ability to achieve these mutually agreed upon outcomes. For Microsoft some of the biggest outcomes were around achieving a single, global finance solution with effective, consistent processes across the world.

In February 2007, Microsoft signed an outsourcing agreement with Accenture, with an original contract term of seven years at a value of $185 million. In just two years, Microsoft was realizing its transformational goals, including:

- Reducing the number of systems used to manage its finance operations from 140 to less than forty.
- Prior to launching OneFinance, financial controllers, for example, spent more than 75% of their resources supporting transactions, compliance activities, and local reporting—some 530,000 hours annually worldwide. After just the first two years of OneFinance, this dropped to 23%.
- Service levels miss rate of only 0.43%. This is remarkable given the complexity and scale of the Microsoft procure-to-pay process. While hitting SLAs is important, the real benefit to Microsoft comes in looking at the bigger picture. For example, Accenture delivered a 20% increase in first time pass on accounts payables.
- Satisfaction levels amongst finance operations' customers (finance and procurement community) substantially increased. While the overall satisfaction increased, the proportion of customers either "dissatisfied" or "strongly dissatisfied" moved from 33.3% to 3.4%
- Increasing coverage of SOX compliance from just fifteen "large" countries in the pre-outsourcing era to all irrespective of size or complexity following outsourcing with zero un-remediated S-Ox 404/302 and audit control deficiencies.
- Microsoft has already neared a 20% reduction in the cost of the contract and the expected reductions are estimated to exceed 35% by the end of the contract.

A vested sourcing business model has led Microsoft and Accenture to award-winning status in the world of outsourcing. In 2008, the Outsourcing Center awarded the OneFinance contract the "Most Strategic Outsourcing Contract for 2007".[67] In March 2010, the Shared Services Outsourcing Network awarded the Microsoft-Accenture outsourcing relationship as the "Best Mature Outsourced Service Delivery Operation." In February 2011, the team won its third award from the International Association for Outsourcing Professionals.

Case Study—Shared Services— Bell Canada/PSI

In 1995 Bell Canada's distribution operations were operating at service levels at 10% to 15% below industry average and at a cost base of $100 million. Bell Canada (the largest telecom services company in Canada) decided to spin off the assets and the staff of the distribution business into a stand-alone, wholly-owned subsidiary known as Progistix Solutions Inc. (PSI). The idea was that by creating a separate shared-services entity with their own profit and loss (P&L), PSI would be driven to operate more efficiently. PSI was chartered to provide a full range of order management and inventory management business processes for all of Bell's operating businesses, and a new CEO was brought in to turnaround the business.

At its inception PSI had an estimated revenue stream (benchmarked by Deloitte) of $55 million against its cost base of $100 million. Progistix had a mandate to achieve a financial breakeven state and to meet industry-average service levels. The new CEO chose to judiciously blend new talent with experienced incumbent managers. This combination ensured that the valuable learnings embedded in the corporate history would not be lost and that best practices from outside could be introduced by new managers with direct experience in the new practices.

With the team in place, PSI put in place the basics of a business:

- Transactional services contracts were negotiated and executed between PSI and its client groups.
- A financial management system was built to support the business.
- Distinct HR policies and systems were built to manage the employee base of over 1000 of which over 75% were unionized.
- A client management organization was assembled to better understand and meet client needs.

With its own P&L, the shared services group carefully reviewed where it needed to invest in business processes and technology to meet its charter of becoming a profitable business unit and raising service levels to its Bell counterparts. PSI invested in three key areas:

- Replaced the aged technology infrastructure and outdated applications.
- Renegotiated the four collective agreements to align wage rates and work rules with the logistics services market.
- Commenced the long process of culture change from an entitlement-based telecom services company to a market-focused logistics services competitor.

Clearly the cultural change would be the most difficult. By moving non-core functions to an organization dedicated to enhance quality in their respective field (shared services or outsourcing), these employees gain respect and self-confidence enabling them to perform at much higher levels.

In addition to the attention to the key priorities above, the management team was driven through profit-sharing incentives to dramatically reduce costs in all parts of the organization. As a result of their efforts, PSI reduced its costs by $45 million yielding a breakeven position in 1998. In addition systematic improvements raised service levels to industry standards: over 95% of the orders processed during the day were picked, packed, shipped, and delivered to customers by the end of the next day.

During the next two years, PSI was able to generate industry standard profits and to grow the revenues by 15%. By the end of 2000, PSI's shareholders at Bell Canada made a decision that they no longer needed to own PSI to benefit from its services. Bell Canada sold Progistix for $40 million to Canada Post Corporation in June 2001 and continues to provide services to Bell Canada—as well as many other customers.

Case Study—Joint Venture—Samsung and Sony

The consumer electronics giants Samsung Electronics and Sony established a 50–50 joint venture in 2004 for the production of liquid crystal displays for flat panel televisions. The companies formed a new company near Seoul, South Korea, S-LCD Corp., with an initial capital budget of nearly $2 billion.

The two tech giants—and fierce industry rivals—structured the venture so that stocks in S-LCD were held by South Korea's Samsung at 50 percent plus one share of stock and 50 percent minus one by Japan's Sony. "The two companies will invest evenly, but Samsung has the ultimate initiative," said a Sony spokeswoman.[68]

The upstart Samsung had begun construction of an LCD production facility in 2003 at a large projected capital expenditure over the next decade for what was then a relatively new technology and market, while Sony had no production base for large LCD panels. A joint collaboration was thus advantageous for both companies.

The deal was also controversial. Sony had pulled out of a Japanese-state-backed LCD-panel development group to close the deal with Samsung. In 2006 Bloomberg Business Week described the venture as a win-win: "They have pulled off one of the most interesting and fruitful collaborations in global high-tech by jointly producing liquid-crystal display (LCD) panels. And it's an alliance that is reshaping the industry."[69]

The venture was instrumental in Sony's introduction of the hugely successful Bravia LCD-TV lineup. It also put Samsung's own LCD-TV business on the map, with the company emerging as a trend-setter in the LCD-panel industry, aided by Sony technology that helped ensure high-quality, sharp TV pictures. "The Sony-Samsung alliance is certainly a win-win," said Lee Sang Wan, president of Samsung's LCD unit.[70]

The alliance had industry-wide impact in the TV market for large screen sets. It also changed the pecking order among LCD-TV makers. In 2008 the companies strengthened the venture by committing another $2 billion to build a new facility to produce so-called eighth-generation panels. In the intervening years, despite global economic and financial turmoil, currency fluctuations, heavy competition, and new entrants in the LCD and electronics market, and more recently the earthquake and tsunami in Japan, the S-LCD venture has survived.

The earthquake and faltering global demand in the LCD market did force S-LCD to reduce capital by $555 million in April 2011. There were even rumors that the joint venture might be dropped due to losses in Sony's TV business, but Sony quashed that idea in August.

"Televisions are a core business for Sony and it would be unthinkable for us to shrink that business," said Kazuo Hirai, Sony's executive deputy president. When asked about the Samsung partnership, Hirai asserted: "We are absolutely not thinking of abolishing the joint venture, and it's not something that would be easy to do."[71]

The venture is unusual and remarkable in terms of its scope and duration. Two fierce competitors put their rivalry aside to achieve the win-win in an emerging market.

Business Model Summary

Today, virtually all businesses use the same transaction-based approach for procuring complex services (i.e., outsourcing) as they do to buy more simple commodities and supplies. Unfortunately, many business professionals wrongly assume that a transaction-based sourcing business model is the only sourcing business model. For simple transactions with abundant supply and low complexity, a transaction-based sourcing business model is likely the most efficient model. But the real weakness of a transaction-based approach emerges when any level of complexity, variability, mutual dependency or customized assets or processes are part of the transaction. Simply put, a transactional approach cannot produce perfect market-based price equilibrium in variable or multidimensional business agreements and instead increases transaction costs.

As companies strive to transform their operations through outsourcing or seek innovation from their suppliers, they will most certainly need to better understand their business environment and the various sourcing business models that are available. It is important that today's businesses leaders understand that the fundamental differences of each type of sourcing business model and consciously strive to pick the right model for the right environment, ultimately picking the right approach to use for the right job.

As you embark on your journey to outsource more effectively, the authors urge you to consider the fact that outsourcing is more than a make-buy decision—it is a continuum. As a sourcing, contracting, or outsourcing professional, it is your job to understand your business environment and use the right sourcing business model that will best accomplish your objectives. We also challenge companies that have created shared-services groups to explore the concept of vested outsourcing as a way to help better align and bring market-based thinking to a captive insourced environment.

Summary

Strategic ideas and thinking with regard to sourcing/acquiring were the focus of this chapter. This chapter focused on relationships between supply and buyer (manufacturer/distributor/GPO, and the health organization), models to utilize to improve supply-chain relationship decisions, and strategic business models that influence those supply-chain relationships. What models and what level of compatibility are required between supply and buyer to create, increase, and maintain value in healthcare supply-chain operations? Strategic decisions of business models and whom to partner with strategically in the healthcare supply chain are critical and of increasingly greater salience amid health industry change.

Sarah Says: A Student's Perspective

This chapter focuses on relationships between suppliers and buyers, models to utilize to improve supply-chain relationship decisions, and strategic business models that influence those supply-chain relationships. There are multiple models to help increase and maintain value in healthcare supply-chain operations. The first model, the Kraljic model, is a more traditional structure and tends to be one sided when considering strategic relationships. The second model, the CAAVE model, answers and tangibly validates Williamson's queries of the supply-chain domain by specifically embedding organizational behavior and theory into the framework of Nash's and Williamson's constructs, proposes strategic partnership or relationship styles of mutual benefit.

Understanding transaction relationships helps position organizations for the implementation of strategic relationships between suppliers and buyers. Three types of transaction-based sourcing relationships have evolved over time. The three types are simple transaction providers, approved providers, and preferred providers.

As companies strive to transform their operations through outsourcing or seek innovation from their suppliers, they will most certainly need to better comprehend their business situation and the various sourcing business models that are available. The models and concepts presented in this chapter facilitate the systems and relationship thinking required in the industry today.

Discussion Questions

1. Describe the concept of value in strategic relationships in healthcare supply-chain sourcing/acquiring.
2. Describe and provide an example of the Oliver Williamson statement: "There are many hidden transaction costs associated with performing work that is non-core to the organization."
3. Apply the compatibility and trust assessment and model to an ideal hypothetical healthcare supply-chain relationship and to a less-than-ideal hypothetical healthcare supply-chain relationship.
4. Explain and assess the importance of the differences between the CAAVE and Kraljic models.
5. Synthesize the concepts of business models and relationship compatibility and trust with regard to sustainable healthcare supply-chain management practices.
6. Evaluate the application of the different sourcing business models in the context of the healthcare supply chain.

Exercises

1. Describe the concept of value in strategic relationships in healthcare supply-chain sourcing/acquiring in a half page or less.
2. Describe and provide an example in one page or less of the Oliver Williamson statement: "There are many hidden transaction costs associated with performing work that is non-core to the organization."
3. Apply the compatibility and trust assessment and model to an ideal hypothetical healthcare supply-chain relationship and to a less-than-ideal hypothetical healthcare supply-chain relationship in two pages or less.
4. Explain and assess the importance of the differences between the CAAVE and Kraljic models in one page or less.
5. Synthesize the concepts of business models and relationship compatibility and trust with regard to sustainable healthcare supply-chain management practices; in one page, develop your model for sourcing.
6. Evaluate the application of the different sourcing business models (select three different models) in the context of the healthcare supply chain in one page or less.

Journal Items

Answer the following:

Describe the CAAVE and CaT assessment models in two pages or less.

What business model would you use and why: to lead, manage, and plan within the context of the healthcare supply chain with regard to sourcing?

Considering the Value Chain and the function of acquiring, what did you find most helpful in this chapter to develop your thinking about leading, managing, and planning within the healthcare supply chain?

References

1. Luitzen de Boer, Eva Labro, and Pierangela Morlacchi, "A Review of Methods Supporting Supplier Selection," *European Journal of Purchasing & Supply Management*, 7, (2001), 75–89.

2. Wars of the Roses (n.d.). Retrieved from http://en.wikipedia.org/wiki/Wars_of_the_Roses, (accessed 1 May 2012).

3. Craig R. Carter and P. Liane Easton, "Sustainable Supply Chain Management: Evolution and Future Directions," *International Journal of Physical Distribution & Logistics Management*, Volume 41, no. 1, (2011), 46

4. Marjolein C. J. Caniels and Cees J. Gelderman, "Purchasing Strategies in the Kraljic Matrix: A Power and Dependence Perspective," *Journal of Purchasing & Supply Management*, 11, (2005), 141–155.

5. Oliver E. Williamson, "Outsourcing: Transaction Cost Economics and Supply Chain Management," *Journal of Supply Chain Management*, 44, no. 2, (2008), 8.

6. Oliver E. Williamson, "Outsourcing: Transaction Cost Economics and Supply Chain Management," *Journal of Supply Chain Management*, 44, no. 2, (2008), 8.

7. Oliver E. Williamson, "Outsourcing: Transaction Cost Economics and Supply Chain Management," *Journal of Supply Chain Management*, 44, no. 2, (2008), 8.

8. Oliver E. Williamson, "Outsourcing: Transaction Cost Economics and Supply Chain Management," *Journal of Supply Chain Management*, 44, no. 2, (2008), 8.

9. Oliver E. Williamson, "Outsourcing: Transaction Cost Economics and Supply Chain Management," *Journal of Supply Chain Management*, 44, no. 2, (2008), 8.

10. Wendy L. Tate and Lisa M. Ellram "Offshore Outsourcing: A Managerial Framework," *Journal of Business and Industrial Marketing*, 24, no. 3/4 (2009), 256–268.

11. Joseph P Cannon et al., "Building Long- Term Orientation in Buyer-Supplier Relationships: The Moderating Role of Culture," *Journal of Operations Management*, 28, (2010), 506–521.

12. de Boer, Labro, and Morlacchi, "A Review of Methods Supporting Supplier Selection."

13. de Boer, Labro, and Morlacchi, "A Review of Methods Supporting Supplier Selection."

14. Anna Dubois and Ann-Charlott Pedersen, "Why Relationships do not Fit into Purchasing Portfolio Models: A Comparison Between the Portfolio and Industrial Network Approaches," *European Journal of Purchasing and Supply Management*, 8, (2002), 35–42.

15. Paul D Cousins and Robert Spekman, "Strategic Supply and the Management of Inter – and Intra-organizational Relationships," *Journal of Purchasing & Supply Management*, 9, (2003), 19–29.

16. Dubois and Pedersen, "Why Relationships do not Fit into Purchasing Portfolio Models."

17. Cees J. Gelderman and Arjan Van Weele, "Handling Measurement Issues and Strategic Directions in Kraljic's Purchasing Portfolio Model," *Journal of Purchasing and Supply Management*, 9 (2003), 207–216.

18. Dubois and Pedersen, "Why Relationships do not Fit into Purchasing Portfolio Models."

19. Carter and Easton, "Sustainable Supply Chain Management: Evolution and Future Directions,"

20. Oliver E. Williamson, "Outsourcing: Transaction Cost Economics and Supply Chain Management," *Journal of Supply Chain Management*, 44, no. 2, (2008).

21. Williamson, "Outsourcing: Transaction Cost Economics and Supply Chain Management."

22. Carter and Easton, "Sustainable Supply Chain Management: Evolution and Future Directions,"

23. Williamson, "Outsourcing: Transaction Cost Economics and Supply Chain Management."

24. Carter and Easton, "Sustainable Supply Chain Management: Evolution and Future Directions,"

25. George A Zsidisin et al. "Evaluation Criteria Development and Assessment of Purchasing and Supply Management Journals," *Journal of Operations Management*, 25, (2007), 165–183.

26. Tate and Ellram "Offshore Outsourcing: A Managerial Framework."

27. Jukka Hallikas et al. "Risk-based Classification of Supplier Relationships," *Journal of Purchasing & Supply Management*, 11, (2005), 72–82.

28. Frederik Zachariassen, "Negotiation Strategies in Supply Chain Management," *International Journal of Physicial Distribution & Logistics Management*, 38, no.10, (2008),. 764–781.

29. Williamson, "Outsourcing: Transaction Cost Economics and Supply Chain Management."

30. Hallikas et al. "Risk-based Classification of Supplier Relationships."

31. Williamson, "Outsourcing: Transaction Cost Economics and Supply Chain Management."

32. Williamson, "Outsourcing: Transaction Cost Economics and Supply Chain Management."

33. Tate and Ellram "Offshore Outsourcing: A Managerial Framework."

34. Tate and Ellram "Offshore Outsourcing: A Managerial Framework."

35. Williamson, "Outsourcing: Transaction Cost Economics and Supply Chain Management."

36. Tate and Ellram "Offshore Outsourcing: A Managerial Framework."

37. Caniels and Gelderman, "Purchasing Strategies in the Kraljic Matrix: A Power and Dependence Perspective."

38. Caniels and Gelderman, "Purchasing Strategies in the Kraljic Matrix: A Power and Dependence Perspective."

39. Cousins and Spekman, "Strategic Supply and the Management of Inter – and Intra-organizational Relationships."

40. Cousins and Spekman, "Strategic Supply and the Management of Inter – and Intra-organizational Relationships."

41. Cousins and Spekman, "Strategic Supply and the Management of Inter – and Intra-organizational Relationships."

42. Cousins and Spekman, "Strategic Supply and the Management of Inter – and Intra-organizational Relationships."

43. Cannon et al., "Building Long-Term Orientation in Buyer-Supplier Relationships: The Moderating Role of Culture."

44. Tate and Ellram "Offshore Outsourcing: A Managerial Framework."

45. Cannon et al., "Building Long-Term Orientation in Buyer-Supplier Relationships: The Moderating Role of Culture."

46. Desmond Doran, Peter Thomas, and Nigel Caldwell, "Examining Buyer-Supplier Relationships within a Service Sector Context," *Supply Chain Management: An International Journal*, 10, no. 4, (2005), 272–277.

47. Cousins and Spekman, "Strategic Supply and the Management of Inter – and Intra-organizational Relationships."

48. Gelderman and Van Weele, "Handling Measurement Issues and Strategic Directions in Kraljic's Purchasing Portfolio Model."

49. Xinxing Luo et al., "Supplier Selection in Agile Supply Chains: An Information-processing Model and an Illustration," *Journal of Purchasing and Supply Management*, 15, 249–262, (2009), 249.

50. Glenn Parry, Andrew Graves and Mike James-Moore, "The Threat to Core Competence Posed by Developing Closer Supply Chain Relationships," *International Journal of Logistics, Research and Applications*, 9, no. 3 (2006), 295–305.

51. The quote is widely attributed to these men. It is unclear who said it first, but likely Peters did in *In Search of Excellence (*New York: Harper & Row, 1982). Drucker's quote retrieved from: www.qualitywriter .com/about-us/famous-quotes-deep-thought -humorfun-politics-sayings. Harold Waterman was also a proponent of outsourcing core functions, see David Souden, Ingenuity and Engineering: The Waterman Story (2002), www.watermangroup.com /brochures/get_file?id=34.

52. There are a variety of reasons why companies may choose not to outsource non-core activities. Companies cite different reasons, but a primary reason is that service providers do not have the capabilities to provide unique or highly integrated services.

53. The legal scholar Ian R. Macneil was instrumental in developing a wider view of the contract, known as relational contract theory. He said that most contracts are ill-equipped to address the reality

of business needs. In his 1968 work, Contracts: Instruments for Social Cooperation, Macneil wrote, "Somewhere along the line of increasing duration and complexity [the contract] escapes the traditional legal model." He argued that contracts are rooted in the classical approach to contract law and thus crafted to address transactions and legal protections such as pricing and price changes, service levels, limitation of liability, indemnification, and liquidated damages. He said business-to-business contracts should be "instruments for social cooperation."

54. Catch-22 generally is regarded as a no-win situation that uses self-contradictory circular logic. For instance, you may need a pass to enter a particular building, but in order to get a pass you have to visit an office in the same building.

55. "Contract Negotiations Continue to Undermine Value," International Association of Contracting and Commercial Management Ninth Annual Top Ten Terms Report, April 2010.

56. It is the authors' opinion that incentives work better than penalties and create a more positive working relationship with service providers.

57. Behavioral economics is the study of the quantified impact of individual behavior or of the decision makers within an organization. The study of behavioral economics is evolving more broadly into the concept of relational economics, which proposes that economic value can be expanded through positive relationships with mutual advantage (win-win) thinking rather than adversarial relationships (win-lose or lose-lose).

58. Shared value thinking involves entities working together to bring innovations that benefit the parties—with a conscious effort that the parties gain (or share) in the rewards. Two advocates are Harvard Business School's Michael Porter and Mark Kramer who profiled their "big idea" in the January–February 2011 *Harvard Business Review* magazine. The article states that shared value creation will drive the next wave of innovation and productivity growth in the global economy. Porter is renowned for his Five Forces model of competitive advantage. Due to his prominence,

it is likely that his take on shared value, although focused on society, likely will cause practitioners to embrace shared value approaches.

59. J. D. Power press release, www.jdpower.com/autos /articles/2010-Sales-Satisfaction-Index-Study (accessed Dec. 2010).

60. Benchmarking statistics courtesy of APQC. To learn more about APQC visit www.apqc.org

61. Peter Kraljic first described his Kraljic model or matrix in "Purchasing Must Become Supply Management," *Harvard Business Review* (September-October 1983). The model can be used to analyze the purchasing portfolio of a company with regard to two factors: profit impact and supply risk.

62. "Reflections of a Pioneer," CPO Agenda (Autumn 2008). http://www.cpoagenda.com/previous-articles /autumn-2008/features/reflections-of-a-pioneer/

63. Michelle E. Bernson, "The Value of a Common Approach to Lean," MIT (2004) http://dspace.mit .edu/bitstream/handle/1721.1/34753/56607252 .pdf?sequence=1

64. Vitasek et al. *The Vested Outsourcing Manual*. Palgrave Mamillan. 2011.

65. See Kate Vitasek, Mike Ledyard, and Karl Manrodt, *Vested Outsourcing: Five Rules That Will Transform Outsourcing* (New York: Palgrave Macmillan, 2010).

66. Department of the Navy, Commander, Naval Supply Systems Command, Nominations for the Secretary of Defense Performance-Based Logistics Award, June 5, 2005

67. "Growing the Business to Drive Value," Outsourcing Center, August 1, 2008. http://www.outsourcing -journal.com/aug2008-moststrategic.html

68. Yoshiko Hara, "Samsung, Sony complete LCD joint venture deal," EE Times-Asia, March 11, 2004.

69. "Samsung and Sony's Win-Win LCD Venture," *Bloomberg Business Week*, Nov. 28, 2006.

70. Ibid.

71. "Sony rules out exiting TV business or LCD panel venture," *Reuters*, August 4, 2011.

CHAPTER 12

LESSONS TO TRANSFORM HEALTHCARE CONTRACT PERFORMANCE: TRANSACTION-COST ECONOMICS

LEARNING OBJECTIVES

1. Describe the importance of Williamson's work for the healthcare supply chain.
2. Explain transaction-cost economics (TCE) and how this concept relates to supply-chain management.
3. Demonstrate an understanding of the ten key insights from Oliver Williamson's TCE model.
4. Categorize the types of supply chain present in a typical healthcare organization in terms of their associated risk to the healthcare organization.
5. Integrate healthcare supply-chain principles with TCE tenets to develop a list of considerations for a typical transaction in the supply chain.
6. Evaluate TCE in the context of the supply chain using the Value Chain model.

Introduction

Without a doubt, healthcare costs continue to rise. In the United States, healthcare costs are expected to reach $4.8 trillion by 2021.[1] According to the World Bank, healthcare costs were approximately 17.9% of GDP in 2011.[2] Supply-chain management in hospitals can account for as much as 30% of total hospital costs.[3] One expert, Bruce Johnson, CEO of GHX, states: "The supply chain is the second largest and fastest growing expense for healthcare providers; with only labor costing most providers more".[4] Approximately one-third (31%) of annual operating expense can be attributed to the healthcare supply chain.[5]

The technology of healthcare delivery is heavily dependent on supply-chain decisions, operations, and status. Adding to the concern of the healthcare supply chain are the tensions on reduced reimbursements for healthcare services, inflationary pressure of pharmaceuticals, high-preference supply items, high-volume supply items, and the move to "accountable care organizations." According to Vance Moore, CEO of ROi (the supply chain entity within the Sisters of Mercy Health System based in St. Louis, Missouri), in a 2008 presentation in Chicago, the trend in the cost of the healthcare supply chain continues to grow such that, if the trend continues, supply chain could equal labor cost for annual operating expenses for hospitals and health systems between 2020 and 2025.[6] Clearly, maximizing efficiency of the healthcare supply chain is an increasing concern. From an analysis of charges for fiscal year 2003, approximately 36% of inpatient nursing floor unit supply charge capture items were actually being charged correctly.[7]

Other industries have mitigated their market risks and cost increases through the use of strategic partnerships and outsourcing.[8] Firms like McDonald's, Proctor & Gamble, and Microsoft have obtained cost saving, flexibility, transformation, and innovation by developing key strategic partnerships.[9] This chapter explores the possibility of reducing costs, increasing flexibility, and transforming the work processes in healthcare through strategic relationships.

One way to view these strategic relationships is through the lens of TCE. This lens has been used by several researchers in the healthcare field over the past two decades.[10, 11, 12, 13, 14]

Specifically, we focus on a single article written by Williamson in 2008 for several reasons. First, the article describes various types of relationships firms can have with their suppliers, ranging from transactions to strategic partnerships. Second, his focus is on improving the performance of the supply chain. Finally, while our analysis provides insights on how these lessons relate to healthcare, many of them can also apply to other disciplines and industries as well. We begin with a brief overview of TCE, then apply insights from Williamson into ten specific lessons for healthcare professionals and discuss future implications. This chapter was prepared by James Stephens, Ph.D., Karl Manrodt, Ph.D., Gerald Ledlow, Ph.D., Richard Wilding OBE, Ph.D., and Christopher Boone, Ph.D. The authors would like to thank several individuals for their assistance on this chapter; these include Kate Vitasek and Tim Cummings.

What Exactly is TCE?

Transaction costs are the costs that occur when participating in a market. To use a very simple example, when buying a book, there is not only the purchase price of the book but also the costs you incur in purchasing the item. These could include your energy and effort in selecting the book, the costs of traveling to the store or using the Internet, the time waiting, and the effort and costs of making the payment. The costs that go beyond the book's price are the transaction costs. Transaction costs include actual monetary costs, expertise, flexibility, risk, asset specificity, the cost of managing the relationship, and supplier set up and switching costs, to name only a few that must be considered.

TCE adopts a contractual approach to the study of economic organizations. Briefly, TCE is best thought of as accounting for all the costs of a deal or contract, both the obvious and hidden costs.

Williamson (2008) notes there are transaction costs whether a firm decides to make or buy a product or service.[15] A company should strive to use TCE as the basic unit of analysis to determine these costs to make better, more meaningful decisions. A firm has to decide whether to do the work internally (make) or procure the service (buy), and it should consider all of the transaction costs—taking special care to identify hidden transaction costs. If a company does decide to outsource, it should work to reduce transaction costs with regard to how the companies work together—including the remaining internal transactions. That is, there is still a cost associated with managing the relationship that needs to be accounted for.

It is important to understand that there are transaction costs ranging from the simplest one-on-one commodity contract to the costs associated with vertical integration. There is no such thing as a zero transaction cost: there is a cost for bureaucracy and there is a cost for operating in the market. The goal then becomes to identify and quantify these and optimize for how you do business.

Ten Key TCE Lessons for Healthcare Practitioners

A key element of Williamson's work is to explain how behaviors and approaches to the contract can impact transaction costs. This section of the chapter examines ten key lessons that are directly applicable to outsourcing and supply-chain professionals. Each lesson is discussed, and is illustrated by an example drawn primarily from the healthcare field.

Lesson 1: Outsourcing Is a Continuum, Not a Destination

In 2004, Peter Drucker said, "Do what you do best and outsource the rest!" Most companies jumped on the outsourcing bandwagon and used conventional procurement methods for negotiating often large and complex outsourcing deals. For the most part the conventional approaches meant using contracting philosophies and approaches that were used for buying supplies and commodities.

Under conventional thinking about outsourcing there are basically two approaches: one is going to "the market" and the other is building "corporate hierarchies" and bringing the capability within the organization. Companies have generally made a make-versus-buy decision when it comes to outsourcing, and if they outsource they use conventional free-market economy and market-based approaches for developing the contract.

The market (buy/outsource) mode has an incentive for its use. There is little administrative control and well-established contract law to rely on. The market mode assumes an unrestricted market, or basically an ideal transaction featuring an absence of dependency and with governance accomplished through competition. Neither the buyer nor the supplier relies on the other. If one acts poorly, the other can easily exit the relationship.

The downside to the market mode is that service providers are often "competed" into outsourcing agreements that pose hidden risks. For example, Williamson points out that service providers might have "specialized investments" that can easily expose the business to significant loss if the contract fails and for which no safeguards have been provided. When this happens service providers will raise their price to reflect the level of risk they have taken on. To counteract this and thus provide a more acceptable price to the customer, service providers will often negotiate heavily for contract safeguards in the absence of certainty. For each safeguard that is put in place, the service provider typically reduces the price charged. This "give and take" is a normal part of market-based negotiations.

The other traditional choice, the corporate hierarchy (make/insource) is exactly the opposite: low incentives, high administrative control, and a legal system that is "deferential to the management." As a consequence, innovations that might come from the market or third parties are not shared or developed. Because there are additional bureaucratic costs involved in taking a transaction out of the market and organizing it internally, it is usefully thought of as the "organizational form of last resort," (Williamson 2008, p. 5). In other words companies should not insource services that are not core unless they absolutely have to.

Perhaps the best way to think of Williamson's work is to consider outsourcing in terms of a continuum with free-market force on one side and corporate hierarchies on the other.

Williamson (2008) advocates for a third "hybrid approach" to contracting as the preferred method for dealing with complex services that need to be performed under an outsource arrangement. Under a hybrid-contracting approach (where the

---

FIGURE 12.1	Two Basic Approaches to Ensuring Supply

Two Basic Choices

The Market (Outsource)

Corporate Hierarchies (Insource)

Reproduced from Vitasek, Manrodt, Wilding and Cummins, Unpacking Oliver - http://www.vestedway.com/wp-content /uploads/2012/09/unpacking_oliver_6.14.pdf, p. 8, Figure 1.

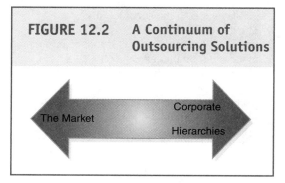

FIGURE 12.2	A Continuum of Outsourcing Solutions

The Market

Corporate Hierarchies

Reproduced from Vitasek, Manrodt, Wilding and Cummins, Unpacking Oliver - http://www.vestedway.com/wp-content /uploads/2012/09/unpacking_oliver_6.14.pdf, p. 9, Figure 2.

majority of outsource contracting resides), added security and contractual supports "take the form of interfirm contractual safeguards." Unfortunately, he also notes that when companies have taken the hybrid approach, it works well—"but not surpassingly well"—because often companies do not approach contracting as wisely as they should. Williamson (2008) states, "The viability of the hybrid turns crucially on the efficacy of credible evidence (penalties for premature termination, information-disclosure and verification mechanisms, specialized dispute settlement, and the like), the cost-effectiveness of which varies with the attributes of transactions."

Insight

Insourcing does have its costs—and consequences—for poor performance. These costs are not just monetary, as this example highlights.

One of the authors served as an executive vice president and chief operating officer of a large 560-bed regional medical center. The organization made a decision to outsource the dietary services to an international hotel corporation. The purposes of outsourcing this service were the following:

A. To increase the quality satisfaction level of meals from our inpatients, employees, medical staff members, and outside families and guests.
B. To decrease the cost of providing meals to this large customer base.
C. A significant portion of our patients and employees were Hispanic; therefore, special dietary meals needed to be considered.
D. The group purchasing through the international hotel corporation allowed for significant rebates in dietary food purchases.
E. The contract with the international hotel chain allowed for the recruitment of qualified and experienced department directors, service-line managers, and dietitians.

The medical center was a complex organization that provided approximately 1,500 meals to inpatients each day, three daily meals to an employee group of 3,000, a medical staff of 700, and over 500 volunteers. We believed there could be significant

cost reductions associated with providing dietary services for all these constituency groups. Not only was total cost of dietary services extremely important, but the satisfaction of patients and the morale of the various internal work groups were also at stake.

Before we contracted with an international corporation for dietary services, our cost per meal was significantly high compared to benchmark standards in our industry; and the satisfaction level of patients through patient surveys was low, as were the employee satisfaction surveys. The decision to outsource this nonclinical area resolved both cost and quality issues.

Before we made the change, our dietary department director decided to change the morning breakfast menu. With about 50% of our employees being Hispanic, we had provided on the breakfast menu beans, tortillas, peppers, etc. He removed those items from the breakfast menu, and the medical center almost had an employee uprising. Even though the department director did not directly report to me, I felt a need to step in and request that all items taken off the menu be placed back and that breakfast be provided free to employees for a week. Now we knew that changes were needed for this department.

Clearly, there were several costs that were hard to quantify based on the current insourced solution. Employee satisfaction and customer service were not being met. By moving to the other end of the continuum, we were able to meet the needs of both parties and reduce many of our apparent and less visible costs in dietary services.

Lesson 2: Develop Contracts that Create "Mutuality of Advantage"

Once a company has answered the make/buy decision, an organization must determine the strategy for working with its suppliers. Williamson (2008) cites fellow economist James Buchanan, who stated that the notion of economics as a "science of contract" rather than as a "science of choice" is underdeveloped. Buchanan writes that "Mutuality of advantage from voluntary exchange…is the most fundamental of all understandings in economics."[16]

Williamson (2008) points to the power of win-win approaches, which in the realm of performance-based and vested outsourcing includes game theory, behavioral economics, solutions concepts and the non-zero sum game. A game in the context of outsourcing includes a set of companies, a set of moves (or strategies) available to those businesses, and details of the payoffs for each combination of strategies applied.

Win-win/game-theory thinking has grown in popularity among academics studying mathematics and economics. To date eight Nobel Prizes have been awarded to game theorists, the first being John Nash in 1994 for his famous "Nash Equilibrium." However, it is important to understand that win-win thinking is more than just a popular phrase saying that companies need to collaborate better. Win-win thinking should be a key strategy for companies. What most practitioners do not realize is that droves of economists and mathematicians have simulated and strategically proven that agreeing to play a win-win game enables individuals and organizations to come out ahead.

In outsourcing, achieving equilibrium among the parties by committing to a win-win strategy through collaboration, flexibility, and foresight can grow both organizations' businesses. As Nash demonstrated, the key lies in players working together toward a mutually beneficial strategy that optimizes for the cumulative payoff. The idea is not to optimize for the status quo, but to look for ways to change the game, or the contract process, to achieve a larger payoff for everyone. In other words, work to create more opportunities to grow profitable work for both organizations. Companies can and should work together to find ways to create more opportunities. By working together they can identify opportunities to reduce costs, increase services, expand into new markets, or develop new products or services for the marketplace.

Our collective experiences have shown that even when companies talked win-win they often still contracted under typical win-lose thinking. For example, we often hear business people talk about "collaboration" and the "long term" but their contracts would clearly spell out 30- or 90-day terms for convenience clauses. A panel of shippers described how important their carriers were to their success, yet none of these contracts lasted longer than a single year. That is like telling a five-year-old to sit still for an hour in order to get a treat. That's a strategy that won't work very well for the short or the long term.

Insight

As a large health system with an embedded supply-chain operation, consolidated service center, and distribution system for twenty hospitals and eighty-three clinics across five states, creating an environment of "mutuality of advantage" was critical to reduce costs for high-cost and high-volume purchases. In the cardiology service line, for cardiac rhythm management items such as pacemakers and drug eluding stents, the health system was spending over $109 million. These manufactured items were necessary to meet the standard of care of the service line.

Approximately five vendors were being used to procure the items for the health system. A team consisting of the clinical staff, cardiologists, and cardiac surgeons were consulted to reduce the vendors and SKUs of the service line in an attempt to discount current pricing. After a considerable amount of effort, two vendors were adopted as the primary vendors for the service line. This reduced costs, with compliance of purchasing from the health system, but it became clear that further costs could be reduced for both the vendors and the health system.

To this end, the health system adopted a strategy of being the vendors' "low-cost but high-margin/profit" partner. Contract negotiation resulted in finding elements that would reduce vendor and manufacturer costs, reduce distribution/shipping costs while meeting the needs of the health system. The result was an annual reduction in cost to the health system of approximately $20.1 million as long as compliance to the contract, that included a high percentage of exclusivity, was at 90% or above. The vendors and manufacturers reduced their costs by approximately 7% while improving their margin/profit by 4.3 to 4.8%. The "mutuality of advantage" principle was used in this partnership to advantage of all parties.

Lesson 3: Understand the Transaction Attributes and their Impact on Risk and Price

Once a company understands that outsourcing should be seen as a continuum instead of a simple insource versus outsource decision, the question then should become: "What is the best approach for structuring the relationship and contract" to drive out non-value-added transaction costs?

Williamson (2008) points out that companies need to understand three attributes of their business environment in order to help them have better discussions with outsource providers and ultimately lead to better contracts. Each of the attributes is identified in **Table 12.1**.

Understanding these three attributes and how companies view them can and does have a direct influence on how a company and a service provider will "behave" when it comes time to write a contract because each element can and does add risk to a service provider.

In a perfect world, a company and the service provider can take a snapshot of the business and create an agreement that allows for the service provider to price the work under a set of given circumstances. The service provider clearly understands the task and the attributes of the work and provides a "price" to the company.

Unfortunately, the world of business is not perfect. Williamson (2008) says that the more an outsource agreement contains higher risk in the three attributes (asset specificity, uncertainty, and variable frequency), the more a service provider will feel potential risks and will want to put in "safeguards" into a contract to protect them from the risk of changes. It is recognized by Williamson that many firms are opportunistic and act with self-intent. Therefore he advocates safeguards to protect against opportunism.

Williamson (2008) suggests that if asset specificity is high, and disturbances are high, one can assume that transaction costs are at their highest. In these instances it would be less expensive—from a TCE perspective—to keep things in-house. If the asset specificity is low and disturbances are minimal, then transaction costs are much more predictable and therefore lower.

His logic is fairly simple. The higher a customer's need for asset specificity, the more uncertain and the less frequent the work, the higher the transaction costs, or price that they should expect to pay. From a service provider's perspective, the greater the degree that these attributes are present, the higher the risk for the

TABLE 12.1   Impact of Attributes On Risk to a Service Provider

Attribute Impacting Risk	Risk To Service Provider	
	Low	High
Asset specificity	Widely available and generic assets can be used to provide services	High degree of customization and investment needed in order to provide services
Uncertainty of work	Static environment; little likelihood of the work changing or be eliminated	Dynamic environment; high degree of work scope changing or being eliminated
Variable frequency	Consistent levels of work to amortize over assets	Inconsistent levels of work to amortize over assets

service provider. As a result the service provider will need to charge a premium for the work.

As mentioned previously, companies should consider the total costs of all transactions—not just the price paid. Organizations should address these attributes in a transparent and open dialogue and work towards optimizing the best way to mitigate the risks associated with each attribute. In other words, by reducing the degree that these attributes are present, the team can minimize risk and costs associated with the work.

Let's look at two real world examples to put this into perspective.

Example 1: There is a significant risk associated with the uncertainty of currency fluctuations for a back office procure-to-pay BPO (business process outsourcing) project between Microsoft and Accenture. In this example, the contract originally stated that Accenture would manage the currency fluctuations associated with the accounting processes it managed. However, after monitoring the impact of the currency fluctuations, it was determined that this was causing Accenture to bear too much risk. Rather than raise the price to cover this risk, the two companies agreed that Microsoft would be better suited to bear the risk of currency fluctuations. Accenture still manages the procure-to-pay process under the outsourcing agreement, but Microsoft manages the currency fluctuations and "hedges" in order to beat the market and create further value. By recognizing that currency fluctuations were an uncontrollable risk, the companies could evaluate which one was best suited to bear the risk. In the end, Microsoft was able to use its hedging skills to best manage the risk while still leveraging Accenture's skills in managing the actual accounting process.

Example 2: A conventional way to price for transportation is on a per-mile basis. Trucking companies must pay for the fuel. If fuel costs rise, the trucking company bears the risk and the cost increase eats into their profit. As such, most trucking companies will impose a "fuel surcharge," which is often the cause of contentious debate and negotiations. Rather than fall back to negotiating, one company looked at fuel rates and the impact on the trucking rates

and then created an outsourcing arrangement whereby the cost of fuel was removed from the transportation costs. With non-controllable costs burdened by the company, the company's carrier agreement was then centered around having the carrier manage and optimize transportation efficiency and service levels.

Anticipating network cost improvements also leads to contentious negotiations, often resulting in complex management protocols to ensure the cost savings are shared between the parties. This drives up transaction costs, often outweighing the savings to both parties.

A more successful approach was to place the telecommunications costs outside of the contract and provide incentives for the service provider to improve network utilization and implement management and technology innovation to reduce costs.

Insight

In the healthcare supply-chain world, medical and surgical supplies are different from pharmaceutical and biological supplies. As health systems and hospital networks attempt to reduce costs, understanding price and risk is paramount.

A large health system in the Midwest analyzed the composition, transaction costs, inventory and management costs, quality control costs, information system costs, and operational costs of the entire supply chain. Based on the pricing/costs and risks of the myriad of supply items, the health system determined that insourcing the medical and surgical supply chain to a great degree while outsourcing the pharmaceutical and biological supply chain was in the best strategic interest of the health system. This accounted for approximately 3,500 to 5,000 SKUs in the medical and surgical side of the equation and 500 to 1,500 in the pharmaceutical and biological arena.

Given the volatile nature of the pharmaceutical and biologicals pricing and availability, directly linked to pricing and risk, and the regulatory nature of the pharmaceutical aspect of the supply chain, partnering with a well-respected pharmaceutical company was the best approach. Over time, synergy of the partnership created a superior working relationship where costs are reduced for both partners while margins and profit have improved. The decision to insource (much directly from the manufacturer and not using a distributor) the medical and surgical supply chain and to outsource the pharmaceutical and biological supply chain was based on pricing and risk.

Lesson 4: The More Bilateral Dependencies, the More the Need for Preserving Continuity

Unfortunately, the world of business is not static or perfect and companies and their service providers will try to develop a relationship that can best address a dynamic environment. This can create a bilateral dependency that makes it difficult to "undo" an outsource agreement. For example, often a service provider invests, develops, or creates assets or skill sets to be used specifically for a specific customer. This could be the purchase of a facility near the client's site, or hiring specialized labor to manage specific needs of the customer. The cost of redeploying these assets to alternative uses becomes increasingly difficult, placing the service provider at risk should the contract expire.

This came home to one of the authors who was interviewing a large high technology firm on a different research project. During the discussion the firm noted that it needed a software link to be written between themselves and a third-party logistics firm. The third-party logistics firm offered to write the software; this offer was flatly and quickly turned down. This would have meant that the program would have been owned by the supplier. As a result, it would have been harder to undo the relationship if either party needed to do so in the future.

Alternatively, service providers gain additional information about the processes that are performed and at some point may be more skilled at performing work than the customer. This places the customers at risk, as they could fall victim to predatory pricing. Care is taken to make sure the service provider is good, but not too good.

In other cases, both service providers and customers increase their asset specificity over time as well, such as by creating interdependent processes and systems. These bilateral dependencies can make it costly to undo a relationship if things go wrong over time. Williamson (2008) argues that contracts should have a "preserving governance provision." In other words, there should be a governing structure in place to avoid a loss in the first place. The governance structure should be flexible enough to account for "disturbances" or "maladaptations" when things go wrong.

Unfortunately, a recent International Association of Contracting and Commercial Management[17] study highlights the problem of these dependencies and how opportunistic behavior can take place. According to the report, "Many powerful organizations simply ignored inconvenient terms and insisted on their renegotiation. Others made unilateral, non-negotiable changes, in particular in areas such as payment terms (interestingly, the fact that suppliers felt forced to accept such changes led buyers to see "increased collaboration," whereas the suppliers felt that collaboration had taken a hefty negative blow)."[18]

Insight

At a large integrated health system in the Midwest, it was our corporate policy to develop and preserve long-term agreements with major vendors for either operating and/or capital purchases. I will never forget one year when a healthcare entrepreneur made an appointment to meet with me about a major outpatient center proposal. It included an outpatient surgery center, rehabilitation facility, and a radiology center, which included the installation of an open-end MRI unit (which at this time was new technology to the market).

The entrepreneur's offer to our corporation was 50% of the enterprise if we agreed to up-front 50% of the capital cost. He mentioned that he had negotiated an agreement for the purchase of the open-end MRI unit. Our market area had yet to acquire such a unit because the technology was so new. In our health system, we already operated an outpatient surgical center and were building a major rehabilitation and cancer center. However, it was our strategic goal to be the first in the market with an open-end MRI unit. The entrepreneur gave me his business card and stated we had a week to decide on his offer. After that, he would approach one of our rivals in our healthcare market.

I contacted our main vendor for radiology equipment, which happened to be one of the world's largest corporations in this specific technology market for MRIs, CATs, and other radiological equipment. They advised me it would take 18 months to deliver a new open-end MRI, and I stated we needed one in 8 weeks or I would lose market share and significant revenue stream. Because we were a member of a multiple-billion dollar national health system and had a long-term working relationship with this corporation, we were able to receive the delivery of an open-end MRI unit in 12 weeks. The unit was $1.3 million and the preparation of the room to install was at a cost of $400,000 in addition to sending radiologic technicians to training on the new technology.

Such reactions to market changes in technology would never have happened if we had a history of frequent transition of new suppliers each year. The long-term relationship with a major supplier of high level radiology technology preserved continuity of maintaining our position as the market leader in healthcare services.

Lesson 5: Use a Contract as a Framework—Not a Legal Weapon

Ian Macneil was ahead of his time when he professed that business-to-business contracts should be instruments for social cooperation.[19] Unfortunately, many companies have lawyers that are creating outsourcing contracts that are so tightly defined with self-interested terms that their contracts are legal weapons instead of instruments of social cooperation.

Yet the world of business is not static; it changes and evolves over time. As such, Williamson (2008, p. 6) argues that organizations "need to come to terms both with bounds and rationality." He points out that "all complex contracts will be incomplete—there will be gaps, errors, omissions and the like." And as human actors we are bound by our inability to know everything. For this reason he advises that a contract should provide a flexible framework and a process for understanding and managing the parties' relationship as the business world changes.

A common mistake that companies make today is that they create a detailed statement of work (SOW) and try to define too tightly the work to be done.

Williamson (2008) advises that the contract should have "the effect of which is to facilitate adaptation, preserve continuity and realize mutual gain during contract implementation." Contracts should be structured with flexibility to deal with unanticipated disturbances so as to relieve potential maladaptations.

IACCM's research also supports this finding.[20] According to the previously cited IACCM study, today's contracts are filled with terms designed to protect self-interest rather than promote collaboration between companies. Their study found the terms receiving the most emphasis are about self-protection, indicating that companies are using their contracts as legal weapons to protect themselves from unforeseen risks. Table 2 highlights the terms that are negotiated with the greatest frequency.

It is difficult to see how focusing on these terms will provide the framework needed to be adaptable in a changing environment. Instead, these terms—coupled with overly prescribed SOWs—create a rigid operating environment. When the business does change (as it always does) the parties begin to get uncomfortable creating tension between the parties. A simpler approach is to realize that the business environment can and will change—and that companies need to address how to best mitigate the risk versus trying to shift it to the partners.

TABLE 12.2	Terms That Were Negotiated with the Greatest Frequency

Limitation of liability

Indemnification

Price/charge/price changes

Service levels and warranties

Payment

Intellectual Property

Warranty

Performance/guarantees/undertakings

Termination

IACCM, Top Negotiated Terms 2015: No News Is Bad News, p. 4. © 2015 IACCM. All Rights Reserved.

What makes this more interesting is that using a contract as a legal weapon is something that is done by choice—not by law. That is, in business contractual obligations are undertaken by the parties, and not necessarily imposed by the law. In other words, companies choose to design contracts with terms that defeat collaboration; they are not required by law to do otherwise. If we have chosen the contractual obligations we are imposing on ourselves, shouldn't they be beneficial to everyone involved?

Insight

One of the authors was new to our healthcare system, where he served as CEO. Prior to joining the system, there had been an ongoing issue with the contracted radiologist group. The radiology group had ten radiologists and a contract with the health system for over twenty years. The previous system CEO would not challenge the radiologist group on issues relating to poor working relationships with the medical staff—especially the surgeons for night and weekend emergency coverage—and poor working relationships with the health-system employees and the health-system executive team. Finally, the radiologists had little interest in technological advancements in their own specialty. For these reasons the strategic future of this major clinical service was at jeopardy and unclear. After a year of little success in working with the group, the entire radiology group was given a ninety-day notice of contract cancellation.

The medical staff leadership and system executives had to determine a new contract process to successfully recruit a technologically advanced and highly motivated radiology group who would be shared partners in our mission. The new contract was designed where the radiologist group would focus all their attention on the needs of the medical center patients and medical staff and not have other outside contractual relationships. This had not been the case with the previous radiology group. The second major change in the process was that the new radiology group would meet regularly with leaders of the medical staff and the executives of the medical center to resolve issues and to assist in the development of strategic initiatives for the health system. Finally, we agreed to be the most advanced radiology department in the market by purchasing the newest and most advanced radiology equipment and by recruiting radiologists and radiology technicians with advanced training.

The new radiology contract increased the medical center radiology department's revenue by a million dollars in their first year of the contract with continued increases each year afterward. Because the health system focused on the process and tools to be used in a new contract, there was significant increase in patient, physician, and health system employees' satisfaction level, which allowed us to cement a dominant position for radiological services in the market.

Lesson 6: Develop Safeguards to Prevent Defection

A flaw in human nature is that people (and organizations) are often tempted to act in a self-interested manner. We tend to deflect responsibility when risks are high or when things go wrong. In laymen's terms, organizations will defect from a contract if the advantage from defecting is better than staying. Williamson (2008) notes that, due to bounded rationality, costly breakdowns continue in spite of efforts to develop sound contracts. A key reason for contractual breakdowns is that business and market dynamics can and do change the economics of the agreement. What was once a viable contract may become a burden to all.

Many have heard of the horror stories of suppliers closing up shop or companies that outsource invoking their "terms of convenience" clauses. In either case, one party is left holding the proverbial bag and feels the pain associated with defection. The conventional approach is to negotiate safeguards to "protect" each party's interest. Suppliers do this by increasing their price. Companies that outsource protect their interests with terms of convenience clauses.

Rather than be fearful of the risks associated with a bad contract, organizations should work to develop proper safeguards that allow for organizations to disentangle their relationship in a fair and equitable manner without harming the other party. We like to think of this as an off-ramp or exit management clauses. Whatever you call it, the purpose is to develop safeguards that protect either party in the event that one of the parties no longer wants to continue to do business under the contract. By addressing the transaction costs associated with exiting the business arrangement, companies can address the risk and costs head-on rather than hide the costs. Typically off-ramps and exit management clauses will tend to make one of the parties "whole" if the contract is terminated prematurely. For example, if a service provider invests in a specific piece of equipment or other asset, and their client invokes their term of convenience, the off-ramp would likely have a provision to pay back part of the supplier's investment.

Where should the work go when business relationships go sour and need to be terminated? Williamson (2008, p. 9) warns companies against the temptation of bringing the work back in-house. This is due to the additional "bureaucratic costs" involved in taking a transaction out of the market and organizing it internally. He warns that an "internal organization is usefully thought of as the organization of last resort."

Insight

Our primary market began to experience heightened competition. There was a new strategic entrance to our patient market area by the two largest health corporations in the state. One was the twelfth largest hospital in the United States, which had recently merged with the state's only medical school/medical center in addition to being a very prominent children's hospital, and the second was the largest insurance not-for-profit healthcare payer in the state. Both of these health organizations had the same strategic intent, which was to acquire forty to sixty primary care physicians associated with our health system. If either healthcare organization was successful, or even if they split the physician acquisitions among them, it would have serious long-term consequences for our health system's revenue streams and existing market share. Even though our health system did not believe purchasing physician practices was the best strategic and/or financial initiative, it was important for us to realize that drastic market changes were going to occur with severe consequences if we failed to respond.

The acquisition of the primary care physicians by the state's largest insurance payer was our biggest concern. While both corporations had the capital funds to purchase forty to sixty physician practices, we could not allow the insurance payer to have this leverage during our annual contract negotiations. If we did not agree to specific contract terms, then changes in patient flow to other rival hospitals might occur. The second health organization interested in acquisition of our primary care physicians became less of an external threat as time went by because our physicians did not like their arrangement offer or the centralized structure of their existing physician practice.

Because the majority of our primary care physicians were young in age (the health system had spent five years in a successful major physician recruitment plan), we already had a significant investment in this physician group. Our health system then developed a three-stage approach into acquiring physician practices. The first was to quickly execute contracts with the multiple physician groups; the second was to encourage those physicians in private practice to form group practices; and the third was to acquire those who wanted to remain in a private practice environment. We researched and obtained consulting advice in determining fair and equitable acquisition cost of the practice, salaries and bonus incentives, benefit plans, and office operations by specialty (general practice, internal medicine, OB-GYN, and pediatrics). We were particularly interested in the general practice, internal medicine, and the GYN part of the OB-GYN physicians because of payment reimbursement for these physician types.

The first concern relating to this significant strategic development and change in our market was to assure our health system that cost was clearly identified with any termination of the contracts and that the terms of the contract were fair and equitable so the physicians would remain associated with our health system even if the contracts were terminated in the future. After capital acquisition of the practices, salary, benefits, etc. was finalized for each physician group and/or private practice, the contract had a clause whereby the physicians had an exit plan that occurred at the eighth year of the contract. The exit term allowed each party to have safeguards to remain "whole" at the contract conclusion.

The health system was quite particular about which physicians were targeted for our acquisition. Such targeted acquisition was based on evidence-based medical practice, the quality of the practice, cost focus, and long-term loyalty to the mission of the health system. We did not want to acquire all the sixty primary care physicians but only those whom we had designated as solid and effective partners. The market was changing at a fast rate, so we planned to acquire forty-eight practices in eighteen months. The actual result was forty-two physician practices acquired, which were organized into a new physician group practice corporation (the health system having a fifty-fifty ownership structure).

As a result of the quick response, the health system kept its primary care physicians intact, the two larger healthcare organizations lost interest in the primary market, and we had an exit plan agreeable to all physician practices. A real win-win situation had just occurred for all parties associated with our organization.

Lesson 7: "Predicted Alignments" Can Minimize Transaction Costs

As mentioned in Lesson 3, Williamson writes that transactions have various attributes that operate in different governance structures. One of the goals of TCE is to minimize transaction costs. To do this Williamson (2008, p. 9) points to a concept called "predicted alignment." Here the goal is to create an alignment that results in the economizing or minimizing of transaction costs to the largest extent possible, given the uncertainties inherent in market dynamics and forecasts. In simple terms, this means the business and the contracting approach need to be in sync. This is described in detail in **Figure 12.3**.

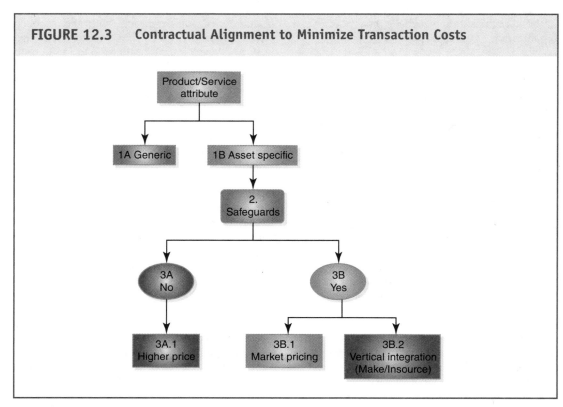

FIGURE 12.3   Contractual Alignment to Minimize Transaction Costs

Data from Williamson, O. (2008). Outsourcing: Transaction Cost Economics and Supply Chain Management. Journal of Supply Chain Management. 44, (2): 5-16.

The first decision a company must make when aligning the business with the right type of contracting approach is to determine if what is being sourced is generic or asset specific. If there are no specific assets involved and the parties are "essentially faceless," then the product/service is generic (depicted as 1A). A company can buy the product from one supplier that is no different than buying it from another. In the case of a generic product/service, there are virtually no transaction costs because switching suppliers is very easy.

In cases where some specific assets are required (depicted as 1B), transaction costs will increase because of the inherent risks associated with investments in the assets that are needed to perform the service. This creates a "bilateral dependency" between the buyer and the seller, and both parties are inherently incented to promote continuity of supply to avoid transaction costs associated with switching suppliers. It is at this stage of the decision process that organizations begin to discuss safeguards that reduce their risk. This is depicted as 3. For example, in the case of the supplier, the supplier will want to rely on contractual safeguards such as minimum order quantities or a long-term contract to help protect against their investments in the specific assets.

Companies that enter into contracts requiring specific assets and do not use safeguards should expect higher prices from their suppliers because the suppliers will use pricing as a way to hedge against their risk in order to protect their investments in their assets (depicted in 3A1). To mitigate from higher prices (or to protect their risk), companies should include safeguards into their contract (depicted as 3B).

The conventional approach a company uses to negotiate asset-specific contracts is a market-pricing approach under a competitively bid environment (depicted in 3B1). The rationale is that frequent competitive bidding will regulate cost and risk by pitting suppliers against each other to drive down the price with suppliers absorbing risk in hopes of winning the work. Once market prices are known, a company can then decide if it wants to buy (outsource) as depicted in 3B1 or make (vertical integration) as depicted in 3B2.

To demonstrate Williamson's (2008) model, let's suppose a supplier is asked to make a part

requiring them to make a special dye. The cost of the tooling has to be added to the price charged by the supplier. If no safeguards are put in place, such as a year-long contract or a guarantee on a minimum of parts ordered, the company can expect to pay more for the part. The supplier can only cover their risk (making a special dye) by increasing the price of the part. If, however, safeguards are put in place, such as a minimum quantity, or a multi-year contract, the risks borne by the supplier are minimized and the cost of the dye can be spread out over all of the parts to be produced.

However, what if the part is of strategic importance to the company? Or the costs being charged by the potential supplier are far too great? In these cases the company may decide to keep the work internal and integrated with the rest of the firm, assuming that the firm has the ability to perform the work. Or, to refocus on Lesson 1, where outsourcing is a continuum, it may be beneficial for the firm to own the dye and allow the supplier to use it.

Williamson's (2008) insights point companies to work through the options to help them select the most logical path to solve their product/supply requirements. Using Williamson's (2008) framework, complex outsourcing agreements should absolutely rely on safeguards for protecting both the service provider and the customer because the complexity drives unknowns. Organizations should *transparently* discuss the risks and how to deal with the risks through properly defined safeguards. Our field research shows that the most successful outsource arrangements openly discuss risk and work collaboratively to determine how to mitigate the risk (see Lesson 2). Failure to have transparent discussions about risks and safeguards will result in higher prices from the supplier as well as higher transactions costs.

Insight

Our market area began to experience many changes as the result of the federal government's Medicare/Medicaid Prospective Payment System using the Diagnosis Related Grouping (DRG) as the reimbursement structure for all Medicare patients. The initiation of this new payment plan began to be duplicated by both the for-profit and non-profit health-insurance payers. Therefore, our health system began discussion with our medical staff leadership to develop a corporate entity where both the health system and its medical staff could enter into contracts with insurance carriers and large employers. The new corporate structure was called a Physician/Hospital Organization (PHO) with joint corporate ownership between the health system and the physician group. It was the intent of the health system to only ask the physicians, both primary care and specialty, who had demonstrated in the past the highest quality and most cost-effective practice to be partners. This resulted in 310 physicians out of a total medical staff of 450 that became partners in the new corporation.

Needless to say, there were many physicians not pleased with this decision, but in order to successfully manage insurance health contracts, it was critical to only enter into partnership with physicians who practiced evidence-based medicine and controlled their costs by reducing length of stay for inpatients and appropriate utilization of clinical services.

A twelve-member governing board was appointed with the health system and the physician group each holding six seats. There were two people (one from the health system and one from the physician group) as co-chairmen. The payment system had incentives designed to financially reward physicians who demonstrated efficient and quality practice. This was determined by standards developed by the PHO members and by acquiring nationally recognized performance standards established for each physician specialty. For medical services not provided in the health system (organ transplants, pediatric trauma, burn cases, etc.), an outsourcing agreement with a tertiary medical center 40 miles from our primary market was signed.

The success of the PHO was to allow the health system and the medical staff to develop a "shared vision" that not only reduced transaction cost of providing medical care more effectively and at less cost to payer groups, but also gave us the structure and confidence to develop other new strategic ventures. The PHO successfully negotiated and executed ten major contracts with payer groups for medical care in our primary market.

Lesson 8: Your Style of Contracting Matters: Be Credible

Williamson (2008) describes in some detail the three styles of contracting, which he refers to as muscular, benign, and credible. This can be found in **Figure 12.4**.

Muscular

The muscular contracting approach has one of the parties holding the balance of power, and does not hesitate to exercise it. While both buyers and suppliers in theory can hold power positions, more often than not it is the buying organization that demonstrates its power, and tells a service provider what it wants and expects.

Williamson (2008, p. 10) calls the muscular approach to outsourcing of goods and services "myopic and inefficient." Our research found examples of companies we termed "800-pound gorillas" that would use a heavy-handed approach in dealing with their supplier simply because they could. Companies using this approach typically have war stories of bankrupt suppliers, or worse, a dwindling number of suppliers willing to work with them.

A classic example was an organization known for poor relationships with their transportation carriers. The customer's reputation was so bad that soon none of the major carriers bid on any of their business, even though it was worth several million dollars. In one instance, the firm partnered with a carrier on a special project; this required an investment of both time and assets on the part of the carrier. As an incentive, the carrier was told that this part of the business would not be bid out to competitors. Yet after a three month trial run—with great results—the customer reneged and bid the business. A lower-cost carrier won the business.

Williamson (2008, p. 10) writes that "muscular buyers not only use their suppliers, but they often 'use up' their suppliers and discard them." When this happens the company will need to bear the cost of switching suppliers—or worse, have the risk that their supplier leaves them high and dry when they go out of business.

Yet this risk is not borne just by the muscular party. Increasingly it is recognized that competition is no longer between individual companies

---

FIGURE 12.4   Contractual Alignment And Contracting Styles

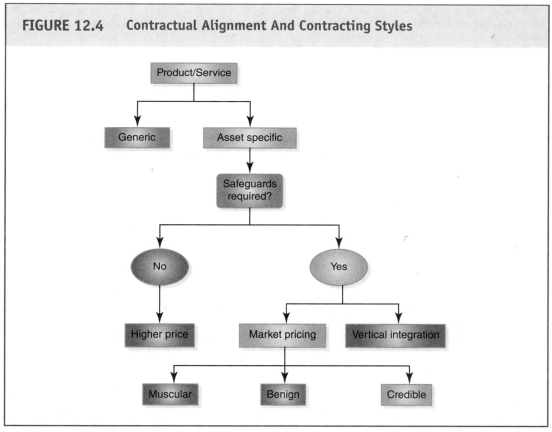

Data from Williamson, O. (2008). Outsourcing: Transaction Cost Economics and Supply Chain Management. Journal of Supply Chain Management. 44, (2): 5-17.

---

but rather between their respective supply chains. Forcing a supplier into bankruptcy can not only destroy the company; it can also create the seeds of destruction for the customer by potentially making the entire supply chain noncompetitive in relation to the supply chains of its competitors. Companies also risk paying more when a market consolidates, when suppliers merge with one another or if they leave the market entirely. We contend that a weak global economy has given companies far too much of an excuse to adopt muscular behaviors that will result in higher costs for all.

Williamson adds that when organizations adopt this muscular approach, the suppliers really have two choices for defense in the contract negotiation. They can charge higher prices and try to recoup their costs that way, or they can ask for safeguards in a contract. Safeguards could include longer contracts or guaranteed volume, just to name a few.

Williamson's point is that bullied suppliers will come up with overt and covert options to protect themselves—and this approach is bad for the company because no matter what countermeasures the suppliers take to protect themselves—it will ultimately result in higher overall total costs.

Benign

The benign approach assumes that both parties will cooperate; both parties will give and take in the relationship. This works well until the stakes are raised. In other words, the temptation becomes too great and one party will take advantage of the other. The impact that such behavior will have on the offending party may help to deter this behavior. However, that is part of the transaction cost thus taken into account. This cooperation "eventually gives way to conflict and mutual gains are sacrificed unless countervailing measures have been put into place."

The benign approach does not work well for long-term agreements, as the risks (transaction costs) are too high. Being too nice can lead to being taken advantage of. The benign approach blindly assumes too much trust on the part of all or some parties. It also assumes that cooperation to deal with unforeseen contingencies to achieve mutual gains will always be there.

Our field research found evidence of organizations that were too trusting in the initial stages of the relationship and were taken to the cleaners as a result. One example (which we saw repeatedly) was when service providers would extend too much trust by developing a "gain-share" with their customers. If the service providers found savings, they would receive a share of the benefits. The agreement was clear in most cases—a 50-50 split. The problem was defining the rules of how to split the savings. In several cases a service provider identified and implemented ideas that drove savings for a client and the client would come up with excuses as to why they did not have to pay.

Clearly a company should not be gullible. To avoid this, Williamson recommends companies use a third approach, which he calls a credible contracting approach. The fundamental philosophies outlined in a vested outsourcing approach follow Williamson's credible contracting style.

Credible Style

Williamson (2008, p. 13) describes credible contracting as "hardheaded and wise." It is hardheaded because it strives for clear results and accountability, but it is not mean-spirited, as in the muscular type. It is also wise because it arises out of an awareness that complex contracts are "incomplete and thus pose cooperative adaptation needs" and require the exercise of feasible foresight, meaning that "they look ahead, uncover potential hazards, work out the mechanism and factor these back

into contractual design." To address these potential risks, Williamson (2008) argues that credible commitments should be introduced to effect hazard mitigation.

Credible contracting is not new. Contract safeguards can take unconventional forms, as discussed by Williamson (2008) with respect to ancient Mesopotamia, where self-inflicted curses were used to deter breaches of treaties. The key point is that a good hybrid contract for a complex outsourced service will be above all fair and equitable to both parties in the agreement and it will challenge the organizations to focus energy on unlocking inefficiencies rather than negotiate for the win at the other party's expense.

Insight

Our health system experienced a very unusual situation with a large employer who was 40% of our corporation's net profit. The employer was, at the time, the largest corporation in the world. This corporation had a history of flexing their "muscle" with not only suppliers of the automobile industry but also with healthcare providers to their 800,000 employees. The health system typically increased its medical charge rates (12,000 different charges) on January 1 of each calendar year. The process of changing rates for a health system is quite difficult and involves intensive negotiation with the state's major health insurance payer. All charges then are changed in the health system's information system which has computer-to-computer billing structures.

The customer requested that the CEO of the health system travel to its corporate headquarters in Detroit for a meeting in the late part of November. Accompanying the CEO were several financial and contract executives, all who would meet with several of the automobile's health plan executives. The meeting was quite short and the health system was politely asked not to raise their medical charges to employees of their corporation for the next year. They were bluntly advised if they did not the customer would sign an "exclusive contract" with a rival healthcare provider. The CEO and his team were not only in a state of shock but also had a serious problem with only thirty days to resolve it.

The CEO advised them that their demands were unfair and maybe unrealistic. In addition, the CEO offered to provide information that their customer's would face higher market costs in switching contracts to an exclusive healthcare provider in our market because their charge rates were higher than ours. The automobile corporation's health plan executives were not in any negotiating mood and maintained their position of no rate changes to their employees for the next calendar year or else. Needless to say, the health system got the message.

Upon returning to the office, they immediately began to develop a new fiscal budget, strategic plan, and the renegotiation of agreements with their suppliers. The team based their planning philosophy on the belief that they would have to "bite the bullet" for the coming fiscal year. However, the year after that was the period when the large automobile corporation's contract with their employee's union expired. We believed this situation would occupy their complete attention and priority. It was a risky plan, but it worked to their prediction and to their best interest.

While the health system was forced to freeze a pay raise for its 3,000 employees, decrease the size of both the operating and capital budget, and recruit help from several of our larger supplier companies, the health system survived the fiscal year without a negative net income. The following year, as predicted, the automobile corporation was focused on potential shut-down of their plants. As a supplier to this large employer customer, the health system was forced to use conventional negotiation with its own employees and supplier groups; however, such contractual provisions and behavior in future years eventually drove up higher costs to our largest customer because of delayed operating and capital purchases.

Lesson 9: Build Trust: Leave Money on the Table

Williamson (2008) also says that TCE does not necessarily embrace "user-friendly" concepts such as the "illusive concept of trust." He wonders what benefits might come from the more widespread use of trust among outsourcing buyers, and at what cost. Trust should not necessarily supplant

power entirely and indefinitely, he argues, and that is where the credible part of contracting comes in.

We would propose that the most effective and collaborative contracts, the ones that are truly credible, must include trust. The idea of vesting, or committing, oneself or a company in a contract arrangement implies a large degree of initial trust in the value of the enterprise, a large degree of give-and-take to achieve mutual goals, and a large degree of good faith during the course of the relationship.

Trust is implicit in Williamson's (2008) suggestion that it's often better to leave money on the table, or not insist on winning every negotiating point. It's an idea that goes against the usual low-cost, transaction-based grain in a traditional contract.

In a new and potentially long-term arrangement constructive and strategic contractual intentions are sometimes hard to differentiate. What exactly are the parties' intentions going into the negotiation?

If there is a strategic rather than constructive purpose that skews the contract in one party's favor "and if real or suspected strategic ploys invite replies in kind, then what could have been a successful give-and-take exchange could be compromised," Williamson (2008, p. 13) explains.

If each party, or even one party, has a strategic agenda and wants to gain an upper hand—or go muscular—asymmetry will result. This "could plainly jeopardize the joint gains from a simpler and more assuredly constructive contractual relationship," he says.

"Always leaving money on the table can thus be interpreted as a signal of constructive intent to work cooperatively, thereby to assuage concerns over relentlessly calculative strategic behavior (Williamson, 2008, p. 13)." What can result is a pragmatic and ultimately wise outsourcing contract with credibility from start to finish.

Insight

As the CEO of a 300-bed hospital, our medical facility had undertaken a $35 million construction project to develop a new women's center, new emergency room department, new radiology department, and renovation of other support areas.

The general contractors had three years to complete the project and a "liquidation damage" clause if they did not meet the completion date. The damage clause would assess a penalty of $10,000 per day for each day after the contract completion date. The general contractor was a very respectable corporation and had successfully completed other projects for the hospital.

The general contractor had chosen to use subcontractors who hired only union employees. During the construction period, the hospital had experienced a very cold and snow-related winter, and, unfortunately for the contractor and the hospital, the construction project had eight labor union strikes. Both situations were pushing the contractor into a serious situation with the contract completion date and possible enforcement of the liquidation damage clause in the contract. If this was not enough of a concern for all of us, the hospital architectural firm tested one side of the wall for a five-story new tower, which did not meet contract specifications and would have to be torn down and rebuilt. Now the construction contractor was in serious trouble in meeting the contract completion terms.

In a meeting with the president of the construction company, it was estimated that the bad weather, union strikes, and rebuilding a five-story tower wall would place the completion of the project approximately 300 days beyond the construction terms and would initiate a $3 million liquidation damages penalty to be paid to the hospital by the general contractor. Such a financial impact to the construction company stability plus overrun cost of the project would potentially bankrupt them and end employment for all of the company employees.

It was important to the management philosophy of the hospital to build strong and long relationships with suppliers and develop intent to work cooperatively with them so there is a credible understanding among all parties from start to finish. We finally negotiated with the construction company that they would have up to 200 extra days after the original contract to complete the entire project, and we would only execute liquidation damages for days after the first 200 days. The general contractor accepted these new terms under the condition that they were also willing to hire additional construction workers to complete the project.

The construction company completed the project under the new terms and protected its financial viability. The hospital was able to have access to the new and renovated areas; therefore, generating new revenue to pay the debt service of the construction project. Both parties continued their long-term relationship for future projects even though the hospital left money on the table for this specific project.

Lesson 10: Keep It Simple

Williamson points out the importance of trying to keep things as simple as possible.

"Keeping it simple is accomplished by stripping away inessentials, thereby to focus on first order effects—the main case as it were—after which qualifications, refinements and extensions can be introduced (Williamson, 2008, p.6)."

Getting it right entails working out the logic, and making it plausible. Plausibility means to preserve contact with what is actually occurring in the market and in the contract while avoiding what he calls "fanciful constructions (Williamson, 2008, p.7)." Getting it right and keeping it simple also entails translating economic concepts into accurate mathematics or diagrams or words.

Conventional thinking is that the "best practice" for outsourcing is to create more detailed statement of works and tightly defined service level agreements to monitor the business in great detail. This trend is often coupled with complex pricing models and associated penalties for service providers that do not meet the metrics. Unfortunately, too many organizations are focusing on measuring for measurement's sake and they are often perplexed to find out that their scorecard is "green" but the business is not as profitable and customers are not as happy as they would like.

Our field research found that some of the most successful outsourcing arrangements bucked conventional best-practice thinking and instead chose to focus on few (five or less) clearly defined and measurable desired outcomes. While the parties agreed that measuring the business was essential, the contract itself focused on creating a shared vision and how to measure success against desired outcomes, not on defining and micro-managing day-to-day operational metrics. The outsourcing agreement then focused on leveraging a governance structure that used data to drive business improvements jointly rather than point over whose fault it was when a service level agreement was missed.

The complexity of life, systems, and business interactions make simple models in each case attractive and necessary. Simplicity is simple to say but can be quite complicated to achieve. It requires knowledge, the ability to prioritize, and a high degree of flexibility and pragmatism.

Insight

We developed as one of the key components of our strategic plan to be the healthcare provider of emergency medical care. Therefore, it was quite important to contract with an emergency room (ER) physician group that would strive to keep such a relationship pragmatic, plausible, and in the best interest of all parties. We kept this relationship simple, functional in terms of the contract provisions, and highly professional. Of all the physician contracts the health system had executed, the ER physician contract was the shortest in number of terms, contract pages, and requirements. We had the best working relationship between the health system and them as compared to any of the other physician contracts. The health system's emergency department had the largest patient volume in the primary market, which was important to us because 40% of all inpatient admissions to our medical center came from this area.

In similar hospitals, it is typical for emergency services to be major problems to the health system because of patient complaints, wait time, and poor working relationships between the medical staff and the emergency staff in addition to other departments of the medical center. All of this was absent from our contract relationship with this specific ER physician group. We had a very good business relationship and supported each other when necessary because we kept it simple and focused on the needs of both parties.

Future Implications

The bottom line on Williamson's work is that the bottom line is not always apparent at first look; you have to look at the hidden costs of doing business as well as the price of what you are buying. This includes understanding the costs of poorly structured contracts and bad behavior such as using a muscular approach for negotiating with your service providers.

Williamson's work shows how businesses can address conflict resolution. He takes the concepts of game theory and focuses them on the contracting process itself—looking through the "lens of the contract" and how organizations behave when it comes to the contract and how people behave during contract negotiations.

Williamson's (2008) thoughts on outsourcing go beyond the numbers and substantiate the value of a collaborative, win-win approach to outsourcing and third party logistics (3PL) contracts. It is some of the best academic work to show how the contract and governance structures need to be addressed in developing outsourced relationships.

The main reason Williamson's (2008) work is so useful to us is that his work with mathematical and economic models aligns nicely with what we have learned in our applied case-based research on vested outsourcing, performance-based outsourcing and collaborative supplier relationships:

- Win-win relationships are a must when there are complex requirements. Not only is win-win a common sense thing to do but applying "muscular" win-lose thinking actually increases the cost of outsourcing. We call this establishing a WIIFWe (What is in it for We) versus WIIFMe (What is in it for Me) foundation.
- An effective outsourcing arrangement should include a shared vision and a "predicted alignment" with clearly defined and measurable desired outcomes that guide the decisions of how the companies work together.
- Focusing on price alone only provides a partial picture of the true TCE of an outsourcing relationship. Companies need to establish transparent pricing models with incentives that optimize for cost/service trade-offs. These pricing models should include a well-thought-out exit management plan with the desire to drive continuity of service.
- Putting in place a good governance structure is essential. The contract should be seen as a flexible framework, augmented with well-thought-out governance structure designed to manage the business with the understanding that the business environment will likely change.

Williamson's (2008) lessons are simple and profound when you reduce them to their core essence. We hope more people will understand the contribution of his work after reading this chapter.

Healthcare as an industry and the supply chain with specific consideration of strategic sourcing can benefit much from the principles set forth by Williamson. Known for years, there are many opportunities for improving efficiency and effectiveness in the healthcare supply chain. Williamson provides insight on a culture of knowledge and application to support better decisions, implementation, and performance oversight on a core business of healthcare.

Summary

Consideration of TCE is vital to understanding the cost and operational improvements for the healthcare supply chain. This chapter presented a strategic view of TCE with practical examples. Understanding TCE is important to lead people and manage resources in the healthcare supply chain.

Sarah Says: A Student's Perspective

Transaction costs are the costs that occur when participating in a market where exchanges of goods and services take place. Transaction costs include actual monetary costs, expertise, flexibility, risk, asset specificity, costs of managing the relationship, time, and supplier set up and switching costs (to name only a few that must be considered). Williamson explains how behaviors and approaches to contracts can impact transaction costs. He focuses on ten major lessons to help manage the transaction costs. The following are the summaries of the lessons:

- The first lesson is "outsourcing is a continuum, not a destination." There are two basic approaches to outsourcing: going to "the market" and building "corporate hierarchies."
- The second lesson is "develop contracts that create 'mutuality of advantage.'" In outsourcing, achieving equilibrium among the parties by committing to a win-win strategy through collaboration, flexibility, and foresight can grow both organizations' businesses.
- The third lesson is "understand the transaction attributes and their impact on risk and price." Williamson (2008) points out that companies need to understand three attributes of their business environment in order to help them have better discussions with outsource providers and ultimately lead to better contracts.

- The fourth lesson is "the more bilateral dependencies, the more the need for preserving the continuity." Unfortunately, the world of business is not static or perfect and companies and their service providers will try to develop a relationship that can best address a dynamic environment. This can create a bilateral dependency that makes it difficult to "undo" an outsource agreement.
- The fifth lesson is "use a contract as a framework, not as a legal weapon." Unfortunately, many companies have lawyers that are creating outsourcing contracts that are so tightly defined with self-interested terms that their contracts are legal weapons instead of instruments of social cooperation.
- The sixth lesson is "develop safeguards to prevent defection." Rather than be fearful of the risks associated with a bad contract, organizations should work to develop proper safeguards that allow for organizations to disentangle their relationship in a fair and equitable manner without harming the other party.
- The seventh lesson is "'predicated alignments' can minimize transaction costs." Here the goal is to create an alignment that results in the economizing or minimizing of transaction costs, to the greatest extent possible, given the uncertainties inherent in market dynamics and forecasts.

- The eighth lesson is "your style of contracting matters: be credible." Williamson (2008) describes in some detail the three styles of contracting, which he refers to as muscular, benign, and credible.
- The ninth lesson is "build trust: leave money on the table." We would propose that the most effective and collaborative contracts, the ones that are truly credible, must include trust.

- The tenth and final lesson is "keep it simple." Williamson points out the importance of trying to keep things as simple as possible.

Understanding total cost economics is imperative in order to be able to better lead subordinates as well as effectively manage resources within an efficient, effective, and efficacious health organization.

Discussion Questions

1. Describe the importance of Williamson's work for the healthcare supply chain.
2. Explain transaction-cost economics and how this concept relates to supply-chain management.
3. Demonstrate an understanding of the ten key insights from Oliver Williamson's TCE model.
4. Categorize the types of supply chain present in a typical healthcare organization in terms of their associated risk to the healthcare organization.
5. Integrate healthcare supply-chain principles with TCE tenets to develop a list of considerations for a typical transaction in the supply chain.
6. Evaluate TCE in the context of the supply chain using the Value Chain model.

Exercises

1. Describe the importance of Williamson's work for the healthcare supply chain in one page or less.
2. Explain TCE and how this concept relates to supply-chain management, especially the function of acquiring, in one page or less.
3. Demonstrate an understanding of the ten key insights from Oliver Williamson's TCE model using healthcare supply-chain examples.
4. Categorize the types of supply chain present in a typical healthcare organization in terms of their associated risk to the healthcare organization in two pages or less.
5. Integrate healthcare supply-chain principles with TCE tenets to develop a list of considerations for a typical transaction in the supply chain and explain why you have each item on the list.
6. Evaluate TCE in the context of the supply chain using the Value Chain model in two pages or less.

Journal Items

Answer the following:

Describe TCE in one page or less.

What considerations would you have, and why, to lead, manage, and plan within the context of TCE of the healthcare supply chain?

Considering Chapters 11 and 12, what did you find most helpful in your thinking about leading, managing, and planning within the healthcare supply chain?

References

1. Centers for Medicare and Medicaid, National Health Expenditure Projections 2010–2020, (2013), https://www.cms.gov/Research-Statistics-Data-and-Systems/Statistics-Trends-and-Reports/NationalHealthExpendData/downloads/proj2010.pdf (accessed 5 Jul. 2013)

2. Health expenditure, total (% of GDP). *World Bank Indicators.* http://data.worldbank.org/indicator/SH.XPD.TOTL.ZS (accessed 15 Jul. 2013)

3. D Schwarting, et al. "The Transformative Hospital Supply Chain: Balancing Costs with Quality," (Boston, MA: Booz and Company, 2011) http://www.booz.com/media/file/BoozCo-Transformative-Hospital-Supply-Chain.pdf (accessed 15 Jul. 2013)

4. B Johnon "5 Ways Supply Chain Can Reduce Rising Healthcare Costs." http://hitconsultant.net/2013/05/13/5-ways-supply-chain-can-reduce-rising-healthcare-costs/ (accessed 25 Aug. 2014).

5. H. Nachtmann, E. Pohl, "The State of Healthcare Logistics: Cost and Quality Improvement." Center for Innovation in Healthcare Logistics, University of Arkansas, (2009, July).

6. Vance Moore, "Clinical Supply Chain," A presentation at the American College of Healthcare Executives National Congress, (Chicago, 2008)

7. S. Bacon, and C. Pexton. *Improving patient charge capture at Yale–New Haven,* (2010), http://www.isixsigma.com/implementation/case-studies/improving-patient-charge-capture-yale-new-haven/ (accessed 9 Apr. 2010).

8. K. Vitasek, M. Ledyard and K. Manrodt, *Vested Outsourcing.* (New York: Palgrave Macmillan, 2010).

9. Vitasek, Ledyard and Manrodt, *Vested Outsourcing.*

10. T. Ashton, "Contracting For Health Services In New Zealand: A Transaction Cost Analysis." *Social Science & Medicine,* 46, no. 3 (1998), 357–367.

11. J. Coles and W. Hesterly, "Transaction costs, quality, and economies of scale: examining contracting choices in the hospital industry." *Journal of Corporate Finance,* 4, no. 4 (1998), 321–345.

12. R. Donato, "Extending transaction cost economics: Towards a synthesized approach for analysing contracting in health care markets with experience from the Australian private sector." *Social Science & Medicine* 71, no. 10 (2010), 1989–1996.

13. D. Parker and K. Hartley, "Transaction costs, relational contracting and public private partnerships: a case study of UK defence." *Journal of Purchasing and Supply Management* 9, no. 3 (2003), 97–108.

14. N, Pelletier-Fleury et al. "Transaction costs economics as a conceptual framework for the analysis of barriers to the diffusion of telemedicine," *Health Policy* 42, no. 1 (1997), 1–14.

15. Oliver E. Williamson, "Outsourcing: Transaction Cost Economics and Supply Chain Management," *Journal of Supply Chain Management,* 44, no. 2, (2008), 5–16.

16. J. Buchanan, "Game theory, mathematics, and economics." *Journal of Economic Methodology,* 8, no. 1 (March 2001), 27–32.

17. IACCM, (2010, April/May). Contract Negotiations as a Source of Value. Ridgefield, CT.

18. IACCM, (2010, April/May). Contract Negotiations as a Source of Value. Ridgefield, CT.

19. I. Macneil, *Contracts: Instruments For Social Cooperation.* (South Hackensack, NJ: F B Rothman,1968).

20. IACCM, (2010, April/May). Contract Negotiations as a Source of Value. Ridgefield, CT.

CHAPTER 13

THE HEALTH LEADER, INFORMATION, DECISIONS, AND CREATING A KNOWLEDGE CULTURE IN THE SUPPLY CHAIN: THE FOUR PS OF HEALTH ANALYTICS ADOPTION

LEARNING OBJECTIVES

1. Describe the significant changes in the health industry that prompt an integrated approach for utilizing health information from multiple areas to make good decisions for health services delivery and improved health status of communities.
2. Explain how health-industry reform and policy changes impact the rate of health analytic adoption within health organizations and what changes require analytic adoption in the health industry.
3. Demonstrate how applicable models associated with health information and technology improve efficiency, effectiveness, performance, and efficacy of health services and healthcare delivery.
4. Compare and contrast methods to effectively use analytic models to integrate raw data and develop knowledge to improve health-system performance and equity within a community.
5. Categorize health organizations in technology adoption, analytics adoption (information utilization), and information integration using the integration of the HIMSS Delta model and the 4 Ps of Health Analytics models and provide examples.
6. Appraise and evaluate the integration of population, patient, process, and profitability (net margin for not-for-profit businesses (NFPs)) information in solving community health challenges and/or strategic planning for a health organization.

Introduction

Changes in healthcare and the need to integrate community and population factors into the considerations and decisions for healthcare service delivery impact the healthcare supply chain. Leaders need actionable information to positively influence the delivery of care, and that includes the supply chain in the mission to provide the technology of care to the caregivers. Health leaders need information to effectively guide and direct their organizations. Starting with raw data gathered from various operational, governmental, and other systems, how do health leaders create an organizational culture based on knowledge utilization? How do health leaders take data, place it in context, integrate information from multiple domains, take action based on the information, and have the organization learn from those actions and improve strategies and operations of the health organization? With the changes in the health industry that require closer connections to the communities health organizations serve and require more assumption of risk for the health status of those communities, what model can health leaders utilize to achieve a knowledge-based organization? Complicated ideas are often shown as a model. A **model** is a simplified substitute for an event or situation that is being studied or predicted. Models can be used in multiple ways. The most common are describing a situation or proscribing course of action. A **descriptive model** describes *how a system should function* according to the model. A **prescriptive model** shows *how to make a system function* according to the model. The most useful type of model is a combination of the two concepts, a model that is both prescriptive and descriptive. Models of this type describe how something works and how to make it work as described.

Due to the complex nature of the health industry there are many models regarding the operation of health organizations. This is true of health analytics, health information for analysis and decision making, and supply-chain management because they are exciting, rapidly evolving fields—even by health-industry standards. The implication of change is relevant; the health industry is a dynamic industry. Recent changes from health reform, policy changes, and the need to demonstrate value in health services delivery have created an environment where new models of health analytics, health information utilization, and health technology are required. In this chapter we will discuss the need, basis, creation, and usage of the 4 Ps of Health Analytics. The 4 Ps of Health Analytics model integrates well with the knowledge management and learning organization construct and strategic planning process construct of the dynamic culture leadership model. The 4 Ps of Health Analytics

model, a model concerned with how information is efficiently, effectively, and efficaciously utilized in an integrated manner, describes conceptually *how* data flows, and from what data domain in the health organization, and prescribes integration of data from crucial domains to develop knowledge in the health organization. Health leaders need to be competent in the philosophy and utilization of information as it develops into useful knowledge. This chapter explains this process within the 4 Ps of Health Analytics model and how to achieve success; combined with other valuable models, the integrated model is the 4 Ps of Health Analytics Adoption model. Success is coupling technology with integrated information to build knowledge that improves strategic and operational planning, improves health outcomes, improves health equity, and improves community health status. This chapter was prepared by the textbook authors and J. Tyler Croft, MHA.

Analytics models such as the 4 Ps of Health Analytics Adoption have a growing importance for the healthcare supply chain. The complexity of the healthcare supply chain comes from the four distinct supply lines: capital equipment, medical/surgical, pharmaceutical, and commodities and their unique requirements. Managing this complexity is a cumbersome process that can be significantly improved through the use of technology. The 4 Ps of Health Analytics Adoption provides a framework for an organization to gain knowledge by providing context to the raw data found in the master supply chain files.

Situational Analysis: Catalyst to Integrated Information Necessity

Patient Protection and Affordable Care Act (PPACA)

The Patient Protection and Affordable Care Act of 2010, commonly referred to as the Affordable Care Act (ACA, or "Obamacare" after President Barack Obama who signed the bill into law March 23, 2010). The ACA is the largest and most significant change to the United States healthcare system since the passage of Medicare and Medicaid in 1965 with the Social Security Amendments

18 and 19. The ACA is still very controversial with multiple challenges waiting to be heard by the Supreme Court; operational challenges within the health industry will require changes to the law, the system, and to the leaders of health organizations.

The ACA puts a greater focus on prevention and cost-effective care while increasing the number of individuals insured through mandatory insurance coverage. This insurance can be purchased directly from private companies, or the purchase can be facilitated by the federal government or state governments through health insurance exchanges or marketplaces. **Health insurance markets** are exchanges for consumers to buy health insurance plans that meet the ACA guidelines. These exchanges have been set up by both the state and federal governments.

ACA-compliant healthcare plans must meet certain standards set by the federal government. These plans are rated according to the "metal" system: Bronze, Silver, Gold, and Platinum. Companies offering plans on the health exchanges must provide plans that meet at least the Silver and Gold level. The reason behind this is to give consumers choice in their health insurance. Individuals that earn between 138% and 400% of the Federal Poverty Level are eligible for subsidies of their health insurance premiums; below this level an individual is eligible for Medicaid. The **federal poverty** level is the level below which an individual is said to be living in poverty. As of 2014, this is $11,600 for an individual or $23,850 for a family of four.[1] The Silver plan is considered the standard for calculating which subsidies will be available to individual beneficiaries.[2] Purchasing insurance plans through the healthcare marketplace is done during a period of open enrollment. **Open enrollment** is a period of time in which individuals are able to apply for or change their current health insurance plan. For the qualified health plans in the marketplace this time period is November 15 through February 15 each year.[3]

Individuals are required to show that they have health insurance on their taxes or pay a fine. The tax will gradually increase from 1% of an individual's yearly household income or $94 dollars per person to 2% household income or $695 per person (whichever is greater). Individuals earning less than $10,150 per year do not have to pay a penalty. Under the income percentage method, the maximum tax is the same as the national average premium for a bronze plan.[4] This was done to encourage individuals to purchase health insurance through the exchanges.

In addition to requiring individuals to purchase health insurance, the ACA has provisions aimed at improving the quality of care provided. One of these provisions calls for the **meaningful use** of electronic health records (EHR). **Meaningful use** is the use of EHRs to improve quality, safety, efficiency, and reduce health disparities. The meaningful use requirements include a reward/penalty system to compel hospital compliance. The payment adjustments associated with the meaningful use of EHR began in federal fiscal year 2015. This grace period of a few years from the passage of the ACA has allowed hospitals the opportunity to implement an EHR system and avoid a penalty.[5] The meaningful use requirement is a strong incentive to install an EHR system for health organizations that have not yet moved to at least a partial electronic system. For those facilities who already have electronic medical records, the program, along with other ACA provisions, provides encouragement to improve EMR systems. Whether installing, maintaining, or upgrading an EHR system, there is a need to measure its effectiveness. As mentioned in the introduction, this measurement is best done through the use of a **model.** With a large increase in insured individuals, many without a history of insurance coverage, how do health organizations gain insight into services needed by this newly insured group? Consider the disease profiles, cultural differences, and health system understanding levels of the newly insured, how do health organizations deliver quality care of needed services to improve community health status, improve patient care outcomes, and serve those who historically were medically underserved? How does a health organization provide outreach, education, screening for health indicators to a group of individuals without established access to care? How do health organizations provide demonstrated value to existing patients and to new patients? Will these answers mitigate and allow health organizations to manage risk effectively?

American Hospital Association Perspectives

Your Hospital's Path to the Second Curve Framework: Integration and Transformation:

In response to regulatory and environmental factors, payment systems, and changing demographics, health organizations have begun to transition from volume-based systems to value-based systems. Volume-based systems involve providing more services to a greater population with little focus on outcomes. Value-based systems focus on maximizing outcomes while reducing costs. Hospitals that use volume-based systems are considered to be on the "first curve."[6] Hospitals that have undergone organizational transformation and utilize a value-based system are considered to be on the "second curve."[7] Many hospitals are currently located in the gap between the curves as they try to evolve under the pressure of dynamic change. It is necessary for leaders of these healthcare systems to develop strategies to accomplish the second curve. To reach the second curve requires swift movement to acquiring greater clinical, financial, operational, and cultural integration.[8] Waiting to "evolve" is a very dangerous approach for health systems given the changing landscape of the industry. Developing the capacity to take risks is necessary for healthcare systems to survive "life in the gap." Healthcare leaders will need to consider the following key issues:[9]

- Healthcare is moving to new performance models in which organizations are integrating financial risk and care delivery.
- There is no "one-size-fits-all" model, as provider capabilities and community needs are different everywhere.
- The status quo is not a viable strategy because the environment is changing rapidly.
- Each hospital and care system can consider multiple paths.
- Each path has its own distinct risks and rewards.[10]

As these organizations make short-term and long-term plans, the changing landscape, environment, and trends must be identified and analyzed thoroughly. Health leaders will need to be aware of the following pressures:[11]

- Patient demographics will shift significantly throughout the next decade.
- Enhancing care coordination during hospital-to-home transitions has consistently shown beneficial effects on cost and care quality, requiring hospital leaders to focus on care after patients leave the hospital.
- Political and regulatory pressures are compelling hospitals and care systems to provide efficient and optimal patient care and address market volatility.
- Hospitals need to serve multiple patient populations effectively.[12]

Paths to Transformational Change

Organizational transformation can be a daunting task for many health organizations; however there are five transformational paths that can be used: [13]

1. **Redefine** to a different care delivery system.
2. **Partner** with a care delivery system or health plan for greater horizontal or vertical reach, efficiency, and resources for at-risk contracting.
3. **Integrate** by developing a health insurance function or services across the continuum.
4. **Experiment** with new payment and care delivery models.
5. **Specialize** to become a higher performing and essential provider.[14]

There is not one specific path that health organizations must adhere to; instead a combination of these paths can be used in conjunction with one another. The paths chosen must best fit the needs and goals of the health organization.

Health Equity: AHA Equity Care Report

Value-based health organizations will need to work to improve the quality of care to the patients and populations by improving and refining data collection and assessment. Risk management is also greatly enhanced by thorough and quality data collection and assessment. It is projected that by the year 2043, racial and ethnic minorities will account for the majority of the population in the United States. Successful health organizations must adapt to accommodate these changes and must begin collecting and analyzing race, ethnicity, and language data, also referred to as REAL data.[15] The REAL data can "identify high cost drivers, develop interventions to improve care for vulnerable population, and appropriately deploy resources."[16] Despite the usefulness of REAL data, only about 14–25% of hospitals and health systems are utilizing this data to improve the quality of care and the outcomes; there are four steps that should be used when using REAL data:[17]

1. Determine appropriate data categories—acquiring census data, distributing surveys, forming focus groups with important community organizations, and utilizing data that has already been acquired.
2. Develop a methodology for data collection— deciding who collects the data, how often, processes, methodology standardization, monitoring data collection progress, and assigning accountability.[18]
3. Train staff members on methodology for data collection.
4. Assign accountability and monitor progress of data collection efforts—identify appropriate measures, references points, risk adjustments, and sample size.

Organizations that utilize this four-step approach will clearly identify where disparities exist, allocate resources, and create effective and efficient interventions. Benefits of collecting and using REAL data include "reducing costs, reducing disparities in health outcomes, reducing hospital readmissions, receiving incentive payments, and meeting Patient Centered Medical Home (PCMH) certification requirements."[19] Effective collection and use of REAL data will position hospitals and care systems for success in an environment where regulators, payers, employers, and, most importantly, patients are looking for more differentiated and individualized healthcare.[20]

One Size Does Not Fit All: Meeting the Healthcare Needs of Diverse Populations

Effective data collection will allow health organizations to better assess and analyze information related to diverse populations. Demographic data will provide a greater understanding of the population and lead to better resource allocation, identification of health inequities, and greater communication and community interaction.[21] Demographic data includes race, language, socioeconomic status, gender, and age. Identifying the unique and different populations will allow organizations to respond to changing demographics, health needs, market-based demands, and be able to forecast future service needs.[22] Once this data has been thoroughly evaluated, the organization can then begin implementing policies tailored to suit the needs of the populations they serve.

Accommodating the needs of specific populations includes promoting staff awareness through training, dialogue, and support to cultural competence; enhancing the hospital's physical space; adapting services to address cultural beliefs; and helping patients to manage their care.[23] Staff members are given incentives to be culturally sensitive in order to accommodate the patient population they serve, which includes compensation for cultural training. The development of cultural competence among staff requires training to be continuous and tailored to patient needs.[24]

The fourth theme discusses the need to establish internal and external collaborations.[25] Internal collaborations include different stakeholders being brought together to develop, implement, evaluate, and improve initiatives aimed at meeting the needs of the diverse patients.[26] The stakeholders of the health organization should be as diverse as the population they serve; thus, organizations should include individuals from different departments, ethnic backgrounds, positions, and professional levels.[27] Stakeholders are also excellent sources for data associated with the community that may otherwise be unattainable. External collaborations can be with other hospitals, health organizations, governmental agencies, and community groups that have the same patient needs, patient base, and educational institution affiliations.[28] External collaborations will be important to address challenges such as limited resources and high costs of developing new materials. The health organizations can share information and materials to reduce expenses. The community collaboration strategy should include community leaders, educational institutions, health-related governmental officials, and patients. Including patients and community members will be important to bring a more diverse perspective while increasing the likelihood of bridging cultural barriers, thus allowing the health organization to become more active in the community.[29]

The Joint Commission Perspectives

The Joint Commission Road Map

Through data collection and research, it has been discovered that non-clinical needs of patients can shape how patients view, receive, and participate with health organizations.[30] Health organizations must integrate effective communication, cultural competence, and patient and family-centered care practices into its core activities.[31] As discussed earlier, each health organization is unique and there exists no "one-size-fits-all" solution. The *Roadmap for Hospitals* was created to assist health organizations, specifically hospitals, in deciding which directions and methods should be used to meet the specific needs of their patients. The Joint Commission uses the care continuum to illustrate

changes that must be made to patient care to better connect and serve communities.[32] Hospitals should address the following components of the care continuum:[33]

1. Admission.
2. Assessment.
3. Treatment.
4. End-of-life care.
5. Discharge and transfer.
6. Organization readiness.

The admission phase of the care continuum offers opportunities to identify the needs of each patient during both emergencies and scheduled appointments.[34] Patients and their families share information regarding their background, physical requirements, and family history that can be accessible to all departments in the hospital.[35] Assessments are often collected during the admission process to help staff members address sensitive issues.[36] Some of these include the patient's health literacy level, mobility, sexual orientation, gender identity and expression, cultural, religious, spiritual, lifestyle, or dietary needs.[37] It is crucial to address the needs of the patient during admission and during assessment. However, it is important for the hospital to address the needs of their patients while providing appropriate diagnostic services, care, treatment, and other services.[38]

Treatment stage hospitals should integrate communication and cultural competence with patient and family-centered care in order to address treatment options, as well as risks and alternatives for patients.[39] The initial treatment for the patient should address any communication barriers through patients' medical records such as language, culture, those with sensory impairments (ear or eye).[40] Consent can only be given if the patient fully understands the information provided. Alternative communication resources (translator or interpreter) should be provided, if necessary.[41] The interpreter should always be someone who is not affiliated with the patient or family so the potential for miscommunication is reduced.[42] Materials should also be modified so the patient can understand despite education level. Addressing a patient's cultural, religious, or spiritual beliefs and practices is another large part of the treatment process; as best as possible, those beliefs should not be violated during treatment.[43] Dietary needs or restrictions should also be noted.[44] The last aspect of the treatment process is to make sure all the needs of the patient are directly communicated to the entire care team.[45] This requires integration of data, in the context of the patient, to provide actionable information to the care team members across the care continuum.

Supportive care should be given to the patient during their final stages of life. It is essential that patient communication needs are addressed and that any communication barriers are noted.[46] Changes in the patient's ability to communicate should also be addressed during each stage of health so appropriate communication methods

are sought and employed.[47] Additionally, involving the decision maker, noting the mobility needs, and recognizing religious or cultural beliefs should be noted and incorporated into the care plan and processes.[48] This element also requires integrated and actionable information.

In the discharge and transfer process, there is a concern with patients and their families feeling overwhelmed by the amount of healthcare information included in the discharge-and-transfer plan.[49] When hospitals plan to transfer or provide referrals for follow-up care and treatment, appropriate providers should be identified.[50] Nurses and other discharge planners must efficiently deal with the discharge-planning services, and nurses must be the cornerstones for in-home healthcare services.[51] It is increasingly evident that effective hospital discharges can only be achieved when there is quality collaboration between the care providers, primary care providers, and others involved in the care of the patient, including a clear understanding of respective services required post institutional care.[52] Without this, the diverse needs of local communities and individuals cannot be met.[53] This element also requires integration and access to information across the care continuum. There are five domains for organization readiness to serve diverse patient groups: leadership; data collection and use; workforce; provision of care, treatment, and services; and patient, family, and community engagement.[54]

- Leadership discusses how leaders must clearly articulate a hospital's commitment to meet the unique needs of its patients to establish an organizational culture that values effective communication, cultural competence, and patient- and family-centered care.[55]
- The second domain of data collection and use discusses how the hospital must define what types of data to collect, how to collect data, and how to use data for service planning and resource allocation to advance effective communication, cultural competence, and patient- and family-centered care.[56]
- The third domain of workforce discusses how the hospital and its staff, including the medical staff, must commit to meeting the unique needs of the patients they serve.[57]

- The fourth domain of provision of care discusses how the hospital, in striving to meet the individual needs of each patient, must embed the concepts of effective communication, cultural competence, and patient- and family-centered care into the core activities of its care delivery system.[58]
- The final domain of patient, family, and community engagement discusses how the hospital must be prepared to respond to the changing needs and demographics of the patients, families, and the community served. The hospital can identify the need for new or modified services by being involved and contributing to the overall engagement of patients.[59]

Each domain represents a key area that health organizations, specifically hospitals, should address to make sure necessary systems and processes exist to meet the unique needs of each patient. The hospital can use the domains as a framework for exploring the organization's readiness to address patient needs throughout the care continuum. Recommendations for increasing the readiness of health organizations for innovation should include key organizational strategies for embedding innovation: development of incentives; sophisticated knowledge management; inter-functional and inter-organizational coordination and collaboration; and development of an innovation infrastructure.[60]

Governmental Imperatives

IRS Policy Guidance

The Internal Revenue Service (IRS), in its oversight of not-for-profit (NFP) organizations with IRS Code 501 (c) 3 status, has revised policy guidance. The guidance change reflects the requirement that NFP health organizations improve service and connection with the communities they serve. One major element is the requirement for NFP health organizations to conduct community health needs assessments, integrate findings of those assessments into the strategic decision making of the organization, and monitor effectiveness of community health needs initiatives. The organization will have to write and publish a fee assistance policy,

a policy written for actions taken in emergency medical conditions, and perform a community needs assessment once every three years.[61] These requirements will require resources to establish but will soon become part of the culture and can be administered seamlessly.[62]

This movement toward more community connection requires the integration of community and population data into the flow of information that leads to actionable information and knowledge within the health organization.

Centers for Medicare & Medicaid Services (CMS): Medicare Value-Based Purchasing

Value-based purchasing (VBP) is an initiative from CMS designed to reward acute care hospitals with incentive payments for providing high-quality care to people insured by Medicare. It is important to note that, historically, commercial health insurance providers have followed the federal government's efforts to implement quality improvement programs within a few months to a few years of federal program implementation. CMS measures the quality of care provided on how well the facility enhances the patient experience during their hospital stay and how closely clinical best practices are followed. This is a change from previous systems which simply paid based on the number of procedures performed. The VBP program was established with the passage of the ACA and was initiated with payments starting October 1, 2012. The launch of the program included 2,985 hospitals across the country.

Through the VBP program, incentive payments are made based on:

- How well a facility performs on a given measure.
- How much improvement in performance on each measure compared to the baseline time period, two years prior (2015 versus 2013, for example).

The categories of performance measures under VBP are clinical process of care, patient experience of care, outcomes, and efficiency. Under each category are standard practices such as stopping certain medications related to a surgical procedure at the correct time, doctor communication, as well as reporting of key measures such as mortality due to heart failure. Hospitals are given a score based on their results in these categories, with patient experience of care and outcomes being weighted most heavily.

The VBP program is funded by reimbursement payments withheld from hospitals for care provided to Medicare patients. When the program started in 2013, the bonus money available was 1% of Medicare payments, and when the program is in full effect in 2017, the applicable percentage will be 2.0% of Medicare payments.[63] Hospitals that fail to improve under VBP lose their applicable percentage from Medicare payments. Through this, the VBP system is cost neutral in terms of payments; the "reward" payments given to high performers are covered through the payments withheld from low performers.

Healthcare supply chain directly impacts all four areas of VBP; however, it is most evident within the clinical processes and efficiency domains. Within clinical processes, an efficient supply chain ensures that the items necessary for patient care are available. This directly affects SCIP-Card 2 and SCIP-VTE-2 by ensuring that the correct medication is available and on hand when needed.[64]

Hospital Compare

Hospital Compare is a website, launched in 2005, that has information about the quality of care provided at over 4,000 Medicare-certified hospitals across the United States. The system can be used to, as the name suggests, find and compare the quality of care provided at different hospitals. The information on Hospital Compare is provided in an easy-to-use format targeted for consumers.[65]

Physician Compare

The **Physician Compare** website displays information on physicians and other healthcare practitioners which participate in the program. Recently, the physician compare system began including information on physician practices as well as for individual physicians.[66]

In addition to comparing physicians and hospitals, CMS also collects data on nursing homes, home health, and dialysis facilities. All of these websites are interconnected with each other for ease of use. However, ranking services such as these provided by CMS are not unique; there are many others run by professional groups, private companies, or industry watchdog groups. You may have seen advertisements for hospitals proudly announcing that "one of the best hospitals in the country is just around the corner." The ranking of hospitals is typically not consistent between various best hospital lists and this holds true for data on the Hospital Compare system; however, over time the data and consistency of that data should improve. A likely cause of this discordant ranking between the myriad of quality indicator-based systems is a direct result of the methods used by each ranking service, constructs used and the utilization of geographic and volume modifiers with the analyses; the variance in these rankings can lead to confusion for consumers.[67]

Integrated Information Required: Need for Technology and Informatics Solutions

Healthcare is rapidly evolving industry, but has been slow to adopt advances pioneered in other fields related to information technology. The use of electronic medical records (EMR) began in the early 1970's as computer systems became sophisticated enough to perform the tasks required. From the start, the use of EMR was controversial and the industry was resistance to change. EMR is different from paper charting of medical records and often requires changes in caregiver workflow.[68] Even though the technology has been available for nearly fifty years, many facilities are slow to adopt EMR systems. The costs associated with the systems and return on investment are often of concern.[69] However, the use of these solutions has increased quickly due to a requirement by the federal government that medical facilities show meaningful use of EMR by 2015 or face a 1% penalty on their Medicare reimbursement; this penalty will increase over time.[70]

As health organizations begin to transition to EMR in ever increasing numbers, the need for effective and reliable methods of measuring the level of utility that health institutions are receiving from their implementation is evident. Effectively measuring how something is used or implemented is accomplished through benchmarks defined in a **Model**.

HIMSS Analytics Adoption Model for Analytics Maturity (AMAM)

The HIMSS Analytics AMAM is an 8 stage model (stages 0-7) that helps healthcare organizations understand their analytics maturity and plot a course to data-driven decision making. **Analytics** is the use of information to form insights (actionable information) resulting from the analysis of data. Data which advance clinical decision support and clinical care are collected and managed through an (EMR). Analytics of that data are used to manage and improve financial and operational activities of the healthcare organization. The AMAM advances data-driven decision making by providing a roadmap that systematically improves analytics of clinical, financial, and operational data.

The AMAM model indicates that the foundation of analytics is to build a centralized location for amassing data and establishing governance. Maturity in the capability oriented model advances to its pinnacle at stage 7 in four focus areas: Data content; Infrastructure; Data governance; and Analytics capability. HIMSS Analytics benchmarks healthcare organizations against AMAM compliance statements that outline critical capabilities in each of these four focus areas. Assessment results help organizations develop and implement a customized analytics strategy.

Stage 0 is the starting point for every organization. At some point in time every organization started from ground zero, having little or no resources to work with, an inconsistent version of the truth, and realizing there was a need to improve insights and analytics capabilities.

FIGURE 13.1 HIMSS Analytics Adoption Model for Analytics Maturity

STAGE	Adoption Model for Analytics Maturity Cumulative Capabilities
7	Personalized medicine & prescriptive analytics
6	Clinical risk intervention & predictive analytics
5	Enhancing quality of care, population health, and understanding the economics of care
4	Measuring & managing evidence based care, care variability, and waste reduction
3	Efficient, consistent internal and external report production and agility
2	Core data warehouse workout: centralized database with an analytics competency center
1	Foundation building: data aggregation and initial data governance
0	Fragmented point solutions

HIMSS Analytics Adoption Model for Analytics Maturity. Reproduced with permission from HIMSS Analytics.

Stage 1 organizations are just beginning to accumulate and manage data. They may or may not have a formal database for storing this data, but are accumulating it into an operational data store or data warehouse for historical reference and consolidated access. The location could be a shared drive, within the organization or in the cloud, or a specific server or a common electronic shared library. The storage method could be as simple as a spreadsheet, a set of reference tables, or a simple SQL or graphical database tool. The main concept of stage 1 is to document and begin execution of an analytics strategy that brings basic data together from appropriate systems of record and begin to understand how to manage (data governance) and define the data (development of metadata) so that it can be used and referenced by a broad cross section of analysts.

Stage 2 is where the foundation for analytics activities is strengthened and expanded. It is to a large degree a continuation of stage 1, but with more purpose and progress. Stage 2 is designed to extend the concepts and capabilities introduced in stage 1 and expand them in a broader context across the enterprise and in the depth of their capabilities. It is a core workout for building strength and experience.

The organization expands from having data centrally located to having it in a formal data warehouse as an enterprise resource (as opposed to a silo oriented and narrowly used resource) with master data management (MDM) that supports ad-hoc queries and descriptive reporting. The enterprise begins maturing data governance while leveraging this environment in support of basic clinical and operational tasks, such as patient registries. All activities should be aligned with the organizations' overall strategic goals. Analytic skills, standards, and education are managed through an analytics competency center.

Stage 3 describes an organization that has mastered descriptive reporting broadly across the enterprise. Varying and different parts of the organization are able to effectively coral data, work with it, and produce historical and current period reporting with minimal effort. Data quality is stable and predictable, tools are standardized and broadly available, and data warehouse access is managed and reliable.

In Stage 4 the organization begins to direct analytical data assets, skills, and infrastructure developed in previous stages squarely towards improving clinical, financial, and operational program areas. This includes a concerted effort to understand and optimize by honing analytics resources that support evidence based care, track and report care and operational variability, and identify and minimize clinical and operational waste.

Organizations in stage 5 expand point of care oriented analytics and the support of population health. Data governance is aligned to support quality based performance reporting and bring further understanding of the economics of care.

Stage 6 pushes the organization to mature in the use of predictive analytics and expands the focus on advanced data content and clinical support.

Stage 7 represents the pinnacle of applying analytics to support patient specific prescriptive care. This stage demonstrates how healthcare organizations can leverage advanced data sets, such as genomic and biometrics data to support the uniquely tailored and specific prescriptive healthcare treatments of personalized medicine. This is the mass customization of care combined with prescriptive analytics.

The 4 Ps of Health Analytics: An Informatics Framework

The 4Ps of Health Analytics is a descriptive model of how data is used within a health system. It is also a prescriptive model; this will be discussed later in this chapter. Unlike the HIMSS Delta model, the 4Ps breaks data into four categories which are depicted in the following figure.

The 4 Ps of Health Analytics describes the interconnections between the four major categories of data found in health organizations: patients, populations, processes, and profitability (called "net margin" for NFP organizations). Traditionally, these four types of information have been used separately. When data is not easily accessed or integrated with other data from complementary domains, it is referred to as being in an **information silo**. As computer systems evolved, it became

FIGURE 13.2   4 P's of Health Analytic Framework

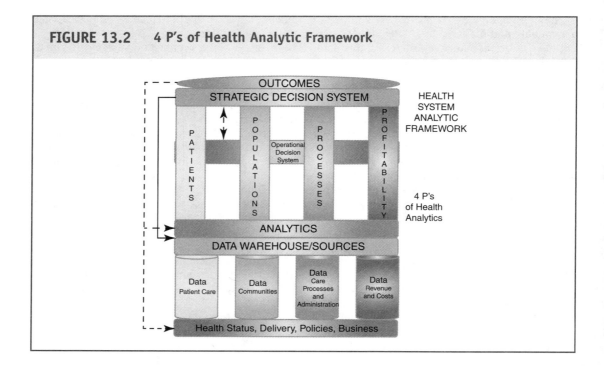

possible to store data in an electronic database which, when properly implemented, allows for information that, previously in a silo, can be used with other data sources. Another term for these electronic databases is a data warehouse or enterprise data warehouse. A **data warehouse** is a system which creates a central repository of data and makes that data available for reporting and data analysis.

As the HIMSS Delta Model is oriented toward "technology," the 4 Ps Model is oriented to "information." To reduce complexity, the 4 Ps model is presented in its component parts and what is included in each type of data, before explaining the interconnectivity within the model.

Patient data is data pertaining directly to the demographic information, history, diagnostics, treatment, care plans, and outcomes of care of the patient; this data is contained in the EMR system.

Population data refers to the communities where health organizations are located. The data in this category are related to improving community health status, and to the health and well-being of the community as a whole.

Process data includes information on the way business is conducted within the health organization; this data (or elements of the data) can be found in ERP systems and organizational documents.

Profitability data ("net margin" for NFP health organizations) includes data on the ability of a health organization to generate income such as cost of services, amount billed, and expected reimbursement along with expenses; this data can be found in ERP systems and organizational documents.

Profitability

Ensuring profitability (another way to consider this is financial viability) requires organizations to properly measure and assess all the financial components continuously. Financial ratios such as operating margins, days cash on hand, debt to capitalization, and capital spending are some important metrics that can be pulled from a health organization's financial statement to measure profitability, liquidity, and capital structure.[71] The transition to value-based payment, narrowing margins, and focus on reducing costs will require health organizations to look further into operations, expenses, and reimbursement to maintain profitability or net margin. The Health Research & Educational Trust, in partnership with the American Hospital Association (AHA), published metrics for high-priority strategies to evolve to the "second curve." As previously noted, one of the top four strategies is improving efficiency through productivity and financial management; this is crucial to profitability.[72]

The first metric is expense-per-episode for each care setting established by analysis with a broad range of episodes of care (volume of patients). This data gives insight and understanding to the true cost of care for specific episodes by service line (cardiology, labor, and delivery, etc.), which is necessary for financial planning and improvement strategies. Metrics should be in place to measure, manage, model, and predict risk, using a broad set of historical data from multiple sources.[73] Measuring risk is necessary when entering into partnerships with payers and can be assessed with possible financial gains and savings.[74] Cost-reduction goals can be created for specific departments or services in order to increase profitability and meet the needs of patients. Organizations must use these metrics to establish specific yet attainable goals.[75] Similarly, results from quality-improvement initiatives and process re-engineering should be measurable.[76] In order to meet these goals and assess profitability, these changes must be demonstrated and monitored through a series of metrics. Lastly, the impact of managing future Medicare payment levels must be considered. Projecting the financial impact is necessary to cut costs in order to manage the organization at the forecasted reimbursement level for all payments while monitoring expenses.[77]

Effective financial management will require more comprehensive data sources, integrated information, and appropriate analytical methods for assessment and evaluation. Implementing appropriate technology, coupled with an informatics framework, facilitates metrics to be utilized in cutting costs, increasing efficiency, and boosting revenues.[78]

The profitability of a health organization is critical to its continued operation. A hospital may provide the best care in the country with superior outcomes in patient care and high levels of satisfaction, but if the staff salaries and bills cannot be paid, the doors will close. Health organizations want the latest medical technology and the highest qualified physicians and staff. This will attract patients, but this achievement is unreachable without the availability of financial resources. However, NFP health organizations, considering the IRS policy guidance, may lose tax-exempt status if the culture becomes overly focused on reputation and profit while ignoring the community.

An indicator of a financially healthy organization is its ability to earn a profit or net margin and achieve a return on their investments. The financial stability of health organizations are measured by gross profit margin. The gross profit margin is defined as the percentage of money remaining after goods and services have been paid. Focusing on a healthy or high gross profit margin will reflect favorable potential earnings. This in turn mirrors profitability. A net profit margin highlights pricing, cost structure, and efficiency of an organization. All three of these components dictate the potential success and future direction of any organization. How money is spent, costs must be managed as well. An organization must be efficient in order to leverage the most from purchases of labor, equipment, facilities, and supplies. Inefficiency can reduce the ability to leverage costs into productive activity that leads to profitability.

Making adequate use of resources that an entity has can be measured by looking at the return on assets. Every resource is valuable. Not using an available resource to its highest efficacy is a waste and a drain on the potential improvement. Before taking on any new ventures or investments, a review of the organization's return on equity should be an additional measure.[79] This allows the health organization to see the returns, if any, gained on the investments that were made.[80] The healthcare organization must also track the return on investments to determine whether or not resources should remain allocated to a particular aspect of the operation.[81] Positive returns on an investment may control decisions on future investments. A decrease in profitability will result in a decline in the return on assets and return on equity. Each of the previous measures is important to sustain a financially healthy status.[82]

In order to sustain profitability, health-organization revenue must be safeguarded. This can be achieved through internal audits.[83] Internal audits can mitigate the potential for revenue loss through denied or recovered payments.[84] Changes in coding and qualified bundle payments will only increase the amount of denied claims.[85] Through an internal audit, mistakes can be caught before a loss of time and money ensues or prolongs. This in turn allows health organizations to improve billing and coding.[86] As a result the health organization can seek entitled revenue knowing its system is above reproach even during payer audits.[87]

Profitability is a key element in maintaining state-of-the-art technology needed to attract and keep highly trained healthcare professionals[88]. This is also a crucial component to providing high-quality care for patients. For-profit hospitals can raise equity by issuing shares. In order to maintain not-for-profit status for tax purposes, a hospital in this category cannot issue shares.[89] They can, however, build equity on internal operations supplemented with donations and gifts to manage financial investments.[90] Singh's study looks at the relationship between patient revenue in relation to its assets and the time it takes on collection of patient revenue.[91] Other important factors include financial performance indicators: operating and total profit margins, free cash flow, and equity capital of the health organization. Managing the patient revenue cycle successfully can lead to increased profitability. Of course higher patient revenue amounts per total assets and quicker collection times are associated with improved operating and profit margins.[92] The research noted faster collections reduced the balance in accounts receivable, and as a result, the health organization's need for short-term financing and, thus, interest expenses were

lessened.[93] Effective revenue cycle management also allowed for higher "free cash flows." This facilitated an increase in cash flow from operations.[94] The research provides firsthand evidence that significant improvements can be achieved in each health organization's revenue cycle performance.[95] Likewise, effective financial management, expense management, and productivity coupled with quality revenue management are imperatives for health organizations and directly linked to their survival. Integrated, multi-domain information is required to achieve this level of leadership.

Patients

At the heart of the health industry is the patient and their family. Several data sources and metrics should be used to evaluate the patient domain: readmissions, patient satisfaction surveys, awards, occupancy rates, and average length of stay.[96] Readmissions are important because these numbers can help determine whether or not appropriate care was provided to the patient in a previous visit to the health organization within a 30-day period and the effectiveness of discharge plans[97]. This evaluates if treatment methods were effective or not. Patient satisfaction surveys determine if the medical staff communicated appropriately with the patient when providing care. Awards are a way of determining the effectiveness of patient care in comparison to other medical facilities. It also provides feedback for health organization performance.[98] Another way of measuring patient care is through occupancy rates, which indicate the health organization's census.[99] Patient satisfaction can be measured through occupancy rates; for example, if the census of the health organization remains high, perhaps it is an indication of success and/or quality throughout the organization.[100] Finally, the average length of stay (AVLOS) is the fifth metric used to measure patients; it determines the type of patients treated in the hospital.[101] For example, if most AVLOS are high, it shows a greater number of patients with severe illnesses or higher acuity or patients with more complex or multiple procedures per episode of care.[102] Patient outcomes and satisfaction are essential to understand before a leader can develop a knowledge culture; integrated information is required to firmly grasp patient outcomes and satisfaction levels.

Populations

A population can be measured in various ways but understanding the population, groups within the population and special groups within the population is the basis for community linkage and serving that community. How can you best understand a community's population? Some of the metrics that can be used to measure the population include census, school data, state and federal health data sources, focus groups with important community organizations, surveys, and the use of REAL data patients.[103] These metrics can be utilized to acquire reliable, accurate, and useful information on the surrounding community.[104] As previously stated, assessing the needs of the population can help deliver a higher quality of care but the care that is needed.

EHRs contain a considerable amount of health information. EHRs, once data is pulled out from individual patient records, can provide insight into health needs and may offer solutions to improving population health. EHRs can be used for research integration and patient care.[105] Realizing this potential will require understanding what EHRs can realistically offer in efforts to improve population health, the requirements for obtaining useful information from EHRs, and a plan for addressing these requirements.[106] Potential contributions of EHRs to improving population health include better understanding of the level and distribution of disease, function, and well-being within populations.[107] Being able to utilize EHRs allows for better understanding of the patient and how to access patient needs, while providing insight into improving services.[108]

With the advancement of EHRs, population health is a high priority for health information management and for health information management professionals. A shift in population health management (PHM) must occur in the near future, as medicine becomes the spotlight for managing the long-term health effects of patient populations.[109]

"Population health management (PHM) lowers costs by refocusing healthcare on not just the sick but also the well." The goal of PHM is to keep a patient population as healthy as possible and reduce the need for expensive interventions like tests, emergency department visits, hospitalizations, and procedures. While most healthcare providers see the critical importance of PHM, they do not have the information technology, the required understanding of PHM, or the data management skills and resources that are required to successfully utilize population health management. Some of the first things that must be understood when launching a PHM program is what a population of healthy people looks like, how clinical risk is defined, how financial risk is measured, and what will be the metrics used to analyze how sick patients with chronic disease do and do not get sicker. PHM programs also track and trend inpatient, ambulatory, and emergency department patients."[110]

Understanding the usage of PHM and all its functions is important in addressing all the risks related to a population of non-healthy people versus healthy people.[111] PHM makes use of patient data registries and data banks to create a portrait of a certain population and analyze trends to find solutions to problematic behaviors and connect care gaps that may leave certain segments chronically underserved.[112] Using population health data to its fullest extent and achieving complete data integration will "redesign the way providers approach and deliver care" while taking advantage of existing health IT initiatives, such as EHRs and health-information exchanges (HIEs) that represent huge investments for hospitals and physicians.[113] Drawing from recent data and analytics, health-information management (HIM) professionals must be the trend setters in quality data analytics by gathering proper information, maintaining the integrity of clinical documentation, HIE information governance and EHRs, and analyzing data to be effective in the way patients of diverse populations are perceived and treated.[114]

Processes

Previous studies show that medical errors due to lack of communication among the medical staff are estimated to be the chief causes of death for

44,000 and 98,000 patients every year. Therefore, the productivity of health organizations and improvement of patient health rests upon the implementation of health-information technology (HIT) in health organizations. Defining HIT can be challenging because it can be composed of multiple administrative and clinical applications that may vary across different organizations and medical settings. HIT is not an application that can be applied to the health organization and be expected to run smoothly by itself; HIT needs the commitment of the leadership and staff of the organization for it to work effectively and efficiently.[115] Focusing only on the technology and not on the reasons for the technology to provide information that is actionable to develop a knowledge culture would be unwise. Why you have the technology, what you get from that technology, and how you use the output (in this case, information) is critical.

Health leaders are the spearhead of this operation, and therefore must advocate for the implementation of HIT in their organizations.[116] Health leaders must focus on what the HIT provides: information. Of equal importance, leaders must understand that HIT implementation is a process and may take years to have an optimal and operational system.[117] Thus, the loss of productivity in the "project" years is expected and must be taken in consideration.[118] Moreover, having a successful operating HIT not only helps productivity within the organization, but it also helps the organization's profitability, patient's quality of care/outcomes, improves processes, and improves population health.[119] Along with all the pros of HIT adoption, there are also cons. The cons include cost and loss of productivity in the project phase due to learning and adjustment processes.[120] Health leaders must keep their eyes on the reason for HIT, the actionable and integrated information that can inform high-quality decisions across the organization in pursuit of a knowledge culture.

HIT will increase productivity after the initial two years of implementation by allowing smoother communication with supply chain management, accounting, and billing.[121] It will also reduce transaction costs and improve resource allocation.[122] The rising cost of healthcare and the presence of inefficiencies in health organizations can lead to the loss of resources (dollars, time, high-quality physicians and staff, and opportunities). HIT can satisfy many functions to include monitoring physician behavior and how resources are allocated;[123] a clinical information monitoring system can be used to identify any overuse of laboratory and radiology resources, for example.[124] This reduction in transaction costs attributed to inefficiency of production and resource allocation will increase overall profitability, improve patient care outcomes (to include increased safety), enhance processes and community health status by allowing the health organizations to keep more of its profits or net margin,[125] and use those funds for improvements. This requires integrated and actionable information.

HIT, such as EMR, will also improve the quality patients' care by allowing better communication between physicians and staff throughout the health organization and its external support structures.[126] Patient care requires coordination of many activities across multiple and various departments in which communication among the staff is critical; human errors can be costly to both the organization and its patients.[127] HIT implementation allows for a reduction of redundancy of treatment and communication errors among medical staff.[128] This improves patient care by allowing the patients to manage their health alongside the physician.[129]

The main deterrent to the adoption of HIT is cost. Many inefficient health organizations struggle to survive; having to adapt to a brand new clinical and administrative HIT system may seem daunting.[130] Productivity in the overall operation can be increased due to HIT, such as when electronic medical records are introduced (once the learning curve is overcome), with the benefits likely outweighing the costs of adoption.[131] Moreover, improving health through the process of health information technology takes more than just integrating the technology into the organization's system[132] but the technology must provide pertinent information to realize these desires. Training is an important part of HIT implementation; more importantly, making post-implementation maintenance training available to the staff is critical.[133]

HIMSS Electronic Medical Record Adoption Model

There are several constructs models related to the Delta model that fall under the category of analytic maturity models. An analytic maturity model offers a more detailed description of an organization at each level of analytic usage. Of particular interest for our purposes is the Electronic Medical Record Adoption Model (EMRAM). The EMRAM model categorizes analytic maturity based on the capabilities of the EMR system utilized by the organization. HIMSS has conducted several studies using the EMRAM model in the United States and Canada that revealed interesting results that are summarized in the tables below.

As can be seen from the results, high levels of analytic adoption are rare in the sample from the United States and non-existent in the Canadian sample. When the results were repeated in 2014 Q2, the adoption rates had not changed from Q1 in Canada while there was moderate improvement in the United States health organizations.

The survey reveals that there is great potential for improvement with regard to the use of analytics in health organizations across the country as well as in Canada. Additionally, the increasing levels of EMR utilization in the United States shows that EMR adoption and system improvement is an issue important to US-based health systems today. The reasons for this improvement could be related to the PPACA requirements, the timeliness of the technology, or competitive factors. Regardless of the reason, health organizations will need to adapt and grow their EMR systems to keep pace with industry-wide adoption of the technology.

TABLE 13.1   US Electronic Medical Record Adoption Model

United States EMR Adoption Model [SM]

Stage	Cumulative Capabilities	2013 Q4	2014 Q1
Stage 7	Complete EMR; CCD transactions to share data; Data warehousing; Data continuity with ED, ambulatory, OP	2.9%	3.1%
Stage 6	Physician documentation (structured templates), full CDSS (variance & compliance), full R-PACS	12.5%	13.3%
Stage 5	Closed loop medication administration	22.0%	24.2%
Stage 4	CPOE, Clinical Decision Support (clinical protocols)	15.5%	15.7%
Stage 3	Nursing/clinical documentation (flow sheets), CDSS (error checking), PACS available outside Radiology	30.3%	27.7%
Stage 2	CDR, Controlled Medical Vocabulary, CDS, may have Document Imaging; HIE capable	7.6%	7.2%
Stage 1	Ancillaries - Lab, Rad, Pharmacy - All Installed	3.3%	3.2%
Stage 0	All Three Ancillaries Not Installed	5.8%	5.6%

Data from HIMSS Analytics® Database © 2014 http://www.himssanalytics.org/emram/emram .aspx, Retrieved July 30, 2014.   N = 640   N = 640

TABLE 13.2   Canada Electronic Medical Record Adoption Model

Canada EMR Adoption Model [SM]

Stage	Cumulative Capabilities	2013 Q4	2014 Q1
Stage 7	Complete EMR; CCD transactions to share data; Data warehousing; Data continuity with ED, ambulatory, OP	0.0%	0.0%
Stage 6	Physician documentation (structured templates), full CDSS (variance & compliance), full R-PACS	0.6%	0.6%
Stage 5	Closed loop medication administration	0.0%	0.5%
Stage 4	CPOE, Clinical Decision Support (clinical protocols)	3.8%	3.6%
Stage 3	Nursing/clinical documentation (flow sheets), CDSS (error checking), PACS available outside Radiology	32.2%	32.5%
Stage 2	CDR, Controlled Medical Vocabulary, CDS, may have Document Imaging; HIE capable	29.1%	28.9%
Stage 1	Ancillaries - Lab, Rad, Pharmacy - All Installed	14.5%	14.5%
Stage 0	All Three Ancillaries Not Installed	19.8%	19.4%

Data from HIMSS Analytics® Database © 2014 http://www.himssanalytics.org/emram/emram .aspx, Retrieved July 30, 2014.   N = 640   N = 640[134]

The EMRAM model can be used for other types of data as well, not just the EMR or patient-related data. If this type of scale is used to measure the effectiveness of all four information types, it can provide a score for how all data types are utilized. Although EMRAM does an excellent job of categorizing the utilization of analytics, it does not address the actionable information, knowledge, or meaningful use components.

Integration of 4 Ps, HIMSS Delta and EMRAM Models

Efficiency, Effectiveness, and Efficacy

The efficiency, effectiveness, and efficacy of a model are important considerations to take into account when selecting a method to pursue in the domain of informatics. **Efficiency** is how much time, effort, or resources are required to implement the model divided by the output or utility of the model. **Effectiveness,** in this context, is how well the model works to achieve a set of goals or objectives in real world situations. **Efficacy** is how much value or "good" the model brings to the problem or improvement effort; in essence, what positive outcomes can you attribute due to using a particular model? At first glance it may appear that effectiveness and efficacy are measuring the same attribute; this is a common point of confusion. Models with high efficacy must be effective when applied to real world situations. Regardless of the efficacy and effectiveness of a model, if it's not efficient to use, the model will be less useful in the fast-paced environment of health organizations. Let's explore some models.

TABLE 13.3   US EMR Adoption Cumulative Capabilities

US EMR Adoption Model^{SM}

Stage	Cumulative Capabilities	2014 Q1	2014 Q2
Stage 7	Complete EMR; CCD transactions to share data; Data warehousing; Data continuity with ED, ambulatory, OP	3.1%	3.2%
Stage 6	Physician documentation (structured templates), full CDSS (variance & compliance), full R-PACS	13.3%	15.0%
Stage 5	Closed loop medication administration	24.2%	27.5%
Stage 4	CPOE, Clinical Decision Support (clinical protocols)	15.7%	15.3%
Stage 3	Nursing/clinical documentation (flow sheets), CDSS (error checking), PACS available outside Radiology	27.7%	25.4%
Stage 2	CDR, Controlled Medical Vocabulary, CDS, may have Document Imaging; HIE capable	7.2%	5.9%
Stage 1	Ancillaries - Lab, Rad, Pharmacy - All Installed	3.2%	2.8%
Stage 0	All Three Ancillaries Not Installed	5.6%	4.9%

Data from HIMSS Analytics™ Database © 2014   N = 5,449   N = 5,447

Data from HIMSS Analytics® Database © 2014 http://www.himssanalytics.org/emram /emram.aspx, Retrieved July 30, 2014.

For illustration purposes, each of the models, EMRAM, Delta, and the 4Ps describe a different aspect of an EMR system. Since each model emphasizes a different important element of the EMR, combining the models will allow a more comprehensive picture to emerge concerning EMR; actually, the combination of the models will create a more robust picture of any technologically enabled informatics situation. Used in conjunction or integrated, all of these models are effective, efficient, and have high efficacy.

Integration

By combining the 4 Ps, Delta, and EMRAM models, a new model that is both prescriptive and descriptive emerges. The 4 Ps describes the type of data

and how the four types of data in each domain, patients, populations, processes, and profitability work together. The HIMSS Delta model ranks the utilization of data analytics. The HIMSS EMRAM gives an in-depth description of each level of utilization. Combining the three models creates a complete picture of how data should be used at each stage of analytic adoption and gives a roadmap for improvement. The combined model, for purposes of discussion, is the 4 Ps of Health Analytics *Adoption*.

The 4Ps of Health Analytics Adoption is both a prescriptive and descriptive model that is an extension of the 4Ps of Health Analytics Model and incorporates the valuable HIMSS Delta and EMRAM Models. At each level of analytics utiliza-

TABLE 13.4   Canada EMR Adoption Cumulative Capabilities

Canada EMR Adoption Model[SM]

Stage	Cumulative Capabilities	2014 Q1	2014 Q2
Stage 7	Complete EMR; CCD transactions to share data; Data warehousing; Data continuity with ED, ambulatory, OP	0.0%	0.0%
Stage 6	Physician documentation (structured templates), full CDSS (variance & compliance), full R-PACS	0.6%	0.6%
Stage 5	Closed loop medication administration	0.5%	0.5%
Stage 4	CPOE, Clinical Decision Support (clinical protocols)	3.6%	3.6%
Stage 3	Nursing/clinical documentation (flow sheets), CDSS (error checking), PACS available outside Radiology	32.5%	32.5%
Stage 2	CDR, Controlled Medical Vocabulary, CDS, may have Document Imaging; HIE capable	28.9%	28.9%
Stage 1	Ancillaries - Lab, Rad, Pharmacy - All Installed	14.5%	14.5%
Stage 0	All Three Ancillaries Not Installed	19.4%	19.4%

Data from http://www.himssanalytics.org/emram/emram.aspx, Retrieved July 30, 2014. [1]   N = 640   N = 640
HIMSS (2014). The EMR Adoption Model - HIMSS Analytics. Retrieved July 24, 2014, from
https://www.himssanalytics.org/stagesGraph.asp.

tion, data is unified through the data warehouse. The extent of this utilization is what determines the effectiveness and efficacy of the data; this combined effectiveness and efficacy can be quantified by a score in the model. The utilization levels are loosely based on the scores associated with the EMRAM developed by HIMSS.

Data used incorrectly, even if the electronic systems are fully utilized, will not help an organization and can actually negatively impact organizational decisions. To measure the effectiveness at which the data provided by analytical systems is converted into knowledge, the 4Ps of Health Analytics Adoption assigns a letter grade, the same as one would expect to receive in a class. The knowledge scale in the 4Ps Adoption model consists of a four letter range: A, B, C, and D. Note that a high knowledge score is essentially

measuring the meaningful use of the electronic systems and EMR combined with continuous learning and feedback loops using the information. When the score is combined with the knowledge score, a matrix of possible values can be created. As an example, this point is illustrated in **Table 13.5**.

While an "X" in the above table is the most common score, any value within the table is possible, although much less likely to occur. The reasoning behind this becomes apparent when the extreme scores of "1A" and "7D" are examined. A score of "1A" means that only fragmented bits of information are available and what is available is converted to high levels of knowledge spanning the patient, the population in which the patient lives, the processes that support the patient's treatment, and the financial implications. A score

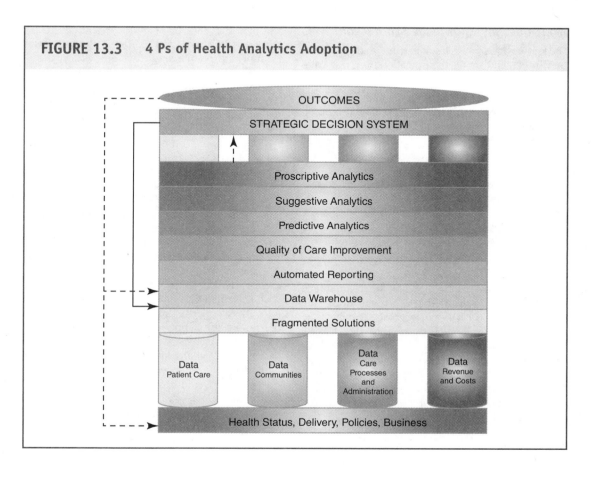

FIGURE 13.3   4 Ps of Health Analytics Adoption

TABLE 13.5   4 P's of Health Analytic Adoption and HIMSS Delta Model Integration

	1	2	3	4	5	6	7
A				X	X	X	X
B			X	X	X	X	X
C	X	X	X	X	X		
D	X	X	X				
Information Score (4 Ps)/Technology Adoption Score (HIMSS)	1	2	3	4	5	6	7

of "7D" is still unlikely to occur. "7D" would be assigned to an organization that has full utilization of all possible analytic solutions and adoptive technologies but is unable to use those systems to generate anything beyond raw data. With this framework, individual scoring can be explored.

What Does my Knowledge Score Mean?

The knowledge score is a single letter grade between "A" and "D" and shows the transition from raw data to knowledge.

- A = knowledge; actionable and integrated information is used for improvement in a continuous feedback loop. Knowledge-based organizational cultures operate in this environment for most strategic and operational decisions.
- B = actionable information is integrated across the 4 Ps and prompts action.
- C = Data in context or information that is minimally integrated across the 4 Ps.
- D = Raw data without integration; data in its "silo."

It is noteworthy that raw data could be further broken down into incomplete, fragmented, and clean. The reason the 4P model does not do this is because it is not relevant to what the 4 Ps is describing. The purpose of the model is to move organizations to higher levels of utilization so while it is acknowledged that further categorization of raw data is possible, moving past this state of informatics utilization is prudent since most health organizations are beyond this state of development regarding informatics.

What Does my Utilization Score Mean?

The utilization score is a number between 1 and 7 and describes the adoption of analytical tools within a health organization. The integration of the knowledge scores with the utilization scores becomes clear with an explanation that follows:

1. Fragmented data with multiple sources available.
   - A score of 1 means that an organization is in the planning stages of adopting analytical tools. At this stage data is most likely to be stored in separate systems with no integration or unified fields. Any available data is likely to be fragmented with multiple versions of "the truth" available at any one time.
2. Data warehouse with patient, population, process, and profitability data stored in a standardized system. The standardization of this system is important because it is what

allows the data from multiple sources to be utilized in a meaningful way. If the data was simply stored in a single system without standardization the data is still effectively in an **information silo**.

3. Automated internal dashboards and external reporting using the data available from the data warehouse.
   - Dashboards and scorecards define modern business. In health organizations these tools are used, some would say overused, every day. By automating the creation of these tools, analysts are able to spend their time analyzing data instead of building reports. As a result it is possible to have more effective meetings and allow decision making to keep pace with the healthcare environment.
4. Waste reduction and quality of care improvement.
   - The reduction of waste and quality of care improvements can be done through streamlining the supply chain through analysis of supply usage. By understanding how much is used when, inventory on hand can be reduced and space that was once used for storage can be converted to patient care areas.
5. Predictive analytics to manage clinical outcomes.
   - Predictive analytics to manage clinical outcomes takes into account how patients behave in their communities. Predicting how patients will behave once they leave the facility allows case managers to effectively manage risks for readmission and other target areas.
6. Suggestive analytics to manage population health.
   - Suggestive analytics go beyond what is offered by predictive analytics in that they suggest potential treatment options to providers based on patterns in existing information.
7. Prescriptive analytics to personalize medicine.
   - This is the ultimate goal of analytics in healthcare. Prescriptive analytics does not necessarily translate to a knowledge score of "A." Having such an analytic system and not fully understanding it would result in a score of less than an "A."

When Should my Organization Work to Increase Our Utilization Level?

A health organization and its leadership team will receive the most benefit of an increase in the level of analytic utilization if the knowledge score for the current level is maximized. Increasing utilization before the knowledge score is maximized will most likely result in no change to the knowledge score without improvements to the adaptive (or human ways of using information) processes and organizational culture. The reason behind this is that the addition of new systems when the current ones are underutilized shines a light on business processes and adaptive/human issues. This can be countered through additional training on existing systems and providing intensive training on new features as they are added. It can also be beneficial to provide periodic review courses to essential team members and creating understanding of why information is needed and how it is utilized.

Examples of 4 Ps of Health Analytics Adoption Model in Practice

Next, we will look at some examples of how the 4 Ps can be used in common situations within a health system. The examples used are simple yet demonstrate the initial basic assessment that using the 4 Ps Health Analytic Adoption Model can provide without a large investment in time or other resources. Our first example is a small rural hospital and the second is within the context of a large health system. The examples follow.

Example 1: Using the 4 Ps in a Small Rural Hospital to Determine the Need for an Analytic Solution

As the CEO of a critical-access hospital, your organization is struggling to make payroll and investment in new capital equipment that is not possible at this time. With the EMR meaningful use requirements looming on the horizon, VBP increasingly causing stress, and net margin narrow, you must act quickly so that your Medicare reimbursement is not effected. This is especially important to your organization because you are

dependent on Medicare reimbursement payments to pay your employees since Medicare comprises nearly 40% of your payer mix. Many vendors want to install an EMR system in your hospital, but you are not sure which product is the correct choice for your hospital. Additionally, you want to make sure that your staff is effectively using their available analytic resources. The supply chain implications are especially important to your crucial access hospital where the efficient care of Medicare patients is the difference between growing your business and closing the doors. The proper EMR system will enable efficient charge capture and empower your director of materials to negotiate better pricing for the top use items, an area that is currently unexplored by your organization.

The 4 Ps of Health Analytics Adoption is the perfect model to use in this situation because it accounts for the needs of small facilities as well as large. Under the 4 Ps a utilization score of "7" is not necessarily the "best." Rather, the usage of the information available is the most important and whether that information gives your decision support that you need to operate and lead successfully. A small facility may have their analytic needs met at a score of 3 B, 4 B, or 4 A, for example.

Knowing this, you and your team complete the 4P assessment process and find that your current score is 2 B. This score shows that while actionable information is available, the information that is available is being utilized rather effectively at the utilization level of 2. This result, combined with other research, gives you the confidence to select an EMR system that would move your utilization to a 3 or 4 level with the option to expand capabilities in the future. In this example, you know that your facility is ready for the basic EMR system because the information available was already being highly utilized; advancing the technology utilization level and increasing the level of information available will most likely be utilized to improve your organization. The investment in EMR will most likely result in a positive return on that investment. Let's assume, for example, that the 4 P assessment returned a score of 1 D for this small hospital. This score would tell the CEO that additional basic comprehensive training on the use of information systems was needed before and during the EMR implementation process and that an update of the business processes of the organization must be made prior to that implementation. If this update of business practices (adaptive changes) and training did not occur, the EMR system would be severely underutilized and for a hospital on a tight budget this will likely be a wasted investment.

Example 2: Using the 4 Ps in a Large Health System With an Existing EMR and Data Warehouse System

Imagine that you are the CIO of a large healthcare system. Your organization has been using an EMR system with an associated data warehouse for about ten years. Overall, physicians with whom you speak are happy with the current EMR system and operational leaders/ managers feel that they have the tools they need to assess the risks of patients, improve processes in the operation, and connect better with the populations in the community. Your organization is growing at a rapid pace; there is need for expanded technological and informatics systems. Due to the cost associated with changes or additions to the information systems, you want to see how well the current systems are being utilized. Your team completes the utilization and knowledge assessments and presents the findings to you. Under the 4 Ps Adoption model, your health system received the score of 4 C. This score means that while your health system has advanced analytic capabilities to automate reporting, improve some operational processes, and streamline supply chain with Electronic Data Interchange (EDI) transaction processing, the data available within your systems are not being effectively converted to integrated actionable information, not to mention consistently achieving the knowledge level. Since the current systems are not being fully utilized, an expansion of the information system may not be as effective without enhanced training, improvements to business operations, utilization of metrics, and professional analysts to interpret and use the data correctly.

With the results of the 4 P Adoption model assessment, a business process reengineering and update process was initiated, a training program begun on utilizing data/information/knowledge for improved operations and services, and a thorough assessment of business and clinical-analyst needs was launched. These efforts were started before expanding the information systems at your organization. When the 4 Ps Adoption model assessment was completed again eighteen months later, your organization received the score of 5 B, showing a growth in utilization and knowledge. As the 4 Ps Adoption Model is a prescriptive and assessment model, this re-evaluation has also shown areas for further growth.

4 Ps of Health Analytics Adoption and Supply Chain

So how does this apply to the healthcare supply chain? Health organization supply chain is often overlooked when thinking in terms of process and system improvement. Commonly, this is due to misaligned incentives for change or a lack of education on the process.[135] Supply-chain management (SCM) is managing the flow of goods; this includes the delivery and storage of supplies used to treat patients. Many of the excess costs associated with the supply chain are caused by inefficient processes related to transport and delivery to health organizations from suppliers[136]. The use of a model such as the 4 Ps of Health Analytics Adoption provides health leaders with a new way of looking at supply-chain-related data. Reorganizing data into patients, populations, process, and profit can break down existing barriers. With traditional barriers removed, factors can be addressed that collectively affect, for example, profitability of the health organization. For those organizations that do not use some sort of ERP system, the 4 Ps of Health Analytics Adoption shows that by grouping processes together efficiencies can be created.

Example

Suppose a hospital has 100,000 square feet of patient-treatment areas and 50,000 square feet of support

Example **361**

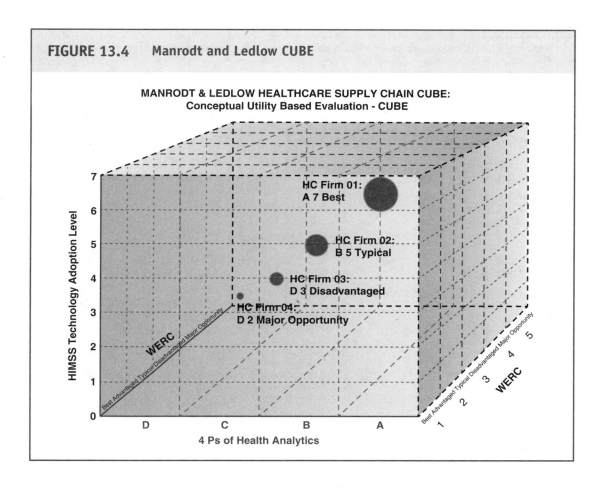

FIGURE 13.4   Manrodt and Ledlow CUBE

MANRODT & LEDLOW HEALTHCARE SUPPLY CHAIN CUBE:
Conceptual Utility Based Evaluation - CUBE

services, including a 25,000 square foot warehouse. The CEO of this hospital wants to expand in order to better treat the growing population within the community. This is important to him because as the population grows, wait times in the emergency room (ER) have increased greatly, affecting the quality of care. However, the costs associated with increasing the number of beds in the ER is prohibitive because all 100,000 square feet within the hospital is being fully utilized. The alternative to expanding to a new space is to optimize the utilization of currently available space. In order to do this, a team at the hospital completes the Manrodt & Ledlow CUBE model assessment. The CUBE assessment allows the team to determine that current warehousing practices

for medical products put them at a disadvantage when compared to other facilities. By improving these processes, they are able to reduce the size of the warehouse to 15,000 square feet. The space formerly used to store equipment can then be converted to patient-treatment areas.

Manrodt & Ledlow CUBE

Manrodt and Ledlow's CUBE model utilizes the 4 Ps of Analytic Adoption model by including a healthcare supply-chain component. The addition of this supply-chain component, specifically warehousing and inventory management, allows the CUBE model to accurately benchmark and measure improvement in a wider range of business activities of supply-chain functions or warehousing and inventory management. The supply-chain component is scored on a five point categorical scale from major opportunity to best-in-class based on multi-industry standards and benchmarks.

Major Opportunity

Processes that score as a major opportunity are severely handicapping an organization and should be improved immediately. Failure to improve processes in the major opportunity category will eventually result in an organization no longer being competitive.

Disadvantage

A score of disadvantage means that an organization is performing below the industry average for the process being measured.

Typical

Processes that rank as typical are relatively close to the average level of efficiency for the process being measured.

Advantage

Processes in this group are performing better than the average for a given industry.

Best-in-class

A score of best-in-class shows that the process being measured is leading the industry for efficiency.

The cube model is a natural extension of the 4 Ps of Health Analytics because supply chain falls under the processes data silo.

4 Ps and Supply Chain

The healthcare supply chain is an integral component (core business function) of the delivery of healthcare services. Information systems, technology, and data are necessary to lead and manage the healthcare supply chain successfully. The level of data, information, and knowledge available to the leader and manager, at every level, to improve the supply chain is a critical factor. The use of the 4 Ps of Health Analytics Adoption, coupled with the HIMSS models and the WERC Models, can assist in strategic improvement decisions for the supply chain as well as benchmarking performance against other health organizations in similar situations. A major aspect of leading and managing the healthcare supply chain is mastering the data, information, and knowledge of the operational systems that integrate with the supply-chain operation.

Summary

In this time of rapid change and the absolute necessity for health leaders to understand how information and technology can evolve health organizations, one way for health organizations to continue to advance is to adopt technological advancements such as the EMR, SCM systems, and administrative HIT systems. Within the supply chain, the adoption of EMR systems will greatly increase charge capture efficiency, allowing for more efficient patient care. This is especially important given recent reform, policy guidance, and reimbursement changes along with new expectations placed on health systems by patients and the community. Managing risk and serving the needs of a population is a very new requirement for health-service delivery organizations; this challenge is a leadership responsibility to migrate the culture to a knowledge-enabled organization. A health leader must make informed decisions with integrated information in the patient, process, population, and profitability domains. To assess current utilization of analytics and other tools that create knowledge from raw data, a model such as the 4 Ps of Health Analytics Adoption is a starting point.

The 4 Ps of Health Analytics is a descriptive model which describes the ideal use of mission critical data into actionable information with emphasis on creating a knowledge culture. With the valuable HIMSS models integrated with the 4 Ps of Health Analytics model, the 4 Ps of Health Analytics *Adoption* is both a prescriptive and descriptive model; it describes and assesses the current state of utilization of technology and knowledge in information systems, coupled with business practices. Successful health leadership requires selecting the correct model to inform, guide, and improve health organizations. With the dynamic industry evolving, knowledge from the four basic domains will equip the health organization to embrace challenges and improve health status one patient at a time and the entire population of the communities the organization serves.

Sarah Says: A Student's Perspective

This chapter discusses three major models. The first model is the HIMSS Delta Powered Model and the second is the 4 Ps Analytic model. The HIMSS Delta Powered Model is a five-level model that categorizes the maturity level of a health organization's analytics system. The model measures the usage of analytics over five core competences: data, enterprise, leadership, targets, and analysts. The healthcare supply chain is integrated into the informatics infrastructure of most health organizations; thus, understanding the relationship between the models is important.

As the HIMSS Delta Model is oriented toward "technology," the 4 Ps Model is oriented to "information." The 4 Ps of Health Analytics is a descriptive model of how data is used within a health system. The 4 Ps of Health Analytics describes the interconnections between the four major categories of data found in health organizations: patients, populations, processes, and profitability.

The EMRAM model can be used for other types of data as well, not just the EMR or patient-related data. If this type of scale is used to measure the effectiveness of all four information types, it can provide a score for how all data types are utilized.

The efficiency, effectiveness, and efficacy of a model are important considerations to take into account when selecting a method to pursue in the domain of informatics. This is true for healthcare supply-chain information systems as well.

Discussion Questions

1. Describe the significant changes in the health industry that prompt an integrated approach for utilizing health information from multiple areas to make good decisions for health services delivery and improved health status of communities.
2. Explain how health-industry reform and policy changes impact the rate of health analytic adoption within health organizations and what changes require analytic adoption in the health industry.
3. Demonstrate how applicable models associated with health information and technology tools improve efficiency, effectiveness, performance, and efficacy of health services and healthcare delivery.
4. Compare and contrast methods to effectively use analytic models to integrate raw data and develop knowledge to improve health-system performance and equity within a community.
5. Categorize health organizations in technology adoption, analytics adoption (information utilization), and information integration using the integration of the HIMSS Delta Model and the 4 Ps of Health Analytics Adoption models and provide examples.
6. Appraise and evaluate the integration of population, patient, process, and profitability (net margin for NFPs) information in solving community health challenges and/or strategic planning for a health organization.

Exercises

1. Describe the significant changes in the health industry that prompt an integrated approach for utilizing health information from multiple areas to make good decisions for health-services delivery and improved health status of communities in one page or less.
2. Explain how health-industry reform and policy changes, based on AHA and other associations, impact the rate of health-analytic adoption within health organizations and what changes require analytic adoption in the health industry.
3. Demonstrate how applicable models associated the health information and technology tools improve efficiency, effectiveness, performance, and efficacy of health services and healthcare delivery. Visit http://svi.cdc.org: How can the 4 Ps of Health Analytics Adoption be used with social and vulnerable populations using the SVI Index?
4. Compare and contrast methods to effectively use analytic models to integrate raw data and develop knowledge to improve health system performance and equity within a community.
5. Categorize health organizations in technology adoption, analytics adoption (information utilization), and information integration using the integration of the HIMSS Delta Model and the 4 Ps of Health Analytics Adoption models and provide examples.
6. Appraise and evaluate the integration of population, patient, process, and profitability (net margin for NFPs) information in solving community health challenges and/or strategic planning for a health organization. Utilize the 4 Ps of Health Analytics Adoption model as if you are working for one of the organizations used in example 1 or 2 from the text and discuss your results.

Journal Items

Answer the following:

Describe the 4 Ps of Health Analytics model in one page or less.

What considerations would you have and why, to lead, manage, and plan within the context of the healthcare supply chain?

References

1. https://www.healthcare.gov/what-if-i-dont-have-health-coverage/ (accessed 23 Jul. 2014) HHS (2014). 2014 Poverty Guidelines, *ASPE*, http://aspe.hhs.gov/poverty/14poverty.cfm (accessed 19 Jul. 2014).
2. ObamaCare Subsidies, *ObamaCare Facts*, (2013), http://obamacarefacts.com/obamacare-subsidies.php (accessed 19 Jul. 2014).
3. Open Enrollment Period, *HealthCare.gov*. (2013). Retrieved July 19, 2014, from https://www.healthcare.gov/glossary/open-enrollment-period/ (accessed 19 Jul. 2014).
4. Fees You Pay If You Don't Have Health Insurance Coverage, *HealthCare.gov*, (2014), https://www.healthcare.gov/what-if-i-dont-have-health-coverage/ (accessed 23 Jul. 2014).

5. Meaningful Use Stage 1 Requirements, *CMS*, (2012). 29–30 , https://www.cms.gov/Regulations-and-Guidance/Legislation/EHRIncentivePrograms/downloads/MU_Stage1_ReqOverview.pdf (accessed 23 Jul. 2014).

6. American Hospital Association, Committee on Research. *Your hospital's path to the second curve: Integration and transformation* (Chicago: Health Research & Educational Trust, 2014, January), 4.

7. American Hospital Association, Committee on Research. *Your hospital's path to the second curve: Integration and transformation*, 4.

8. American Hospital Association, Committee on Research. *Your hospital's path to the second curve: Integration and transformation*, 4.

9. American Hospital Association, Committee on Research. *Your hospital's path to the second curve: Integration and transformation*, 4.

10. American Hospital Association, Committee on Research. *Your hospital's path to the second curve: Integration and transformation*, 4.

11. American Hospital Association, Committee on Research. *Your hospital's path to the second curve: Integration and transformation*, 6.

12. American Hospital Association, Committee on Research. *Your hospital's path to the second curve: Integration and transformation*, 6.

13. American Hospital Association, Committee on Research. *Your hospital's path to the second curve: Integration and transformation*, 16.

14. American Hospital Association, Committee on Research. *Your hospital's path to the second curve: Integration and transformation*, 16.

15. Health Research & Educational Trust. *Reducing health-care disparities: Collection and use of race, ethnicity and language data*. (Chicago: Health Research & Educational Trust. 2013b) August). 2 www.hpoe.org

16. Health Research & Educational Trust. *Reducing health-care disparities: Collection and use of race, ethnicity and language data*. 2

17. Health Research & Educational Trust. *Reducing health-care disparities: Collection and use of race, ethnicity and language data*. 3-5

18. Health Research & Educational Trust. *Reducing health-care disparities: Collection and use of race, ethnicity and language data*. 3-5

19. Health Research & Educational Trust. *Reducing health-care disparities: Collection and use of race, ethnicity and language data*. 6

20. Health Research & Educational Trust. *Reducing health-care disparities: Collection and use of race, ethnicity and language data*. 6

21. A. Wilson-Stronks et al. One size does not fit all: Meeting the healthcare needs of diverse populations, (2008), 7 http://www.jointcommission.org/assets/1/6/HLCOneSizeFinal.pdf

22. Wilson-Stronks et al. One size does not fit all: 7

23. Wilson-Stronks et al. One size does not fit all: 7

24. Wilson-Stronks et al. One size does not fit all: 8

25. Wilson-Stronks et al. One size does not fit all: 40–44

26. Wilson-Stronks et al. One size does not fit all: 40–44

27. Wilson-Stronks et al. One size does not fit all: 40–44

28. Wilson-Stronks et al. One size does not fit all: 40–44

29. Wilson-Stronks et al. One size does not fit all: 40–44

30. Advancing effective communication, cultural competence, and patient- and family-centered care: A roadmap for hospitals, *The Joint Commission*, (2010), 3 http://www.jointcommission.org/assets/1/6/aroad-mapforhospitalsfinalversion727.pdf

31. Advancing effective communication, *The Joint Commission*, 3

32. Advancing effective communication, *The Joint Commission*, 3

33. Advancing effective communication, *The Joint Commission*, 3

34. Advancing effective communication, *The Joint Commission*, 3

35. Advancing effective communication, *The Joint Commission*, 9

36. Advancing effective communication, *The Joint Commission*, 13

37. Advancing effective communication, *The Joint Commission*, 13

38. Advancing effective communication, *The Joint Commission*, 13

39. Advancing effective communication, *The Joint Commission*, 17

40. Advancing effective communication, *The Joint Commission*, 18–23

41. Advancing effective communication, *The Joint Commission*, 18–23

42. Advancing effective communication, *The Joint Commission*, 18–23

43. Advancing effective communication, *The Joint Commission*, 18–23

44. Advancing effective communication, *The Joint Commission*, 18–23

45. Advancing effective communication, *The Joint Commission*, 18–23

46. Advancing effective communication, *The Joint Commission*, 25–26

47. Advancing effective communication, *The Joint Commission,* 26

48. Advancing effective communication, *The Joint Commission,* 26

49. Advancing effective communication, *The Joint Commission,* 29

50. Advancing effective communication, *The Joint Commission,* 29–30

51. Advancing effective communication, *The Joint Commission,* 29–30

52. Advancing effective communication, *The Joint Commission,* 29–30

53. DH (Department of Health) (2003) Discharge from Hospital: Pathway, Process and Practice. Page v

54. Advancing effective communication, *The Joint Commission,* 33–34

55. Advancing effective communication, *The Joint Commission,* 33–34 http://www.jointcommission.org /assets/1/6/aroadmapforhospitalsfinalversion727 .pdf

56. Advancing effective communication, *The Joint Commission,* 33–34

57. Advancing effective communication, *The Joint Commission,* 33–34

58. Advancing effective communication, *The Joint Commission,* 33–34

59. Advancing effective communication, *The Joint Commission,* 33–34

60. Williams, I. "Organizational readiness for innovation in healthcare: some lessons from the recent literature." *Health Services Management Research*, 24, no. 4 (2011, January 1). 213–8. http://www.birmingham.ac.uk /Documents/college-social-sciences/social-policy /HSMC/publications/2011/organisational-readiness -health-care.pdf (accessed 22 Apr. 2014)

61. Sarah H. Ingram, Department of the Treasury, Internal Revenue Service. (2012). *Additional requirements for charitable hospitals* (2012-15537)

62. Ingram, *Additional requirements for charitable hospitals* (2012-15537)

63. "Hospital Value-Based Purchasing Program," *cms,* (2015), 1–8 http://www.cms.gov/Outreach-and-Education /Medicare-Learning-Network-MLN/MLNProducts /downloads/Hospital_VBPurchasing_Fact_Sheet _ICN907664.pdf (accessed 23 Jul. 2014).

64. "Hospital Value-Based Purchasing Program, " *cms.*

65. Medicare Hospital Compare Overview, *Medicare.gov*, http://www.medicare.gov/hospitalcompare/About /What-Is-HOS.html (accessed 23 Jul. 2014).

66. About the data. *Medicare.gov,* (2013), http://www .medicare.gov/physiciancompare/staticpages/data /aboutthedata.html (accessed 23 Jul. 2014).

67. L. K Halasyamani and M. M. Davis, "Conflicting measures of hospital quality: ratings from 'Hospital Compare' versus 'Best Hospitals'." *Journal of Hospital Medicine*, 2, no. 7, (2007), 128–134.

68. Mather, B. S. (1973). Problem Oriented Medical Record. *British medical journal*, 4(5883), 49.

69. Jha, A. K., DesRoches, C. M., Campbell, E. G., Donelan, K., Rao, S. R., Ferris, T. G., ... & Blumenthal, D. (2009). Use of electronic health records in US hospitals. *New England Journal of Medicine*, 360(16), 1628–1638.

70. Congress, U. S. (2009). American recovery and reinvestment act of 2009. *Public Law*, (111-5), 111.

71. S. Rodak, "5 key financial ratios healthcare providers should track," *Becker's Hospital Review*, (2012), http ://www.beckershospitalreview.com/finance/5-key -financial-ratios-healthcare-providers-should-track.html

72. American Hospital Association, Committee on Research. *Your hospital's path to the second curve: Integration and transformation.* (Chicago, IL: Health Research & Educational Trust, 2014, January), 18.

73. American Hospital Association. *Your hospital's path to the second curve.* 2.

74. American Hospital Association. *Your hospital's path to the second curve.* 2.

75. American Hospital Association. *Your hospital's path to the second curve.* 5.

76. American Hospital Association. *Your hospital's path to the second curve.* 6.

77. American Hospital Association. *Your hospital's path to the second curve.* 2.

78. L.E.K. Consulting. *Hospitals adopt new strategies to boost profitability, but still face deep challenges: A new imperative for medtech.* Executive Insights, 15, no. 4 (2013) http://www.lek.com/sites/default/files/2013_L.E.K. _Hospital_Priorities_Study.pdf

79. D. C. Benton et al. "Use of Open Systems Theory to Describe Regulatory Trends." *Journal of Nursing Regulation*, 4, no. 3 (2013), 49–56. Page 51

80. Benton et al. "Use of Open Systems Theory to Describe Regulatory Trends."

81. Benton et al. "Use of Open Systems Theory to Describe Regulatory Trends."

82. Benton et al. "Use of Open Systems Theory to Describe Regulatory Trends."

83. B. Allen, "Internal audits can safeguard hospital revenue." *Hfm (Healthcare Financial Management)*, 67 no. 9, (2013), 106–112. Page 106

84. Allen, "Internal audits can safeguard hospital revenue."

85. Allen, "Internal audits can safeguard hospital revenue."

86. Allen, "Internal audits can safeguard hospital revenue."

87. Allen, "Internal audits can safeguard hospital revenue."

88. S. Rauscher Singh and J. Wheeler, "Hospital Financial Management: What Is the Link Between Revenue Cycle Management, Profitability, and Not-for-Profit Hospitals' Ability to Grow Equity?" *Journal Of Healthcare Management*, 57, no. 5 (2012), 325–339. 326

89. Singh and Wheeler, "Hospital Financial Management." 326.

90. Singh and Wheeler, "Hospital Financial Management." 326.

91. Singh and Wheeler, "Hospital Financial Management." 325.

92. Singh and Wheeler, "Hospital Financial Management." 325.

93. Singh and Wheeler, "Hospital Financial Management." 335.

94. Singh and Wheeler, "Hospital Financial Management." 333.

95. Singh and Wheeler, "Hospital Financial Management." 327.

96. D. Cosgrove et al. "A CEO Checklist for High-Value Health Care. Discussion paper. Washington, *DC: Institute of Medicine*, (2012). http://www.iom.edu/Global/Perspectives/2012/CEOChecklist.aspx (accessed 7 Jul. 2014).

97. Cosgrove et al. "A CEO Checklist for High-Value Health Care."

98. J. Sorra et al. "Hospital Survey on Patient Safety Culture" *User Comparative Database Report.* (Prepared by Westat, Rockville, MD, under Contract No. HHSA 290201300003C). Rockville, MD: Agency for Healthcare Research and Quality; March 2014.

99. Sorra et al. "Hospital Survey on Patient Safety Culture."

100. Sorra et al. "Hospital Survey on Patient Safety Culture."

101. Health Research and Educational Trust. *Improving Health Equity Through Data Collection AND Use: A Guide for Hospital Leaders.* (Chicago: Health Research & Educational Trust, 2011). http://www.hret.org/health-equity/index.shtml Page 2

102. Health Research and Educational Trust. *Improving Health Equity Through Data Collection AND Use:* Page 2

103. Health Research and Educational Trust. *Improving Health Equity Through Data Collection AND Use:* Page 4

104. Health Research and Educational Trust. *Improving Health Equity Through Data Collection AND Use:* Page 3

105. D.J Friedman, R. Parrish and D.A. Ross, "Electronic Health Records and US Public Health: Current Realities and Future Promise." *American Journal of Public Health*, 103, no. 9, September 2013, 1560–1567. doi: 0.2105/AJPH.2013.301220 Page 1560

106. Friedman, Parrish and Ross, "Electronic Health Records and US Public Health" Page 1561

107. J. Bresnick, "Population health is the new frontier for HIM, says AHIMA." *EHR Intelligence.* (2013, July 30), http://ehrintelligence.com/2013/07/30/population-health-is-the-new-frontier-for-him-says-ahima/ (accessed 22 Apr. 2014).

108. Bresnick, "Population health is the new frontier for HIM, says AHIMA."

109. Bresnick, "Population health is the new frontier for HIM, says AHIMA."

110. Bresnick, "Population health is the new frontier for HIM, says AHIMA."

111. Bresnick, "Population health is the new frontier for HIM, says AHIMA."

112. Bresnick, "Population health is the new frontier for HIM, says AHIMA."

113. Bresnick, "Population health is the new frontier for HIM, says AHIMA." Pg. 1

114. Bresnick, "Population health is the new frontier for HIM, says AHIMA." Pg. 1

115. N. Zhang, et al. "Health Information Technology Adoption in US Acute Care Hospitals." *Journal of Medical Systems*, 37, no. 2, (n.d.) Page 8

116. Zhang, et al. "Health Information Technology Adoption in US Acute Care Hospitals." *Journal* Page 8

117. N. Zhivan and M. Diana, "U.S. hospital efficiency and adoption of health information technology." *Healthcare Management Science,* 15, no. 1 (2012), 37–47. doi:10.1007/s10729-011-9179-2 Page 38

118. Zhivan and Diana, "U.S. hospital efficiency and adoption of health information technology." Page 38

119. Zhivan and Diana, "U.S. hospital efficiency and adoption of health information technology." Page 38

120. Zhivan and Diana, "U.S. hospital efficiency and adoption of health information technology."

121. Zhivan and Diana, "U.S. hospital efficiency and adoption of health information technology."

122. Zhivan and Diana, "U.S. hospital efficiency and adoption of health information technology." Page 40

123. Zhivan and Diana, "U.S. hospital efficiency and adoption of health information technology." Page 37

124. Zhivan and Diana, "U.S. hospital efficiency and adoption of health information technology."

125. Zhivan and Diana, "U.S. hospital efficiency and adoption of health information technology." Page 45

126. Zhivan and Diana, "U.S. hospital efficiency and adoption of health information technology." Page 45

127. Zhivan and Diana, "U.S. hospital efficiency and adoption of health information technology." Page 42

128. Zhivan and Diana, "U.S. hospital efficiency and adoption of health information technology." Page 45

129. Zhivan and Diana, "U.S. hospital efficiency and adoption of health information technology." Page 45

130. Zhivan and Diana, "U.S. hospital efficiency and adoption of health information technology." Page 45

131. Zhivan and Diana, "U.S. hospital efficiency and adoption of health information technology." Page 45

132. Zhivan and Diana, "U.S. hospital efficiency and adoption of health information technology." Page 45

133. Zhivan and Diana, "U.S. hospital efficiency and adoption of health information technology." Page 38

134. The EMR Adoption Model - *HIMSS Analytics*, (2014), https://www.himssanalytics.org/stagesGraph.asp (accessed 24 Jul. 2014).

135. K. E. McKone-Sweet, P. Hamilton, P., and S. B. Willis, "The ailing healthcare supply chain: a prescription for change." *Journal of Supply Chain Management*, 41, no. 1 (2005), 4–17.

136. C. D. Brennan Integrating the healthcare supply chain. *Healthcare financial management: journal of the Healthcare Financial Management Association*, 52, no. 1 (1998), 31–34.

CHAPTER 14

A SYNTHESIS OF HEALTHCARE SUPPLY CHAIN VALUE

LEARNING OBJECTIVES

1. Describe the path a cotton ball takes through the healthcare supply chain from identifying a need for the item to the utilization of that item by a clinician for the care of a patient.
2. Outline the basic steps based on the Value Chain for a typical healthcare supply chain and how supply chain operations can integrate in clinical operations and/or building/facility operations.
3. Calculate the economic order quantity and the safety stock for a healthcare supply chain item.
4. Assess how the importance of metrics in supply-chain management supports the clinician in the care process and what metrics are most important from a clinical perspective.
5. Integrate concepts of leadership, management, and planning to create a vision for excellence in the healthcare supply chain. How can supply-chain operations integrate with tools such as geographical information systems?
6. Determine fundamental tenets of performance evaluation for the healthcare supply chain.

Introduction

This chapter will provide a concluding overview of the previous chapters to allow reflection and thinking focused on supply-chain excellence in healthcare. The Value Chain sets the context for the concluding healthcare supply-chain overview. How will you improve the healthcare supply chain to be a valuable core function of healthcare organizations that provide care to patients? How will you provide the "technology of care" to the caregivers, physicians, surgeons, nurses, and other clinical staff to improve the quality of care and efficacy to the care process? How can you develop, improve, and

hold to high standards of healthcare supply-chain efficiency, effectiveness, and efficacy? Every health professional serves an important role in healthcare supply-chain operations and management.

Important Details

Healthcare supply chains have similarities and differences from other industries, yet it is these differences that significantly impact the cost and delivery of care to the patient. Four basic differences were summarized in Chapter 1: consequences, regulatory pressures, variation, and assets out of control of the hospital.

What are some of the consequences of these differences? Primarily, increased cost within the supply chain when compared to other industries, especially the cost of holding additional inventory. While some additional inventory in the form of safety stock is necessary, this doesn't mean that there isn't room for improvement. Inventory levels should be realistic, and take into account the high level of service available in an unforeseen event like a stock-out. Like in other industries, management of the supply chain is viewed as a support function in healthcare; more progressive firms view their supply chains as a means of creating a strategic advantage.

Because of the complexity and variety of supply chains utilized in healthcare, purchasing in healthcare is significantly different than other industries. In healthcare, purchasing is typically dependent on group purchasing organizations (GPOs). Forming a partnership with a supplier instead of working with a GPO to purchase goods directly is not common in healthcare. In other sectors, group purchasing is not used and it is common for partnerships to form between suppliers and customers.

Finally the challenges covered in Chapter 1 encourage the use of metrics to evaluate performance.

However, in healthcare, organizations are usually benchmarked against their peers whereas in other industries benchmarks and best practices are compared regardless of industry. For instance, a bank may study a retailer to benchmark and measure customer service. In addition, other industries use scorecards and other tools to manage supplier performance. Process improvement such as lean Six Sigma or other tools are commonplace.

In the healthcare sector logistics is often referred to by an older name: materials management. Materials management in healthcare is the procurement, storage, inventory control, quality control, and operational management of supplies, pharmaceuticals, equipment, and other items used in the delivery of patient care or the management of the patient care system.

Any discussion of logistics, transportation, or supply-chain management would be incomplete without discussing the importance of creating value for the ultimate customer. Value is an underlying reason and theme to the actions of logistics and supply-chain managers. Firms that do not create value will not stay in business very long.

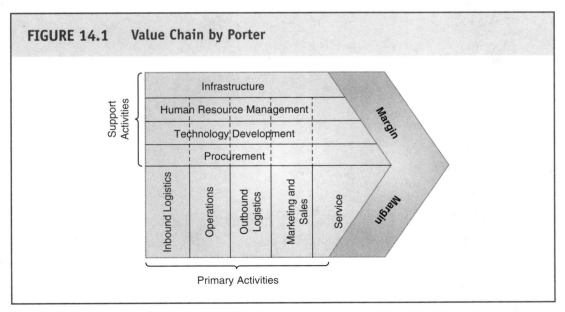

FIGURE 14.1   Value Chain by Porter

Value is generated through a chain of actions or processes. The concept of a Value Chain was first introduced by Michael Porter in his 1985 book *Competitive Advantage: Creating and Sustaining Superior Performance*. The central idea is that a chain of specific activities, when done correctly, can add more value to an organization than the cost of each activity individually. The value added to the organization is in the form of competitive advantage. Due to the potential to generate a competitive advantage, the Value Chain can be used as a tool for strategic planning and process improvement.

Reconnecting with the Value Chain

As we learned in Chapter 2, the Value Chain is thoroughly integrated with healthcare supply-chain sourcing and purchasing, also known as procurement.

Procurement is a business activity which includes all the activities and processes to acquire goods and services.[1] Procurement is just as important in a service industry, like healthcare, as it is in a manufacturing business. Both types of businesses need certain items to continue to operate. In manufacturing, these items can be raw materials or components which are assembled into a new product. In a service industry, equipment and tools used by the business to provide the service need to be procured. Understanding the perspectives and incentives of various stakeholders within the supply-chain process, specifically considering procurement, is critically important to efficiently, effectively, and efficaciously utilize the scarce resources of a healthcare organization. To make quality decisions about your healthcare organization's supply chain, it is important to understand the mission, process, goals, and incentives of these

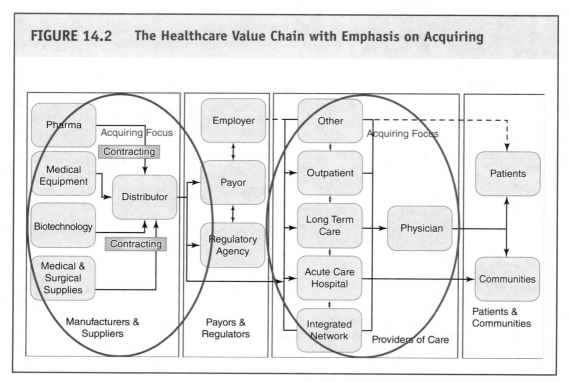

FIGURE 14.2 The Healthcare Value Chain with Emphasis on Acquiring

Acquiring / Procurement =

Sourcing = Need and Vendor Assessment + Value Analysis

+

Purchasing = Value Analysis + Business Transactions + Vendor Management stakeholders: Manufacturers; distributors; GPOs; transportation organizations; and healthcare organizations (also known as provider organizations) are presented.

In order to determine the correct amount of a product to order, demand forecasting tools are used. Perhaps one of the most well-known is economic order quantity (EOQ). This method calculates the most cost-effective amount to purchase at a time. Also, EOQ can be combined with a safety level for crucial items, so the health organization always has that item available. The formula is:

$$EOQ = \sqrt{\frac{2UO}{hC}}$$

Where U = annual usage rate, O = ordering cost, C = cost per unit (each, package, box, carton, etc.) and h = holding cost per year as a percentage of unit cost. An example would be, if an item, say a package of cotton balls, has an annual usage of 1200, a fixed cost per order of $3.00, a unit cost of $2.50 and an annual holding cost of 20% per unit, the calculation is:

$$EOQ = \sqrt{\frac{2*1200*3.00}{0.2*2.50}} = \sqrt{\frac{7200}{0.5}} = \sqrt{14400} = 120$$

Taking the square root = 120 packages of cotton balls to order. To add a simple safety level method, determine the time it will take to receive the cotton ball packages order, say 1 week, and divide the annual usage by 52 weeks (52 weeks per year) for 1200/52 = 23.077 packages and rounding up = 24 packages. So, using this method, you would order 120 packages of cotton balls, and if you use a simple safety level method with EOQ on this item, you would purchase 144 cotton ball packages.

Inventory Management

In Chapter 3, we learned how to manage our inventory once it enters into our organization.

There are cost trade-offs associated with storing and transporting items as well as other "hidden costs." Total logistic costs include storing, shipping, administration, and order-processing costs. The administration and order-processing costs are typically related to the volume of items being handled. Depending on the logistics strategies

being used, the cost to transport and warehouse items will vary for the same volume of items. A strategy to minimize cost and maximize return on purchases is classifying the items stored or used by an organization.

The **single-period model** is used for one-time orders such as purchasing items for a one-time event.

A **fixed-order-quantity model** can be used to maintain a specific level of an item in stock. Under this system, inventory levels are monitored and when they reach a certain level, the item is reordered.

The **fixed-time-period model** is similar to the fixed-order-quantity model but the key difference is that instead of monitoring the inventory level and reordering when the inventory reaches a critically low level, the item is ordered regularly on a specific day regardless of the quantity needed.[2]

Inventory is important to all businesses, including those using just-in-time (JIT) ordering, for three main reasons. First, inventory allows businesses to maintain independence in their operations. This is because there are costs associated with changing processes due to running out of supplies. Second, inventory allows an organization to continue operating during sharp increases in demand for their product or service. In healthcare, increases in demand may be associated with the seasonality of disease or natural disaster. Inventory also allows for flexibility in production scheduling. Having items on hand in a manufacturing business means that there is less pressure on the production system when orders increase. In healthcare, and other service industries, it allows for flexibility in ordering products. Inventory also allows for bulk purchases which can increase order costs due to pricing discounts as well as the costs associated with placing the order. Examples of costs associated with placing orders are equipment required to place the order such as phones, additional office space, salaries for employees, and transportation costs.[3] Storage and inventory management also include warehouse or consolidated service-center cost based on the model utilized.

Warehouses have three basic, yet different, approaches to formation: stock keeping unit (SKU)

FIGURE 14.3   Storing or Inventory Management Focus

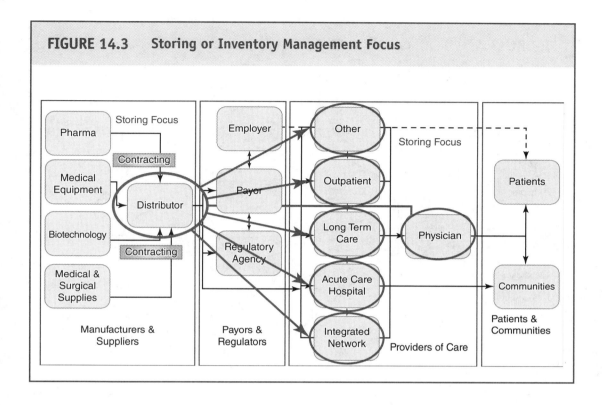

storage, job lot storage, and cross-docking. In SKU storage, products are separated by specific type and stored together, thus reducing confusion and increasing efficiency. Job lot storage employs the idea of storing products related to a certain job together, providing a more efficient picking and packing method. The cross-docking approach uses a different system where the warehouse does not store the product; instead it is where trucks from suppliers drop off large quantities of a given product and it is then broken down into smaller lots and repackaged "on the dock" and not brought into inventory or storage but rather immediately shipped to the final location. These production and warehousing approaches create the beginning of the supply chain at the distributor or warehouse or consolidated service center (which is a warehouse with multiple product storage). A basic principle is "increase throughput while simultaneously reducing both inventory and operating expense."[4]

Distributing Items Within the organization

Dispensing or distributing healthcare supply-chain items to the care providers and patients, or at points of care, is an essential continuation of the healthcare Value Chain. In essence this is stocking of supplies used in patient care. To keep the supply items available to care providers, restocking is accomplished to replenish supplies used in the care process. The healthcare supply chain provides the "technology of care" in a variety of methods and models. Healthcare organizations can either insource (provide the functional capability within the organization by employing supply chain technicians, equipment, and facilities) or outsource (hire an organization outside of the healthcare organization to provide the functional capability) the distribution of supply-chain items to points of care within the health organization. There are several models of distribution of supply chain items; the different models are

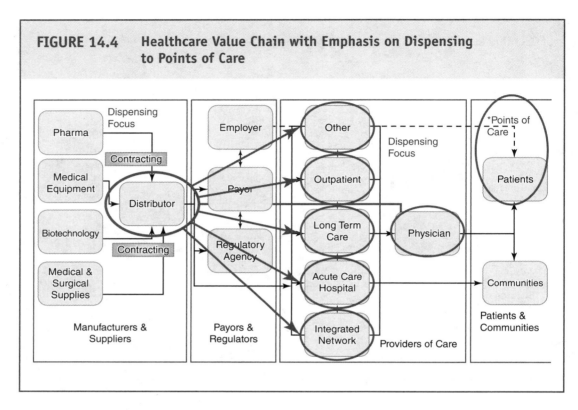

FIGURE 14.4   Healthcare Value Chain with Emphasis on Dispensing to Points of Care

selected based on the point of care (medical and surgical ward, clinic, operating room, etc.) and the operational needs of the health organization. In addition, security and compliance within the supply chain is essential in healthcare in order to provide care with the highest level of efficacy and safety for patients while meeting legal requirements and statutes. These statutory or legal or law requirements include chain of custody of sensitive, high-pilferage, or highly addictive items through the components of the supply chain. Due to the complexity of the items used within most healthcare facilities, there are a myriad of regulations and protocols for the storage, chain of custody (that is who is in control of the items), and dispensing of medications/pharmaceuticals and medical supplies.

Dispensing

There are different systems for dispensing items within an organization. General purpose inventory

dispensing systems such as PAR, JIT, perpetual inventory, or kanban systems are commonly used. It can be a myriad of "alphabet soup" but the overview provided will explain the different models. Outsourced or vendor-specific solutions are often used as well. The most common dispensing or distribution outsourced/vendor solutions were discussed in Chapter 4 after a brief introduction to PAR, JIT, Perpetual Inventory, and kanban dispensing models. These models have widespread use in healthcare.

Pharmaceutical-Specific-Solution Models

Many inpatient and outpatient (to include retail pharmacies) pharmacies utilize cabinet systems integrated with the patient-care process and the supply-chain system. These are computerized systems, in most cases, that are linked to computerized order entry (called CPOE systems) where physicians order/prescribe pharmaceuticals to patients as per the patient's plan of care. The CPOE system alerts the pharmacy where the computerized cabinet decrements the pharmaceutical item stock on hand (such as a tablet or pill) in the cabinet when the pharmacist prepares the prescription for the patient. The system links to the supply chain system to electronically "order" the item that was used for the patient for resupply of that item.

Information Systems in Healthcare Supply Chain

Computers and information technology have an important role in healthcare. This is especially true for complex systems that integrate with all other functions within the healthcare organization. However, due to the rapid changes that occur in both the healthcare and computer technology industries, it can be difficult to take full advantages of the opportunities for process improvement that occur through a partnership between healthcare and information technology. Today there are a multitude of information systems available with applications for the healthcare industry, ranging from process simulation to metric tracking, and supply chain optimization. As the scope and complexity of the healthcare industry continue to increase, the appropriate use of information technology will continue to be important for health systems to remain profitable.

Data Management and Information Flow

Managing data and the flow of information in the healthcare supply chain is a continuous challenge. There are a variety of data types that need to be tracked for daily activities in the supply chain. Information flows in the organization are affected by both the functional layout of the organization and the task at hand. Managing this flow of information through the organization is important in the healthcare supply chain in order to prevent stock-outs or excess inventory. With process improvement plans methods such as lean that push inventory levels down, problems with information flow in the supply chain are quickly uncovered. Some basic information that can prevent supply-chain issues is easily communicated across the supply chain through some variation of three questions:

- What needs to be ordered next?
- What has not yet been delivered?
- What types of products will we need in the future?

How Does Information Flow in the Organization?

The information flow in a typical organization can take several forms, both informal and formal. For the purposes of communicating information related to the supply chain, we will concentrate on formal communication channels. The formal communication network includes all communication along official lines of authority within an organization. These formal channels typically have certain functional communication barriers.[5] These functional barriers to communication result when information needs to pass between various divisions of the supply chain. For example, without the aid of an information system, passing information about a stock-out from departmental storage to central storage and then to acquisitions is a slow process that moves forward step-by-step. Through the use of an information system, the level in the departmental storage area can be remotely monitored and restocked from central storage without risk of a stock-out. The same is true for central storage; items and their use can be monitored electronically and an order placed automatically without risk of stock-out or the use of a large number of employees to hand count stock. Information systems in the healthcare supply chain merge with the use of an interface with clinical, revenue management (reimbursement for services or payment), financial, and human resource systems. Interfaces connect one information system with another and share data. A one-direction (uni-direction) interface sends information from one system to another while a two-direction (bi-direction) interface sends and receives information from one information system to another.

What Data Should Be Managed?

Information to be managed within the supply chain includes inventory, vendor information, transaction history, and contract-related information. This information is usually managed through the use of an enterprise resource planning software package or ERP. ERP technology is currently more popular in industries not related to healthcare such as financial accounting, human resources, and supply-chain management outside of the healthcare arena.[6] For those healthcare organizations that have an ERP system, there is a tendency for organizations to focus on their clinical systems while ignoring their older support system such as ERP. There are multiple vendors for ERP software solutions that specialize in different types of business with the major players in the general business ERP industry being SAP and Oracle. Some examples of healthcare ERP vendors include McKesson, SYSPRO, QAD, and Lawson.

Clinical Operations and Healthcare Supply Chain Integration

The important link between the healthcare supply chain and the care process is the connection with the clinical operations of the health organization. The service lines and clinical processes in health organizations are where the diagnosis, treatment and care giving and support are provided to patients and their families. At this salient link, the clinical operation, the healthcare supply chain must deliver the technology of care on time, in the right quantities and with high quality. In most health organizations there is a link or interface between the healthcare supply chain and the clinical information systems. The business or "people" part of the link is what is important to understand with regard to integration. Part of this integration involves maximizing clinical professionals and staff, physicians, surgeons, nurses, pharmacists and technicians, time on patient care, and associated processes.

The healthcare supply chain must provide the technology of care with as little interference as possible and with as little clinician time as possible on the supply chain tasks. This is a leadership challenge since clinical professional time is required on item selection, sourcing decisions, knowledge concerning upgrades in supply-chain items and similar aspects of a modern healthcare supply chain. For example, spending clinical professional time on cardiac rhythm management supply chain items (such as pacemakers) manufacturer selection and item quality is well worth the clinical professional's time away from patient care, but taking inventory and restocking supply chain items on the shelf may not be a good utilization of a clinical professional's time. It is a balance that leadership must master.

Physicians and surgeons diagnose and treat patients and that is what earns reimbursement to pay everyone and resupply the supply items used; the more time those professionals take away from patient diagnosis and treatment, the less the reimbursement or pay to the health organization.

Why is clinical integration with the healthcare supply chain so important? First, over 770,000 injuries and deaths occur each year as a result of adverse drug events (ADE) with over 400,000 preventable ADE-related injuries that occur in hospitals each year where the cost of each ADE requires hospitals to spend approximately $8,750 per incident.[7] The potential increase in efficiency, effectiveness, and efficacy for better clinical-to-supply-chain integration could reduce these incidents. This is pronounced since 90% of medical errors are due to failed procedures and systems.[8] Stinson, Roycroft, and Moore suggest a clinically integrated supply chain[9] needs to be a strategically led project of change that is characterized by:

- Physician satisfaction.
- Mission critical product support.
- Utilization criteria and best practice.
- Therapeutic generic substitutions.
- Patient demand forecasting and matching.
- Strategic sourcing.
- Balanced scorecard measures.
- Procedural fulfillment.
- Automated replenishment (of supply items).
- Point of use services.
- Elimination of hoarding and shrinkage.
- Single e-catalog and information system integration.
- Fewer SKUs.
- Supplier relationship management with fewer but more strategic suppliers.
- Remove process variation (six and lean sigma).
- Committed volume (90%+) to strategic contracted suppliers.
- Leverage contracts for [efficiency, effectiveness, and efficacy].
- Supplier enhancement of their market share.
- Utilization of contract management metrics.

Analysis of the entire system, from demand forecasting and acquiring to restocking at points of care to supply-item use for patient care, is required to create an efficient, effective, and efficacious supply chain with emphasis on the core mission. That mission is patient diagnosis, treatment, and care with a very high level of quality and no errors. That is the challenge.

Putting It All Together – Supply Chain Management Operations

Turning to operations, leadership, and management of the healthcare supply chain as a core business of healthcare, we focused on acquiring the "technologies of care" for health organizations. Business operations are the process through which an organization gains value from assets controlled by the organization and in turn provide value to customers. Customers are patients, family members of those patients, and the community the health organization serves. In a hospital setting, this includes all aspects of the business that provide care or support the care of patients with focus on the supply chain. From day-to-day management of the supply chain to strategic integration of supply chain operations into the health organization, the essential knowledge of important functions of the supply chain will serve you well in your career. Leading and managing to be "high performing" individually, and more importantly, as a unit or team must be the mindset of the health professional. Many organizations, in various industries, leverage (remember the discussion on competitive advantage) their supply chain operation to add greater value to customers; that means delivering items of quality, proven performance, and durability at reasonable costs and in mass quantities. You have that opportunity in health organizations as well and this opportunity, if implemented successfully, can be a lasting cornerstone to your career and legacy as a professional in the health industry.

High-performing organizations are focused on achieving results and outcomes. These organizations have a result-oriented organizational culture which fosters and reinforces their focus.[10] Moving an organization from low to high performing requires a shift in culture that moves from:

- Outputs to results.
- Stovepipes to matrixes.
- Hierarchical to a more flat, horizontal structure.

- An inward to external focus on clients, customers, partners, and other stakeholders.
- Moving from micromanagement to employee empowerment.
- Reactive behavior to proactive approaches.
- Avoiding new technologies to embracing and leveraging them.
- Moving from hoarding knowledge in data silos to sharing knowledge.
- Avoiding risk to managing risk.
- Protecting "kingdoms" to forming partnerships.
- Moving from adversarial to constructive leader-member relations.[11]

A resource commonly used by high-performing healthcare organizations is GPOs, which save the US healthcare industry more than $36 billion dollars a year. This savings is accomplished through discounts offered for bulk purchases that GPOs make possible because they are purchasing for multiple facilities. GPOs typically charge a small administrative fee to the vendors who provide services to hospitals, although some GPOs charge fees to the hospitals. There are even GPOs that charge a fee to both the vendor and hospital. Whatever the selected fee structure, the fees are used by the GPOs to fulfill their mission to encourage competition and reduce overall costs for healthcare organizations.[12] In addition to the leverage and bulk-buying power provided by GPOs, they also allow healthcare organizations to save time and money that would normally be spent negotiating and executing, potentially, thousands of individual contracts. Hospitals are able to select the most cost-effective GPO available, and this produces a strong incentive for GPOs to be as efficient as possible.

Once items are purchased, decisions must be made as to their storage location. This is a multi-faceted decision that begins with deciding if the primary distribution center for the organization will be insourced or outsourced.

Pros and Cons of External Distribution Centers

External distribution centers are able to fulfill orders at all levels of the supply chain, including PAR, operative, and central storage. The argument for outsourcing supply chain activities is that outsourcing supply chain activities can result in a competitive advantage for the healthcare organization because supply-chain management is a multifaceted system that requires wide-ranging expertise to be efficient. Just as the outsourcing of transportation fleets to companies such as DHL and UPS allowed organizations to focus on their primary business activities, outsourcing of distribution will further allow organizations to focus on their primary business activities.[13]

A major argument against the use of an external distribution center is the control given up over the supply chain by the organization when it is outsourced. This loss of control can result in anticipated fees and potentially increased shipping costs from the distribution center to the hospital. These problems can be magnified if the organization handling the supply chain creates unrealistic timelines with regard to distribution. The worst case scenario is the potential for stock-outs of key items due to missing shipments.[14]

This being said, outsourcing high-level supply-chain functions is becoming an economically effective strategic option for organizations. In order to facilitate decision making with regard to outsourcing, a decision making framework can be utilized. An example of such a framework is as follows:

Prior to deciding to outsource, the following four questions should be carefully examined:

1. Is the function a core competency?
2. Is the knowledge-management strategy associated with the function fully understood and aligned with the goals of the organization?
3. Who will improve the function most in the future?
4. What is the externalization risk?[15]

Based on the answers to these questions, the decision to outsource or keep supply-chain activities in-house can be made. If it is decided that the organization will operate its own distribution centers, the next step is to ask:

What Does Your Own Distribution Center Look Like?

There are three primary types of distribution centers:

1. Conventional.
2. Mechanized.
3. Automated.

A conventional distribution center moves materials round the facility through the use of people and mobile equipment. A mechanized distribution center has equipment that helps move materials throughout the facility such as sorting or conveyer systems. Finally, an automated distribution center moves materials totally, or in part, through the use of robotics.[16]

About 20% of healthcare organizations have their own distribution center. The advantages to owning the distribution center are primarily long-term cost savings, simplified ordering, and logistics. As you may have guessed, building a distribution center is extremely expensive. Due to the costs, typically only large organizations or a group of smaller organizations build their own distribution center. In the wake of the Great Recession, a group of four healthcare organizations in Washington State decided to take advantage of the potential cost savings associated with running their own distribution center. Swedish Medical Center in Seattle and Providence Health and Services, Multicare Health System in Tacoma, and Central Washington Hospital worked together on the distribution center. The health systems expected to order about $10 million per month in supplies through the distribution center.[17] Due to the large quantities of supplies used by these four organizations, senior leadership decided that designing and building a distribution center would be more economical than continuing to contract services to a third party.

In addition to potential cost savings, there are some considerations that go along with operating, expanding, or building a distribution center. Examples of things to consider include machinery to move pallets, types of pallets, how high to stack the pallets, and the overall layout of the facility.

Internal Distribution

The distribution of supplies throughout the healthcare organization is perhaps the most complex portion of the supply chain. Distribution is also a key component to the culture of patient safety. Earlier stages of the supply chain, from manufacturer to distributor to central storage, are generally linear in nature, and all supply lines converge upon central storage within each hospital in a healthcare organization. From this point, the supply lines become much more complicated, with medical/surgical, pharmaceutical, and capital equipment interwoven throughout the facility. The types of methods used to distribute supply chain items to the points of care are heavily dependent on the needs of the end user or customer (namely the clinician and patient) and how a particular service operates in the healthcare organization. Rather than creating a "one-size-fits-all" approach, the supply-chain operation must attend to the needs of the particular service of care in the healthcare organization.

Simulation is a powerful tool for modeling the distribution of items within the supply chain and is particularly helpful with the complexities of internal distribution. The most common options for managing internal supply chain issues may not be the best choice for your particular organization or situation. Even if your organization chooses to use consignment, kanban, or PAR, how is that solution best implemented? These questions come as a result of a fundamental problem in supply-chain management, performance evaluation. How do we choose the best solution and monitor its performance over time against alternatives to ensure we remain competitive? There are three main approaches to performance evaluation:

- Analytical methods.
- Physical experimentations.
- Simulation or emulation.[18]

For today's complex supply chain, the use of analytical methods is considered to be impractical because a mathematical model for a realistic case is too complex to be solved in any realistic time period.[19] Actually implementing all possible scenarios is also impractical due to the time and cost associated with not only running the test but lost productivity due to testing of sub-optimal choices. Simulation is the clear option of the three main approaches because it gives an organization the ability to test out many scenarios and choose the best option according to the simulation to implement within the facility.

Some considerations when designing a simulation are the location of storage, capacity, what items are supplied at each level of fulfillment, policies governing the system, and collaboration with stakeholders.[20] Finally, it is important to stress the simulation during testing to ensure that the model holds up in a "worst-case" scenario.

Leadership

Whether in a worst-case scenario or routine activities, it is important to lead people and manage resources within the healthcare supply chain. In the healthcare supply-chain leader's array of knowledge, skills, and abilities, motivation and inspiration rank high on the list. Carnevale states that "creating a climate that enhances motivation, with the commensurate increase in productivity, is a requirement."[21] Motivation is all about getting a person to start and persist on a task or project. Inspiration is the emotive feeling of value a person experiences while performing a worthy task or project.

Motivation and inspiration in the present day are rooted in the concepts of influence, and to some degree, power. Leaders use motivation and inspiration to influence subordinate actions. Traditionally, leadership thinking rested in the concepts of power and influence. However, the modern-day art of leadership requires a more subtle approach to the misconception of aggressive power and "arm-twisting" influence. The well-educated and complex health workforce will resist the use of errant influence and positional power.

Perhaps not surprisingly, many leaders, academics, and scholars disagree about the best use of power and influence. "There is more conceptual confusion about influence processes than about any other facet of leadership.[22] First this section presents a brief discussion of where influence "exists" for a person; it is followed by a discussion on group affiliation, and then influence as a concept is explored.

Subordinates in health organizations look to leaders, and especially senior executives, as champions and sources of inspiration. Inspirational motivation in health organizations can be achieved when the leader passionately believes in the vision and is able to motivate others through this passion. The leadership team plays an important role in ensuring the success of the organization. This team determines the direction of the organization, while also ensuring that the details behind each event are managed well. Leaders have the responsibility of being concerned about the task of the organization and the support of the organization's stakeholders. Successful health organizations have leaders who not only provide the overall vision for the organization but also step in and play a pivotal role by motivating and recognizing the efforts of subordinates that contribute to success.[23]

Ethics and morality play a key role in motivating others as well; collectively, they represent a crucial characteristic for a leader to possess. The success of the organization may rise and fall on the perception of the community regarding the morals of the organization. Subordinates and the community expect leaders to use their best judgment and to do what is right. Although leadership distinctions may depend on the execution of skills and abilities, such as charisma, the distinction of authentic leadership rests heavily on perceptions of morality.[24] To gain widespread support, the organization must demonstrate the sincerity of its mission and stay true to the values it supports as an organization.

Managing Regulatory Compliance

Managing regulatory compliance is a top concern for healthcare supply-chain professionals according to a study by UPS.[25] Interestingly, regulatory compliance concerns have ranked as the number one issue for survey respondents three years in a row. The continued concern among supply-chain executives is also reflected in another result of the survey: 78% of those surveyed said regulatory compliance and increasing regulation are a top trend driving both business and supply chain changes.[26]

In the 1990s regulatory compliance on the supply chain was minimal. However, the FDA began to increase oversight after a series of high-profile recalls removing items from the market that were damaged after being shipped from the manufacturer. The result of this oversight was an in-depth assessment of the distribution practices of medical devices and other items. These assessments resulted in regulatory increases designed to increase consumer safety.[27]

Some healthcare organizations are having success in addressing regulatory requirements through partnering with other organizations that have expertise in regulatory compliance. Of supply chain executives surveyed by UPS, only 12% said that they were happy with their companies' performance with meeting regulatory challenges.

Metrics

Metrics are used to drive performance within an organization. A lack of informative, unified metrics is often cited as a common pitfall of supply-chain management.[28] The performance of the supply chain depends on the joint performance of all aspects of the supply chain. However, even in a vertically integrated supply chain, each site is typically managed in a fairly autonomous way. As such, each site has its own objectives and mission which may not always be completely aligned with the goals of the organization as a whole. The end result is that each site in the supply chain is striving to meet individual goals that, when met, may achieve suboptimal results for the chain as a whole due to created inefficiencies.[29]

Follow the Cotton Ball

With the healthcare supply chain elements, operations, strategies, and concepts explained, can you follow the cotton ball through the healthcare Value Chain? Does your healthcare supply chain provide an efficient, effective, and efficacious "cotton ball?" Can you envision and follow other items such as sutures, pharmaceuticals, equipment, and instruments?

Sarah Says: A Student's Perspective

The final chapter is a concluding overview of the previous chapters. You as a healthcare professional should now be able to answer the following questions: How will you improve the healthcare supply chain to be a valuable core function of healthcare organizations that provide care to patients? How will you provide the "technology of care" to the caregivers, physicians, surgeons, nurses, and other clinical staff to improve the quality of care and efficacy to the care process? How can you develop, improve, and hold to high standards of healthcare supply-chain efficiency, effectiveness, and efficacy? The healthcare Value Chain plays an important role as well. Understanding how everything works together and how you can use that to your advantage in your healthcare organization will give you, the healthcare professional, an advantage. Getting the technology of care to the clinical caregivers is the essence of the healthcare supply chain.

Discussion Questions

1. Describe the path a cotton ball takes through the healthcare supply chain from identifying a need for the item to the utilization of that item by a clinician for the care of a patient.
2. Outline the basic steps based on the Value Chain for a typical healthcare supply chain.
3. Provide an example of the EOQ and the safety stock for a healthcare supply chain item.
4. Assess how the importance of metrics in supply-chain management supports the clinician in the care process and what metrics are most important from a clinical perspective.
5. Integrate concepts of leadership, management, and planning to create a vision for excellence in the healthcare supply chain.
6. Determine fundamental tenets of performance evaluation for the healthcare supply chain.

Exercises

1. Describe the path a cotton ball takes through the healthcare supply chain from identifying a need for the item to the utilization of that item by a clinician for the care of a patient in a flow diagram.
2. Outline the basic steps based on the Value Chain for a typical healthcare supply chain in one page or less.
3. Explain with an example the EOQ quantity and the safety stock for a healthcare supply chain item.
4. Assess how the importance of metrics in supply-chain management supports the clinician in the care process and what metrics are most important from a clinical perspective in one page or less.
5. Integrate concepts of leadership, management, and planning to create a vision for excellence in the healthcare supply chain in one page or less.
6. Determine fundamental tenets of performance evaluation for the healthcare supply chain in one page or less.

Journal Items

Answer the following:

Integrate concepts of leadership, management, and planning to create a vision for excellence in the healthcare supply chain and determine fundamental tenets of performance evaluation for the healthcare supply chain.

Does your model from the question immediately above maximize clinician time for the care process? Discuss and explain your answer.

References

1. (2010). Definition of Procurement - Purchasing Insight. http://purchasinginsight.com/resources/what-is/definition-of-procurement-procurement-vs-purchasing/ (accessed 17 Sep. 2014).

2. Chapter 11 - Inventory Management - *McGraw-Hill Education*, (2014), http://highered.mheducation.com/sites/dl/free/0073525235/940447/jacobs3e_sample_ch11.pdf (accessed 16 Oct. 2014).

3. Chapter 11 - Inventory Management - *McGraw-Hill Education*.

4. Michael H. Hugos, *Essentials of Supply Chain Management*, 3rd ed. (Hoboken, NJ: John Wiley and Sons, 2011)

5. 8.5 Communication Channels, *Flat World Knowledge*, (2012), http://catalog.flatworldknowledge.com/bookhub/7?e=collins-ch08_s05 (accessed 8 Dec. 2014).

6. A Few Thoughts on ERP in Healthcare – *Tribridge*, (2013), http://www.tribridge.com/knowledge-center/tribridge/posts/p2/2013/06/09/a-few-thoughts-on-erp-in-healthcare (accessed 8 Dec. 2014).

7. Stinson et al. "The Clinically Integrated Supply Chain." Presentation at the American College of Healthcare Executives Annual Congress, Chicago, IL, March 14, 2008.

8. Stinson et al. "The Clinically Integrated Supply Chain."

9. Stinson et al. "The Clinically Integrated Supply Chain."

10. U.S. Government Accountability Office. High-Performing Organizations: Metrics, Means, and Mechanisms for Achieving High Performance in the 21st Century Public Management Environment. (2004, February). (Publication No. GAO-04-343SP). GAO Reports Main Page via GPO Access database: http://www.gpoaccess.gov/gaoreports/index.html

11. U.S. Government Accountability Office. High-Performing Organizations.

12. Understanding Administrative Fees - Healthcare Supply, (2011), http://www.supplychainassociation.org/resource/resmgr/research/admin_fees.pdf (accessed 19 Jan. 2015).

13. C. Alvarenga, Core Competency 2.0: The Case For..., *Accenture*, http://www.accenture.com/SiteCollectionDocuments/PDF/282Accenture_Core_Competency_20_The_Case_For_Outsourcing_Supply_Chain_Management.pdf

14. The Risks and Benefits of Outsourcing Supply Chain ... Retrieved February 25, 2015, from http://www.businessbee.com/resources/operations/supplier-management/the-risks-and-benefits-of-outsourcing-supply-chain-management/ (accessed 25 Feb. 2015).

15. The outsourcing of even high level supply chain functions are become an economically effective strategic option for organizations.

16. Distribution Center Design Concepts Explained ... – *MWPVL*, (2012), http://www.mwpvl.com/html/distribution_center_design_concepts_explained.html (accessed 21 Feb. 2015).

17. Washington hospitals join forces to launch distribution center. http://www.healthcarefinancenews.com/news/washington-hospitals-join-forces-launch-distribution-center (accessed 21 Feb. 2015).

18. C. Thierry, The Role of Modeling and Simulation in Supply Chain, *scs.org*, (2010), http://www.scs.org/magazines/2010-10/index_file/Files/Thierry.pdf.

19. Thierry, The Role of Modeling and Simulation in Supply Chain.

20. Thierry, The Role of Modeling and Simulation in Supply Chain.

21. A. P. Carnevale, *America and the new economy.* (Washington, DC: Department of Labor, 1991).

22. G. Yukl, *Leadership in organizations*, 3rd ed. (Englewood Cliffs, NJ: Prentice Hall, 1994), 193.

23. M. Sorcher and J. Brant, "Are you picking the right leaders?" *Harvard Business Review* (2002, February), 78.

24. T. L. Cooper, *The responsible administrator: An approach to ethics for the administrative role* (San Francisco: Jossey-Bass, 1998).

25. G. Degun, Regulatory compliance top supply chain concern among healthcare professionals. (2014, September 23), http://www.supplymanagement.com /news/2014/regulatory-compliance-top-supply -chain-concern-among-healthcare-professionals (accessed 22 Mar. 2015).

26. Degun, Regulatory compliance top supply chain concern among healthcare professionals.

27. Quality Assurance and Regulatory Compliance. (n.d.), http://www.genco.com/Healthcare/regulatory -compliance.php (accessed 23 Mar. 2015).

28. A. Gunasekaran, C. Patel, and R. E. McGaughey, "A framework for supply chain performance measurement." *International journal of production economics*, 87, no. 3 (2004), 333–347.

29. Gunasekaran, Patel, and McGaughey, "A framework for supply chain performance measurement."

GLOSSARY

810 Transaction: 810 is the EDI x12ID code for an invoice used in the following way: the vendor sends an invoice back to their trading partner as a bill for the products ordered.

832 Electronic catalog: 832 is the EDI x12ID code for an electronic product catalogue defined in the following way: an electronic catalog of products and items from a manufacturer, distributor, or vendor.

Class I recalls: Class I recalls are situations where there is a reasonable probability that the use of or exposure to a volatile product (product in violation of FDA regulations) will cause serious adverse health consequences or death.

Class II recalls: Class II recalls are situations where the use of or exposure to a volatile product may cause temporary or medically revisable adverse health consequences or where the probability of serious adverse health consequences is remote.

Class III recalls: Class III recalls are situations in which the use of or exposure to a volatile product is not likely to cause adverse health consequences.

Consolidated service center: Consolidated service centers are warehouse operations that handle and store multiple types of healthcare supply-chain items and are most usually owned or internal to the healthcare system (insourced versus outsourced).

Cross-docking: The cross-docking approach uses a different system where the warehouse does not store the product; instead it is where trucks from suppliers drop off large quantities of a given product and it is then broken down into smaller lots and repackaged "on the dock" and not brought into inventory or storage but immediately shipped to the final location.

Dis-intermediated supply chain: In contrast to the traditional or non-integrated healthcare supply chain is the vertically integrated supply chain, also called the dis-intermediated model. The vertically integrated model uses insourcing to a much greater extent than the traditional model. The vertically integrated model maintains an internal group purchasing, distribution, transportation, and hospital supply-chain organization where the goals and work are coordinated to derive the greatest value for the organization.

Dispensing: The process of delivering the technology of care (supply-chain items) to the points of the care process, where those items are utilized efficaciously for patient diagnosis, treatment, and care.

Distributor: An agent who supplies goods to stores and other businesses that sell to consumers or use those products to provide a service.

Economic order quantity: Economic order quantity (EOQ) is a method to calculate the most cost-effective amount to purchase at a time. EOQ can be combined with a safety level for crucial items, so the health organization always has that item available. The formula is:

$$EOQ = \sqrt{\frac{2UO}{hC}}$$

Where U = annual usage rate, O = ordering cost, C = cost per unit (each, package, box, carton, etc.) and h = holding cost per year as a percentage of unit cost.

Enterprise resource planning systems: Enterprise resource planning (ERP) systems are a set of software applications that organize, define, and standardize the business processes necessary to effectively plan and control an organization so the organization can use its internal knowledge to seek external advantage.

Group purchasing organization: A group purchasing organization (GPO) is an entity formed by its members to leverage their combined purchasing power to obtain discounts from vendors. Forming a partnership with a supplier instead of working with a GPO to purchase goods directly is not common in healthcare. In other sectors, group purchasing is not used and it is common for partnerships to form between suppliers and customers.

Information system interface: A shared connection across two separate components of a computer system where information is exchanged. This exchange can be between software, hardware, people, or any combination of these.

Intermediated supply chain: This model uses GPOs for contracting of manufactured items, distribution organizations, and transportation organizations that are outsourced. Once the supply items reach the hospital or health system, the internal distribution and management of supplies can be either outsourced or managed by internal labor (insourced). To grasp the full extent of the utilization of this or some form of this model, 98% of healthcare organizations use GPOs to some extent and a vast majority of hospitals rely on them heavily.

Just-in-time delivery: Just in time (JIT) is a system to reduce inventory and minimize spoilage while still meeting the needs of customers. The central theme of JIT is essentially "items in inventory is wasted cash that cannot be used for other activities." Items in inventory do not add value to the company until they are sold, used for manufacturing, or provide a service. In addition, items in inventory are subject to damage, loss, or spoilage while in storage. The JIT system was developed in the 1970s to address these issues. Taiichi Ohno of Toyota developed the system for manufacturing to minimize waste and improve quality. The key benefits of the JIT system are:

- Low inventory
- Low waste
- High quality production
- High customer responsiveness

Manufacturer: A business involved in the manufacturing or the production of merchandise.

Medical/surgical supplies: Medical and surgical supplies such as sutures, gauze, cotton balls, and syringes, sometimes called "Med/Surg."

Metrics: Tool derived from data used to measure an activity. The metric is informed by data from the supply-chain operation and usually is associated with a measure of efficiency and is set within parameters of operation.

PAR: The PAR system is a method of managing inventory that requires items to be restocked to a specific level. In a PAR system, each of the items stored in central storage and the department storage areas are assigned a stock requirement or PAR level. At a certain time, sometimes continuously, through the use of automation, or every few days, the items are counted and restocked, from a central storage location, based on the number of items used. Often, the process is facilitated by using handheld scanners to read product barcodes. PAR systems are best suited for patient care units and for high-use, low-cost items.

Perpetual inventory: This is accomplished through electronically requesting supplies from the materials management department and automatically receiving the supplies requested in the correct quantities. When done optimally, the perioperative supply chain can be converted to a perpetual style system.

Pharmaceutical supplies: Pharmaceuticals (medicinal and biological treatments such as tablets, pills, injections, and the like, called "pharma").

PPIs: Physician preference items.

Privileging: Physicians diagnose, treat, and care for patients in hospitals that give physicians "practice rights" at their facility.

Receipt lines: Receipt lines are the number of items [lines] processed or received into inventory in that particular warehouse of consolidated service center.

Restocking: Replenishing a location with supplies.

Safety level: Safety levels can be the amount needed to cover the days it takes to order and ship to your location or it can be a percentage of use of that item. A safe level of stock is necessary to provide coverage for unexpected customer/patient demand, damage in the warehouse, or quality issues found in production.

SKUs (in supply-chain context): Stock keeping unit (SKU) products are separated by specific type and stored together, thus reducing confusion and increasing efficiency.

Strategic sourcing: An organized approach or method that allows a supply-chain function to systematically work on spending areas or processes that can result in cost-saving benefits.

Strategic sourcing: The strategic sourcing process consists of a number of formal steps: identification of need, analysis, sourcing, negotiation and contracting, implementation, measurement, and management.

Supply chain – clinical integration: Integrating the supply-chain information systems to optimize clinical item availability and reduce stock-outs.

Supply chain – revenue management integration: Integrating the supply-chain information systems to optimize product availability and maximize revenue growth.

Supply-chain management: Supply-chain management is the integration of the flows of products, information, services, and finances from the point of origin to the final customer.

Value Chain: The Value Chain categorizes activities as primary and support. The primary activities include inbound logistics, operations, outbound logistics, marketing and sales, and service. The support activities include infrastructure, human resource management, technology development, and procurement.

Value Chain analysis: Using the Value Chain as a tool for strategic planning and process improvement.

INDEX

Page numbers followed by *f* or *t* indicate material in figures or tables, respectively.